Deeper Than Reason

Deeper than Reason takes the insights of modern psychological and neuroscientific research on the emotions and brings them to bear on questions about our emotional involvement with the arts. Robinson begins by laying out a theory of emotion, one that is supported by the best evidence from current empirical work on emotions, and then in the light of this theory examines some of the ways in which the emotions function in the arts. Written in a clear and engaging style, her book will make fascinating reading for anyone who is interested in the emotions and how they work, as well as anyone engaged with the arts and aesthetics, especially with questions about emotional expression in the arts, emotional experience of art forms, and, more generally, artistic interpretation.

Part One develops a theory of emotions as processes, having at their core non-cognitive 'instinctive' appraisals, 'deeper than reason', which automatically induce physiological changes and action tendencies, and which then give way to cognitive monitoring of the situation. Part Two examines the role of the emotions in understanding literature, especially the great realistic novels of the nineteenth century. Robinson argues that such works need to be experienced emotionally if they are to be properly understood. A detailed reading of Edith Wharton's novel *The Reef* demonstrates how a great novel can educate us emotionally by first evoking instinctive emotional responses and then getting us to cognitively monitor and reflect upon them. Part Three puts forward a new Romantic theory of emotional expression in the arts. Part Four deals with music, both the emotional expression of emotion in music, whether vocal or instrumental, and the arousal of emotion by music. The way music arouses emotion lends indirect support to the theory of emotion outlined in Part One. While grounded in the science of emotion, *Deeper than Reason* demonstrates the continuing importance of the arts and humanities to our lives.

Caspar David Friedrich, *Large Enclosure at Dresden*, c.1831. Photograph
© AKG London.

Deeper Than Reason

Emotion and its Role in Literature, Music, and Art

JENEFER ROBINSON

CLARENDON PRESS·OXFORD

OXFORD

UNIVERSITY PRESS

Great Clarendon Street, Oxford OX2 6DP

Oxford University Press is a department of the University of Oxford.
It furthers the University's objective of excellence in research, scholarship,
and education by publishing worldwide in

Oxford New York

Auckland Cape Town Dar es Salaam Hong Kong Karachi Kuala Lumpur
Madrid Melbourne Mexico City Nairobi New Delhi Shanghai Taipei Toronto

With offices in

Argentina Austria Brazil Chile Czech Republic France Greece
Guatemala Hungary Italy Japan South Korea Poland Portugal
Singapore Switzerland Thailand Turkey Ukraine Vietnam

Published in the United States
by Oxford University Press Inc., New York

© Jenefer Robinson 2005
First published in paperback 2007

The moral rights of the author have been asserted
Database right Oxford University Press (maker)

First published 2005

British Library Cataloguing in Publication Data

Data available

Library of Congress Cataloging in Publication Data

Data available

Typeset by SPI Publisher Services, Pondicherry, India
Printed in Great Britain
on acid-free paper by
Biddles Ltd,
King's Lynn, Norfolk

ISBN 978–0–19–926365–3 (Hbk.)   978–0–19–920426–7 (Pbk.)

1 3 5 7 9 10 8 6 4 2

To John,
Jane, and Neil

Acknowledgements

I HAVE been working on the issues in this book for over twenty years. My first published paper on the emotions appeared in 1983. It was a piece of armchair theorizing and I have changed both my views and my methods quite a bit since then. Nevertheless the foundations of the 'anti-judgementalist' view I defend here were already partly in place at that time. More recent papers from 1995 and 1998 reflect the influence of the empirical research that I studied in the intervening years and especially the influence of my colleague, the psychologist Bill Dember, with whom I co-taught courses on the emotions over a long period. My interest in aesthetic questions goes even further back, starting with a Ph.D. dissertation on representation and expression in the arts. Indeed I was led into emotion theory when I began to question exactly what was meant by saying that works of art express and arouse emotions, that artistic style is an expression of temperament or personality, or that the meaning of music is its emotional content.

Because my thinking on these questions has evolved over such a long period, it is inevitable that I won't remember everyone who has helped me along the way; but I hope I have remembered those who had the most important influence. There are several people I'd like to thank who have had a global influence on my thinking since the beginning of my career. Unfortunately Monroe Beardsley and Richard Wollheim are no longer with us, but I can at least thank my former teacher at the University of Toronto, Francis Sparshott, who set me on the road that led to this book.

Among those who have been the most supportive and helpful to me are some whom I have singled out for criticism. In particular, everything I have ever written on emotion theory begins by a critique of the views of Bob Solomon, someone who has been unfailingly generous and supportive of me over the years. I am also consistently critical of the views of Peter Kivy who has been equally helpful and kind for a very long time. Other friends who come in for attack include Noël Carroll, Stephen Davies, Jerrold Levinson, and Kendall Walton. I hope these friends will remain so.

On emotion theory, my biggest debt is to my friend and colleague William Dember, who introduced me to the psychological literature on emotion and continues to be a source of wisdom. John Bickle and Bob Frank helped me with the neuro-science, and David Ricks gave me a clinical perspective on emotion. I have also learnt from exchanges with Ronald de Sousa, Patricia Greenspan, Paul Griffiths, Jesse Prinz, and Robert Solomon. On literature, my biggest debts are to Michael Atkinson and Ellen Peel, from whom I learnt a lot both when I co-taught courses with them and subsequently, and to Cathryn Long and Don Bogen with whom I regularly discuss literary questions. On the literary-philosophical front, I have also learnt from Peter Lamarque and Bob Stecker. On music, I am particularly grateful to Steven Cahn, Gregory Karl, Severine Neff, and Edward Nowacki. Jennifer Judkins, Andrew Kania, Jonathan Kramer, Fred Maus, Mary Sue Morrow, Frank Samarotto, and Allen Sapp helped me on specific points. Others to whom I am indebted in various and sundry ways include Rose Bianchi, Donald Gustafson, John Hancock, Diane Haslam, Van Quinn, Earl Rivers, and Jim Young. I owe a special debt to Cathryn Long and Taffy Ross who have for years listened sympathetically and offered helpful suggestions as I mulled over these topics.

Several people made the ultimate sacrifice of actually reading and commenting on parts of the book: I would like to thank especially Noël Carroll, William Dember, Stephen Davies, Susan Feagin, Christopher Gauker, Gregory Karl, Jerrold Levinson, Ellen Peel, Stephanie Ross, and Michael Sontag. John Dilworth, Jennifer Judkins, Andrew Kania, Jerrold Levinson, and Sarah Worth commented on versions of chapters that I gave at meetings of the American Philosophical Association and the American Society for Aesthetics. Numbers of students have also been exposed to my work and have often given helpful feedback. They include Zac Cogley, Fred Harrington, Gregory Johnson, Jon Lang, and Michael Sontag.

Some people read huge chunks of manuscript. I am particularly indebted to Malcolm Budd, Gregory Currie, and Ronald de Sousa who read the whole thing and made numerous useful suggestions, as well as to Cathryn Long and Alex Neill, who each read and commented on substantial portions.

Audiences at various presentations I have given have also indirectly improved the manuscript. They include audiences at the University of British Columbia, University of Bristol, California State University at Fullerton, California Polytechnic State University at Pomona, College of Charleston, the College Conservatory of Music at the University of Cincinnati, Duke University, Florida State University, University of Leeds, University of Southampton, Sussex University, University of Texas at

Arlington, Victoria University, University of Virginia, Virginia Polytechnic University, the University of York, various meetings of the American Philosophical Association and the American Society for Aesthetics, and the meetings of the International Society for Research on Emotion in Quebec City, and the British Society for Aesthetics in Oxford. I have tried to take account of most of the comments I received in one way or another, but I do not expect to have satisfied everybody.

In the summer of 2002 Jerrold Levinson directed a National Endowment for the Humanities Institute on Art, Mind, and Cognitive Science, which Dominic Lopes and I co-directed. I would like to thank the members of the Institute for helpful discussion, especially Amy Coplan, Stacie Friend, James Harold, Jerrold Levinson, Dominic Lopes, Shaun Nichols, Laura Perini, Miles Rind, Stephanie Ross, and James Shelley.

During the academic year 2002–3 I was a National Endowment for the Humanities fellow at the National Humanities Center. The Office of the Vice-President for Research, the Charles Phelps Taft memorial fund, and the Dean of the McMicken College of Arts and Sciences at the University of Cincinnati also provided some support. The National Humanities Center was an ideal place to work and I'd like to thank the Endowment, as well as the fellows and staff for a very happy and profitable year. Sigrun Svavarsdottir and Sue Hirsch in particular were constant sources of encouragement.

I am also grateful to Peter Momtchiloff and his excellent staff at Oxford University Press, and to Greg Johnson who helped enormously with the index.

Finally, and most warmly of all, I thank my husband, John Martin, for loving support over a period of almost thirty-five years, and my children Jane and Neil Martin, who have also helped to keep me emotionally sane. This book is dedicated to the three of them. They have provided a rich source of fieldwork on the emotions, and among the many happy experiences we have had together, some at least have been aesthetic. As I said at the beginning, this book was over twenty years in the making, and perhaps would have been written sooner if I hadn't had a family to think about. But both my life and this book would have been much the poorer.

CHAPTERS 1, 2, and 3 draw on material in 'Emotion: Biological Fact or Social Construction?' in Robert C. Solomon (ed.), *Thinking About Feeling: Contemporary Philosophers on Emotion* (New York: Oxford University Press, 2004), 28–43; 'Theoretical Issues in the Role of Appraisal in Emotion:

Cognitive Content Versus Physiological Change', in Robert R. Hoffman, Michael F. Sherrick, and Joel S. Warm (eds.), *Viewing Psychology as a Whole: The Integrative Science of William N. Dember*, (Washington, DC: American Psychological Association, 1998), 449–69; and 'Startle', *Journal of Philosophy* 92 (1995), 53–74.

CHAPTERS 4 and 5 had their origins long ago in 'Experiencing Art', *Proceedings of the Eleventh International Congress in Aesthetics* (Nottingham Polytechnic, England, 1988), 156–60.

CHAPTER 6 is a much revised and expanded version of 'L'éducation sentimentale', *Australasian Journal of Philosophy* 73 (1995), 212–26 (used with permission of Oxford University Press), reprinted in Stephen Davies (ed.), *Art and Its Messages* (Pennsylvania State University Press, 1997), 34–48.

CHAPTER 7 has appeared in abbreviated form as 'The Art of Distancing: How Formal Devices Manage Our Emotional Responses to Literature', *Journal of Aesthetics and Art Criticism* 62 (2004), 153–62 (used with permission of Blackwell Publishers).

CHAPTER 9 discusses an earlier paper of mine, 'Art as Expression', in Hugh Mercer Curtler (ed.), *What Is Art?* (New York: Haven, 1983), 93–121.

Careful readers of Chs. 10, 11, and 12 might discover some overlap between them and previous work on the philosophy of music, especially 'The Expression and Arousal of Emotion in Music', *Journal of Aesthetics and Art Criticism* 52 (1994), 13–22, reprinted in Peter Lamarque and Stein Olsen (eds.), *Aesthetics and the Philosophy of Art: the Analytic Tradition* (Oxford: Blackwell, 2003), 470–9; 'Shostakovich's Tenth Symphony and the Musical Expression of Cognitively Complex Emotions' (with Gregory Karl), *Journal of Aesthetics and Art Criticism* 53 (1995), 401–15, reprinted in Jenefer Robinson (ed.), *Music and Meaning* (Cornell University Press, 1997), 154–78, and the introduction to *Music and Meaning*.

Many of the themes in this book are adumbrated in 'The Emotions in Art', in Peter Kivy (ed.), *The Blackwell Guide to Aesthetics* (Oxford: Blackwell, 2004), 174–92.

I am grateful for permission to draw on all this previous work.

The photographs in Ch. 2, Fig. 2.1, are from Paul Ekman, *Emotions Revealed* (New York: Henry Holt, 2003), 9. Reprinted by permission.

J. R.
Cincinnati
October 2004

She felt a warning tremor as she spoke, as though some instinct deeper than reason surged up in defense of its treasure. But Darrow's face was unstirred save by the flit of his half-amused smile.

Edith Wharton, The Reef

Contents

List of Figures

Part One

What Are Emotions and How Do They Operate?

For thousands of years people have assumed that that there is some special deep connection between emotion and the arts. In the *Republic* Plato famously complained that one reason why poetry often has such a bad moral influence on people is that it appeals to their emotions rather than to their reason, the 'highest' part of the soul. The idea that the emotions are intimately connected to the arts was taken up by Aristotle and given a more sympathetic twist. Almost ever since, there has been a widespread conviction among Western thinkers that there is some special relationship between the arts and the emotions.[1]

Until very recently, however, there was little consensus about what the emotions really are and how they actually operate, and so it has been hard to adjudicate exactly how they function in relation to the arts. This situation has now begun to change. Within the last thirty years or so there has been an upsurge of research into the emotions in disciplines as diverse as experimental and clinical psychology, neurobiology, anthropology, sociology, and philosophy. We now have a much better idea of what emotions are. Not that there is a complete consensus: far from it. Competing theories are rife. But none the less there is growing agreement about emotion and what its most important ingredients are.

I wrote this book in order to bring to bear the insights of modern psychological and other empirical research into the emotions on questions about our emotional involvement with the arts. So I begin by laying out a theory of emotion, one that is supported by the best evidence from current empirical work, and then in the light of this theory I examine some of the ways in which the emotions function in the arts. The book is intended for anyone interested in the emotions and how they work, as well as anyone interested in the arts and the philosophy of the arts, especially questions about emotional expression in the arts, the emotional experience of the arts, and, more generally, interpretation in the arts.

Part One is about the emotions, what they are, why we have them, and how they function. We need to have a firm grasp of what emotions are before we go on to tackle more difficult questions about emotions and the arts. Part Two is about literature and the emotions, especially about the emotional reactions that people have to poems, plays, novels, and other types of literature. Do we have to respond emotionally to poems and novels in order to understand them properly? Can good novels educate us emotionally about life? What is the role of structure in a novel or poem in guiding our emotional responses? Part Three deals with emotional expression. It moves the discussion away from the emotional reactions of audiences and turns instead to the expression of emotions by artists: writers, composers, painters, choreographers, film-makers, and so on. The idea that the arts are expressions of emotion in their creators was axiomatic in the Romantic movement at the end of the eighteenth and for much of the nineteenth century, and it is still an idea with many adherents. I show how the way people think about artistic expression today cannot be disentangled from its roots in Romanticism. The last part of the book is about music, both the expression of emotion in music and the emotional reactions of audiences to music. It is often thought paradoxical that apparently content-less 'pure' instrumental music can express or arouse emotions. I explain how a proper understanding of the emotions can help us to solve this apparent paradox.

I begin, then, with the emotions: love, anger, fear, jealousy, grief, shame, and many more. My goal in Part One is to establish a theory of emotion that draws on recent work in experimental psychology, neuroscience, and other empirical disciplines. The theory I outline and defend is a theory that I think *best accounts for the currently available evidence on emotion*. In other words, things may change as more results come in from the empirical sciences, but right now the best available evidence suggests that my theory or something very like it is the most plausible on offer.

Chapter 1 is devoted to theories of emotion that emphasize cognition or 'judgements'. The insights of the cognitive theory have to be preserved in any satisfactory theory of emotion, but there are many reasons why cognition or judgement cannot be the essential ingredient in emotion, as the judgement theory maintains. Chapter 2 examines results from psychology and neuroscience and lays the groundwork for the theory I develop in Ch. 3, where emotion is treated as essentially a *process*, in which a special kind of automatic 'affective appraisal' induces characteristic physiological and behavioural changes and is succeeded by what I call 'cognitive monitoring' of the situation. Although there is usually lots of cognitive activity going on in the course of an emotion process, the process itself is always initiated by an automatic affective appraisal that occurs prior to reflection. It is because emotions are triggered by an automatic affective appraisal that they are in some important ways immune to assessment as rational or irrational: they are, as Edith Wharton suggests in the epigraph, 'deeper than reason'.

1

Emotions as Judgements

The emotion is a specific manner of apprehending the world.

Jean-Paul Sartre, *Sketch for a Theory of the Emotions*

What Are Emotions? Are They Feelings, Behaviour, Physiological Symptoms, or Judgements?

For many people the answer to the question 'what is an emotion?' is straightforward: emotions are *feelings*. After all, when I am in the throes of an emotional experience, it's natural to say that I *feel* angry or elated or nostalgic or jealous. One way to explain this way of talking is that emotions simply *are feelings*: a feeling of anger, a feeling of elation, a feeling of nostalgia, or a feeling of jealousy. We tend to think of our feelings as our own private mental states or states of *consciousness*, and we are inclined to believe that only we ourselves have access to our feelings of joy and fear, our inner surges of anger or jealousy. If emotions are nothing but feelings, this would mean that our emotions are private mental states or states of consciousness, and that I find out what my emotions are by introspection.

However, a very little reflection shows that even if experiencing emotions does involve having feelings, we can't simply identify emotions with feelings. After all, there are lots of feelings that are not emotions: we feel hunger pangs, sexual urges, and various itches and tickles, to say nothing of feelings of hot and cold, of heartburn and lower back pain. And at the same time, it just seems wrong to reduce such a lofty emotion as love to an inner feeling such as butterflies in the tummy. However trembly I get when my beloved comes into view, it doesn't seem right to say that my love is nothing but the trembly feeling. After all, I may get the trembly feeling when I am nervous or when I have run too fast up the stairs. I may get a warm glow inside not just when I see my beloved but also when I have just finished exercising. I can have a sharp burst of indigestion as well as a sharp burst of irritation.

In a marked reaction against the view that emotions are simply inner feelings, and under the pervasive influence of behaviourism, some philosophers and psychologists in the mid-twentieth century argued that emotions should be analysed as characteristic bits of behaviour or as dispositions to behave in a certain way. In this way of thinking about things, my love is not my trembly feeling but my caring behaviour. My anger is not my turbulent inner feelings; it is my vengeful behaviour. One problem with this conception of emotions is that sometimes emotions don't seem to have any accompanying behaviour at all: It seems as though I can be secretly in love or annoyed or afraid without there being any sign of it in my overt behaviour. Proponents of the behaviour view therefore usually prefer to say that emotions are *dispositions* or tendencies to behave in certain ways. Anger is thought of as a disposition to revenge or to aggressive behaviour, love as a disposition to care for and cherish the object of love, and so on. In other words, if I am angry or in love I will tend to exhibit my emotions in the way I behave if the opportunity arises: if the object of my anger or my love is far away, there may be long periods when you can't tell just from looking at the way I behave whether or not I am angry or in love. It is only when I am put into the right circumstances that my tendency to behave a certain way will be activated.

There are several reasons why thinking of emotions as pieces of behaviour, or even as tendencies to engage in certain pieces of behaviour, is a bad idea. For one thing, the behaviour associated with two different emotions, such as shame and embarrassment, or regret and remorse may be the very same: behaviour or tendencies to behave in a certain way cannot distinguish between two closely related emotions. A second consideration is that although my caring behaviour may indeed be a symptom of my love for you, I may act in the same way simply out of a sense of duty. So the behaviour all by itself cannot be the same thing as the emotion of love. Consequently, although behaviour may be an important component of at least some emotions, we cannot identify emotions with behaviour or tendencies to behave, any more than we can identify emotions with inner feelings.

Another striking feature of emotion consists in physiological responses of various kinds. When we see a man who is angry, we may notice that his face is getting red and his hands are trembling; that he is beginning to sweat, and his face is contorted. These are all physiological symptoms of his emotional state, but once again it doesn't seem right simply to identify emotion with physiological changes. After all, each of the marks of anger just listed may be nothing more than symptoms of strenuous exertion. A man lifting heavy weights may have a contorted, red face, and typically he will sweat and tremble. Like behaviour, physiological symptoms may be an important component of emotion but they cannot be all there is to emotion.

Currently, the most widely accepted theory of emotion is probably the 'cognitive' or 'judgement' theory of emotion. What, after all, is the big difference between the trembly feeling I get when I am in love and the trembly feeling I get when I run up the stairs too fast? In the one situation my feeling is caused (partly) by a rapid heartbeat brought on by a sudden burst of strenuous exercise; in the other situation my feeling may also be (partly) caused by a rapid increase in heartbeat, but in this case the increased heartbeat appears to be caused not by some physical activity I am engaged in—such as running too fast—but by a judgement that I make, the judgement that my beloved has arrived and that he is the darling of my heart. Similarly, whereas a sharp burst of indigestion may be caused by eating too many raw onions, a sharp burst of annoyance seems to be caused by a judgement, the judgement that something has happened or someone has done something to thwart my plans or interests.

The judgement theory also explains why the same piece of behaviour or tendency to behave in a certain way is sometimes the result of an emotion and sometimes not. If I care for you and cherish you out of love, then my behaviour is plausibly construed as a result of my judgement that you are the darling of my heart, a wonderful person, and a joy to be with. Alternatively, if I care for and cherish you solely out of a sense of duty, then my caring for and cherishing you is caused by my sense of duty; I do not judge you to be the darling of my heart; I may be indifferent to you or even dislike you.

Furthermore, the judgement theory explains how the same behaviour may be characteristic of two different emotions. Shame and embarrassment are both typically associated with withdrawal and hiding behaviours; the difference between them seems to be cognitive. When I am ashamed, I seem to be judging (in part) that I have been degraded in some way that casts doubt on my sense of self-worth, whereas when I am merely embarrassed, I judge that I am in a socially awkward situation but not one that is necessarily degrading to me or that impugns my sense of self-worth. The difference between remorse and regret also seems to be cognitive:[1] when I experience regret, I judge that something untoward has occurred for which I may or may not be responsible and that I wish had not happened, whereas when I experience remorse, I judge that I have performed some action that I think is morally bad and for which I am responsible, and I wish very much that I had not done it.

The Judgement Theory of Emotion

In their discussions of emotion, the great philosophers from Aristotle to Descartes, Spinoza, and Hume, have typically emphasized the cognitive content of emotions. Thus Aristotle famously defined anger as 'a desire for revenge accompanied by pain on account of (dia) an apparent slight to oneself or to one's own, the slight being unjustified'. Descartes is often caricatured as having a 'feeling' theory of emotion, but in fact his theory is extremely sophisticated; it includes an analysis of the physiology and even the neurophysiology of emotion, the connection between physiological response and feeling, and the way in which cognition interacts with physiology. Descartes also gives wonderfully subtle accounts of the cognitive content of many emotions. Hume, too, is not adequately describable as merely a 'feeling' theorist. His analyses of pride, love, and other complex emotions have generated a lot of interest among cognitive theorists today. And Spinoza is also a 'judgement theorist' after his own fashion. He envisaged emotions as a species of thought, although he identifies emotion with 'inadequate or confused ideas'.[2] Despite the fact that many of these older accounts of emotion are very subtle, I am going to focus in this book almost entirely on contemporary writers on the emotions. Today the judgement theory is defended by some of the best-known psychologists and philosophers writing on emotion, including the philosophers Robert M. Gordon, Gabriele Taylor, Robert C. Solomon, William Lyons, Martha Nussbaum, and Peter Goldie, and the psychologists Richard Lazarus, Andrew Ortony, and Phoebe Ellsworth.

Some philosophers treat the topic of emotion within the framework of cognitive science. According to Robert Gordon, for example, it is the cognitive aetiology of an emotional state that makes it the state that it is. Emotions are mental states identified by means of the particular structures of beliefs and desires that *cause* them. All the emotions Gordon studies are directed at some kind of proposition, anger or delight or fear *that* something or other is the case. A 'factive' emotion—such as your delight, anger, or resentment that Jones has insulted you—is based on your knowledge that Jones has insulted you and either the satisfaction of a wish (you are delighted that he insulted you) or the frustration of a wish (you are angry or resentful that he insulted you). By contrast an 'epistemic' emotion, such as your fear or hope that Jones will insult you, is caused by the satisfaction or frustration of a wish (that Jones insult you) together with an epistemic state of uncertainty. (You do not know whether or not Jones will insult you.) Gordon is clearly giving an account of emotions that treats them as very much like cognitions. He wants to bring emotion into the orbit of cognitive science by producing computer simulations of emotions that treat them as belief–desire structures that explain and predict our actions. But it is noteworthy that most of Gordon's examples are very 'thinky'. They are all propositional, as I have said, and they include such 'unemotional' examples as 'fear that it will rain' and 'regret that one has stepped on a pine cone'. Few, if any, of the emotions he describes could be attributable to a rat or even a monkey. And as for human beings, it seems perfectly possible to be in a 'factive' or 'epistemic' emotional state without actually feeling emotional at all.[3] In contemporary American urban culture, it is only in exceptional circumstances that people get very worked up about whether or not it will rain. Even if our emotional states are caused by beliefs and wishes in the way

Gordon describes, it seems that something else must be present in the causal chain that leads to genuine emotional experience.

Gabriele Taylor has given cognitive analyses of shame, pride, and guilt that are similar in style to Gordon's analyses. For example, she gives the following analysis of 'pride the passion' (as opposed to pride the character trait):

a person who experiences pride believes that she stands in the relation of belonging to some object (person, deed, state) which she thinks desirable in some respect. This is the general description of the explanatory beliefs. It is because (in her view) this relation holds between her and the desirable object that she believes her worth to be increased, in the relevant respect. This belief is constitutive of the feeling of pride. The gap between the explanatory and the identificatory beliefs is bridged by the belief that her connection to the thing in question is itself of value, or is an achievement of hers.[4]

In other words the feeling of pride is itself constituted by a belief, the belief that *identifies* the emotion pride. This belief in turn is grounded upon a belief that *explains* why the person holds the identificatory belief. Suppose, for example, that I am proud of my beagle, Bobby. For Taylor this means that I believe Bobby to be a splendid beagle who belongs to *me*, and it is in virtue of the fact that I own this spectacular creature that I believe my self-worth to be increased. This is an interesting analysis, but, like Gordon's, it doesn't get to the heart of what makes an emotion such as pride *emotional*.

The same cannot be said of the philosopher, Robert C. Solomon, who comes to the topic of emotion from a background in existentialism. In his groundbreaking 1976 book *The Passions*, Solomon argues that an emotion is a special kind of judgement, or set of judgements: an emotion always involves 'a *personal evaluation* of the *significance* of [an] incident'. It is an evaluative judgement about 'our Selves and our place in the world'.[5] An emotion is a judgement that concerns matters that are very important to oneself, and one's interests, values, and goals. Thus the emotion of anger is at its core an evaluative judgement that someone has wronged or offended me. It involves both a personal evaluation, and a *moral* judgement, an appeal to moral standards. 'My anger *is* that set of judgements.'

Central to Solomon's account of emotion is that emotions, like judgements, are—usually, at least—*about* something or other. Emotions, as philosophers say, have _intentionality_: they are directed towards something. It seems to make no sense to say that I am envious but I don't know what I'm envious about, or that I am in love but not with anyone in particular. Similarly, judgements are _about_ something and have intentionality: I judge that Jones has wronged me or I judge that Joe is loveable. So both emotions and judgements have content, and both seem to involve cognitions. Of course this does not prove that an emotion _is_ a judgement, but it shows that it could be. It also suggests that an emotion cannot just be a twinge or a pang, an increased heart rate or a change in the facial musculature, or the tendency to run away or weep. Emotions can't be reduced to feelings or physiological states or bits of behaviour.

Solomon likes to make the point[6] that a change in an evaluative judgement that I make may _ipso facto_ produce a change of emotion. I cannot be angry that you have insulted me if I learn that you did not in fact insult me. If I thought you said 'You cow!' and then I discover that you really said 'Oh wow,' my anger is likely to change to relief and amusement. A change in the judgement seems to entail a change in the emotion, and/or the abandonment of the emotion.

The view that emotions simply _are_ evaluative judgements might be thought extreme, since other things seem to be important to emotion too, such as action tendencies and physiological changes. But it seems eminently reasonable to think that emotions must at least _include_ some kind of judgement. Being angry that you have called me an insulting name seems to entail that I judge what you said to be an insult: I judge that you were 'calling me an insulting name' and 'wronging me by calling me an insulting name'. Likewise, it seems to be impossible for me to be ashamed or remorseful about neglecting my children unless I acknowledge that I did neglect them and evaluate my neglecting them as a bad thing to do.

Furthermore, we argue with people about their emotions; we say that I _should not_ be angry with you, because you did not insult me at all. We say that I _ought_ to feel ashamed for neglecting my children, because what I did was immoral. This suggests that we are arguing about evaluative judgements: you are trying to convince me that I am right or wrong to make a particular evaluative judgement. If emotions were nothing but feelings or physiological changes, argument would be beside the point: normally you would not try to argue somebody out of a twinge, a pain, or an accelerated heart-rate.

William Lyons hails from the tradition of analytic philosophy but he too holds a version of the judgement theory. In his 1980 book, *Emotion*, which has had a big influence on philosophers writing about emotion, including especially those who write about the theory of the arts, Lyons defended what he called the 'cognitive-evaluative' theory of emotion, which emphasizes both judgement and physiological change. More precisely, emotion is defined as 'a physiologically abnormal state caused by the subject of that state's evaluation of his or her situation'.[7] For Lyons, then, emotion is not identified with a judgement but with a physiological state that is caused by a judgement. However, like other cognitive theorists, he believes that emotions are caused by 'cognitive evaluations' of a situation, and that different emotions are distinguished by their characteristic evaluations. 'Generally speaking,' he says, 'an emotion is based on knowledge or belief about properties.'[8] For example, love is based on the (loveable) properties the beloved is believed to have; anger is based on an evaluative belief that someone has done me wrong.

Whatever their differences, Gordon, Taylor, Lyons, and Solomon all agree on one important point: they all stress that the 'judgements' that are involved in emotion are *evaluative* judgements about a situation in terms of one's own wants, wishes, values, interests, and goals. It is an evaluation of the personal significance of something going on in the (external or internal) environment, either the external environment of other people, things, and events, or the internal environment of one's own thoughts, memories, and imaginings. As Lyons puts it, an emotion involves 'an evaluation of some object, event or situation in the world about me in relation to me, or according to my norms'.[9] Solomon even goes so far as to say that our emotions are 'the very core of our existence, the system of meanings and values within which our lives either develop and grow or starve and stagnate'.[10] Even Gordon, whose theory is so very 'thinky', notes the crucial importance to emotion of our wants and wishes.

We find similar themes among psychologists who defend a cognitive theory of emotions.[11] Richard Lazarus, for example, has claimed that the relevant 'judgement' that forms the 'core' of an emotion is always an '[a]ppraisal of the significance of the person-environment

relationship'. Indeed he claims that such an appraisal 'is both necessary and sufficient' for emotion to occur; 'without a personal appraisal
(i.e. of harm or benefit) there will be no emotion; when such an
appraisal is made, an emotion of some kind is inevitable'.[12] Psychologists are interested in systematizing the emotions and so have tried to
come up with typologies of these appraisals. Lazarus has identified
what he calls 'core relational themes' for each type of 'basic emotion',
which essentially identify the evaluations necessary for each basic
emotion type. Thus the theme for anger is 'a demeaning offense
against me and mine', that for envy is 'wanting what someone else
has', and that for sadness (sorrow and grief) is 'having experienced an
irretrievable loss'.[13] The 'basic emotions' for Lazarus are anger, anxiety, fright, guilt, shame, sadness, envy, jealousy, disgust, happiness,
pride, relief, hope, love, and compassion. He bases his list on the
different relationships between person and environment that underlie
each emotion. 'A core relational theme is simply the central (hence
core) relational harm or benefit in adaptational encounters that
underlies each specific kind of emotion. . . . Each individual emotion
or emotion family is defined by a specific core relational theme.'[14]

In a somewhat different research strategy, the psychologist Andrew
Ortony has distinguished three classes of emotion based on the different kinds of appraisal that produce them: 'appraisals rooted in goals',
'appraisals rooted in standards and norms', or 'appraisals grounded in
tastes and attitudes'.[15] Ortony and his colleagues identify different
types of 'valence' such as the desirability or undesirability of events,
the praiseworthiness or blameworthiness of agents, and the appeal or
lack of appeal in objects. They speculate that emotions serve to
represent in a conscious and insistent way (through distinctive feelings
and cognitions) the personally significant aspects of construed situations. Throughout his account, Ortony—like Gordon—emphasizes
the 'eliciting conditions' for emotion, the 'appraisals' that set in
motion an emotional experience.

Despite their differences, both Lazarus's theory and Ortony's emphasize that the appraisals central to emotion are of harm and benefit.
Given the kind of creatures that we are, if an event is evaluated as 'a
demeaning offense against me and mine', or as 'an irretrievable loss',
it is evaluated negatively, as in different ways productive of harm to
me. Similarly, Ortony has essentially distinguished three different

ways in which emotional evaluations can have an impact on one's well-being: one can evaluate a person, situation, or event as promoting or conflicting with one's goals, one's standards and norms, or one's tastes and attitudes.

What's Wrong with the Judgement Theory?

As we have seen, the judgement theorists disagree about exactly how to characterize the relation between emotion and judgement. Some think that emotions are identical to judgements, others that judgements are *sufficient* for emotions, and others again that judgements are a necessary condition for emotions but not sufficient.

The most obvious objection to the view that an emotion should be *identified* with an 'appraisal' or evaluative judgement is the fact that you can make the relevant judgement without feeling the corresponding emotion. Solomon asserts that my anger at Jones for stealing my car *is* the judgement that Jones has wronged me by stealing my car. 'Similarly, my embarrassment *is* my judgement that I am in an exceedingly awkward situation. My shame *is* my judgement to the effect that I am responsible for an untoward situation or incident. My sadness, my sorrow, and my grief *are* judgements of various severity to the effect that I have suffered a loss.'[16] But of course I can judge that I am in an awkward situation without being embarrassed: I might be amused or depressed, or simply unmoved and dispassionate about the situation. Similarly, I can judge that I have suffered a loss without being sad, sorrowful, or grieved.

The same objection can be made to the view that an evaluative judgement is sufficient for an emotion, i.e. that once you have made the judgement that's all you need for the emotion to occur. Lazarus, for example, claims that an appraisal of the personal significance of the person–environment interaction is both necessary and sufficient for emotion. If I appraise the situation as one in which a demeaning offence has been committed against me or mine, then anger is inevitable. But all the examples of appraisal that Lazarus gives, like those of Solomon, are open to the same objection: I can judge dispassionately that a demeaning offence has been committed against me or mine, yet philosophically shake my head and murmur forgivingly: 'It's the way of the world.' Even if I make the 'right' judgement, anger is not inevitable. It is hard to resist the conclusion that—at least as far as concerns the examples typically given by judgement theorists—a judgement is not sufficient for an emotion to occur.

Solomon has recognized this objection and tried to rebut it. On occasion he has argued that an emotion is not a single judgement, but a system of judgements. So my anger is not just the judgement 'you have insulted me', but it is this judgement in the context of a set of other judgements. For example, these judgements might include 'calling me a cow is anti-feminist, vulgar, and demeaning', 'it is a personal insult and personal insults are immoral', 'insults are immoral in that they risk damaging self-esteem', and so on. However, merely multiplying judgements in this way is not by itself a solution, since it is conceivable that I could make all the judgements in the system of judgements identified with anger, and yet make them in a dispassionate way without actually 'getting angry'.

At other times, Solomon says that an emotion is a judgement of a special kind: emotions are 'self-involved and relatively *intense* evaluative judgments. . . . The judgments and objects that constitute our emotions are those which are especially important to us, meaningful to us, concerning matters in which we have invested our Selves.'[17] Elsewhere he characterizes emotions as 'urgent' judgements: 'emotional responses are emergency behavior'. An emotion is 'a necessarily hasty judgement in response to a difficult situation'.[18]

However, to call a judgement 'intense' seems odd unless you are already convinced that some judgements are emotions: emotions may be intense, but judgements are not normally thought of as the sorts of things that admit of degrees of intensity. And to define emotions as 'urgent' judgements is also problematic. I may start to be *afraid*—say, about the state of my stock portfolio—only after months of painstaking statistical analysis. Similarly, if my anger is identified as a judgement that a demeaning offence has been committed against me or mine, this too may be a judgement that results from long and careful study.

Some judgement theorists concede that judgements are not sufficient for emotion. Gordon, for example, thinks that a belief that the government has raised taxes and a wish that the government had *not* raised taxes, *together with certain other conditions*, are sufficient for anger, resentment, or indignation that the government has raised taxes. But Gordon says nothing at all about what these other conditions might be.

Lyons has a more concrete suggestion: that while an evaluative judgement all by itself is not sufficient for an emotion to occur, if the evaluation causes an 'abnormal physiological response', this *is* sufficient for emotion to occur. This is a valuable suggestion which will in a certain sense turn out to be accurate. The trouble with this suggestion is that it does not explain why sometimes an evaluative judgement leads to physiological change and hence emotion, while at other times what appears to be the very same evaluative judgement *fails* to lead to physiological change and emotion. Thus, to appeal to one of Lazarus's examples, the judgement that a demeaning offence has been committed against me or mine sometimes produces anger, but sometimes it produces anxiety, sometimes sadness, and sometimes merely a philosophical shrug of the shoulders. The very same judgement with the same propositional content sometimes produces physiological change and sometimes not. This is something that needs to be explained. Nevertheless, Lyons's suggestion is a good one.[19] Essentially he is arguing that emotion requires an evaluative judgement but that this is a necessary, not a sufficient condition for emotion.

Emotions as Ways of Seeing the Environment

All the judgement theorists I have been discussing agree that making an evaluative judgement is necessary to having an emotion: without a judgement there can be no emotion. All these theorists also believe that the kind of evaluation that is so important to emotion is an evaluation of the environment in terms of one's own interests, desires, goals, and so on. How can I be afraid without evaluating something as a threat, or ashamed without evaluating my deeds as morally wrong?

Furthermore, it seems like a reasonable supposition that emotions can be distinguished from one another by means of the evaluations they require. Different theorists characterize these evaluations with more or less precision and subtlety. Solomon's and Taylor's accounts of emotions explain in great detail what evaluations must be made if one is truly to be said to be ashamed, or proud, or whatever.[20] Other theorists with different agendas are less exact. Gordon's analysis of positive and negative factive emotions lumps together many different emotional states. Thus, where 'p' stands for any proposition, anger, indignation, and resentment that p all involve a belief that p and a wish that not-p. Lazarus, who, as a psychologist, is presumably less interested in the nuances of conceptual analysis than in a workable framework for experimental research and clinical practice, gives fairly crude accounts of the different evaluations he deems necessary to each emotion. For example, one can presumably be sad without experiencing 'an irrevocable loss', and 'taking in or being close to an indigestible object (metaphorically speaking)' is at best a clumsy analysis of the evaluation necessary to disgust.[21] Like all psychologists, Lazarus is trying to come up with a framework for the scientific study of the emotions, and so he is naturally more interested in a general account of the cognitive appraisals that he thinks are necessary to basic *types* of emotion rather then coming up with accurate accounts of how to use English words such as 'angry', 'sad', or 'disgusting'.

Philosophers have a tendency to think of emotions as mental states directed at propositions. This makes an emotion seem like a purely internal mental phenomenon. By contrast, the psychologist Lazarus does not describe his 'core relational themes' in terms of *propositions* that a person judges to be true, but rather in terms of *situations* in which people interact with the environment. Lazarus is not very clear about how he thinks of these interactions, but it would seem that if my anger is evoked by 'a demeaning offense against me or mine', I must be reacting to a situation that I 'see' as 'a demeaning offense', whether or not I actually have a firm *belief* that such an offence has occurred. And in grief I am reacting to a situation that I see *as* 'an irrevocable loss'. In other words, I see the environment under a particular description—demeaning offence, irrevocable loss—although I don't necessarily have a considered opinion that the environment really is the way that it currently *appears* to me.

Emotions are broadly categorizable in terms of what are sometimes called 'formal objects'. When I am afraid, for example, I regard the situation as threatening; when I am in love, I regard the person in question as amiable and/or desirable. Fear is necessarily directed at a threatening situation; anger is necessarily directed at a demeaning offence; adult sexual love is necessarily directed at a desirable person (or perhaps we should say a person-like creature, since, according to the novelist Marian Engel, it is possible to fall in love with a bear[22]). We don't have to describe what emotions are directed towards as propositions (I am angry *that I have been offended*). Indeed I do not think I have ever been in love with a proposition (or a bear, for that matter). Instead, we can characterize these formal objects as the environment-considered-or-viewed-under-a-certain aspect (threatening, demeaning, loveable). As Lyons puts the point:

An emotional state . . . is labeled as 'fear' rather than 'love' or 'grief' because [it is] believed to be the result of an evaluation that something is dangerous rather than that it is appealing (or good in the eyes of me, the lover), which would be the evaluation typical of love, or that it is a grave loss or misfortune, which would be the evaluation typical of grief. The categories 'the dangerous,' 'the appealing,' . . . and 'the grave loss or misfortune' are what is called the formal object of fear, love, and grief respectively.[23]

Lyons is treading on treacherous ground here. Just as it is inadequate for Lazarus to define the core relational theme of sadness in terms of 'having experienced an irrevocable loss', so it is inadequate to describe fear as always directed towards 'the dangerous'. Notoriously I can be afraid of my own shadow. But the general point is a useful one: the evaluations that help to define the various emotions are evaluations of the environment considered or viewed under various different aspects: as a threat or as an offence, as friendly or hostile, as tragic or comic.

Because philosophers tend to talk about emotions as private conscious mental states directed towards propositions, they also tend to think of emotions as quintessentially human phenomena. But emotions are essentially ways in which organisms interact with their environments. As we shall see, fish and even insects respond emotionally to their environments, and some non-human mammals have a fairly rich emotional life. Human beings, with their capacity for language, enjoy more diverse and subtly differentiated emotional states than do fish or monkeys, but their emotions too are not essentially private events but interactions with the environment, ways in which people deal with the characteristic situations in which they find themselves, situations arising from the nature of their physical limitations, as well as their physical and social environment. Emotions are ways of evaluating the environment in terms of how it affects the organism, and this is just as true whether we are thinking of crayfish, frogs, cats, chimpanzees, or human beings. So for this reason alone I think it is wise to think of emotional states not as directed towards propositions (*the fact that* Jones has offended me by stealing my car or *the thought that* I have suffered an irrevocable loss) but as provoked by the environment, whether internal (our thoughts and imaginings) or external (Jones and death and taxes), viewed under a particular *aspect*, as threatening, as amiable, as offensive, etc. Emotions are provoked when frogs, cats, or humans interact with the environment, viewed in terms of its effect upon their wants, interests, and goals.

What Are the Judgements in the Judgement Theory? The Greenspan and Rorty Critique

It looks as if there is general agreement that making an evaluation is a necessary condition on emotion in general, as well as essential to distinguishing one emotion from another. The trouble is that an 'evaluation' may not always be the sort of evaluative *judgement* discussed by the judgement theorists. A number of arguments have been advanced by philosophers to cast doubt on the idea that emotions entail evaluative *judgements*. Some have argued that although the evaluations involved in emotion have propositional content, as evaluative judgements do, in emotion this content is not *judged* or *believed* to be true; in emotion we take an attitude to propositional content that is less exacting than belief or judgement. Other philosophers have taken a more extreme position and argued that in some cases emotions do not have propositional content at all, and that to experience an emotion is more like perceiving or paying attention to something in a certain way—a kind of 'seeing-as'—than it is like judging or believing something to be the case.

Patricia Greenspan[24] has come up with an ingenious argument designed to show that emotions cannot be judgements or beliefs, because they have different criteria of rationality from judgements or beliefs. More generally, she shows that emotions have different formal logical properties from judgements or beliefs. Greenspan imagines a situation where a close friend (let's call her Jane) and I are vying for some coveted good such as a prize. When Jane wins the prize I experience 'mixed feelings': on the one hand I am *happy* that she won, because she is my friend and I love her, but on the other hand I am *unhappy* that she won, because I wanted to win myself. Greenspan argues that if emotions were judgements, then in the imagined case I would be simultaneously judging that it is good that Jane won and that it is not good; but these judgements are inconsistent and to maintain them both simultaneously would be irrational. If I am to be rational about these judgements, I would have to either *qualify* them, judging that in some respects it is good that she won and in some respects not good, or alternatively I would have to *sum up* my judgements, judging that it is on the whole good that she won or on the whole not good.

However, Greenspan argues, this is not true for the corresponding emotions. If I am happy that Jane won the prize and simultaneously unhappy that she won, I am not obliged to either qualify or sum up my emotions in order to be a rational person: it is perfectly rational for me to maintain both my happiness and my unhappiness. Of course I *could* qualify my emotions or sum them up, being happy about my friend's winning while unhappy that I failed to win, or feeling on the whole happy or on the whole unhappy that she won. But Greenspan's point is that I don't *have* to do this in order to be rational, whereas in the case of the corresponding judgements, I do have to do this in order to be rational.

Greenspan argues that whereas an impartial judgement has to be assessed for rationality on the basis of *all* the available evidence, an emotion, by contrast, 'is appropriate as long as there are adequate reasons for it, whatever the reasons against it'. Emotions 'are based on reactions to particular facts, as they come into consciousness, rather than consideration of all the relevant reasons'.[25] So my simultaneous happiness and unhappiness that Jane won the prize are based on different subsets of the available evidence and so are not inconsistent in the same way as an impartial judgement based on a consideration of *all* the relevant data would be. Greenspan's conclusion sheds some light on Solomon's idea that emotions are 'self-involved' and directed towards matters that are especially meaningful or important to us, for if an emotion is based on only a subset of the available evidence, this may be because it is focused only on those aspects of a situation that are particularly significant to our 'Selves'. In this particular case, one subset of the evidence concerns the situation as it affects me, and another different subset of the evidence concerns the situation as it affects one of 'my own', namely Jane.

Interestingly, these features of emotion that Greenspan points out link emotion not with beliefs or judgements but with desires. My simultaneous happiness and unhappiness that Jane won the prize are due to two simultaneous desires, on the one hand the desire that my friend win, and on the other hand the desire that I win. Like emotions, desires are resistant to qualification and to summing. It is perfectly rational to maintain both these desires without summing them and arriving at a summary desire that on the whole one of these actions carries the day over the other.[26] After all, it is an adaptive feature of human beings that they act to satisfy their own desires, but it is just as important for human well-being that we act to satisfy the desires of other people, especially those in our closest social group, so it is also adaptive for me to act to satisfy the desires of my close friend Jane. Hence, as Greenspan points out, it would not necessarily be rational for me to sum up my desires, judging that on the whole Jane's winning the prize is good (or bad). Similarly, it is not necessarily rational that I qualify my desires, judging that in some respects one desire is more important than the other.

In later work on emotion Greenspan has described emotions as states of 'comfort or discomfort directed towards evaluative propositions'. In other words, she thinks that there is an 'evaluative component' of emotion, but denies that this evaluative component is necessarily a judgement. In her view, emotions are always directed at some proposition, but the relevant 'propositional attitude' does not have to be a belief. When I am in a particular emotional state, I may merely entertain the relevant proposition; I do not have to endorse it. For example, I may be afraid of Fido, a loveable and harmless old dog, perhaps because of some traumatic incident with a dog when I was a child, but I do not necessarily believe or judge that Fido is dangerous. I may merely have a '*thought* of danger' in his presence. Greenspan agrees with the judgementalists that there is an evaluative component of fear, but she wants to deny that this evaluation has to be an evaluative *judgement* or a belief. When I am afraid of poor old Fido, Greenspan says that I 'feel as though' danger is at hand. I am evaluating Fido as dangerous in some sense, even though I sincerely believe that he is not.[27]

In another example, Greenspan says that she herself has a 'somewhat phobic fear of skidding, ever since a car accident in a blizzard'. On a later occasion when travelling with someone who is driving slowly and safely along an empty road, a slight skid caused her to 'gasp audibly for a second out of fear'. Greenspan says that she 'felt for a second as though danger were at hand' but did not act as she would have if she *believed* or judged that she was in danger. She didn't alert the other passengers, for example. Greenspan interprets this situation as one in which I make an unconscious 'danger-evaluation' (as she calls it) without *believing* I am in danger, without consciously judging that I am in danger.[28]

The cases Greenspan focuses on are examples of irrational fear: a person fears Fido or a skid even though she knows neither is harmful. In these cases, it is not at all obvious that 'thinking' in any normal sense is going on at all: the response seems to be automatic, like a reflex. They are cases of what Lyons calls 'Pavlovian' emotions, and these examples are problematic for any view that insists that some type of belief or judgement or 'cognitive evaluation' is essential to emotion. Greenspan's solution to the problem, however, is equally problematic. If in fear I merely have a 'thought of danger' rather than a belief that I am in danger, it is mysterious why this would *motivate* any behaviour in me at all. If Fido merely makes me feel as though danger were at hand, why do I avoid him with the same care that I take to avoid younger, larger, and fiercer dogs? It is true that Greenspan acknowledges that after the skid she is not motivated to alert her fellow passengers to any danger, but if the skid brings merely a *thought* of danger, why does she cry out? On the face of things, it would seem that I can think about danger all day long without ever becoming afraid or acting to avoid it. And by the same token a thought of danger does not seem sufficient to produce any of the physiological symptoms of fear.[29]

Another problem with her theory is that since she wants to insist that emotions are directed at propositions, it follows on her view that non-human animals do not have emotions. A cat, for example, cannot be said to be genuinely angry unless we can 'attribute to it at least some evaluation of the situation'. Without a propositional object, the cat's state cannot properly be termed 'emotional'; it is rather a 'pure feeling of arousal' which people, thinking anthropomorphically, and finding in the cat's behaviour the same kind of perceptual causes and behavioural effects that we find in human anger, mistakenly term 'anger'.[30]

Some philosophers have gone further than Greenspan and have argued that emotions do not have to have propositional content at all, not even a content that is 'held in mind' rather than believed. Amélie Rorty has drawn attention to the way in which emotions sometimes persist even though the corresponding judgement or belief is rejected.[31] She tells the tale of Jonah who for deep reasons going back to his childhood and his relationship with his mother, resents Esther, his female boss. But he does not judge or believe that Esther is unfair and dictatorial; indeed he sincerely denies that she is. His emotion persists even while the judgement on which it appears to rest is rejected.

As we have seen, Solomon argues that I cannot be angry that Jones has stolen my car if I discover that it is false that Jones has stolen my car. However, although it is strictly correct in these circumstances to say that I am no longer angry *that Jones has stolen my car*, I may still (perhaps irrationally) be angry and even angry with Jones. I may search around for something to be angry with Jones about, remembering or inventing other instances of Jones's turpitude. Or I may no longer be angry with Jones, but I am angry with my child for failing to put her tricycle away! If anger is prevented in one area, it has a way of spilling over into others, as in James Joyce's story, 'Counterparts', from *Dubliners*.

Rorty suggests that rather than looking for a judgement in every case of emotion, the 'intentional component' of emotions can sometimes take the form of 'patterns of intentional salience' such as a 'pattern of focusing on aspects of women's behavior construed as domineering or hostile rather than as competent or insecure'.[32] Jonah pays selective attention to what Esther does, and perceives it in a particular way: certain of her actions are salient to him and others not, and he interprets these salient actions negatively. He does not *judge*

Esther to be a tyrant; he simply cannot help *seeing* her that way. Interestingly enough, however, even in this example Jonah seems to be *evaluating* his boss—as dominating and hostile—even though he does not *believe* her to be dominating and hostile. As in Greenspan's examples, there is a disconnect between Jonah's emotional evaluations and his beliefs. Rorty's way of thinking has an advantage over Greenspan's however, in that if emotion involves some kind of seeing-as it would seem that many non-human animals are just as capable of emotion as human beings. All organisms pay selective attention to the environment, depending upon their needs, wants, and interests. Perhaps it will be objected that Jonah's interests are not served by the way he sees Esther. But as Rorty tells the story, we can infer a plausible explanation for his seeing Esther in the way that he does. In the story he *is* (indirectly) trying to satisfy his wants and interests. Because he is afraid of yet again being denied his mother's love, he defends himself against women in authority by seeing and treating them as tyrants. This satisfies his intense desire not to be hurt by a mother-surrogate (even though it cannot achieve his real goal, which is his mother's affection).

Like Rorty, Robert Kraut also emphasizes the relationship between emotion and perception.[33] Kraut points out that a cognitive-evaluative theory of emotion like that of Lyons is implausible with respect to many emotional phenomena. Love is especially recalcitrant to an analysis in terms of one's evaluative beliefs about the object of one's love. As Kraut shows, love is directed towards particular people, not sets of properties. If Walter loves Sandra solely on the basis of her properties—perhaps, he suggests, it is her marvellous piano-playing that attracts him—then he doesn't really love Sandra. For a doppelgänger of Sandra (Sandra 2) would have all Sandra's properties and so ought to be equally loved by Walter. However, it is a defining feature of love, according to Kraut, that it's not true that if Walter loves Sandra, he also loves Sandra 2. It certainly doesn't follow from the fact that Walter loves Sandra that he also loves Sandra 2. Indeed, if perchance Walter did love Sandra 2 as well as Sandra, it would have to be the case that he loved her on the basis of *different* properties. What Kraut is emphasizing is that love is an emotion that is not grounded upon a judgement or set of judgements; it is intentionally directed not at a proposition but at a particular irreplaceable individual. Kraut, in a way similar to Rorty, suggests that a better model for emotion would be perception rather than belief or cognition. At the same time, Kraut, like Rorty, seems to assume that emotions are based on some kind of evaluation: Walter sees the particular individual, Sandra, as loveable. Perceptions, after all, are value-laden, just as beliefs are.

Both Rorty and Greenspan want to maintain a principle of 'logical charity', according to which we assume rationality and consistency among beliefs unless there is good reason not to. However, given the many recent studies about the irrationality of what people believe and the lack of evidence on which they base their beliefs,[34] it may be that we cannot distinguish between the evaluations central to emotions and other evaluative beliefs we might have on the grounds that the latter, unlike the former, obey laws of rationality. Rorty and Greenspan may just be wrong in insisting that people's beliefs are in general consistent and based on a survey of all the evidence rather than just a subset of the evidence. It seems as though people's beliefs are frequently inconsistent and irrational and based on inadequate evidence. If this is true, then the insistence that the fear of Fido cannot be based upon a *belief*—even an unconscious belief—that Fido is a threat seems ill-founded. The person who's afraid of Fido may also—inconsistently and irrationally—believe that Fido is not a threat. Similarly, Jonah may *say* that he doesn't believe Esther is a tyrant but, unconsciously perhaps, he *does* believe that she is.

Despite these problems, however, Greenspan, Rorty, and Kraut have provided a valuable commentary on the judgement theory. They have demonstrated that even if emotions essentially involve some kind of evaluation, it is not at all obvious what that evaluation is. Must an evaluation be embodied in a *belief*? Can it be *unconscious*? Can it be merely a *thought*? Is it a type of *perception* or seeing-as? Can it be present in what looks like a reflex reaction? We will return to these questions in Ch. 2.

Some Conclusions

We can draw a number of conclusions from this discussion. First, the theory that says that emotions simply *are* judgements is false. We cannot define emotions in terms of judgements since however we describe the relevant judgement, it is always going to be possible to make the judgement yet fail to be in the corresponding emotional state: I can judge that you have wronged me or 'see you as' wronging me without being angry. I can judge that you are amiable and desirable, or view you as amiable or desirable without loving you. At the same time it seems as *if some kind of appraisal or evaluation is necessary for emotion* and that *we distinguish one emotion from another by reference to the different kinds of appraisal they require.* My anger requires some kind of assessment roughly to the effect that someone has wronged me or mine. My love for you requires that I find you amiable or desirable in some respect or other.

Secondly, it is important to notice that all the theorists I have discussed emphasize *the connection between emotion and our interests, wants, wishes, values, and goals.* Among judgement theorists, Gordon analyses emotion in terms of beliefs and wishes, and Ortony and Clore in terms of goals, norms, and attitudes. Solomon, Lyons, and Lazarus all talk of the relevant judgements being appraisals of the personal significance of an event or situation. Moreover, even those theorists who question whether emotion involves belief or judgement rather than a thought or a kind of seeing-as nevertheless emphasize that in emotional encounters with the environment a person thinks about or sees the environment in terms of what's important to that person. For Greenspan the evaluative thoughts in emotion are the object of a person's states of comfort or discomfort. Rorty argues that the evaluative component of emotion can be thought of in terms of 'patterns of salience'—of paying attention to the world under some particular aspect—rather than judgements, but in her examples she too seems to acknowledge that what we pay attention to in emotion are precisely those aspects of the world that we see as important to our own interests, wants, and goals. In short, whatever the evaluations in an emotion are, they are evaluations in terms of what we want, what we care about, what our interests are. If this is true, then it helps to explain why emotions are in general adaptive and why we have emotions at all in addition to dispassionate beliefs. For emotions seem to be ways in which an organism appraises the environment as satisfying or failing to satisfy its wants and interests.

Thirdly, although there is wide agreement that some kind of evaluation is present in every emotional encounter, yet *there is major disagreement about what these evaluations are*. According to the judgement theorists, the relevant evaluations are judgements or beliefs. According to their critics, the relevant evaluations may be evaluative thoughts, modes of paying attention, or even an uncomfortable sense that danger is nigh. Do emotions require a complex judgement with propositional content, or is some kind of more primitive 'unthinking' seeing-as or focus of attention all that's necessary? We will take up this question again in Ch. 2.

Finally, if emotion requires more than merely some kind of evaluation, then we need to figure out what is this something more. Lyons suggests that the other necessary element in an emotion is some kind of physiological change. This is an old idea in emotion theory and one that has been extensively explored by psychologists. In this chapter I have mainly talked about philosophers and their arguments. In the next chapter we will turn to the psychologists and see what light they can shed on the question of emotion.

2

Boiling of the Blood

But the natural philosopher and the dialectician would give a different definition of each of the affections, for instance in answer to the question 'What is anger?' For the dialectician will say that it is a desire for revenge or something like that, while the natural philosopher will say it is a boiling of the blood and hot stuff about the heart.

Aristotle, *De Anima*

The Central Importance of Physiological Changes in Emotion

William James, the father of modern psychology, argued that physiological change is essential to emotion. In his epoch-making *Principles of Psychology*[1] he famously pronounced that 'the bodily changes follow directly the perception of the exciting fact, and . . . our feeling of the same changes as they occur *is* the emotion'.

James was almost certainly wrong to say that 'every one of the bodily changes, whatsoever it be, is *felt*, acutely or obscurely, the moment it occurs', for it is not true that we are consciously aware of all the physiological changes that occur during emotional experience. Many visceral changes in particular take place below the level of awareness: we have no idea of most of the goings-on in our stomachs and intestines. Moreover, many non-human animals appear to evince such emotions as fear, rage, and contentment, yet it is unclear whether and to what extent such animals can be consciously aware of their bodily states. However, in his main points about emotion, James, as so often, is right on target. As we shall see, he is correct to

note that 'objects do excite bodily changes by a preorganized mechanism', and he is right to say that '*If we fancy some strong emotion, and
then try to abstract from our consciousness of it all the feelings of its bodily
symptoms, we find we have nothing left behind*, no "mind-stuff" out of
which the emotion can be constituted, and that a cold and neutral
state of intellectual perception is all that remains.'

James is often taken to be arguing for the view that an emotion is
nothing but a feeling of bodily changes. But in this quotation what he
seems to be saying is that there has to be an 'intellectual perception'
before there can be any emotion. It's just that an intellectual perception all by itself is not *sufficient* to produce an emotion. Physiological
changes are essential to turn an intellectual perception into an emotional state. In short, James makes the important observation that
without physiological changes there might be an intellectual perception that here is a dangerous situation, but there will be no fearful
emotional response.[2] In the terminology of Ch. 1, 'evaluations' are not
enough for emotion; there have to be physiological changes as well.
Notice that James is obviously not talking about long-term emotions
such as my enduring love for Joe or my nagging envy of Julia; he is
talking about emotional *responses*, which are short-term responses—
although, as we shall see, they may occur one after another.

Largely due to James's influence, there has been a long tradition in
psychology of studying the physiological symptoms of emotion. But
there is controversy over whether emotion involves a kind of generalized arousal, or whether there are distinct physiological changes
characteristic of particular emotional states. James's position was that
each emotion has a distinctive 'feeling' caused by distinctive physiological symptoms. However, he does not produce any hard empirical
evidence that different emotions exhibit different patterns of physiological activity. His old student turned critic, Walter B. Cannon, by
contrast, thought that emotion involves a generalized pattern of
arousal in the sympathetic nervous system, which he called the
'emergency reaction', and which he considered to occur not only
in emotional but also in non-emotional states such as pain, hunger,
and cold.

The emergency reaction—sometimes referred to as the 'fight or
flight' reaction—is a pattern of physiological activity that mobilizes
energy, 'either directly or by inhibiting physiological activity that

does not contribute to energy mobilization'. NicoFrijda describes the responses that comprise the pattern of arousal as follows:

increase in heart rate and heart stroke volume: increase in muscular blood flow; bronchial dilation; increase in activity of the sweat glands that results in the psychogalvanic skin response; increase in blood glucose level; constriction of the blood vessels in the skin, stomach, intestines, and sexual organs; decrease of gastric and intestinal motility; decrease of saliva flow; contraction of anal and urinary sphincters; pupillary dilation; increase in epinephrine secretion, which in turn triggers a number of the responses just mentioned. In addition deeper and faster respiration serves to meet increased oxygen requirements.[3]

This pattern is supplemented by characteristic hormonal changes, such as the release of ACTH (adrenocorticotropic hormone), the so-called 'stress hormone', which is responsive to stressful events and mobilizes energy to resist stress. For example, it stimulates the adrenal cortex to increase production of cortisol, which generates the production of glucose into the bloodstream. When an animal is under stress, the catabolic hormones (those that enhance metabolism) tend to increase, and the anabolic hormones tend to decrease. When the stressful situation is over, the anabolic hormones (those that restore energy) tend to rebound.

Although Cannon's 'emergency reaction' does occur in situations of stress, it is not true that this very same reaction is present in all emotions. Most obviously, while sympathetic activity is associated with arousal and stress, the parasympathetic system is associated with rest and tranquility. Calm or passive emotional states reflect the dominance of the parasympathetic nervous system rather than the sympathetic nervous system. Secondly, even among emotional states of arousal, there seem to be differences in the pattern of arousal between one emotion and another. As far back as the 1950s, A. F. Ax found that 'fear and/or anxiety is associated with increased secretion of epinephrine [adrenaline] and anger with increased secretion of norepinephrine [noradrenaline]'.[4]

One of the marks of the emergency reaction is an increase in the electrical conductivity of the skin (a rise in its ability to conduct electricity); it is best measured on the palms of the hands or the soles of the feet, where there is a high density of sweat glands. Skin conductance is not the same thing as sweating, but they are strongly correlated.[5] Interestingly, different emotions can to some extent be distinguished by means of differences in skin conductance. In the 1950s, studies by Ax found that fear as compared with anger showed greater average skin conductance, 'more muscle tension peaks, higher heart rate, and faster respiration'.[6] Other studies by Averill, Schwartz et al., and Ekman respectively have demonstrated that imagined sadness or sadness induced by films showed strongly increased skin conductance as compared with either imagined anger or imagined fear.

More recently, one of Ekman's collaborators, Robert Levenson, has asserted that we can identify 'four reliable differences among the negative emotions of anger, disgust, fear, and sadness' and a possible fifth.

These are: (a) anger produces a larger increase in heart rate than disgust; (b) fear produces a larger increase in heart rate than disgust; (c) sadness produces a larger increase in heart rate than disgust; and (d) anger produces a larger increase in finger temperature than fear. . . . The possible fifth difference is that sadness produces greater peripheral vascular dilation and greater speeding of blood to the periphery than the other negative emotions.[7]

In sum, the evidence suggests that Cannon's emergency reaction is not a mark of *all* emotions, and that different emotions exhibit different patterns of physiological activity.[8] But the evidence for emotion-specific physiology is hardly mind-boggling. As yet, I think, we are not entitled to infer that each 'basic' emotion has a uniquely identifying physiological profile. The differences that Levenson and others have found, while intriguing, are not sufficient to pick out each emotion uniquely.

Nico Frijda takes a different approach. After exhaustively cata-loguing what is known about the various physiological signs of different emotions, he concludes that responses differ both from one study to another and from one kind of 'fear' or 'pleasure' to another. In general, he argues that

physiological response patterns correspond to the functional requirements of dealing with the environment rather than to different emotions. . . . Physiological response in emotion, in Cannon's view, is functional for preparation of active, energy-requiring response. Other modes of dealing with the environment—other modes of activity or activity control, or of coping response—can be expected to correspond to other physiological response patterns, or of variations within some given pattern.[9]

In other words, for Frijda different patterns of physiological activity correspond to the action requirements of a given emotion-eliciting situation. In some instances different emotions such as fear and anger will exhibit the same pattern of activity, but sometimes they will not. By the same token, the same emotion (i.e. anger, fear, or sadness) will not always show the same pattern of physiological activity: 'There is calm joy and active joy, there is rigid and mobile fear, there is active and blocked or inner-directed anger, and so forth.'[10] In short, for Frijda physiological changes are associated with particular states of action-readiness, rather than particular emotional states.

So far, then, the reasonable conclusion to this discussion would seem to be that, although some distinctions can be made—in skin conductance and heart rate especially—among some 'basic' emotional responses, yet in 'standard' cases where there is no suppression of the response or other defeating conditions, no uniquely identifying physiological profiles have been discovered that would unambiguously distinguish every case of one emotion from every case of another. At this stage it looks as if emotions are going to have to be individuated not by some specific pattern of physiological changes but by means of some sort of evaluation.

Emotion and Facial Expression

That conclusion, however, may be too hasty. There is one particularly interesting set of evidence that shows that for at least some emotions, we can distinguish one emotional state from another by means of a particular kind of physiological change, namely changes in the facial musculature. Even more surprisingly, perhaps, it seems as if at least some emotions can be evoked without there being any kind of appropriate evaluation being made at all.

The pioneer in the study of emotional expression in human faces is Paul Ekman, who has conclusively demonstrated that for several emotions, there are universal facial expressions.[11] He has shown that there is remarkable agreement among different researchers using different methods about the facial expressions of anger, fear, enjoyment, sadness, and disgust. In his most recent book he expresses confidence that there are also universal facial expressions for surprise and contempt.[12] At the same time, Ekman does not think that there is one unique expression for every instance of these emotions. Rather, there are identifying expressions for every emotion *family*. 'Anger, for example, can vary in *strength*, ranging from annoyance to rage, and in *type*, such as sullen anger, resentful anger, indignant anger, and cold anger, to mention just a few,'[13] and these differences are written on the face. Ekman and his associate W. V. Friesen found more than sixty anger expressions. However, what is important is that each of the anger expressions shares particular muscular patterns, by means of which they can be reliably distinguished from the family of fear expressions, disgust expressions, and so on. 'For example, in all members of the anger family the brows are lowered and drawn together, the upper eyelid is raised and the muscle in the lips is tightened.' Other muscular actions may or may not be evident in anger expressions, such as 'a tightened lower eyelid, lips pressed together tightly or tightly open in a square shape, tightening of the lip corners, pushing the lower lip upwards, etc.'[14] Ekman is responsible for the best-known measuring device for facial expressions, which distinguishes each muscle movement in a given expression.

The evidence for universal facial expressions of Ekman's seven 'basic emotions' is based not just on 'high agreement across literate and preliterate cultures in the labelling of what these expressions signal', but also from 'studies of the actual expression of emotions, both deliberate and spontaneous, and the association of expression with social interactive contexts'.[15] Ekman has carried out several different sorts of experiment. Typical is one study focused on people in New Guinea who had had no prior contact with Westerners. In one set of experiments, subjects were told a story and asked to pick out from photographs the facial expression most appropriate to the story. In another set of experiments, subjects were asked to pose the expression itself; their facial expressions were then videoed and shown to students in the United States, who were asked to identify the expressions.

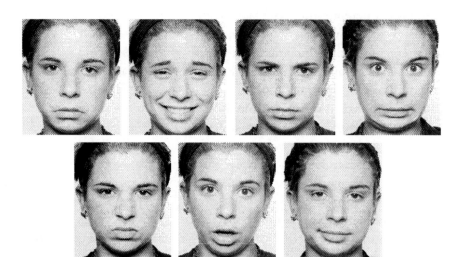

Fig 2.1. Examples of facial expressions of emotion, © Paul Ekman 2004

If Ekman is right, then there *is* emotion-specific physiology at least for some emotions, or families' of emotions.[16] We can tell different 'basic emotions' apart by their distinctive facial expressions.

If the facial expressions for the basic emotions are universal, how come people in different cultures exhibit different facial expressions in the same circumstances? Ekman conducted an ingenious experiment designed to show that despite appearances, there *are* universal facial expressions for the basic emotions, and that cultural differences are to be explained in terms of different 'display rules' in different cultures. American and Japanese students (in America and Japan respectively) were shown a gory and unpleasant film and their facial expressions were monitored without their knowledge. Each group of students responded with the same facial expression of disgust and revulsion. Then the students were told that a scientist would be present while they watched. In this scenario, the Americans continued to express revulsion, but the Japanese smiled politely: in the presence of an authority figure the display rules for their culture dictated that they should not exhibit any negative emotion.[17] However, when people are following display rules, there is almost always some 'leakage' of the emotion they are *really* feeling, even if it is only for a split second (what Ekman calls a 'micro-expression').

Ekman has shown that there are significant differences between unplanned spontaneous emotional expressions and deliberate, voluntary expressions.[18] Deliberate smiles, for example, are more often asymmetric than spontaneous smiles; they have different timing from spontaneous smiles, being either too short or too long; and they tend not to involve the muscle around the eyes.

Interestingly, there is good evidence that different neural pathways are employed in spontaneous and in deliberate expressions of emotion. Antonio Damasio has noted that patients in whom a stroke has destroyed the motor cortex in the brain's left hemisphere cannot produce a normal smile deliberately: the muscles cannot act and the mouth tends to be pulled towards the side that can still move normally. But when the patient smiles or laughs at a joke (i.e. spontaneously) the facial expression is completely normal.[19] By contrast, patients with a different neural deficit can smile only deliberately, not spontaneously.

Ekman has also studied the polygraph—i.e. the 'lie-detector'—and in his most recent book, *Emotions Revealed*, he notes that his work on lying has brought him into contact with 'judges, police, lawyers, the FBI, CIA, AFT, and similar agencies'.[20] It is often vitally important to know what someone's facial expression signifies, especially when it conflicts with other indications of what emotion the person is feeling. Not only are some people better than others at reading other people's facial expressions, but apparently some people—such as CIA agents and well-trained terrorists—are better than others at concealing their emotions, both facially and in other ways. In his book *Telling Lies*, Ekman points out some of the consequent dangers of relying too heavily on polygraph tests.[21]

Emotions Revealed is partly practical in its intent. Ekman painstakingly demonstrates the various positions of the face in the spontaneous expression of the various basic emotions as well as blends of those emotions, and at the end readers are invited to take a test to see how well they can discriminate facial expressions. His results also shed light on the possible consequences of the recent craze for Botox.[22] Injections of Botox paralyse the muscles of the face so that the price of beauty turns out to be inexpressiveness and consequent problems in personal relations!

In other research, Ekman has produced some fascinating results from studies of the facial expressions and autonomic nervous system

changes characteristic of emotion. There is evidence that physiological changes characteristic of specific emotions can be induced
directly by the manipulation of the facial musculature. Ekman has
found that when subjects moved their facial muscles without knowing what expression they were being asked to configure, there was
activity in both skin temperature and heart rate distinctive of the
particular emotion.[23] In other words, facial expression all by itself is
sufficient to produce autonomic nervous system changes characteristic of particular emotions. Ekman comments that although cognitive
mediation could not be ruled out, he believes that there is a direct,
central connection between the pathways from the motor cortex
which directs the facial musculature and hypothalamic areas involved
in ANS activity.[24] Both belong to an automatically induced system of
reactions, including autonomic, facial, and vocal expressions, which
are part of what Ekman refers to as an 'affect program',[25] a set of
responses that is 'complex, coordinated, and automated'.

To sum up our results so far. We have now got ample reasons for
believing that an 'evaluation' is not all that's necessary for emotion,
and Ekman's results suggest that perhaps an evaluation isn't even
necessary in some cases. Bodily changes of various sorts, however,
appear to be essential ingredients in emotion. As William James
suggests, it is physiological change that puts the 'emotionality' into
emotion. James seems to be right about this on both conceptual and
empirical grounds. Conceptually, there is nothing we can identify as
an emotional response unless there is marked physiological activity of
some sort or other. Indeed an emotional response *is*, at least in part, a
set of physiological responses. When—at the sight of my lost 2-year-
old toddling towards me out of the crowd—I respond by running
towards him, crying out, gasping, laughing, trembling, and turning
white, in a heady mixture of fear and joy, that set of gestures,
behaviour, and physiological responses *is* my emotional response.
Moreover, James's ideas have been empirically confirmed to the
extent that there are physiological changes characteristic of some
particular 'basic' emotions, especially changes in facial expression,
although it looks as if he was wrong to think that each and every
emotion with a distinct name has a distinct physiology.

In Ch. 1 we saw good reason for thinking that some kind of
evaluation is necessary to emotion. Now we find that physiological

changes are also necessary to emotion. Perhaps, then, we should accept Lyons's suggestion that emotions are—at least in most cases—'abnormal' physiological changes caused by a cognitive evaluation of something in terms of its importance to our wants, interests, and goals? However, we also saw in Ch. 1 that there are powerful arguments by some philosophers to the effect that the evaluations characteristic of emotion are not *cognitive evaluations* if that means ordinary dispassionate evaluative judgements. Psychologists have also provided good grounds for doubting that cognitive evaluations or 'cognitions' are what set off an emotional response. I turn now to their evidence.

Can Affect Precede Cognition?

There are several different types of evidence that psychologists have come up with, all tending to demonstrate that *cognitive evaluations* are not what induce emotion. One kind of evidence that casts doubt on the thesis that emotion is or entails cognitive evaluation comes from developmental psychology. There is good evidence that our earliest emotions or affects do not require complex cognition. The founder of behaviourism, John Watson, performed some notorious experiments on newborn babies.[26] He found that restraining the new-born's ability to move its head was a universal stimulus for rage, that sudden loss of support (dropping the baby) was a universal stimulus for fear, and that gentle caresses universally elicited pleasure (although Watson dubbed this response 'love'). Yet newborn babies do not seem to have the cognitive resources necessary to make cognitive evaluations such as 'That was an offence!' More recently—and more ethically—Andrew Meltzoff and Tiffany Field have studied the inborn ability of newborn infants to mimic the mother's smiling face and other expressions.[27]

Alan Sroufe has studied the way various emotion systems develop over time with the development of cognition. For example, at birth the infant shows 'intense crying and flailing, which may be considered the prototype of *rage*', due to 'covering the face, physical restraint' or 'extreme discomfort'; at about the fifth month rage can be due to 'disappointment',[28] i.e. the interruption of some specific ongoing activity, such as being unable to reach a visible object. What Sroufe considers anger proper emerges later, when, for example, the infant can perceive the *cause* of the interruption. In other words, at least 'proto-types' of emotion are present at birth, before the cognitions typical of anger are present. Klaus Scherer agrees. He argues that emotions depend on a sequence of what he calls 'stimulus evaluation checks', the most elementary of which he thinks are probably at least partly independent of higher cortical functions and may be a direct result of neural firing patterns. The most elementary, present at birth, are the check for novelty and the check for intrinsic pleasantness or unpleas-antness. One of the many interesting features of Scherer's research is that it shows how particular emotions evolve in the infant and young child in parallel with the evolving ability to make certain sorts of cognitive evaluation.[29] Sroufe and Scherer concur that full-blown cases of adult anger, love, and fear arise out of and require as precondi-tions primitive emotions (or affects) of infantile rage, pleasure, and fear.

What this research shows is that there are certain emotional states that are inbuilt in human beings and which do not appear to require cognition. The same is true of other species as well. Nico Frijda, in a discussion of 'unlearned stimuli', points out that many species—including human beings—respond 'instinctively' to the strange and weird. For example, dogs and apes are afraid of people dressed or behaving in unfamiliar ways; horses are afraid of flapping plastic bags; and Rhesus monkeys are terrified of mechanical moving monsters.[30] Moreover, other fear responses, while not inbuilt or present at birth, are easily acquired with very little learning, such as human fear of spiders and snakes.

The person who has done most to question the primacy of cogni-tion over affect, however, is the social psychologist, Robert Zajonc, who, in a series of articles,[31] has argued that, at least in primitive cases of emotion, 'affect' can occur without any prior cognitive appraisal. Psychologists tend to talk about 'affect' and 'cognition', rather than 'emotion' and 'judgement', but both philosophers and psychologists are talking about more or less the same thing. In claiming to show that affect precedes cognition, Zajonc is mounting a direct threat to the judgement theory, whether in its more extreme form in which emotions are said to be identical to judgements or in the less extreme form according to which cognitive appraisal is a necessary (but not sufficient) condition for emotion. Zajonc has accumulated a great deal of data designed to show that affect can precede and therefore does not require cognitive activity. In my view, the most compelling evidence comes from four sources in particular.

1. In the 'mere exposure effect' experiments, Zajonc and others have convincingly established that people prefer stimuli to which they have been exposed more often, even when the stimuli are presented so fast that the subjects cannot consciously recognize what they are seeing. For example, in one experiment, Zajonc and his colleague W. R. Wilson (later, Kunst-Wilson) flashed slides of irregular polygons to a group of subjects, which—it was independently established—appeared too fast for recognition. The subjects were asked to discriminate which of two polygons they liked better and which they had seen before. In this study the rate of recognition was virtually equivalent to chance, but the liking responses reliably distinguished between those polygons that were 'old' or (in some sense) 'familiar' and those which were 'new' or 'unfamiliar'. Kunst-Wilson and Zajonc conclude: 'Individuals can apparently develop preferences for objects in the absence of conscious recognition and with access to information so scanty that they cannot ascertain whether anything at all was shown. The results thus suggest that there may exist a capacity for making affective discriminations without extensive participation of the cognitive system.'[32]

2. More recently, Zajonc has undertaken a series of experiments designed to show that new affective reactions can be induced apparently without the intervention of cognition. In these experiments he and his colleagues have studied what he calls 'nonconscious affective priming', that is, inducing an affective reaction to a neutral stimulus such as a Chinese ideograph (presented to someone who does not know Chinese!) by priming the stimulus with an affective picture, such as a picture of a happy or an angry human face. The prime is exhibited to the experimental subjects so briefly that they are unaware they have seen anything, and yet the Chinese ideographs that have been primed by a smiling face are much preferred to those primed by an angry face. However, when the primes are presented more slowly so that they can be consciously recognized, this effect vanishes. Zajonc summarizes his results as showing that: 'suboptimal

[i.e. too fast for awareness] affective primes—in the form of facial expressions presented for only 4ms [milliseconds]—generated significant shifts in subjects' preferences for the target ideographs, whereas the same primes presented at optimal exposure durations [i.e. not too fast for awareness] did not'.[33]

3. Some of the most compelling data that Zajonc cites comes from classic experiments carried out in the early 1950s by Richard Lazarus (the appraisal theorist) and his associate R. A. McCleary, called the 'subception' experiments.[34] In these experiments people were presented with ten five-letter nonsense words. The subjects' galvanic skin responses were then conditioned to five out of the ten, using electric shock as the unconditioned stimulus. In other words, five out of the ten 'words' were associated with a shock, and when the subjects saw those words they responded with a heightened galvanic skin response. As we have just discussed, such a reaction is part of the 'emergency' response posited by Walter Cannon. All ten stimuli were presented an equal number of times, so that the subjects would be equally familiar with all ten. After the subjects had been conditioned in this way, a test was administered in which the words were presented at tachistoscopic speeds (too fast for recognition) and the subjects were asked to say what the word was that they had 'seen'. In the test itself no shocks were administered, but the subjects were not told this. The remarkable result of this experiment was that the galvanic skin response was much higher for words associated with shock than for those associated with non-shock, *even when the subjects were unable to identify* the words that had been presented to them. Lazarus called this effect 'subception', indicating a kind of perception that occurs below awareness: the subjects did not know which word had appeared to them, but their skin did! In Zajonc's terms, the subjects *disliked* certain words even though they had not cognitively processed them: they did not know what they were.

4. Zajonc also cites a number of studies by other people that he thinks lend weight to his conclusions. For example, he cites a 1980 article by John Garcia and his colleague K. W. Rusiniak about the relative merits of smelling and tasting as means of conditioning to poisoned food.[35] Garcia reports that in one experiment rats were presented with a new taste (a flavoured solution), and then fifteen minutes later with a nauseous substance. After imbibing the nauseous

substance (we are not told what it was), the rats developed an aversion to the previously presented taste. What is interesting about this experiment is that the nauseating substance was administered while the animal was anaesthetized. From Zajonc's point of view, the important point is that if the rat were making any 'appraisal', such an appraisal would have to make 'a rather remote connection between the ingested food and the nausea that occurred during anesthesia (and has probably been only vaguely registered)'. Zajonc concludes that it is 'highly unlikely that any sort of appraisal process, even unconscious, could have been involved when the animal rejected the [new taste] following conditioning'.[36]

Affective Appraisals

We saw in Ch. 1 that philosophers who maintain a judgement theory of emotion are widely in agreement that the relevant judgements concern matters of great importance to our needs and goals. Psychologists who are appraisal theorists concur. Richard Lazarus stresses that the judgement that forms the 'core' of an emotion is always an appraisal of 'the significance of the person-environment relationship'. He maintains that 'without a personal appraisal (i.e., of harm or benefit) there will be no emotion; when such an appraisal is made, an emotion of some kind is inevitable'.[37] Ortony and his colleagues agree that the appraisals central to emotion concern the way in which the environment can have an impact on one's well-being: in their terms the relevant appraisals are those which have an impact on one's goals, values, or tastes and attitudes.

However, as I emphasized in Ch. 1, a mere cognitive evaluation is not enough to generate an emotional response. One can cognitively evaluate the situation as one in which one finds oneself in an awkward position, and yet fail to feel embarrassment; one can cognitively evaluate the situation as a dangerous one without responding fearfully. How can this be?

The answer suggested by Zajonc's research findings is that there is an *affective appraisal* that concerns those things that *matter* to the organism and that occurs very fast, automatically, and below the threshold of awareness. This affective appraisal is *non-cognitive* in that it occurs prior to and independently of any cognitive evaluation. It serves to pick out and focus attention on those things in the internal or external environment that matter to the animal or human being and to appraise or evaluate them in terms of *how* they matter, for example, whether they are a good or a bad thing, a threat or an offence. The affective or non-cognitive appraisal causes physiological changes that then serve as feedback reinforcing the appraisal of threat or liking or whatever, and helping to fix attention upon its object.

Zajonc himself interprets his results as evidence that affect precedes cognition and that cognitive evaluation is therefore not necessary to emotion. Yet the data he cites can just as plausibly be construed as showing that at least some emotions involve primitive evaluations that occur below consciousness and independently of higher cognitive processing. Examples would include the preferences evinced by subjects in the mere exposure experiments, in which subjects 'evaluated' the tones or polygons they had been exposed to more often as pleasanter than the others. Similarly, in the subception experiments, subjects 'evaluated' some syllables as threats. In the experiment mentioned by Garcia, the rats 'evaluated' as disgusting the flavoured drink that they had been conditioned (under anaesthesia) to connect to a nauseating substance: they didn't like it. Similarly, the work by Scherer and Sroufe on infantile emotions such as fear, rage, and attachment, can be regarded as showing not that 'primitive' neonate emotions do not involve evaluations, but that they involve evaluations of a special kind, specifically, evaluations that do not involve any higher cognitive processing.

The kinds of affect that Zajonc has emphasized occur very fast and automatically. If we think of these affects as involving fast, automatic *appraisals*, then these appraisals include appraisals of liking or disliking, of disgustingness, and threat. (More of this in Ch. 3.) From an evolutionary perspective it seems plausible to speculate that fast, automatic appraisals are adaptive just because they take place more quickly than higher cognitive processes. Perhaps this explains why we need *emotional* appraisals as well as cognitions: emotional or non-cognitive appraisals can occur very fast because it is often important for us to respond very fast to what we perceive. It may be very important to us to know instantly whether something in the environment is friendly or hostile, is conducive to our well-being or not. It seems likely that

swift emotional appraisals are processed differently from slow, deliberate, dispassionate appraisals where truth and accuracy are more
important than a prompt response. Furthermore, as we have seen,
there is widespread agreement among appraisal theorists that emotional appraisals concern matters that are of significance to us, to our
survival, and/or our well-being. When we make emotional appraisals
of the environment, we are not asking questions of it in a spirit of
philosophical inquiry or intellectual curiosity. Again, it makes sense
that such appraisals may, at least sometimes, need to be made rapidly
because an urgent response is required for self-preservation.

We should also remember that emotions serve as signalling devices.
Those psychologists, such as Zajonc and Ekman, who have emphasized the role in emotion of motor activity and autonomic nervous
system changes, have noted that motor activity, including movement
of the facial musculature, plays an important role in emotion as signals
to others (and perhaps oneself) that one is in a particular state, and also
to subserve patterns of motor behaviour adaptive for a particular
emotion, preparing the organism for appropriate action (such as
fight or flight). It may well be that such signals often need to be both
made and recognized very quickly, perhaps before there is time to
deliberate over either one's own state of mind or that of the perceived
other person (or other organism). Facial expressions are crucial signals
to others: if you are threatening me with bared teeth and laid-back
ears, then I know immediately I had better back off and look humble.
My appraisal of your expression may be very rapid and hence unreliable. But it is better to have an organism that responds fast and mis-
takes your smile for a snarl than one that pauses to reflect and gets
attacked. The idea that emotional appraisals can be fast and automatic,
and use different neural pathways from cognition, combined with the
idea that emotional appraisals are ways of narrowly focusing on those
particular aspects of the environment that are crucial to our survival
and/or well-being suggests the idea that emotions should be concep-
tualized as special kinds of information-processing devices, and that
central to emotion is what I have called a non-cognitive or affective
appraisal.

It is ironic that Zajonc cites Lazarus's subception experiments in
support of his own position that affect precedes cognition, because
Lazarus himself, as we have seen, is a leading exponent of the theory

that emotion requires appraisal. In the 1980s Zajonc engaged in a
fairly acrimonious dispute with Lazarus, during which Lazarus
claimed that since emotions require appraisal, Zajonc's examples
were not of emotion at all, while Zajonc in turn accused Lazarus of
simply defining emotion in such a way that it necessarily requires
appraisal and any phenomena that do not cannot for that very reason
count as emotions. More recently, however, Lazarus seems to have
accepted that Zajonc's examples *are* examples of affect, while still
maintaining that affect entails appraisal.[38] His solution is to posit two
kind of appraisal, one conscious and deliberative, the other unconscious and automatic.

In his 1991 book, *Emotion and Adaptation*, which represents the
summation of over forty years of research on the emotions, Lazarus
claims that 'there are two different modes (perhaps systems) of appraisals: one *conscious, deliberate, and under volitional control*, the other
automatic, unconscious, and uncontrollable'. For example, the subception
experiments 'leave little doubt that discrimination between threat and
no threat had occurred at a preconscious or unconscious level. . . . Put
differently, subjects were making an automatic appraisal without
awareness.'[39] In short, Lazarus concedes that the subjects were experiencing 'affect', but he maintains that they are nevertheless 'appraising'
the stimuli in a simple, automatic way: 'it is not so outrageous to
argue that meaning is *always* (a high-risk word) involved in emotion,
because most if not all mammalian creatures are capable of simple,
learned evaluations of elemental categorical distinctions of harm,
threat, and benefit. There is no logical or empirical reason why
cognitive activity should not be regarded as a necessary condition of
emotion'.[40]

As Lazarus points out, because we can process the same bit of the
environment in two different ways, it is possible for us to believe
contradictory things simultaneously about it. For example, as a result
of conscious rational deliberation, including a study of the relevant
statistical data, I may conclude that flying is safe. But at the same
time, as I am about to take off in a plane, I make the uncontrollable,
non-conscious, automatic appraisal that it is very dangerous. In my
terms, I appraise the situation 'non-cognitively' as fearful, while
cognitively I appraise the situation as safe; I know that rationally
I should not be afraid. Lazarus points out that 'preconscious evalu-

ations' make only crude distinctions, such as 'good or bad', rather than the 'finely grade analogical distinctions'[41] that consciousness and language permit.

Interestingly, however, Lazarus still clings to the idea that these two kinds of appraisal are both based on cognitive activity, whereas Zajonc wants to insist that affect can precede any cognitive activity. However, as Phoebe Ellsworth, among others, has pointed out,[42] whether affect can precede cognition depends on what you mean by affect and cognition. Most theorists agree that we should keep the term 'cognition' for higher processes, although what counts as 'higher' and 'lower' is not very precisely definable, given our current state of knowledge. I think I am on the side of the majority in using the term 'cognition' only when we are talking about processes localized in the neo-cortex. Lazarus, by contrast, evidently thinks that even evaluations made at a subcortical level count as cognitions. The bottom line, however, is that whether these fast emotional appraisals are cognitive or not depends on how you define 'cognition'. The substantive point is that such fast emotional appraisals exist and that they do not require any higher processing. If an automatic appraisal of pleasure, aversion, or novelty counts as affect, virtually everyone now agrees that affect can occur prior to any higher cognitive processing. I will call such appraisals 'affective appraisals', and I shall assume that they are 'non-cognitive', in the sense that they occur without any conscious deliberation or awareness, and that they do not involve any complex information processing.[43]

Other theorists have made a similar distinction between two kinds of appraisal, one swift and automatic and vital to emotion, and another slower, deliberative, and conscious. Keith Oatley makes what I think is essentially the same distinction, although he makes it less clearly than Lazarus. Oatley contrasts what he calls 'semantic messages', which have propositional content, with 'control messages', which 'need not be parsed or interpreted',[44] but which function merely to activate particular cognitive and/or motor systems. Oatley claims that emotion signals are a kind of control message. One such message might prepare one to attack; another might activate fearful vigilance. Oatley describes 'basic emotion signals' in a way that suggests he thinks of them as the kind of 'non-cognitive appraisal' that I have tried to describe.

First, they make the system capable of rapid and unified response, interrupting ongoing activity and causing transition to readiness for a new one, without parsing, interpretation, or other computations that could be lengthy and may not reach completion. Second, longer-term maintenance becomes possible so that the system can stay in one of the organized states, or moods, that resist further transitions or the intrusions of other concerns.[45]

In short, 'emotion control signals' focus attention on some situation or event in the environment which is crucial to our own wishes, wants, and concerns; they keep attention so focused as long as that situation prevails; and they 'appraise' the situation in a rapid automatic way, without 'semantic content'.

Now, it might be objected that while paying selective attention to certain events in the environment and assessing them rapidly and automatically may be essential to emotion, they are also present in non-emotional situations. A carpenter surveying a newly constructed house will doubtless pay selective attention to those things that interest him and that he knows about, but he need not be in what we would normally consider an emotional state. The answer to this objection is that the 'non-cognitive appraisals' present in emotion *always result in physiological arousal, change in facial expression, or some other physiological response*, whereas the carpenter may be quite dispassionate. People in an emotional state not only automatically 'appraise' the situation as important to their wants, wishes, values, goals, interests, and concerns, but also respond physiologically to the situation. They are in a changed physiological state, which serves to reinforce the appraisal and maintain attention, and which signals to others (and maybe themselves) what state they are in.

The biological function of a human emotion is to alert the person to something in the (internal or external) environment which is of vital importance to the organism's interests, goals, wants, or values. Insects and fish presumably do not have values and goals, at least no values and goals that can be articulated in propositional form, but their emotions serve much the same biological function as human emotions do for us. The affective appraisal picks out from the multitude of competing stimuli those that are important to the organism and need to be dealt with. Physiological changes help the organism prepare for appropriate action. Indeed some theorists believe that action tendencies are the most important aspect of the emotion process.

Physiological changes play two other important roles, however, which should not be forgotten. First, many such changes affect the organism's appearance, which acts as a signal to others that the organism is in a particular state. The baby smiles in response to the mother's smile, thereby reinforcing the mother's affection. The angry gorilla's facial expression alerts other gorillas that they had better back off if they want to avert being attacked. A sad expression—whether in gorilla or human—lets the other members of the group know that an individual needs comforting. An expression of shame lets the members of the group know that the individual has done wrong; perhaps it is also a signal that the individual accepts group standards and sanctions, and is requesting reintegration into the group.

Another important role of the physiological changes that constitute the emotional response is that they act as feedback to the system, reinforcing the affective appraisal and helping to focus attention on it. When a person or other animal is startled by a sudden gunshot or some other very sudden loud noise, there is an immediate automatic response, which helps to fix attention on the stimulus. A mild version of such a response is what psychologists call the 'orienting' reflex. Similarly, when I am joyful the physiological changes characteristic of joy help to fix my attention on all the wonderful things that have happened; in sadness physiological changes reinforce the sad appraisals that I make.

A Perspective from Neurophysiology

In a series of articles culminating in his 1996 book *The Emotional Brain*, the neurophysiologist Joseph LeDoux has argued that there is no unitary phenomenon called 'emotion', but only a variety of emotion systems. Emotions are not peculiar to humans or 'higher' animals; the *basic* emotion systems are to be found in many 'lower' species, even insects and fish. These basic emotion systems are designed so that the organism can cope with fundamental life encounters. It is important to think of a basic emotion system as adapted through evolution to particular sorts of important interaction between the organism and its environment. LeDoux thinks that a list of basic emotions would correspond to a list of 'special adaptive behaviors that are crucial to survival'. His 'working hypothesis' is that 'different classes of emotional behavior represent different kinds of functions that take care of different kinds of problems for the animal and have different brain systems devoted to them'.[46]

The emotion system that LeDoux has studied most extensively is the fear system. The object of his study has been conditioned fear in rats, but his research has wide and important implications for naturally occurring fear—including fear in human beings—as well as for the study of emotion in general. LeDoux thinks that whatever your theory of emotion, the 'core' of an emotion system is 'a mechanism for computing the affective significance of stimuli'.[47] In other words, the organism can somehow 'appraise' or evaluate the emotional significance of a stimulus. As I have explained, Zajonc's results (among others) show that such an 'appraisal' can take place very quickly and prior to any conscious cognition or complex information processing. LeDoux's great contribution to emotion research has been to show how this can happen. He and his colleagues have discovered a fear circuit in the brain that operates very rapidly and without awareness; it can compute the affective significance of a stimulus without the organism's being able to recognize what the stimulus is.

LeDoux conditioned fear in rats to the sound of a buzzer (the conditioned stimulus) by using shock (the unconditioned stimulus). An 'appraisal' of threat unleashes a number of different responses that prepare the organism to deal with the impending danger. Interestingly, LeDoux has found that it does not matter very much which response the experimenter focuses on and measures. The same brain circuitry seems always to be involved. He himself has studied the freezing response, in which a fearful animal will stop all movement, and its concomitant blood pressure changes. Freezing as a response to perceived danger is very widespread among different species. It is often the safest thing to do in the face of danger; it also prepares the animal for subsequent rapid escape or for defensive fighting. Escape and defensive fighting are also very widespread responses, although of course the form that they take will depend on the animal's physical make-up: a bird will fly from danger, a fish will swim. The conditioned fear response also activates the autonomic nervous system: the muscles require extra blood, so there are various cardiovascular and other visceral responses that help maintain the freezing response, and stress hormones are released into the bloodstream 'to further help the body cope with the threatening situation'. Reflexes, such as the startle and the eyeblink reflexes are also 'potentiated', allowing 'quicker, more efficient reactions to stimuli that normally elicit protective movements'.[48] In summary, the conditioned response is an innate response that is artificially induced by conditioning to the buzzer sound.

The key to the fear system in the brain is the amygdala, a small almond-shaped formation in what is often referred to as the 'limbic system', which is where the emotional significance of threat is registered.[49] LeDoux found that when the rat hears the sound of the buzzer, the *auditory thalamus* is activated. The thalamus has been called a 'way station' in the brain, because it receives incoming stimuli and sends them on to different parts of the cortex, responsible for higher processing in the various different sense modalities (vision, hearing etc.). The auditory thalamus receives auditory signals and sends them on to the *auditory cortex* where the sound is 'cognitively processed:' the sound is identified, for example. The auditory cortex then sends signals to the amygdala where the emotional impact of the buzzer sound is assessed. However—and this is the important point—the auditory thalamus also sends signals *directly* to the amygdala, *bypassing the cortex* altogether. The amygdala computes the affective significance of the stimulus *before* the more precise information about what the stimulus is gets received from the auditory cortex. Significantly, for a rat it takes about 12 milliseconds (12 one-thousandths of a second) for an acoustic stimulus to reach the amygdala through the direct pathway from the thalamus, whereas it takes almost twice as long to traverse the cortical route.[50] The thalamo-amygdala and cortico-amygdala routes converge in the lateral nucleus of the amygdala. Once in the lateral nucleus, the signal is dispatched to the central nucleus of the amygdala which controls the characteristic fear *responses*, the freezing response, the release of stress hormones into the bloodstream, and the various cardiovascular and other visceral responses: increased blood pressure, sweating, increased galvanic skin response, etc. If information from the thalamo-amygdala route is co-ordinated with information from the cortico-amygdala route in the lateral nucleus of the amygdala, then presumably it would be possible for the information derived from the auditory cortex to confirm or disconfirm the information received directly from the thalamo-amygdala route; it could confirm whether the 'affective appraisal' is appropriate or not, and whether the responses generated should be maintained or aborted.

Significantly, the auditory thalamus cannot make very fine discriminations in a stimulus. It is in the auditory cortex that fine discriminations are made. LeDoux concludes that he has discovered two different pathways for processing the same sound. On the one hand there is a 'quick and dirty processing system', which responds very fast, warns the organism that something dangerous may be around without identifying it very carefully, and gets the organism to respond appropriately to whatever it is. And on the other hand, there is a slower, more discriminating processing system which operates through the cortex and figures out whether the thalamo-amygdala 'affective appraisal' is appropriate or not.

Imagine walking in the woods. A crackling sound occurs. It goes straight to the amygdala through the thalamic pathway. The sound also goes from the thalamus to the cortex, which recognizes the sound to be a dry twig that snapped under the weight of your boot, or that of a rattlesnake shaking its tail. But by the time the cortex has figured this out, the amygdala is already starting to defend against the snake. The information received from the thalamus is unfiltered and biased toward evoking responses. The cortex's job is to prevent the inappropriate response rather than to produce the appropriate one, Alternatively, suppose there is a slender curved shape on the path. The curvature and slenderness reach the amygdala from the thalamus, whereas only the cortex distinguishes a coiled up snake from a curved stick. If it is a snake, the amygdala is ahead of the game. From the point of view of survival, it is better to respond to potentially dangerous events as if they were in fact the real thing than to fail to respond. The cost of treating a stick as a snake is less, in the long run, than the cost of treating a snake as a stick.[51]

The idea of two different processing mechanisms of the same sensory stimulus is not new. Over forty years ago William Dember proposed that

the perceptual processing of a stimulus takes place at two levels. . . . The first level of perceptual processing engages the emotions. The visual system extracts sufficient information to make out the emotional significance of a stimulus, determining if it poses a threat or signals a reward. An observer's attention can shift to other features of the stimulus once the emotional significance of the stimulus is grasped. Classifying and identifying a stimulus is carried out by a second, higher level of perceptual processing, which many theorists associate with cognition and consciousness.[52]

What LeDoux has done is to discover the brain circuits that are responsible for these two levels of processing, at least in the fear system.

LeDoux cites a fascinating experiment that nicely illustrates the existence of the two different processing systems. In this experiment two similar tones were used, one of them conditioned to shock and the other not. Rabbits were conditioned to respond with increased heart rate to the sound associated with the shock and not to the other sound. Then the experimenters cut the rabbits' auditory cortices, so that the paths from the thalamus to the auditory cortex were severed. What happened was that the rabbits could no longer discriminate between the two similar sounds, so they reacted emotionally to *both* sounds, as if both had previously been associated with shock. LeDoux comments that the neurons in the thalamus that project to the auditory cortex are 'narrowly tuned—they are very particular about what they will respond to'. Neurons in the thalamus that project to the amygdala, however, are 'less picky':[53] they do not make fine discriminations. Consequently, when the rabbits' auditory cortices are damaged, they have only the direct thalamo–amygdala pathway to rely on and the amygdala treats the two (similar) stimuli in the same way.

In summary, LeDoux has shown that 'emotional responses can be rapidly initiated on the basis of crude stimulus properties prior to and independent of more complex stimulus transformations, such as those involved in the recognition of objects as semantic entities'.[54] He proposes that emotion and cognition should be thought of as 'separate but interacting mental functions mediated by separate but interacting brain functions'.[55] The initial response to fear is generated by an 'emotional appraisal' in the amygdala that happens very fast and prior to cognitive intervention. The subsequent slower 'cognitive appraisal' can parse the stimulus more precisely, assess the appropriateness of the prior automatic response, and presumably attempt to modify and control both the initial appraisal and the organism's subsequent responses. Such affective appraisals would require 'the existence of pathways that transmit sensory inputs to the affective system (i.e. amygdala) without first transmitting the inputs to the cognitive system (i.e. hippocampus)'.[56] And, as LeDoux has shown, such pathways do in fact exist. The evolutionary advantage in these mechanisms is that they act very quickly indeed and prepare the organism to take instant action when something of vital importance to the organism is at stake.

Reconsidering the Judgement Theory

In Ch. 1 I discussed the judgement theory of emotion according to which an emotion is or entails a judgement or 'cognitive appraisal.' We have now seen that this theory is false. There are in fact cases of emotion—or at least of 'affect'—that do not require a conscious complex judgement of the sort discussed by Gordon or Taylor. But at the same time, some kind of evaluation does seem to be essential to emotion, although the evaluations in question are not deliberate, conscious judgements with semantic content. They are rather *affective appraisals* requiring no cognitive intervention.

In Ch. 1, we considered the objections that several philosophers had to the view that emotions involve judgements or beliefs. Greenspan holds that the propositional content of an emotion does not have to be believed, but can be merely held in mind or entertained. Rorty thinks that an emotion is more like a pattern of salience than a judgement or belief. Finally, Solomon holds that an emotion is a judgement but a special kind of judgement, an urgent or emergency judgement. I think that the notion of a 'non-cognitive appraisal' makes sense of these various suggestions, because a non-cognitive affective appraisal has many of the features that have been pointed out by philosophers critical of the judgement theory.

Greenspan notes that the judgements involved in emotion are unlike dispassionate judgements in that they are resistant to summing and qualification: in order to be rational I do not have to *sum up* two apparently inconsistent affective appraisals. I do not have to conclude that, all things considered, it is either a good thing or not a good thing that my friend won the prize. Nor do I have to *qualify* my appraisals, judging that in one respect it is good that my friend won the prize and in another respect it is not good. When I am simultaneously happy and unhappy that my friend won the prize, each of my affective appraisals takes note of only a subset of the total available evidence. When I am happy that she won, I am focusing on the fact that she got what she wanted and I like it—and it is important to me—when she gets what she wants. When, on the other hand, I am unhappy that she won, I am focusing on the fact that I did not get what I wanted, and I do not like it—and it is important to me—when I do not get what I want. Greenspan's observation that in each case I am paying attention to only a subset of the total available evidence is nicely corroborated by LeDoux's neurophysiological observations: 'the representations that activate the emotional system can be based on incomplete and fragmented information rather than on veridical perception'.[57] Our emotional pathways are fast and 'dirty', emphasizing the situation as perceived in terms of my interests and desires. I get not a dispassionate picture of the total situation, but a partial picture based on what appeals to my interests. Of course we are not yet in any position to know what is going on in my head in a case of 'mixed feelings', but it is fascinating to observe that LeDoux's findings corroborate Greenspan's idea that emotions are based on partial evidence.

Rorty emphasizes how emotions resist change even when the affective appraisal is faced with a wealth of opposing evidence, and how affective appraisals, far from being identical with beliefs, are often in conflict with our beliefs. Here again it is helpful to remember that there are two processing routes for incoming stimuli, the fast affective route through the amygdala that takes immediate account of anything deemed important to the person, and the slow 'cognitive' route through the cortex. In Rorty's example, Jonah just can't help seeing his boss, Esther, as hostile, although he claims truthfully that he does not believe her to be hostile. As Rorty tells the story, there are deep-seated causes, going back to his relationship with his mother, to account for his tendency to see women in authority as hostile. In the light of Zajonc's and LeDoux's findings, we can say that Jonah's affective appraisal of his boss is that here is an enemy, while the cognitive appraisal is signalling that here is a reasonable person just trying to do her job.[58] Jonah's emotional appraisal is inconsistent with his rational beliefs. Once in a situation of subordination to a woman, certain emotional responses are elicited automatically, which help to fix his attention on the woman's 'dictatorial qualities'. Rorty describes him as having acquired a pattern of responding to women in authority as enemies.

Finally, although Solomon claims that an emotion is a judgement, he also wants to say that it is a judgement of a special kind. Emotions are 'self-involved and relatively *intense* evaluative judgments' that are 'especially important to us, meaningful to us, concerning matters in which we have invested our Selves'.[59] Elsewhere he says that emotions are 'urgent' judgements, and emotional responses 'emergency behavior'. An emotion is 'a necessarily hasty judgment in response to a difficult situation'.[60]

The notion of a non-cognitive affective appraisal accommodates very nicely the features of emotional judgement that Solomon indicates. An affective appraisal operates very fast or 'urgently' in situations where the person or other organism has a vital stake in what's going on: it concerns matters 'which are especially important to us'. The appraisal immediately gets the person physiologically prepared for possible *emergency* action. The whole process is marked by *intensity*: what is happening is very important to the person and demands his or her exclusive attention. But, strictly speaking, what is intense is not so much the appraisal as the physiological activity that it induces. This activity in turn helps keep the attention focused on what is perceived as of *urgent* importance and prepares for emergency action, if necessary.

The idea of a non-cognitive appraisal produced automatically and automatically resulting in physiological changes also explains why traditionally emotions have been treated as passions, as phenomena that act upon us and are not directly under our control, rather than as judgements that we consciously and deliberately make. Non-cognitive affective appraisals are not controllable except indirectly. I can try to programme myself or brainwash myself. I can go to a therapist. But I can't just decide not to react when I see the rattlesnake before me, just as Greenspan cannot just decide not to react when she feels herself skidding.

Conclusion

In Ch. 1 we saw many good reasons for thinking that emotions require complex cognitive judgements, and that it is by means of such judgements that we distinguish one emotional state from another. Now, however, it appears that emotions require only a non-cognitive appraisal. I can be afraid without judging that there is a snake before me; I may merely register a curly stick-shape on the forest floor. Similarly, I do not have to believe 'that Jones has wronged me by stealing my car' in order to become angry with Jones. I can respond angrily in an automatic way without much idea of why I respond as I do. By the same token, Solomon is wrong to argue that a change of judgement *ipso facto* produces a change in emotion: recall that Solomon thinks I cannot be angry with Jones once I discover he has not stolen my car, merely borrowed it for the afternoon. But this is too simple. My anger may refuse to dissipate, even once I know the true situation. My physiological response just keeps on going and my affective appraisal still may insist 'He done me wrong' even though my reason knows he has not wronged me.

However, we now seem to be faced with some difficult questions. First, the judgement that Jones has wronged me by stealing my car (anger) and the judgement that I have neglected my children and ought not to have neglected them (remorse) are not affective appraisals in the sense I have been discussing. They are cognitive evaluations, and, as such, they are not enough to set off physiological responses and hence emotion. Yet at the same time we seem to be able to discriminate one emotion from another by means of complex cognitive contents of this sort.

Secondly, if we turn to the evaluations or points of view that identify emotions in Rorty's and Greenspan's examples, these have some of the marks of an affective appraisal—they rely on only a subset of the evidence and are resistant to change—but they still do not seem to be the same as the rapid, pre-linguistic evaluations that Zajonc and LeDoux are talking about. In Rorty's example, Jonah's evaluation is that women in authority are tyrants. In Greenspan's example, the evaluation is that my friend's winning the prize is a good or a bad thing. These do not sound like coarse-grained appraisals using quick and dirty neural pathways. How, then, do we reconcile the data about non-cognitive affective appraisals as sources of emotion with the fact that apparently the evaluations that define particular emotions are cognitively complex? In the next chapter I will try to solve this puzzle.

3

Emotion as Process

The ways we are moved are as various as the lights in a forest;
and they may intersect, sometimes without cancelling each
other, take shape and dissolve, conflict, explode into passion,
or be transfigured.

Susanne Langer, Problems of Art

A Puzzle Solved

In Ch. 1 we examined judgement theories of emotion, and concluded
that judgements all by themselves cannot explain the occurrence of
emotional responses. At the same time it looked as though some kind
of evaluation may be essential to emotion. Emotions are typically
triggered by some kind of evaluation that an important goal or want
or interest is at stake, and different emotions seem to be distinguished
by different kinds of evaluation. Some philosophers have suggested
that the evaluations in question need not be judgements but are more
like different ways of looking at things, or different points of view on
things, but even with this qualification the judgement theory has
problems. The main problem is that a person can make the right kind
of judgement or 'see' things in the right way and still not respond
emotionally. Something is missing.

In Ch. 2 we explored the possibility that the something missing is
some kind of physiological activity or action tendency. I endorsed
William James's idea that physiological changes of some sort are
essential to emotions, and that indeed we don't call a response
emotional unless it is a physiological response that has been produced

in a certain way. Moreover, there are to some extent distinct physiological profiles for each emotion. We saw that some basic emotions do show distinct patterns of autonomic nervous system activity and identifiable facial expressions. However, it is extremely unlikely that *every* emotional state that can be distinguished in the English language (or the Japanese or any other language) is going to be identifiable by some unique pattern of physiological change. In particular, if we want to distinguish closely related emotions such as remorse, guilt, shame, and embarrassment, it looks as though we have to do it by appealing to the evaluative component of emotion, as the judgement theorists have argued.

Psychologists have shown that the physiological changes characteristic of emotional responses can be triggered by what I called 'non-cognitive appraisals'. In Ch. 2 I presented the evidence that in the primitive cases studied by experimental psychologists a non-cognitive appraisal triggers an emotional response, i.e. a physiological response involving some or all of the following: autonomic nervous system changes, changes in facial and vocal expressions, and action tendencies. These non-cognitive affective appraisals occur very fast and automatically, and seem designed to call attention to and deal urgently with events in the environment registered as significant to the organism's life and/or well-being, and/or that of its 'group'.

The emotional responses studied by experimental psychologists, however, are very primitive and simple and seem to be worlds apart from the complex cognitions studied by the philosophical judgement theorists. Non-cognitive appraisals can be made not only by people but also by frogs and fruit flies and other lower species. Of course human beings are capable of far more complex cognitive evaluations than any other species (so far known to us). Fruit flies presumably cannot be *ashamed* that they neglected their fruit-babies, or *contemptuous* of other fruit flies that neglect their young. Yet both humans and fruit flies make affective appraisals of the environment in the sense that both species make such instinctive automatic appraisals as the appraisal of harm characteristic of fear, and both engage in subsequent avoidance behaviour.

So we are faced with a puzzle. We know that rough and ready, quick and dirty evaluations are enough to trigger emotional responses, but at the same time many human emotions seem to have cognitively complex content: they are reactions to beliefs about morality and politics or responses to women in authority or my friend's winning a prestigious prize. And it also seems as if emotions are distinguished one from another by means of these complex cognitions, since rough and ready, quick and dirty evaluations are not enough to distinguish shame from guilt or jealousy from envy.

LeDoux's model of what happens in a simple episode of emotion suggests an answer to our puzzle. In the simple cases studied by LeDoux there is an affective, non-cognitive evaluation that causes autonomic and motor changes and is succeeded by cognitive monitoring. In other words, even a simple episode of emotion is a *process*, involving a number of different events, and, in particular, involving *both* affective *and* cognitive evaluations. According to this model, it is an affective evaluation that generates the autonomic and motor changes that constitute the emotional response and put the emotionality into an emotion, as James might have said. Affective appraisals also generate action tendencies and behaviour. But all this activity is immediately modified by subsequent *cognitive monitoring*.

Generalizing from LeDoux's results, then, we can say that in the simplest, bare-bones case of an emotion process, there is (1) an initial *affective* appraisal of the situation that focuses attention on its significance to the organism and causes (2) physiological responses of various sorts—especially ANS activity and changes in the facial musculature—and motor responses, which get the organism dealing with the situation as very broadly appraised by the affective appraisal, and which gives way to (3) a further more discriminating *cognitive* appraisal or monitoring of the situation. In other words, emotion is not a thing or a response or a state or a disposition; it is a *process*, a sequence of events. An affective appraisal draws attention to something in the environment significant to me or mine and gets my body ready for appropriate action.[1] Then immediately cognitive evaluation kicks in, checks the affective appraisal to see if it is appropriate, modifies autonomic activity, and monitors behaviour. More complex cases of emotion in human beings might involve affective responses not to a perception but to a thought or belief, and the cognitive monitoring may be correspondingly sophisticated, but at the core of emotion will always be physiological responses caused by an automatic affective appraisal and followed by cognitive monitoring.

We can see this pattern at work in animals all up and down the phylogenetic scale when they are in threat situations. The startle reaction to a sudden loud sound such as a gunshot is a good example of an instinctive appraisal of new and potentially harmful information, resulting automatically in a specific constellation of physiological and behavioural reactions, including the characteristic start or jump.[2] Human beings cannot completely inhibit the startle response or convincingly simulate it because it occurs much too fast.[3] But immediately after responding automatically to the gunshot-sound, human beings adjust their behaviour as cognitive monitoring kicks in:[4] I realize my small son has just let off a firecracker under my feet and I smile in relief or frown in angry disapproval, or I realize that a gunshot has indeed sounded and I throw myself to the ground in terror.

Interestingly, a very similar sequence of events can be observed in much simpler organisms. For example, when neuroscientists studied the neural pathways of startle responses in crayfish, they detected two types of tailflip manœuvre: one is mediated by the two giant axons that fire only in response to stimuli with an abrupt onset, and with very short latency, usually about 3–7 milliseconds. 'These latencies provide little time for evaluation of the nature and location of the stimulus beyond the coding inherent in the receptor fields of the giant axons.' Consistent with this, the tailflip escape movements that invariably follow are stereotyped: the crayfish simply move rapidly away in response to the threat. By contrast, non-giant escape production circuitry generates much slower responses which are 'flexibly structured to provide for accuracy, probably visually guided trajectories away from threats and toward known places of safety'.[5] Often, a giant-mediated response is followed by one or more non-giant responses.

Strong, abrupt threats often cause a giant-mediated reaction followed by a nongiant-mediated swimming sequence, and this is an optimally adaptive strategy for escape given the limitations of each control system. The giant-mediated response gets the animal moving away from the stimulus almost immediately, and by the time flexion and re-extension have occurred (about 100–200 msecs), enough time has passed to prepare for well-directed nongiant-mediated tailflipping.[6]

Something very similar occurs in the case of human fear envisaged by LeDoux which I quoted in Ch. 2. A person walking in the wood hears a crackling sound; the amygdala defends against a rattlesnake; and the person jumps back before the slower cortex reports that indeed there is a rattlesnake and the person should walk around it at a safe distance (or there is no rattlesnake, only a stick, and no special action is required). In short, there is an immediate instinctive reaction, followed by cognitive monitoring of the situation, and behaviour is adjusted accordingly.

It might be objected that crayfish are incapable of cognitive evaluations.[7] However, as LeDoux has pointed out, many lower organisms do have 'areas that meet the structural and functional criteria of neocortex',[8] even though these areas are not in exactly the same place as in mammals. At any rate, what seems to be true throughout the phylogenetic scale is that an emotional startle response is the result of an initial affective appraisal, but that the affective appraisal is then in turn monitored by higher processes. The resultant behavior is in its first stage caused solely by the affective appraisal (**This is strange, new, unexpected, threatening**) but at later stages the behaviour is monitored and controlled by cognition. People, of course, have a great deal more cognitive flexibility at their disposal than crayfish. As we'll see later, in human beings cognitive monitoring of an emotion process can be extensive and sophisticated, ranging from assessing how to cope with a threat or an offence to figuring out the probable causes of the emotional response and reflecting upon its significance in our lives as a whole.

First, however, I want to say a bit more about the affective appraisals that set off the emotion process.

What Triggers Emotions?

As human beings grow up and become cognitively more sophisticated, they are able to make ever more complex *cognitive* evaluations of their environment. People are disgusted not only by someone's vomit but by a person's contemptible behaviour; we are afraid not only of the looming shape in the dark but of a sudden fall in the value of our stock portfolio. How is it that cognitively complex beliefs and judgements—the sort of thing identified by the judgement theorists—apparently provoke emotions just as simple perceptions do? The answer is that I can make an affective appraisal of my stock portfolio in just the same way as I affectively appraise the looming shape in the dark. The affective appraisal is fast, automatic, not directly controllable—'quick and dirty', as LeDoux puts it—and it produces immediate physiological changes. Thus I may feel an emotional response to a realization that my portfolio is performing badly only after having studied long and hard to find out just how the portfolio is behaving. It is only after lengthy cognitive evaluations that I realize how badly I am doing, but once I make this discovery, then all of a sudden I make an affective appraisal that rivets my attention on this discovery and its implications for my well-being: I am suddenly frightened and vulnerable. In such situations, there is cognitive activity prior to the affective appraisal, but it is only after there is an affective appraisal that there is an emotional response. We can think of the affective appraisal here as a kind of 'meta-response', evaluating in a rough and ready way—for example, as **bad for me** or **good for me**—an already existing cognitive evaluation. To put the point dramatically, what turns a cognition into an emotion is an affective appraisal and its concomitant physiological changes.

How should we think of affective appraisals? In Ch. 2 I characterized an affective appraisal as a non-cognitive appraisal, working very fast and automatically through lower brain centres, that fixes attention upon and evaluates in a rough and ready way the personal significance of something in the internal or external environment. An affective appraisal serves to pick out and focus attention on those things in the internal or external environment that matter to the animal or human being and to appraise or evaluate them very broadly in terms of *how* they matter. But it is an open question how we should conceptualize this 'mattering'. As we have seen, many psychologists recognize the existence of something like an affective appraisal in the sense I have just defined, but they tend to think of these appraisals in somewhat different ways. Given that an affective appraisal is by definition not describable in propositional or linguistic terms, it is difficult to know how to describe these appraisals in ordinary language. When in LeDoux's experiments the conditioned rat responds to a sound with the physiological symptoms of fear, should we think of the rat's non-cognitive appraisal as 'I don't like this,' or as 'This is inconsistent with an important life goal of mine,' or 'This is a threatening situation'? Obviously we can't ask the rat, or if we do, we won't get a very helpful answer. The problem is not confined to rats, however. Exactly the same question can be asked of the human being who responds fearfully to the sight of a rattlesnake curled up on the path just ahead: since the appraisal is instinctive—very fast and by-passing cognition—the human being is in no better a position to answer the question than the rat.

The question is vital to emotion research, however, since it is tantamount to the question: what triggers emotion? More precisely, what non-cognitive appraisals produce the physiological changes and action tendencies characteristic of emotional responses? In general, psychologists have answered this question in one of four ways. I call them the preference/aversion approach, the component approach, the goal-orientation approach, and the basic emotion approach.

1. *Preference and Aversion.* If we examine Zajonc's experiments, the evaluations he discusses tend to be characterized in terms of prefer-ence and aversion. In the mere exposure experiments, subjects were described as 'preferring' the more familiar polygons. In the affective priming experiments, subjects are said to 'like' the stimuli primed by the smiling face significantly more than those primed by an angry face. In the experiment cited by Garcia and in turn by Zajonc, in which a new taste was conditioned to induce nausea in rats by the administration of a nauseating substance under anaesthesia, the rats are described as developing an 'aversion' to the conditioned stimulus (the new taste).

These experiments seem to demonstrate that creatures have likings and dislikings that are based on innate programming. For example, we are evidently constructed in such a way that we respond differen-tially to familiar and unfamiliar aspects of our environment, and we tend to prefer the familiar over the unfamiliar. Similarly, rats are constructed in such a way that they respond aversively to nauseous substances, and anything conditioned by their use. We are all bio-logical organisms, programmed to like and dislike certain things, and to respond positively or negatively to various aspects of the environment. So one way to conceptualize an affective appraisal is as 'saying' **I like it!** or **I don't like it!** I use semi-bold letters to render these non-cognitive evaluations, because what I am talking about is not just some dispassionate evaluation of the form 'I like this all right, although I've seen better' or 'I do not like this, but I can live with it,' but rather a fast, automatic, 'hot' evaluation of what is important to me and my wants and values, and which *because of this* leads to physiological activity and action tendencies.

There are, however, difficulties with this way of conceptualizing the meaning of a non-cognitive appraisal. First, there are some states that appear to be emotional but do not in themselves have positive or negative valence. An emotional response of surprise, for example, might seem to be neutral as to whether the surprising stimulus is pleasant or unpleasant: it is merely unexpected. Some theorists have thought that this lack of valence is sufficient to show that surprise is not a bona fide emotion. For example, Lazarus says that surprise is a 'pre-emotion', like curiosity, attentiveness, and the orienting reflex; these states 'prepare the person or animal to evaluate what is happening',[9] but don't actually involve an evaluation. Oatley and Johnson-Laird have argued that surprise may accompany any emotion and so is probably not an emotion in its own right.[10] Of course, these theorists may just be noting a peculiarity of the English language, which has only one word for surprise regardless of whether it is a good or a bad surprise, whereas other languages make a distinction between welcome and unwelcome surprises.[11]

Secondly, there is an ambiguity in the non-cognitive appraisals **I like it** and **I don't like it!** On the one hand they might mean 'This is pleasant or pleasurable' and 'This is unpleasant or displeasurable.' And on the other hand they might mean 'This is conducive to my goals, wants, interests, etc.' or 'This runs counter to my goals, wants, interests, etc.' Many non-cognitive appraisals seem to have little to do with immediate pleasure or displeasure. Anxiety, for example, is an unpleasant or negative emotion, but it does not seem to involve a non-cognitive appraisal 'This is unpleasant!' Rather, it is an appraisal of *possible* unpleasantness, an appraisal of threat. Furthermore, some emotional responses seem to involve a mixture of pleasure and displeasure, as in my mixed fear and joy on recovering my toddler who has wandered off into a crowd. These examples seem to suggest that non-cognitive appraisals have various different dimensions or components, beyond just pleasantness and unpleasantness.

Thirdly, to reinforce this last point, there are to some extent distinct physiological responses for the various 'basic emotions', which are the immediate product of the non-cognitive evaluations I am currently trying to conceptualize. If anger, fear, sadness, and disgust have distinct physiological profiles, then they are almost certainly caused by distinct non-cognitive appraisals.[12]

I conclude that the preference–aversion view is inadequate on its own, although it may be that affective appraisals of preference and aversion are among possible triggers of emotion, including, perhaps, the emotions of love and hate.

2. *The Component Approach.* So-called 'componential' theorists hold that there are a variety of appraisals that generate emotion— not just **I like it!** and **I don't like it!**—but that, like **I like it!** and **I don't like it!**, these appraisals do not correspond one-to-one in any obvious way to specific emotional states. Examples might include **This is weird!** (which could be a component of curiosity, anxiety, or pleased surprise), **This is a friend/enemy!** (perhaps components of love and hate, but also possibly of joy and fear), **This is uncertain! I can't control this! This is an obstacle!** as well as **I like/dislike this!**

As I mentioned in Ch. 2, Klaus Scherer has identified what he calls 'stimulus evaluation checks', some of which are present at birth— such as the checks for novelty (newborns turn their heads towards a novel stimulus) and for intrinsic pleasantness and unpleasantness— and some of which develop later as the child develops cognitively and in other ways. The five stimulus evaluation checks he distinguishes are (1) novelty, (2) intrinsic pleasantness, (3) conduciveness to one's needs and/or goals, (4) one's ability to *cope* with the stimulus, and (5) whether the stimulus is compatible with one's own norms and sense of Self.[13] For Scherer, each emotion is distinguished by the particular cluster of stimulus evaluation checks that it requires. More recently, Scherer has refined his scheme. He now recognizes a total of fifteen 'facets' or 'vectors', which are facets of the original five basic types of stimulus evaluation check. Thus the 'coping potential check' involves checking one's degree of control over an event, one's relative power to change or avoid the outcome of the event, and one's potential for

adjustment to the final outcome.[14] With the probable exception of
the checks that are present at birth, however, these checks clearly
involve cognitive activity. Scherer is not trying to identify specifically
non-cognitive 'evaluation checks'.

Another version of the componential approach is offered by
Ellsworth and Smith,[15] who distinguish a list of 'appraisal features or
components': pleasantness, anticipated effort, attentional activity,
certainty, human agency, situational control, perceived obstacle, importance, and predictability. As in Scherer's scheme, Ellsworth and
Smith are positing basic stimulus evaluations, none of which corresponds to a particular emotion, and each emotion is thought to be
preceded and defined by a particular cluster of stimulus evaluations.
Like Scherer, too, they seem to be analysing the appraisals they
consider vital to emotion, regardless of whether these appraisals are
cognitive or non-cognitive. More importantly, Smith and Ellsworth
get their data from questioning human subjects about the dimensions
they detect in certain current or remembered emotional states. However, there is no reason to think that these dimensions or components
are actually triggering or causing the emotion. In thinking about my
anxiety on being told I have just failed an exam (one of the situations
used in the Ellsworth experiments), I may detect uncertainty and lack
of situational control, for example, but it doesn't follow that an
appraisal of uncertainty and lack of situational control is what caused
the emotional state.

If we are interested in very fast non-cognitive appraisals, it is in any
case unreliable to depend on self-reports by subjects, usually in
answer to questionnaires, for a non-cognitive appraisal typically
occurs very fast and beneath conscious awareness, and there is no
reason to suppose that it can be reliably reported by subjects. Rats, of
course, refuse to answer questionnaires, but adult human subjects are
no better at accurately reporting their non-cognitive—or indeed
even their cognitive—appraisals. As a matter of fact, if we could get
accurate answers when we ask people what non-cognitive appraisals
were causing their emotional responses, we would not have any
difficulty conceptualizing non-cognitive appraisals and I would not
need to be discussing the issue here.

I conclude that componential theories that rely on self-reports are
not fruitfully thought of as theories about what triggers emotional

response. On the other hand, some componential evaluations such as those of novelty, strangeness, and intrinsic pleasantness or unpleasantness may turn out to be triggers of emotional responses.

3. *Goal-Oriented Theories*. Some theorists have defined the crucial evaluations that trigger an emotional response in terms of the goals of the agent.[16] According to Richard Lazarus, emotions are triggered by *primary* appraisals, which have three components: 'goal relevance, goal congruence or incongruence, and type of ego-involvement'.[17] An appraisal that the situation is *relevant* to a goal is necessary for there to be any emotional response at all. An appraisal of *goal congruence* or *incongruence* distinguishes so-called positive from negative emotions: 'this is good for me (given my wants and goals)' versus 'this is bad for me (given my wants and goals)'. And an appraisal of *type of ego-involvement* distinguishes different ways in which the event is appraised as good or bad.

The discussion of ego-involvement is not very satisfactory. The various kinds of ego-involvement that Lazarus distinguishes seem to include anything that might be important to an individual and are a very motley crew. Lazarus lists self-esteem, social esteem, moral values, ego-ideals, 'other people and their well-being', 'meanings and ideas', and 'life goals'. No doubt all these things can be important to the generation of emotion, but they do not help in the specification of non-cognitive triggers of emotion that can be found across all human beings and even in other species. An appraisal that I have successfully lip-synched to Elizabeth Schwarzkopf may make me *proud* but I doubt that this appraisal is a basic, non-cognitive appraisal that can be found in all peoples and maybe a rat or two.

There are various ways in which Lazarus's theory could be amplified. One way is to think of the affective appraisals that trigger emotional response as **This is conducive to my goals, wants, interests**, and **This runs counter to my goals, wants, interests**, or, perhaps, better, **Yes!** and **No!** (or even **Yesss!** and **Nooo!**)

Viewed in this way, the theory seems to be open to one of the same objections that we discussed with reference to the preference–aversion theory. Surprise and curiosity involve appraisals that are not straightforwardly of goal conduciveness or obstructiveness; rather in surprise and curiosity we are faced with something that may or may not turn out to be relevant to our goals. However, if we think of the acquisition of new knowledge as a fundamental goal, then, since surprise and curiosity are both reactions to new information, they do in a sense represent the fulfilment of a goal (or, as Lazarus thinks, a state of *preparedness* for achieving the goal of new knowledge). Similarly, anxiety and hope respectively do not involve an appraisal that something is contrary to or conducive to a goal, but they do involve an appraisal that something *might* be contrary to or conducive to a goal.[18]

The goal-orientation approach shares another problem with the pleasure–aversion hypothesis. Some emotions such as fear, anger, and disgust can be distinguished physiologically. This suggests that we should not conceptualize affective non-cognitive appraisals simply in terms of whether something forwards or thwarts my goals. Our physiology makes more fine-grained distinctions than that. In emotional states our bodies tell us more than simply that something is conducive to (or opposed to) our goals.

4. *Basic Emotions.* The other way of amplifying Lazarus's theory is the one he opts for himself. This is the idea that there are a limited number of what he calls 'core-relational themes' corresponding to specific goals and defined by specific evaluations.[19] As we saw in Ch. 1, these include appraisals that something is 'a demeaning offense against me and mine' (anger), 'wanting what someone else has' (envy), and 'having experienced an irretrievable loss' (sadness). As we also saw, these characterizations are not very satisfactory. Nor does Lazarus think of these appraisals as non-cognitive. But it may be that there is a kernel of truth in this approach.

Many emotion theorists have hypothesized that there is a relatively small set of *basic emotions*. On this view, there are a small number of basic emotion systems, usually identified by means of their uniquely distinguishable physiological symptoms, including facial expressions. In the present context, the idea would be that corresponding to each basic emotion, there is a *basic affective (non-cognitive) appraisal*. An emotional response of fear, for example, is evoked by an affective appraisal: **This is a *threat*.** Disgust is evoked by an affective appraisal, **This is *nauseating*.** Anger is evoked by an affective appraisal, **This *wrongs* me (or mine)** or **This is an *offence*.** Such affective appraisals might be part of what Ekman calls the 'affect programs' that identify the basic emotions.

LeDoux has postulated that there are different emotion systems to deal with different 'fundamental life tasks'. The universality of basic emotion in people stems from the fact that all people (and many other creatures) have the same fundamental life tasks, to reproduce, to be accepted as a member of groups, to ward off enemies, to preserve one's own life and well-being and that of one's group, to avoid poisonous food, and so on. This view incorporates the idea that likes and dislikes prompt emotional responses, as well as the idea that non-cognitive affective appraisals are made in terms of one's goals and interests; it's just that the basic emotion hypothesis suggests that there are particular goals that prompt particular kinds of emotional responses. On the face of things, the basic emotion view seems quite different from the componentialist view, but they may not contrast as much as appears. In some cases, anyhow, the components identified by the componentialist as triggering emotion are the same as affective appraisals identified by the basic emotion theorists. Examples might include: **This threatens me (or mine)!** (fear), **This is a friend!** (love/ attachment), **This is an enemy!** (hate), and **This is strange and unexpected!** (surprise).

One problem with this way of conceptualizing the non-cognitive appraisals essential to emotion is that we do not yet know how many basic emotions there are and what they will turn out to be. As we have seen, LeDoux himself has studied only the fear system. As yet we do not even know if there is an anger system or a disgust system, an attachment/love system or a hate system.[20] Even if there is a system for disgust, anger, and fear, is there also a system for shame? For surprise? Curiosity? Clearly, there are not different emotion systems for every emotion named in the English language, since the whole point of talking about basic emotion systems is that they are biologically based and universal among humans. But identifying all the right basic emotions is a practical, not a theoretical problem. My own hunch is that currently the most promising approach is the basic emotion approach. The other suggestions for how to conceptualize affective appraisals seem to me either too broad (**I like it! I don't like it!**) or too narrowly focused on a particular goal of mine (the Elizabeth Schwarzkopf lip-synching problem) to capture the emotion spectrum as we currently understand it. But the issue remains unsettled. What is *not* unsettled, however, is that there are indeed affective appraisals that initiate the physiological and behavioural changes that we define as emotional. Further, even if it is a cognitively complex thought or belief that *appears* to trigger an emotional response, the response itself is the result of a rough and ready affective appraisal *of* that thought or belief, serving to direct attention to it and to prepare for appropriate action.

How Can Complex Cognitions Provoke Affective Appraisals? The Role of Emotional Memory

How is it that in human beings the very same non-cognitive affective appraisal can be set off sometimes by a stimulus that we are preprogrammed to respond to or which we learn very easily to respond to (such as fear of snakes and spiders) and sometimes by a complex cognition that can only be the result of sophisticated learning processes? How is it that I interpret a quiet remark by my boss as an **offence** (which it may very well be and be intended to be)? Somehow, it seems, my brain categorizes very diverse phenomena as an **offence** and responds to them in the same way. I do not pretend to have a complete answer to this question, and I don't think anyone else does either. What I can do, however, is point to some evidence that we do have the ability to do this and that the neural pathways for doing this exist and have to some extent been studied. I believe that an important clue to understanding this possibility is the existence of an *emotional memory system.*

LeDoux has drawn attention to the fact that memory is not a single system within the brain and that there is an emotional memory system that is independent of explicit or declarative memory.[21] A nice example of the existence of two kinds of memory is provided by Edouard Claparède, a French medical doctor practising in the early twentieth century who had a female patient who in all likelihood had damage to her medial temporal lobe memory system. When Claparède came to visit her, she never recognized him or remembered seeing him before. He could leave the room for just a few minutes, and, when he returned, the woman would greet him as though she had never encountered him before. One day, however, Claparède concealed a tack in his hand and when he shook hands with her, stuck the tack into her hand. The next time he met her she failed to recognize him as usual, but after this incident she always refused to shake hands with him. She had an 'emotional memory' of the incident, although she had no declarative memory of it.

This story illustrates the existence of two distinct memory systems for declarative memory and *emotional memory*. Suppose I have explicit or declarative memories of a situation as traumatic—a car accident, for example. The explicit memory is mediated by the temporal lobe system and has no emotional consequences: I remember such things as whom I was with and what kind of car I was driving. However, according to LeDoux, I can simultaneously have an 'aversive emotional memory' and a current bodily response which is mediated by 'an emotional memory system' such as the implicit fear memory system involving the amygdala. The two memories may be fused in consciousness so that I remember (explicitly) having been emotionally aroused by the traumatic situation; or I may forget the whole thing as far as declarative memory is concerned, and yet a cue, such as the sight of a car exactly like the one I was driving, will trigger an emotional reaction. What this discussion suggests is that anything whatsoever can be imprinted on emotional memory, ready to elicit emotional responses in the right circumstances.

In Ch. 1, I criticized Pat Greenspan's explanation of some examples of irrational fear—her fear of Fido, the harmless old dog, and her fear of skidding on a dry road in summer. We are now in a position to understand these examples. In both cases there is an automatic, instinctive response, based on an emotional memory of the stimulus. In the one case she had a bad experience with a dog and is now traumatized by the sight of tame old Fido. In the other case she was terrified by a skid and now reacts automatically to any skid, however harmless. *In both cases there is a non-cognitive appraisal that she is being threatened* or is in a dangerous situation, which is inconsistent with her cognitive appraisal that there is nothing to be afraid about.[22] Similarly, in Rorty's example about Jonah, he has had programmed into his emotional memory a set of responses to mother figures that are automatically elicited by any old female authority figure, however benign.[23]

For Greenspan it is the traumatic memory of a skid that produces the affective appraisal. For Rorty, it is the trauma of (what he believes is) the loss of his mother's love that causes Jonah's aberrant reactions to female bosses. In a less traumatic kind of example, a memory of many previous encounters with an irritating colleague may produce an affective appraisal of dislike or the need to escape: when I see him coming into view down the hallway, my blood pressure rises and my fists begin to clench, without my forming any conscious thoughts about him. I have been around him for so long that the mere sight of him induces an instant emotional reaction of anger and annoyance: I react 'instinctively', as William James might have said. It seems as if emotional reactions can become programmed into emotional memory, ready to be elicited automatically and resulting immediately in physiological changes once attention is focused on a stimulus that awakens the memory. This focus of attention may be unconscious: my heart begins to race *before* I have consciously registered that it is Jones coming down the hall. Similarly, Greenspan gasps *before* she consciously realizes she is in a skid. And Rorty says that Jonah starts complaining before the new boss has even had time to put her family photos on her desk.

These kinds of cases suggest that neural channels exist that process non-cognitive appraisals of some *category of event or person* and produce automatic affective responses to *any member of that category*. *How* this happens is not clear. But *that* it happens is.

Robert Zajonc once suggested that the fear response might be stored in motor memory and elicited automatically, without cognitive mediation.[24] Recent results from research into the multiple mechanisms underlying different instances of 'procedural memory' (memories of how to perform a task as opposed to declarative memory) would seem to confirm Zajonc's hunch. Motor skills, such as how to swim, ride a bike, mend a burst pipe, and so forth are stored in separate motor memories. Furthermore, one can remember how to ride a bike or swim even if one has lost declarative memory. One possibility, then, is that emotional memories are memories of the motor responses produced by different affective appraisals.

A more elaborate proposal has been made by the neuroscientist, Antonio Damasio. He has found that patients with damage to the ventromedial sectors of the prefrontal cortices are unable to 'generate emotions relative to the images conjured up by certain categories of situation and stimuli',[25] and thus cannot have the appropriate bodily *feeling*—what he calls a 'somatic marker'—that (he thinks) is a feeling of some bodily change that has become associated through learning with specific types of scenario. In my terms, these patients are unable to make non-cognitive affective appraisals and hence do not generate the physiological changes that result from non-cognitive affective appraisals.

In his book, *Descartes' Error*, Damasio is primarily interested in the role of emotion in decision-making and tasks generally thought to be the exclusive domain of rationality. He thinks that good decision-making in matters of personal and social importance requires an emotional component. Specifically it requires that the range of choices of behaviour be narrowed down by the somatic marking of certain envisaged possible outcomes as being beneficial or harmful. When we deliberate we consider only those options that are marked as good or bad somatically, although we usually need to use rational strategies (such as cost–benefit analyses) as well. If Damasio is correct, then the brain is able to classify scenarios as harmful or beneficial, *based on past experience with similar such scenarios*, and it does this by marking these categories of scenario *in a bodily (somatic) way*, which we access by means of the feelings of bodily change.

I do not want to discuss Damasio's theory in any detail, but to focus on his idea that we learn to associate classes of stimuli as good or bad by marking them in a bodily way. In my terms, we learn to classify stimuli as **good** and **bad** and also perhaps as **weird**, as **friend** or **enemy**, as **threat** or **offence** by means of non-cognitive appraisals that immediately result in bodily responses.[26] An emotional memory may then be a juxtaposition of a (type of) scenario with a particular set of bodily responses.

Damasio describes a fascinating series of 'gambling experiments' in which patients with damaged frontal lobes were compared with normal subjects. The subjects played a game in which they were faced with four packs of cards, A, B, C, and D, and invited to turn over cards from any pack. Depending on the card turned over, they would receive money or have to pay the 'banker'. Participants were not told when the game would end and were given no other information about it. It turns out that packs A and B gave larger pay-outs than C and D, but that they also exacted much larger payments to the banker. After a while, the normal subjects drew almost entirely from

C and D while the damaged patients drew almost exclusively from A and B (and continued to do so even after they had to borrow money time and again from the banker to cover their losses). Damasio considers various possible explanations for this behaviour and concludes that the most likely is that the damaged patients are suffering from 'myopia for the future', i.e. although they are still sensitive to both rewards and punishments (for example, they avoided the bad packs immediately after one of the bad outcomes), 'neither punishment nor reward contributes to the automated marking or maintained deployment of predictions of future outcomes, and as a result immediately rewarding options are favored'.[27]

This conclusion is borne out by fascinating studies of skin conductance during the gambling game. Both groups of subjects reacted with skin conductance changes right after turning up an appropriate card, but the normal subjects also gradually began to show a (bigger and bigger) response *before* turning a card from one of the bad decks, whereas the damaged subjects '*showed no anticipatory responses whatsoever*'.[28] This set of experiments cleverly shows that people do classify scenarios as bad or good in a way that is immediately registered in the body (and that this ability is very important to our capacity to make good life decisions). The experiments strikingly demonstrate that these 'bodily classifications' are acquired by *learning* and that autonomic responses to appraisals of **beneficial** and **harmful** are not just responses to specific stimuli that people are preprogrammed to respond to.

Interestingly, the damaged patients knew 'rationally' that A and B were bad decks, but they did not *feel* it emotionally. Such patients respond with what Damasio calls 'flat affect' to all situations that most of us would experience as emotional. In other experiments, for example, they recognize that disturbing images are disturbing, but they are not disturbed by them: both autonomic measures and self-report concur that they do not 'get emotional'.

In short, for my purposes, what Damasio has shown is that normal emotional functioning requires the categorization of *learned stimuli* as having an emotional significance and that this significance is stored in bodily reactions—or, as I surmise, in affective appraisals that cause bodily reactions. In other words, anything whatsoever can be categorized as a 'threat' and whether we perceive or merely think about one of these things, an affective appraisal of **Threat!** is likely to be automatically triggered. Consequently we respond emotionally not only to things that we are innately attuned to appraise affectively as threats, but also to stimuli that have been categorized as threats as a result of our individual experiences. Damasio has also identified some of the neural channels that mediate these capacities.

Monitoring the Emotion Process

So far I have been focusing on the affective appraisals that generate emotional (physiological) responses, and how people can respond affectively to complex learned stimuli as well as to stimuli that we are probably programmed to respond to from birth, such as a loud sound or a large animal bounding towards us. Now I want to turn to the other end of the emotion process, the process of cognitive monitoring that modifies our responses, changes our focus, moderates our behaviour. When discussing the componential theorists, I complained that many of the components they recognize are unlikely to provoke an emotional response. But it seems quite likely that many of the suggested appraisal components are in fact appraisals that occur in the emotional process *after* the initial non-cognitive appraisal. Among the appraisal components identified by Smith and Ellsworth are 'anticipated effort', 'situational control', and 'predictability'. Although these are unlikely candidates for non-cognitive appraisals that trigger emotion, it is entirely possible that such appraisals occur somewhere along the line in the emotion process: I hear the crackling sound; I jump; and I see that indeed there is a rattlesnake; I realize that effort is required to get me out of this situation, that the situation is unpredictable, and that I am not in control of it: this whole process could well be characteristic of fear. In short, once an emotional process has been initiated, there is constant cognitive monitoring of the situation.

Similarly, the psychologist Richard Lazarus believes that subsequent to the primary appraisals that he thinks initiate emotional responses, there are 'secondary appraisals', in which the person assesses blame or credit, whether he or she can cope with the situation, and what his or her future expectations are. He emphasizes

cause all encounters between persons or animals and the
nment change continually and generate feedback, affective
sals also change and so do subsequent cognitive appraisals and
reappraisals, as the person or animal monitors the situation.

Much of this discussion of appraisal and reappraisal is somewhat
speculative. We infer that a cognitive appraisal or reappraisal occurs
because our behaviour changes—from confident to tentative, from
sitting quietly to bursting into tears, from freezing to fleeing, from an
incipient movement of flight to sitting quietly again, depending upon
the circumstances. Even though LeDoux has found that cognitive
appraisal in fear takes place more slowly than affective appraisal, it still
occurs pretty fast, and, if he is right, cognitive appraisal or something
very like it occurs in creatures that lack consciousness. It is not surprising, then, that typically human cognitive appraisals and reappraisals,
like affective appraisals, take place below the level of consciousness. So
just as it was difficult to say exactly how to verbalize the non-cognitive
appraisals that trigger emotional responses, so it is also difficult to know
whether there are specific kinds of cognitive appraisals and reappraisals
that typically monitor emotional responses, and, if there are, what the
sequence of such appraisals and reappraisals would be like. It is not
surprising that we cannot tell what we are experiencing when one
emotional response gives way to another so quickly. It seems likely that
most of the mental adjustments we perform take place largely beneath
awareness. Whatever the actual sequence of appraisals and reappraisals
may be, however, it is clear that emotion does involve such sequences.
Emotion is a *process* that unfolds, as the situation is appraised and
reappraised, and as continuous feedback occurs.

In a discussion of William James's theory of emotion, Phoebe
Ellsworth also stresses the idea that emotions are processes. She takes
the idea one step further, however, arguing that the various events that
occur in an emotion process are themselves processes that to some
extent unfold independently. Most theorists agree that interpretation
of a stimulus, physiological arousal, expressive behaviour, action tendencies, and subjective feelings are all involved in emotion, but

[i]nterpretation, subjective feeling, visceral and motor responses are all
processes, with time courses of their own. There is no reason to believe
that all of the bodily feedback should reach the brain before any subjective

feeling results, or that the interpretation of the situation must be completed before the body can begin to respond, or that fully nuanced emotional experience must occur before interpretation can begin. ... The interpretation develops over time, and so does the feeling, in a continuously interactive sequence, often a very rapid one. Neither interpretation, nor bodily feedback, nor subjective experience comes first; at the very most, one can talk about which of these complex temporal processes *starts* first.[29]

Ellsworth suggests that 'very simple appraisals' serve 'as entry points into the realm of emotions: a sense of attention or novelty, a sense of attraction or aversion, a sense of uncertainty'.[30] In my terms, an emotion process is always triggered by a non-cognitive affective appraisal. We would not call a process *emotional* unless there were such an appraisal to trigger the emotional (physiological) responses and associated action tendencies. As we have seen, there is dispute about the exact nature of these non-cognitive appraisals. But however we think of them, the non-cognitive appraisals (in both human beings and 'lower' animals) are themselves monitored or appraised by higher cognitive processes, and the action tendencies initiated by the affective appraisals are modified in accordance with subsequent cognitive appraisals. Ellsworth eloquently describes the process:

At the moment when the organism's attention is aroused by some change in the environment, or the stream of consciousness, certain neural circuits in the brain are activated ... the heart may slow, the head may turn, and the organism *feels different* than it did before the event. Arousal of attention does not necessarily lead to emotion—the novel event may be easily explained as trivial or familiar, and the organism returns to baseline—but attention is very often the first step in emotional arousal. No nameable emotion has yet developed, but already there are cognitive, physiological, behavioral, and subjective changes. If the organism senses that the stimulus is attractive or aversive, the feeling and the bodily responses change again. As each succeeding appraisal is made, mind, body, and feeling change again. The sequence may seem to burst forth all at once, or it may unfold over a much longer period of time. When all the requisite appraisals have been made, quickly or slowly, the person may say he or she is in a state corresponding to one of the familiar emotions catalogued by ancient and modern taxonomists. Nevertheless, such states may be rare ... Often the situation may be ambiguous with respect to one or more of the appraisals, or an appraisal may be variable, or the situation we perceive may change—on its own or in response to our own behavior so that no steady state is possible, at least not until long afterward, when the emotion has been catalogued in recollection.[31]

There are a number of insights in this passage. First, there is the idea that in an emotional process each aspect of the process runs its own temporal course, and that there is continuous feedback of various sorts from one aspect to another. For example, physiological changes may help to fix my attention on something important in the environment: the loud sound that startles me makes my eyes blink and checks my breathing, so that I am alert to this sudden new event in my environment and my attention is focused upon it. If I am instinctively (non-cognitively) surprised or startled or enraged by some occurrence, subsequent cognitive appraisals may confirm or disconfirm the occurrence, and will in any case modify my appraisal of it. ('It's just a firecracker,' or 'Somebody's got a gun!') In an emotional response, the non-cognitive appraisal produces both physiological changes and action tendencies, and both can be modified by subsequent cognitive appraisals and reappraisals. Moreover, actions taken in response to a non-cognitive appraisal, such as freezing in fear or tensing in anger, often alter the situation itself—perhaps the enemy retreats—and so indirectly modify my appraisal of the situation, and thus in turn affect my subsequent behaviour. After responding instinctively by freezing or tensing, I may see that the situation is no longer threatening, so I relax. Feelings, too, which I have said little about, may function in conscious human beings to draw attention to one's physiological state or the evaluations one is making, or both.[32]

The fact that each aspect of the emotion process has its own temporal trajectory is also important. It is noteworthy, for example, that however quickly a sequence of appraisals takes place, the physiological symptoms of emotion may last longer. Suppose I affectively appraise something as a threat but then cognition tells me I am in no danger. Even after I realize I am safe, adrenaline continues to course through my blood for a while. Indeed, hormonal reactions to threat may last hours and even days. By the same token, that's why I can still 'be angry' after discovering I haven't been wronged: my facial expression and physiological reactions may still keep going after the relevant evaluation has been rejected. Again, a course of action embarked upon as a result of an affective appraisal may continue long after the appraisal and its consequent cognitive monitoring have faded from memory. A facial expression may disappear even as the evaluation of a situation persists.[33]

A second important idea derived from Ellsworth is that particular nameable emotional states may be relatively rare, that our emotional life occurs in 'streams' that change all the time in response to ever-changing appraisals, ever-evolving actions and action tendencies, ever-changing bodily states. As William James noted, our emotional processes are in constant flux: we can change quite quickly from fearful to cheerful, from anxious to angry. Particular nameable emotional states in this view are typically recognized after the event 'when the emotion has been catalogued in recollection'. So it is only after the event that we (or our friends) describe a situation as one in which I was sad, angry, or jealous, ashamed, guilty, or merely regretful, or calm, bored, or world-weary. It is by using ordinary emotion words like this that we try to make sense out of and explain our emotional experiences.

Cataloguing in Recollection

Among the reappraisals that human beings often carry out after a non-cognitive appraisal and typically some initial cognitive evaluation has taken place, is an attempt to explain the emotion in folk-psychological terms by *naming* it. Human beings, unlike crayfish and rats, not only respond emotionally to the important events in their lives; they also *reflect* upon them. As we'll see, great works of art frequently encourage us to reflect upon our emotions in a careful and detailed way. But in ordinary life, people tend to appraise their own emotional experiences by applying generalized labels from commonsense or 'folk' psychology. So I may think to myself: 'I see now why I yelled at Bobby: I was *jealous* of Sue who had been monopolizing his attention,' or 'Now I realize why I got so upset; I was *angry* with Bobby and *resentful* of Sue.' In seeking a psychological explanation for my behaviour and for my physiological state, I label my experience with one of the emotion words available to me in my language, and I may also make inferences about what it was that set off my 'jealousy', 'anger,' or 'resentment.' I may decide that it was because Bobby was flirting with Sue and she was receiving his attentions willingly that I was *angry* with Bobby, and *jealous* and *resentful* of Sue. In short, I reflect upon the stream of my emotional responses and try to assess in folk-psychological terms what prompted them and how to categorize them.

Social construction theorists like to point out that different languages carve up the emotion territory in different ways. Some languages have words for emotion states that are supposedly untranslatable into English. Emotion words often mentioned in this regard are Japanese *amae*—described by one source as 'an emotion of interdependence, arising from a kind of symbiosis, from comfort in the other person's complete acceptance' and by another as a 'propensity to depend upon another's presumed indulgence'[34]—and *fago*, an emotion found on the South Pacific island of Ifaluk, that is translated by Catherine Lutz as 'compassion /love/sorrow'.[35] Emotion concepts typically specify a type of situation or context in which the emotion occurs, together with a characteristic type of response. Different cultures have somewhat different emotional vocabularies because different societies have somewhat different values and prize different character traits. It is not surprising that a country such as the United States, which puts a high premium on independence, individuality, ambition, and aggressiveness, does not have such a concept as *amae*, which implicitly recognizes mutual dependency as an important social goal. Similarly with respect to Ifaluk *fago*. The English language has over two thousand words for emotions,[36] yet even English does not have the resources for *naming* all the subtle emotions of which people are capable. Indeed it seems likely that there are many emotions that are nameless in every language. John Benson once speculated that it would be nice to have a word for the emotional state expressed by J. Alfred Prufrock in Eliot's poem.[37] He suggests the word 'prufishness', as in 'I've been feeling rather prufish lately.'

It is important to be clear that in making folk-psychological appraisals (I was jealous, I was *fago*ing, I was resentful, etc.), I am making *after-the-fact assessments* of my emotional state and that such assessments are *prone to error*. In making folk-psychological appraisals, such as 'I was resentful,' I am not reporting on the actual sequence of appraisals and reappraisals that took place in me. The actual sequence of appraisals that occurs changes very rapidly and I am typically unaware of most of it. Indeed it is typically only if I find myself puzzled by the way I am reacting or by the way I feel that I seek an explanation in folk-psychological terms for my emotional reactions and/or feelings. And perhaps it is important to us to name our emotions because it gives us at least an illusion of control when we (think we) understand why we responded as we did.

But whatever the reasons for seeking such explanations, the explanation itself is a *summary judgement*, an appraisal that sums up what I think I must have been attending to, what wants and interests I think I must have registered as being at stake, what thoughts I think I must have had about the unfolding situation. If, as my boss leaves the room, I find myself trembling, with my fists clenching and unclenching, and my heart pounding, I may think to myself 'I must be really resentful. I must have found it really unjust and offensive when he told me I didn't work fast enough.' In formulating these thoughts, I am in effect offering a folk-psychological explanation for my current emotionally aroused state. I hypothesize that I must have seen my boss's behaviour as an **affront**, that **I really didn't like** it, and that it contravened an important goal of mine, such as maintaining my self-respect. In short, I subsume this event or series of events under the folk-psychological concept of 'resentment'. But I do not have access to the entire sequence of appraisals and reappraisals I (appear to) have made.

Because I am making an after-the-fact summary of the sequence of appraisals and reappraisals that probably occurred, my assessment is likely to be unreliable. Suppose, for example, that my long-time husband were to abandon me for a younger woman. In such a situation my emotions are likely to be in turmoil: streams of grief, anger, shame, and despair intermingle and it would probably be hard for me to summarize my experience in a single word: the emotion process would be too complex and too ambiguous. After a while, when I catalogue the experience in recollection, I may *say* that I am *indignant* that my husband abandoned me for a younger woman, but in fact my behaviour and my physiological reactions reveal that my primary emotions are shame and grief. In our culture indignation is treated as a form of anger, which is a 'powerful' emotion and to preserve self-respect I want to avoid appearing as if I have lost control of my life. Indignation also implies that I am occupying the moral high ground. It is not too much of an exaggeration to say that in our culture grief and shame are for the timid and feeble.

Sometimes, as in Rorty's example of Jonah, a person may be completely wrong about why he responded as he did, because he is unconsciously keeping at bay some deep-seated desires. Jonah's hostile reaction to his new boss is all due to a convoluted story about his past relations with his mother of which Jonah is totally (or at least partially) unaware. Jonah *rationalizes* his emotional response as one of indigna-tion with his new boss, let's say, on the grounds that the new boss is a tyrant (even though he is hard-pressed to come up with the evidence). With therapeutic help, perhaps Jonah can be made to realize that his emotional response is actually one of *fear* and *disappointment*, fear of yet again failing to win love from a mother-figure, and disappointment that his actual mother did not (he thinks) cherish him.

These two examples are obviously about complex emotions. But even when we reflect on the ordinary emotional incidents in our everyday lives, we can never be sure we are getting things right. We all want to think well of ourselves, and prefer to think that we act out of love rather than envy, righteous indignation rather than petty jealousy, pride in ourselves rather than shame. And every emotional situation is ambiguous to some degree, so it is easy to see how people come to label their emotions in ways that are comforting rather than accurate.

Interestingly, however, the way we *name* our emotions and the way we *think* of the situation will affect the emotion process itself. We have already seen how every aspect of an emotion process feeds back on the other aspects. It seems likely that the same thing happens when I label my state with an emotion word. If I label my emotion 'sorrow' rather than 'shame', then my action tendencies and behaviour will probably be different, and consequently I will begin to *feel* different than if I label my emotion 'shame'. If I think I'm sorrowful, then I'll act sorrowful, not ashamed, and *acting* sorrowful can actually make me sorrowful, as William James long ago observed.

sit all day in a moping posture, sigh, and reply to everything with a dismal voice, and your melancholy lingers. . . . Smooth the brow, brighten the eye, contract the dorsal rather than the ventral aspect of the frame, and speak in a major key, pass the genial compliment, and your heart must be frigid indeed if it do not gradually thaw![38]

Changing your posture, your facial and vocal expressions, and your action tendencies will tend to change your physiology and the way you feel, and hence—in James's view—your emotional state. And, as we saw in Ch. 2, there is some empirical evidence to suggest that he was right about this. Ekman has shown that deliberately configuring your facial muscles so that they express a particular emotion produces physiological changes appropriate to the emotion modelled as well as self-reports that one is indeed in the appropriate emotional state. In short, naming one's emotional state as 'sorrow' may actually induce the behaviour and bodily states appropriate to sorrow and thus sorrow itself.

It is in the light of these remarks that I think we should understand one of the most famous experiments in emotion theory, the 1962 study by Schachter and Singer, which is cited by so many philosophers of emotion. The ostensible function of the experiment was to resolve the question of whether cognition plays a role in emotion by demonstrating that specific emotions could be induced by 'the interaction of . . . cognitive factors with a state of physiological arousal'.[39] Subjects were injected with adrenaline but were not told that that is what was happening to them. Then some of the subjects were told about the real side-effects of the drug, others were told nothing, and others were given misleading information. (There was also a placebo condition.) Some subjects were then asked to fill out a questionnaire which asked increasingly insulting questions, while one of the subjects—really a stooge—became increasingly upset and angry, or they were left on their own with a cheery stooge who started a series of apparently spontaneous games, such as playing basketball with balls of paper. The subjects were (unbeknownst to them) observed while interacting with the stooge, and their behaviour measured, and after the experiment they were asked questions designed to reveal their emotional state and also to indicate their awareness of physiological arousal. Pulse measurements were taken before the injection of epinephrine and again at the end of the experiment. Those who showed no increase in pulse rate and no visible signs of arousal were excluded from the experiment, thus ensuring that the subjects were all in a state of physiological arousal.

The results of the experiment seemed to show that those subjects who did not understand why their bodies were behaving in a peculiar way (due to the adrenaline)—they were either ignorant or misinformed about the effects of what they had been injected with—were more susceptible to the stooge. When asked at the end of the experiment 'how irritated, angry or annoyed' they felt, people in the anger group reported feeling significantly angry or irritated. When asked 'how good or happy' they felt, people in the euphoria group reported feeling significantly good or happy. Yet both groups were apparently in the same physiological state. Schachter and Singer thought that the subjects made a *cognitive evaluation* that their state was one of anger or euphoria. By contrast, those who had an explanation for the way they were feeling were less inclined to attribute anger or euphoria to themselves. Schachter and Singer concluded that 'emotional states may be considered a function of a state of physiological arousal and of a cognition appropriate to this state of arousal'.[40]

It is an interesting fact that everybody who describes the Schachter and Singer experiment tends to describe it in different terms and as showing different truths about emotion.[41] One of several odd features of the experiment is that the 'cognitions' that Schachter and Singer claim to be essential to emotions are not evaluations of *the environment*, such as 'I have been insulted,' or 'Something good has happened to me,' which most theorists assume are the kinds of evaluation that normally trigger an emotional response, but evaluations of *the subject's inner state*: the subjects are labelling their inner state with the name of an emotion, 'euphoria' or 'anger'. Another oddity is that it is quite unclear what causes the subjects to label their emotional states as they do. Schachter and Singer might be assuming that there is a *social contagion* effect, that the subjects respond the way the stooge does, by virtue of some sort of motor mimicry, but we just don't know what the mechanism was in fact.

From my point of view, the Schachter and Singer experiment is important because it offers a potential counter-argument to the view that emotions are always set off by automatic affective appraisals. Here is a case in which people started off as merely physiologically aroused, and ended up attributing emotions to themselves without apparently making any affective (or cognitive, for that matter) appraisals of the environment. It is no accident that Schachter is one of the pioneers of research into 'confabulation', the way in which people explain their mental states or behaviour in specious ways that they think are socially expected or acceptable.[42] These people 'felt funny', their fellow subject (the stooge) was clearly angry (euphoric) and so it was natural for subjects to become 'angry' or 'euphoric' regardless of 'the facts.'

Now it is true that we do not know how or why these subjects came to be angry or euphoric, whether by contagion or perhaps by confabulation. However, as soon as people begin to think of themselves as angry or euphoric, they begin to make the affective appraisals, and take on the facial expressions, motor activity, and action tendencies characteristic of that emotional state. In short, thinking they are angry or euphoric becomes a self-fulfilling prophecy. Moreover, in this particular case, it would have been easy to affectively appraise the offensive questionnaire as offensive. (For example, the final question asked 'With how many men (other than your father) has your mother had extramarital relationships?' 4 and under——: 5–9——:10 and over——.) And it would have been easy affectively to appraise the jolly basketball-playing as jolly. In other words the subjects may well have begun to be angry or euphoric in actual fact: they made appropriate affective appraisals, engaged in appropriate behaviour, and so on. Unfortunately, the experimenters did not take detailed physiological data at the end of the experiment that might have shown whether the physiological state of those in the anger group and those in the euphoria group had themselves changed differentially as a result of the experiment, thus potentially providing evidence that the two groups ended up in genuinely diverse emotional states.

Another way of describing what happened was that because the subjects were in a physiologically aroused state and were encouraged to think of themselves as in some emotional state or other (they were asked in a questionnaire what emotional state they were in), they were actually in a *mood* state: a *nervous* or *jittery* mood, perhaps. A mood is usually defined in part as a bodily state in which one is more apt or ready to get into an emotional state.[43] Both sets of subjects were *aroused*, and *nervous* or *jittery* because of the shot of adrenaline, and so were more easily induced to attribute emotional states to themselves. And, as I've suggested, once the people in the anger group began to think of themselves as 'angry', they would start *to think angry thoughts* and *to make angry affective appraisals*. Similarly with respect to the euphoria group.[44] As we'll see in Ch. 13, something like this can happen when we listen to music.

I conclude that how we 'catalogue' our emotional responses affects the way in which the emotion process develops. Sometimes, no doubt, we get it right when we catalogue our emotion as anger or fear or whatever, but, especially in ambiguous situations, we may often get it wrong. When I am distraught about my husband's abandoning me, I do not know exactly what emotions I am experiencing. Like Schachter's subjects, I am in a state of arousal, but my state is ambiguous and I cannot tell exactly why I am responding as I am. Perhaps we could say that I am in a turbulent *mood*. But even if I am wrong in saying that my chief emotion is 'indignation' rather than 'sorrow,' the label, once applied, may affect how the emotional process plays out: my sorrow and shame may gradually give way to genuine indignation.

The Emotion Lexicon

So far I have suggested that affective appraisals, physiological changes, action tendencies, and cognitive monitoring are all part of a normal emotion process and that each element in the process functions in feedback loops to influence the other elements in the process. Now I would like to speculate briefly about the various possible ways in which emotions as named in ordinary language folk psychology could be correlated with the non-cognitive affective appraisals that trigger the primitive emotional responses studied by a scientific psychology, such as practiced by Zajonc and LeDoux (among others).

One possibility is that emotion words in ordinary language simply correspond to liking and disliking in a particular situation. So, roughly speaking, happiness is a positive emotion that can occur in any (liked) situation; relief is a positive emotion that occurs in a situation that turns out well where there has been an expectation that it might not; and pride is a positive emotion that occurs when

I contemplate something good that I identify with in some way. Similarly, unhappiness is a negative emotion that can occur in any (disliked) situation; disappointment is a negative emotion that occurs when there has been an expectation that things would turn out better; and remorse is a negative emotion that occurs when I have done something I perceive to be morally wrong. In other words in this analysis all emotion words describe states in terms of valence— negative or positive—and a particular situation. The job of philosophers like Solomon and Taylor is then to sharpen and make more precise than I have done in this summary the situations in which it is correct to apply a term such as 'remorseful,' 'proud', or 'disappointed'.

Another possibility is that emotion terms in ordinary language correspond to different 'componential' non-cognitive appraisals, such as appraisals of strangeness (corresponding to surprise), appraisals of friend or enemy (corresponding to love and hate), appraisals of liking and disliking (as in the suggestion discussed above), and so on.

A third possibility embodies the idea that each emotion word corresponds to some different goal or interest, and that the non-cognitive appraisals which trigger emotion simply appraise the situation as conducive to or thwarting these various particular goals. Jealousy would then be analysed (following Farrell)[45] as a situation in which A wants to be favoured by B but thinks that B is favouring C over A, and this **thwarts A's goals**!

Finally, there is the possibility that all emotion terms correspond to one of the 'basic emotion' systems, in which simple examples of emotional response induced by non-cognitive appraisals are marked by distinct physiological reactions and action tendencies, as well as by distinct neurological pathways. On this view, the cognitively complex emotions of the sort studied by the philosophers would then be divided up into groups corresponding to different basic emotion systems. The anger system would include what in our language and culture we call 'indignation', 'fury', 'rage', 'irritation', 'choler', 'frustration', 'annoyance', as well as some cases of resentment, envy and jealousy, ingratitude, and scorn. The fear system would include fear, fright, nervousness, worry, terror, panic, and so on, as well, perhaps, as horror, anxiety, suspicion, and maybe embarrassment and some cases of jealousy. The happiness system would presumably include pleasure, relief, gladness, cheerfulness, delight, euphoria, happiness, joy, optimism, satisfaction, self-satisfaction, amusement, as well as pride, hope and hopefulness, gratitude and thankfulness. The unhappiness system would include sadness, unhappiness, despair, disappointment, regret, remorse, anguish, dejection, depression, pessimism, and being upset, as well as, perhaps, shame, humiliation, guilt, being sorry, and some cases of resentment. Some English words would mark what Ekman calls 'blends' of basic emotions: consternation would be a response of unhappiness and surprise, horror perhaps a response of fear and disgust, awe perhaps a response of fear, pleasure, and surprise.

It is in fact impressive how many of our ordinary English words for emotions turn out to be analysable in terms of a fairly limited number of basic emotion systems. Note that the argument is not that the concept of indignation, for example, can be analysed without re-mainder as anger, but that there are non-cognitive appraisals trigger-ing emotional responses that correspond to the basic emotions, and that indignation would in this case be triggered by the anger appraisal (not the fear appraisal or the love appraisal). What exactly this means for blends is unclear. Perhaps both the non-cognitive appraisal **This is strange and unexpected!** and the appraisal **I don't like this!** would be necessary for 'consternation'.

One problem with this way of thinking is that noted by James Averill, the social construction emotion theorist. Averill has made an intensive study of how English speakers use the word 'anger', and he concludes that the situations that most commonly evoke anger in ordinary human life are not the situations of physical danger typically discussed in connection with anger, but of 'frustration, loss of self-esteem, or a threat to an interpersonal relationship'.[46] Moreover, angry responses are extremely diverse. He thinks that 'it seems almost meaningless to ask, what is the typical response during anger?'[47] Furthermore, actual physical aggression—and even the impulse to aggression—is rare in actual cases of anger. In self-reports the most common expression of anger was 'a verbal retort or the denial of some benefit'.[48] Non-aggressive responses, such as talking over the anger-provoking incident, were just as common as aggressive re-sponses. If this is right, then we cannot just assume that every case of anger actually proceeds according to the anger 'affect programme', much less that all cases of indignation, annoyance, irritation, frustra-tion, etc. proceed in this manner.

Of course, we can't be certain what is the correct way to interpret Averill's data, which is mainly derived from interviews and self-reports. However I think it is salutary to reflect that cognitive monitoring is very important in all emotional encounters. As Lazarus has emphasized, cognitive monitoring is what enables us to *cope* with an emotion-arousing situation. We control and modify our responses by means of cognition.[49] So it would not be at all surprising if normal adults who, in the normal interactions of some personal relationship, are provoked by something that the other person does or says nevertheless do not engage in aggressive behaviour, which could well put the relationship itself at risk, but instead give a 'verbal retort' or 'deny some benefit'. It is interesting, however, that the only physiological symptom consistently reported by Averill's subjects is 'increase in general tension or arousal',[50] a response consistent with the anger 'affect programme'. (Again, remember Ekman's notion of display rules: how we manifest anger is partly controlled by informal social rules.)

To sum up, I have been arguing that affective appraisals respond automatically to events in the environment (either internal or external) and set off physiological changes that register the event in a bodily way and get the agent ready to respond appropriately. An emotional response is a response set off by a non-cognitive affective appraisal. I speculated that there are probably a limited number of basic emotion systems each identified by a specific non-cognitive appraisal and the particular suite of behaviour it prompts. Cognitively complex emotions are triggered by the same non-cognitive appraisals as 'primitive' emotions, but they are succeeded by complex cognitive activity. In particular, human beings reflecting on their emotion processes give names to their emotions in the words available to them in their language and culture. Like the startle response of the crayfish, human indignation is a three-stage process of affective appraisal, physiological responses, and cognitive monitoring, but unlike the startled crayfish, an indignant person is likely to be indignant about something requiring complex thought, and is also likely to catalogue her emotional state in words: I was 'resentful' or 'indignant', 'ashamed' or 'embarrassed', 'remorseful' or 'regretful'. The affective appraisal may be the same for 'indignation' and for 'resentment'— **Offence!** or **Nooo!** or **Goal denied!** or whatever—but only cognitive monitoring can make the fine-grained distinctions between indignation and resentment.

Different languages have different words for carving up the emotion landscape corresponding to the different values, interests, and goals characteristic of different cultures. Within a culture, children learn a particular emotion vocabulary in the context of types of situation and characteristic responses to that situation. Ronald de Sousa has proposed that such 'paradigm scenarios' can provide the basis for learning an almost unlimited number of emotions. Moreover, there are many emotional states that have never been labelled. 'Prufishness' was unnamed until Benson named it. Likewise, the emotions examined in other literary works may require more than folk-psychological labelling if they are to be properly monitored and understood. As Susanne Langer says in the epigraph to this chapter, our emotions are 'as various as the lights in a forest'.

But am I not now reverting to the judgement theory that I castigated in Chs. 1 and 2? The short answer is 'No.' The judgement theory claims that an emotion either is or is caused by a judgement or a cognitive evaluation with an intentional object. I deny both claims. As I argued at length in Chs. 1 and 2, a cognitive evaluation alone cannot cause, much less *be*, an emotion. But we are now in a position to see what is right and useful about the judgement theory. What the judgement theorists have got right is their idea that cognitive evaluations are what distinguish one cognitively complex emotional state from another. The best judgement theorists give careful analyses of the differences between resentment and indignation, remorse and regret, shame and embarrassment, by clarifying the conditions under which it is appropriate to use a particular emotion term in our culture. These conditions include the situation in which the emotion occurs, the person's thoughts and beliefs *vis-à-vis* the situation, the attitude of the society towards that emotion in that situation, the subsequent behaviour of the person experiencing the emotion, and so on.

In a case of emotional resentment, for example, the thought that I have been badly treated in a situation in which I have been led to believe I will be well treated may be part of the causal chain leading up to an affective appraisal of **Offence!** When I catalogue my emotion as 'resentment', I am implicitly adverting to a situation in which (I think) I have been treated badly and (I think) I don't deserve it, and it well may be that these thoughts play a causal role in the emotion process: indeed my affective appraisal of **Offence!** may be an affective appraisal of the situation *as I thought it to be*. So yes, thoughts and beliefs and ways of seeing a situation can figure in the causal chain that leads to an affective appraisal, but they are never the whole story. There has to be also a 'meta-appraisal' that this is **Bad!** or an **Offence!** or **Thwarts my goals!** And this meta-appraisal is part of an inbuilt mechanism for detecting harm or offence or goal-thwarting and registering it in a bodily way.

If I say I was 'resentful' about the situation, I am endorsing a causal hypothesis: that certain thoughts and/or beliefs or ways of seeing that are characteristic of resentment did in fact play a causal role in my emotional state. But notice that there is nothing privileged about my access to my psychological state. I can always be wrong. In attributing to myself certain thoughts, beliefs or ways of seeing, and consequently in describing myself as 'resentful', I am doing a little after-the-fact folk psychology: I am hypothesizing about what probably contributed to causing my emotional state. But my physiological state, facial and vocal expressions, and subsequent behaviour may reveal that I have mis-labelled the scenario: it is not a resentment scenario after all, but an indignation scenario. Again, however, if I am convinced that I really am resentful, then thinking may eventually make it so.

An Objection

Paul Griffiths has argued that there are at least two independent phenomena going by the name of 'emotion' that have very little to do with one another, on the one hand Ekman-type 'affect programs', and on the other hand 'higher cognitive states' that are less well understood, and may be explicable along social constructionist lines, but cannot, he thinks, be explained in the same way as an 'affect program'.[51] Griffiths claims that commonsense or folk psychology is wrong to imply that fear, anger, and the rest are unitary concepts. He would therefore presumably reject my attempt to generalize about emotion by arguing that all emotional responses are part of the kind of emotion process I have been describing, and that all (or most) emotional responses are initiated by a non-cognitive affective appraisal.

Griffiths argues that the basic emotion systems identified by Ekman—fear, surprise, anger, disgust, joy, and sadness—are correctly describable as 'affect programmes', in which certain inputs always produce a particular set of complex, co-ordinated, and automatic responses or outputs. He then argues that higher or cognitively complex emotions are independent of affect programmes and must be explained in a totally different way. My response to Griffiths is twofold: first, the evidence that there are indeed affect programmes in the way Griffiths describes them is weak; and secondly, there is good evidence that cognitively complex emotions are caused in just the same way as the 'primitive' emotions Griffiths refers to in his discussion of the affect programmes.

1. Griffiths claims that for each affect programme there are distinct facial and vocal expressions, endocrine changes (such as changes in hormone levels), autonomic nervous system changes, and musculo-skeletal changes (such as flinching or orienting). Griffiths thinks that there may be a single neural programme triggered by an appropriate stimulus, which controls all these various sorts of responses. Alternatively, he considers a view defended by Neil McNaughton, who hypothesizes that different systems have evolved for separate evolutionary reasons, and thinks that different programmes respond to different features of the stimulus situation. McNaughton thinks that some elements in a response will trigger other elements (as Ekman found that posing the facial expression characteristic of a basic emotion also produced the ANS changes characteristic of that same emotion), which is why the various responses appear to be co-ordinated even though not directed by a single controlling programme. Griffiths comments that this general approach is quite consistent with his notion of an affect programme: the important point is that the responses are of many different sorts, yet all automatic and co-ordinated.

Griffiths may be right that there are affect programmes in nature, but I think we have to admit that right now the evidence is far from conclusive. As we have seen, although there is evidence of distinct facial expressions for some basic emotions, the evidence of distinct ANS activity is far weaker, and even Griffiths notes that, despite some promising work by Scherer, not much is known about distinct vocal expressions. There is some evidence that 'action tendencies'—musculo-skeletal and endocrine changes—are distinct for each basic emotion, but, as we saw in Ch. 2, Frijda has noted sceptically that distinct action tendencies may not be distinctive of particular emotions but of particular goals which may be common to different emotions and may occur in non-emotional states.

More importantly, what Ellsworth's analysis of emotion suggests is that even if Griffiths is right and a particular kind of non-cognitive appraisal does indeed set in motion a set of distinctive responses (ANS changes, facial expressions, musculo-skeletal responses, expressive vocalizations, endocrine system changes), each of these responses may not only occur independently, as McNaughton suggests, but may also have its own pattern of temporal development. Even more significantly, each one will *feed back* on to the others and will itself be affected in different ways by feedback from each different system. Perhaps most important of all, *subsequent cognitive monitoring will affect the development of each of these responses*, perhaps in different ways and at different times. In other words, even if Griffiths' picture of a programme which dictates the development of a basic emotion is appropriate for some pre-programmed responses, such as the rat's fear of the sound that is conditioned by an electric shock, or the startle response of the crayfish, cognitive monitoring will change everything that happens subsequent to the initial affective appraisal and the initial physiological changes. Depending on the details of the situation, cognitive appraisal and reappraisal will modify the various different responses. I conclude that it is not clear that affect programmes exist in the way described by Griffiths, and even if they do, even if some emotion processes are pre-programmed in the sense that a specific input automatically produces a specific output, these emotion processes will continue and develop in a more flexible way after the 'programme' has run its course.

2. Griffiths thinks that we cannot analyse higher or cognitively complex emotions in the same terms as basic emotions. What I have been arguing throughout this chapter is that we can, indeed that it is possible that *all* emotions can be analysed in terms of basic emotions. I have also explained how a primitive, inflexible, non-cognitive appraisal—**This is bad for me!** or **This is a threat!** or **Here's an enemy!**—can take as input a complex cognition, so that I respond

with fear not only to the large hairy bear that is haring towards and bearing down on me, but also to my boss's quiet ultimatum. Earlier I argued that it is a not unreasonable hypothesis that there are basic emotion systems that evolved to deal with important situations of loss, danger, threat, etc. and that through learning have become capable of being evoked by a vast number of different situations (although all are roughly describable as situations of loss, danger, threat, etc.). As we have seen, a great many—perhaps all—of the emotions identified in folk psychology can be analysed in terms of a very few basic emotions. In complex social contexts, the programmed suite of reactions will often no longer be particularly useful, except as a communication device: screaming and running would be a very unexpected and counterproductive response to the boss. And in any case, each set of reactions—facial, vocal, motor, etc.—to a non-cognitive appraisal of threat (say) will be modified by subsequent cognitive monitoring. When my boss insults me, I may realize that exhibiting fear is not a politically wise response and I will instead smile politely and 'suck it up'. A polite smile is dictated by the 'display rules' of my culture, and only a little fearful or angry 'leakage' from the tightness around my mouth reveals what my affective appraisal of the situation is and what I am really feeling.[52]

If this picture of emotion is correct, then we can explain fear or anger as a unitary phenomenon, always caused by a particular kind of non-cognitive affective appraisal of **Threat!** or **Offence!** which always leads to a typical pattern of bodily responses, regardless of how little or how much cognitive work it takes to detect the threat in question. Fear and anger are basically the same no matter where and when they occur, just as folk psychology assumes they are. It follows that in my view Griffiths is overly pessimistic about the value of folk-psychological theories of the emotions, and the extent to which they can be usefully appealed to in the scientific study of emotion.

How To Be Angry Without Being Emotional

Another objection to my approach might be that if I am right, then emotion words such as 'angry' and 'afraid' will not always refer to bona fide emotional states. But this does not strike me as a serious objection. We often say that people are *angry* about the state of the economy or, like Robert Gordon's farmers, *afraid* that it will rain, but without implying that they are emotionally worked up. When a person makes the cognitive evaluation characteristic of anger or fear or embarrassment but does not 'get emotional' about it, I suggest that the person is not in a bona fide emotional state, but in a related cognitive state. We use the same name for the cognitive state and the corresponding emotional state, because typically the cognitive state leads to (an affective appraisal and) the emotional state, but in this particular case it does not. Saying a person is 'angry' or 'afraid' or 'embarrassed' that, say, the party has been cancelled does not imply that the person is in an emotional state. If the person is an optimist, well fed, well rested, and in a good mood, and the party isn't very important anyway, then he or she may be quite unemotional about the situation.

In short, our emotion words—jealousy, anger, etc.—have derivative uses where they refer not to emotional responses per se but simply to the evaluations themselves which typically but not always produce emotional responses. If I wish I were young again and in the Paris of yesteryear, then we may say that I am *nostalgic for Paris*, even if I am not making any non-cognitive appraisal and I am physiologically unmoved. I am not experiencing an *emotional response* to (my thoughts of) Paris. We can call my state an 'emotion of nostalgia' if we like, but this is misleading because there is no 'emotionality' or emotional upheaval.[53] Similarly, I may be *happy* that I am at home again at the end of a long and busy day, but it is misleading to say that I am experiencing an 'emotion of happiness' unless I am in a suitable physiological state.

Sometimes when I am *angry* about something, I will be emotional about it and sometimes not. Why is this? Why am I emotional about something on some occasions and on other occasions not? Or why does the very same event make *me* emotional and not *you*, although we are both evaluate the event in an angry or fearful way? There are almost certainly a number of variables involved here.

1. For objects, people, or events to make me emotional, I must have some important want, goal, or interest at stake. I will not get emotional about something that is of no importance to me. Even

when I get emotional about something that appears to be trivial, it has to have some significance for me or mine that may be invisible to a bystander. Because you are constantly making off with my property, I blow up when you borrow my pencil. Nevertheless, this does not seem to be a sufficient explanation of emotional states, since although I can sometimes get quite emotional about something trivial, at other times I may not. Why is this?

2. Sometimes I am distracted. I am not paying the requisite attention to an event. Usually when you make off with my stuff, I am deeply resentful and upset. Today I just got a promotion and a big present from my co-workers, and I am not alert to what in other circumstances would offend me. In other words, one has to be alert or paying attention in some sense to the offensive event, in order to register it as an offence.[54]

3. One must be in a state of bodily readiness. Notoriously, if one is short of sleep, it is easier to see the ordinary mishaps of life as wrongs or offences deliberately inflicted by an uncaring world; one is more prone to respond negatively. If one is full of energy one is more likely to think of the world as one's oyster.

4. The emotion states I get into are partly a function of my current *mood*. My moods may vary from one occasion to another, and mood changes bring in their wake changes in our predisposition to be in certain emotional states. Sometimes I am desperately in need of affection and respect, and when you pinch my pencil without so much as a by-your-leave, **I really don't like it**. At other times, I am in a more confident and optimistic mood and I am resigned to your thievery. A mood is a bodily state that lowers the threshold for getting into a bona fide emotional state.[55] In an irritable mood I am more likely to get angry with you about the pencil. In a depressed mood I am more likely to see your action as a sign of your disrespect and my worthlessness.

5. Different people have in any case different thresholds for responding emotionally because of temperamental differences, such as pessimism versus optimism: I am more prone to respond negatively than you are; you are more inclined to positive responses. In short, two people may be entertaining the same thought at the same time— 'she's pinching my pencil'—but only one makes the further non-cognitive appraisal **This is bad**. Again, different emotional responses

can differ in intensity, depending upon the intensity of the physiological symptoms of emotion, and perhaps on the intensity of the
wants and wishes which are deemed to be at stake.

Conclusion

I have been arguing in this chapter that emotions are *processes*, in which
a rough-and-ready affective appraisal causes physiological responses,
motor changes, action tendencies, changes in facial and vocal expression, and so on, succeeded by cognitive monitoring. The function of
non-cognitive affective appraisals is to draw attention automatically
and insistently by bodily means to whatever in the environment is of
vital importance to me and mine.[56] These affective appraisals can be
automatically evoked not only by simple perceptions such as a sudden
loud sound, but also by complex thoughts and beliefs. The reason why
we experience emotions as passive phenomena is that we are never
fully in control of our emotions: once an affective appraisal occurs, the
response occurs too. We can influence our emotions only indirectly
through subsequent cognitive monitoring.

An emotion process involves constant feedback from each of its
elements to the others. More finely discriminating cognitive monitoring affirms or disconfirms the affective appraisal, and probably
assesses such matters as how much control one has over the situation,
whether one can cope with it, and what is likely to happen next. In
human beings, the end of an emotion process—or one stream of a
more complex emotion process—is often marked by a conscious
judgement cataloguing the emotion in recollection: people label
their emotions with one of the emotion terms available to them in
their language and culture. Naming one's emotion and what caused it
is, however, notoriously unreliable.

In chapter one we saw that a judgement, or a set of judgements, can
never all by itself be sufficient for emotion. In order for a cognitively
complex state such as my jealousy of a young rival on the tennis pro
circuit (as discussed by Dan Farrell)[57] or my wary suspicion of a pushy
insurance salesman (as discussed by Pat Greenspan)[58] to initiate emotional responses, there has to be a further affective non-cognitive
appraisal of the situation and subsequent physiological changes. If this

is correct, then it follows that Rorty, Kraut, and Greenspan were right to note that the evaluations central to emotion are not cognitive evaluations. Solomon was right to say that the evaluations central to emotion are of a special, urgent character. And Lyons was right to identify an emotion as a process in which a certain kind of physiological response is caused by an evaluation. But none of these thinkers identified the relevant evaluations correctly as rough-and-ready affective appraisals that happen very fast, serve to focus attention in an insistent way, and automatically produce physiological changes and action tendencies. Moreover, the kinds of cognitive evaluation that the judgement theorists discuss are never necessary to emotion. A belief that I am in danger is neither necessary nor sufficient for fear, for example. All that's needed is an affective appraisal of **Threat!** and once that affective appraisal of **Threat!** occurs, then willy-nilly there's a fearful response.

The judgement theorists are engaged in after-the-fact classification of emotion processes, using the resources of ordinary language and the terms of folk psychology. The beliefs or thoughts or wants that they posit as crucial to some particular emotion may well figure in the causal chain eventuating in an affective appraisal, but the beliefs and thoughts and wants they identify are never *sufficient* to set off an emotion process. At best they figure among the conditions leading up to the affective appraisal that sets off the emotion process. The judgement theorists could also be thought of as explaining what we might call cognitive attitudes: they may make accurate generalizations about when it is correct to say that I am 'afraid that it will rain' or 'regretful about your lost garlic-press'. But they are not explaining emotion. They are not explaining how an emotion process actually unfolds, the sequence of affective and cognitive appraisals that actually characterizes a specific emotion process.

What the judgement theorists are really doing is trying to explain how we should use language, and specifying the general kinds of circumstances when it is appropriate to describe ourselves as 'angry', 'indignant', remorseful', or 'regretful'. When we label our emotions after the fact, we use the classifications that philosophers and psychologists offer us, that make sense of the emotion process in the terms of our language and culture and fit our thoughts and behaviour into recognizable social patterns. Cataloguing our emotions is a form of generalization about emotions. But if we really want to understand emotions in all their uniqueness and individuality, if we want to follow the progress of an emotion process as it unfolds, if we want to understand how the different elements of the process feed into one another and interact, and how the streams of emotional life blend and flow into one another, then we would do better to stay away from the generalizations of philosophers and psychologists, and turn instead to the detailed studies of emotion that we find in great literature.

Part Two

Emotion in Literature

It is a deeply rooted idea in contemporary Western culture that there is some peculiarly intimate relationship between the arts and the emotions. Now that we have a better idea of what the emotions are and how they function, I am going to be looking at the role of the emotions in our encounters with the arts. I begin with literature.

In Part Two I examine the idea that one of the important things that literature does is to evoke emotions in readers. In Ch. 4 I argue that some works of literature—especially realistic novels by the likes of Tolstoy and Henry James—need to be experienced emotionally if they are to be properly understood. There is some interesting work in psychology on narrative, but little has been done on the role of emotion in understanding narrative. I explain how our emotions function to help us understand a novel, focusing especially on *characters*, and I argue that a plausible interpretation of a novel relies on prior emotional responses to it. In Ch. 5 I answer a raft of possible objections to this idea, including the so-called paradox of fiction.

In Ch. 6 I give a reading of Edith Wharton's novel, *The Reef*, in which I argue that reading a morally serious novel such as *The Reef* is a means of education, an education of the emotions or, borrowing from Flaubert, a sentimental education. Again, knowing how the emotions actually function enables us to see more clearly exactly what an emotional education consists in. Here I also address two issues that

I pushed under the carpet in Ch. 4. First, what *is* a 'proper' way of understanding a novel? Different people respond emotionally in different ways to the same novel, play, or movie, but perhaps only some of these responses are 'authorized' by the work itself. Is there any one authorized version of a novel or play? I do not think so. Nevertheless some emotional responses are more appropriate than others. Secondly, what is the role of the author in evoking my emotional responses? Should I be responding as the author intended me to? If I do not, am I fatally misunderstanding what I am reading? I end Ch. 6 by briefly tackling these thorny questions. In general I defend a 'reader-response' theory of interpretation that treats our emotional responses to a novel or play as important data in arriving at an interpretation.

Chapter 7 turns to form in literature. Taking off from some findings about the coping mechanism from the psychologist Richard Lazarus, I develop an account of how form manages and guides our emotional experiences of a literary work, and also enables us to 'cope' with emotionally difficult or highly charged material. I again use *The Reef* as one of my examples, but I also spend some time talking about poetry.

The focus in these four chapters is on literature, but I believe that the ideas I am exploring have much wider application. There are paintings, sculptures, movies, dance pieces, and music which also demand to be experienced emotionally if they are to yield up all their riches. (In Part Four I'll deal with emotion and music.) But I do not want to argue that what I say is true of all art, or that if you cannot appreciate something emotionally then it can't be art at all. Different kinds of artworks have very different goals. Some are mainly concerned with design or form. Others deal mainly with ideas and demand to be appreciated primarily on an intellectual level. I am not arguing that all artworks have to be experienced emotionally if they are to count as art. I am not even arguing that all artworks have to be experienced emotionally if we are to understand them properly. Given the protean nature of art, any such generalization is unlikely to be true.

My main goal in these chapters is not to arrive at hard and fast distinctions about which types of artwork or novel or poetry do or do not merit our emotional engagement, but to clarify with respect to the works—whatever they turn out to be—that do emotionally engage us *how emotion enters into our interpretation* of these works, *how we learn emotionally* from them about human nature and human motivation, and *how emotion manages and guides our responses* to them through the manipulation of form.

4

The Importance of Being Emotional

In every great poem—in Shakespeare's plays, in Dante's *Commedia*, in Goethe's *Faust*—we must indeed pass through the whole gamut of emotions. If we were unable to grasp the most delicate nuances of the different shades of feeling, unable to follow the continuous variations in rhythm and tone, if unmoved by sudden dynamic changes, we could not understand and feel the poem.

Ernst Cassirer, *An Essay on Man*

How to Read a Story

A good story makes us curious and suspenseful about what is going to happen; it makes us laugh and cry; and it may make us feel fear and anger, horror and disgust, love and compassion, indeed the whole repertoire of emotions in our culture. In this chapter I'll explain how the emotions function when we respond emotionally to characters and events in novels, plays, and movies. We'll see that emotion processes actually work just the same way when we respond to characters and events in novels, plays, and movies, as they do when we respond to people and events in real life.[1] In this chapter I'll be explaining how our emotional responses to novels, plays, and movies help us to *understand* them, to understand characters, and grasp the significance of events in the plot. (And in Ch. 6 I'll be explaining how our emotional responses to novels, plays, and movies can also teach us about life itself.) I'll suggest that our emotions help us in the construction of a satisfactory summary reading of the novel or play or movie, or what is often called an 'interpretation'.

This may not be true of *all* novels, plays, and movies, but it is certainly true for realistic novels, plays, and films such as the novels cited by F. R. Leavis as part of the 'Great Tradition' of the English novel.[2] Indeed the great realistic novels of nineteenth-century European and American fiction, that purport to be depictions of 'real life', require to be experienced *emotionally* if they are to be properly experienced and understood. In this chapter I'll be demonstrating how a reader figures out the meaning of a work of this sort in the process of emotionally interacting with the text. In this sense, I'll be defending a version of 'reader–response theory'.

Although some form of reader–response theory is widely accepted among teachers of literature, it is not a very popular view among philosophers who write about literary interpretation. It is true that the theory faces important problems. If people's emotional responses are partly going to determine the meaning of a novel, then since different people respond very differently to the same novel, how can we ever come to agreement about what it means? What if readers determine the theme to be something that the author could not possibly have intended? These problems might not unduly worry a literary critic who is mainly interested in finding bold new innovative and intriguing responses and readings of a work, but they really bother philosophers, because philosophers are always preoccupied with finding clear criteria and general truths. I am going to leave aside this question for the moment, however, and try to show first what goes on when we interact emotionally with a novel, and secondly how having emotional responses generated by reading a novel or watching a play can actually help us to understand the novel or play and can serve as the basis of an interpretation. I'll return to the question of criteria of correctness at the end of Ch. 6.

It might seem puzzling how having our emotions aroused can help us to understand anything at all. After all, if I am very angry or afraid or sorrowful, I am not in a very good state for understanding anything. Moreover, far from helping me to understand the novel I am reading, my own feelings may distract my attention from it. Surely, it might be said, in my encounter with a novel, I should be trying to understand the novel itself and its qualities, rather than focusing on my own feelings, which may be idiosyncratic, leading me away from rather than into the work. There are indeed many times when the emotions aroused by a story do not help me to understand it at all. If I'm watching a film and the hero's appearance reminds me insistently of my beloved Jack, the hero may elicit in me a nice warm feeling that has nothing to do with the character on screen (who happens to be a weasel). Or if I read in a novel a description of my home town where the novel is set and fall into a gloomy reverie about my ghastly childhood in that town, my feelings of gloom may have nothing to do with the way the town is depicted in the novel. What's more, in these cases my attention seems to be mainly directed not at the novel but at Jack or my childhood.

Obviously, then, not every emotion aroused by a novel or movie is relevant to understanding it. There are, however, a number of uncontroversial ways in which emotion *can* contribute to our understanding of works of literature and film. A feeling of curiosity or interest may precede our engagement with a work and may prod us to persist in its study. A feeling of pleasure in our mastery of the work may succeed our experience of it, and perhaps motivate us to experience other works in the hope of achieving a similar reward. What I want to focus on, however, is somewhat more controversial. I believe that, in addition to getting us interested in and repaying with pleasure or displeasure our attention to a novel, our emotional responses can also play a crucial role in the way we actually *understand* and *interpret* it. The emotions function to alert us to important aspects of the story such as plot, characters, setting, and point of view. Especially in reading the great realist novels of the Western tradition, our emotions can lead us to discover subtleties in character and plot that would escape a reader who remains emotionally uninvolved in the story.

Even if you agree with me that an emotional experience of this kind of novel helps us to understand it, you might still think that it's possible to come to the same understanding by a more cerebral engagement with the text. Towards the end of the chapter I'll try to show that this is not true: nothing else can do the job that emotions do. Without appropriate emotional responses, some novels simply *cannot* be adequately understood.

Getting Involved with Literary Characters

In reading a novel, we may not be emotionally worked up all the time, but typically there are moments when we do become emotionally engaged. These tend to be occasions when the author is aiming to impress upon us facts or events that are important to the novel, to establish character, to mark significant developments in the plot, to drive home the theme or moral of the story, or—as often happens—all three. To make my case that emotional responses are often necessary for us to understand a novel, play, or movie, I'll begin by giving some examples that demonstrate how the text often communicates something important by evoking the reader's emotional responses to an incident or a remark or a turn of the plot. For simplicity's sake, I have chosen examples in which it is pretty clear that the emotional responses described are appropriate to the text and were probably intended by the author. In studying these examples, we'll see that they evoke emotion processes in just the same way as emotional situations in real life.

Weeping for Anna Karenina

Anna Karenina is never more an object of sympathy and compassion than when she returns surreptitiously to her old home in order to visit her son Seryozha, whom she has not seen since she abandoned her husband to go away with Vronsky. We know that Anna has longed to see Seryozha and has looked forward joyfully to her visit. She buys a great many toys to take with her for his birthday, and arrives at the house early in the morning before Karenin is up. The boy is half asleep and seems to think that she is part of a happy dream. Seeing and touching him again, she is moved by how much he has grown and how much she has missed him. The visit is short; Karenin wakes up and the servants warn her to leave; she has to go in a hurry. When she has gone, Tolstoy comments poignantly: 'She had not had time to undo, and so carried back with her, the parcel of toys she had chosen so sadly and with so much love the day before.'[3]

In this short episode, the reader's sympathy and compassion are themselves a way of understanding Anna and her situation. An examination of the sources of our emotional responses to Anna reveal important facts about Anna and her situation as described in the novel.

According to Lawrence Blum, compassion characteristically involves 'imaginative dwelling on the condition of the other person, an active regard for his good, a view of him as a fellow human being, and emotional responses of a certain degree of intensity'.[4] Blum's account is thoughtful and persuasive, and I think it is in general consistent with my own view of emotion. Blum's account of compassion includes as an important element the focusing of one's attention: one 'dwells' on the condition of the other person. He stresses the 'strength and duration' of compassion, contrasting the 'distress, sorrow, hopes and desires' of true compassion with mere 'passing reactions or twinges of feeling', which would be insufficient to maintain the focus of attention and disposition to action necessary to compassion.[5] Blum's account also mentions 'emotional responses of a certain degree of intensity'. Interestingly, when he specifies what those emotional responses are he refers to the basic emotion of sadness. Compassion involves (at least) a basic emotional response of sadness evoked by a perception or thought of another person's unfortunate state.

I have stressed that affective appraisals are always in terms of one's own goals, interests, wants, or wishes. I respond emotionally when my interests or those of my group (me or mine) are perceived to be at stake. In most of my discussion of emotion I have stressed the case where my own interests are at stake. A paradigm example of emotion since James has been the situation where I am being threatened by the rampaging bear in the wilderness. However, although I no doubt respond with intense emotion to that situation, I probably react with even more intense emotion when it is not me but my child who is threatened by the bear. I often feel much more bitter towards those who hurt my loved ones than towards those who hurt me. And I am often happier for their successes than for my own. Usually, it is only our nearest and dearest who evoke these powerful emotions, but as we discover from television news coverage of calamities and atrocities in distant lands, we can be brought to experience emotions for other folk if they are presented as connected to us in some way.[6] We may be able to read dispassionately about a flood in Bangladesh, but if we see on the screen drowned babies looking very much like our own babies or those of our neighbours, then dispassion is likely to turn into passion.

When Blum says that compassion involves dwelling imaginatively on the condition of the other person, he is talking about the importance of involving oneself in that condition. Blum emphasizes that while *identification* with the other person is not necessary for compassion (although it often helps), one must be able to reconstruct imaginatively what the other person is undergoing.[7] This involves not only imaginatively taking the other person's viewpoint, and involving oneself in the other person's vision of the world, but also having care and concern for that person as a fellow human being. In other words, one has to connect oneself with the other person and regard her as like oneself in important ways: she is part of my group, whether this be sect or society or language group or ethnic group or gender or species. She is in some sense one of 'my own', the kind of creature who arouses my emotions by virtue of being related to me. Indeed, part of the social value of reading novels arises from the fact that novels expand the list of those with whom we can sympathize. We discover that even *those people* are human beings like us, with the same troubles and problems, the same loves and hates, the same longings and hopes.

In a similar vein, Blum stresses that the compassionate person has 'an active regard' for the 'good' of the person for whom they feel compassion. One of the aspects of emotion that usually seems to be present is an action tendency of an appropriate sort. When engaged with literature, there is no actual action one can perform to help the unhappy heroine, but sensitively responding readers may indeed find themselves wanting to help and feeling frustrated that they cannot. If Blum is right, then compassion 'requires the disposition to perform beneficent actions', that is, an urge or impulse to action of a certain sort, and where this is impossible (as it is impossible for us to help Anna Karenina), then it requires 'hope and desire for the relief of the condition by those in a position to provide it' (for example, by Karenin).

When we read the scene of the visit to Seryozha, we feel an intense urge to help Anna, an intense distress and sorrow at her predicament, an intense desire and hope that her predicament will be resolved. The passage is so poignant indeed that it easily provokes tears and other physiological symptoms of sadness and distress. If, however, we experience the passage emotionally in this way, then we are in a good position to try to discover *why* we respond emotionally as we do, and this in turn can lead us to seek in the work the origins of this response. Our emotional reaction marks this passage as significant in the story: it represents the clearest realization Anna has yet achieved of how much she has lost in abandoning Karenin and how hopeless the possibility of return has become. At the same time she herself does not articulate these thoughts and is perhaps only half-consciously aware of them. Her naiveté together with her suffering combine to give the passage the peculiar poignancy it evokes. It is through responding emotionally to this passage that we are made aware of the poignancy of her situation and thereby acquire a deeper, fuller understanding of the work.

Revulsion for Macbeth

There is a horrifying moment in *Macbeth* when Rosse brings word to Macduff that Macbeth has had Lady Macduff and all their children murdered. When Malcolm seeks to comfort Macduff, he responds:

> He has no children. All my pretty ones?
> Did you say all? O hell-kite! All!
> What, all my pretty chickens and their dam
> At one fell swoop?[8]

Aside for compassion for Macduff, we are also *horrified* and *repulsed* by Macbeth. My apprehension of Macbeth affects me in a personal way: put crudely, he has violated a value-system that is important to me. I can't help but focus my attention on Macbeth's horrific deeds. And I may well respond physiologically, by shuddering, turning cold, and tensing my muscles. I may also experience an impulse to retreat or withdraw from Macbeth (and maybe also a horrified fascination with him that does not permit me to withdraw). In other words, Macbeth evokes in me an emotional response of horror and disgust.

How does all this help me to *understand* Macbeth? The emotional response I have described can, I think, lead to a deeper understanding of Macbeth. If we seek the source of our emotional response of horror and repulsion, we find a man who, in his attempt to secure the throne of Scotland for himself and his chosen successors, has multiplied his crimes until, with the murder of Lady Macduff and her children, he is spreading evil not simply for some definable goal—as in the initial murder of Duncan—but out of a generalized fear of and hatred for anyone who opposes him. The horror and repulsion we feel for Macbeth is an emotional reaction to a man who has put himself outside the norms of human conduct, denied his humanity, and isolated himself from the rest of mankind. He is in danger of becoming a *monster* and hence an object of horror and disgust.[9] We feel ourselves personally involved in this view of Macbeth, because of our own concerns, interests, and values: we are human; we fear and dislike a man whose actions show such contempt for our fundamental human values. Macbeth threatens us because he too is human and yet he is capable of denying his humanity. Perhaps, too, this raises the possibility that in the right circumstances we might be capable of becoming like Macbeth ourselves. For this reason, while Macbeth, unlike Oedipus, may not arouse our pity, he does arouse our fear. (Later in the play he also evokes a grudging admiration for his courage and for the clarity of his self-knowledge.)

Laughing at Strether

My third example is less depressing than the first two. There is a moment at the beginning of Henry James's novel, *The Ambassadors*, when Maria Gostrey and Strether are just getting to know each other. Miss Gostrey has just learned that Strether's full name is 'Mr. Lewis Lambert Strether', and she comments that she likes it.

'particularly the Lewis Lambert. It's the name of a novel of Balzac's.'
   'Oh, I know that!' said Strether.
   'But the novel's an awfully bad one.'
   'I know that too.' Strether smiled. To which he added with an irrelevance that was only superficial: 'I come from Woollett, Massachusetts.'

The remark amuses us not just by its apparent inconsequence but also because Strether is so anxious to avow his origins, as though, as Maria Gostrey points out, he wants to prepare her for 'the worst'. There is also the comic incongruity between the reference to Balzac and the reference to Woollett. As Maria Gostrey reflects: 'Balzac had described many cities, but he had not described Woollett, Massachusetts.'[10]

In this incident we perceive Strether as faintly comic, we focus on the comic elements in him and we are provoked to mild laughter or a smile; we relax; perhaps we also feel a mild urge to give Strether an affectionate and reassuring pat on the shoulder. How does this emotional perception help us to understand the incident? In seeking the source of our response, our attention is drawn to Strether's good nature, to a mildly priggish side he has (I'm from Woollett, not evil Paris!) and to his insularity. It reinforces the impression we already have of Strether as a good, well-meaning, intelligent man who is also a naive and rather strait-laced traveller. But although Strether comes off in this passage as faintly comic, we laugh *with* him rather than *at* him. After all, it is through Strether's eyes that the reader sees the action of the story, and we trust his honesty, even if—as we discover—his psychological understanding is unreliable.[11]

What is 'Emotional Involvement'?

What does it mean to become *emotionally involved* in the characters, situations, and events recounted in a novel such as *Anna Karenina* or *The Ambassadors*? In the first part of this book I argued that in general an emotion is a *process* of interaction between an organism and its environment. When human beings have an emotional response to something in the (internal or external) environment, they make an *affective appraisal* that picks that thing out as *significant to me* (given my wants, goals, and interests) and requiring *attention*. This affective appraisal causes *physiological changes*, *action tendencies*, and expressive gestures, including characteristic *facial and vocal expressions*, that may be subjectively experienced as *feelings*, and the whole process is then modified by *cognitive monitoring*. The various aspects of the emotion process are interconnected in various ways. For example, physiological responses reinforce attention. Expressive gestures, action tendencies, and behaviour may change the environment so that the emotional situation changes or dissipates. Cognitive monitoring may confirm or disconfirm affective appraisals. In short the process is constantly modulating in response to feedback from the various elements in the process.

This analysis has a number of important implications for what it means to get emotionally involved with the events and characters in a novel.

1. First of all, it is clear that I won't experience any emotional response to a novel unless I sense that my own interests, goals, and wants are somehow at stake. The story has to be told in such a way that the reader cares about the events it recounts. If I am going to respond emotionally to the character Anna Karenina, what happens to her has to be important to me in some way. When I read *Anna Karenina* I find myself deeply caring about the fate of the characters, especially Anna herself: I don't want her to fall under that train. I don't like Karenin's silly friend who devotes herself to him and leads him into superstition. I want Karenin to be more understanding, less sensitive to his self-image, less rigid and bitter. I react to the characters in a way that suggests I feel my own wants and interests to be at stake in what happens to them.

2. Emotions are *bodily* responses, that reinforce attention on the emotional situation, prepare us for appropriate action, and signal to others what state we are in. If I am in an emotional state, that means I get emotionally or physiologically worked up: perhaps my heart rate accelerates, perhaps I weep. If I am genuinely feeling sorrow for Anna, then I experience physiological changes, especially autonomic changes. In addition, perhaps my facial expression will be characteristic of sorrow and perhaps I may weep. These physiological changes reinforce my focus of attention on Anna and her painful situation. I may also experience action tendencies: perhaps I want to help Anna and have a *tendency* to act to achieve this.

3. If I am truly in an emotional state, then it is non-cognitive affective appraisals that fix my attention on those aspects of the story that are of significance to me and mine. An emotional response is a physiological response initiated by a non-cognitive affective appraisal which evaluates the world instinctively and automatically in terms of my wants and wishes, my goals and interests, or, possibly, in terms of certain basic appraisals corresponding to some set of basic emotions: **This is a threat! This is an offence! This is wonderful!** and so on.

If we are watching a play or movie, what are appraised in the first instance are the people and the actions before our eyes. I perceive various goings-on, and, if the play or movie appeals to some deeply held interest or goal or value of mine, then I will react automatically and physiologically: my heart may pound and I may find my palms are clammy. Some of what we react to, however, is reported by the actors or implied by what they say and do, rather than presented before us on the stage or screen. In ancient Greek drama the worst news—that Jocasta has hung herself and Oedipus blinded himself, that a monstrous bull from the sea has killed Hippolytus—is always reported by a luckless attendant or messenger, rather than graphically portrayed on stage.[12] In such cases, if we respond emotionally, we are responding to thoughts about the events unfolding, rather than the situation itself. In novels, where nothing is presented before our eyes, our responses are always to what we are thinking about rather than to anything directly perceived. What we perceive are words on a page; what we respond to are their content, the thoughts and images that they provoke.[13] In either case if there is a genuinely emotional response, it is generated by an affective (non-cognitive) appraisal.

4. Emotional involvement also entails that my attention is absorbed in the events of the novel. As we have seen, there is good evidence that affective appraisals focus attention on those things in which we have a personal stake or interest, and the resultant physiological changes reinforce that focus of attention.

5. But an emotion isn't just a physiological response caused by an affective appraisal. Even in the most primitive cases, the fast automatic appraisal gives way immediately to a cognitive appraisal that monitors the affective appraisal and modifies subsequent behaviour and physiological responses. For example, after an affective appraisal of Threat! a cognitive appraisal may confirm the affective appraisal (yes, danger is nigh; that's a mugger over there in the dark) or it can deny the affective appraisal and abort the physiological changes (there's no danger: that's not a mugger lurking in the darkness; it's the shadow of a tree), or it can lead to a new affective appraisal (that's not a mugger; it's my beloved come home unexpectedly from the war) and a new sequence of physiological and motor changes.

The cognitive appraisals and reappraisals of my affective appraisal influence my physiological responses, my focus of attention, and also my actions and action tendencies. If I feel compassion for a neighbour, there is probably something I can do to help her or him, but if I feel compassion for the flood victims in Bangladesh, I may want to help but be unable to. Similarly, there is nothing I can do to help Anna Karenina.

Most readers of the novel make a cognitive appraisal that this is a *story* we are engaged with and that there is no appropriate action to take. Even if I weep over Anna Karenina's fate, and I want to help her, and have a tendency to lecture her in my head ('Don't do it,' 'You'll regret it'), I know perfectly well that I cannot help her, cannot lecture her, cannot rescue her from her fate. Indeed, part of the poignancy in my thoughts about her derives from the cognitive appraisal: 'I am not in control of this series of events.'

Cognitive monitoring has other important roles too, in readjusting attention and in reflecting on initial affective appraisals. As I'll argue later, in reading a complex novel such as *Anna Karenina*, we don't just emote about Anna. We use our emotional responses towards her as data in arriving at an interpretation of her character. And although of course there are many other aspects of the novel, I think we will all agree that an interpretation of Anna's character lies at the heart of the novel, its plot and its theme. Cognitive monitoring of our emotional responses to Anna provides crucial data for an interpretation of the book as a whole.

6. As we have seen, there is evidence from LeDoux and others that there are special emotional memory systems, independent of declarative memory. Some believe that emotional responses are stored in motor memory; indeed, if Antonio Damasio is right, then the brain is able to classify scenarios as harmful or beneficial, based on *past experience* with *similar* such scenarios, and it does this by marking these categories of scenario in a *bodily* (somatic) way, which we access by means of feelings of bodily change. If this is right, then the characters and events in the novel may elicit bodily responses based on our own emotional memories. But more importantly, if my emotional reactions to the novel are strong enough, then they in turn may become encoded in emotional memory, making new connections between affective appraisals and bodily responses (somatic markers) and influencing my thoughts and beliefs long after I have finished the novel.

7. Finally, I have stressed that an emotion is a *process* in which emotional (physiological) responses are activated by an affective appraisal that is instinctive and automatic, but that gives way to cognitive monitoring of the situation which reflects back on the instinctive appraisal and modifies expressive, motor, and autonomic activity accordingly as well as actions and action tendencies.

In short, in reading a skilfully constructed realistic novel, my initial affective responses to the events and characters treat them much as if they were in fact real. When I am emotionally engaged with a novel, I find *my own wants and interests to be at stake*, I make *affective appraisals* of what I read, and these affective appraisals *affect me physiologically*, focus my attention, and perhaps lay down emotional memories. Finally I *cognitively monitor* these affective appraisals and the bodily changes they set off. At the same time, however, as we'll see later, I know that Anna is a character, not a real Russian noblewoman, and that the events Tolstoy relates are fictional. Indeed even as I react to Anna as a person, I may also be enjoying the way in which the story unfolds, admiring Tolstoy's craftsmanship, and taking pleasure in its complex structure.

Filling in the Gaps

Emotion isn't everything. Clearly, you have to understand the meanings of the words in a literary work before you can get off the ground at all. And if you are reading a novel, you also have to understand the conventions of the genre, including the characteristic literary patterns and themes found therein, and you should maybe know something about literary history, the author of the novel, and so on.[14] You also have to make appropriate *inferences* as you read.

Wolfgang Iser, the reader-response theorist and critic, has emphasized that an author cannot tell us everything in a story.[15] A text is always and necessarily full of *gaps*, and understanding a text is necessarily a matter of *filling in the gaps*. A fairy story begins: 'Once upon a time there was a boy called Jack.' It doesn't say: 'Jack had two arms, two legs, a head, a liver, a pancreas, two kidneys, and a heart,' but the reader assumes that if he is a boy, then he has all of these things: we make the appropriate inferences and fill in the gaps accordingly. It would be to wilfully misunderstand the text to think of Jack as having one leg or a heart condition. (With only one leg and a heart condition he wouldn't be able to shin up the beanstalk.) In short, an author relies upon our making *inferences* all the time as we read, in order to fill in the gaps that the text does not explicitly cover. On the other hand, some things are left open in the story and are not important to its proper understanding: the story does not say 'Jack was curly-haired and had brown eyes.' This is a fairy tale and details of the hero's appearance are not relevant to understanding it. Readers are free to imagine he is curly-haired if they wish but it doesn't matter to the story if the matter is not resolved.

The psychologist Richard Gerrig has summarized a body of empirical evidence that confirms that 'readers are routinely called upon to use their logical faculties to bridge gaps of various sizes in texts'.[16] Psychologists tend to study very brief narratives of only a few sentences, but their findings have interesting implications for the more complex narratives we find in novels and movies. The evidence suggests that there is a 'core of automatic processes'[17] for the cognitive processing of narratives. According to McKoon and Ratcliff's 'minimalist hypothesis', for which there is considerable empirical support, as we read a narrative 'only two classes of inferences, those based on easily available information and those required for local coherence, are encoded during reading, unless a reader adopts special goals or strategies'.[18] For example, if we are told that Jack's mother sends Jack to bed without any supper, we do not automatically imagine Jack lying in his bed, although presumably that's what he'd be doing (rather than watching the Late Show). The idea is that we imagine only so much as we need to make sense of the ongoing narrative. Unless the fact that Jack is in his bed turns out to be vital to the plot, we won't ever think about it as we read.

However, although there is this 'core of automatic processes,' there are other processes which are 'under the strategic control of the reader'. In other words, different readers fill in the gaps in different ways.[19] Individual differences can be explained partly by the ways in which differences in readers' background knowledge affect how those readers process a text. For example, 'enhanced knowledge enables readers to direct their attention toward the more informative aspects of narratives'. Unsurprisingly, people who already know a lot about baseball recall far more information about a baseball-related passage that those who are less knowledgeable. A reader may have relevant knowledge, but in order to influence narrative understanding, it must become 'available at the appropriate time'. For example, we may all know what it's like to wash clothes, but experimenters found that a particular passage was hard to interpret until the reader finds out that it is about washing clothes. Finally, 'the knowledge must be represented in a fashion that is accessible to comprehension processes', for example, by drawing on associations that the reader has previously internalized.[20]

One of the most important ways in which readers fill in the gaps is by making *causal* inferences. Many theorists *define* narrative partly in terms of causal relations. Noël Carroll, for example, says that 'in narrative, causal relations are standardly the cement that unifies the subject of the story'. He defines 'the narrative connection' partly in terms of the notion of causation: 'the earlier event in the narrative connection must be causally relevant to the effect event'.[21] But often the story itself is not explicit about causal relations; it is the *reader* who has to make the appropriate causal inference. The story says 'Jack's mother threw the beans out of the window. The next morning a giant beanstalk was growing in the garden.' Readers have to make the causal inference that the magic beans are the *cause* of the giant beanstalk.

In a similar vein, Tom Trabasso and his colleagues have endorsed the idea that understanding a narrative consists in understanding 'a *causal network* that represents the relationships between the causes and the consequences of events in a story'. As readers read moment to moment in a text, they 'derive a main *causal chain* for the story, which preserves the sequence of causally important events that serves as the backbone for the story'. Gerrig reports that in experiments using several short texts, Trabasso has 'demonstrated that the *importance* and *memorability* of the clauses in these texts can be predicted by the causal connectedness of each clause as well as by whether it lies along the main causal chain'.[22]

Other researchers have suggested that 'readers build causal networks by strategically deploying the resources of working memory' and that 'the causal structure of a narrative controls the allocation of attention as it is read'.[23] Fletcher and his associates advocate a model they call the 'current state selection strategy', designed to use working memory to best advantage. Readers identify 'the most current clause with causal antecedents—but no consequences—in the preceding text. All propositions that contribute to the causal role of this clause remain in short-term [working] memory as the following sentence is read.'[24] The idea is that the reader assumes that 'any clause that has not yet yielded causal consequences is likely to do so as the text continues',[25] and so readers should keep it in working memory. Some clever experiments suggest that this is indeed what happens as readers process a text. Fletcher and his associates have shown, for example, that if we read a series of sentences, each one describing an event in a causal series, p, q, r, we tend to push out of working memory the steps in the causal chain as their consequences become known. If it turns out that some future event s relies causally on some step q that came earlier in the causal sequence, it takes longer for the reader to understand it and make the causal connection.

$$t_1 \qquad t_2 \qquad t_3 \qquad t_4$$
$$p \; \longrightarrow \; q \; \longrightarrow \; r \qquad s$$

The gap-filling activities I've described so far are all *cognitive*: we fill in the gaps by making causal inferences or inferences about the way the world is. But in addition to making causal inferences, readers also fill in the gaps, I suggest, through their *emotional* responses. When we respond emotionally to a text, our attention is alerted to important information about character and plot that is not explicitly asserted in the text. And just as different readers process a narrative differently depending on how they make causal and other inferences, based on cognitive processing, so different people understand a text differently partly because of their different emotional responses to it.

Gerrig does not focus on emotional responses in general, but he does discuss what he calls 'participatory responses' which he characterizes as responses that 'arise as a consequence of the readers' active participation'[26] or involvement in a narrative, some of which are emotional. 'Participatory responses', he says, are heterogeneous 'non-inferential responses' that include the readers' emotional responses to a suspenseful situation in a thriller or the kinds of hopes and fears that readers entertain for a character as the plot develops. Gerrig notes that since causal relations are so important in narrative, readers devote a lot of attention to goals and outcomes, and each time a character is in a position where a goal may or may not be met, the reader has a chance to 'express a preference'.[27] He reports one of his own experiments which demonstrated that if a story induced a preference for a negative outcome—the kind of outcome one would not welcome in the real world—then readers found it difficult (it took them longer) to verify whether the negative outcome had in fact occurred in the story, when they were asked about it later, even if they were asked about it right after reading the passage in question. This demonstrates, he says, that the 'mental expression of hopes and preferences [can] directly affect the representations of textual information',[28] and that 'the creation of unusual preferences altered ... readers' experiences of the stories' in the experiment. In particular, expressions of hope and preferences have 'measurable consequences for the memory representations constructed in the course of experiencing a narrative world'.[29] Extrapolating from the experiment, we can say that outcomes that we find troubling are harder to process.

Gerrig also discusses readers' reactions to suspenseful narratives. He suggests that suspense involves the emotions of hope and fear together with a cognitive state of uncertainty about something deemed significant,[30] and he points out that even when we reread a story, so that we ought to know what will happen, the information is in some sense inaccessible to us as we read, so that we are always in a state of uncertainty. It would be inappropriate to digress here on a long discussion of suspense, but I would like to note in passing that my theory of emotion has a ready explanation for this phenomenon (sometimes called the 'paradox of suspense'). Our affective appraisals are instinctive, automatic appraisals of a perception or thought: they fix attention on the uncertain event and appraise it as threatening, regardless of the fact that a moment's reflection would tell us that we are just reading a story. Even if we have read the story before and reflectively 'know just what is going to happen', our automatic affective appraisals fasten attention on each situation or event as it is presented and induce responses to it *before* cognitive monitoring kicks in.

In general, Gerrig says that participatory responses, although closely connected to inferences, 'do not fill gaps in the text' and so 'do not fit the classic definition for inferences'.[31] Contrary to Gerrig, however, I think it is clear that many emotional responses *do* fill in gaps in the text, although perhaps not in quite the same way as when we make causal inferences. Henry James does not say 'Strether is a mildly comic character.' He induces us to laugh at Strether. Similarly, Tolstoy does not say that Anna Karenina is in a poignant situation: he describes her situation and lets us experience it emotionally for ourselves. It is through our emotional responses that we gather important information about characters and plot. If this is right, then our emotional responses are a vital part of *understanding* a narrative text.

If I have an instinctive affective reaction to Anna and her fate, this provides me with information that is not explicitly in the text. Indeed, Gerrig himself notes that sometimes a 'gut reaction' will give us the same information as a (cognitive) inference. So I would argue that emotional responses can and do fill in gaps in texts, that they give us information about the characters and events described, and furthermore, that the different ways in which different readers assess characters and events is partly a *function* of the different emotional responses of those readers to the characters.[32]

Interpretation as Reflection on Emotional Responses to a Text

I have said that understanding a narrative is a matter of filling in the gaps and that we fill in some of the gaps in a text by means of our emotional experiences of it. But experiencing a narrative is not the same thing as interpreting it. It is important to distinguish among *experiencing* the work, *reflecting* on our experiences of it as they occur, and *interpreting* it by reflecting on and reporting our experiences of the work after finishing it, by summing it up as a whole.[33] When we respond emotionally to some incident in a story, there is an initial unthinking or instinctive appraisal (**Oh no! This is a threat! I don't like this!** or whatever), which fixes attention and produces a physiological response and is then succeeded by cognitive evaluations of the incident. There is then likely to be extensive reappraisal in the light of succeeding events in the novel. When we *reflect* about our experience of the novel, one of the things we are doing is engaging in *cognitive monitoring* of our earlier responses. Finally, when we have reflected enough so that we think we have made sense of the incident in the light of preceding and succeeding events in the novel, we may report on our reflections about our experience of the work by offering an *interpretation* of the work as a whole.

On this way of thinking about how we come to understand a novel or play, our emotional experience of the novel or play is itself a form of *understanding*, even if it is an inarticulate or relatively inarticulate understanding: if I laugh and cry, shiver, tense, and relax in all the appropriate places, then I can be said to have understood the story.[34] If, however, I want not only to have a rich emotional experience while reading the novel but also to give a critical account—a reading or interpretation—of it, this requires *reflecting* on my emotional experience. I need to reflect upon my affective appraisals, figure out what they were, what it was in the story that provoked them, and whether they were justified. In this way I may arrive at an overall interpretation of the novel, which is the result of affective responses and subsequent cognitive monitoring of them, including judgements about whether my initial responses were appropriate. The initial affective appraisals of the work are part of the data that the critic draws upon when giving a reflective interpretation of the work as a whole.

In my earlier examples I talked about experiencing Anna Karenina as pitiable, Macbeth as horrifying, and Strether as mildly amusing. If I weep for Anna, shudder at Macbeth, and smile at Strether, then I am expressing in an inarticulate way my *understanding* of the incidents I have described. If I want to discover *why* Anna is pitiable, Macbeth horrifying, and Strether amusing, I can examine the source of my responses to these characters. To discover the source of my compassion for Anna Karenina, for example, is to discover the pitiable nature of her situation in all its details. If I then go on to articulate my emotional experience of the novel, the words I use will reflect that experience: I will describe Anna as pitiable and Macbeth as horrifying. My interpretation of a work is partly a meditation on my emotional responses to it.

If I experience compassion for Anna and respond to Karenin with, say, a mixture of pity and contempt, even in an inarticulate or subconscious way, then I am in a much better position than the disinterested observer to reflect upon these characters and the role they play in the novel as a whole. I am in a better position to give a critical interpretative account of it. For what I am reflecting upon is not just a set of words and their literal descriptive meanings but my experience of what is described, my feelings about the characters, my emotional responses to them. These experiences, feelings, and responses can then form the basis for a critical reading of the work. 'The work' is not just a set of words and their literal meanings, but descriptions, dialogue, etc. as experienced by the reader. A critical interpretation of a work becomes a reflection upon one's emotional experience of the work.

An emotional encounter with *Anna Karenina* involves an initial affective appraisal, followed by physiological changes, action tendencies, and cognitive monitoring of the situation, together with feedback from each of these different systems. In real life, we often reflect upon our past emotional experiences in an effort to understand them. Usually we do this using terms from folk psychology, including the emotion terms of our language. In attempting to give a critical analysis of Tolstoy's characters, I am engaged in the same kind of activity: I am summarizing my emotional experience of them over many chapters. I may summarize by saying that Tolstoy presents Anna as an object of *compassion*. We experience her predicament from her own perspective as well as that of the other people around her. We grasp how she feels trapped in her marriage, yet devoted to her young son Seryozha, passionately in love with Vronsky, yet terrified of her complete dependence upon him. Given the sort of woman that she is and the society in which she lives, there are no easy answers for her. That is why the reader is likely to feel compassion for her. In other words, a critical assessment of the characters and the plot involves *cognitively monitoring our responses* as we read, and then *giving an overview of those responses* in folk-psychological terms.

It seems to be true that people *like* a work of narrative more when they are emotionally involved in it. There is evidence, for example, that people like suspenseful narratives. One explanation for this is that such narratives produce a rise in arousal—either a succession of moderate increases or a temporary sharp increase—followed by a reduction of arousal.[35] It is reasonable to think, too, that people *appreciate* a narrative more when they are emotionally involved with it.[36] If we respond emotionally to the scene between Seryozha and his mother, we are better able to appreciate how skilfully Tolstoy describes the scene and the telling details he includes, how he builds up the suspense, and how he induces the reader's compassion. But I am not just saying that emotional involvement is necessary for liking or for appreciating a work. What I have been suggesting is that responding emotionally is a form of understanding and that an interpretation, which claims to give an overall critical reflective understanding of a novel as whole, is partly the result of reflection upon our emotional responses to the novel.

As we have seen, emotion isn't everything: you have to understand the meanings of the words in a literary work, and if you are reading a novel you probably need some background information such as its place in the history of literature and how it fits or fails to fit the general conventions of the genre of novel. You also need to be able to make appropriate inferences: an author relies upon our continually making inferences as we read in order to fill gaps in the text. But what I am insisting is that our emotional reactions to a novel are also a means of filling in the gaps, and hence also an important part of *understanding* the novel, and that they are an important source of data for an interpretation.

Are Emotions Necessary to Literary Understanding?

Even if it's granted that responding emotionally to a literary work can be a mode of understanding that can give us data on which to rely in arriving at an interpretation of the work, yet someone might object that the information we get via emotional involvement with a work could equally well be gathered by purely cognitive means. Why, for example, do I *have* to be amused by Strether or feel compassion for Anna in order to understand the episodes I discussed earlier? Cannot I have a dispassionate understanding of Strether's predicament and see it as comic but without actually being amused by it? Cannot I grasp dispassionately that Anna's predicament is tragic and that she is pitiable, without myself feeling compassion for Anna? Why do I need to become personally emotionally involved in order to understand what is going on? More generally, why does a critic have to rely on a prior emotional experience of a work in order to come up with a convincing interpretation of it?

There may be different ways of meeting this challenge, but in keeping with my emphasis in this chapter on the importance of character in literary interpretation, I want to stress that understanding character is essential to understanding the great realist novels I've mainly been discussing, that understanding character is relevantly like understanding real people, and that understanding real people is impossible without emotional engagement with them and their predicaments.

Consider first the way in which emotions focus attention.[37] I might not even notice that Strether is a comic character unless I smile (or snicker) at Strether. I might not notice Anna's vulnerability unless I respond with sadness and compassion to her. The emotions are ways of focusing *attention* on those things that are important to our wants, goals, and interests. In responding with amusement to Strether, with sadness and compassion to Anna, and with disgust to Macbeth, I am focusing on important aspects of their characters, aspects that either endear the character to me or repel me. Indeed if I do not notice that Strether is a comic character or Macbeth a horrifying one, then I have missed a very important aspect of the literary work in question.

In general, our emotions let us know what is important to us by focusing attention through affective appraisals and consequent physiological responses. Anna is described as a person in deep distress and my emotional responses to her register this fact in a way that holds my attention willy-nilly: I make an affective appraisal that one of 'my own' is suffering **Loss**! and is faced with **Threat**! Physiological changes also reinforce the focus of my emotion; action tendencies and expressive gestures keep my body alert to how I am thinking of her. I *feel* my compassion for Anna in a bodily and instinctive way that is hard to eradicate. So although it might seem that an unemotional point of view can serve the same purpose as a bona fide emotional response, in fact those who fail to respond emotionally to Anna won't be focused on her vulnerability with the same urgency and sense of its importance.

Similarly, if I don't laugh affectionately with Strether, I may not notice his mildly comic innocence and lack of worldliness. Unlike

Anna's vulnerability, it is not so easy to detect James's subtle comedy, so unless I am amused by Strether, it is quite possible that this important aspect of his character will be completely lost on me. I suppose someone could just *tell* me that he is a comic character. But unless I am actually amused by Strether so that I laugh or smile at the description of his conversation with Maria Gostrey, do I really *understand* that he is comic? And if I don't understand why he is comic, why should I believe it when someone tells me I ought to find him funny? Perhaps I admit that *this other person* for some reason finds him funny, but I could attribute that to some quirk of this person's personality rather than to anything about Strether. On the other hand, if this other person is a friend on whose testimony I often rely, then perhaps I might bow to her superior understanding and grant that Strether is indeed a comic character, but still without understanding *why*. If my friend then explains—it's the comic incongruity between Balzac novels and Woollett, Massachusetts—I may still remain mystified: what's funny about *that*? In some sense I do now understand *why my friend finds Strether comic*, but that is not the same thing as my understanding *why Strether is comic*. The same thing is true in real life. You can tell me that some comedian is hilarious, and try to explain why, but unless I laugh myself, I do not really understand why he is funny; at best I begin to understand why *you* think he is funny.

This is related to a second point, that understanding a novel or the characters in a novel is not the same thing as understanding a proposition. There is a difference between smiling at Strether and understanding that we ought to smile, between feeling compassion for Anna Karenina and figuring out cognitively that she's in a bad way. In general, there's a difference between cognitive understanding of propositions—that Strether is comic, that Anna is suffering—and understanding how people feel, and the emotional significance of a situation, event, or setting. *Emotional understanding is in the first instance a kind of bodily understanding*: my affective appraisals of characters, events, and situations are automatic and instinctive, and they immediately produce physiological and behavioural responses that reinforce these emotional appraisals. Consequently I *feel* my compassion for Anna in a bodily and instinctive way. And although the bodily responses in question may be less violent, I *feel* Strether's amusing qualities when I smile, however weakly, at his remarks.

Thirdly, emotional understanding 'regestalts' the world in a global way: in responding emotionally to Anna Karenina, I see the whole world of the novel through the prism of that emotion. My feelings for her affect my feelings about the harshness of the marriage laws, the difficulties of Vronsky's professional position, the heartlessness of polite society, and so on and so on. Feeling compassion for Anna is not just a response to her but a response with wide implications for my understanding of the novel as a whole. Similarly, being amused by Strether colours my understanding of the whole structure of the novel, and of the moral balance among the characters: it contributes to my sense that Strether is a good and intelligent man who is also in some ways an 'innocent abroad', out of his depth in the situation in which he finds himself.

When emotions regestalt the world in line with our wants, goals, and interests, they do this by affective appraisals of the world, re-inforced by bodily changes, which register the world under a par-ticular aspect, so that, for example, I register the world of *Anna Karenina* as difficult, painful, and threatening to its heroine. I don't just dispassionately notice the emotional implications for Anna of Vronsky's position or the attitudes of high society: if I'm responding emotionally, then I feel these implications in a bodily way, which reinforces my sense of their importance to Anna (and thus to me). Recognizing cognitively that Anna's world is difficult and painful is not the same as feeling it to be so.

But someone might still object that I can figure out that Strether is comic and Anna vulnerable without actually experiencing any emo-tion for these characters, and that I can figure out the ramifications of Anna's vulnerability for the wider context of the novel without any emotional prism to look through. Why insist that the proper under-standing of a novel requires emotional understanding? The answer is that people who lack this kind of emotional understanding in real life have a serious deficit that shows up in various social inadequacies. It seems that in real life we *need* emotional understanding and fellow-feeling if we are to understand other people properly, and that cognition without emotion simply does not do as good a job. If this is true for our understanding of people in real life, it is likely to be true of fictional characters as well, at least when they are richly and realistically portrayed.

In ordinary life we all agree that it is important to be capable of fellow-feeling for others. People who lack this ability have an emotional deficit, a lack of emotional intelligence, and they behave insensitively as a result. Fellow-feeling is fellow-*feeling*, not just an intellectual recognition that someone is in trouble, say, but a 'gut reaction' of compassion, an emotional or bodily response, a response consisting in autonomic and motor changes. So-called 'intuition' about people is probably just this kind of emotional sensitivity to others, and it is a valuable capacity.

To see what happens when people lack this capacity, I'd like to look briefly at a range of examples. In general, I think that people who lack *emotional* understanding are unable to understand other people very well, and that this is true not just for understanding our neighbours and friends but also for understanding the characters encountered in novels and plays. First, imagine a reader who doesn't notice that Strether is comic because the subtle Jamesian emotions are outside her emotional experience. For example, a precocious little girl reading 'The Ambassadors' might understand what she reads in a sense if she understands the literal meaning of the words, but in another, deeper sense she won't understand because she won't understand the characters or their motivation. The book is 'too old' for her in that it describes experiences outside her emotional range. She understands the words 'I come from Woollett, Massachusetts,' but the emotional implications are most probably beyond her reach. Here cognition is clearly not enough. The little girl needs emotional sophistication as well.

But perhaps such an example will be deemed irrelevant to my case, since a little girl probably would not be able to grasp what is going on in a Henry James novel either emotionally or cognitively. So consider next those who have a low 'EQ' or *emotional intelligence*. One of the marks of such people is that they fail to register other people's emotional gestures and expressions and consequently fail to understand other people's feelings and motivations. Peter Salovey reports that there are 'individual differences in people's ability to perceive accurately, understand, and empathize with others' emotions' and suggests that 'individuals who are best able to do so may be better able to respond to their social environment and build a supportive social network'.[38] People who are relatively lacking in the ability to have or to access or interpret gut reactions of the sort I have described are much more likely to fail to perceive what emotions other people are experiencing and what motivations they have for their behaviour.[39] This same ability to understand emotionally what other people are experiencing would seem to be an asset in our attempts to understand fictional characters as well as actual people.

Finally, we saw earlier how Antonio Damasio has suggested that our brains are able to classify kinds of stimuli and link them with a particular kind of bodily feeling, or 'somatic marker'. His idea is that when faced with a stimulus of the right sort, our body responds automatically with what I would call an affective appraisal of **Good!** or **Bad!** So when we read Tolstoy's description of Anna's visit to Seryozha, we focus attention on what's happening, and register it as important to me and mine and as **A Bad Thing!** In Ch. 3 I suggested that these pairings of groups of stimuli and somatic markers are stored in what LeDoux calls emotional memory. If this is right, then when my emotions for Anna Karenina, Macbeth, or Strether are evoked, I may be drawing on associations from emotional memory, and, since these associations are stored in emotional memory, they are particularly insistent and hard to eradicate. It seems not unlikely that these gut reactions stored in emotional memory are necessary for my grasp on what people are like and how they are likely to act, and that they respond to fictional people as they would to any other people.

Damasio's patients with damage to the frontal lobe (probably to the ventromedial prefrontal cortices) lacked 'somatic markers' linking specific emotional responses and feelings to specific kinds of scenario, and so failed to make sensible decisions in the gambling experiments. It may be that some deficit of this sort is also responsible for pathological failures to respond with appropriate emotions to the way other people behave and express themselves.[40] That such pathologies exist is itself suggestive that mere cognition is not enough for understanding other people and that *emotional* understanding is crucial. If this is right, then it seems reasonable to think that it is also crucial to understanding the 'people' who populate well-crafted realistic novels.

Some of what I have been saying here is admittedly speculative. In particular, Damasio is discussing people's ability to make plans and decisions, not their ability to understand other people.[41] Nevertheless, I hope I have said enough to show that understanding other people in real life most probably requires a special kind of emotional or bodily understanding. We know this is so, because people who lack the ability to respond in a bodily, emotional way to other people—their expressions, behaviour, and gestures as well as their thoughts and attitudes—simply don't understand other people very well. Further, I suggest that it is reasonable to think that understanding characters in great realist novels requires the same kind of bodily understanding. And of course understanding characters is a *sine qua non* of understanding the works in which they figure.

Dispassion and Disinterestedness

We have been used to thinking of the dispassionate person as an epitome of reason and detachment. If I am a dispassionate reader, presumably I do not let my feelings sway me one way or another. This sounds like a good thing: if I want to arrive at a fair and balanced interpretation of a novel, surely I ought to assess the characters and events independently of my particular feelings about them.[42] Similarly, generations of theorists have claimed that the proper 'aesthetic attitude' to take to a work of art is *disinterest*, an attitude in which I have no personal stake in the work. I put myself 'out of gear' with the practical world and focus on the work 'for its own sake alone': I have no special 'interest' or stake in the work. These theorists point out that I am not appreciating a work if I am focused on learning what I can from it about the politics of Victorian England or if I am thinking constantly of the fact that it was written by my brother or if I am the impresario in the audience at a play, focused only on the size of the audience and the consequent box-office takings.[43]

Disinterestedness is a much-contested idea, one that goes back to Shaftesbury and is very important to the work in aesthetics by Hutcheson, Hume, Kant, and other major figures. Among modern scholars, Jerome Stolnitz[44] describes the 'aesthetic attitude' as 'disinterested and sympathetic attention to and contemplation of any object of awareness whatever, for its own sake alone'. He then amplifies these ideas. When in the aesthetic attitude, the object we are contemplating *absorbs our attention*. We contemplate it *sympathetically*, i.e. we 'accept the object on its own terms' and 'relish its individual qualities'. This entails inhibiting any responses that are unsympathetic to the object. For this reason, he says, a Muslim with an 'animus against the Christian religion' may not be able to take the aesthetic attitude to a picture of the Holy Family. When we are *disinterested* we 'do not look at the object out of concern for any ulterior purpose which it may serve'.[45] Similarly, J. O. Urmson[46] contrasts aesthetic satisfaction with moral satisfaction (the novel promotes the right moral values), economic satisfaction (it's on the best-seller list), personal satisfaction (it was written by my brother), and intellectual satisfaction (I figured out whodunit by page 43).

It would seem, then, that to be a good reader requires being disinterested, having no personal stake or *interest* in the narrative. And disinterestedness might seem to imply *dispassion*, reading without passion, or emotionless reading.[47] Emotion researchers now generally agree that emotions are evoked when some interest, goal, or want of mine is at stake. If I do not sense my interests to be at stake about something or other, I do not get emotional. Hence if I have no personal stake in the narrative I am reading, I will not get emotional about it. An emotionless understanding of *Anna Karenina*, for example, would presumably be one in which the words are literally understood, the plot is grasped and we can tell roughly why the characters behave as they do, but we don't care what happens in the story.

When deliberating about something, the dispassionate person will try to be impartial, to look at all sides of the question, and to give due weight to all the relevant considerations. However, as we saw in the discussion of Greenspan towards the end of Ch. 1, emotional evaluations are by their nature *partial* in both senses of that word: they do not consider all the evidence, only part of it, and they look at a situation with partiality, from the point of view of the interests, wants, and goals of the person themselves and those with whom they identify. In reading literature, impartiality is often just inappropriate. We are encouraged to identify with certain of the characters, to despise others, to mock, to pity, to be amused or irritated as the case may be. Indeed, a disinterested, dispassionate reader who is out of gear with the practical world would be incapable of fully understanding a novel with the scope and power of *Anna Karenina*. Such a reader would not be emotionally involved in the story and so would not be sympathetically engaged with Anna and her fate. The most sensitive readers are likely to be those who do feel they have something at stake.

Of course to say that the best reader is one who has a personal interest in the work means that the reader has an interest in its *content*. While I am watching *Macbeth* I am not gauging the size of the house and calculating my profits; I am not preoccupied by the splendid performance by my daughter as the Third Witch. But I do and should have an 'interest' in the content of the drama, in the course of Macbeth's quest for power, in whether he achieves his ambitions. Similarly, a sensitive reader of Henry James's novel *The Ambassadors* has an interest in whether Strether will escape untainted by the sophisticated immorality of the Old World. I have a stake in these outcomes because my own interests and wants have been invoked.

There is another side to the issue, as well. Today many people think that disinterestedness is an impossible ideal, and that we cannot help but bring to a text our own state of knowledge, our own attitudes, and our own biases. From this perspective, those who defend the principle of aesthetic disinterestedness are simply defending an 'interested' view, which happens to be that of the dominant culture, or a dominant set of people within a culture.

I have been arguing that in many cases—and most notably in the great nineteenth-century realistic novels—people need to have a stake in the novels they read in order to understand them properly, and that our emotional responses give us important information about a novel, information that is not available to someone who does not respond emotionally. For this reason interpretations of certain kinds of works *have* to be based on emotional responses if they are to be compelling. But this does not mean that disinterestedness and dispassion have no role to play in interpretation, or that they represent an unattainable ideal. As I have also argued, when we interpret a work we are not usually just emoting; we are reflecting back on our emotional responses and using them as data in arriving at an interpretation. Dispassion and disinterest should be construed not as *lack* of passion or *lack* of interest but in terms of rational reflection on our passionate, interested, emotional responses.

In short, dispassion and disinterestedness in criticism should not mean lack of feeling or personal interest, but rather a fair, balanced (cognitive) assessment of the many different emotional reactions provoked by the work and the various personal interests we feel to be at stake in it. In this respect, Tolstoy's novel is a splendid model. For part of the greatness of *Anna Karenina* lies in the fact that *all* the main characters are presented as individuals; they are all treated with the same understanding and affection. (By contrast, Flaubert seems to dislike all his characters, even those who might have been quite tolerable in real life!) If Tolstoy seems to be dispassionate, it is because he shows us every character—even the most unlikeable—from a compassionate point of view; we emotionally experience every character sympathetically. This is 'disinterestedness' on the part of the author. What I am suggesting is that it is a kind of disinterestedness that should be emulated by the reader. Disinterestedness does not mean lack of passion or lack of any interest or stake; it means a dispassionate assessment of our many and varied personal emotional responses to a work.

Those who think that disinterestedness is an impossible ideal focus on the fact that an interpretation of a literary work is always by a particular person from a particular class, gender, and ethnic group, who has a particular set of interests which may be at stake in the work. But I disagree that disinterestedness is an impossible ideal. If understood correctly, it is useful as an ideal, even if it may be difficult to achieve. Disinterestedness and dispassion should not be understood as lack of any interest or stake in a work or lack of passion or emotion in one's responses to a work. A critical overview or interpretation is an attempt to make sense out of our emotional responses. Interpretation is 'dispassionate', then, only in the sense that it involves constant *cognitive monitoring* of our initial instinctive affective responses—assessing them for appropriateness and consistency—as well as a cognitive overview of the whole work, which takes into account all one's emotional experiences of the work as far as that is possible, and attempts to mediate among them.[48] Dispassion in the sense of lack of passion is simply inappropriate; a passionless encounter with a work of art, far from being the proper aesthetic way to proceed, may in fact prevent us from understanding it at all.

In cognitively monitoring our responses we may discover that we have been misled by our emotions in some ways, or we may discover that the author has induced incompatible emotional responses to the same events or characters. Cognitive monitoring may lead us to realize that the conclusions we reached on the basis of our emotional responses as we move through the early parts of a novel need to be revised in the light of later responses to later parts. But however things turn out, the interpretation we ultimately arrive at will be partly a function of those initial non-cognitive appraisals that set off our emotional responses.

5

Puzzles and Paradoxes

Problems

In Ch. 4 I explained how and why our emotional responses are a way of understanding a novel (or other narrative) and how they can—and often should—serve as the basis of interpretations. To have one's emotions evoked as one reads a realistic novel is often not only desirable but also necessary to a proper understanding of the novel. But in laying out this view, I ignored a number of potential problems with it. In the present chapter I will address some of those potential problems. Readers who are not interested in the detail of the philosophical arguments, and who are already convinced of what I say, can skip this chapter if they wish.

First Objection: Lots of Novels Don't Require Emotional Involvement

I gladly acknowledge that many novels do not require intense emotional investment in the characters. I can read a 'stock' detective novel or Harlequin romance without getting emotionally worked up about the characters, simply because I understand it as just a characteristic member of a particular genre. There is no need for me to enter into the feelings of the detective or the country squire or the butler: they are just stock characters behaving in a stock way. On the other hand, even stock genres evoke some emotions, although they may be stock emotions. It would be an unsuccessful detective story that did not make us curious and suspenseful about what is going to happen, and a failure for a Harlequin romance to arouse no feelings of satisfaction when the heroine is rescued by the mysterious dark and handsome hero.

More interesting are those novels that deliberately attempt to prevent the reader from getting emotionally involved even in the development of the plot. Italo Calvino is a master of this sort of thing, haranguing the reader as if she were a misbehaving character and then turning her into just such a character. The reader is never allowed to forget herself and enter emotionally into the trials and tribulations of (other!) characters. Another trickster author, Robert Coover, fragments his narrative as Calvino does, and also invents characters that are quintessentially 'characters', comic constructions, seen from the outside. These novels are written as a reaction against the kind of work that I have been discussing: they foreground the formal aspects of the novel and downplay the content of the story. (I'll have a lot more to say about form in Ch. 7.)

A different kind of trick is played by Ian McEwan in his best-seller, *Atonement*. The novel encourages the reader to get emotionally involved with the story and the characters, only to reveal at the end that the denouement of the story is a lie: it turns out that (in McEwan's fiction) the story has been written by one of its characters and that she has manipulated the ending, so that what was supposed to have 'really happened' in fact did not. In seeking atonement for a crime she committed as a child, this character/author has 'made things right' in the fiction even though in 'real life' they went horribly wrong. McEwan ends the novel with a meditation in the mind of his fictional author on the power of an author to manipulate the reader: 'how can a novelist achieve atonement when, with her absolute power of deciding outcomes, she is also God?' The novel is profoundly unsettling just because McEwan is so good at writing what is apparently a realistic novel and at evoking his reader's emotions. It is disturbing to discover that one has 'wasted' all that emotional energy on a fiction, only of course we always knew it was a fiction; we just didn't know that fictionally it was a fiction!

All these examples are of novels that deliberately play with the conventions and traditions of the realistic novel, and deliberately subvert our tendency to get emotionally involved with narrative fiction. I am also happy to acknowledge that such novels exist and that indeed today they tend to be among the most interesting being written. What I am suggesting is that an emotionless reading of Tolstoy or Henry James or other traditional realistic novels, while no doubt revealing some of the important aspects of a novel, is seriously inadequate, and that a personal emotional involvement with the characters and the story is essential to a proper understanding of novels *of this sort.*

Second Objection: Do We in Fact Respond to Novels in a Bodily Way?

Do we in fact sweat and swear and weep and groan as we sit in the theatre watching a play or in the living-room curled up with a novel? In other words, given my insistence that an emotional response is a *physiological* response, it could be objected that we never or hardly ever respond with genuine emotion to works of literature. One response to this objection would be to point to the audience in the nearest movie theatre during a suspense film, a love scene, a comic routine, or a horror film. All kinds of subdued groans and curses, sobs, chuckles, and sudden intakes of breath would be heard. And if we could turn up the lights and examine pulses and galvanic skin responses, we would find many pounding hearts, sweating palms, and the like. Some audiences show even clearer symptoms of emotional involvement, calling out 'You go, girl,' to Beatrice when she gets the better of Benedick, or, as Leonardo di Caprio takes the poison at the end of *Romeo and Juliet,* crying spontaneously 'Oh no! Is he going to *die?*'

Better still, there is now empirical research that shows people do in fact experience the physiological changes characteristic of emotion when reading a text. For example, Vrana and his associates showed that 'recall of sentences that describe fearful situations resulted in greater heart rate increase than recall of less affectively arousing text'.[1] Paul Harris reviews a number of studies by Peter Lang and his group also showing that when reading a text that describes a frightening encounter, 'some of the visceral accompaniments to fear (i.e. heart-rate acceleration and skin conductance) are triggered.'[2] Interestingly, fearful reactions to a passage about snakes produce a more powerful reaction in people who have a phobic fear of snakes.

Perhaps it makes sense for people to respond fearfully to thoughts about critters that they fear in real life. But why get all excited about Anna Karenina? After all, none of us is acquainted with a nineteenth-century Russian noblewoman. Why should we respond physiologically to her troubles? There is some empirical evidence to shed light on this question. In an experiment by Jose and Brewer, for example, children read stories and were then asked to rate 'how similar they were to the main character, how much they liked that character and how much they worried about the character when he or she was in danger'.[3] The experiment showed that the children were most anxious about the good characters in a story, that they liked those characters the most, and also that they judged themselves to be most similar to those characters. Jose and Brewer suggested that it was *identification* with the characters that made the children worried about them, but even if we do not make this assumption, the experiment suggests a connection between emotional involvement with a character and thinking of them as in some respect 'like me' or, as I have put it previously, as like 'me or mine'. So it makes sense that we would respond emotionally to Anna if we are responding to her as in certain respects someone like me (or my dear old mum).

It may be that movies evoke more powerful physiological responses than novels. It would be interesting to know the truth about this empirical matter. Vrana's heart-rate results are suggestive in that increased heart rate was found both in subjects who silently articulated the fear-inducing sentence and in those who were asked to form appropriate mental pictures, but heart responses were more marked in those subjects who formed mental pictures.

On the other hand, I don't want to be committed to asserting that full-blooded emotional, i.e. physiological, responses are always present when we witness a film or read a novel. Maybe we can form the point of view appropriate to a particular emotional state *without* any physiological changes. Whether that's possible is an empirical matter. But there are at least two ways of explaining this possibility: either I don't care enough about what's going on in the novel or movie for my point of view to have registered in bodily changes, or I exhibit bodily changes that are suppressed.

First, as we saw in Ch. 3, it is possible in ordinary language or folk-psychological terms to be *angry* about something without becoming *emotional* about it. Similarly, perhaps a novel or movie may succeed in getting us to form appropriate thoughts about the events and characters depicted but without our actually becoming emotional about them. There are many reasons why this could happen, from inadequacy on the part of the author to distraction and fatigue on the part of the audience. In these cases, for whatever reasons, I presumably do not care enough about the characters, or—which is much the same thing—I do not feel my own interests and wishes to be sufficiently at stake to evoke an emotional (physiological) response. I am not reacting to Anna Karenina as one of my own. I have compassionate thoughts about her but without the physiological concomitants of sadness. Or I fear for Romeo (or Leonardo) without increase in heart rate or skin conductance. Having said that, however, I would like to stress that having a compassionate or fearful point of view on someone or something typically *does* produce a physiological response, just because of the way we have been designed. And it remains to be seen whether it is empirically possible to have sad or fearful thoughts without any physiological disturbance.

Secondly, as Paul Ekman has shown, emotional expressions are often suppressed, in accordance with the *display rules* for one's culture. It may be that in the case of responses to fiction, the non-cognitive appraisal **I don't like this** produces an emotional response, but that this is quickly *suppressed* because of a succeeding cognitive appraisal: *It's only a story.* Although some of us will admit to reading a novel with tears streaming down our faces, or cracking up with laughter over a story while all-alone in our living rooms, many people no doubt just feel silly sitting all by themselves in tears for 'no good reason'. By the same token I suspect that, at least in our culture, women will have fewer inhibitions in this respect than men. Interestingly, in an experiment on music listening, Carol Krumhansl has shown that emotional responses to music are closer to the suppressed emotion condition in a study by Gross and Levenson.[4]

Third Objection: I'm Ignoring Authorial Manipulations

Another objection to my picture of emotional involvement with characters in novels is that my responses may not in fact reflect my own interests, goals, wants and wishes, likes and dislikes. The author has manipulated me into abandoning my usual interests, goals, and wishes and adopting some new set just for the purposes of the novel.[5] A disturbing example occurs in the movie *Pulp Fiction*, when in one incident we are encouraged to find the sight of the John Travolta character shooting someone in the face amusing. If we laugh, we may be appalled later on when we reflect on our emotional response and perhaps angry at Tarantino for manipulating us in this way. We resent being encouraged to act in ways that we deem on reflection to be immoral. On the other side of the coin, Susan Feagin has pointed out that there are 'selfish sentimentalists' who weep over fictional characters while ignoring their own families, the poor, the homeless, etc.[6] Such folk are manipulated by the author to be (albeit briefly) better people than they really are, whereas in the *Pulp Fiction* example we are encouraged to be worse.

This phenomenon is a genuine concern, and one that raises the whole question of the role of the author in guiding our emotional responses. For now, let us simply note that while reading a novel or watching a movie or play, my interests, wants, and goals might indeed differ from those I have when I am not reading or watching. This does not affect my basic point. We respond emotionally to what we perceive and think about, especially if it is presented in vivid images. We affectively appraise the situation presented as terrible, wonderful, or whatever, because it is presented to us as either thwarting or facilitating what *at the time* are our goals, wants, and interests. It is important to remember that emotional reactions are automatic and instinctive: we do not pause to wonder whether, all things considered, we regard the heroine as suffering or the Travolta action as amusing (although later on, of course, we may do just that).

Fourth Objection: What About Inappropriate Emotional Responses?

One corollary of a reader-response theory of interpretation is that different readers will come up with different interpretations based on their different emotional experiences of the work in question. This is a welcome result, I think. (As we'll see at the end of Ch. 6, this is true even if we accept the idea of an 'implied reader' who gives a 'correct' interpretation of a text.) Most people agree that great works of art admit of a wide range of 'valid' interpretations. My view explains how this can be. Because interpretations are the result of cognitive monitoring of our non-cognitive affective appraisals, and because those non-cognitive appraisals are likely to be different for different people with different goals, wants, and interests, there is likely to be disagreement about the resulting cognitive overview of plot, character, and theme.

But what about responses that seem to be plain inappropriate: implacable hatred for Strether, say, or amused enjoyment at Macbeth, or loathing and disgust for Anna Karenina? One can imagine situations in which a person might have such responses. For example, loathing and disgust for Anna might be experienced by a woman who thinks that a mother's most important job in life is protecting her sons and who is appalled by adultery whatever the situation. In order to allow these feelings to colour her entire interpretation of the novel, such a reader would have to refuse to experience Anna's suffering; she would have to ignore or reject large parts of what Tolstoy wrote. Can I argue someone out of such an interpretation? It depends. The person may be uninterested or unwilling to experience the novel in any other way; she may refuse to open herself to the aspects of the novel that she is missing. But what I *can* do is to show that this reader *is* ignoring large parts of the novel.

An interpretation claims to be an overview, making sense of as much of the work as possible in a consistent way.[7] This remains true even when the basis for our interpretations is a series of emotional experiences. Again, if I hate Anna from the word go, just because she's a Russian or a noblewoman (or both), then I will be unable to respond sympathetically to her, and once again much of the significance of her story will pass me by. If I have no idea what it is like to live in another country or another culture, I may be simply bewildered by Anna's story or bored by my incomprehension: I do not have enough in common with the work for my emotions to get involved at all. If such readings sound so bizarre as not to be worth talking about, we should remember that most people respond to novels in personal ways. It is not necessarily a bad thing for people to respond in a personal way, connecting up what they read with their own experiences and able to respond emotionally because their own wants and interests have been successfully appealed to. It would be a bad thing, however, if our own lack of awareness or our own idiosyncratic personal interests forbid or prevent us from enlarging our emotional horizons by sympathetically engaging with people who are different from us in significant ways. If the reader is unable to treat these people as part of 'our own', then they may miss the significance of the novel altogether.

It is not hard to root out all the interpretations that ignore huge chunks of the novel, or which do not show a basic understanding of the words on the page. But of necessity every interpretation can be shown to ignore *some* aspect of a work. Different interpretations necessarily emphasize some aspects and underemphasize others.[8] That is why there will always be different interpretations that are all valid in that they account for the work as a whole (give or take a little). In the academy readings of novels often suffer not from a naive or dogmatic emotionalism, but from a different kind of problem: not enough emotional involvement. Cognitive ingenuity is often more prized than emotional insight. But a meaningful encounter with a great work of art is often a highly emotional set of experiences. In the view I have outlined here multiple interpretations of the same work of art are not just possible but to be encouraged and celebrated; for they represent reflections about a genuine emotional involvement with the work in question.

Fifth Objection: The Paradox of Fiction

I turn now to the most celebrated objection to the idea that we respond emotionally to characters and events in novels, plays, and movies: the so-called paradox of fiction. How can we feel compassion for Anna, amusement at Strether's expense, and revulsion for Macbeth if we know perfectly well that none of these people really exist? Almost none of the people who have written on this topic have had much of a theory of emotion, yet how one responds to this issue will depend very largely on what one thinks an emotional experience is.[9] The problem arose because people thought that the judgement theory of emotion was true: if compassion for Anna necessarily involves a belief that she is in some terrible distress, then obviously there is a problem if at the same time I know perfectly well that she doesn't exist. How can I feel compassion for a woman because she felt her life to be so intolerable that she threw herself under a train, when I know at the same time that there is no woman, no intolerable situation, and no train?

In general, the answer to this question is that knowing we are emotionally engaged with imaginary or fictional characters and events does not alter our non-cognitive affective appraisals. An emotional response to something-or-other does not require a belief that the something-or-other exists. If this is right then the paradox of fiction is not really a paradox at all. Let me explain.

We have emotional responses to all sorts of things, both real and imaginary, both perceived and merely thought about, both possible and impossible. I can smile to myself with love and tenderness as I think of my husband working away in his lab (which he is), but I can also make myself weep by imagining him dying in a plane crash (which he hasn't). I can feel compassion for my troubled next door neighbour, who exists, as well as for Anna Karenina, who doesn't, but whose story could conceivably turn out to be non-fiction: after all Tolstoy based it on an account he read in the newspaper of a young woman who really did throw herself under a train. But I can also feel compassion for somebody whom I know cannot possibly exist, as when I feel compassion for Little Grey Rabbit who is captured by the wicked weasels and forced to keep house for them. I feel compassion for her, even though I have no inclination to acknowledge the possibility of the existence of a rabbit who wears a blue apron and keeps a neat little house with a squirrel and a hare.[10] I suspect that we can view *anything* emotionally, present or absent, existent or non-existent, concrete or abstract. After all, it seems that certain individuals can even view numbers emotionally: 'The mathematician Wim Klein has put this well: "Numbers are friends for me, more-or-less. It doesn't mean the same for you, does it—3,844? For you it's just a three and an eight and a four and a four. But I say, 'Hi! 62 squared!' "'[11]

We respond emotionally not just to what is happening in front of us but to whatever we are paying attention to, whether in the external environment or in the internal environment of our minds. All that's minimally required for an emotional response to occur is a non-cognitive, affective appraisal followed by physiological changes of a certain sort, followed in turn by a cognitive appraisal of the situation (each aspect of the process feeding back upon the others). This emotion process is set off when we sense that our wants, goals, interests, etc. or those of our family or group are at stake. When I am emotionally involved with Anna Karenina, I am focused upon her, I appraise what I read about her affectively (non-cognitively) and this appraisal results in physiological symptoms and action tendencies (which in turn reinforce my focus of attention), followed by cognitive appraisals and reappraisals. Following Blum's analysis of compassion, when I respond to Anna with an emotional reaction of compassion, I am imaginatively dwelling upon her fate, I have an active regard for her well-being, I view her as a fellow human being, and I respond to her with 'emotional responses of a certain degree of intensity'. None of this entails that I believe that Anna exists. I can imaginatively dwell upon her fate and have hopes and wishes for her even while firmly convinced of her non-existence.

Some philosophers think it is absurd to say that I am responding emotionally to Anna Karenina since she does not exist and I know she does not exist, so maybe I am responding to some real-life counterpart of Anna Karenina: I am responding to a person who is just like Anna in all details except for the fact that *this* person, unlike Anna, exists. But then other philosophers counter with the argument that it's not some counterpart of Anna that we pity, but *Anna herself*. Again, some people say that our pity is directed at a *thought* of Anna, not a flesh-and-blood woman, but the reply to this argument is that we aren't compassionate towards a *thought* (whatever that would mean), but towards a *woman*. And so on and so forth for the past thirty years.

What all this discussion ignores is the fact that although philosophers make their living by making these kinds of distinctions, our psychology does not. Pre-cognitive affective appraisals do not discriminate between real and imagined scenarios: I respond emotionally to whatever seems to have a bearing on my interests and on those to whom I am close (my family, my group, my fellow humans). It does not matter to my emotion systems (fear, anger, sadness, etc.) whether I am responding to the real, the merely imagined, the possible, or the impossible. A sculpture of the grieving Mary or a novel about the sad fate of a Russian noblewoman can evoke compassion just as easily as a perceived or thought-about real-life situation. Indeed, sometimes a vivid thought can evoke emotion more powerfully than a seriously held belief. After the initial response, however, there will be cognitive monitoring, which tells us right away whether we are weeping over a block of marble or a flesh-and-blood woman, whether we are pitying a real or an imagined person. This cognitive monitoring will feed back on the original response and modify the physiological symptoms and action tendencies set off. We may weep, but we won't recommend grief counselling to the Holy Mother, or suggest to Anna that she get herself a good lawyer.

Recent empirical evidence has backed up this conclusion. Paul Harris has studied how children respond emotionally to make-believe situations even when they know that the situations are only imaginary.[12] There are other studies that show that people respond affectively (as I would put it) even when they know the response is rationally unjustified. Some good examples come from the literature on disgust: people refuse to eat fudge in the shape of a dog turd or to drink from a glass of juice into which a sterilized cockroach has been dunked. And if you pour sugar into two brand-new empty bottles, one of which is labelled as sugar and the other as poison, and then make sugar water in two beakers, one with sugar from the bottle marked as such and the other from the bottle marked 'poison', people much prefer to sample the sugar water made from the contents of the bottle marked as sugar.[13]

Is it Irrational to Respond Emotionally to Fictions?

Even if I am right about the paradox of fiction, however, Colin Radford's original point could still be true: our emotional reactions to fictional entities could still be *irrational* (just as the behaviour of the sugar-water subjects is irrational).[14] Is this so? Many people have been unwilling to agree that such a normal, socially accepted, and widespread activity as reading (or hearing) stories should turn out to be irrational. But, strictly speaking, Radford is right. It *is* irrational to want to meet the perfect man, when I know or strongly suspect that there are no perfect men; it *is* irrational to weep over the imagined scenario of my husband's death in a plane crash; it *is* irrational to feel one's own interests at stake when Little Grey Rabbit is kidnapped by the weasels; perhaps it is even irrational to love the number 3,844 (since there is not much one can do to prove one's love and the beloved probably doesn't repay one's affection). But the fact of the matter is that we *do* sense our wants, interests, and values to be at stake when we think about certain people, things, situations, and events, even when we know that they do not actually exist, or have not actually occurred.

However, even if from a strictly cognitive point of view it is irrational to have wants and goals with respect to Anna Karenina and her ilk, it is not 'emotionally irrational' and it is certainly not maladaptive. As we saw in Ch. 1, Pat Greenspan has argued that there are different criteria for 'emotional rationality' than for rationality of belief.[15] Remember that in her case of 'mixed feelings' each conflicting emotional response relies on only a subset of the total evidence available. When I simultaneously feel happiness and unhappiness that my friend Jane won the prize (which I wanted to win), these 'contrary emotions' are both 'appropriate' and hence ' "basically" rational'.[16] Furthermore, she argues, if we think of the 'basic rationality' of emotions as 'not determined by cognitive criteria', as if emotions should be treated as judgements or beliefs, then the case of mixed feelings turns out to be rational after all, although not on cognitive grounds. 'On a standard of rationality that evaluates emotions according to their behavioural consequences—which takes into account, for instance, the social value of identification with others—ambivalence might sometimes be *more* rational than forming an "all things considered" emotion that resolves the conflict.'[17]

Greenspan emphasizes the motivational aspect of emotions and points out that it is a more adaptive outcome if I maintain both my sense of my own interests and also my identification with my friend's. An all-things-considered reaction to Jane's victory might perhaps turn out to be 'a somewhat tempered negative reaction'. But in this case 'I would no longer participate in [my friend's] emotion, and share [her] point of view.' Similarly, a neutral reaction 'would also fail to express my identification' with my friend's interests: 'I simply would not care who happened to win.' Greenspan comments:

The philosopher's ideal of 'perfect' rationality is often an ideal of *detachment* from particular points of view. But with emotions taken as motivating attitudes, whose behavioral effects are ordinarily open to control, I think it is clear that conflict between emotional extremes may sometimes serve a purpose that would not be served by moderation. Commitment to different points of view, in short, can motivate behavior unlikely to arise from emotional detachment.[18]

Greenspan's point is that it is more adaptive—and hence 'basically' more 'rational'—to sympathize with my friend's feelings, whatever my overall view of the situation turns out to be, since I am then more likely to behave in ways that will further, rather than damage, the friendship. Moreover, in general, behaviour based on this kind of sympathy furthers the social good. 'Genuine emotional identification with others, then, motivates spontaneous sympathetic behavior, behavior that expresses our concern for others' interests for their own sake. ... [Such] behavior facilitates social relations, and thus promotes an important human end, in a way that detached behavior, or behavior arising from tempered self-interest, would not be likely to.'[19]

Greenspan is here focusing on a case of 'mixed feelings' and using it to make a case for the 'basic rationality' of emotions, even when they seem to be in conflict on cognitive grounds. But her conclusion has wide ramifications. In particular, it has implications for the 'basic rationality' of responding emotionally to fictions. For it is one of the important purposes and rewards of engaging emotionally with stories and other fictions, that it encourages us to sympathize and even identify with fictional characters. What Greenspan's argument demonstrates is that it is 'basically rational' and certainly adaptive to respond emotionally to the trials and tribulations, the joys and triumphs of other people (and even rabbits). It is adaptive to be able to sense one's wants and wishes, interests and goals to be at stake when reading and thinking about Anna Karenina. This is because it is adaptive to respond to her as though she were one of my 'own kind', just as in Greenspan's example, it is adaptive to respond to my friend as if she were truly a friend. When I respond compassionately to Anna, I am sympathizing with her fate in a way that is socially adaptive.

Further Complications

In an introductory article to a volume of essays called *Emotion and the Arts*, Jerrold Levinson surveys the many and various proposals that have been proffered over the years as solutions to the paradox of fiction. He characterizes the paradox as generated by accepting three apparently inconsistent propositions:

(a) We often have emotions for fictional characters and situations known to be purely fictional;

(b) Emotions for objects logically presuppose beliefs in the existence and features of those objects;

(c) We do not harbor beliefs in the existence and features of objects known to be fictional.[20]

It might help to situate my own proposal if I show how it fits into Levinson's taxonomy of possible solutions. In general, in terms of how Levinson has described the paradox, my own solution takes the form of denying (b).

1. The 'non-intentionalist solution' claims that emotional responses to fiction 'are not, despite appearances, instances of emotions as such, but rather of less complex states, such as moods (e.g. cheerfulness) or reflex reactions (e.g. shock), which lack the full intentionality and cognitivity of emotions per se'. Levinson comments that this proposed solution, even if valid, would apply to only 'a small portion of the full range of developed responses to fictions'.[21]

My own rejoinder would be that emotional responses to fiction, as to anything else, are always based on a non-cognitive and automatic appraisal, and so in this respect all emotional responses are rather like certain reflex reactions such as the startle mechanism: they follow willy-nilly from automatic affective appraisals.[22] The idea that emotions properly speaking have to have 'full intentionality and cognitivity' is just wrong.

2. The 'suspension-of-disbelief solution', due originally to Coleridge, asserts that while reading a novel or watching a play we 'temporarily allow ourselves to believe in the non-existent characters and situations of the fiction'. Levinson comments that the solution 'turns on a denial of (c)' but that 'it unacceptably depicts consumers of fiction as having a rather tenuous grip on reality and an amazing ability to manipulate their beliefs at will'.[23]

The solution is not quite as silly as this description makes it sound. Emotional responses do involve a selective focus of attention, and it is true that while focusing on Anna and her trials, I am not paying attention to the fact that she is Not Real. My attention can flicker back and forth, as I focus now on Anna as a person and now on Anna as a 'character', a fictional device in a structure of such devices.[24]

Roughly speaking, realistic novels such as *Anna Karenina* try to keep our attention firmly fixed on characters as people, whereas postmodern stories, such as Coover's *The Babysitter* or even Sterne's *Tristram Shandy*, deliberately try to prevent our attention becoming absorbed by the characters and keep reminding us that we're reading a *novel* (for Heaven's sake). So although I would not agree with Coleridge that we 'suspend disbelief', or that we harbour beliefs in characters we know to be fictional, there is a sense in which he is right if we take him to be pointing out that temporarily we stop *paying attention* to the fact that characters are fictional.

3. Another possible type of solution is the 'surrogate-object' solution, one version of which sounds a bit like my solution: it is the idea that 'the objects of response' are not actual individuals, but 'the descriptions, images, propositions, or thought contents afforded by the fiction'.[25] This solution involves denying (b) rather than (a) and to this extent I am in agreement with it. Levinson criticizes this view on the grounds that our responses have 'characters and situations as their evident objects, and not . . . the thoughts through which they are delineated'.[26]

In this book I have tried to avoid all talk of the *objects* of emotion, as I find it an ill-defined and unhelpful idea.[27] Obviously when I am feeling sorry for Anna Karenina, I am not feeling sorry for a thought, whatever that might mean. What I am feeling sorry for is not *the thought* that she is in a painful situation, but *the content* of that thought. And it is *the content* of the thought to which my emotional response helps to draw my attention. But it is indeed the thought that Anna is in a painful situation—or something like it—that *provokes* my emotional response of compassion for her. It is the vivid representations I form, on the basis of Tolstoy's words, that prompt my emotional responses to Anna.

A more literal version of the surrogate object solution is the 'shadow object' solution, according to which 'the objects of response are real individuals or phenomena from the subject's life experiences, ones resembling the persons or events of the fiction, and of which the fiction puts the subject covertly or indirectly in mind'.[28] As I have already suggested, this is an unsatisfactory solution, because we are responding to thoughts about Anna Karenina, not to thoughts about some real person who happens to be just like Anna. Having said that, however, it is perhaps worth pointing out that our emotional involvement with Anna Karenina is not explicable independently of our propensity to get emotionally involved with people in our group who have a rough time in real life. The reason why we get upset about Anna is that we normally get upset about those in our group who find themselves vulnerable in some similar type of situation.

4. Of all the possible solutions Levinson discusses, the 'antijudgmentalist solution' comes closest to my own. This solution states that: 'Emotional responses to objects do not logically require beliefs concerning the existence or features of such objects, but only weaker sorts of cognitions, such as seeing a certain way, or conceiving in a certain manner, or regarding as if such and such.'[29] This proposal questions the truth of (b), as I do.[30]

Levinson argues that there is a continuum of emotional states ranging from the primitive and non-cognitive, such as startle, to the highly cognitive, such as compassion, and he thinks that only the primitive emotions could possibly fit the antijudgementalist solution. Pity and other more complex emotions 'are centrally mediated by representations of various sorts . . . that serve to characterize the object of response':[31] thus, Anna Karenina is judged to be, or conceived of as, in a painful situation. Furthermore, even if—implausibly— cognitively complex emotions such as pity for Anna Karenina do not require 'characterizing' beliefs, i.e. beliefs about the properties that Anna has, still 'we must, on pain of incoherence, be taking [Anna] to exist or be regarding [her] as existent'.[32]

I have argued at length that affective appraisals are always primitive and speedy and always and immediately productive of physiological changes. In this sense, emotional responses do not require any cognitions at all, weak or otherwise, although of course cognition enters in at a later stage of the emotion process. So it is just empirically false that we have to take something to exist before we can respond emotionally to it. When I begin to weep because I'm thinking of Little Grey Rabbit kidnapped and far from home, I do not believe that Little Grey Rabbit exists. The emotion systems respond when one feels one's wants and interests to be at stake, regardless of whether they really are or even whether one truly believes them to be. Emotions do not require belief in their 'objects' to get off the ground. To say that we must believe in Little Grey Rabbit's existence 'on pain of incoherence' simply means that, as we have seen, the emotions are not governed by the same standards of rationality as are beliefs.

On the other hand, as we have also seen, human emotions are often set off by complex thoughts. If I have a genuine emotional response of compassion for Little Grey Rabbit, this is a response to a complex mental representation of her and her characteristics. My emotional response of compassion is set off—fast and automatically—by a thought or mental representation of a good little rabbit-person stolen away by the wicked weasels and suffering far from home. Of course my thoughts about Little Grey Rabbit must be of the right sort to qualify as compassionate. As we learned in Ch. 4, compassion requires a conception of the other person as suffering in some way and it characteristically involves dwelling on the other person's state, having an active regard for her good, viewing her as a fellow person (even though not a fellow rabbit-person), and responses of distress and sorrow.[33] But if I have the right kind of conception of Little Grey Rabbit, and the right kind of regard for her as a fellow person and so on, then it is quite appropriate to say that I pity her, even though I know perfectly well that she is a fictional character.

5. The 'irrationalist' solution, that 'while caught up in fictions, consumers of fiction become irrational, responding emotionally to objects that they know do not exist',[34] is therefore, as I argued earlier, in a sense correct.

6. The 'surrogate-belief solution' is the idea that some emotional responses to fictions 'require belief only that, *in the fiction*, the character exists and is or does such and such'.[35] This solution has always seemed to me to face an insuperable objection: there is no plausible mechanism whereby believing that someone suffers *in the fiction* can generate physiological disturbances in real life.[36]

7. The 'make-believe, or imaginary solution' is Levinson's final and favoured solution to the paradox. According to this solution, emotional responses to fiction are 'instances of imaginary, or make-believe, emotions'.[37] Or, in Kendall Walton's somewhat more careful way of talking, it is fictional or make-believe *that* we experience fear of the green slime in the horror movie or compassion for Anna Karenina.

The make-believe view relies on the supposed fact that, unlike the 'standard emotions of life', making-believe that one is in a particular emotional state such as compassion does not require having a belief or making a belief-like assumption that what one is emoting about *exists*, and does not have behavioural consequences. But as I have explained, these supposed facts are not facts at all. First, as I've just argued, emotional responses prompted by a thought of something-or-other do not require that the something-or-other exists. And secondly, the fact that emotional responses to novels, plays, and movies do not normally motivate us to take action to help the heroine or to punish the villain is the result of *cognitive monitoring* that succeeds the initial affective appraisal and results in the suppression of the relevant action tendencies. The emotion *process* is just the same in both the real life and the fictional case.

To conclude: I take it as indirect support for my view that it not only solves the paradox of fiction but also explains why various other solutions have seemed attractive in various ways.[38] One final note. I have not used the term 'simulation' at all in this discussion. The term has been used in such widely different ways by different people that it is hard to know what it means any more.[39] Moreover, it often carries the implication that readers imaginatively *identify* with the characters of fiction. Throughout my discussion, I have talked about how we respond emotionally to people and events in both life and fiction without making any assumptions about whether we actually identify with them or not, and what it would mean if we do. This omission has been deliberate.

6

A Sentimental Education

All these questions may be asked. First, have poetry and elo-
quence the power of calling out the emotions? The appeal is to
experience. Experience shows that for the vast majority of men,
for mankind in general, they have the power. Next do they
exercise it? They do. But then, *how* do they exercise it so as to
affect man's sense for conduct...?

Matthew Arnold, 'Literature and Science'

Learning from Literature

It is often claimed that great novels can teach us important truths
about the world. Certainly there is a relatively unproblematic sense in
which novels can teach us facts about the Napoleonic Wars or
Victorian London or Gladstone. But in addition to such factual
information about particular historical events, places or people,
novels are often also thought to provide more profound knowledge
of human nature and morality. Several writers have stressed that the
most important learning we achieve through reading great novels is
emotional: we learn both through watching the emotional development of the characters and through responding emotionally to them.
Martha Nussbaum, for example, has argued that much of what is
psychologically important and morally profound in a novel is learned
through our emotional involvement with it.[1]

Nussbaum comes to the emotions from a background in classics,
and in this respect she is a follower of Aristotle rather than Plato.
Despite his own love of poetry and the literary language in which he
couched his philosophical dialogues, Plato notoriously argued that the

arts are never, properly speaking, a source of knowledge. Instead, they appeal to the emotions, a lower part of the soul. His most famous pupil, Aristotle, however, while writing in dry, scientific prose, expressed views about the arts that are infinitely more sympathetic and persuasive. Aristotle agrees with Plato that the arts arouse our emotions, but he thought that we can learn from works of literature *through* having our emotions aroused by them. A tragedy, such as *Oedipus Rex*, elicits a *katharsis* of pity and fear, and in so doing it teaches us about our own limitations and potentialities. We learn through our emotional experience of the drama. What we learn is not theoretical knowledge, but practical: experiencing literature can help us become more perceptive and astute in our understanding of human motivation, human frailty, and human achievement. In her work on literature Nussbaum has explored the ethical implications of this perspective.

Now, it is a striking fact about the many recent discussions of emotional responses to fiction, including Nussbaum's, that virtually all of them endorse without argument the view that emotions are or entail beliefs or judgements, and that this cognitive component is the most fundamental aspect of emotion.[2] Learning about life through reading fiction would then seem to consist in the acquisition of beliefs. There are a number of serious problems with this idea, however. One problem, as we saw in the last chapter, is that the view that emotions entail beliefs and that we respond emotionally to characters in fiction might well ensnare us in the 'paradox of fiction'. In this chapter I will focus on a second problem, which is that the idea that learning emotionally through fiction consists primarily in the acquisition of beliefs does not do justice to the experience of reading a novel. I will try to show that it is the process of reading that is emotionally educational, not just the eventual acquisition of beliefs.

If we are genuinely engaged emotionally with a novel, we are frequently unsure until the end what exactly we *believe* about the characters and what they should and should not do. It is often only after we have finished a novel that we can look back at it, reflect on the significance of its various episodes, and arrive at an interpretation of it that we can say we believe. As we read, we receive a series of impressions or points of view on the characters that are often conflicting, and it is not until all the evidence is in, as it were, that we acquire *beliefs* about them as opposed to entertaining multiple, often conflicting, and changing *thoughts* about them. Of course, I am not suggesting that we have to be emotionally engaged in the novel from start to finish before we are allowed to reflect upon it, only that—as I argued in Ch. 4—the process of reflection succeeds and depends upon the process of emotional involvement. We can pause and reflect after every page if we wish, but if we try to arrive at beliefs too quickly, before we are emotionally involved in the novel, we are likely to arrive at mistaken beliefs.

Significantly, if we do arrive at beliefs about what we have read after we have finished reading, those beliefs depend essentially upon the emotional experience of reading the novel. We will never be able to abstract a 'message' from a great novel by means of an after-the-fact summary of it. To be told that *Anna Karenina* teaches us that betraying your husband can lead to misery is no substitute for reading the novel. One important reason why this is so is that it is only through an emotional experience of a novel that one can genuinely learn from it. The message of a great novel is inextricable from the reader's experience of the novel.

In this chapter I argue that although the emotional experiences we have in reading a novel do not entail having beliefs, nevertheless we do learn about life from novels and our learning is emotional. I shall try to demonstrate that the emotional process of engaging with characters and situations in a novel is part of a 'sentimental education', an education by the emotions. First of all, if we have a rich emotional experience of a novel, then when we reflect back on that experience we will be in an excellent position to arrive at true, or at least plausible, *beliefs* about the characters and situations we have experienced. The acquisition of these beliefs is, then, a *result* of our emotional experience of the novel. Secondly, what I want to focus on here is how the emotional experience itself, although not necessarily involving beliefs, is educational in other ways, particularly in *focusing attention* on certain aspects of situations and characters, in *making affective appraisals* of them that appeal to our *wants and interests* and affect us *physiologically*, and in *formulating thoughts* about them from a 'partial' point of view. Finally a good novel encourages us to cognitively monitor or reflect back upon the whole emotion process, including affective appraisals, physiological responses, action tendencies, points of view, and foci of attention.

I will try to demonstrate my thesis by reference to Edith Wharton's *The Reef*, a novel that not only tells how its characters gradually come to new emotional awareness of their own situations, but also induces a similar learning experience in the reader. I will show that the emotional education of characters and readers alike takes place via a series of emotional episodes in which *beliefs* are less important than such things as unexpected physiological responses, non-cognitive affective appraisals, shifts in focus of attention, the perception of new aspects of situations, and the revelation of previously hidden wants and interests. After reflecting on their emotional experiences, both characters and readers may acquire new beliefs, but the acquisition of those beliefs depends essentially on the emotional experiences that precede it. And the educational value of this experience consists not just in the fact *that* it may eventually lead to new beliefs, but also in *how* it does so.

As we saw in the opening chapters, an emotional response is a physiological response that is caused by a non-cognitive affective appraisal. An episode of emotion is best thought of as a *process*, consisting minimally in a non-cognitive affective appraisal succeeded by physiological changes of specific sorts, action tendencies, and cognitive monitoring of the non-cognitive appraisal and the other elements of the response. The physiological response helps to focus attention on whatever it is that is affectively appraised (whether this be real or imaginary, an object of thought or an object of perception), as well as to alert others and perhaps oneself to the state one is in; it may also help prepare the person or organism for action. This whole process gets going only when one senses one's wants, interests, goals, values, etc. to be at stake in some encounter with the (internal or external) environment. Specific emotions (compassion, anger, fear, parental love, sexual love) involve specific kinds of cognitive and non-cognitive appraisal. Sometimes I make the appraisals appropriate to compassion (say) but without any ensuing physiological response. In these cases, I am making a compassionate appraisal of somebody or other, but I am not experiencing a full-fledged *emotion* of compassion. I am in a cognitive or attitudinal state of compassion, but without being *emotional*. However, I have previously pointed out that such cases might turn out to be relatively rare. Whenever we sense our interests really to be at stake, we do tend to respond physiologically, although of course cognitive monitoring may suppress the physiological changes almost as soon as they have begun.

Whereas my illustrations in Ch. 4 were of small snippets from much longer works, in this chapter I will be emphasizing the unfolding of a novel over time, the experiences of the characters over time and the unfolding experience of the reader over time. In this way we shall see not only how each episode of emotion unfolds as a process, but also how one emotional episode often transforms into another, as appraisals change, as attention is refocused, and as physiological and motor changes adapt to changing circumstances.

In the next two sections I will examine the process of sentimental education as Edith Wharton describes it in her novel *The Reef*. I shall try to demonstrate how the careful reading of a novel of this sort can educate our emotions. This happens in at least two ways: one is by careful description of the emotional states of the characters and how they are educated through their emotions. A novel does this by showing (1) the characters' focus of attention; (2) their thoughts about or point of view on the situation on which they are focused; (3) how this point of view and focus of attention reflect their desires, interests, and values; (4) the affective appraisals that they make; and (5) how their physiological states serve to maintain their focus of attention on whatever it is that they are affectively appraising. Further, by reflecting on their responses, characters can be brought to understand and form beliefs about themselves and their situations. The reader watches the education of the characters' emotions, and is thereby given a lesson in how the emotions function as teachers.

The second way in which we can have our emotions educated is more direct: we can have our own emotions aroused as we read, so that we too, like the characters, are made to focus attention on certain situations and to see them in a certain way. We too are influenced in how we respond by our desires, interests, and values, and we too may have our attention fixed by physiological means. Finally, we too are encouraged by a novel such as *The Reef* to reflect on our emotional experience while reading and to form beliefs about the significance of what we have read. The experience of a serious reader of *The Reef*, therefore, has the same form as that of the main characters: both have emotional experiences in which they have their attention focused on situations affectively appraised as personally significant in some way.

Both are, as a result of these experiences, then led to reflect on them and to discover their significance. Both will, if all goes well, eventually reach understanding and acquire new beliefs.

Novels are not just illustrations of principles of folk psychology. They introduce both characters and readers to emotional states for which there are no one-word descriptions in folk psychology. Much of the interest in a good realistic novel comes from watching the characters change and develop over time. This means that their focus of attention, their desires and interests, and their thoughts and conceptions about people and things may change. In the best realistic novels these changes are subtle and not easily put into words. They may occur gradually or in fits and starts or as the result of a sudden revelation. The characters expand their emotional repertoires, experiencing 'new' shades of emotion for which there are no good one-word descriptions such as 'happy' or 'sad'. And by observing the characters, readers also expand their emotional horizons and learn about the possibility of new emotional states.

The reader's 'sentimental education' is guided by the author. As we read, we respond to the characters and events emotionally, but when we reflect upon our emotional experiences as readers, we make inferences based partly on our sense of who the author is. In short, we construct an implied author even as we respond under 'her' tutelage to the characters, plot, setting, and so on. As we saw in Ch. 4, an interpretation of a realistic novel is the result of reflection about our emotional experiences of the novel. But we have to remember that although our own personalities and emotional experiences will affect how we respond to a novel (as indeed to anything else), our emotions are also to some extent guided by the author. Indeed one of the aspects of a novel that requires interpretation is the attitude of the implied author, the author as we construe her to be. I'll return to these difficult issues after my discussion of *The Reef*.

Before turning to that discussion, let me say again what I stressed in Ch. 4. Not all novels invite the kind of serious, sustained emotional attention I am about to discuss. There are bad novels that try to teach us something and fail, there are genre novels that merely aim to entertain, and there are novels that are more like intellectual puzzles or games. Again F. R. Leavis's 'Great Tradition' of morally serious, realistic works are the kinds of work I mainly have in mind. Leavis does not discuss Edith Wharton in his book, but he does discuss Henry James, and *The Reef* is in many ways a Jamesian novel, repaying the same kind of emotional and intellectual absorption that James demands of his readers.

The Emotional Education of George Darrow

Edith Wharton's novel *The Reef* tells the story of two expatriate Americans, Anna Leath and her suitor George Darrow. When the story begins, Darrow is on his way from London to visit Anna in her country house in France, Givré, where she lives as a widow with her mother-in-law, her adolescent stepson Owen, and her small daughter Effie. Darrow had been intending to propose to Anna, but just as his train is about to leave London, he receives a telegram from her asking him to postpone his visit. At Dover he runs across Sophy Viner, a pretty young woman whom he knows slightly, and he continues his journey to Paris in her company. She is poor and friendless; Darrow is kind to her and they end up having a brief affair. So ends Book One of the novel. At Givré some months later, when Darrow eventually pays his visit, he discovers first that Sophy Viner has become governess to Effie, and second that Owen is engaged to her. On seeing Darrow again, Sophy realizes that she has been in love with him ever since their affair and she breaks off her engagement to Owen. Anna eventually discovers the truth about Sophy and Darrow, and is torn between her revulsion at his infidelity and her love for him.

The interest of the story lies not in its rather melodramatic plot, but in the intricacies of the inner lives of the protagonists, especially Anna herself and Darrow. The unfolding events are seen through their eyes, the narrative point of view switching between the two of them throughout the novel. The story is about how Darrow gradually comes to understand the significance of his casual liaison with Sophy and how Anna struggles to understand its significance to herself. Both Anna and Darrow are engaged in learning about themselves and the significance of their conduct. In this section I will confine my attention to Darrow. In the next I will discuss Anna.

Darrow's 'education' takes place largely through a series of emotional episodes at Givré, as he is gradually led to realize the significance of his liaison with Sophy. The book opens with a description of his emotional state as he travels from London to Dover after receiving Anna's telegram. He is focused obsessively on the words of the telegram.

'Unexpected obstacle. Please don't come till thirtieth. Anna.' All the way from Charing Cross to Dover the train had hammered the words of the telegram into George Darrow's ears, ringing every change of irony on its commonplace syllables: rattling them out like a discharge of musketry, letting them, one by one, drip slowly and coldly into his brain, or shaking, tossing, transposing them like the dice in some game of the gods of malice; and now, as he emerged from his compartment at the pier, and stood facing the windswept platform and the angry sea beyond, they leapt out at him as if from the crest of the waves, stung and blinded him with a fresh fury of derision. 'Unexpected obstacle. Please don't come till thirtieth. Anna.'[3]

Anna's apparent rejection of him is dramatized by the way in which everything around him—the sound of the train, the cold unwelcoming sea, the wet gloomy weather—seems to echo her words: they too seem to reject him and to be either hostile or indifferent to his fate. The very waves are 'derisive' of him, and he even feels himself 'obscurely outraged' by the crowd on the pier, who seem to be 'contemptuously bumping and shoving him like the inconsiderable thing he had become. "She doesn't want you, doesn't want you, doesn't want you," their umbrellas and their elbows seemed to say.'[4]

In describing Darrow's emotional state, Wharton is *not* describing his *beliefs*. Darrow does not *believe* that Anna is too cold and formal to be worth marrying; he does not *believe* that the waves and the weather are deliberately rejecting him. Rather he is focused obsessively on the telegram and on certain thoughts about Anna that it induces. He is thinking of her as cold-hearted and as chillingly over-influenced by convention, and the waves and the weather strike him as her accomplices in rejecting him. His resentment towards her prepares the way for the affair with Sophy, who is pretty, charming, informal, glad to see him, and in need of help and friendship. Darrow's feeling of humiliation has been compounded by his being made to feel passive. With Sophy's arrival on the scene his vigour returns: he can help Sophy, impress himself upon the situation, and regain self-esteem. He can try to end the discomfort of his cross feelings by seeking consolation with Sophy.[5]

At Givré several months later, Darrow discovers that Sophy has become Effie's governess. Wharton describes his first reaction to this revelation as he walks in the woods with Owen. He is so focused on this piece of news that he can pay scarcely any attention to Owen's conversation. The revelation is seen or felt by him as a blow to his interests and desires, but he has no clear idea of how it affects him as yet, and his thoughts are so turbulent that he has no clear idea what to do either. Although occasionally he notices the beauty of the woods, it is only enough 'to fill the foreground of his attention'.[6] In his 'secret consciousness' there is turmoil: 'His sensations were too swift and swarming to be disentangled. He had an almost physical sense of struggling for air, of battling helplessly with material obstructions, as though the russet covert through which he trudged were the heart of a maleficent jungle ... '[7]

In his first meeting alone with Sophy he discovers that she is terrified he will betray their liaison and she will be forced to leave Givré. His immediate reaction is emotional: a mixture of compassion for her, admiration for her 'absolute candour, her hard ardent honesty'[8] and shock that she should think him capable of such a betrayal. 'She was *afraid*, then—afraid of him—sick with fear of him! The discovery beat him down to a lower depth ... '[9] Again Wharton describes his initial emotional response in terms of his focus of attention and how he 'sees' the situation: he feels under attack, set about by obstacles, and 'battling helplessly', and he feels the beginnings of shame: he is beaten down 'to a lower depth'. He is confused and bewildered, however, and none of these vague feelings of being trapped and shamed amounts at this point to a belief about himself. He feels as if the situation is 'whirling him about so fast that he could just clutch at its sharp spikes and be tossed off again'.[10] Similarly, although he certainly feels a variety of emotions towards Sophy, he is not described as having beliefs about her: his compassion, admiration, and shock are all different ways of seeing her, but none of them amounts to a belief. He does not yet know what he believes about Sophy.

Later, however, in his room, he has an opportunity to 'think the complex horror out, slowly, systematically, bit by bit',[11] and he then discovers for the first time that he has never before thought seriously about Sophy or the implications of their relationship. For him Sophy had been but the 'chance instrument' of his lapse from 'his own preconceived ideal of his attitude toward another woman'.[12] As he reflects on the situation, he realizes with 'humiliating distinctness' that for him the affair had been emotionally cheap. He had not given up anything significant of himself to it: his real emotional commitments were elsewhere. 'He would have liked to be able to feel that, at the time at least, he had staked something more on it, and had somehow, in the sequel, had a more palpable loss to show. But the plain fact was that he hadn't spent a penny on it; which was no doubt the reason of the prodigious score it had since been rolling up.'[13]

The following day it is revealed that Sophy is not only Effie's governess, but is engaged to Owen. Darrow's troubles are now multiplied.

Hitherto he had felt for Sophy Viner's defenseless state a sympathy profoundly tinged with compunction. But now he was half-conscious of an obscure indignation against her. . . . Assuredly he did not want to harm her; but he did desperately want to prevent her marrying Owen Leath. He tried to get away from the feeling, to isolate and exteriorize it sufficiently to see what motives it was made of; but it remained a mere blind motion of his blood, the instinctive recoil from the thing that no amount of arguing can make 'straight.'[14]

In this striking passage Wharton characterizes Darrow's response not as embodying a belief about the situation but as 'a mere blind motion of his blood'. His 'view' of the situation is not thought out but is signalled by an 'instinctive recoil', an immediate physiological response (what Damasio would call a 'somatic marker'). What dominates his consciousness is what he *wants*: to avoid betraying Sophy but also to prevent her from entering the family he is about to enter himself. Wharton suggests that there is also a tinge of jealousy in his response: he would 'rather [she] didn't marry any friend of [his]', as Sophy shrewdly points out. Again, the process of understanding begins with emotional responses—compunction towards Sophy giving way to indignation, jealousy, and revulsion—and again these responses do not entail beliefs about her. Darrow is still working out his beliefs about Sophy and about himself. At present he has only a vague sense of his own emotional state, signalled by a physiological disturbance. Wharton describes Darrow's emotional state partly by describing his physical state and his sensations. He 'plunged out alone into the rain' with his thoughts 'tossing like the tree-tops';[15] as at Dover, the tempestuous weather reflects his tempestuous inner state. Darrow is emotionally excited and this is helping him to learn an important moral lesson by focusing attention on certain significant events and by presenting them from a certain point of view, but it has not yet taught him full understanding.

When Sophy avows her love for Darrow and exults in the sacrifices (of Owen and a secure future) she is willing to make to it, Darrow can only bow 'his humbled head' and mutter 'Poor child—you poor child!'[16] Once again Darrow's emotional response leads him to reflection. It is only now that he comes to understand how the affair with Sophy occurred and what his beliefs about it really were. Interestingly, it is only now that the reader finds out too. We have never been told how Darrow and Sophy progressed from frank good-fellowship to sexual liaison. Darrow now realizes that the affair developed because he was physically attracted to Sophy while at the same time intellectually and emotionally bored by her:

Perhaps it was because, when her light chatter about people failed, he found she had no other fund to draw on, or perhaps simply because of the sweetness of her laugh, or of the charm of the gesture with which, one day in the woods of Marly, she had tossed off her hat and tilted back her head at the call of a cuckoo; or because, whenever he looked at her unexpectedly, he found that she was looking at him and did not want him to know it; or perhaps, in varying degrees, because of all these things, that there had come a moment when no word seemed to fly high enough or dive deep enough to utter the sense of well-being each gave to the other, and the natural substitute for speech had been a kiss.[17]

The kiss is better than talk: Darrow feels that 'she would never bore him again'. Moreover, he now no longer has to listen to her: he just lets 'her voice run on as a musical undercurrent to his thoughts'.[18] And perhaps the kiss would not have led to a full-fledged liaison if it had not been for the bad weather that made them both irritable and tired and confined them to the hotel.

Darrow's emotional education about the affair with Sophy is completed in this meditation. Now at last he understands what he did and its moral and emotional implications. Measured by Anna's standards—her confidence in and love for him, her sensitivity, her integrity, her care for the feelings of others, her devotion to her family, her sense of justice, and her penetrating mind—Darrow finally grasps that he has betrayed both Anna and Sophy. He has betrayed Anna, because, although supposedly devoted to her and about to become engaged to her, he has an affair with another woman while on his way to see her; and more importantly he has betrayed Anna's love for and trust in him, her confidence that he has the same high standards of feeling and behaviour that she does. He has also betrayed Sophy because she has fallen disastrously in love with him, and he could and should have prevented this. Whereas for Sophy the affair and its consequences are momentous, for him it was just a minor escapade. Interestingly, Darrow realizes that his failure has been an emotional failure: 'a case of not feeling'.[19] Despite his actions, he did not have any strong feelings for Sophy: she was *not* significant to him; his desires and interests were *not* much at stake; he did *not* focus attention on her; and he did not notice or care much about what Sophy's feelings were for him. Earlier in the book Wharton has described how Darrow sees Sophy at the end of the affair. She has become simply an irritating bodily presence. She is a footfall, a voice, a hand, a face. 'Suddenly he felt the presence of the hand on his shoulder, and became aware that the face was still leaning over him, and that in a moment he would have to look up and kiss it ... '[20]

We can perhaps formulate what Darrow learns in the course of the novel as beliefs. He comes to believe that he mistreated Sophy and that his mistreatment was the result of failing in his emotional response to the situation. He tells Anna:

when you've lived a little longer you'll see what complex blunderers we all are: how we're struck blind sometimes, and mad sometimes—and then, when our sight and our senses come back, how we have to set to work, and build up, little by little, bit by bit, the precious things we'd smashed to atoms without knowing it. Life's just a perpetual piecing together of broken bits.[21]

However, Darrow's sentimental education which the book traces cannot be adequately captured simply by capturing the beliefs that he acquires. What the novel demonstrates is the process by which he arrives at those beliefs, and this process, as we have seen, is in important ways emotional. Darrow's education is initiated by his emotional responses to the situation as it unfolds at Givré. His emotional responses in turn lead him to reflection. His responses to Sophy and to Anna at Givré alert him to the undistinguished role he had earlier played in Paris. It is by reflection that Darrow comes to understand his past conduct, but his reflection is prompted by his unfolding emotional experiences in the present, including affective appraisals and physiological and motor responses, and the way they focus attention on particular thoughts about or points of view upon Sophy, Anna, and himself that are of striking significance to him and his wants, interests, and values.

It is noteworthy that there is no easy way to describe Darrow's complex emotional state in the last part of the novel. There is first of all shame at how he has treated Sophy and a finely shaded regret for his affair with her, together with a conviction that although more important than he realized, the affair is not ultimately as important as Anna thinks it is; there is also deep affection and love for Anna, and some penitence towards her, a mixture of admiration and impatience for her attitude towards him and the affair, as well as fear that he may yet lose her; there is also pride in himself, and courage that makes him argue in his own defence. However, none of these words—shame, regret, affection, love, penitence, admiration, impatience, fear, pride, or courage—conveys the particularities of his emotional states. His developing emotional states, as Wharton describes them, are much more finely tuned. The novel teaches him—and through him the reader—the peculiarities of the shame and pride, the love and fear, as Darrow experiences them. Folk psychology generalizes; literature particularizes.

The Emotional Education of the Heroine

Anna's sentimental education is very different from Darrow's. We learn when we first meet her that she is a person of sensitivity, refinement, and upright character, whose reflections on her emotional states are honest and penetrating. But she has had few powerful emotions to reflect about: her life has been sheltered and, with the exception of her passion for her daughter Effie (and to a lesser extent her affection for her stepson Owen), she has never had deep desires or 'cared' passionately about anyone or anything. Her relationship with Darrow brings her an ecstatic joy that she has never before known, the joy of an intellectual, emotional, and physical union with a man who reciprocates her own passionate devotion. She learns that life can be infinitely more fulfilling than hers has ever been. At the same time she learns that in order to grasp the happiness Darrow offers her, she also has to suffer unpleasant emotions that are new to her: doubts and fears about the past and the future, sorrow and revulsion for what Darrow has done. And in the midst of her almost obsessive reflections about what she ought to do, she also learns that her emotions—her instinctive 'affective appraisals'—are just as important guides to right conduct as rational reflection.

Anna Summers spent her girlhood in the sheltered, conformist atmosphere of upper-class New York society. 'In the well-regulated well-fed Summers world the unusual was regarded as either immoral or ill-bred, and people with emotions were not visited.'[22] She has a brief flirtation with Darrow, to whom she is powerfully attracted, but she does not know how to encourage him, and he—while retaining his admiration and liking for Anna—goes on to liaisons with women who are more experienced in the ways of the world. Finally, she marries Fraser Leath, a lover of art and collector of snuffboxes, a man whom she thinks will release her from conventionality but who in fact is rigidly conventional himself in his own way. Life for Fraser Leath was 'like a walk through a carefully classified museum, where, in moments of doubt, one had only to look at the number and refer to one's catalogue'.[23] There is no passion in him and Anna is vaguely aware that something is missing 'in the rare moments when Mr. Leath's symmetrical blond mask bent over hers, and his kiss dropped on her like a cold smooth pebble'.[24]

They settle in Givré, a chateau bequeathed to Mr Leath's mother, Madame de Chantelle, by her second husband, and Anna stays on there with Owen and Effie and her mother-in-law after Fraser Leath's death. She has made a quiet, orderly life for herself in this beautiful old chateau set in its own park in the calm French countryside. The house is lovingly described and in some ways is perhaps an apt symbol for Anna herself: the chateau reflects her physical and moral beauty and refinement, quiet, mellow, untouched by gusts of passion, and harmonious like the perfectly attuned colours and textures of a Chardin painting. But it also represents confinement and rigid adherence to social convention. At the end of the novel the only people left at Givré are the 'innocents', Effie and her grandmother. When Darrow re-enters Anna's life (they meet by chance in England), her passion for him is revitalized, deepened by the intervening years, her lifeless marriage, and her sense that, except as a mother, her life at Givré has been emotionally empty.

The first 'emotional discovery' that Anna makes is that this joyful passion has transformed her world. On the day when she expects Darrow to arrive at long last at Givré, she finds herself running in sheer exuberance.

> She only knew that run she must, that no other motion, short of flight, would have been buoyant enough for her humor. She seemed to be keeping pace with some inward rhythm, seeking to give bodily expression to the lyric rush of her thoughts. The earth always felt elastic under her, and she had a conscious joy in treading it; but never had it been as soft and springy as today. . . . The air, too, seemed to break in waves against her, sweeping by on its current all the slanted lights and moist sharp perfumes of the failing day.[25]

Wharton here describes how Anna's emotion finds expression in action and action tendencies as well as in a joyful conception of the world. She is not particularly conscious of why she feels this way; she 'finds herself' running; we are made aware of her 'affective appraisals' of the earth as unusually springy, the air as unusually soft and beautiful.

When Darrow arrives and they take their first walk alone together to the river, all her senses are alert and she is 'intensely aware'[26] of his physical presence. At the same time, however, she feels impelled to question him about the woman whom Owen saw him with at the theatre in Paris. Wharton tells us that she is physiologically worked up. 'Her heart was beating unsteadily'[27] and 'her heart trembled'.[28] Darrow turns aside her worries. He does not tremble or blanch or show any other signs of physiological distress. As I have explained, this is because, prior to his sentimental education, he is unemotional about the whole Sophy episode; he lies about it because it is meaningless as far as he is concerned. He embraces Anna, and 'she sat as if folded in wings'.[29]

This scene captures in microcosm Anna's emotional experiences in the period leading up to her discovery of Darrow's affair with Sophy. Her dominant emotion is joy in her new-found love, but she also feels half-consciously an undercurrent of anxiety, jealousy, and uncertainty. Thus when she and Owen announce to Darrow that Owen and Sophy are engaged, she has 'an unaccountable faint flutter of misgiving', the 'eerie feeling of having been overswept by a shadow which there had been no cloud to cast'.[30] Here Wharton nicely acknowledges that the appraisal is non-cognitive: Anna has not yet cognitively evaluated how she feels and does not understand why she reacts that way.

After the announcement of Anna's engagement, Sophy Viner asks permission to go away for a few days. Owen accuses Sophy of going away in order to break their engagement, and Darrow of holding the key to Sophy's unexpected decision. Anna's emotional response is described in physiological terms, as a 'tremor of alarm',[31] because Owen has given voice to her own vague doubts. When she taxes Darrow yet again with having some secret understanding with Sophy, he still calmly denies it, but her pride is piqued by his insinuation that she is worrying about nothing, and she still feels a 'warning tremor', as if 'some instinct deeper than reason surged up in defense of its treasure'.[32] As in the subception experiments, her body knows enough to be afraid, but cognitively, consciously, she is still ignorant.

The actual discovery eventually occurs after Darrow's final interview with Sophy, when Sophy joyously declares that she is in love with him and because of this cannot or will not marry Owen. As we saw earlier, this interview is what leads Darrow to understand at last the full implications of the affair he had entered so lightly. After Sophy has gone, he continues to sit in Anna's sitting room reflecting on the past and experiencing powerful emotions of shame, sorrow, and compassion. When Anna enters the room and sees his facial expression, she knows instantly that he is experiencing some kind of anguish. Interestingly, this episode is told first from Darrow's point of view, and then from Anna's. This double view of it makes it perhaps the central scene in the book.

First we are shown Anna from Darrow's perspective. When she turns lovingly to him for an embrace, he 'looked at her through a mist of pain and saw all her proffered beauty held up like a cup to his lips; but as he stooped to it a darkness seemed to fall between them ... '[33] Darrow's physiological symptoms have given him away and Anna can tell he is struggling with some terrible truth: finally he is compelled to admit that he had indeed been with Sophy at the theatre in Paris. As he struggles to find a plausible reason why he has been concealing this fact, he sees 'a tremor' go through Anna, but 'she controlled it instantly and faced him straight and motionless as a wounded creature in the moment before it feels its wound'.[34] Here from the 'outside' we see Anna's intense focus on the situation, her bodily gestures and posture, her physiological symptoms, together with the cognitive control that she exerts but that is not sufficient to conceal the bodily state that reveals the threat she senses to her 'wants and interests'.

Then we are shown Anna from the 'inside'. When Darrow leaves the room, Anna reflects upon the scene that has just passed. She had come into the room with a newfound sense of security.

All the spirits of doubt had been exorcised, and her love was once more the clear habitation in which every thought and feeling could move in blissful freedom. And then, as she raised her face to Darrow's and met his eyes, she had seemed to look into the very ruins of his soul. ... It was as though he and she had been looking at two sides of the same thing, and the side she had seen had been all light and life, and his a place of graves.[35]

Significantly, Anna learns the crucial fact that Darrow has been lying to her through emotional communication: she sees in his facial expression what he has been trying to conceal. At the same time she begins to get an inkling that her love for Darrow has two aspects, at once full of 'light and life' and 'a place of graves'.

It is not until her own interview with Sophy that she discovers the whole story—that Darrow and Sophy have had an affair in Paris, and that Sophy is in love with Darrow—and again it is through her rapidly changing emotions that she grasps the various implications of this revelation. When Sophy reiterates that she can't marry Owen, 'Anna stood motionless, silenced by the shock of the avowal. She too was trembling, less with anger than with a confused compassion. But the feeling was so blent with others, less generous and more obscure, that she found no words to express it, and the two women faced each other without speaking.'[36] Here we see Anna feeling emotions that she can identify, such as anger blended with compassion, but also emotional states for which she has no words. We can infer that she is experiencing envy of Sophy's experience with Darrow, together with bitterness and jealousy that Sophy has lived with Darrow experiences which she, Anna, has not. At the same time she is sorry for Sophy who is sacrificing a great deal to her love for Darrow, and she admires Sophy's courage in avowing her love and in acting on it both during the affair and now in its aftermath. The situation calls forth a range of different points of view on the situation, and focuses her attention on several of these different, incompatible ways of seeing what is going on. Anna cannot speak probably because she is trying to understand her complex emotional reactions, to reconcile irreconcilable ways of seeing things, and to keep from expressing the 'less generous and obscure' emotions she is dimly aware of. What she does realize, however, is that she has never before understood the complexities of sexual passion. As Darrow says, 'almost harshly' and with 'sudden bitterness',[37] Anna is 'too high . . . too fine . . . such things are too far'[38] from her understanding. She cannot grasp how the affair between Sophy and Darrow occurred, because it is too far outside her own emotional experience and her moral norms.

Once Anna knows about the affair, and that it happened while Darrow was on his way to propose to her, a new stage in her emotional education begins. When she is reflecting (cognitively), she thinks that she cannot possibly marry a man who has betrayed her and lied to her. But when she is in Darrow's presence, her instinctive, affective appraisals predominate: she is overwhelmed by her physical attraction to him and her sense of the terrible sorrow she would feel if she lost him. Her initial reaction is simple pain and suffering, an affective appraisal: **No! No! No!** Earlier, we have seen, she is like 'a wounded creature in the moment before it feels its wound'. Now the image of the wounded animal returns: 'She had suffered before—yes, but lucidly, reflectively, elegiacally: now she was suffering as a hurt animal must, blindly, furiously, with the single fierce animal longing that the awful pain should stop . . .'[39] In my terms, suffering that is 'lucid' and 'reflective' is suffering that has been consciously reflected upon and understood. It is not the result of an immediate non-cognitive affective appraisal that her whole life's meaning is threatened with annihilation.

In her first encounter with Darrow after her discovery of his infidelity, we witness her shifting emotions, as different desires, values, and goals come to the forefront of her attention in turn. For example, she feels 'animal anguish', then a 'thrill of resentment'[40] that Darrow won't leave when she begs him to, then 'courage'[41] when he exhorts her to look things in the face, then coldness and bitterness, followed by a 'sudden rush of almost physical repugnance'[42] at the thought of the affair, then 'speechless misery',[43] while Darrow is explaining how it happened, 'resentment and indignation',[44] jealousy and sorrow that, if she gives him up, she will never experience with Darrow what Sophy has, and finally a renewed sense of her passion for Darrow followed by the 'pride' to conceal it. The scene ends with Darrow committed to leaving Givré, presumably for ever. He reminds her that she always wanted to 'look at life, at the human problem, as it is, without fear and without hypocrisy', but now she has to realize that 'it's not always a pleasant thing to look at'.[45]

After all this inner turmoil, Anna quietly reflects upon her emotional reactions. She realizes that her 'sense of honor' is no longer 'her deepest sentiment',[46] since she still 'worships' Darrow, despite his infidelity. When Darrow rushes back from London to see Anna in Paris, she succumbs to her physical passion to him: 'All her fears seemed to fall from her as he held her. It was a different feeling from any she had known before: confused and turbid, as if secret shames and rancours stirred in it, yet richer, deeper, more enslaving. . . . She knew now that she could never give him up.'[47] Wharton does not name this 'different feeling', but she vividly explains its various components. In folk-psychological terms, Anna is experiencing a blend of shame and bliss: she is focused upon two conceptions, the shameful and the blissful, of a situation that completely absorbs her attention, in which **I want it!** and '**I don't want it!**'—or pleasure and pain—conflict, but in which the pleasure is too powerful to resist. It involves not just action tendencies but actions: she shuts her eyes and gives herself up to physical passion. Anna is 'enslaved' by this emotion and by Darrow.

She recalled having read somewhere that in ancient Rome the slaves were not allowed to wear a distinctive dress lest they should recognize each other and learn their numbers and their power. So, in herself, she discerned for the first time instincts and desires, which, mute and unmarked, had gone to and fro in the dim passages of her mind, and now hailed each other with a cry of mutiny.[48]

In this remarkable image, Wharton conveys Anna's 'enslavement' to Darrow, as well as the way in which her unconscious desires—revolutionary desires, from Anna's point of view—are rebelling against cool cognition and insisting that they should have their way. The image also conveys that her new-found joy has revealed to her a whole host of desires which she had hitherto kept unacknowledged and out of sight. We can infer that they include sexual desires as well as perhaps the desire for a more exciting life, for travel, for intelligent adult companionship, for a home of her own, for the freedom to be herself at last, and so on. But Wharton does not say explicitly. She does not *name* Anna's emotion by reference to some term of commonsense psychology. She expresses its unique and peculiar quality in her imagery.

When Anna and Darrow return to Givré for a few days, Anna fluctuates between her 'inextinguishable bliss'[49] and her dislike of not being able to trust him. On what bids fair to be their last night together she once again resolves to tell him that they must part, but as she is saying goodnight, she is overpowered by the prospect of losing him, and the prospect of being left 'alone among her shrunken thoughts'.[50] Even after they have spent the night together and 'she was his now, his for life',[51] she still has moments when she cringes from him and Darrow feels that he fills her 'with aversion'.[52] But whenever she attempts to free herself, she cannot.

Her last attempt comes when she tries to find Sophy to announce that she will give up Darrow after all, but Sophy has gone off to India with her disreputable former employer Mrs Murrett. Sophy's sister receives Anna in a squalid and vulgar apartment which presumably symbolizes Sophy's return to her origins. Wharton does not explain to us how Anna greets the news of Sophy's departure and the end of the novel is ambiguous,[53] but the implication is that, with Sophy safely out of the way, Anna has finally run out of reasons for refusing to marry Darrow.

Like Darrow, Anna learns her most important lessons by emotional means. We might summarize what she learns in the form of new beliefs that she acquires: (1) she learns that Sophy and Darrow had an affair; (2) she learns that passionate love can transform one's life; (3) she learns that the enjoyment of a happy love may involve a compromise with one's 'high' and 'fine' principles. But the most important part of her education comes in the experience of a whole series of new emotions, that eventually lead to the acquisition of these beliefs. Thus it is the actual ongoing experience of her passionate love for Darrow that teaches her what a fulfilling life can be like. It is because this passionate love has transformed every aspect of her life—intellectual, sensual, and emotional—that she cannot bear to give him up. But as soon as her love has taught her what a fulfilling life can be like, she discovers Darrow's untruthfulness and infidelity, and her consequent repulsion proceeds to teach her that the enjoyment of her love will require that she is—perhaps for ever after—a prey to this repulsion and to anxieties and jealousies that are foreign to her previous experience. Anna also learns from the emotional conflicts she suffers: attraction versus repulsion for Darrow, pity versus jealousy of Sophy, pride in her own uprightness versus shame at her lack of experience. Each emotion involves different conceptions of the situation, and they teach her complexities that her narrow, conventional life has never exposed her to before.

The conflict that occupies the whole of the last part of the book can also be couched, however, as a conflict between reason and 'instinctive' (non-cognitive) emotional appraisals. Anna not only learns emotionally that she has to endure imperfection and compromise in order to achieve a happier, richer life; she also learns that relying on affective appraisals, rather than always engaging in refined and careful cognitive monitoring of one's experiences, is not necessarily a bad thing. Anna has relied too heavily on cognitive reflection; she has to give more weight to instinctive emotional appraisal. It is instinctive emotional appraisal that initially guided her to Darrow and the joy she has found with him. It is instinctive emotional appraisals that are largely responsible for uncovering the secret about Sophy Viner. And it is by reflecting on her instinctive emotional appraisals that she ultimately learns that refined sensibility, a sense of honour, and adherence to principle do not by themselves ensure happiness. Reason and moral principle tell Anna to sacrifice her love; emotional experience suggests that such a sacrifice is pointless. Perhaps Anna's emotions are 'basically rational' in Greenspan's sense, despite the fact that they involve incompatible ways of seeing the world. Her emotions and her reason focus on different aspects of the same situation, and Wharton seems to endorse the view that her emotions are in the right: Anna *should* resist reason's demand to engage in a pointless sacrifice.

Both Darrow and Anna demonstrate the importance of a sentimental education. Both experience a stream of changing emotions, and both reflect upon their changing emotions: they engage in extensive cognitive monitoring of their emotional experiences. In their very different ways each of them develops from lack of feeling to feeling, Darrow because he failed to feel the significance of his affair with Sophy, and Anna because her 'sweet reasonableness' and lack of emotional experience prevented her from feeling deeply at all. Wharton has demonstrated that an emotional education takes place through a sequence of shifting emotional states, which cannot be adequately conveyed in the terminology of everyday or 'folk' psychology. Eventually both Darrow and Anna arrive at beliefs, but only after a complex sequence of shifting thoughts and foci of attention, of physiological changes and action tendencies. Appropriately one of the beliefs they both acquire is that emotional experience is an important means of learning and growth.

The Reader's Emotional Education

As we read *The Reef* we too undergo an emotional education like that of Darrow and Anna. If we are reading seriously and attentively, we become emotionally engaged with the characters and we experience a stream of changing emotions as we read. Our own emotional experiences evolve as we follow the evolving emotional experiences of the main characters. Different readers may have different experiences. Doubtless, too, the same reader will have different experiences on rereading the same novel.

At the beginning of the novel perhaps I sympathize with Darrow's disappointment, his mild indignation against Anna, and his irritation that everything seems to be conspiring against him; I might even share these feelings myself. Then my feelings are likely to shift to a faint feeling of disgust and disapproval when I learn that he and Sophy have begun an affair, although I notice that Darrow already regrets having embarked upon it. When I encounter Anna for the first time 'from within',[54] I am drawn to her joyful exuberance at the prospect of Darrow's arrival, especially since it leads her to tell Owen that she will support him in his own love affair. I become a little anxious when Anna taxes Darrow with Owen's story of the pretty lady in the pink cloak whom he saw with Darrow at the theatre in Paris, and I feel a little nervous when I find that Darrow just brushes aside the story. I am startled by the discovery that Sophy Viner is the governess, and startled again when it is revealed that she is Owen's fiancée. I begin to pity Darrow and to fear for Anna. At the same time, I am much less involved with Sophy's and Owen's feelings, because I am never allowed to see them from the inside. My focus of attention moves back and forth between Anna and Darrow, and I find myself sympathizing with each in turn. As I read, I move from pleasure in Anna's happy love to anxiety about what the future holds for her, to surprise and shock when Sophy Viner turns up as the governess, to sympathy for Darrow's emotional turmoil, and finally through many shifts and slides[55] of attention and emotion, to sympathy for Anna's anxious conflict between love and principle. By the end of the novel, however, I want her just to stop fretting and marry Darrow.

In other words, I, like the main characters, experience a continuing stream of changing emotional responses in which my attention is focused on the characters and their predicaments by means of non-cognitive appraisals and the physiological activity and action tendencies that they produce. I become tense and nervous when Darrow is lying to Anna about his 'slight acquaintance' with Sophy, I start with surprise when Sophy shows up as the governess, my heart begins to race as Anna nears discovery of the truth. And so on. Wharton keeps me emotionally involved because the various aspects of the story and characters appeal to my own wants, interests, and values. I make non-cognitive appraisals about what is going on in the novel and my attention is focused on the objects of those non-cognitive appraisals. My emotional responses may sometimes mirror those of the characters and at other times not.

Perhaps not all readers will become physiologically worked up about Anna and Darrow, but as I have pointed out before, if we are emotionally engaged with the characters, our attention is focused on them and we have appropriate thoughts about them, then usually there will be some corresponding physiological reaction. However, it is possible to have anxious thoughts—to be in an anxious cognitive or attitudinal state—about the events in a story without *getting emotional* about them.

After I have finished the novel, I may, just like the characters, sit down in the privacy of my sitting room to reflect about my emotional experiences and try to figure out what, if anything, I have learned from them. I may then formulate the results of such cogitation in the form of beliefs that I have acquired: I may conclude, for example, that Darrow wronged Sophy, but that Anna is nevertheless doing the right thing in marrying him, despite his moral failings. More generally, in reflecting on Darrow's affair with Sophy, I may acquire the belief that moral sensitivity must include careful attention to and emotional awareness of the details of a situation. In reflecting upon Anna's experience I may formulate the belief that emotional experience is just as important as abstract moral principles in determining the proper course of one's life. These reflections, however, are the result of cognitive monitoring of the series of emotional experiences I have had over the course of reading the novel. I am reflecting back on these experiences and giving a reflective overview of the novel, based on my experiences.

The education I receive in reading the novel is not just a matter of acquiring these beliefs (or perhaps, if I already have these beliefs, of having them reinforced). The emotional experience is itself educational. It is the series of emotional episodes, which constitute my emotional experience of the novel, that little by little changes my focus of attention, my points of view, my thoughts about the characters, my wants with respect to them, and so on. If I genuinely *learn* something important about human conduct from the novel, it will not simply be the bald belief that moral principles without sensitive perception of the feelings of others is insufficient to ensure good conduct, or that emotional experience is as important as abstract moral principles in determining the proper course of one's life. The series of emotional episodes that constitutes my emotional experience of the novel will little by little change my conceptions and my focus of attention. It is in the process of experiencing emotionally the sequence of episodes described in the novel that my sentimental education occurs.

My argument here is reminiscent of the argument in Ch. 4. There too I emphasized the importance of actually responding emotionally to literary works. But what I emphasized there was that emotional experience is often necessary to understanding the novel. Here I want to emphasize that my emotional experiences can teach me not just about the novel but about life itself. It is no accident that I have chosen to discuss *The Reef* in this chapter, because *The Reef* provides a model or exemplar of what an emotional education could and should be. The characters exemplify the emotionally rich reflective life that Wharton is implicitly endorsing. Both Darrow and Anna struggle with their emotions and emerge as better, more thoughtful people as a result. And we in turn are encouraged by the book to engage in the same kind of reflection about our own emotional experiences in reading it: is Darrow justified in thinking that his crime is not so very bad? Should Anna marry Darrow? Is it right that Sophy should be sacrificed to Anna and Darrow's long-term happiness? The book raises these questions but does not answer them unambiguously. It leaves room for readers, too, to engage in rich reflections on their emotional experience and its ethical implications.

Who Does the Educating? 'Edith Wharton' as the Implied Author

If the reader learns emotional lessons from her encounter with *The Reef*, then presumably her teacher is the novelist, Edith Wharton. I have been writing all this while as if my emotional responses to the novel are just like my emotional responses to a slice of life, and in a sense this is right. A narrative about Anna Leath can evoke emotions in just the same way as a narrative about a real woman with similar problems. But a novel is also a carefully crafted work of art. If I can really be said to learn emotionally from a novel, it can only be because Wharton has provided the lessons. It might seem, therefore, that if I am to learn the emotional lessons provided in a novel, I must respond emotionally in the way intended by the author. If I guffaw all through the climactic scene in which Anna learns of Darrow's infidelity, then, although I am responding emotionally all right, I am not responding with the right or appropriate emotions.

If I am to learn what Wharton teaches, then presumably I must respond as she wants me to. It is Wharton, after all, who directs our attention, and who gets us to focus on certain aspects of the characters and situations she describes by making those aspects *salient* to us. It is Wharton who startles us with the appearance of Sophy at Givré, saddens us by the way she describes Anna's suffering, and pleases us by making Darrow remorseful for his conduct. Wharton focuses our attention in very specific ways, and sometimes her story evokes physiological responses to reinforce our focus of attention, as when we start with surprise at the unexpected appearance of Sophy Viner at Givré, or when our hearts begin to race as Anna nears discovery of the truth. Wharton manages to invoke these emotional responses by appealing to our wants, values, and interests, by presenting her characters and situations from particular points of view, and encouraging us to have particular thoughts about them.[56]

When I read *The Reef*, I respond emotionally to the thoughts and images it provokes, and on reflection I make inferences about how appropriate my reactions are and whether Wharton intended me to respond emotionally in the way that I do. But although it is important to know what the author probably intended, it is not as straightforward as some people have thought to figure out what that is. In assessing the appropriateness of my reactions, I am implicitly construing the author as a certain sort of person. I am responding emotionally to *the author as she seems to me to be*: in other words, I am responding to the implied author 'Edith Wharton'. A different reader will respond emotionally to a slightly different implied author.

My own take on the beginning of the book, for example, is that 'Wharton' shows us the situation as it appears to Darrow, so that we are encouraged to feel some compassion for his disappointment at being turned away by Anna. At the same time, I am mildly amused by how sharply he feels this blow to his self-esteem. Wharton gets me to feel this way by showing the situation mostly from Darrow's point of view but at the same time injecting a point of view of her own.[57] For example, she has Darrow thinking: ' "Please don't come till thirtieth." The thirtieth—and it was now the fifteenth! She flung back the fortnight on his hands as if he had been an idler indifferent to dates, instead of an active young diplomatist who, to respond to her call, had had to hew his way through a very jungle of engagements!'[58] In my view the author is poking gentle fun at Darrow and wants us to feel mildly amused too.

Similarly, during Darrow's emotional education at Givré, Wharton shows us the situation from Darrow's point of view in an effort to ensure that we never entirely lose sympathy with him even as we learn of his shortcomings. Wharton seems to want us to want Darrow to marry Anna, and so she is careful to focus our attention on Darrow's shame, remorse, and inner torment, rather than on the shabby way that he treated and continues to treat Sophy. Again, the author tries to get the reader to feel sympathy for Anna partly by showing us the unfolding events from Anna's perspective; we feel for her because we have been persuaded to have her interests at heart. Wharton tries to get the reader to care about Anna, so that we want her to be happy with Darrow and to be able to forgive him.

I am aware of the way Wharton wants us to react chiefly because of the way she describes her characters, especially the way she describes their inner lives. When Darrow is trying to explain about the affair, for example, Wharton has him sitting down 'with a groan', and acknowledging that ' "It seemed such a slight thing—all on the surface—and I've gone aground on it because it *was* on the surface. I see the horror of it just as you do. But I see, a little more clearly, the extent and the limits, of my wrong. It's not as black as you imagine." '[59] Here Wharton shows us Darrow's remorse and his reflective understanding of what he has done, and so I feel with him in his shame. But at the same time, Wharton wants Anna to agree that his wrong is not as black as all that, and she wants her readers to agree too.

At times, however, as in her comment on Darrow's 'jungle of engagements', Wharton inserts herself more assertively in the story. Another occasion comes in her description of Fraser Leath, Anna's first husband, the snuffbox collector. Ostensibly it is Darrow's thoughts about him that we are hearing, but there is a moment when Darrow clearly gives way to Fraser Leath's own thoughts, as ironically presented by Wharton herself. 'He was blond and well-dressed, with the physical distinction that comes from having a straight figure, a thin nose, and the habit of looking slightly disgusted—as who should not, in a world where authentic snuffboxes were growing daily harder to find, and the market was flooded with flagrant forgeries?'[60] Here Wharton is having her fun at the expense of the would-be aesthete. And if we too smile, we are responding to the implied author.

We construct a sense of the author as we read.[61] As we read, we make assumptions about how Wharton wants us to react, for example. But there is a difference between hypothesizing how the author wants us to respond and actually responding that way. We can understand how an author seems to want us to feel without actually feeling like that. Sometimes, for example, the author intrudes a little too blatantly and we feel ourselves manipulated. Perhaps the moment when I am most aware of Edith Wharton intruding into the narrative is at the end, when she bundles Sophy off to India with the disreputable Mrs Murrett so that (as I see it) there can no longer be any obstacle in Anna's mind to her union with Darrow. Mrs Murrett is something in the nature of a *dea ex machina*, and I think that Wharton 'cheats' as a novelist in so far as Sophy gets a fate she does not deserve so that Anna can marry Darrow with a clear conscience. It is interesting to note, however, that my emotional response to this turn of events is probably not intended by the author. My *disgust* at the unceremonious way Sophy is bundled off to India is unlikely to be a response that Wharton intended. Yet it is one of the emotional responses on which I base my interpretation of the novel.

Noël Carroll has described the way the author elicits emotional responses from readers (or movie-goers) in terms of what he calls the 'prefocusing' of the text.

Certain features of situations and characters will be made salient through description or depiction. These features will be such that they will be subsumable under the categories or concepts that . . . govern or determine the identity of the emotional states we are in. Let us refer to this attribute of texts by saying that the texts are criterially prefocused.[62]

Carroll distinguishes two steps in the proper elicitation of an emotional response by a text. First, the text must be 'structured in such a way that the description or depiction of the object of our attention is such that it will activate our subsumption of the event under the categories that are criterially relevant to certain emotional states'.[63] Thus Darrow is described as inconvenienced and mildly exploited by Anna's putting him off, so readers are directed to *pity* him (mildly), since 'enduring suffering' is the correct category for the application of the emotion of pity. Secondly, the audience 'must be invested with concerns—certain pro and con attitudes—about what is going on in a story'.[64] Wharton has to induce in me a pro attitude towards Darrow if I am to feel pity for him and not disdain or indifference.

Carroll suggests that 'the implied reader' of a novel is one who has the emotions intended by the author to be elicited by the text. In general, authors can rely on knowing how to invoke the 'right' emotions because they share a common biological and usually a common cultural background with their readers. When an author gets it wrong—assumes that readers will be falling about in gales of laughter when in fact they remain stony-faced and bored—this is 'the exception rather than the rule'.

There is much that I endorse in Carroll's view,[65] but in general he subscribes to much too mechanical a model of what goes on in the emotional experience of novel-reading. First of all, not all the emotions that are evoked by reading *The Reef* involve subsuming an event under a category that is criterially relevant to a particular nameable emotional state. According to Carroll, once we recognize an object under the 'right' category—horrifying, say—then we will feel the right emotion: our skin will crawl and our attention will be riveted on the object. But many of the shifting states that are evoked in the ongoing experience of reading *The Reef* do not have neatly categorizable names. Sometimes on reflection I can put a name to the emotional responses I have: I feel disgust for Darrow, anxiety for Anna, compassion for Sophy. In other words, I describe my emotional experience in the terms of folk psychology. But this is not always possible. I experience a hundred different shades of emotion, one state continually shifting and sliding into another, and it is only the broad outlines of my emotions that I can 'catalogue in recollection'. Thus at the beginning of Book Two when we first encounter Anna, I feel a mixture of emotions including what I later may classify as 'affection', 'empathic exuberance', and 'anxiety' about what will befall, but these folk-psychological terms are at best an after-the-fact approximation of my experience. As I have remarked before, works of art and literature typically both describe and cause readers to experience hitherto unexplored blends of emotion, for which there are no handy folk-psychological labels.

A second problem with Carroll's analysis is that we respond to things emotionally *before* we classify or evaluate them cognitively. Our affective appraisals are what alert us to what's going on before cognition kicks in. So although what our attention is drawn to may be 'subsumable' under some emotion category, we do not actually subsume it under a category until *after* our attention has been fixed upon it. Moreover, the initial affective appraisal appraises in a coarse-grained way: **this is good/bad, friend/enemy, strange and threatening/safe and familiar.** It is only *after* the affective appraisal that we appraise in a more fine-grained way: 'this is a horrific monster', or 'this is a suffering heroine'. These cognitions are not what directly evoke the emotion. It is the affective appraisal that does that job. More generally, Carroll's assumption that there's a cognition followed by an emotion and focus of attention is a gross oversimplification of what actually happens. When engaged with sophisticated literary narratives, our emotional responses shift constantly as we read, so that there is a succession of affective and cognitive appraisals going on all the time, of which we are largely unconscious. It is in subsequent reflection on our experiences that we catalogue them in recollection, using words from the vocabulary of our folk psychology.

A third problem with Carroll's notion of 'prefocusing' is that it assumes that the writer can succeed in a relatively straightforward way in fixing the reader's attention on certain aspects of a scene, character, or event, and that she can describe these aspects in such a way that a particular emotional response is more-or-less assured. Carroll does acknowledge that we may need some historical understanding if we are trying to engage with a work from the distant past or from an alien culture, but thinks that 'historians can supply us with the background necessary to make the emotive address of texts from other cultures and other periods in the history of our own culture emotionally accessible to us'.[66]

This seems to me a little too blithely optimistic. When we are emotionally engaged with a work of art or literature, there is always an *interaction* between the reader and the text. This is one of the important insights of phenomenological reader–response theories such as Wolfgang Iser's.[67] As Iser points out, when we read a novel, we are always 'filling in the gaps' in the text. For example, Wharton describes the 'instincts and desires, which, mute and unmarked, had gone to and fro in the dim passages of [Anna's] mind, and now hailed each other with a cry of mutiny'.[68] Wharton does not tell us what these 'instincts and desires' are, but when I was giving an interpretation of this passage earlier on, I suggested what some of them might be. In doing so, I was 'filling in a gap' left by the text, and I filled it in my own way, based on my interpretation of what Anna was probably feeling at that point in the novel, given my overall interpretation of the development of the novel as a whole. Similarly, I suggested that at the end of the novel Anna can marry Darrow with a clear conscience, but Wharton does not say this anywhere. She ends the book with Anna leaving Sophy's sister's apartment, as the sister lies in bed and tells Anna she should ask 'Jimmy Brance' to call the elevator for her. Here, too, I am 'filling in the gaps' left by Wharton, and to some extent *constructing* my version of the story. I am making inferences about the development of the plot and the motivation of the characters. Clearly, then, when I come to interpret 'the theme' of the novel, I will rely on my experience of the novel as I have in part constructed it. When I say that Anna has learned that emotional experience is as important as abstract principle in determining the course of one's life, I am relying in part on my own understanding of the 'instincts and desires' that Anna newly recognizes and on my own understanding of what the end of the novel signifies.

Philosophers in the Analytic tradition often write as though 'the meaning' of a text is something that is in principle stable and determinate, even if it is difficult actually to arrive at it. Thus we find Jerrold Levinson, for example, arguing that 'the core meaning of a literary work is utterance meaning—that is, what a text says in an author-specific context of presentation to an appropriate, or suitably backgrounded, reader'.[69] The meaning of a text should be thought of as 'properly tied' to 'our best construction, given the evidence of the work and appropriately possessed background information, of the artist's intent to mean such-and-such',[70] for an ideal audience. An ideal audience for a particular work is one who has the proper background to understand the work in question. Levinson illustrates his thesis by reference to 'an interpretation' of Kafka's 'A Country Doctor' according to which it is 'a stylized dream report', the content of which is basically 'the conflict between ordinary, sensual life, as represented by the servant girl Rose and the doctor's comfortable home, and one's calling: to heal, edify, spiritually succor. The doctor is in effect an artist, as is, more transparently, the hunger artist of Kafka's later tale.'[71] What Levinson is doing here is summarizing the inferences he (or the critic, Sokel, on whom he draws) made after reading the story; he is stating what he takes to be 'the theme' of the story.

Levinson claims that his interpretation is 'our best informed-reader construction of what this specific writer, Kafka, was aiming to convey'. A suitably backgrounded reader, he says, 'might readily come up with this interpretation'. What is it, then to be 'suitably backgrounded?' Such a reader, he says, is one who knows at least that 'Kafka regularly worked at night', that 'Kafka thought of writing as "medicinal", "thera-peutic", "a calling,"' that 'Kafka did not separate his writing and his life', that 'Kafka was familiar with Freud's *Interpretation of Dreams*', and that Kafka's 'A Hunger Artist', written five years after 'A Country Doctor', is 'about a man who starves himself publicly as both an artistic performance and an admission that ordinary food had no appeal for him'.[72] But of course, as Levinson has described him, the 'suitably backgrounded reader' is one who has just exactly the knowledge required to come up with the interpretation that Levinson has given us. He has specified his appropriately backgrounded reader in such a way that this postulated reader corresponds exactly to his favoured interpretation.

The trouble is, as countless critics have pointed out, that differently backgrounded readers will have different, equally plausible interpret-ations. Moreover, it seems to me that the example is particularly ill-chosen: Kafka's works are notorious for the number of irreconcilable interpretations they have spawned, and although doubtless some are better than others, to say that any particular one is 'readily come up with' is unduly optimistic. Another way to put the point is to note that there is no *one* 'best informed reader-construction' of what the author intended to communicate: readers with different background assumptions, focusing on different aspects of a work, will come up with different, possibly inconsistent, interpretations of what the author intended, and in so doing they will construct different versions of what the author is like. The person who seems to have authored the text (its *implied author*) is in part a *construction* of the reader.

In interpreting a text a reader construes the author as being a certain sort of person, and in turn the kind of person the author is construed as being partly determines how the reader interprets the text. Since the author's intentions are never transparent, we are always interpreting when we try to assess what the author probably intended. Philosophers dispute whether we should say that readers should *interpret as the author intended* or *interpret as an ideal reader would rationally believe the author intended*, but in practice the two principles are equivalent and both are equally misguided.[73] We shall never know exactly what the author intended and there are no 'ideal readers' with special access to the author's intentions. All we can do is to construct a picture of what the author seems to be like (the implied author), figure out what such an author probably means in particular passages, and modify our picture of both author and meaning as best we may as we read further along in the text and perhaps in other texts by the same author.

Of course, Carroll and Levinson are right to point out that if we want to understand a novel, it usually helps if we have some idea of its genre, its style, the period in which it was written, and the genesis of the novel itself. Knowledge about the real author, too, often functions to constrain how we construe the implied author. After all, the author as she seems to be (the implied author) is likely to be consistent with the author as she really is (although even this principle is not impregnable, since an author might deliberately try on a new persona in a particular novel). In Ch. 5 I observed that there are some readings of a novel that can be ruled out as inappropriate because they fail to fit large parts of the novel in a consistent way. Construing the implied author so that she is consistent with what is known about the real author is a further plausible constraint on what counts as an appropriate interpretation.[74] People are fascinated with the biographies of real authors with good reason: they contain clues to the interpretation of their works.

It is anecdotally interesting to know, for example, that the real Edith Wharton reportedly said of *The Reef*, 'I put most of myself into that opus,' and to speculate that the book represents a working-out of her attitude to her own lover, Morton Fullerton, who seems to have been an interesting, talented, sensitive man like Darrow, but, also like Darrow, a bit of a philanderer. More relevant to interpretation, however, is the evident Jamesian influence on the novel: Wharton was a good friend of James, and they admired each other's work. Like James's novels, *The Reef* is (to this reader) a meditation on morality, proceeding by means of a precise and sensitive characterization of the thoughts and perceptions of the characters.

But knowledge of the author and her times is never going to be enough to determine every aspect of the implied author's personality and attitudes, and hence never enough to determine uncontroversially what the implied author communicates in a particular passage. One problem is that a text often *betrays* aspects of the author or implied author of which she herself may be unaware.[75] For example, the implied Wharton, in my view, has attitudes to class and gender that are probably beyond the reach of her premodern consciousness. She is too harsh on Sophy in seeming to suggest that a fate with the dreadful Mrs Murrett is fitting for a person of her vulgar origins, and not harsh enough on Darrow who in a crucial passage attributes to general human nature what are in fact his own weaknesses and failings.[76]

It would clearly be wrong to construe 'Edith Wharton' as a Marxist or as a follower of Jacques Lacan. We should remember that the author hails from the upper echelons of 'Old New York' at the turn of the last century. At the same time, however, a reader may discover that from a Marxist perspective, Wharton is not acutely aware enough of the systemic inequalities implicit in the class system of her world, although she sees its effects on certain individuals such as Lily Bart in *The House of Mirth* or Charity Royall in *Summer*,[77] or that from a Freudian perspective she is unaware that, as we will see in the next chapter, *The Reef* turns out to be a shocking family psychodrama. These readings interpret the novel in ways that Wharton would probably not consciously endorse, yet they rely on an interpretation of what Wharton, the implied author *is like*: she *betrays* her attitudes and traits to a reader who approaches the text with the appropriate background knowledge.

Notice that I am talking here about the implied author or *the author* as she seems to me to be, and not about *the narrator* or narrators of a story.[78] James Joyce's *Ulysses*, for example, contains sections narrated by different particular individuals with different personalities, as well as a section ('Aeolus') in the style of a newspaper, and a section ('The Oxen of the Sun') in which there is a succession of different styles.[79] The implied author, however, is not identical to any of these narrators: 'he' can be detected in the Irish themes, the exuberant language use, the originality of conception, the use of stream-of-consciousness techniques, and so on.

Both Carroll and Levinson tend to downplay the reader's role in interpretation and to write about the author's intentions as though there were some relatively straightforward procedure for discovering what they are. Discovering the author's intentions is indeed important but interpretation also requires discovering what the author is like—not just the intentions she avers but also the unconscious attitudes and beliefs she has—and how 'she' is construed to be will necessarily depend on the sensitivities and background assumptions of the reader. An implied author is in an important way a construction of the reader. Put another way, implied authors and implied readers dance hand in hand in a hermeneutic circle.

Who Gets Educated? Real and Implied Readers

Louis Auchincloss begins his introduction to the Collier Books edition of *The Reef* by saying that

> the reader must be prepared for a moral climate in which extra-marital physical love is considered damning to a woman and only mildly reprehensible to a man. If Anna Leath is going to strike the reader as a prude for opposing her step-son's engagement to a woman who has been another man's mistress, and as a fool for attempting, for the same reason, to break off her own pending marriage to that other man, then *The Reef* is not for him [*sic*][80]

I should not have put the question in just this way. It is not so foolish to dislike it when the man who is going to propose to you stops off en route for a quick affair, or to be offended when it turns out that one's beloved stepson is about to marry one's future husband's ex-mistress! Be that as it may, however, in this quotation Auchincloss nicely raises the question that must be faced by any form of reader-response theory: can there be incorrect or inappropriate readings or interpretations of a work of art or literature?

Iser stresses that readers 'fill in the gaps' in a text, but often seems to imply that there is an ideal way of doing this, an ideal reader who will fill in the gaps in the right way. Other reader-response theorists, however, have emphasized that gap-filling necessarily leads to different interpretations by different readers coming to the text with different attitudes, interests, and wants, and different background assumptions. I myself have stressed that different interpretations depend partly on readers' different emotional experiences, and the emotional experiences we have will certainly be affected by our different personalities and attitudes. I have argued that there can be no one set of 'right' background beliefs and values that readers must have if they are to interpret a novel properly, and that there are many possible interpretations that are equally appropriate to the text, even if inconsistent with each other. But are there any interpretations that we can dismiss as simply incorrect or inappropriate to the text? Are there emotional responses that are inappropriate, that *we ought not to have*? Even if there is no one ideal reader of a novel, are there readers whose interpretations are incorrect or inappropriate because based on incorrect or inappropriate emotional responses?

Norman Holland, whom I will return to in more detail in the next chapter, has argued that different readers give different and mutually inconsistent interpretations of the same text because of their different personalities or 'identity themes'. He has studied, for example, how different readers' interpretations of Faulkner's short story, 'A Rose for Emily', apparently depend on their different personalities.[81] For Holland differences in interpretation are differences among individual readers and their individual personalities. He has little to say about inappropriate responses, and given his theoretical assumptions, I do not think he recognizes that there can be any such thing.

In a series of essays in his collection, 'Is there a Text in this Class?' Stanley Fish defends a less individualistic position.[82] Fish thinks that in a sense interpretation is always indeterminate and undecidable, since there are endless different ways in which the same sentence or set of sentences can be construed. What makes an interpretation 'acceptable' is its acceptance by a literary community or sub-community.

Fish illustrates his point with some deliberately outrageous examples: a reading of 'A Rose for Emily' in which the tableau of Emily and her father in the doorway of their home describes an Eskimo, and a reading of Jane Austen's *Pride and Prejudice* in which the treatment of Mr Collins is totally serious and lacking in irony. (He takes his examples from other critics, who say surely *here* is a reading that the text will not support!) Interestingly, Fish makes his case by suggesting in both cases that hitherto unknown evidence is uncovered about the author. A letter from Faulkner is discovered in which he 'confides that he has always believed himself to be an Eskimo changeling'.[83] And new evidence about Jane Austen is discovered—'a letter, a lost manuscript, a contemporary response'—showing that her intentions were never ironic; she was 'celebrating' not 'satirizing' the 'narrow and circumscribed life of a country gentry'.[84]

In making his case, Fish is relying on the principle I have already discussed, that we should interpret a work in a way consistent with what the author probably intended. On these grounds we can rule out the Eskimo reading of 'A Rose for Emily' and the serious reading of Mr Collins, since no such letters as Fish imagines have been discovered and we have a pretty good idea of what both Faulkner and Jane Austen were like as people and as writers. In other words, Fish's position, although ostensibly radical, rests on a rather conservative critical principle.

But Fish's wider point that there are many inconsistent but equally legitimate interpretations made by different 'interpretative communities' or groups of readers with similar theoretical assumptions, is no doubt correct. Readers who are intentionalists or Marxists or deconstructionists will find different sorts of interpretative practice acceptable and will produce different, possibly incompatible, interpretations as a result. Indeed I hinted as much in my discussion of Edith Wharton: it is possible to read *The Reef* as a story about class or a story about gender, as a Marxist cautionary tale, or (as we'll see in the next chapter), as a Freudian psychodrama. If I'm a feminist, I'm more likely to be irritated by Darrow and maybe also by Wharton for being so soft on him. If I'm a Marxist, I may find Sophy's treatment unforgivable. If I'm a postmodernist, I may dismiss the whole novel as hopelessly traditional and uninteresting. All such readings could be consistent with what is known about Edith Wharton, but they focus on different aspects of the text and of the implied author, including what she unwittingly communicates as opposed to what she consciously wants to get across.

As I have already pointed out, in interpreting a text readers construct the implied author, not only by reference to what she probably intended but also to what she may not have intended, to characteristics she has of which she is probably well aware as well as to characteristics she has of which she probably remains unaware. Some of the most interesting interpretations by reader-response theorists rely on drawing out hitherto unnoticed traits in the implied author. I am thinking, for example, of Judith Fetterley's feminist readings of some of the great American novels. Her reading of Hemingway's *A Farewell to Arms* is a model of its kind, pointing out how self-serving Hemingway's descriptions of the hero are and how, behind the novel's 'surface investment' in the ideal of romantic love, 'is a hostility whose full measure can be taken from the fact that Catherine dies and dies because she is a woman'.[85]

In a not dissimilar way, many so-called deconstructive readings of texts draw out implications of which their authors were probably unaware. Derrida's account of Rousseau's use of the concept of a 'supplément' in the *Grammatologie* is a case in point.[86] I don't want to discuss this difficult text in detail, merely to note that one of Derrida's points is that there is slippage in the significance of the word 'supplément' as it appears in Rousseau's writings: it seems to mean one thing—a supplement is something *added*, unnatural, and inessential, as writing is supposedly an unnatural, inessential supplement to speech—but it can be shown to mean what it was not *intended* to mean: a supplement is also a *replacement* for speech, a substitution of one set of signs for another. Thus a supplement doesn't signify one pole of a binary opposition—nature–culture, speech–writing, etc.— but shows the limits of such oppositions, and suggests a replacement of the idea of binary oppositions with that of a chain of signifiers. My point here is not to defend deconstruction but to point out that it often consists in a demonstration that an intended meaning is undermined by other implications of a text, that were not apparent to its author.

These interpretations are not free associations by clever readers. They are attempts to make sense out of a text, taking seriously the fact that the text was authored by a particular person writing at a particular time and place.[87] In general, as I have already argued, the reader is constrained by what is known about the author as well as by the need to produce an interpretation that is internally coherent and that takes account of as much of the text as possible.[88] These constraints are not enough to produce a single correct interpretation, but they are enough to rule out the Eskimo reading of 'A Rose for Emily' and other readings that take no account whatsoever of the origins of the text. But once we have ruled out the inappropriate readings of a text, there are multiple appropriate interpretations left, answering to different interests and stemming from different theoretical perspectives.[89]

What I want to emphasize in this book are individual differences in interpretation that result from *different emotional experiences* of a text. Different foci of attention, different attitudes, interests, wants, and goals will inevitably produce interpretations that differ at the very least in what they find emphasized.[90] And as in any learning experience, 'Wharton' can teach us only what we are prepared to learn. If our goals and wants and interests are too remote from those of the characters, we may be unable to become emotionally involved in the story at all, and so unable to learn emotionally from it. But if the reader engages emotionally with a novel such as *The Reef*, then what the reader takes away from it is partly a function of one's own emotional experiences of it, including, importantly, one's emotional experiences of its implied author.

If learning from a novel is a matter of responding to it emotionally, then it is inevitable that different readers with different degrees of knowledge, interests, and values, will respond differently to the same work. They will fill in the gaps in the text according to their own interests and tendencies. To me, for example, an important aspect of *The Reef* is that it seems to be told from a distinctively feminine—in some ways even feminist—point of view.[91] I respond to it as Anna's story more than Darrow's, and I think that the moral norms assumed are close to those ascribed to Anna. In this respect I find the novel distinctly un-Jamesian. If James had written this novel, I suspect that Anna would have taken the high moral road and given up her claim to Darrow. But I agree with Louis Auchincloss when he says that 'Mrs. Wharton knew Anna Leath too well to allow her to give up

Darrow. Anna simply would not have done it. She is too much a woman of flesh and blood, so much so that there are moments when we wonder what she is doing in Givré, what she is doing in France, what she is doing in a late Jamesian novel'.[92]

My own response is to want Anna to marry Darrow, which is the reading I think Wharton would like us to endorse. It is perhaps a conformist, conservative reading, taking seriously what Wharton seems to have intended. Other readers, however, may say that although they can tell that on balance Wharton wants us to approve of Darrow, they cannot like him but persist in finding him to be a self-serving male chauvinist who refuses to take full responsibility for Sophy's predicament and Anna's anguish. They will say that Wharton conveys these qualities in Darrow even though she may not have consciously meant to. Both readings are to my mind appropriate. One can understand the novel in many different ways, coming at it from many different directions, and taking away from it many different lessons.

If I am merely reporting my emotional experience, then I am not making any claims about what anyone else should experience on reading the work, but if I am offering 'an interpretation', then presumably I want other people to endorse it too. But it is not always easy to convince another person how they should experience a text. With reference to a novel such as *The Reef*, it is easy to imagine readers who would find the book as well as the main characters unbelievably stuffy and boring. Sophisticated readers who prefer the detached irony of many contemporary writers (Calvino, Coover, DeLillo) may find Edith Wharton's style hopelessly old-fashioned, and her interest in psychologically probing her characters tediously out-of-date. At the other end of the scale, unsophisticated readers may be willing to try to relate to the characters but find themselves unable to do so because they find the social mores described by the book unrecognizable. Thus many teenagers and young twenty-somethings who 'hook up' for the night at parties are unlikely to relate to Anna's repulsion for Darrow's infidelity or to Darrow's remorse at his treatment of Sophy. As Anna reflects interminably upon her passion for Darrow and whether she should yield to it, one can almost hear the cries of 'Get a life!' If interpretation rests upon emotional involvement, however, such readers cannot interpret because they cannot experience the novel emotionally in the way the author seems to intend.

A reader's interaction with a text is guided by the author but the author cannot 'intend' every response of the reader. If readers are emotionally involved in a novel, then their emotional responses will be changing all the time, and these responses will vary from one reader to another, depending not just on how much background they have in the novelist and her times, but also on the particularities of their own interests, wants, and values. The author tries to guide us through the text, but she can lead us only so far. We also have to be open to the novel, emotionally ready for the experiences it can offer us. Something has to draw us in emotionally for us to proceed with a novel at all. For this reason I would not recommend *The Reef* as required reading for high-school students.

The State of Ohio requires sophomores in advanced high-school English classes to read both *Ethan Frome* and *Silas Marner,* novels that are respectively about an ancient passion that ends up causing an elderly *ménage à trois* living together in a state of permanent bitterness, and an old miser who adopts a small child. I suppose the motivation is that these books are short. The direful result is that many kids are permanently alienated from two of the greatest novelists in the English language. There is virtually nothing in these novels for the average 15-year-old American (regardless of gender or ethnic background) to relate to his or her own experience. Both these books are largely about being old and lonely and sick and miserable in what must seem like a far-off land at a far-off time in history.[93] Authors who try to guide their readers describe characters and events from particular points of view so that we will care about them and respond to them emotionally in predictable ways. But the author can never be sure of 'uptake'. Different cultural assumptions can be barriers to understanding. And readers have to have certain attitudes before they can even begin to become emotionally involved in a story.

The strategies by means of which authors guide their readers are *formal* strategies, ways of structuring the novel so as to encourage particular responses at particular points in the story. We can also call them *rhetorical* strategies, uses of imagery, sentence structure, and so on that direct our attention in particular ways and focus our responses on particular emotional conceptions of what is being described. These formal or rhetorical strategies are the subject of my next chapter.

7

Formal Devices as Coping Mechanisms

Cyrano satisfies, as far as scenes like this can satisfy, the requirements of poetic drama. It must take genuine and substantial
human emotions, such emotions as observation can confirm,
typical emotions, and give them artistic form; the degree of
abstraction is a question for the method of each author.

T. S. Eliot, *'Rhetoric' and Poetic Drama*

The Function of Form

The discussion of our emotional responses to literary works has been
dominated by the question of whether we can in fact have genuine
emotional responses to literature such as we have in life, or whether
we can have only quasi-emotional or some other truncated form of
emotional response. There has also been much discussion of whether
and how we can respond emotionally to fictional characters, whether
we empathize or sympathize with them, whether we simulate their
experiences or infer to what they feel, and so on and so forth. In this
chapter I want to talk about an issue that has not so far received very
much attention, namely the role of form and formal devices in our
emotional experiences of literature. Theories about the aesthetic tend
to emphasize that successful works of art—unlike life—have formal
properties as well as (usually) some kind of formal coherence or unity.
Artworks are typically structured in such a way that we can enjoy
their unity or harmony or proportion in a way that is rarely possible in
life. But those who emphasize the importance of form in the arts are

often those who deny or downplay the idea that we have genuine life emotions when we respond to works of art. Extreme formalists, such as the early twentieth-century art critic, Clive Bell,[1] assert that paintings should arouse a special aesthetic emotion and that to the extent that artworks evoke life emotions, they are not worthy of aesthetic attention.

I have already argued that we do indeed respond with 'life emotions' to works of art, and, in particular, to the great novels of the realist tradition—Tolstoy, George Eliot, Henry James, Flaubert. What I want to do now is to examine the role of form and formal devices in guiding and managing our emotional responses to literature. In this context I shall be thinking of form not so much as an object of our aesthetic admiration in its own right, but as a means of guiding and managing our emotional experience of a work of literature.

First I will briefly revisit the theory of emotion, and explain how real-life emotions characteristically involve a sequence of appraisals and reappraisals. I will focus on one important kind of 'reappraisal', the 'coping' appraisal, in which initial appraisals are assessed and regestalted in such a way that the person can deal with or manage them. I will then describe some experiments that illustrate the coping mechanism.

Secondly, I will argue that formal or structural devices in literature play the role of coping mechanisms. Formal devices direct the sequence of appraisals and reappraisals that we engage in as we read, and in particular, they act as coping strategies for the reader. I borrow Norman Holland's idea that formal devices act as defensive strategies by the reader which enable us to manage or deal with the explosive fantasies that he thinks are to be found in the content of a work. In terms of contemporary emotion theory, I prefer to say that our emotional responses to literature are guided or *managed* by the formal devices in the work in such a way that we are enabled to *cope* with what we encounter emotionally in a literary work.

Finally, I illustrate this idea by reference to specific literary examples, including Matthew Arnold's 'Dover Beach,' Edith Wharton's *The Reef*, and a sonnet by Shakespeare.

My conclusion will be that, although we respond emotionally to literary works in a way very similar to the way we respond to people and events in real life, there is at least one major difference: in responding emotionally to literature, our responses are guided and managed—through the form or structure of a work—much more carefully than is possible in life, and this is an important source of our pleasure in literature.

Primary and Secondary Appraisals: The Coping Mechanism

As we saw in Part One, the function of an affective appraisal is to alert the agent very fast and automatically to whatever in the (external or internal) environment is of significance to the agent's well-being, and to produce instantly a physiological state that readies the agent for appropriate action and signals to others the state of the agent. However, the process rarely stops there. Almost always—even in non-human animals—there is subsequent *cognitive monitoring* of the situation. Indeed in human beings, these affective appraisals are usually both preceded and succeeded by cognitive appraisals. Human beings not only respond automatically to whatever seems to be important to their well-being; they also have the cognitive ability to monitor and modify their responses. Darwin gives a good example of this (see Fig. 7.1). He tells of his initial 'instinctive' (affective) appraisal of harm and reaction of fear to seeing a puff adder at the zoo. He instinctively flinched and jumped back.[2] But this affective appraisal is immediately moderated first by the recognition that this is indeed a deadly snake, and secondly by a subsequent cognitive appraisal that the snake is safely behind plate-glass. The immediate appraisal gets the adrenaline going and the emotional process under way. But although cognition confirms that indeed he is very close to a deadly snake, the emotion of fear is nipped in the bud by the *re*appraisal that he is safe after all, so that the response eventually peters out or—more likely—changes to relief or embarrassment. Similarly, when my mother dies, my instinctive affective appraisal is that I have suffered a terrible loss, an appraisal that is confirmed by cognition. But I may then *re*appraise the situation, telling myself she hasn't really been annihilated, or that now she's out of her misery, or that 'Death comes to all things,' or I may

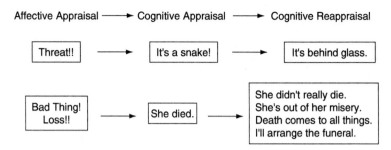

Fig. 7.1. Appraisals and reappraisals: the coping mechanism

refocus on aspects of the situation that are easier to deal with, and start fussing about the funeral arrangements.

The psychologist who has examined coping mechanisms in most detail is Richard Lazarus, whose early work dealt with how people cope with anxiety and stress. He is not alone, however, in recognizing the existence of a 'coping' appraisal. Componential theorists, such as Smith and Ellsworth[3] and Klaus Scherer,[4] also recognize 'coping' as an appraisal that often occurs in the emotion process. Among the various appraisal components in emotion that Smith and Ellsworth have identified are 'certainty,' 'situational control' (or 'situational coping'), and 'predictability.' Similarly, Scherer lists 'coping potential' as one of the appraisal components in emotion.

Lazarus takes the view that emotions should be thought of as transactions between the organism and its environment and that each particular emotion—anger, fear, envy, shame, and so on— corresponds to a unique 'core relational theme', which 'summarizes the personal harms and benefits residing in each person–environment relationship'.[5] Examples include 'a demeaning offense against me and mine' (anger), 'facing uncertain existential threat' (anxiety), 'facing an immediate, concrete, and overwhelming physical danger' (fright), and 'having failed to live up to an ego–ideal' (shame).[6]

One important aspect of Lazarus's theory is the idea that the appraisals that define particular nameable emotions are of two general kinds. On the one hand there are 'primary appraisals' that address 'whether and how an encounter is relevant to a person's well-being' and are 'based on the personal relevance of what is happening, which in turn depends on goal commitments and transactional stakes in a particular environmental context'.[7] Instead of distinguishing components as Scherer and Ellsworth do, Lazarus categorizes primary appraisals in terms of their relevance to a person's goals or concerns. The three components of primary appraisals are said to be 'goal relevance, goal congruency or incongruency, and type of ego-involvement'.[8] In my terms these primary appraisals play the role of the initial affective appraisals that set off an emotional response and the emotion process as a whole.[9] Indeed Lazarus recognizes that these primary appraisals may be rapid, automatic, and unconscious.

On the other hand there are 'secondary appraisals' which 'have to do with the options for coping and expectations.' The three components of secondary appraisals are said to be 'blame or credit, coping potential, and future expectations'.[10] Each nameable emotion is then defined by a core relational theme which is constructed by a particular pattern of primary and secondary appraisals.

We do not need to examine Lazarus's theory in detail. The aspect I want to focus on is his idea that emotions involve a sequence of appraisals, in which a primary appraisal of how some situation is relevant to our well-being gives way to a reappraisal or secondary appraisal of that situation as appraised by the primary appraisal. I am particularly interested in the secondary appraisal about how well I can *cope* with the situation.

Lazarus defines 'coping' as consisting of 'cognitive and behavioral efforts to manage specific external or internal demands (and conflicts between them) that are appraised as taxing or exceeding the resources of the person'. Coping may 'flow from the emotion and be aimed at changing the conditions of the emotion or the emotion itself', but it also 'directly and indirectly affects subsequent appraisals (reappraisals), and it is therefore also a causal antecedent of the emotion that follows'.[11]

Coping can alter emotions in three fundamental ways: first by actions on the environment or person which changes the troubled relationship, hence the relational meaning, and the resulting emotion; second, by affecting attention deployment, as in psychological avoidance, which takes one's mind off the trouble even if only temporarily—without changing the relational meaning; third, by changing the way the relationship is appraised, and hence the relational meaning, and the resulting emotion.[12]

The first kind of coping is 'problem-focused': it involves action designed to change the person–environment interaction and solve the problem posed by the emotion: the dog is threatening me, but I speak gently to it and calm it down. I am not sure it is very perspicuous to include action taken to deal with a primary appraisal as 'coping'. In any event I will have nothing to say about problem-focused coping which takes the form of changing the actual encounter between person and environment.

The other kinds of coping—those I am concerned with in this chapter—are '*emotion-focused* or *cognitive coping* strategies'. They take the form of avoidance or 'internal restructuring', that is, not changing the person–environment interaction itself, but changing its meaning. Even though these cognitive coping strategies

do not change the actual relationship, they change its meaning, and therefore the emotional reaction. For example, if we successfully avoid thinking about a threat, the anxiety associated with it is postponed. And if we successfully deny that anything is wrong, there is no reason to experience the emotion appropriate to the particular threat or harm—say, anxiety, anger, guilt, shame, envy, or whatever.[13]

In general, coping 'directly follows an initial appraisal of harm, threat, or challenge and can modify the subsequent appraisal, thereby changing or even short-circuiting the emotional reaction'.[14] Thus in my earlier example, the various reappraisals of my mother's death exemplify different ways in which I cope with my loss and attempt to decrease my sadness.

Some of Lazarus's early experiments on the coping process in the 1960s used subjects' responses to a silent film depicting a primitive puberty ceremony, in which incisions were made with a piece of flint in the penis and scrotum of adolescent boys. Lazarus and his colleagues performed various simple manipulations that nicely demonstrated that people could *manage* their emotional reactions to this troubling film. One easy way to get people to reappraise the situations they were watching was to just *tell* the subjects to detach themselves from the emotional impact of the film, or to involve themselves more fully. A somewhat more complex way to get people to reappraise the situation and to regestalt it was to add a soundtrack. One was a 'denial' soundtrack ('These boys really enjoy participating in this important tribal ceremony...'), and another was a 'distancing' soundtrack that intellectualized what was being shown in scientific or anthropological terms.[15] These various coping strategies were shown to moderate the emotional response, decreasing 'negative emotions such as anger and anxiety', and increasing 'positive emotions such as happiness and confidence'.[16]

In other experiments, Lazarus's collaborator Folkins told subjects they were about to receive an electric shock and specified different waiting periods for different groups of subjects. At the outset each group of subjects received a flashing sign, saying 'shock in 30 seconds', 'shock in 1 minute', etc. The subjective distress and psychophysiological reactions of each subject was recorded as they waited.

Stress reactions were found to be greatest in the briefest waiting-time period, but less in 3- or 5-minute waits. Interviews showed that alarm was generated in those subjects with the short waiting periods and that this alarm was mitigated by all sorts of reappraisals when enough time was given. For example, subjects in the groups with 3- and 5-minute waiting periods used the longer time to reappraise what was going on in the experiment, saying to themselves that the professor conducting the study would not dare to truly injure them and that shock from an inductorium couldn't be a valid cause for alarm. In effect, when time was short, subjects felt an elemental dread, but with sufficient time for deliberation and reappraisal, they considered all sorts of realistic and reassuring thoughts, which reduced the experienced stress and distress. There is a great temptation now to call this *cognitive coping*.[17]

Lazarus notes the connection between his idea of 'defensive reappraisals'[18] or cognitive coping and Freud's concept of 'ego-defences' against unconscious anxiety. On the other hand, Lazarus denies that there is such a thing as unconscious anxiety, in the way that psychoanalytic theories tend to assert. He thinks that to trigger cognitive coping all that's required is a primary appraisal of threat.[19] Although this *appraisal* may be unconscious, it does not follow that the whole process of anxiety is unconscious. He is surely right about this. On the other hand, I do not want to speculate about how much of the emotion process is available to consciousness. Certainly it seems likely that often coping reappraisals will themselves be unconscious. For my purposes in this chapter, all we need to note, however, is that coping procedures function very much like ego-defences and that Lazarus refers to procedures of *avoidance*, *denial*, and *intellectualization*, all of which are classic Freudian defence strategies.

Interestingly, some emotions can be distinguished chiefly by differences in secondary appraisal. Thus both fear and anger may occur when someone has done something to us which we regard as a wrong or a threat. Fear is associated with an appraisal that one is unable to deal with the situation, as when I have been insulted by my boss, and anger is associated with an appraisal that I can deal with the situation, perhaps by exacting revenge, as when I have been insulted by an underling or subordinate. Fear and anger are usually proposed as totally distinct emotional states, but this analysis suggests that they might be quite closely related. In the situation where I have been insulted by my boss, I am likely to engage in a sequence of appraisals, some characteristic of fear, others of anger. How I emerge at the end of the process will crucially depend on how successfully my coping mechanisms—avoidance, denial, and the rest—have functioned.[20]

Form as Defence Mechanism

One of the hallmarks of most great literature is an emphasis on form. The structure of a novel by Henry James or Marcel Proust is remarkably subtle and complex, quite unlike the stereotyped development of a Harlequin romance. In great poetry form is perhaps even more important, and the reader's responses are guided by the way the author has structured the imagery and other formal devices in the poem. It is my main contention in this chapter that form not only controls the initial affective appraisals made by the reader, but can also serve the function of reappraisal or coping identified by Lazarus as so important to real-life emotional processes. If I am right, the basic emotional process of appraisal and reappraisal is common to our experience of both art and life.[21] The major difference is that in art our experience is guided and managed by the form of the work, so that in a successful literary work, however painful its subject matter, the form will organize the experience into a harmonious whole that *brings pleasure*. In a way this is a very old idea. What is new is the linking of this old idea to new research into the coping mechanism.

One way in which an experience of literature *manages* our immediate emotional responses is simply by being literature rather than life.
To quote Phoebe Ellsworth: the events in a movie or novel 'trigger
responses that are initially identical, or at least highly similar, to those
triggered by real events'. When we see the monster apparently lurch
towards us out of the screen, the ' "higher cognition" that we are not
in danger, that the events are not real, comes into play only after the
process has been set in motion, modifying the experience and inhibiting the associated action tendency.'[22] As we saw in Ch. 5, this is a
particularly apt description of what happens in the horror movie
when a nasty green slime seems to surge towards the viewer. When
we perceive the slime as heading fast straight for us, we form a nonconscious affective appraisal automatically which is succeeded by
cognitive appraisals of various sorts, one of which is the reappraisal
that we are in fact in the movie theatre. The initial affective appraisal
sets in motion the characteristic physiological symptoms of fear, but
the realization that I am in the movie theatre normally stops me from
heading for the exit. However, there are many more interesting and
particular ways in which literary works first evoke immediate emotional responses and primary affective appraisals and then help us to
cope with them, to reappraise the initial situation and to manage our
initial emotional response.

In *The Dynamics of Literary Response*, the literary critic Norman
Holland offers a psychoanalytic take on form and content in literature. Holland believes the content of a literary work always involves a
central unconscious fantasy, such as the Oedipal fantasy in *Hamlet*.
Readers find meaning in literature through a 'dynamic process' in
which some unconscious fantasy, 'charged with fear and desire', is
transformed into 'the conscious meanings discovered by conventional
interpretation'.[23] In fact it is not really the story that 'means', according
to Holland, but rather the reader who generates meanings through the
transformation of unconscious fantasy into 'a total experience of
aesthetic, moral, intellectual, or social coherence and significance'.[24]
This transformation is what gives us pleasure in the story.

One reason why we can get pleasure out of literature that embodies
painful and troubling fantasies is that the text provides *defences* against
the powerful and volatile subconscious material of fantasy. Holland
thinks that we would not be able to accept the uncomfortable fantasy

material unless it were transformed defensively. And it is his contention that these defensive manœuvres are enacted by the *formal* devices
in the work. For Holland the literary work 'embodies and evokes in
us a central fantasy; then it manages and controls that fantasy by
devices that, were they in a mind, we would call defenses, but,
being on a page, we call "form." And the having of the fantasy and
feeling it managed give us pleasure.'[25] Readers find in literary works
what they characteristically both fear and desire, but, at the same time,
the work provides resources to the reader for defending against these
frightening yet appealing unconscious fantasies. It is the formal or
structural devices in a literary work that serve as 'defensive modifications of unconscious content',[26] and permit the reader to accept the
threatening content.

Holland relies on a basic Freudian taxonomy. In life we develop
defence mechanisms, notably repression, denial, and displacement of
various kinds—including reversal, reaction formation, undoing, projection, introjection, regression, splitting or decomposing, symbolization, sublimation, and rationalization.[27] Literary works 'handle' the
fantasies they embody by formal techniques that function as defensive
strategies. Irony corresponds to reversal and reaction-formation,
omission to repression and denial, pointing a moral to rationalization,
and so on. 'Very loosely,' he says, 'form in a literary work corresponds
to defense; content to fantasy or impulse.'[28]

In later writings Holland stresses how different readers interpret the
same work in different ways partly because individual readers find in
literary works their own peculiar fantasies—what they characteristically fear and desire—and partly because individual readers seek their
own characteristic defensive strategies in the work for dealing with
these fears and desires. Different readers respond differently to the
same text because of differences in their 'identity themes', which are
revealed in the fantasies they find, the adaptive strategies they use, and
even in the diverse ways in which the raw fantasies are transformed
into respectable interpretations fit for presentation at academic con-
ferences. In other words, there is no one structure—*the* form of the
piece—that controls every reader's responses: 'Each reader, in effect,
re-creates the work in terms of his own identity theme.'[29] Readers
respond in individual ways to a text and what they experience as the
form of the text, and they differ in the coping mechanisms they

employ: 'all of us, as we read, use the literary work to symbolize and finally to replicate ourselves'.[30]

It might be objected that it is authors who construct formal devices whereas it is readers who deploy coping strategies. Holland notes that authors, like readers, have an 'identity theme', which includes characteristic ways of managing or coping with reality that are manifested in the author's works. In order for a reader to become emotionally involved in a text, there must be a good fit between the characteristic adaptive strategies of reader and author (or—as I would say—*implied author*).[31] Indeed Holland seems to think that there has to be an *exact* match or the reader will not achieve emotional access to the work, but this seems too strong a requirement. I can get emotionally involved with authors whose 'identity themes' are somewhat different from my own. Nevertheless, there has to be a reasonably good fit between the reader's characteristic strategies of adaptation and those provided by the author in the text, or the individual will reject the literary experience.

I do not want to endorse Holland's theory of interpretation in its entirety, because I think it is open to question on both conceptual and empirical grounds. Conceptually, for example, the idea that everyone has an identity theme is questionable: it may be that many personalities are fragmented and inconsistent. Empirically, it is hard to know how one would confirm or disconfirm Holland's thesis that readers find deep unconscious fantasies in literary works. The same is true, of course, for many Freudian hypotheses that rely on the concept of the unconscious.

On the other hand, there is much that is perceptive and valuable in Holland's account, especially if we replace his heavy-handed Freudianism with a more empirical psychology. First, even if you deny that everyone has to have an identity theme, it is not implausible that there has to be some emotional congruence between author—or implied author—and reader in order for the reader to get emotionally involved in a work. Second, the general idea that readers respond differently to the same text, depending upon characteristic differences in their emotional style and ways of dealing with the world emotionally is also a very plausible idea, as we saw in Ch. 6. True, it is the author who originates the work and so—consciously or unconsciously—deploys any defensive strategies that may be in the work, but different readers may nevertheless find different strategies available to them in the same work. 'My' Matthew Arnold may not be yours.[32] Third, as we will see, it is a very suggestive idea that in literature it is formal devices that play the role of defence mechanisms and that form enables us—in our different ways—to *cope* with troubling content.

The idea that form organizes content is, of course, a very old one. What Holland brings to this idea is a psychological interpretation. Whether or not you believe that deep fantasies are evoked by literary works, I think it is true that our experience of the content of a literary work is indeed managed by the way we experience the form or structure of the work. First, at the simplest level, 'the sequence or ordering of content . . . shapes a response by controlling what we are aware of at any given moment',[33] and secondly, the rhetorical devices in a work—metaphor, irony, and so on—control how content is presented and how it is experienced by the reader. We may be more or less aware of these formal devices at work. Holland thinks that whereas an 'entertainment', such as a Harlequin romance or a popular horror movie, appeals on a subconscious level, a literary masterpiece requires more conscious intellectual interpretation.

In the last three chapters I have been emphasizing that if we are to be involved with the content of a literary work, we need to be emotionally stirred by it: we must feel our wants, interests, values, and so on to be at stake in the encounter. So even if we reject the idea that deep unconscious wishes and fears are always at stake, the content of a literary work is indeed often highly charged and it is not always pleasant. Why, then, do we enjoy reading about the tribulations of Anna Karenina or Anna Leath? Holland's idea that form functions as defence is, I think, both interesting and promising. Even if you reject Freudian categories, many of the defensive manoeuvres that Holland describes have been recognized by recent, more empirically minded psychologists, as we have seen. Repression, denial, and displacement are all strategies that Richard Lazarus and his colleagues invoked to manage the unpleasant experiences of the puberty ceremony film. They are familiar strategies from emotional experiences in everyday life. It would not be surprising if our emotional experiences of literary works were managed in the same way as our emotional experiences in real life.

However, since good literary works are so highly structured, we would expect structural devices to manage our responses in a much more controlling way than in real life. We would expect them to engage our coping mechanisms so that we are able to defend success-fully against highly charged or painful emotional content. And this is indeed what happens. Formal devices, as experienced by the individual reader, guide the reader through a work, both encouraging initial emotional responses to characters and events, and also managing those responses by helping the reader to defend against them. More-over, this picture of what goes on in the emotional experience of a literary work helps to explain why we enjoy such works: we have successfully defended against threatening material.

But why not avoid unpleasantness altogether? Why take time to engage with threatening material at all? Briefly, my answer is that highly charged content is highly engrossing, and it is useful to us for various reasons to get practice in dealing with it. Thus audiences enthralled by the tragedies of *King Lear*, *Othello*, or *Macbeth*, are both engrossed by human tragedy and at the same time learning to come to terms with and manage this painful material. In general, it may be that it is coping devices that explain why we take such delight in tragedies, even though they deal with painful material. Perhaps we have here the seeds of a solution to the 'paradox of tragedy', the paradox that people enjoy tragedies, despite their often bloody and macabre subject-matter.[34]

In general, then, formal devices guide our emotional responses to literary works, focusing attention and influencing both our initial affective appraisals and subsequent cognitive evaluations of content. But in addition they guide our cognitive *reappraisals*, helping us to *cope* with the unpleasant aspects of the content. They help to redirect attention and to change our conceptions of or beliefs about the content so that it becomes *less painful*, or we feel our own goals and interests to be *less at stake*, or we find the content to be *less in conflict with our own goals and interests*, so that we are *less saddened or disturbed* by otherwise troubling content. Formal devices help us to focus attention on positive aspects of the content, to divert our attention from painful aspects, and to modify our wants and goals as well as our thoughts or beliefs with respect to the content of what we read.

The best way to demonstrate the plausibility of this idea is to show it in action. So let me now illustrate with respect to some literary examples.

Matthew Arnold's 'Dover Beach'

The sea is calm tonight,
The tide is full, the moon lies fair
Upon the straits;—on the French coast the light
Gleams and is gone; the cliffs of England stand,
Glimmering and vast out in the tranquil bay.
Come to the window, sweet is the night air!
Only, from the long line of spray
Where the sea meets the moon-blanched land,
Listen! you hear the grating roar
Of pebbles which the waves draw back, and fling,
At their return, up the high strand,
Begin, and cease, and then again begin,
With tremulous cadence slow, and bring
The eternal note of sadness in.

Sophocles long ago
Heard it on the Aegean, and it brought
Into his mind the turbid ebb and flow
Of human misery; we
Find also in the sound a thought,
Hearing it by this distant northern sea.

The Sea of Faith
Was once, too, at the full, and round earth's shore
Lay like the folds of a bright girdle furled.
But now I only hear
Its melancholy, long, withdrawing roar,
Retreating, to the breath
Of the night-wind, down the vast edges drear
And naked shingles of the world.

Ah, love, let us be true
To one another! for the world, which seems
To lie before us like a land of dreams,
So various, so beautiful, so new,
Hath really neither joy, nor love, nor light,
Nor certitude, nor peace, nor help for pain;
And we are here as on a darkling plain
Swept with confused alarms of struggle and flight,
Where ignorant armies clash by night.

I begin with one of Holland's examples from his early book where he is discussing his own responses rather than speculating about the different responses of other readers. The example is Matthew Arnold's 'Dover Beach', the unconscious content of which for Holland is the primal scene, the mother's withdrawal from the child, and her turning to a separate adult life with the father, in which she engages with him in violent acts of passion. By the very nature of Holland's thesis, we cannot confirm or disconfirm the presence of such an unconscious fantasy either in Holland or in the poem. Much of his reading seems to me idiosyncratic (and even batty), as when he associates the white cliffs of Dover with Mother's breasts, the movement of waves on the shore with a 'naked clash by night', and the night-time clash of armies with warlike acts of passion by Mum and Dad. Of course, part of Holland's point is that we find in a poem our own characteristic fantasies, which may not be shared by other readers. However, the associations have to be more generally accepted, I think, if his reading is to be *of the poem* rather than a piece of free association. (Literature as Rorschach text, as I once heard Holland's theory described!) At the same time, as we shall see, Holland is clearly right to interpret the poem as about a terrible sense of insecurity and fear of loss, as well as a desire for love and protection. It is not at all implausible to read the poem as concerned with highly emotional issues of this general sort.

If we look at two critics who give a more literal reading of the poem, it is interesting to note that they both acknowledge that it is in some sense about the fear of insecurity. William A. Madden sums up 'the content' nicely: 'Situated in a particularized landscape and dramatic context, the speaker appeals to his beloved for loving fidelity as the one stay of humanity in a world which seems beautiful, but in reality has "neither love, nor joy, nor light,/Nor certitude, nor peace, nor help for pain." '[35] Somewhat more explicitly but in similar vein, J. D. Jump writes:

Precisely because it is no longer possible to believe that the universe is in some degree adjusted to human needs, that it is informed by a divinity which sympathizes with men in their joys and sorrows and in their hopes and fears, the poet must seek in human love for those values which are undiscoverable elsewhere. Moreover—and this is the primary meaning of the last paragraph—the lovers must support each other if they are to live in the modern world without disaster.[36]

How is it that the overall experience of the poem is deeply pleasurable, yet its content is largely about being alone and insecure in a hostile world? Holland's explanation is that the poem provides us with a peaceful and satisfying experience because it 'offers such a heavy, massive set of defenses'.[37] Even though it deals with a powerful disturbance, the poem defends against this disturbance.

There are examples in the poem of denial or repression, splitting, rationalization, and symbolization. The poem attempts to *deny* disturbance by focusing the reader's attention on other things, such as the sea, the shingles, and Sophocles, in order to keep us from focusing directly on the disturbance itself. The poem uses *symbolization* or *rationalization* when it introduces the intellectual, allegorical reference to 'the Sea of Faith' or the historical reference to Sophocles or the Battle between the Athenians and Sicilians at Epipolae. (The 'ignorant armies' are supposedly an allusion to Thucydides.) The poem is full of the device of *splitting*. There is a sharp distinction between reality and the 'land of dreams', between images of sound and sight, between night and day, between Faith and Love, and so on. Strikingly, the lovers themselves who are at the centre of the poem are *denied*: up until the end of the poem they occupy an ambiguous position at the edge between sound and sight, reality and illusion, disillusion and hope; we do not see them face to face, for they are looking out of the window, away from the land to the sea. In the final stanza we at last see them clearly for the first time as 'being *here* and . . . being *we*'.[38] In general, the repression of disturbing thoughts and feelings '[prevent] unpleasure',[39] and at the same time positive pleasure is provided by the image of the lovers 'true to one another' at the end.

Some critics might argue that the poem does not invite this kind of interpretation because its message is positive: it holds out the hope that we can overcome lack of faith, loneliness, and insecurity by relying on ourselves and our capacity for love. There is no need to deploy any defences in reading it. Others might say that the poem's beauty and economy of expression, its vivid imagery, pleasing onomatopoeias and so on are enough to explain our pleasure in it.[40] But these suggestions do not give a satisfying explanation of the peculiar effect of this poem. On the one hand, the overall vision of the poem is pessimistic. Although the dramatic speaker apostrophizes the beloved—'Ah, love, let us be true | To one another!'—it is because 'the world . . . Hath really neither joy, nor love, nor light | Nor certitude, nor peace nor help for pain': there is no security for the lovers in the outside world. The emphasis is all on loss and struggle and darkness, not on the faint hope that a faithful love might overcome these things. And on the other hand, the felicity of expression can be enjoyed wholeheartedly only by ignoring what the imagery and the sounds and the rhythms are conveying. For example, some of the most famous lines in the poem describe the 'grating roar | Of pebbles which the waves draw back, and fling, | At their return, up the high strand, | Begin, and cease, and then again begin, | With tremulous cadence slow, and bring | The eternal note of sadness in.' The lines mimic the movement and the sound of the waves on the shore, but the ultimate effect of those waves is to bring in 'the eternal note of sadness', and this is the *point* of these lovely lines. In short, it seems eminently reasonable to think that the pleasure we get from this poem must have something to do with how we defend against or manage our initial responses to this material which is in fact deeply melancholy.

Let us put aside Holland's insistence on Freudian fantasies and the primal scene, and focus on the way in which (as Holland puts it) 'the form of the poem . . . acts out' the 'defensive and transforming manœuvers' and 'lets us experience for ourselves the experience the poem describes'.[41] If we examine the sequence of images, we find that at the very beginning the poem makes us feel secure, with its images of calm sea, tranquil bay, and so on, before it introduces 'the eternal note of sadness'. The beauty of the lines may distract us from what they are actually asserting, because when the eternal note of sadness is first mentioned it comes as a surprise. Right away, however, the poem proceeds to intellectualize and distance the disturbing influence, with the reference to Sophocles and Ancient Greece. The 'turbid ebb and flow of human misery' then follows but gives way to the intellectual, allegorizing reference to the 'Sea of Faith'. But these defensive tactics eventually fail and the disturbing influence comes back with the reference to the 'melancholy, long, withdrawing roar' of this Sea, building up tension in the reader. The fourth stanza returns from the wider world to the small enclosed world of the lovers and shows the lovers clearly to us for the first time, when the dramatic speaker turns to the beloved and speaks to her directly: 'Ah, love, let us be true to one another!' This image of a stable loving relationship allows the reader to focus attention away from the 'vast edges drear | And naked shingles of the world', and thus to defend against this terrible image. The poem ends with struggle, alarms and the clash of armies, but in giving us a glimpse at the possibility of secure and faithful love, Arnold enables us to deal with a conclusion that is both disturbing and pessimistic.

In general terms, then, Holland is right to say that the *purely formal devices*—such as the positioning of the references to the lovers at the centre of the stanzas and the sequencing of images—'serve to modify defensively the unconscious content of the poem'. In my terms, the purely formal devices 'manage' the uncomfortable—even threatening—theme of the poem and enable us to experience it without discomfort, indeed with pleasure. The formal devices allow us to 'cope' with the 'primary appraisals' we make in reading the poem and the emotional responses that they prompt. Instead of threat, the reader feels pleasure; instead of the terror of abandonment, the reader vicariously experiences the security of love. The form or structure of the poem organizes and guides the reader's responses; the order of events, the sequence of imagery, the patterns of sound and rhythm together control the way in which the reader responds to the work, both in terms of 'primary' immediate affective appraisals and in terms of 'secondary' coping appraisals that allow us to deal with our initial emotional reactions to the poem.

Edith Wharton's The Reef

Holland, following Simon Lesser, characterizes form as 'the whole group of devices used to structure and communicate expressive content', and distinguishes between 'form-in-the-large', i.e. 'the ordering and structuring of parts', and 'form-in-the-small', i.e. verbal form, which includes both syntactic and rhetorical devices: parallel-isms, asyndeton, rhyme, rhythm, imagery, irony, metaphor, metonymy, and so on.[42] In talking about 'Dover Beach', I was mainly focusing on form-in-the-small. In my discussion of *The Reef*, I will focus on form-in-the-large, and, in particular, the plot, the narrative point of view, and the treatment of setting. The events of the plot, the characters, and the setting described in the novel are in one sense the *content* of the novel—what the novel is about—and as such they evoke emotional responses. But the events and characters and setting are not just 'slices of life'. The (implied) author organizes the structure of the novel around her treatment of plot, character, theme, narrative point of view, and setting. So these things also play important roles as structural devices. And it is the structures that we find in the novel that manage or guide our emotional responses to content.

Plot: Histoire *and* Récit

In his study of narrative discourse, Gérard Genette makes a helpful distinction between 'histoire' or 'story'—the sequence of events as they 'really' occurred—and 'récit' or 'discourse'—the sequence of events as they are related by the story.[43] In Ch. 5 I described the *histoire* of *The Reef* but only lightly touched on the *récit*. In fact, the order of recounting is very different from the order of actual events. For example, the earliest event that is relevant to the story is the friendship between Anna and Darrow in New York while she was a girl, but although this is briefly referred to in the early pages of the book, we do not find out the details of Anna's early history, her short, unsatisfactory relationship with Darrow, her marriage to Fraser Leath, and the birth of her daughter, Effie, until the beginning of Book Two. Book One tells about Darrow's journey to Paris and his affair with Sophy Viner. There is a gap of some months between Books One and Two, and during that time Sophy Viner becomes Effie's governess and gets engaged to Owen. But neither Darrow nor the reader finds out about these things until later in the book. Once the main mysteries have been revealed, *histoire* and *récit* come close to coinciding for a while: we learn about Anna's visit to Paris, Darrow's finding her there, and their return to Givré together in the order in which they 'actually' occurred, and we learn about Anna's uncertainty and self-torture as it happens. At the very end, there is another surprise, however, when Anna discovers that Sophy has gone to India the previous day.

The order of events in the *récit* is designed partly to create *suspense*. Given that we care about the characters and what happens to them, we want to know how events will turn out and we want to have the various mysteries cleared up: we keep reading in order to find out what happens and to solve the various mysteries. This reading strategy—this way of structuring the novel—is what Roland Barthes calls the code of the *enigma* or the *hermeneutic* code[44] and it is very important in maintaining the reader's curiosity and desire to read on.

But in addition to creating suspense, the *récit* also functions as a defensive strategy. The order in which the events of the plot are recounted enables us to deal with the unpleasanter aspects of the *histoire*. For example, we are told virtually nothing about Anna until *after* we have been introduced to Darrow and learned about the affair with Sophy. Consequently we do not feel bad for Anna in Book One, as she is merely a cipher at this point. What's more, even after we have met Anna and grown to like her, because we do not learn any details of the affair between Darrow and Sophy until *after* Darrow has become suitably remorseful about it, we do not judge him as severely as we might otherwise.

Perhaps most striking is the conclusion of the novel, where this reader's dominant emotion is pleasure or satisfaction; yet events have actually turned out quite badly for almost everybody. Sophy has given up the man she loves and gone away with a woman who has mistreated her in the past. Owen has lost the woman he loves and has gone away to Spain to forget; Darrow is still unsure whether Anna will marry him; and Anna herself is torn between her passion for Darrow and her lack of trust in him. But with Sophy's exit, the novel (to me) implies that Darrow and Anna will find a way to be happy together, that perhaps will involve Anna in the compromise of some of her 'high and fine' principles and Darrow in a commitment to a life of greater integrity. It encourages the reader to be happy in the prospect of the lovers' union. At the same time the novel *distances* us from Owen and Sophy: it encourages us to avoid thinking about them by having them 'off-stage' throughout the last part of the novel.

Theme, Character, and Point of View

In discussing *histoire* and *récit*, I treated the 'actual' sequence of events as 'content' and the order of their recounting (*récit*) as 'form'. In this sense 'content' is simply 'the events that happened in the order in which they happened', and 'form' is 'the order in which the implied author recounts the events'. But most literary works of any serious-ness and quality also have 'content' in a deeper sense: they convey a *message* or they have a *theme*. If we look more deeply at what happens in *The Reef*, we discover some powerful and disturbing material. It is useful to approach the theme through character. Like plot, character has a double function. In Ch. 6, I examined the characters and our emotional responses to them as if they were real people. But character is also an important principle of *structure* or form. In *The Reef* this structure is particularly interesting, and if we think of it as the underlying structure of the novel, we find that it instantiates a deeply troubling theme. From the point of view of character as a formal device or structuring principle, the main characters are organized in such a way as to form a square of opposition (Fig. 7.2).

Anna is both mother to Owen and potentially wife to Darrow, who would then become Owen's father, and if Owen marries Sophy, Sophy's father too. So the father has had an affair with the daughter and has betrayed her. Anna similarly betrays her son, Owen (by preferring Darrow's interests over his, by not giving up Darrow, and by refusing to admit to Owen that Darrow has any special relationship with Sophy). And there are two pairs of rivals: Darrow

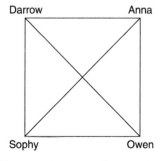

Fig. 7.2. A square of opposition

and Owen are rivals for Sophy; Sophy and Anna are rivals for Darrow. In a sense, Owen and Darrow are also rivals for Anna. The mother must betray the son in order to gain the father. The father must betray the daughter in order to gain the mother. All in all, it is as neat a family drama as any Freudian could wish.

I do not want to venture far onto Freudian terrain. But anyone—whether Freudian or not—can see that Wharton is dealing here with disturbing and potentially explosive material. It is about sex between a father and a daughter, and rivalry between a husband and a son and between a mother and a daughter. Wharton acknowledges these themes occasionally, as when, for example, Darrow sits with the rest of the family in the drawing room at Givré watching Sophy as she listens to Owen playing the piano. She has the same rapt expression as when she was at the theatre with him.

The accident of her having fallen into the same attitude, and of her wearing the same dress, gave Darrow, as he watched her, a strange sense of double consciousness. To escape from it, his glance turned back to Anna; but from the point at which he was placed his eyes could not take in the one face without the other, and that renewed the disturbing duality of the impression.[45]

But for the most part we are not invited to dwell on these Freudian themes, and I must confess that when I first read the novel I did not notice them. Instead we are encouraged to want Darrow to win out over Owen, and Anna to win out over Sophy. We want Darrow and Anna to come together and be happy. We do not like Darrow's betrayal of Sophy or Anna's betrayal of Owen, but somehow we do not care that much about these betrayals: they do not loom large in our awareness of the novel. Certainly we are not encouraged to dwell on the fact that the father betrays the daughter and the mother the son in order to gain their own happiness.

How does the form or structure of the novel manage our emotional responses so that we respond to this troubling material with pleasure rather than anxiety? One strategy or formal device that I have already mentioned is the order of recounting of the events. Our attention and emotional responses are manipulated in such a way that we are not encouraged to dwell on these sexual complexities. But the main reason, I think, that we respond as we do is that the story is structured by means of what Genette calls 'narration' or *narrative point of view*. Our emotional responses to the characters are guided and controlled as we read by a narrative point of view that switches back and forth between Darrow and Anna, with occasional intrusions by the implied author. However, the novel never shows us events from the point of view of Sophy or Owen. As a result, Owen, for example, is always a shadowy figure whose thoughts and feelings are never revealed 'from the inside', and who consequently is never a source of much interest or concern to the reader. Darrow describes him as 'a faun in flannels', which in context is not meant as a slighting phrase—nor does Anna interpret it as such—but it has the effect that Owen is presented to the reader as less than fully human. Since we see him through Darrow's more manly and sophisticated world-view, Owen is never presented as much of a rival to him. The novel thus manages to suggest that it is entirely understandable that Sophy would reject Owen the minute that Darrow reappears in her life. Sophy herself, although viewed more sympathetically and getting more air time, as it were, is also always viewed from the outside. We are frequently told that she arouses admiration in both Anna and Darrow, but she never wins their love, and since everything is presented through their eyes, she never wins the reader's love either.

By the same token, because we follow Darrow's 'emotional education' *from his own point of view*, as he responds emotionally to unfolding events and learns to reappraise his conduct as damaging to both Sophy and Anna, we remain sympathetic to him. Wharton focuses on his sorrow, guilt, and remorse as well as on his thoughtful appraisals and reappraisals of the situation after it has unfolded, rather than on his shameful treatment of Sophy. Similarly we always see Anna either from Darrow's point of view or from her own, and since we care about her more than anyone else in the novel, we follow her emotional education sympathetically, and ignore its implications for Sophy and for Owen. In Holland's terminology, Sophy and Owen are denied, and with them the Freudian family drama. At the same time, the reader's interest is focused on the more overt moral 'message' of the novel, that emotion is necessary to morality, and that high moral principle without emotion is insufficient. There is also a moral theme about the competing claims of liberty and constraint, of duty and pleasure. Here is the defence of intellectualizing or moralizing in a very obvious form. If the overt moral is construed as emphasizing the role of emotion in the virtuous life, the underlying 'moral' is perhaps not inconsistent with the overt moral, but puts it in a much darker perspective. In this version, the moral is that to lead a life of integrity and fulfilment requires acting on one's darker emotions and betraying those who would prevent one's happiness.[46] Clearly this is not a message to bring contentment to the reader, but the structure of the novel allows us to cope with this message by moralizing and intellectualizing, and by denying it.

Setting

The setting of a novel is, like character, part of the content of the novel, in the sense that the novel represents or is about the characters and the setting. So the action of *The Reef* begins at Dover, moves to Paris, then to Givré, then back to Paris, and so on. At the same time, just as character is a principle of structure, so very often is setting.[47] This is certainly true of *The Reef*, where the setting plays an important formal or structural role. Like the characters, the various settings are in structural opposition to one another, a form of *splitting*. They also play an important *symbolic* role in the novel, and thereby serve to underline some of its important themes.

As I see it, Givré is a powerful symbolic presence in *The Reef*. It represents on the one hand beauty, order, serenity, openness, and high principle, all the things that Anna herself instantiates. At the same time it represents constriction, narrow-mindedness, and prejudice, as instantiated by Madame de Chantelle. Contrasted with Givré are on the one hand the muddled, wet, unpleasant, transitory scenes at Dover and in Paris, where there is liberty and lack of constraint, but a corresponding lack of order and civility, and on the other hand, the urban sophisticated world that Darrow inhabits in London and Paris, where there is a casual immorality but also broad-mindedness, intelligence, culture, and indeed—civility. The challenge for Anna is to learn liberty and sophistication without sacrificing principle and orderliness. The challenge for Darrow is to remain civilized and sophisticated while rejecting libertinism and acquiring serenity and principle.

All of these issues appeal to the reader's emotional engagement. In responding positively to the calm beauty of Givré, I thereby respond emotionally to Anna and to her love of principle, order, and serenity. Similarly, my response to Paris is a response to her emotional conflict: it is both a centre of culture and broad-mindedness and also the Paris that she visits when in emotional turmoil: dark, unpleasant, and somewhat chaotic. In reacting emotionally to it in different ways, I am mirroring Anna's reactions to Darrow: she is attracted to some aspects of it and of him, and repelled by and afraid of others. In other words, the reader's emotional reactions to the various settings are also reactions to the conflicts that underlie what I called the moral or theme of the story.

At the same time, however, I am able to cope with these emotional themes because I am *displacing* my emotional responses, or, in my terms, I am coping with them by responding not directly to Anna's lack of experience and liberty, or Darrow's treading the line between liberty and libertinism, but by reacting to the house at Givré, the weather at Dover, the rain in Paris, and so on. We respond emotionally to setting by making affective appraisals—this is **good**, this **bad**, perhaps—but we are thereby responding to deeper questions. Our responses are controlled by being directed at harmless entities— houses and weather—instead of at the disturbing themes that these harmless entities symbolize.

To sum up: we respond emotionally to literature as we do to life; we feel anxious, bewildered, relieved, amused, sympathetic, and so on just as we do in real life. But there is an important difference between our emotional responses to life and to literature. In life we do not know what is coming next or whether things will work out; we cannot control our environment, and we cannot predict what is going to happen to us. We have evolved strategies for dealing with the vagaries of life, however, notably coping mechanisms. When things go wrong or become unbearable, we intellectualize, or we moralize, or we deny, we deal with the problem by splitting it into parts that we can deal with, or we displace our energies onto other things. Reading literature always has the potential for creating anxiety or uncertainty, but literature, unlike life, often provides us with the coping strategies that we need to deal with its deep and possibly troubling content. The formal or structural devices in a novel allow us to cope with its themes and ultimately to derive pleasure from the very fact that we have successfully coped with a piece of reality.

So far I have been discussing form-in-the-large, which is most easily studied in large-scale narratives such as novels. When we discuss form-in-the-small, it will be convenient to return to poetry.

Shakespeare's Sonnet Number 73

In his book on Shakespeare's sonnets, Stephen Booth, like Holland, is interested in the reader's responses as he or she reads along, but the responses that interest Booth are very different from those that Holland discusses. Booth says little or nothing about emotional responses to the poems. Instead he focuses on the way Shakespeare demands the mind of the reader to be forever active in making connections between different parts and different aspects of a sonnet, and always searching for principles that will organize and unify the reader's experience as she reads. Booth stresses that the reader has to notice connections all the time; what is required is described as a kind of perception or discrimination rather than as an emotional experience.

Booth's main thesis is that in each sonnet (with some possible exceptions, notably the last sonnet) there are a multiplicity of organizing principles, too many for the reader to grasp consciously, yet the reader is constantly looking for these principles so that her mind is constantly alert as she reads. Moreover, because we are, even if dimly, aware of so many different organizational principles at work in it, a sonnet gives us a great deal of satisfaction and pleasure: the reader *senses* a coherence even though the sources of this coherence are not completely available to the reader as she reads.

In the individual sonnets the multiplicity of patterns . . . gives a sense that the poem is an inevitable unity. However, as one reads through a Shakespeare sonnet, the different patterning factors come into focus and out of it constantly, rapidly, and almost imperceptibly, 'each changing places with that which goes before.' The mind of the reader is kept in constant motion; it is kept uneasy as it is made constantly aware of relationships among parts of the poem that are clear and firm but in an equally constant state of flux.[48]

Booth is talking about various different kinds of pattern in the sonnets, for example the formal pattern of rhyme scheme and rhythm, the syntactical pattern of sentence structure, and the rhetorical pattern—the development of the thought of the poem—which may proceed, for example, as a set of examples followed by the statement of a general principle, or as a sequence of steps in a demonstration or argument. In addition there are patterns of imagery, and phonetic or sound patterns. These different kinds of pattern or structure are all present simultaneously, but, says Booth, they do not typically go together and reinforce one another.

Booth's idea is that even though we are unable to focus consciously on so many different structures, they none the less deeply affect the reading process. The reader is dimly aware of these multifarious patterns, although probably many of them register only at subconscious levels, and feels the need to seek out the various connections which she vaguely senses as she reads. At the same time, the presence of so many different structures, all at work more-or-less independently, conveys to the reader a sense of order. Booth points out that even after reading a detailed analysis of patterns of sound in a sonnet we cannot, as we read the poem, hold all these relationships in our head. They are all there and they are all encouraging us to make connections of meaning among the similar-sounding words, but the patterns of likeness are far too complex for us to be aware of them as we are actually reading the poem.

A 'defining peculiarity' of the sonnets is that

as the line in which it appears is read, any given word is likely to slide imperceptibly from one system of relationship into another. The shifting of the contexts in which the reader takes the meaning of a given word is [such that] in making the shifts from one context to another, the reader's mind is required constantly to act.[49]

One might think that so many different, shifting 'systems of relationship' would produce an effect of disorientation, but the ideas fuse together so effortlessly that they do not confuse the reader. When reading a particular line in a Shakespeare sonnet, the mind 'does not puzzle as it does when it tries to understand an obscure line, but neither does it receive the stimuli of the poem passively'. The sonnets are not hard poems and they are not easy ones: 'They are uneasy: the relationships within the poem are in flux and the reader's mind is too.'[50]

Interestingly for my purposes, Booth draws an analogy between coping with life and coping with Shakespeare's sonnets. All art imposes order on experience, he says, and for that very reason it makes it hard for works of art to expand the mind, to grasp 'more of experience than the mind can comprehend'.[51] The most satisfying kind of order is that which seems to be there in reality, not an imposed, 'artificial' order:

what we want of art is the chance to believe that the orderliness of art is not artificial but of the essence of the substance described, that things are as they look when they have a circle around them. We don't want to feel that art is orderly. We want to feel that things are orderly. We want to feel that art does not make order but shows it.[52]

Booth claims that Shakespeare is uniquely capable of conveying the broad possibilities of real life and experience in an orderly way.

In nonartistic experience the mind is constantly shifting its frames of reference. In the experience of the sonnet it makes similar shifts, but from one to another of overlapping frames of reference that are firmly ordered and fixed. The kind and quantity of mental action necessary in nonartistic experience is demanded by the sonnet, but that approximation of real experience is made to occur within mind-formed limits of logic, or subject-matter, or form, or sound.[53]

The sonnets are 'full to bursting not only with the quantity of different actions but with the energy generated from their conflict,' but at the same time the 'multitudinous organizations' in a sonnet provide 'the comfort and security of a frame of reference' even though 'the frames of reference are not constant, and their number seems limitless'. In short, 'the sonnets are above all else artificial, humanly ordered; the reader is always capable of coping'.[54]

> That time of year thou mayst in me behold
> When yellow leaves, or none, or few, do hang
> Upon those boughs which shake against the cold,
> Bare ruin'd choirs, where late the sweet birds sang.
> In me thou seest the twilight of such day
> As after sunset fadeth in the west,
> Which by and by black night doth take away,
> Death's second self, that seals up all in rest.

In me thou seest the glowing of such fire
That on the ashes of his youth doth lie,
As the death-bed whereon it must expire,
Consum'd with that which it was nourish'd by.
  This thou perceiv'st, which makes thy love more strong
  To love that well which thou must leave ere long.

Booth gives a detailed account of Sonnet 73, 'That time of year thou mayst in me behold', focusing mainly on its syntactic and rhetorical patterns, rather than its phonetic patterns or patterns of rhyme. He points out that syntactically the sonnet is organized in three quatrains, together with a couplet which is a single summary sentence. Rhetorically the poem describes three exempla illustrating what old age is like, one in each of the three quatrains, followed by the moral which is drawn in the couplet. The syntactic pattern reinforces the rhetorical pattern: 'the three quatrains compare the speaker to a tree, twilight, and fire respectively; each quatrain is a single sentence; and the first lines of the second and third quatrains echo line 1'.[55]

In terms of imagery, Booth notes that in the three quatrains there are 'several coexistent progressions'. Time gets 'measured in progressively smaller units', as the poem homes in on death, as it were: 'a season of a year, a part of a day, and the last moments of the hour or so that a fire burns'.[56] The light grows dimmer, from daylight to twilight to night, again suited to the approach of death. But the colours become more intense, from yellow leaves to twilight after sunset to the fire. At the same time the 'space constricts, from the cold windy first quatrain to the hot suffocating grave of ashes in the third'. Moreover, 'in a progression concurrent with all these the metaphors give up an increasingly larger percentage of each succeeding quatrain to the abstract subject of the sonnet, human mortality'.[57] The images of autumn, twilight, and fire become less and less vivid, as the speaker looms correspondingly larger to our attention than what he is being compared to. Finally, in the couplet the beholder of the quatrains becomes the actor: it is the beholder who has to leave the speaker, rather than the reverse.

Although these 'orderly progressions' in thought and imagery help to reinforce the careful structure of the poem as a whole, there are so many other factors that obtrude on this organization that 'the poem provides the artistic security and stability of predictable pattern without allowing its reader the intellectual repose that predictability can entail'. For example, the different progressions are 'not mechanically parallel and do not lump together in the mind: the time units get smaller; the speaker looms larger; the color gets brighter; the light gets dimmer; the temperature gets hotter.'[58] Moreover, the reader's mind has to be constantly alert or it will be misled by the syntax. Thus, to give just one of many possible examples, since lines 5 and 9 are exactly parallel, we expect line 10 to begin with 'as', like line 6, but instead the 'as' is delayed until line 11, and when it appears it has a different grammatical form from the 'as' in line 6. Again, the beginning of the couplet (line 13) sounds like the beginning of each quatrain: it is addressed to the observer and describes what the observer perceives when observing the speaker. But whereas 'the bulk of each quatrain is devoted to metaphoric statements of the impending departure of the speaker',[59] in the last line it is the beholder who has to 'leave' the speaker. This reversal 'brings the threat of mortality closer to the beholder, completing the reader's sense that mutability is universal'. Booth comments that 'the change itself and the reader's need to follow it provide one more demand for the reader's activity, commitment, and participation in the process of the poem'.[60]

Because Booth is primarily interested in the structural patterns he detects in the sonnets, he has less to say about their subject matter. But it is striking that the sonnets he discusses are about emotionally highly charged issues. Sonnet 73 is about the inevitability of old age and death, and the poignancy of human love, which must always live with the knowledge that it is necessarily transient. This is obviously emotional material: the tone is poignant, even melancholy. But the poem demands so much intellectual work that we are encouraged to follow the argument and ferret out the various patterns rather than dwell on the unpleasant aspects of the subject matter. In short we are encouraged in an *intellectualizing* defensive strategy, a form of *distancing*. The poem also employs the defence mechanism of *symbolization*. Old age is compared in a series of beautiful images to autumn leaves, the twilight, and the glowing of a fire. This is a type of *displacement*, but it is not a *denial* or *avoidance* of death, but rather a way of emphasizing its positive aspects. The poem prepares us for the last two lines, by making death seem palatable.

Most of all, as Booth's analysis suggests, the poem helps us to cope with the painful aspects of death by means of the many systems of *order* it contains. The order in the poem gives the reader a sense of control even when we are not sure what the source of the order is. What's more, the poem is *about* the orderly progression of life into death that all of us must face: it is about the *pattern* of life itself. The order in the poem reinforces the message that death is not a terrible and unnatural cataclysm, but the supremely natural conclusion to an orderly progression of life.

Although the speaker of the poem is ostensibly addressing the reader, the focus of the poem for the first twelve lines is on the speaker and *his* imminent death. The reader's own death is *denied* throughout most of the poem. Only in the final couplet is attention focused on the reader, when the speaker says that '*your* love' will be more strong, because *you* must leave it 'ere long'. What was denied is suddenly revealed, and the reader is implicated in the 'message' of the poem. The word 'leave' takes us back to the beginning of the poem and reminds the reader that she too will travel the same path from the yellow leaves of life's autumn to the consumed fire of death.

There is an interesting lesson to be drawn from the many ways in which this poem allows or encourages the reader to cope with its painful subject matter, death. Coping strategies vary in their effectiveness, and also in how much dishonesty they demand. As we saw earlier, 'cognitive coping' takes the form of the strategic deployment of attention or of the strategic regestalting of unpleasant events, by changing its 'subjective meaning'. In changing the meaning of an unpleasant situation, we can deny its existence (which may work in the short term but is less likely to be effective in the long term), or we can distance ourselves from the situation or emphasize its positive aspects. These strategies typically work better in dealing with unpleasant situations that we are powerless to change. Similarly, in attention deployment, we can cope by avoiding thinking about the unpleasant situation, or by what Folkman and Lazarus call 'vigilant strategies', that is, by focusing more attention on the source of distress. Vigilance may be counter-productive in a situation where nothing can be done to make things better, but it may also 'reduce distress by increasing understanding and a sense of control'.[61] In other words, some coping strategies are better than others both in how much they require us to deny and in how effective they are in improving our emotional state.

The Shakespeare poem is a good example of how cognitive coping can be both intellectually demanding and intellectually honest. Yes, it shows us death in a pleasant light, and encourages us not to focus on the unpleasant aspects of death, but it does not seek to give an unrealistically rosy view of death, and indeed the couplet at the end forces us to confront death rather than avoid it.[62] But at the same time the orderly patterns that Booth identifies enable us to feel a sense of control. As Booth says, we want to feel that 'art does not make order but shows it'.[63] Sonnet 73 allows us to cope with death by giving us a sense of control. The images of death evoke melancholy even as they delight us with their beauty, but we are prepared for the final devastating couplet by all the defensive strategies that Shakespeare sets up for us. Even as we face death, our emotional responses are not anxiety or terror but acceptance: the poem has enabled us to cope emotionally with the reality of death.

Some Implications

I have already briefly suggested that the paradox of tragedy may be resolvable by focusing on how tragedies both present painful material and at the same time provide the resources for us to cope with this material. There are particularly obvious uses of coping strategies in tragic works. For example, the comic scenes in Shakespeare's tragedies—the porter in Macbeth, the grave-diggers in Hamlet, the annoying Captain Macmorris in Henry V—exemplify *avoidance* strategies: they distract our attention from the tragic events taking place in the main part of the play. Other writers of tragic tales engage in *intellectualization* or *pointing a moral*. For example, when Thomas Hardy at the end of *Tess of the D'Urbervilles*, comments: ' "Justice" was done, and the President of the Immortals, in Aeschylean phrase, had ended his sport with Tess,' he is intruding himself on the story and pointing the moral for us so that we disengage from and cope with the macabre events of the story and meditate instead on its intellectual significance. Hardy's intrusion is ponderous and heavy-handed, and perhaps for this reason less than effective. By contrast, George Eliot often uses a similar strategy to *divert* us (in both senses of that word), as for example in *Middlemarch* when she comments on those who give

unwanted, superfluous advice: 'But a full-fed fountain will be generous with its waters even in the rain, when they are worse than useless;
and a fine fount of admonition is apt to be equally irrepressible.'[64]

My discussion of the coping mechanism also sheds light on another
thorny issue in aesthetic theory, the issue of 'aesthetic distancing'. In a
well-known article, Edward Bullough claims that an aesthetic experience differs from real life in that it involves an act of 'distancing'.[65] He
says that when caught in a fog at sea you may focus on the beautiful
milky whiteness of the fog instead of the fact that a large vessel could
be bearing down on you. But his idea of distancing has been roundly
criticized, notably by George Dickie in an influential article called
'The Myth of the Aesthetic Attitude'.[66] Dickie says he doesn't know
what psychological 'act' distancing is supposed to be, implying that it
is a made-up concept with no content. But Lazarus's theory of coping
in effect answers this objection. In appreciating the fog aesthetically
I am *coping* with the situation by focusing on a non-threatening aspect
of it.

Bullough is talking about an experience of nature, where there is
no structure or form to guide our response, but, as we have seen, in
our encounters with literary works we routinely engage in similar
coping strategies. In 'Dover Beach,' we focus attention away from the
pessimistic message and instead dwell happily on the lovers 'true to
one another'. And in Shakespeare's tragedies and Hardy's gloomy
moral tales, formal devices also enable us to *distance* ourselves from
disturbing material.

Finally, I return briefly to the subject of postmodernism. A short
story, such as Coover's 'The Babysitter', evokes some 'life-emotions'
as we read, perhaps anxiety for the characters as well as amusement at
their shenanigans, but on the whole a reading of 'The Babysitter' is
not a very emotional experience. I suggest that this is because form is
so foregrounded that almost our every response is controlled and
managed by the master manipulator who relates the story.[67] Our
ordinary emotional processes have very little chance of getting
going before they are nipped in the bud by assertive reminders that
the (implied) author is firmly in command and that readers are
responding to an artfully constructed story that celebrates not life
but the supremacy of form and structure. The story is more like a hall
of mirrors than a slice of life. Postmodern stories of this sort may still

228 EMOTION IN LITERATURE

appeal to our emotions in a sense—they can be funny or disturbing—but the emotions evoked are managed to such a high degree that we are mainly aware as we read of the cognitive pleasures of intellectualizing and distancing than of the rewards of deep emotional engagement with the characters or situations described.[68]

Is a novel or play or poem better if it is highly controlled and manages our emotional experience very carefully? Not necessarily, although 'Dover Beach' is a great poem, and *The Reef* is a great novel and both are full of displacement and denial. Perhaps it is a matter of stylistic differences: realistic novels and poems, which try to teach us something of what the world is like, need to protect us against or to help us to confront those aspects of the world that are hard to deal with; whereas highly stylized works such as 'The Babysitter' do not pretend to be teaching us about life. I will not attempt to solve this thorny issue here, however.

To conclude: in all my main examples we have genuine emotional experiences of great literature, and we cope with whatever is unpleasant in these experiences using the same strategies as we do in life. The main difference between coping with life and with literature is that the author (or implied author) guides and helps us with our coping strategies by structuring the sequence of experiences—including the sequences of appraisals and reappraisals—that we make as we read. It follows that although we respond emotionally to literary works in a way very similar to the way we respond to people and events in real life, there is at least one major difference: in responding emotionally to literature, our responses are guided and managed—through the form or structure of a work—much more carefully than is possible in life, and this is an important source of our pleasure in literature.

Part Three

Expressing Emotion in the Arts

The next two chapters deal with the expression of emotion in the arts. Chapter 8 gives an account of Collingwood's theory of expression which embodies the Romantic idea that the main function of art is to express the artist's emotions. I don't agree that this is the main function of all art or that it is correct to say that art is expression, as the Romantics did. The arts have many purposes above and beyond expressing emotions. However, I do think that Collingwood's theory—suitably modified—is an insightful theory of what it *means* for works of painting, literature, music, and so on to express emotions.

Hardly anyone takes Collingwood's theory very seriously these days, however, because it's assumed that the theory has already been demolished by various analytic philosophers, chief amongst whom is Alan Tormey. In Ch. 8 I explain that Tormey's Collingwood bears little relation to the real thing. Then in Ch. 9 I examine two more recent theories of expression that are more-or-less in the spirit of Collingwood, including an old theory of my own. Finally, I articulate and defend a new Romantic theory of artistic expression. I show what it means for the various different art forms to 'express emotions' now that we have a better idea of what emotions are, and I give specific examples drawn from a number of different kinds of artwork.

8

Pouring Forth the Soul

Now more than ever seems it rich to die,
To cease upon the midnight with no pain,
While thou art pouring forth thy soul abroad
In such an ecstasy!
John Keats, 'Ode to a Nightingale'

Romanticism and the Genesis of Expression Theory

There is a long tradition dating back to Plato and Aristotle that emphasizes that for better or worse the experience of art is often an emotional one. In the last four chapters I have been talking about the *emotional effects* of art on the reader, listener, or viewer. There is another more recent tradition, however, that also emphasizes the importance of the emotions in the arts, but this time from the point of view of the creator of the artwork rather than the audience. This is the tradition associated with Romanticism according to which art-works are *expressions of emotion* in their creators. In the next two chapters I will be focusing on artistic expression and after that I will turn to the narrower topic of expression and expressiveness in music.

Few terms are as ubiquitous in discussions of the arts as the term 'expression', and in my view few terms are as poorly understood. Different writers use the term to mean quite different things, which may explain the proliferation of theories of artistic expression: we need a different theory for each different usage of the term. Things are not made any easier by the fact that there are a number of different but related terms all somehow connected to expression. Some works seem to *express* their author's emotions; others which are not expressions of anyone's emotions nevertheless have *expressive qualities*; some works are simply *expressive* without expressing anything in particular; or perhaps they are played or performed *expressively* whether or not they are themselves expressions of anything. To complicate matters further, some works are known as *expressionist*. Finally, there is disagreement about the range of things that can be expressed. Is it only emotions that artworks express, or can they also express ideas or themes? Some people think that strictly speaking neither emotions nor ideas can be expressed, but only qualities. Among these folk there is further disagreement about which qualities count: some think only emotional qualities—sadness, cheerfulness, nostalgia—count, whereas others think virtually any quality can be expressed: power, angularity, movement, and maybe other things as well, such as the state of the nation or the interrelationship of colours.

The core notion of expression in the arts is derived from Romantic artists—primarily poets, composers, and painters—who thought of themselves as expressing their feelings and emotions in the artworks that they produced. The poet Wordsworth in his 1802 preface to the *Lyrical Ballads*, a revolutionary work in its day, wrote that poetry is 'the spontaneous overflow of powerful feelings', which are 'recollected in tranquillity'.[1] Caspar David Friedrich pronounced: 'The painter should not just paint what he sees before him, but also what he sees inside himself.'[2] His works should express the movements of his heart: 'The heart is the only true source of art, the language of a pure, child-like soul. Any creation not sprung from this origin can only be artifice. Every true work of art is conceived in a hallowed hour and born in a happy one, from an impulse in the artist's heart, often without his knowledge.'[3] And Beethoven is reputed to have said in conversation with Louis Schlosser that 'stimulated by those moods which poets turn into words, I turn my ideas into tones which resound, roar and rage until at last they stand before me in the form of notes'.[4]

The Romantic movement greatly increased the status of the artist. No longer just a skilled craftsman able to represent reality in paint, words, or tones, the artist was a *genius*, a special person with special insight into the nature of reality. Kant stressed the importance of the imagination in art: a genius was somebody who through his imagination was able to come up with 'aesthetic ideas', metaphors or pictorial images that suggest a 'rational idea' (an idea for which we can form no good sensuous representations) such as God, angels, Heaven, and immortality. Hegel developed Kant's thought by identifying art as that particular mode of consciousness whereby ideas are presented in sensuous form rather than through myth or theology (religion) or through conceptual thought (philosophy). Like Schelling and the Romantics, Hegel argued forcefully that art is not the mere imitation of an inert nature, but a means to a special kind of understanding: 'the work of art stands in the middle between immediate sensuousness and ideal thought.'[5] Hegel's formulation emphasizes that the artist is a source of knowledge, and that the knowledge conveyed by a work of art cannot be abstracted from how it is conveyed. The separation of a work of art into what is represented (content) and how it is represented (form or style) is henceforth rejected. The artist is no longer merely a skilled craftsperson who learnt his trade and can teach it to others. The true artist is one who goes beyond the rules of art. As Delacroix wrote in 1824, 'rules are only for people who merely have talent, which can be acquired. The proof is that genius cannot be transmitted.'[6]

Here is not the place to examine Hegelian Idealist philosophy or to rehearse the many changes in world view embodied in the Romantic movement.[7] I mention here one or two of the most prevalent themes of Romanticism and Idealism simply to show that the idea of art as the expression of emotion is only part of a much wider conceptual shift. Today, many Romantic preoccupations strike most of us as decidedly odd—for example, the idea that nature and spirit are one and that the artist is the special person who can express the organic unity of man and nature through his works[8]—yet at the same time many Romantic ideas have become accepted as obvious truths, the currency of modernism. One of the remnants of Romanticism that we still live with—despite all that the postmodernists have been able to accomplish—is the idea that artists are special people with special insight, people of imagination and genius who in their artworks are primarily trying to express their emotions. Although practising professional artists may not all share this vision of the artist, it is a view that is widespread in popular culture and something like it is believed by most of the art students whom I encounter daily in my classes.

My task in these next two chapters is not to defend the view that all art is the expression of the artist's emotions. This theory is manifestly false. It leaves out of account too many works that most of us would want to include in the category of art, ranging from religious sculpture from African and pre-Columbian cultures, Byzantine mosaics, and Chinese vases, to contemporary works, such as hard-edged abstract paintings, minimalist music, and postmodern works by the likes of Cindy Sherman or Don DeLillo. What I will be saying is true only of some artworks and not all. My main aim in this chapter is to outline a classic statement of expression theory and to defend it from various attacks upon it by recent analytic philosophers. But I will not be defending it as a theory of *art* but as a theory of *expression*. Then in Ch. 9 I will present a new theory of artistic expression that is true to the Romantic insight that art can be the expression of emotions in its creator, and that is also consistent with current thinking about the emotions. The theory has, I believe, general application to all the arts, at least to all those artworks that have some claim to be called *expressions*.

The main reason why I have begun by talking about Romanticism is that I do not think we can understand the concept of artistic expression without seeing it, at least initially, in its historical context. To my mind many recent theorists have distorted the concept of expression by ignoring its roots in Romanticism and Idealism. I shall focus my discussion on the expression of *emotion* since I believe it is the central case of artistic expression, and also because I am interested in discovering how much truth there is in the doctrine that art expresses emotions, once we take a look at contemporary emotion theory.

Classic Expression Theory: Collingwood's The Principles of Art

A great many thinkers of different philosophical persuasions have argued that art is in some sense expression. In his book on expression Alan Tormey lists John Dewey, Curt Ducasse, R. G. Collingwood, E. F. Carritt, D. W. Gotshalk, George Santayana, Leo Tolstoy, and

Eugene Véron as all subscribing to the 'Expression Theory' of art.[9] I will not attempt to discuss whether all these thinkers held the same theory, but will confine my attention to the classic exposition of expression theory in Collingwood's great work on aesthetics, *The Principles of Art*, published in 1938. Collingwood was a twentieth-century philosopher, not a nineteenth-century poet, but his views are firmly in the Hegelian tradition, mediated by the Italian Hegelian philosopher Benedetto Croce.

According to Collingwood, art is an expression of the artist's emotions in the sense that it is the elucidation and articulation of the artist's emotional state. Expression is an imaginative activity, the production of an 'imaginative vision',[10] and it is the expression of emotion in this imaginative vision that marks the true work of art, not skill and technique alone. One of Collingwood's main goals is to distinguish true art ('art proper') from mere skill and technique. He wants to get away from the classical idea that art is a kind of *technē* or craft, an activity in which a pre-existent plan is the means to a predetermined end. Art is never preconceived; it always involves the working out of some feeling or thought which evolves as the artist works.

Collingwood seems to be describing the Romantic artist *par excellence* in the famous passage where he characterizes the process of artistic creation:

When a man is said to express emotion, what is being said about him comes to this. At first, he is conscious of having an emotion, but not conscious of what this emotion is. All he is conscious of is a perturbation or excitement, which he feels going on within him, but of whose nature he is ignorant. While in this state, all he can say about his emotion is: 'I feel... I don't know what I feel.' From this helpless and oppressed condition he extricates himself by doing something which we call expressing himself. This is an activity which has something to do with the thing we call language: he expresses himself by speaking. It has also something to do with consciousness: the emotion expressed is an emotion of whose nature the person who feels it is no longer unconscious. It has also something to do with the way in which he feels the emotion. As unexpressed, he feels it in what we have called a helpless and oppressed way; as expressed, he feels it in a way from which this sense of oppression has vanished. His mind is somehow lightened and eased.[11]

Collingwood distinguishes expression from various other phenomena with which it could be confused. It differs from Aristotelian *catharsis* in that the emotion that has been purged is 'thereafter no longer present to the mind', whereas in expression the emotion is still present but now accompanied by a 'sense of alleviation which comes when we are conscious of our own emotion'.[12]

There is also a difference between expressing an emotion and 'describing' it.

Expressing an emotion is not the same thing as describing it. To say 'I am angry' is to describe one's emotion, not to express it. The words in which it is expressed need not contain any reference to anger as such at all. Indeed, so far as they simply and solely express it, they cannot contain any such reference.... A genuine poet, in his moments of genuine poetry, never mentions by name the emotion he is expressing.[13]

By the description of emotion, Collingwood seems to mean the labelling of emotion or the categorization of an emotion by a general emotion term recognized in folk psychology, such as 'sadness' or 'anger'. The expression of emotion cannot be accomplished by naming the emotion in question, because expression, unlike description, individualizes. To become 'fully conscious' of 'the peculiar anger' which 'I feel here and now, with a certain person, for a certain cause' means 'becoming conscious of it not merely as an instance of anger, but as this quite peculiar anger'.[14] 'The poet, therefore, in proportion as he understands his business, gets as far away as possible from merely labelling his emotions as instances of this or that general kind, and takes enormous pains to individualize them by expressing them in terms which reveal their difference from any other emotion of the same sort.'[15]

At the same time, Collingwood notes that artists should not live in an ivory tower, expressing esoteric emotions accessible only to the poet and his coterie, since this flouts the 'real function' of art. 'If artists are really to express 'what all have felt,' they must share the emotions of all. Their experiences, the general attitude they express towards life, must be of the same kind as that of the persons among whom they hope to find an audience.'[16]

One of the tenets of a Romantic theory of expression is that in order to understand an artwork, the audience must be able to recreate for themselves what the artist has expressed in the work. In attempting to understand the artist's work the audience is 'attempting an exact construction in its own mind of the artist's imaginative experience'.[17] Collingwood comments that

In so far as the artist feels himself at one with his audience ... it will mean that he takes it as his business to express not his own private emotions, irrespectively of whether any one else feels them or not, but the emotions he shares with his audience. ... [The artist] will conceive himself as his audience's spokesman, saying for it the things it wants to say but cannot say unaided.[18]

In experiencing an artwork properly, then, the audience is experiencing the emotions expressed by the artist in the work and these emotions are or become the audience's own.

From the artist's point of view, however, there is a big difference between expressing one's own emotions in such a way that they can be shared by an audience, and deliberately setting out to arouse the audience's emotions while remaining unmoved oneself. Collingwood thinks that the expression of emotion by an artist is quite different from the deliberate arousal of emotion in an audience:

A person arousing emotion sets out to affect his audience in a way in which he himself is not necessarily affected. ... A person expressing emotion, on the other hand, is treating himself and his audience in the same kind of way; he is making his emotions clear to his audience, and that is what he is doing to himself.[19]

Audiences, in coming to understand a work of art that is an expression, have to be able to experience the work for themselves. This point has been obscured by an overemphasis on Collingwood's idealism and his suggestion that some works (a short poem, for example) can exist in the artist's mind without being realized in a physical medium and hence without being accessible to anyone else.[20]

Finally, Collingwood distinguishes the expression of emotion from what he calls the 'betrayal' of emotion, or the exhibition of 'symptoms' of an emotion, such as clenching one's fists and reddening in anger or turning pale and stammering out of fear.

The characteristic mark of expression proper is lucidity or intelligibility; a person who expresses something thereby becomes conscious of what it is that he is expressing, and enables others to become conscious of it in himself and in them. Turning pale and stammering is a natural accompaniment of fear, but a person who in addition to being afraid also turns pale and stammers does not thereby become conscious of the precise quality of his emotion. About that he is as much in the dark as he would be if (were that possible) he could feel fear without also exhibiting these symptoms of it.[21]

A true artist 'never rants' or writes or paints to 'blow off steam'.[22] Expression is, as we might put it today, a *cognitive* process, a process of becoming conscious of one's emotion in all its particularity and specificity. Notice that this reflects the Romantic idea that, as Wordsworth said, poetry is the spontaneous overflow of powerful feelings which are *recollected in tranquillity*. Collingwood constantly reverts to this crucial point: 'It is only because we know what we feel that we can express it in words,' and 'it is only because we express them in words that we know what our emotions are'.[23]

It is pretty clear from the way Collingwood defines 'expression' that he is using the word in a quasi-technical sense. In ordinary folk psychology, saying 'I love you' or 'I am very sad,' would seem to be a paradigmatic way to *express* one's emotion, but for Collingwood one would have merely described or labelled one's emotion, not expressed it. Similarly, in ordinary language we talk about the physiological symptoms of emotion as *expressions* (remember Ekman's studies of facial *expressions*, for example), but for Collingwood, such spontaneous and unconscious symptoms are betrayals (sometimes he calls them 'psychic expressions'), not expressions in his sense of the word. Expression is conscious and deliberate, and its crucial characteristics are 'lucidity and intelligibility'. On the other hand, the artist isn't getting clear about his emotions as he might on the therapist's couch when he says: 'I thought I was just sad but now I realize I was actually jealous.' There's a big difference between art and therapy. If I discover I was 'jealous' rather than merely 'sad', I am categorizing my emotion using the vocabulary of folk psychology. I am not individualizing the emotion. Nor is an emotion 'individualized' in the right way if it is described as, for example, 'that peculiar emotion which I felt when the mayor playfully dropped an ice cube down the back of my neck'. In thus describing my emotion I am still using general terms. I am not *expressing* it in such a way that an audience could recreate my experience in imagination.

For Collingwood the expression of an emotion takes place in 'language', i.e. in tones, paint, stone, gestures, words, or some other symbolic medium. The artist elucidates his or her emotion by creating a work of art and the emotion expressed is unique and individual because its expression is unique and individual. Only *this* sequence of lines with *this* rhyme scheme, *this* imagery, *this* rhythm, and so on will express *this* exact emotion. Change an image and the emotion expressed will change too. Emotion and expression are one.

The idea that art is expression in Collingwood's sense was widely accepted in the first half of the twentieth century even among those who in other respects had little in common. John Dewey,[24] for example, agrees with Collingwood almost to the letter on the issue of art as expression, although Collingwood is an idealist and Dewey one of the founders of American pragmatism. But like Collingwood, Dewey is steeped in Romantic ideas about the nature of art, and both have abstracted from Romantic and Idealist sources philosophically rich accounts of art as expression which have a great deal in common.

Alan Tormey and the Abandonment of Expression Theory

In the 1950s, however, a change was under way in the discipline of aesthetics in the English-speaking world. As a branch of analytic philosophy, aesthetics sought to distance itself from Idealism and Romanticism and other obscure and dubious nineteenth-century movements and theories, and as part of this reaction, the Expression Theory of art came in for widespread and formidable criticism. Critiques included O. K. Bouwsma's 'The Expression Theory of Art' (1954) and John Hospers's well-known 1955 article, 'The Concept of Expression', as well as Alan Tormey's 1971 book, *The Concept of Expression*.[25] Hospers describes and rejects three ways of thinking about expression. Very broadly, there is (1) expression as a process undergone by the artist, (2) expression as the evocation of emotion in an audience, and (3) expression as communication between artist and audience, a combination of (1) and (2). Hospers rejects all three, instead advocating a fourth theory of expression, 'expression as a property of the work of art'.

It is neither the artist nor the audience that matters here; it is the work of art itself. It is *the music* which is expressive; and the music may be expressive even if the artist had no emotions when he wrote it, and even if the audience is composed of such insensitive clods that they feel nothing when they hear it. The expressiveness of the music is dependent on neither of these things.[26]

In Hospers' scheme of things, 'Expression Theorists' such as Collingwood and Dewey are examples of the first way of thinking about expression. Collingwood is interpreted as proposing that what makes something a work of art is the process by means of which it came into being *rather than* anything about the work itself. Hospers comments that the genesis of the work is irrelevant: 'what we must judge is the work before us, not the process of the artist who created it'.[27]

Alan Tormey's book *The Concept of Expression* is an elegant and persuasive essay that is widely agreed to have demolished the Expression Theory once and for all.[28] While a good deal more subtle than Hospers' treatment, it hews to a very similar line. Tormey sketches a generic Expression Theory (E-T) which he claims is common to Dewey, Ducasse, Collingwood, Carritt, Gotshalk, Santayana, Tolstoy, and Véron, 'whatever their further differences may be'.[29] His very formulation of the theory proclaims the victory of careful analytic philosophy over Romantic muddleheadedness:

> (E-T) If art object O has expressive quality Q, then there was a prior activity C of the artist A such that in doing C, A expressed his F for X by imparting Q to O (where F is a feeling state and Q is the qualitative analogue of F).[30]

Tormey claims to be characterizing the theory in a way designed to call attention to the intimate relation that the Expression Theorists thought holds between 'the activity of the artist and the expressive qualities of the work'.[31] He then argues that the fundamental mistake in the Expression Theory is its assumption that 'the existence of *expressive qualities* in a work of art implies a prior act of *expression*'.[32] Tormey thinks that E-T is committed to the view that if a work of art expresses an emotion, this implies that the composer or poet or painter is actually experiencing the emotion expressed. For example, it follows from E-T, he thinks, that if we discover that Mahler wasn't actually in a state of 'despair or resignation' during the period of the composition of *Das Lied von der Erde*, the Expression Theorist has to deny that any part of the work itself expresses despair or resignation. He comments that this is implausible 'since it implies that statements ostensibly about the music itself are in fact statements about the composer'.[33] Whether a work has certain 'expressive qualities' is a matter of the melodies, harmonies, rhythms, and so on in the work itself; it has nothing to do with the state of mind of the artist: 'statements about the expressive qualities of an artwork remain, irresolutely [sic], statements *about* the work, and any revision or rejection of such statements can be supported only by referring to the work itself'.[34] Statements attributing expressive properties to works of art are 'statements about the works themselves' and 'the presence of expressive properties does not entail the occurrence of a prior *act* of expression'.[35] In other words, artworks may have *expressive qualities* but they are not *expressions* of any emotional states in their creators in anything like the way that Collingwood and Dewey thought.

According to Tormey, there are two defining characteristics of anything that counts as an 'expression'. First of all, 'expressions are always of intentional states',[36] states that have 'intentional objects', something or other that they are directed towards or are 'about', such as a belief or desire *that* it will rain or *that* Bobby will return safely from the war, or an emotion such as relief *that* it is about to rain or sadness *about* the war and Bobby's fate.[37]

Secondly, expressions always warrant certain kinds of inferences. In general, 'A is expressing ϕ' implies that 'A is (or has) ϕ'.[38] Thus, if Fred's behaviour is an 'expression of ϕ', then there is a 'warrantable inference' from Fred's behaviour to some intentional state ϕ in Fred. If, for example, Fred's slumping posture, downturned mouth, and fits of tears are an 'expression of gloom', then we are warranted in inferring from Fred's expression that he himself is feeling gloomy. But in Tormey's view there is a world of difference between saying that Fred's behaviour is an 'expression of gloom' and saying that it is a 'gloomy expression'. If his behaviour is merely a 'gloomy expression', we are not entitled to make any inference about Fred's inner states.

He wears a gloomy expression, but maybe that's just the way he is made. A basset-hound may have a similarly 'gloomy expression', but we cannot infer that the basset-hound is feeling gloomy. He just comes with a face like that.[39]

Tormey's main accusation against E–T is that it fails to distinguish between being an 'expression of ϕ' and being a 'ϕ expression'. He thinks that E–T treats artistic expression as the expression of ϕ, where ϕ stands for some psychological state in the artist, poet, or composer, whereas it ought to be treated simply as a ϕ expression or the possession of expressive properties such as 'gloomy' or 'nostalgic.' Just as Fred's gloomy expression need not be the expression of any gloom in Fred, so a work of art—a poem or symphony or painting—can be a gloomy, resigned, joyful, or despairing *expression* without its being an *expression of* any gloom, resignation, joy, or despair in the creator of the work. Tormey argues that if we claim that a piece of music is expressive of or an expression of ϕ, this proposition should be understood as 'containing "expression" or "expressive" as syntactic parts of a one-place predicate denoting some perceptible quality, aspect, or *gestalt* of the work itself'.[40] In other words, to say that music is expressive of ϕ is simply to say that the music has certain expressive qualities; it does not imply anything about the inner states of the composer.

So what are 'expressive qualities?' Tormey proposes that 'expressive properties are those properties of artworks (or natural objects) whose names also designate intentional states of persons. Thus "tenderness", "sadness," "anguish," and "nostalgia" may denote states of persons that are intentional, and thus expressible in the fullest and clearest sense.'[41] He acknowledges that this stipulation limits what can count as an expressive property, since it follows that works of art cannot express power or weight or the ideas of republicanism, but he wants to preserve the idea that what works of art can correctly be said to express are fundamentally psychological properties. Expressive qualities are 'constituted' by the non-expressive properties of an artwork, so that, for example, the gloom in a melody is constituted by the sequence of tones, key, dynamics, harmonic progressions, rhythm, timbre of the instruments, and so on.[42] It has nothing to do with the internal states of the composer.

Tormey also thinks that E–T has confused two different ways of using the term 'expressive'. He points out that it can be used 'transitively', as when we say that a face or a piece of music is expressive of some quality such as gloom. In this usage to be 'expressive of' is equivalent to being 'an expression of', and so implies that the owner of the face or the maker of the music is indeed gloomy. Or 'expressive' can be used 'intransitively', as when we say a face or a piece of music is simply 'expressive', without thereby making any inferences about the particular psychological states the owner of the face or the maker of the music may or may not be experiencing. In music, for example, the intransitive use of the term 'expressive' or *espressivo* has a quasi-technical meaning: it is 'an adverbial characterization of a manner of performance'[43] and has no implications whatsoever for the inner states of the performer (or the composer). Tormey, however, assumes that, according to E–T, to call a piece or a performance 'expressive' must be to attribute to the composer or performer a particular state of mind which is being expressed. 'It would follow from the E–T that we might always be mistaken in thinking that a performer had played a phrase expressively, since the correctness of this belief would depend on the truth of some psychological statement about the performer's inner states'.[44]

Finally, Tormey discusses whether a piece of music can ever be an 'expression of φ' in the correct sense that inferences are warranted to the state of mind of some 'expresser'. He acknowledges that the music I write—like everything else I do—may indeed express something about me, such as my personality, character, or emotional traits, but he thinks that this fact 'does nothing to support E–T, and further, that it does nothing to distinguish art from any other product of human activity'.[45] Thus, according to Tormey, Nielsen's Symphony Number 6, Second Movement, is an expression of Nielsen's exasperation, bitterness, and disappointment (due to, among other things, his seeming failure to gain an international audience), but Tormey thinks that this is irrelevant to what the music itself expresses. He claims that E–T requires that the creative artist 'imparts a quality' to an artwork 'which is "*descriptively analogous*" to the feeling state expressed by him (sadness—"sadness")' and so should be recognizable as such without any 'extra-perceptual sources of knowledge'. However, according to Tormey, whereas the Nielsen movement expresses the composer's exasperation and bitterness, the music itself sounds *humorous*: the 'prevailing impression left by the music itself is that of light-hearted buffoonery'.[46] The problem for E-T is that 'the qualities of the music here are not, and *cannot* be analogues of the intentional state of the composer. The music is humorous, the composer is disappointed.'[47] Hence we cannot 'warrantably infer' from the expressive character of the music to the intentional states of the composer. 'There is no direct, non-contingent relation between qualities of the work and states of the artist as the E-T supposes:'[48] Nielsen's music can only be heard as an expression of bitterness once we know something about his private life; we cannot infer the bitterness just from the expressive qualities of the music alone.

Tormey concludes that artists 'do not "express" themselves in their work in any sense that is intelligible, consistent, and aesthetically relevant'.[49] The theory that art is the expression of emotion is either trivial (since all human products can be expressions of their makers in some sense) or false (since we cannot infer from what is expressed to inner states of the artist). The only 'residue of truth' in E-T is that 'works of art often have expressive qualities'.[50]

Classic Expression Theory Defended: A Critique of Tormey

The most fundamental problem with Tormey's analysis is that he mischaracterizes the expression theory. His version of E-T would be unrecognizable to both Collingwood and Dewey. First of all, neither of them would accept the idea that the process of artistic expression is an activity 'prior' to the making of the artwork, and secondly, neither of them would accept the idea that the process of artistic expression is a process of 'imparting' expressive qualities to art objects. Even if during the process of expressing an emotion in an artwork the artist does as a matter of fact 'impart' an expressive quality to the work, the quality is fairly unlikely to be a 'qualitative analogue' of the 'feeling state' being expressed. Finally, I think that both Collingwood and Dewey would reject the suggestion that they are confusing expressions of φ with φ expressions. They are explicitly defending the idea that works of art can—and should—be expressions of the artist's emotion (expressions of φ) and not just φ expressions. Moreover, they would both question whether Tormey's Nielsen example is a *bona fide* example of an artistic expression of emotion in their sense.

1. It is a mistake to think that for the Expression Theorists expression is a 'prior activity of the artist' that then (later) results in the 'imparting' of expressive qualities to the work, because according to Expression Theorists, it is *in* writing the poem or painting the picture that the artist 'expresses his emotions'. The artist expresses his own psychological states in an artwork in the way in which he manipulates a medium, and describes, portrays, or characterizes a content.[51] For example, Keats's 'Ode to a Nightingale' is an *expression* of the poet's longing for a timeless world of art and beauty far away from the misery and tedium of the actual world. The poet expresses this emotion in his descriptions of the actual world ('the weariness, the fever, and the fret'), in his evocation of the nightingale as songster, the creator of timelessly beautiful melodies ('Thou wast not born for death, immortal bird'), and so on and so forth. In short, it is *in writing* the poem that the poet expresses his emotions; expressing is not some activity that occurs before the poem is created. Moreover, the Expression Theorists are certainly not saying what Hospers seems to accuse them of: that artistic expression is a psychological process undergone by the artist which consists in creating a work of art while in some emotional state or other, so that the expression by Keats of an emotion of longing means *only* that the poet felt longing as he was writing the poem.

2. The Expression Theory would also roundly reject the idea that expression consists in the 'imparting' of 'expressive qualities' to artworks. Keats's Ode expresses longing for a timeless world of art and beauty far away from the misery and tedium of the actual world, but this does *not* mean that the poem possesses an *expressive quality* called 'longing'. What the poem does is to articulate in a unique and original way the speaker's very particular emotion of longing in such a way that we in reading the poem can come to understand this feeling for ourselves. Even if in the process of expressing longing in his Ode, Keats does in fact 'impart' expressive qualities to it, the qualities need not be 'qualitative analogues' of the 'feeling state' being expressed. The poem expresses longing, but it does not possess any expressive quality called 'longing'. The poem doesn't long for

anything; it is the poet who does that (or, as we shall see, the poet's 'voice', the implied speaker of the poem).

Furthermore, even if there are expressive qualities in the poem such as wistfulness or melancholy, this is not what makes the poem an *expression* of wistfulness or melancholy. There are lots of melancholy, wistful poems that don't express anything in the Romantic sense. Here is an example:

> As I sit upon this log,
> Crying softly all alone,
> I wish I had a little dog
> To love me when I'm on my own.

This is wistful and melancholy, I suppose, but it does not *express* anything in the Romantic sense. If anything it betrays (rather than expresses) sentimentality. This doggerel does not articulate and clarify a peculiar unique wistfulness and melancholy belonging to the speaker; it is trite, banal, and even comical. Similarly the smiley face is *cheerful* and its opposite is *glum* (see Fig. 8.1), but neither expresses anything much.

For the Expression Theorists, when a poet expresses an emotion in a poem, the expression is original and so therefore is the emotion expressed: the poet brings into being a new emotion/expression. Keats's poem has moments in it that are wistful and melancholy, but this is not what makes it an expression of emotion. Expression is a cognitive process, the articulation of a hitherto confused emotional state. A poem can be melancholy or wistful without clarifying or articulating, hence without *expressing*, the emotional states of melancholy, wistfulness, or anything else.

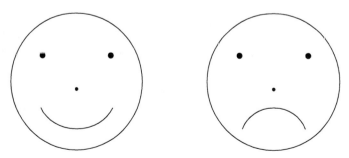

Fig. 8.1. Smiley face and its opposite

3. Tormey says that the only truth salvageable from the Expression Theory is the idea that works of art often have expressive qualities such as tenderness, anguish, sadness, and the rest. But the Expression Theory is not about expressive *qualities* such as the sadness or gloom in a piece of music or a poem. As I have just argued, a melancholy poem may or may not be an expression in Collingwood's sense, and if it is an expression, the fact that it is melancholy is not what makes it one.

Although they do not *analyse* 'expression' as the possession by a painting or song or poem of 'expressive properties'—angry colours, sad melodies, and the like—both Collingwood and Dewey stress that artists make use of 'emotionally charged material' when they express emotions in their work. They would no doubt agree with Tormey that what makes a piece of music sad is its melody, rhythm, harmonic progressions, timbre, dynamics, orchestration, and all the other aspects of 'the work itself', and not some psychological process that the composer undergoes. The Expression Theorists are not denying that expressive qualities are emergent properties of art objects, dependent upon such non-aesthetic qualities as harmony, melody, and rhythm. What they are talking about is a different issue altogether. They are not directly addressing the question of how expressive qualities are grounded in 'non-aesthetic properties' (colour, line, melody, harmony). What they are interested in is what artistic expression *is*, what it consists in. Expression is the articulation and elucidation of an individualized emotional state in a work of art, such as the articulation of Keats's very particular emotion of longing—in just the way described in the poem—which is (or seems to be) the poet's own. In other words, they are implicitly denying Tormey's main point, that artistic expression should be identified with the possession of expressive qualities.

4. Tormey's main accusation against E–T is that it confuses expressions of φ with φ expressions, but I think that both Collingwood and Dewey would reject this idea. They are both explicitly defending the idea that works of art can—and should—be expressions of the artist's emotion (expressions of φ) and not just φ expressions. In their view we *can* infer from what is expressed in a poem to a state of mind in the 'speaker' of the poem (although, as I shall argue shortly, we may not always want to infer to the actual author's state of mind rather than to

an implied speaker). Furthermore, the Romantic theorists have nothing to say about the 'intransitive' use of the term 'expressive'. They are not analysing what it means to play the piano or the violin *espressivo*. Nothing they say implies that a performer who plays in an *espressivo* manner is thereby manifesting his own psychological states. What they are talking about is expressiveness in *art objects*, not styles of performing, and when they say that an art object is 'expressive', they seem to mean that it is an expression in the sense of an expression *of* the artist's emotion. As I have already said, if φ expressions are merely φ properties of artworks, then the Expression Theory is not concerned with them.

If I am right and the Expression Theorists do hold that artworks are or can be expressions of emotions in their creators, why then do I question whether the second movement of Nielsen's Sixth Symphony is an *expression* of the composer's bitterness and exasperation? In his discussion of this example, Tormey's only explanation for why anyone would think that the movement is an expression of the composer's bitterness, disappointment, and exasperation is that the composer is thought to have been experiencing these emotions at the time he was writing the piece. However, if that is all that is meant, and if, furthermore, Tormey is right to say that the music itself is humorous and buffoonish, then clearly the piece is *not* an expression, in Collingwood's or Dewey's sense, of any bitterness, disappointment, or exasperation in the composer, for the music itself fails to *manifest* any bitterness, disappointment, or exasperation, much less to articulate or elucidate these states, as the Expression Theorists require. Merely being in a particular psychological state while composing a piece is not sufficient for expression of that state in the piece.

Let us look a little more closely at this example. Tormey says that the quality of the music is humorous, and he claims that therefore 'There is no direct, noncontingent relation between qualities of the work and [intentional] states of the artist, as the E-T supposes'.[52] Now, Tormey misconstrues the nature of this supposed 'noncontingent relation'. E-T is not saying that 'qualities of the work' are due to—independently characterized—states of the artist, since, as I have reiterated, E-T is not talking about expressive *qualities* at all (in Tormey's sense), but rather the way the artist describes things or manipulates the medium so as to express some new and complex emotional state in the work of art (such as the particular kind of longing for a timeless world of art and beauty, articulated by Keats's poem). Tormey seems to assume that E–T requires that we can pick out the 'expressive qualities' in a work independently of knowing anything about the artist's private life, and he objects that we can hear Nielsen's music as an expression of bitterness, disappointment, and exasperation only if we have 'extra-musical knowledge' of the composer. But what a work expresses (for Expression Theorists) may well be 'manifest' only to those who have some grasp of what the artist is like. It is now a commonplace that what a work can be seen to express is—like its content, form, or style—dependent partly on the context in which it is viewed. As Gombrich long ago pointed out, even the expressive qualities that a work of art seems just to have are not independent of the period in which the work was made.[53] The artist who made it, the individual style of that artist or the general style within which he worked, as well as facts about the artist's class, race, gender, and individual psychology may all be relevant to determining what is expressed by the work. So it's hardly surprising that we cannot tell a work is an expression of bitterness, disappointment, and exasperation in its author just by paying close attention to 'the work itself' independently of its wider context.

If we take a closer look at the Nielsen example, we can see that there are two alternative explanations for the puzzle Tormey identifies: either the piece has the expressive quality 'humorous' and fails to express the composer's bitterness in the sense of the Expression Theory, or it *is* an articulation and elucidation of Nielsen's bitterness and so on, and the 'humorous' expressive quality contributes to that expression, in that it is, for example, humorous in a biting, satirical sort of way. In fact, most commentators on the movement hear it as a bitter parody rather than a piece of light-hearted buffoonery. Certain passages in the movement can, I think, be heard as 'humorous,' when heard in isolation, but in the context of the whole movement and of the symphony itself, they are clearly grotesque and ironic somewhat in the manner of some of Shostakovich's manic scherzi.

Jonathan Kramer calls the movement 'a bitterly sardonic non sequitur.'[54] He points out that after beginning in a 'disoriented, atonal manner', it eventually 'achieves the simplicity of diatonicism and tonality', but this apparent simplicity is 'soon compromised' and almost immediately 'all semblance of innocent simplicity is gone',[55] never to return. Kramer comments on the movement's many 'imaginatively grotesque touches': 'Percussion sonorities, extreme registers, jagged atonal fragments, trombone glissandos and wide intervals give the movement a gallows humor. The few pockets of diatonic simplicity and tonal harmonies...are foils, brief respites, before the onslaught.' The 'insistent trombone glissando' is said to be '(apparently with precedent from the composer himself) the "yawn of contempt"'.[56]

It is reasonable, then, to hear this movement—and indeed the piece as a whole—as an *expression* of Nielsen's bitterness and pessimism (although it is unclear if there is anything in particular he is pessimistic about).[57] Nielsen is articulating pessimism, perhaps bitterness, through music that has marked expressive qualities (it's grotesquely humorous and bitterly sardonic), but these expressive qualities are not 'descriptive analogues' of what the composer is expressing.

To reiterate, then: a work of art can be an expression of ϕ in the artist without necessarily having ϕ-ish expressive qualities, as when a poem expresses the poet's longing but itself does not long for anything, or Nielsen's music expresses bitter pessimism but the music is grotesquely humorous. And a work of art can have expressive qualities without expressing anything in the artist: it can be sad without expressing anyone's sadness and without even being expressive.

Francis Sparshott describes Tormey's version of E-T as 'a causal theory about the genesis of aesthetic properties'[58] in a work of art, or, more precisely, of *expressive* properties. Tormey—like Hospers—is quite right to point out that a work of art can have the expressive quality of sadness without being the expression of any sadness in the creator of the work. But the expression theory is not a theory about the genesis of expressive properties. It is not *about* expressive properties at all. The Expression Theory is a theory about what art *is*, which, according to the theory is *expression*, and about what expression *is*, which according to both Dewey and Collingwood is the articulation and clarification of emotion in a medium. The E-T says that an artwork is an expression and gives an analysis of what expression is; it is not a theory about the causal origins of expressive qualities.

Expressive Qualities

Despite the fact that Tormey misreads the 'Expression Theory', much of what he says about 'expressive qualities'—sadness, happiness, and the like—is perfectly true.[59] Expressive qualities are emergent properties of artworks, dependent upon non-expressive qualities but not connected to them in very tight, rule-governed ways, so that we can never be sure that every large orange and purple painting is 'aggressive' or that every grey painting with wispy lines in it is 'melancholy'. A question that Tormey does not address head-on but that has exercised many thinkers on this topic is why we attribute human psychological qualities to inanimate art objects. Hospers draws an analogy between the 'expressive character' of music and 'human facial expressions and gestures'[60] which also have an expressive character, and suggests that a theory of artistic expression must rest on some *resemblances* between expressive human gestures and expressive artworks, citing Bouwsma who noted that 'sad music has some of the characteristics of people who are sad. It will be slow, not tripping; it will be low, not tinkling. People who are sad move more slowly, and when they speak, they speak softly and low.'[61]

This explanation will not do for all expressive qualities, however. There is no obvious connection between a melody in the minor key and a human expressive gesture of sadness, yet a minor melody might very well have the 'expressive property' of being sad.

There has been some interesting work by musicologists on how conventional associations contribute to expressiveness in music. Some music reminds us of weddings and other music of funerals; some music is pastoral (maybe it's got bagpipes in it), military (it's full of brass), to do with hunting (it's got a horn call or so), or religious (it sounds vaguely like Gregorian chant). Leonard Ratner[62] has described the various *topoi* that occur in 'Classic Music' of the eighteenth and early nineteenth centuries, including the various dance forms with their associations, and various styles such as the 'Turkish' style or the 'Storm and Stress' style. Certainly, these sorts of convention have a role to play in what music expresses.

Another interesting and problematic case is that of colour. An angry man may turn red (although he may also turn white), but in general the expressiveness of colours does not seem to be grounded in similarities between the various colours and the various ways human beings express their emotions. Human beings obviously have a tendency to anthropomorphize the world, to associate the natural world with their own emotions and other states of mind, but the bases upon which they do this are probably extremely various.[63] Sometimes there seems to be a physical basis for these associations. Kandinsky identified the expressive character of some colours as deriving from their effects upon our visual system: since blue tends to recede, it appears to be cool and ethereal—it is 'the typically heavenly color'[64]—whereas yellow appears to come towards the spectator and is described by Kandinsky as 'impudent and importunate'.[65] There may also be a physical basis for the expressiveness of certain musical timbres and dynamics.

However, although there is no doubt some physical basis for some of the connections we experience between colours, shapes, tones, and so on and the emotions, there are many cases where the associations are clearly cultural.[66] Sometimes the associations are general in the culture. In the west, green is the colour of jealousy, for example, and black is the colour of death. Other associations may be more specific to a time, a place, and a particular social world. Many of Watteau's pictures express nostalgia for a graceful Arcadian world. Watteau tends to depict that world in tones of pink, yellow, and violet, the colours of ball gowns and draperies at elegant court soirées, and he thereby evokes the world of eighteenth-century *galanterie*. By contrast, Corot's depiction of a solid, prosperous, rural world that is domesticated, serene, and abundant relies partly on content and partly on the use of earth colours, dull greens and browns. Sometimes the associations are hard to decipher: Richard Wollheim mentions Sassetta's picture of St Francis giving up his cloak to a poor knight, in which 'for the saint's cloak the painter has used lapis lazuli, which is the costliest of pigments',[67] a fact that would have struck a contemporary audience but today we need to be told about. As Wollheim suggests, the association between the colour and the value of the cloak is important to what the picture expresses.

When artists are expressing emotions in their work, they necessarily draw on a web of social, religious, and cultural associations surrounding the objects they depict and the sounds, shapes, and colours they use. Many of these associations and conventions carry emotional significance. Colours, shapes, images, tones, textures, and materials may all have various emotional associations. Artists always work with an awareness of these associations, and of course they may also draw on such associations unwittingly.

I agree with Sparshott's view that it is unlikely that there is any *general theory* that will account for the myriad ways in which bits of the environment become labelled with emotion terms such as 'sad' or 'cheerful'. As he puts the point:

No doubt 'cheerful' is always used by virtue of something somehow relatable to the kind of human feeling, behavior, and intercourse to which the word 'cheerful' may be presumed to have its primary application; but it is likely that the implied relation will be sometimes of one sort and sometimes of another sort and most often of no definite sort at all . . . the property of cheerfulness in art is a complex one, that of pertaining to, and somehow manifesting something relatable to, good cheer.[68]

Similarly with regard to sadness. We talk about sad news, a sad business ('It was a sad business about Nora's abortion'), a sad day ('It was a sad day for America when Kennedy was assassinated'), a sad letter, a sad face, a sad song, a sad time, sad weather, a sad attempt at a joke, and so on and so forth, but we do not call all these things 'sad' for the same reason.[69] In short, yes, it is true that there are 'correspondences'[70] between emotion and the way the world appears to us, but there is no general explanation for such correspondences. Artists draw on many associations between emotions and the world in their choice of colours and shapes, images and tones, and all the rest of it. But drawing on such associations or correspondences is not what expression is. It is one of the means by which expression is accomplished.

Modifying the Expression Theory

Despite my defence of the Expression Theory against Tormey's attack, I am not about to endorse traditional Expression Theory in its entirety. There are a number of standard objections to the theory that seem to me to be decisive. First of all, it is indisputable that the

Expression Theory does not offer a very good definition of art in general. It is rather, as Weitz put it, an 'honorific' definition, meant by its defenders to define *good* art, and, as such, it privileges one aspect of art—albeit an important one—over others.[71] Just as Clive Bell argued that 'significant form' was the one defining mark of true art, probably because he was trying to justify the apparently unrealistic art of the post-impressionists, so the Expression Theorists were promoting a particular type of art, namely Romantic art and its heirs such as Expressionist art. Just as there are acknowledged works of art that are not particularly strong by the standard of significant form, so there are major works that do not seem to be expressions. Albers's *Homage to the Square* series, Ad Reinhardt's giant hard-edged abstractions, and Vasarely's op art paintings come to mind. Or, going back in history, West African votive figures, Ming vases, Persian rugs, the Pyramids of Egypt, and the temples of the Aztecs and Maya are all arguably works of art but are hardly the expression of the artist's personal emotions.

Secondly, one of the main complaints about the Expression Theory is that it assumes that the artist must be *sincere*, in the sense that if he is expressing nostalgia for a lost idyllic past or longing for a timeless world of art and beauty, he must be expressing his own nostalgia or his own longing. But as many people have pointed out, when we are reading a work such as Keats's 'Ode to a Nightingale', we are not primarily interested in whether Keats himself longed for a timeless world; we are interested in the poem as an expression of the poetic *speaker* whether or not he should be identified with the actual poet Keats. We might say that the emotions expressed are those of a *persona*, which may or may not be one of Keats's own personae.[72] A Romantic lyric poem is often in the first person so that it is natural to read the poem as an expression of emotion (as well as ideas and attitudes) in the poetic speaker, the apparent utterer of the words in the poem. But we can generalize the idea of expression in literature to narrators of stories and novels, and to characters in plays. In these cases there is no good reason to think of the utterer as identical to the writer himself. Perhaps a playwright may sometimes be expressing his emotions in a play, but if so, then one of the ways he achieves expression of *his* emotions is by intentionally creating utterances by characters that seem to express *their* emotions. Similarly, in a novel,

the author may be expressing her own emotions or she may be
creating an authorial 'voice' that is expressing its own emotions.
Often one is aware of the authorial voice as distinct from the narrator
in a novel. This is perhaps easier to detect when there is an unreliable
narrator, as in Nabokov's *Pale Fire*, or when, as in *Wuthering Heights*,
there is more than one narrator. In a novel the emotions expressed (if
any) may be those of the overall authorial persona, or they may
belong to a narrator. There are also, of course, characters that express
their emotions as well. In a play, it is only the characters who express
their emotions, although the way the author manipulates these expressions of emotion may be one of the means whereby his own
emotions (or those of his persona) are expressed in the work.[73]

Having said this, however, it is important to remember that
Expression Theory has its home in Romantic artworks, and in
particular in lyric poetry,[74] whereas most novels and plays are not
primarily meant to be interpreted as expressions of the author (or his
persona) in the way that the Expression Theory describes.[75] Another
point worth making is that we should not be too quick to assert that it
doesn't matter whether it is the author or his persona who is expressing his emotions in a poem. It seems to me that we are often quite
interested in the fact that Keats himself probably yearned for a
timeless world of art and beauty, and that it is perfectly appropriate
to identify the poetic voice with that of Keats himself, or of Keats in
one of his guises (one of his personae). As the Expression Theory
emphasizes, a work of art that is also a successful expression enables
the audience to recreate in themselves whatever is expressed by the
work. It is not unreasonable to enjoy the feeling that one is engaging
with the actual emotions of a great poet, that one is not just being
manipulated but is 'overhearing' the poet himself. Moreover, there is
no question that artists often are attempting to express their emotions
sincerely and that this quest is important in the creation of the work.
That an artist is often exploring his own emotions, as Collingwood
suggests, may be one reason why he produces a powerful work.

This brings us to a third objection to the Expression Theory. It is
often asserted that all sorts of bad and/or amateur artists explore their
emotions in their works, but that what they produce is barely art at
all, let alone good art. This objection should be rejected, I think. The
trouble with it is that it does not take seriously what the Expression

Theorists meant by 'exploring one's emotions'. For the Expression Theory expression is an *achievement*. It is only a *good* work of art that succeeds in clarifying and articulating an emotion in a medium. Bad artists just do not achieve this kind of clarity and articulation. To justify this claim, however, I need to examine further what it means for a work of art to be an articulation or clarification of emotion, something I will return to soon.

The last standard objection to the Expression Theory I will consider is that in large-scale works that take a long time to complete, the artist cannot be continually experiencing the emotions that he is expressing in the work. If a large-scale symphony expresses extreme anguish, say, the composer cannot possibly be experiencing that all the time he is working on the symphony: for one thing it is hard to work when you are in the throes of powerful negative emotion. Similarly, a painter painting a huge picture that expresses his defiance towards fate surely doesn't have to be defying fate the whole time he is painting. This objection is so standard that it even has a standard reply: the artist may be remembering past emotion rather than exploring new and present emotion.

This reply is partly correct: the artist in struggling to express some emotion may be trying to articulate an unclear emotion he is feeling right now or some unclear emotion he remembers feeling in the past. But the artist can also surprise himself and us by succeeding in expressing emotions he has not felt hitherto, or at least not in exactly the form in which he expresses them in his work, and in doing so he can cause both himself and us to feel these new emotions too. Moreover, as we shall see later, the expression of emotion in art and language is not just a spontaneous outburst of an occurrent emotion. Rather it represents the results of what I earlier called 'cognitive monitoring' of emotional experience. A lyric poem may seem to be a spontaneous outburst, but it is of course carefully crafted in such a way that it represents a *reflection upon* an emotional experience. It is not an expression of emotion in exactly the same way as is a spontaneous change in facial expression. That would be a 'betrayal' of emotion, in Collingwood's view.

To summarize: the Expression Theory as a general theory of art has a number of serious flaws. I do not want to defend the theory as a theory of *art*. What I do want to do is to argue that—with some important qualifications—the Expression Theory gives us a frame-work for a plausible theory of *expression*. There are a number of truths in Expression Theory that any version of it should, I think, seek to preserve. (1) Expression Theorists stress that in artistic expression the emotion expressed comes into being with the expression. This is because the emotion expressed is 'individual': no other emotion quite like this one has ever been identified because its identification is dependent on the exact words (tones, lines, colours, etc.) used to express it. (2) Part of the motivation of Expression Theory is to distinguish between works of genuine art and works of mere *technē* or skill. The expression of an emotion is at the same time the production of an imaginative 'vision', and it is the artist's ability to articulate a vision that distinguishes him from the rest of us. (3) The expression of emotion is a process of elucidating or articulating that emotion, of becoming clear about it. (4) Understanding the emotion expressed in a work requires the audience to engage in an imaginative process of 'recreating' it and, like the artist, getting clear about it. (5) It follows that artists in expressing themselves and audiences in recreat-ing those expressions for themselves are acquiring a special kind of knowledge: expression is a *cognitive* process.

Recent theories of artistic expression divide into those that are more-or-less true to the spirit of the Expression Theory and think of artworks as expressing emotion in something like the sense that people do in ordinary life, and those that think that to say a work of art expresses some emotion is merely to attribute to it a particular kind of appearance or emergent aesthetic property. In the next chapter I will outline and defend a theory of what artistic expression is that is in the spirit of the traditional Expression Theories and tries to preserve the insights I have identified above. My view takes as central the idea that artistic expression is a kind of elucidation and articula-tion of emotion, and that it is a cognitive process of becoming clear about an emotion. To explain what the articulation and elucidation of emotion consist in I will make use of the emotion theory developed in the first part of this book.

9

A New Romantic Theory of Expression

> from outward forms to win
> The passion and the life, whose fountains are within.
>
> S. T. Coleridge, 'Dejection: An Ode'

Expression Theory Reclaimed

Vermazen's Theory of Expression

In ordinary life, an expression of emotion is a piece of behaviour that manifests or reveals that emotion in such a way that we can not only infer from the behaviour to the emotion but also perceive the emotion in the behaviour. I believe that an artistic expression is just the same: it manifests emotion in such a way that we can infer from the expression to someone's having that emotion and we can perceive the emotion in the expression. It is because artistic expression has the same basic structure as ordinary expression that the Expression Theorists and their contemporary descendants identify artistic expression as *expression* (rather than, for example, the arousal of emotion or the possession of expressive qualities). However, as we have seen, artistic expression also differs from ordinary expression in various ways. In particular, what is expressed is an emotional or other state in an implied author or persona rather than the real author.

In a 1986 article, Bruce Vermazen develops a theory of 'Expression as Expression', in which he explains expression in art as the same general kind of phenomenon as expression in ordinary behaviour, rather than a matter of the possession by works of art of 'expressive properties'. Vermazen follows Tormey in identifying 'the basic notion of expression' as that of 'providing evidence for'.[1] As we have seen, facial expressions, properly understood, are very good evidence for the presence of a particular emotion: a Duchenne smile, for example, is known to be good evidence for happiness. Similarly, if my weeping and groaning expresses my misery, it is evidence of my misery. If my flamboyant way of dressing expresses my confident, extrovert personality, it provides evidence for my confident, extrovert personality. And so on.[2]

Vermazen thinks that what is expressed in an artistic expression is some emotion (or attitude or idea) in a *persona* rather than in the actual artist (although the persona may be the artist's own). In 'a quick summary' of his theory he says: 'An object expresses a mental property if and only if the object is evidence that an imagined utterer of the object has that mental property.'[3] When 'faced with a putative expressive object', the interpreter 'imagines that the object has been uttered by someone . . . and then asks himself what mental economy would be behind such an utterance, what properties of an utterer would make it appropriate to utter just such an object as this'.[4]

In other words, Vermazen's basic notion of expression is that of an *object* or *utterance* expressing something by providing evidence of the mental economy that seems to have produced it. But he avoids attributing intentional states to an imaginary person. Any talk of the putative actions and passions of a persona 'can be translated back into talk about imagining that some speaker or other performs those actions and undergoes those passions'. The persona is partly constructed by the interpreter, and there may be as many personae posited for the work as there are different interpreters of it: 'The persona is made to order for whatever mental property the interpreter finds the work to express.'[5]

Vermazen contrasts expression by an object or a work with expression by a person. A *person* can express something if 'he intentionally *puts* the evidence [i.e. the object or utterance] where others can take it in, and intends it to be taken as evidence of this sort,'[6] but imaginary personae are not capable of *putting* evidence anywhere. Artistic expression is therefore defined in terms of expression by a work of art, not expression by an artist.

For Vermazen, if a work of art expresses some mental property (such as an emotion), it is evidence that the 'imagined utterer' of the work has that property or emotion. In his discussion, the 'imagined utterer' or 'persona' is usually what I have called the implied author of the work, which, as I explained in Ch. 6, is constructed by the interpreter in interaction with the work understood as created by some particular real author. At the same time, like me, Vermazen recognizes 'layers of personas',[7] at least in literature, as when—in his example—the character of the duke in Browning's 'My Last Duchess' expresses (in Vermazen's sense) his thoughts and emotions about his late wife, but the poem as a whole expresses the thoughts and emotions of 'Browning', the implied author, about the characters and situations dramatized in the poem.

Vermazen's theory has several important advantages. First, as he points out, 'it makes expression of thought and expression of emotion two varieties of the same phenomenon'.[8] We might add that it also treats the expression of attitudes, desires, beliefs, and points of view in the same way. Vermazen couches his definition in terms of 'mental properties,' but he means this phrase to include properties of believing and desiring things as well as thoughts and emotions. Although he does not stress this possibility, he leaves room for the expression of complex states of mind such as the 'longing for a timeless world of art and beauty beyond the actual world which is so full of sickness and other troubles' which we find in Keats's 'Ode to a Nightingale'.

Secondly, Vermazen gives us a *univocal* account of expression, an account that applies across the various arts, and does not treat expression in one art as different in kind from that in another.[9] True, Vermazen says little about *how* a work serves as evidence of a mental property in a persona, but he does comment briefly on how poems, paintings, dances, and music express thoughts as well as emotions with varying degrees of specificity. As he notes in a footnote: 'Works in different media express what they express in different ways, but "express" is univocal in application to all of them.'[10]

Thirdly, his emphasis on artistic expression as the expression of psychological states in a persona avoids the problems of attributing what is expressed in a work directly to the author of that work. Since the implied author is partly constructed by the interpreter, author and interpreter in interaction together determine what the work expresses. Since I have been emphasizing the interaction of author and audience in interpretation, this is a conclusion that I welcome.

Finally, and most importantly, Vermazen's theory captures the idea that expression in art is fundamentally the same kind of phenomenon as expression in everyday life. Expressions in both artistic and non-artistic contexts are construed in terms of providing evidence for a psychological state of some kind. The theory explains why the word 'express' is 'the right word to use', about the phenomenon under discussion, and not just 'a holdover from an erroneous theory'.[11] His theory seems to me to be the right sort of theory: it is a theory that tries to explain what expression actually *is*—rather than simply focusing on the grounds of the attribution of so-called expressive properties—and it does so in a way that captures important insights from the Romantic notion of expression.

At the same time, Vermazen's theory ignores some of the central aspects of the Romantic concept of emotional expression in the arts. (1) The expression of emotion is no longer something that the artist intentionally sets out to do. (2) Vermazen does not specify that the character of the expression itself should manifest whatever psychological state is being expressed; for Vermazen the expression of emotion can but need not involve the articulation and elucidation of the emotion expressed. (3) Expression in Vermazen's sense need not be perceived or experienced by the audience. Keats's 'Ode to a Nightingale' expresses longing just as long as I can *deduce* from the poem that it is a symptom of longing in the dramatic speaker of the poem; I don't have to actually detect or experience any longing in the poem itself.

1. For the Romantics expression is the main function of art and it is something that the artist deliberately sets out to accomplish. An expression of emotion is an achievement by the artist, not something that occurs by happenstance. But according to Vermazen's theory, a work of art expresses an emotion if 'attributing that [emotion] to an utterer of the [work] would explain the [work's] having the features it has'.[12] It follows that works of art can express emotions of which their authors are unaware; they can express emotions even if the author of the work had no intention of expressing anything. In this respect what Vermazen is analysing is closer to what Collingwood would call

the 'betrayal' of emotion. When we say that a work expresses an emotion in Vermazen's sense, we are not implying that the real author of the work is expressing anything or even that the work is a deliberate act of expression by some implied 'utterer'.

In Vermazen's sense of 'expression' we can say that the Ancient Egyptians expressed their sense of the godlike nature of the pharaohs in their works, or that Pheidias's sculptures expressed his love of perfection, or that the Byzantine icon-makers expressed their worshipful admiration for the Virgin. But all this means is that the works are evidence of these 'mental properties' in their 'imagined utterers'. Strictly speaking Pheidias himself is not expressing anything; it is just his works that do the expressing. After all the Ancient Egyptians, Ancient Greeks, and Byzantine artists did not have the 'concept of expression' in the Romantic sense. Romantic artists had a different conception of their task from that which probably motivated the Ancient Egyptian, Ancient Greek, or Byzantine craftsmen.[13]

In Vermazen's sense works of art can also 'express' attitudes, points of view, and so on that seem to be those of the period, place, or culture in which the work originated. We can infer from the way the work looks or sounds that it is the product of these attitudes. Works of architecture are not usually thought of as expressions of personal emotion in an architect, but even works of architecture can express, in Vermazen's sense, ideas, points of view, and values current in the culture that produced them. Vermazen's use of the word 'expression' is perfectly reasonable and even useful and enlightening. However, it is not how the Romantic theorists used the term, and it does not quite capture what the Romantics thought was special about works of art that set out to be 'expressions' in their sense.

2. The reason why a Romantic artist who is trying to express emotions in his work cannot do so unwittingly is that, whether the artist is trying to express his own emotions, the emotions of a persona, or the emotions of a character or narrator in the work, he is always trying to *articulate* and *elucidate* those emotions, and articulation and elucidation—unlike spontaneous expression or betrayal—are intentional activities. So in his 'Ode to a Nightingale', Keats is intentionally expressing his poetic speaker's feelings about the nightingale and this means he is exploring them and trying to articulate them. The Romantic artist is intentionally making something that he intends

both to provide evidence for and to *manifest* an emotion in an 'utterer'. For the Expression Theory and the Romantic artists they have in mind, expression is an intentional activity of exploring an emotion and bringing it to consciousness. An artistic expression is not just evidence that some person or persona is in a particular emotional state: a genuine expression teaches us something about what it's like to be in that emotional state.

We need to be careful, however. When Keats wrote his Ode, he probably intended to express his (or his persona's) emotions and attitudes about art and beauty. The expression of emotion was in all likelihood one of Keats's goals in writing the poem. As a Romantic poet, he had the concept of expression: in his era it was one of the things that artists thought of themselves as doing. However, according to the Expression Theory, he could not have intended to express the exact emotion that he ended up expressing, because that emotion didn't come into being until the poem was complete and could not have been foreseen in all its peculiarities until it had been expressed. Keats may well have intended to write a poem about a nightingale. He may have intended to write a poem about a nightingale which, as it turned out, expressed his (or his persona's) attitude towards art and beauty, and it is quite likely that he intended to express his emotions and attitudes (or those of his persona) towards art and beauty by writing a poem about a nightingale. But the critical requirement, as I see it, is that in his poem Keats *intended to express* (that is, explore and elucidate) *some emotion or other* (even though he did not know exactly what it was until he succeeded in expressing it).

There is an apparent paradox in this way of conceiving of expression. On the one hand, I have emphasized that it was crucial to the Romantics that the emotions expressed in a work of art came welling up in the author himself: expression was the expression of emotions in the artist. But on the other hand, if it is an implied author or persona that is doing the expressing of emotion, then different readers will attribute different emotions to the implied author. As we saw in Ch. 6, the reader constructs the implied author as she interacts with the work. Part of what the reader does in interpreting a poem, if it is an *expression* in the sense I am trying to extrapolate, is to experience the poem as an expression of emotion in the implied author: she perceives the poem as manifesting an emotion and as warranting an inference to the presence of that emotion in the implied author. This is an important part of how the reader builds up a sense of who the implied author is. As we have seen, the particular background that a reader brings to this task will also affect her sense of the implied author and what emotional states 'he' is expressing in the work.

It now begins to sound as if expression is not something brought off by an author but something detected by a reader.[14] But as I have stressed throughout this book, experiencing and interpreting artworks is a two-way process. However much work the reader has to do, the actual author has a big say in how the reader experiences the work. In particular, if the Romantic theorists were right, then the actual author is the one who *articulates* and *clarifies* the emotion expressed in a work of art. Of course I am now denying that the emotions articulated and clarified had to be the artist's very own emotions. However, when Wordsworth says that poetry expresses emotions 'recollected in tranquility' or Keats talked about the artist's need for 'negative capability', they are emphasizing that poetic expression involves not the spontaneous betrayal of the artist's very own emotion but *reflection* upon an emotion that may or may not have been personally experienced by the artist. In my terms, artistic expression, as described by Expression Theory, is a process of *cognitive monitoring*, which brings an emotion to consciousness.

3. Jerrold Levinson complains that Vermazen's theory is 'too intellectualized': expressiveness 'must be perceivable, not just inferable, in order to deserve that appellation'.[15] If you smile a Duchenne smile that expresses your happiness, I am able to *see* your happiness *in* your smile; I don't just make inferences from your behaviour to your state of mind. Similarly, the argument goes, I must be able to see expression in painting or hear it in a piece of music; I don't just *deduce* that what I'm encountering is a symptom of some state of mind. Some people make the point by saying that an expression is not just a *sign* of the presence of some state of mind.[16] If Uncle Fred always pulls on his moustache when he's in a good mood or Auntie Maisie always blinks a lot when she's angry, these behaviours are supposedly only signs or symptoms of emotion, not expressions, because we allegedly cannot perceive any emotion *in* the behaviour or experience the blinking *as* angry or the moustache-pulling *as* good-humoured.

I suspect there may not be such a sharp distinction between signs and expressions as is sometimes thought. It's not as if people's expressions are completely transparent, so that all I have to do is look at your face or posture and I'll know exactly what you're feeling. People's ordinary expressions are often hard to read so that it's not straightforward at all to know what the expression is an expression of.[17] Alfred Hitchcock makes good use of ambiguous expressions to create tension in such movies as *Suspicion*, where the young wife reads her husband's ambiguous expressions as expressing sinister intentions—and the audience is encouraged to as well—but where it turns out that his expressions have a very different meaning. Similarly with respect to other works of art: it is often not at all obvious what a work is expressing, and we have to make inferences from the character of the work to what emotion or other state of mind it is an expression of. And on the other hand we can learn to read idiosyncratic or conventional signs of emotion such as Uncle Fred's pulling on his moustache, so that we respond to them just as we do to more 'natural' expressions.

Probably, however, what Levinson means is that Vermazen makes the audience's knowledge of what a work of art expresses sound more like the comprehension of some conventional connection than a direct encounter with someone's expression of emotion. And certainly we do need to see or hear the emotion expressed *in the expression*, even if this requires some inference-making along the way. Notice, however, that Levinson couches his complaint in terms of 'expressiveness' rather than 'expression'. The implication is that, even if we need to infer from an expression to what it is an expression of, its 'expressiveness' must be visible or audible. Thus even if Uncle Fred's tugging on his moustache is a reliable guide to his good humour, it is not an *expressive* piece of behaviour. In my view, that's because it doesn't get us to feel what it's like to be in a state of good humour. If, as I'll argue shortly, expressing an emotion in art involves articulating and individuating that emotion, then certainly we have to perceive what's expressed in its expression. But more than that, the expression should communicate something of what it's like to be in the emotional state expressed.

'Art as Expression'

In an earlier essay, 'Art as Expression',[18] I argued that artistic expression is just like expression in ordinary contexts in that it satisfies the following two conditions: if a work of art expresses an emotion, then (1) it exhibits, or, as I have said here, manifests the emotion, and (2) the emotion expressed causes the work of art to have the emotional quality that it does. Although I did not stress this point, it follows that we can infer from an expression to the emotion in the artist that caused it. The 'central' cases of expression were said to be those in which an artist sincerely expresses his own emotion, which I thought implied that the artist's own emotion *caused* its expression, and that this emotion is *exhibited* in the artwork. This was my attempt to unite the two crucial aspects of expression: an expression issues from an emotion in a person and it communicates this emotion to other people.

I then claimed that ordinary behavioural expressions of emotion such as weeping and laughing are directly caused by the emotion they express, whereas, unlike cases of expression in ordinary life, the causal link between an emotion and its expression in art is an indirect link: the emotion causes the artist to choose—whether consciously or unconsciously—certain shapes, sounds, images, and so on, so as to produce a finished work that will be expressive of the emotion. The artist does this by choosing shapes and sounds and so on that 'correspond' to that emotion.

As Richard Wollheim has stressed, the natural world appears to us as imbued with emotional qualities; we have a natural tendency to anthropomorphize the natural world, perceiving a gnarled and twisted tree as anguished, the sound of a rippling brook as cheerful, the sight of a dark wood as gloomy. Wollheim says that these natural phenomena 'correspond' to various human emotions. My idea was that in artistic expression 'what the artist does is create phenomena which may serve as expressions of human emotion in much the same way that non-human phenomena in the natural world do'.[19] These expressive elements—sounds, colours, verbal images, etc.— correspond to the emotion in question. In what I claimed were the 'central cases' of artistic expression, it is the artist's own emotion which 'causes him to select the expressive elements that he does': 'the artist who attempts to express his emotions in his artistic products intentionally searches out sounds, words and images which seem to "embody" these emotions in a way similar to that in which some object or condition in nature might "embody" them'.[20] In 'secondary' cases the emotion expressed is not the artist's own but only seems to belong to the artist himself. In such cases the artist paints as if from a certain attitude or emotion and still 'makes vivid' the emotion by an appropriate choice of correspondences. Expression is always, therefore, an intentional activity, that of choosing 'correspondences' to an emotion within some medium.[21]

I also argued that this process is in fact a process of 'articulating' and 'individualizing' an emotion, so that my interpretation of 'artistic expression' was able to capture an important aspect of Expression Theory, as developed by Collingwood. I argued that the artist individualizes and articulates this emotion in the process of manipulating his medium, not merely by choosing colours, lines, images, and so on that are 'naturally' expressive—they correspond to some emotion— but also often by emphasizing or even distorting and exaggerating the aspects of these sights and sounds which make them correspond to emotions, in order to express the emotion in question even more clearly. Thus the shapes of a row of tormented-looking trees in nature may correspond to anguish, but Van Gogh in painting his cypresses can exaggerate and distort those shapes in such a way as to emphasize the trees' look of torment.[22]

It might sound as if this account describes the artist as manipulating a medium in order to express some preconceived emotion. But my theory did not envisage the artist as simply choosing an emotion to express and then choosing among materials that are already imbued with that particular emotion. Rather the artist can pick and choose his materials in order to articulate or individuate an emotion that has not been previously articulated or individuated. True, he is aware of the 'inherent' expressiveness of colours and lines, tones and harmonic progressions, but in a work of art context is all: no particular colour, line, tone, or harmonic progression is inherently expressive of this or that; it all depends on how the artist treats his material. As the Expression Theorists said, the artist himself doesn't know what he will express until he's expressed it.

My earlier view did have a number of advantages that I would like to preserve in my current version of Romantic Expression Theory. First, if a work of art is an expression of emotion in a persona, then we can infer from the work to the presence of that emotion in the persona.[23] As Vermazen says, an artwork that is an expression provides evidence for the presence of an emotion (in a persona) and we can infer from the work to the presence of that emotion. Secondly, if a work of art is an expression of emotion, the emotion expressed is *exhibited* or *manifested* in the character of the work: the work of art articulates and individuates the emotion. Thirdly, expression is an intentional activity. The artist does not intend to express a particular emotion that he can characterize ahead of time, but he does intend to express some emotion or other. The intention to express an emotion is an intention to articulate, elucidate, and individuate an emotion, and in individuating an emotion in an artwork, artists make use of emotionally charged material.

Nevertheless, there are at least three problems with my earlier account. First, the idea that the 'central' cases of artistic expression are those in which the artist sincerely expresses his own emotions when he expresses emotions in an artwork is overstated. It is true that Romantic artists and Expression theorists talked that way and it is likely that Romantic artists often thought of themselves as expressing their own emotions in their works. Nevertheless, if we are to expand the notion of Romantic expression beyond those artists who explicitly thought of themselves as expressing their very own emotions, we should allow that many works express emotions in the sense that these emotions *seem* to an audience to emanate from the artist, whether or not they actually do. As Vermazen persuasively argues, works of art that express emotions express the emotions of a *persona*, regardless of whether the persona is to be identified with the actual author. Even in a paradigm of Romantic expression such as Shelley's 'Ode to the West Wind', it is a dramatic speaker who is crying out 'I fall upon the thorns of life! I bleed!' even if in this particular poem we are probably justified in thinking of the dramatic speaker as voicing the poet's own emotions.

Secondly, I would now take issue with the idea that artistic expression is a matter of choosing sounds, colours, shapes, or verbal images that seem to 'embody' emotions 'in a way similar to that in which some object or condition in nature might embody them', or that the artist creates phenomena which 'serve as expressions of human emotion in much the same way that non-human phenomena in the natural world do'.[24] It is not true that 'non-human phenomena in the natural world' express emotions. Trees or brooks may have 'expressive qualities'—they may look melancholy or sound cheerful—based on, for example, similarities between the way they look or sound and the way people look or sound when they are expressing emotion, but strictly speaking trees and brooks can't express anything: it is only human gestures, actions, and behaviour or the results of human gestures, actions, and behaviour that can literally be termed 'expressions of emotion'. As I argued in my discussion of Tormey, expression is not a matter of imparting expressive qualities to an artwork, and nor is it a matter of choosing and putting together expressive materials. Artists do make use of 'emotionally charged' lines, tones, colours, and so on, but, as I have insisted, expression cannot be *defined* as the choosing and putting together of expressive materials.

Thirdly, my early view relies on a false conception of emotion.[25] It is a major mistake to think that emotions *cause* their expressions, because there is no separate event called 'an emotion' that causes behavioural expressions. Rather the behavioural expressions are a normal part of a whole emotion process. As we saw in Ch. 3, an emotion process is set off by a non-cognitive appraisal which appraises the environment in terms of one's wants, goals, and interests.[26] The non-cognitive appraisal in turn causes physiological changes and action tendencies. After subsequent cognitive monitoring of the environment and of the various kinds of feedback one is receiving from one's body, appropriate action is initiated. To be sure, an emotion process is a causal process, but the emotion process itself does not cause its constituents.

In the early essay I did not claim that emotions caused a person to make an artwork, but only that if a person were making an artwork, it would cause them to make one of a certain sort or one having a certain character. But even this is misleading at best. Rather, as we shall see, an artwork that expresses an emotion is a reflection upon the emotion process as a whole, and in a sense represents a kind of summary of the whole process. Expressing emotion in an artwork is a cognitive process, as the Expression Theorists claimed: it is a process of getting clear about an emotion. Artistic expression is not just a matter of *choosing* expressive materials. As we'll see shortly, there is a much more intimate connection between the emotion expressed and the way it is articulated and clarified in an artistic expression.

A New Romantic Theory of Expression

What Expression Really Is

Our examination of Romantic theories of expression has positioned us well to explain what expression in the root Romantic sense is.

If an artist expresses an emotion in a work of art, then
1. the work is evidence that a persona (which could but need not be the artist) is experiencing/ has experienced this emotion;
2. the artist intentionally puts the evidence in the work and intends it to be perceived *as* evidence of the emotion in the persona;
3. the persona's emotion is perceptible in the character of the work;
4. the work articulates and individuates the persona's emotion; and
5. through the articulation and elucidation of the emotion in the work, both artist and audience can become clear about it and bring it to consciousness.

In short, the Expression Theory, suitably modified, suggests a plausible theory of what artistic expression *is*. In its primary sense expression is something intentionally brought about by an artist, just as Collingwood said it was. It is an activity of an artist that consists, roughly speaking, in the manifestation and elucidation of an emotional state of a persona in the expressive character of a poem, a painting, a piece of music, etc., such that the work provides evidence for the emotional state of the persona and the persona's emotional state is communicated to other people (and also the artist himself) through the character of the work. The person's or persona's emotional state is expressed in the character of the artwork, just as the expressive character of a person's face or gestures or tone of voice may express the emotional state of that person. The expression by an artist of an emotion in a work is an intentional act whereby the artist articulates and individuates the emotion expressed. Finally, a successful artistic expression teaches both artist and audience about the emotion expressed, so that they come to understand what it is like to be in that emotional state.

The Romantic theory of expression I have defended is an attempt to articulate a concept of expression that does justice to what the Romantic artists thought they were up to, and that explains how expression functions in the central cases of artistic expression, such as the great lyric poems of Shelley and Keats, and many of the paintings of Delacroix and Friedrich. The theory aims to explain what artistic expression is and to show the connections between the artistic expression of emotion and emotional expression in ordinary life. It is no accident that Romantic theorists called their works *expressions* of emotion.

I have defined artistic expression as primarily an activity by an artist. To arrive at a Romantic theory of expression by an artwork rather than an artist, we have to modify the theory by removing the requirement that stipulates that expression is something that Romantic artists intentionally set out to accomplish. We can also omit any mention of what the artist may learn from the process of articulating and elucidating the emotion. Focusing on the artwork rather than the artist, then, and maintaining our emphasis on the root Romantic concept of expression, we get the following definition.

If an *artwork* is an expression of emotion, then
1. the work is evidence that a persona (which could but need not be the artist) is experiencing/ has experienced this emotion;
2. the persona's emotion is perceptible in the character of the work;
3. the work articulates and individuates the persona's emotion; and
4. through the articulation and elucidation of the emotion in the work, the audience can get clear about it and bring it to consciousness.[27]

Arthur Danto points out that once the term 'expression' has been introduced (by the Romantics) as an aesthetic term, we can look back at the history of art and see that many pre-Romantic (and also post-Romantic) works were expressions even though these works of art were not deliberately created by their makers to be works of expression.[28] Indeed we can now say that the Ancient Egyptian statues express a sense of awe for the godlike nature of the pharaohs or that Pheidias's sculptures express a love of perfection, while saying nothing about the artistic goals of the Ancient Egyptians or Pheidias. These works are not only evidence for the existence of these emotions in their (implied) artists, but to some extent they also articulate these emotions. Works of art and architecture, too, can express attitudes, points of view, and values in much the sense I have just defined for emotions.

How Expression is Achieved

Jerrold Levinson has pointed out that two different questions often get entangled in discussions of expression in the arts. On the one hand there is the question 'What is expression?' And on the other hand there is the question 'How do works of art achieve expression?' or 'What are the grounds of artistic expression?'[29] I have now completed my attempt to state what artistic expression in the full Romantic sense *is*. In my view, it is primarily an intentional activity by *artists*, although the concept is also used derivatively of *works* that may or may not have been intentionally created to express emotions. But this analysis still leaves unanswered the question of how artistic expression is achieved, and in particular how emotions are 'elucidated' and 'individuated' in works of art. What I want to suggest is that this question can best be answered if we consult the theory of emotion I outlined in the first three chapters of this book.

I argued there that 'an emotion' is not a state or a disposition but a *process*, an interactive process or transaction between a person and an environment (which is often another person). The process is typically triggered when my attention is drawn to whatever in the environment is important to my wants, goals, interests, and so forth. An emotional response is a bodily response *caused* by an automatic affective appraisal and occurring as part of a patterned sequence of events, the emotion *process*. An affective appraisal 'appraises' the environment in terms of how my wants, goals, or interests are at stake: whether I am facing a threat, a wrong, a loss, something weird and strange, something especially good, or whatever.

As the process unfolds, the initial affective or emotional appraisal—**This is weird**, or **I like this**, or **This is threatening**—gives way to cognitive appraisals and reappraisals of the situation. In fear or anger I may assess my ability to control or to cope with the situation. In surprise, I may examine the environment for clues about what is happening. And so on. At the same time, the initial affective or emotional appraisal produces in me certain physiological and motor responses, including facial and gestural expressions, which communicate to others and perhaps to myself how I have appraised the environment, whether as strange and threatening, as offensive, as agreeable, or whatever. The angry person frowns, tenses, and prepares in bodily ways for attack; the fearful person trembles, freezes, and then perhaps prepares for flight; the joyful person smiles, relaxes, and possibly skips or jumps for joy. Moreover, there is always feedback of various sorts from each part of the emotion process to the others. Eventually the emotion process will come to an end, or modulate into a different state.

When the process is over, I may label it with one of the folk-psychological terms for emotions in my language: I say I was 'angry', 'sad', 'delighted', or whatever. In other words, I summarize the emotion process with a word. As Phoebe Ellsworth puts it, I 'catalogue' the emotion 'in recollection', using the resources of my language and culture.[30] Ellsworth suggests, however, that particular nameable emotional states may be relatively rare, that our emotional life occurs in 'streams' which change all the time in response to ever-changing appraisals, ever-evolving actions and action tendencies, ever-changing bodily states. As William James noted, our emotional processes are in constant flux: we can change quite quickly from fearful to cheerful, from anxious to angry. On this view particular nameable emotional states are typically recognized only after the event 'when the emotion has been catalogued in recollection'. So it is only after the event that we (or our friends) describe a situation as one in which I was sad or angry, ashamed or guilty, regretful or bored. It is by using ordinary emotion words like these that we try to make sense of our emotional experiences in folk-psychological terms.

Another way in which we might try to make sense of our emotional experiences, however, is by 'expressing' them in works of art.

Here too I am summarizing a sequence of events in reflection; I am *cognitively monitoring* the sequence of events. But a work of art can communicate an emotional state or sequence of emotional states with a detail that is not captured by the categories of folk psychology. For example, if we were forced to name the emotion expressed in Keats's 'Ode to a Nightingale', we might say it is 'longing', but what is really being articulated is a sequence of thoughts, wants, bodily feelings, and so on belonging to the persona in the poem, which defines a particular emotion process that changes and evolves over time. This process can be roughly labelled 'longing'. But what the poem is able to convey is a very particular longing, defined by specific thoughts, wishes, action tendencies, and physiological and behavioural changes. It can also communicate *how* this complex process evolves and how the thoughts, wishes, and physiological and behavioural tendencies themselves change and develop over time (and over the course of the poem). The poem conveys what some situation or series of events is like from the persona's point of view, and the sequence of thoughts, wishes, and so on that articulate how he or she is responding to it *over time*. But it is not just (if at all) a running commentary on a sequence of events, but, crucially, a reflection upon them. The artist presents for us his reflections upon an emotional experience, the result of his cognitive monitoring of it. Unlike facial or vocal expressions of emotion, an artistic expression articulates and clarifies *what it is like* to go through the emotion process and allows the audience to share that experience to some extent,[31] and unlike facial and vocal expressions, an artistic expression is the result of the artist's *reflections* upon this process and an invitation to the audience to share those reflections.

In general, there are two interrelated ways in which a person's or persona's emotions can be expressed (individuated or articulated) in art, corresponding to the fact that emotions are essentially interactions or transactions between the person (persona) and his or her environment (remembering that 'the environment' is often another person). Broadly speaking, emotions in art can be expressed by focusing either on what happens to the person in the interaction or on what happens to the environment.

Focusing first on the environment, works of art that describe or represent the world, such as poems, paintings, and works of photography are able to express an emotion by *articulating the way the world appears to a person in that emotional state*. As a result of an emotional interaction with the environment, the environment takes on a particular *aspect*: to the angry person the world seems to thwart and offend him; to the fearful person the world is threatening. To the sorrowful person the world is a drab and pointless place; to the person in the throes of happy love, the world looks good: a place of welcome, beauty, and manifold satisfactions. Secondly, if we focus on the person doing the expressing, such works of art can express an emotion by *articulating the thoughts, beliefs, points of view, desires, etc. of the person who seems to be expressing the emotion*. To the angry person the world is full of offences, to the fearful person the world is a threatening place. Since the emotional experience is the result of an interaction between person and environment, there is only a difference of emphasis between describing or representing the world from the point of view of an angry or fearful person and simply describing or representing the point of view itself, and/or the thoughts, wants, goals, and interests that shape the point of view.

Earlier I endorsed the idea that in some artworks there are layers of personae, so that in novels, for example, (implied) authors can express their emotions and attitudes partly through the way they portray their narrator or narrators, partly through the way the narrators describe or depict the characters, and partly through self-expression on the part of the characters. In plays the expression of emotion by characters is usually the most salient kind of expression. Thus Shakespeare portrays King Lear on the heath powerfully *expressing* his rage and grief in a way that (1) provides evidence that he is 'genuinely' expressing his own emotions; (2) is perceptible in the words he utters; (3) articulates and elucidates his emotion; and (4) enables the audience to some extent to feel the emotion he is feeling and to reflect upon and get clear about this emotion.[32]

Similarly, many paintings represent the expression of emotion in the sense that they depict people in the act of expressing their emotions. In painting, of course, characters do not express their emotions verbally but via their facial expressions, behaviour, and actions or action tendencies. In the most expressive of such works, the way the artist depicts these things itself helps to articulate the emotions expressed by the 'characters' in the painting, as when violent brushwork and lurid colours help to convey the characters' violent emotions. And at the same time, the way the painter depicts the characters also expresses something of his own attitude towards them (or that of his artistic persona).

Action painting takes this a step further. Even when no characters are depicted, as in the abstract drip paintings of Jackson Pollock, it is the very actions by which the paintings are made that express the artist's (or his persona's) emotions. As Kendall Walton has pointed out, the paintings have the look of having been produced by virtue of these actions.[33]

In this respect action painting is similar to dance. Dance can express the emotions of a persona by *enacting the gestures, behaviour, facial expressions, action tendencies, and actions of a person who is in and manifesting a particular emotional state.* And a song can express emotions in two ways: as poetry it can articulate the thoughts and point of view of a persona—usually the 'protagonist' of the song—who is in a particular emotional state, and as music it can enact the action tendencies, movements, and tone of voice of this persona. (How 'pure' instrumental music can express emotions in the Romantic sense is a topic I address in Ch. 11.)

Part of Collingwood's thesis is that the artist in expressing his or her emotions in an artwork is not just reflecting and reporting on them but is also trying to get the rest of us to understand what is being expressed by causing us to experience those emotions and reflect upon them for ourselves. The idea is that a poem, painting, or song can help us grasp a particular emotional state by causing us to 'recreate' in imagination what it is like to be in that state by actually putting us in that state, or at least encouraging us to *imagine* we are in that state and then to *reflect* about it.[34] A work of art can put us in this state either by showing us the world from the point of view of the emotion or by inducing in us the bodily changes characteristic of that emotion. Interestingly, when an artwork shows us a person in the throes of an emotion, and looking and behaving accordingly, this does induce in us the bodily changes characteristic of the emotions we see (or hear) expressed.[35]

If people engage emotionally with a poem, painting, or song that expresses the emotion of some character and/or expresses the emotion of the artistic persona in the work,[36] then for a while they will have the same wants or goals, experience appropriate bodily changes, and think appropriate thoughts. And because of this, they will also to some degree *feel* as they think the persona in that emotional state feels. At the same time, however, they will also be led to focus on and try to understand what they are feeling (and why) in a reflective way that is rare in ordinary life. In this sense expression is indeed a cognitive process: it teaches us about the emotions expressed and because we ourselves experience those emotions, we thereby learn about ourselves.[37]

The articulation and elucidation of an emotion in art is not an all-or-nothing affair. Some works of art articulate an emotion to some degree but not particularly vividly. An emotion can be more-or-less successfully 'individuated'. The examples I will focus on, however, are mostly paradigms of artistic expression. I will take a brief look at poetry, painting, sculpture, architecture, and dance, and try to sketch how each medium permits and encourages the expression of emotion in its own ways. I will discuss song and instrumental music in Chs. 10 and 11. Notice that I am not trying to explain what makes these works *works of art* but what makes them *expressions*, a very different thing.

Expressing Emotions in Poetry

One of the ways in which literary works can express emotions is by carefully articulating the point of view that characterizes the emotion in question. As Collingwood noted, poetry and other literary works are especially good at articulating and clarifying an emotional point of view.[38] Lyric poetry in particular seems to express the emotions of the dramatic speaker of the poem.[39] Instead of merely describing his sense of awe at the song of the skylark and wistfulness that no human being is capable of such a pure, uplifting song, by saying 'I am in awe of the uplifting song of the skylark, and I sure wish human beings could express such pure unadulterated joy,' the poet Shelley *articulates* this sense of wistfulness and awe with precise imagery, rhythms, and rhymes.

> We look before and after,
>   And pine for what is not:

> Our sincerest laughter
>   With some pain is fraught;
> Our sweetest songs are those that tell of saddest thought.
>
> Yet if we could scorn
>   Hate, and pride, and fear;
> If we were things born
>   Not to shed a tear,
> I know not how thy joy we ever should come near.

These lines characterize the thoughts of the poet or the poetic speaker about the skylark (and probably, 'song' or poetry in general) in terms of his own (apparent) interests, values, and wishes. The poet says that he finds this world full of difficulty and sorrow, whereas he views the skylark as experiencing a joy of which people are incapable. We get a sense both of the poet's wishes and values and of how those wishes and values affect his cognitive appraisals about the skylark and the human world. Once the poem is finished, the emotion expressed has been 'brought to consciousness'. Both Shelley and the reader can now, as it were, look back on the emotional process described by the poetic speaker as his ideas and feelings develop through the poem, and we can now grasp exactly what emotion was being articulated.

In articulating his emotion the speaker also conveys in the movement of the verse and the rhythm of the lines how the thoughts he expresses affect him physically. The poem has a 'tone of voice' that reinforces the thoughts, hopes, desires, etc. it articulates. The first line 'Hail to thee, blithe Spirit!', not only articulates a greeting but sounds like one. The line 'Our sweetest songs are those that tell of saddest thoughts' owes its melancholy not only to the thought expressed but also to the length of the line (in comparison to the previous lines of the stanza) which give it weight and seriousness.

In such poems as Keats's 'Ode to a Nightingale' or Shelley's 'To a Skylark' we are given a double view on the emotion expressed: we are shown the way the world looks to the person in the throes of the emotion and we are also told more directly what evaluations the person is making about the world as so viewed. When Shelley says 'I know not how thy joy we ever should come near,' he is straightforwardly expressing one of his thoughts about the skylark. When he says 'Hail to thee, blithe Spirit! | Bird thou never wert,' he is characterizing the skylark. Of course he is characterizing the skylark from *his* particular point of view: to Shelley the skylark is not (simply) a bird. (Probably the skylark would not agree with this sentiment.)

In articulating the thoughts of his dramatic speaker, Shelley is trying to get across what it's like to be in the emotional state he is expressing. He dramatizes his point of view by personifying the skylark and expostulating with the bird, and—partly by the rhythm and sound of the words—he also conveys something of the emotional (bodily) effect the experience has on him: he conveys his breathless awe at the bird's glorious song as well as his downcast feelings on thinking about the world in contrast with the bird's song. Shelley has given us his *reflections upon* his emotional experience as well as a sense of what the experience is like. The poem is the result of his cognitive monitoring of the experience.

Expressing Emotions in Painting

Representational paintings can also express emotions in a double way. On the one hand a painting can convey a point of view by presenting a vision of the world as seen from the viewpoint of a person in the throes of a particular emotion. On the other hand, a picture can also convey something of what it is like for a person to view the world in that way: it can show the person himself or herself and how the emotion affects him or her. Caspar David Friedrich, a Romantic painter *par excellence*, shows us a vision of the world from the point of view of one in awe before the spirituality of the universe. In paintings such as *The Watzmann* or *Morning Mist in the Mountains*, Friedrich eliminates the foreground plane of Renaissance landscape and allows the viewer to float, 'deprived of, thus unanchored by, a central vantage point'. He dissociates linear perspective from atmospheric perspective (that is, the conveyance of distance by indistinctness), 'which produces visual malaise' and 'suggests a law other than that governing empirical experience'.[40] The result is an expression of *awe* at being in the midst of a vast and mysterious Nature imbued with spirituality, and a kind of spiritual *ecstasy* in feeling oneself spiritually at one with Nature.

In many of Friedrich's paintings there is a 'persona', usually seen from behind, whose view of the universe we seem to share as we look at the painting. In some, such as the *Large Enclosure at Dresden* (see Frontispiece), the persona is assumed. He is standing at our shoulder as we gaze at what the painting represents. Richard Wollheim concurs. He sees Friedrich as selecting the high viewpoint in this picture because he was primarily interested in the person who sees the landscape from this perspective, a person Wollheim identifies with the artist himself, 'the nature-artist of early-nineteenth-century Pietism' who 'through study and meditation' arrives at 'the secrets of nature, which are in effect the secrets of its maker'.[41]

The paintings of Delacroix show us a very different facet of Romanticism, but many of them are also quintessential expressions of emotion in the Romantic sense. In Delacroix, however, the artistic persona behind the paintings exhibits a quite different character from that of Friedrich, nor does Delacroix represent himself or imply his own presence as an onlooker at the scenes he paints. Instead we detect Delacroix himself in *the way in which he depicts* his subjects.

Friedrich paints in a relatively realistic, non-painterly style. He expresses a personal vision of the world by showing the way the world appears to his implied spectator. And Friedrich is not known for his figure painting: where there are figures in his picture they tend to be spectators, taking the role of the implied spectator of the scene. Friedrich's feelings about nature are expressed by the point of view on nature that his pictures take. Almost all Delacroix's paintings, on the other hand, are figure paintings and almost all of them tell a story. They express the artist's (or his persona's) emotions partly in the choice of stories to tell but mainly in the way the stories are treated. First of all, Delacroix emphasizes the expression of emotion *by* the characters he depicts: their facial expressions, postures, gestures, and actions or action tendencies express their own emotions, and these emotions are generally emotions felt in moments of extremity. Delacroix's characters are victims of massacre, revolutionaries bestriding the barricades and marching across a field of corpses, or combatants engaged in mortal struggles often with wild beasts. The animals in his pictures are themselves characters, frequently depicted as engaged in combat with other animals or with human beings and as expressing savage and desperate emotions.

However, as we have seen in our discussion of the smiley face and the upside-down smiley face, there are more or less *expressive* ways of depicting the expression of emotions by characters. Just as important to the effect of Delacroix's paintings is his *style* of painting. Delacroix depicts his characters' expressions of emotion in vibrant colours, tumultuous brushwork, and violently swirling compositions, and thereby succeeds in articulating and elucidating the emotions of the creatures he depicts in such a way that it seems that the spectator can actually feel what they are feeling. And this in turn is largely because the way Delacroix depicts his characters' expressions of emotion in turn articulates and expresses *his own* emotions (or those of his painterly persona).

As more than one commentator remarks, Delacroix loves to paint 'transitional moments, moments of uncertainty, tension, and indecision'. The scene that Delacroix chooses to depict typically 'poses the struggle, the conflict, the precariousness, rather than the resolution— the moment when the action could go either way',[42] such as 'the precise instant when the sharp edge of a blade is about to slice into the flesh of an animal or a warrior'.[43] This is certainly true of the *Arab Horseman attacked by a Lion* (1849, Art Institute of Chicago), which is on the cover of this book. Delacroix has chosen to portray the most dramatic moment of the confrontation, as the lion gains a grip of the terrified horse and the horseman poises to thrust his sword into the lion. We see terror, aggression, resoluteness expressed by the characters (both man and beasts). But we do not dispassionately *observe* these emotions in the protagonists; we are also aware of the passionate excitement of Delacroix, the artist or implied artist. As Clay says:

Delacroix laid out upon a blocked, irregular ground a kind of chromatic vortex, an oval and rather flat mass of colour that looks as if it might have been generated by an expanding, girational movement. The strokes, 'plunged deep like sword thrusts' (Théophile Silvestre), reinforce the lightning swiftness of the action. Each one assumes 'the direction of the form itself,' as [Théophile] Thoré noted in 1847, 'and contributes towards a sense of relief. As the modeling turns, the artist's brush turns in the same direction, and the impasto, which follows the direction of the light, never goes against the illumination radiating throughout the picture.'

The impact of the picture is achieved, as Silvestre says, 'by the violence of the artist's hand'. It 'does not derive from details and their treatment but from the furious movement that sweeps them up, distorting the imagery as required in order to subordinate each part to the effect of the whole'.[44] The overall composition consists of a swirling oval in which lion, horse, and horseman are the constituent moving parts. The apparent violence of Delacroix's *treatment* matches the violence of the scene depicted and the violence of the emotions expressed.

At the same time, of course, Delacroix is presenting us with an image that freezes a particular moment in time, a moment that seems to summarize the action of the story, and allows us not only to feel what is expressed but to contemplate it. Delacroix not only expresses the emotions of his characters and his own emotions, but he also *cognitively monitors* all the violence and passion, summing it up into one unforgettable image and allowing the viewer to ponder it.[45] As Baudelaire memorably puts the point: 'Delacroix was passionately in love with passion, and coldly determined to seek the means of expressing it in the most visible way.'[46]

Delacroix's journal confirms that he conceived of painting as the Romantic expression of emotion, both articulating and evoking emotion through colour, light, and shape.[47]

I firmly believe that we always mingle something of ourselves in the emotions that seem to arise out of objects that impress us. And I think it probable that these things delight me so much only because they echo feelings that are also my own. If, although so different, they give me the same degree of pleasure, it must be because I recognize in myself the source of the kind of effect they produce.[48]

Among post-Romantic styles of painting, Expressionism provides especially good examples of how a picture can express an emotion by manifesting the way the world looks to a person in that emotional state.[49] A well-known example is Munch's *The Scream*. Munch represents a 'character', the screaming person in lower right, who seems—from his[50] exaggerated facial expression—to be in thrall to some powerful emotion of anguish, anxiety, and alienation. At the same time, we are shown the way the world appears to this character and the way that he feels in a physical sense: the person is squashed up against and constrained by the picture plane; he is distanced from the indistinct shadowy black figures at the other end of the bridge, who seem to be turned away from and rejecting him; the bridge stretches away behind him at an acute angle which forces him up against the front of the canvas. And then, of course, there is the scream motif: the whole picture echoes and reverberates with the scream, as if the whole world is infected with the screamer's anguish and anxiety. The picture is justly celebrated because it articulates so powerfully a particular state of mind.

Expressionist paintings often use this technique of representing a character who seems to be responding emotionally to something or other, and at the same time showing the something or other that the character is responding to. So in *The Scream*, the person looks anguished and alienated, and the whole picture represents the kind of vision of the world that the character is responding to. Similarly, in a painting called *Street*,[51] Ernst Ludwig Kirchner shows us a city street that embodies an alienated vision of the city as well as some of the city dwellers whose vision of the city the painting presents. Emil Nolde's sensual pictures of people dancing, such as *Wildly Dancing Children* or *Dance around the Golden Calf*, exaggerate the wildness and abandonment of the dancers' gestures. At the same time, the paintings as a whole, with their fiery colours and crude brushstrokes, embody the enflamed vision of the dancers. Clearly the Expressionists were powerfully influenced by the Romantics, and by Delacroix in particular. One difference between them, however, is that Friedrich and even Delacroix still paint in a more-or-less realistic style, whereas Van Gogh, Munch, and the German Expressionists distort their subject matter in order to emphasize the emotions or attitudes they are expressing. Their works are more abstract than their Romantic precursors.

It is not only Romantic and Expressionist paintings that express emotions in the Romantic sense I am trying to delineate. The eighteenth-century painter Chardin is not a Romantic painter in his choice of subjects. No lion hunts or exotic odalisques appear in his work. Yet Chardin articulates his emotions in his pictures by the way in which he depicts the ordinary things and people of everyday life. His careful, harmonious, loving pictures of copper cauldrons and bowls of strawberries, of pipes and jugs and mortars and pestles, articulate an attitude towards life in general: the importance of civility and harmonious living, the importance of beauty in everyday things, loving respect for ordinary labouring folk, and a serene enjoyment in everyday objects and everyday life.

Sometimes it is hard to tell whether an artist is intentionally expressing some emotion in his work or whether the work is merely a 'betrayal' of emotion, in the sense delineated by Vermazen. We can often infer from a work to the presence of attitudes, emotions, thoughts, beliefs, etc. in a persona, without the work being made intentionally to express an emotion and without there necessarily being any careful articulation or elucidation of the emotions or thoughts expressed. Perhaps this is true of Chardin. Richard Wollheim cites the example of Monet's *The Seine in Thaw*, which he interprets as an expression of mourning, and of Monet's ambiguous feelings towards the death of his wife Camille.[52] Arguably, the painting articulates Monet's emotions and attitudes by showing the way the world appears to him: a frozen landscape beginning to melt into springtime. But it is possible that Monet was unaware that this is what he was doing. He may have been 'betraying' rather than expressing his feelings. On the other hand, even if Monet were not intentionally articulating his emotions in this work, it is still true that the painting itself does so, by articulating a point of view on its subject matter characteristic of the emotion in question and by conveying something of what it feels like to be in that emotional state.

Expressing Emotions in Sculpture and Architecture

Many representational sculptures express emotions as paintings do, by representing persons and scenes from the point of view of someone who is in a particular emotional state. But sculptures focus more than any other art form on the human body, and most often, a sculpture expresses emotion in the Romantic sense by displaying how a person in a particular emotional state looks and behaves. When we infer to the state of mind of the persona from whose point of view the sculpture has been made, we usually infer from the way the human body is represented by the sculpture. Thus Michelangelo's *Pieta* shows the grieving mother weeping over her dead son and expressing thereby both her sorrow and her resignation. In showing the mother expressing her emotions for her son in facial expression, gestures, and posture, the work in turn expresses what seems to be the sculptor's own reverence and sorrow.[53] Similarly, Rodin's *Burghers of Calais*[54] shows the six burghers expressing very different emotions, ranging from fear to despair to anguish to heavy-heartedness to painful acceptance of their destiny, none of which are the usual expressions of heroism or courage in a patriotic sculpture. And through his depiction of their expressive postures and gestures as well as their facial expressions, Rodin thereby expresses his own sympathetic fellow-feeling for the burghers.

Architecture is an art form that does not lend itself to the personal expression of emotion. We can perhaps acknowledge that Gaudi is expressing his emotions in the Sagrada Familia complex in Barcelona, but that is about as close as we can come to architecture that expresses emotion in the Romantic sense. One of Gaudi's idiosyncrasies is that he designs as he builds, as a poet might write a poem, adapting and modifying all the time as he creates. For almost all modern architects, the crossing out and starting over stage occurs while designing the plans and/or models for the future building. In the process of creating a design, the architect can indeed express his (it is usually 'his') love of curvilinear shapes, his feeling for intimate spaces, his fondness for natural materials, his concern for texture, his desire to create civilized living spaces, and so on. The design for a church may express the architect's reverence, or secularism; the design for a public building may express contempt for the masses; a design for a mall may express exuberant enjoyment at the fruits of capitalism. On the whole, however, a design for a building is unlikely to express personal emotions such as anger, jealousy, sadness, joy, fear, and so on. Architecture is more often expressive of attitudes or a worldview, and again, it is not always easy to tell whether such attitudes are deliberately embodied in the design or are there as a result of unconscious preferences on the part of the architect. In short, as with other kinds of art, it is often hard to know if a work of architecture is an expression or a Vermazen-type 'betrayal' of attitudes and emotions.

We can infer from the design of a Gothic cathedral, for example, that its makers were in awe of the Almighty and wanted to make concrete (or render in stone!) the yearning of the faithful upwards to heaven. But again, it does not follow that each individual stonemason was expressing a personal feeling towards the Almighty. In the classical period Palladio's Villa Rotunda expresses the architect's admiration for classical restraint and proportion, his desire to make a gentleman's country place a model of civility and gentility. Was this intentional? Probably to some degree. But to what degree exactly it is impossible to know. In our own day, Peter Eisenman's design for the College of Design, Art, Architecture and Planning at the University of Cincinnati *expresses* the architect's interest in making a building that would educate students even as it houses them, his wish to deconstruct the grid patterns of so many modernist buildings, and his love of strange angles and non-standard sizes, and it *betrays* his impish sense of humour and perhaps a certain arrogance.

Expressing Emotions in Dance

The most obvious way in which dance articulates emotion is by means of gesture and behaviour—often in exaggerated versions—that in ordinary life are expressive of some emotion. Dance can express with exquisite nuance the youthful, impulsive love between Romeo and Juliet, or Giselle's despair at being betrayed by her lover, or the religious ecstasy in Nijinsky's *The Rite of Spring* by mimicking—often in a simplified, abstract, or exaggerated way—the actions, action tendencies, and gestures with which people in ordinary life express these emotions. Like sculptures, dance pieces that tell a story or represent in some way may also be expressive in a double sense, giving us characters who express their emotions in gestures and actions and are also thereby expressing the emotional vision of the choreographer. But abstract works of dance may also be expressive, in the sense that the dancers' movements and gestures express various emotions, even if they do not represent characters in a story or narrative. Abstract works can express emotional responses to the world in general, as well as —in some cases—a vision of the sort of world that would prompt such responses.

Here is perhaps a good place to note that an 'expressive performance'—one that is performed *espressivo*—is a performance that emphasizes expressive gestures.[55] As we have seen, there can be expressive gestures in painting, as in the works of Delacroix, Munch, and Pollock. There can also be expressive performances of music, both vocal and instrumental, as well as expressive performances in film and theatre. But perhaps the clearest examples of expressiveness in this sense occur in dance, in which bodily actions and gestures are themselves the main medium of expression.

Romantic Expression Regained

In what sense is the theory I have sketched a *Romantic* theory of expression in the spirit of the old Expression Theories? At the end of Ch. 8 I enumerated five important features of the Expression Theory. I believe that all five features are captured by my modern version of the theory.

1. First of all, a work of art is an expression only if it clarifies an emotion and brings it to consciousness. I have just tried to explain *how* a work can do this. It is important to note that in its primary sense the articulation of an emotion, as I have described it, is an intentional act: the artist must have *intended* to articulate an emotion in the way I have described. This does not mean that he intends to express a particular emotion that he can detail ahead of time, but that his enterprise in writing the poem or painting the picture is in part an enterprise of expression, of expressing the emotions of a persona, whether his own or that of a character or other persona in or behind the work. According to my second definition, however, of expression in a *work* rather than an artist, a work of art can articulate an emotion even if the artist did not think of himself as articulating or expressing anything.

2. The emotion and its expression come into existence together. In my theory, as in the Expression Theory of old, it is in the articulation of the emotion that the emotion itself is identified: a specific point of view (based on some specific interests or desires), that is represented in a poem or painting, constitutes the point of view that characterizes a specific emotion when the artist reflects upon it and 'recollects it in tranquility'. A dance piece consists of a set of behaviours that identifies an emotion by the exact nature of the behavioural tendencies, motor activity, and expressive gestures that it includes. Hence it is only after the poem, the painting or the dance has been finished that artist and audience alike can grasp exactly what emotion

has been expressed. The gestures in dance or music are often simplified and exaggerated, as if to abstract the essence of the expressive gesture in a purified form. (Of course such gestures are often formally pleasing as well as expressive.)

3. Writing a poem, painting a picture, and so on is not just a matter of learning a skill but of creating an original vision. In some cases the vision is what we see on the canvas or what we read in the poem: Friedrich's vision of a spiritualized landscape, or Keats's vision of a timeless world of art and beauty. These are original visions and they are expressions of new and unique emotional states. Sometimes the vision is the original sequence of tones or dance movements, which articulate an emotional state by analogy with action tendencies and vocal and other bodily gestures. Again, the exact sequence of dance movements gives us a vision of young love (*Romeo and Juliet*), or Giselle's despair at her betrayal, or primitive religious ecstasy (*The Rite of Spring*). Nobody can be taught how to express emotions in this way: it is a matter of trial and error and of recognizing when one has achieved an expression.

4. The Expression Theorists insist that the audience does not just perceive what is expressed but recreates the emotion expressed in their imagination. I have suggested how the audience comes to understand a work of art that is an expression. They learn to see the world through the eyes of the persona and consequently to feel some of the feelings that a person in that emotional state is likely to have. Those who learn to look at nature as Friedrich shows it to us will feel a change from their normal orientation to the world. In the *Large Enclosure at Dresden* the convexity of the world appears to reach out to embrace the viewer, as though he or she had become part of that world. We don't just see this; we feel it. Similarly, Keats gives us such a moment by moment account of the way he (or his persona) experiences the song of the nightingale, the thoughts and memories it evokes, the moods it induces, the desires it kindles, that we too are able to experience it in somewhat the same way. As we'll see later, these effects are probably most powerful in music.

5. Expression is a means to knowledge. The artist learns about the emotion expressed and so does the audience in recreating it for themselves. This is a kind of cognitive monitoring of the emotion. How then does the artist 'coming to know' about an emotion differ

from the psychologist or the philosopher? The difference is this. Both philosophers and psychologists in their different ways *generalize* about emotions. Philosophers do folk psychology, attempting to come up with descriptions or generalizations about what emotions are in general, or what love or shame are in general. Psychologists also deal in descriptions, but in a more empirically oriented way. They ask particular subjects how they felt in thus and so situations, or what they think the difference is between shame and guilt. Only the artist individuates and articulates emotions in such a way that we begin to understand what it is like to be in the emotional state expressed. The emotions Keats articulates in his 'Ode' are complex and unique to the Ode. I can describe it as a feeling of longing and I can say roughly what the longing is about, but that is a summary judgement in generalized folk-psychological terms. What Keats conveys in his poem is a sequence of thoughts, wishes, images, and points of view that characterizes his shifting emotional experience in such a way that we can to some extent share it. The rhythm, onomatopoeia, imagery, and so on that he uses help us to feel and thus to grasp what he is trying to express.

Expression and the Recreation of Emotion in an Audience

If an artistic expression of emotion is successful, it is expressive. And this means that it enables audiences to feel something of what it's like to be in the emotional state articulated in the work of art. Significantly, part of the Romantic conception of expression is that our responses to expressive works are themselves *emotional*: it is through having our emotions evoked that we come to understand what has been expressed in the work. In reading Keats's 'Ode to a Nightingale', we can discover something of what it is like to long for a timeless world of art and beauty: we have some idea of the point of view that the dramatic speaker articulates and—through the rhythm and imagery and so on—some idea of the bodily movements and feelings characteristic of this state of longing. In looking at Friedrich's landscapes, we get an idea of the emotional point of view of the painter and the bodily feelings he experiences as he contemplates Nature.

When watching a dance piece (assuming we are not participants), we engage in motor activity and autonomic activity that communicates even more directly what is being expressed: we can really feel what the dancers are expressing on stage. Of course our own bodily activity is to some degree suppressed. Our muscles may tense, our blood may race, and we may feel as if we are extending our arms and flexing our legs, but all the time we are sitting decorously in the theatre. However, because dance evokes bodily responses in us, we get a keen sense of what it *feels like* to be proud and resentful or in the throes of young love or stricken with grief or rage.[56] In Ch. 3 I noted that inducing certain bodily changes characteristic of a (basic) emotion induces other bodily symptoms of the emotion as well as self-reports that one is in that emotional state. One of the most remarkable features of dance is that it is a *bodily* art that is capable not only of articulating emotion by means of postures, action tendencies, and expressive bodily gestures, but also of inducing bodily states in audiences.

A good criterion for the successful communication of an emotion in an artistic expression is that it produces an appropriate emotional response on the part of the spectator, listener, or reader.[57] As I have stressed throughout this book, emotions are interactions between persons (or other organisms) and their environment. An emotional response is a physiological response to something that is affectively appraised as something significant in some way to the survival and well-being of me or mine. One of the most significant aspects of the environment from the point of view of survival and well-being is the emotional reactions of conspecifics. All normal folk are born with the ability to read faces and voices and gestures and to respond emotionally (as the result of fast, automatic affective appraisals) to what they find there. As with any emotional response to a stimulus affectively appraised as significant to me or mine, my bodily response to an expression will alert me to its significance. Paradigm works of Romantic expression have been carefully constructed so as to articulate the emotion expressed and to encourage the audience to respond emotionally to it in order to understand what is being expressed. My gut reaction gives me a clue about what is being expressed but I am also encouraged to monitor cognitively and reflect upon my reaction. In short, an emotional expression will evoke emotion in those who observe or hear or feel it *because of what it signifies about the emotional state of the person expressing the emotion.* And in the standard case of emotional expression in art as in real life, *the response to expression is itself emotional.*

We saw in earlier chapters how an appropriate emotional reaction to Edith Wharton's *The Reef* can help us understand the novel and learn from it about life. In the chapters on expression I have emphasized lyric poetry rather than the novel, since lyric poetry is the natural home for the concept of expression. However, the sorts of realistic novel I discussed in earlier chapters are also in many ways illustrative of Romantic ideas. In *The Reef* Edith Wharton only occasionally intrudes her own voice, and although her attitudes guide the story, the people whose emotions are most vividly expressed are the characters Anna and Darrow. Just as we need to have our emotions evoked in order to understand Anna and Darrow and *The Reef* in general, so we need to respond emotionally to any work that is an expression in the Romantic sense I have defined. It is possible to regard Friedrich's *Large Enclosure at Dresden* as just a pretty picture of an empty German landscape. But it is also a highly expressive work, one that both expresses Friedrich's emotions, and makes us feel what it is like to have those emotions. Delacroix's *Arab Horseman attacked by a Lion* expresses the violent emotions of its protagonists as well as Delacroix's own excitement, and the visceral effect the painting can have on viewers helps them to detect the violent feelings it expresses.

Finally, one question I have left unanswered is the question of how exactly we should think of 'expressive qualities' now that we have a better understanding of what expression is. In Ch. 8, I argued that it was wrong to equate expressive qualities with qualities that are named by emotion words, such as 'happy' and 'sad'. A sad poem is simply a poem that has some connection or other with sadness, and this connection, as Sparshott wisely notes, is 'sometimes of one sort, sometimes of another sort and most often of no definite sort at all'.[58] I would like to suggest that we should confine the term 'expressive quality' to those qualities in an artwork (or other things, such as merry brooks and anguished old oak trees) that are not only named by an emotion word but also arouse appropriate emotions. More particularly, *expressive qualities* are *qualities that can be grasped through the emotions that they arouse.* A 'sad poem' that is inexpressive—that does not have the expressive quality of sadness—may not arouse emotion at all or it may evoke emotions irrelevant to its sadness. My sad poem in Ch. 8 about my desire for a little loving dog is meant, if anything, to make you laugh.[59] If a sad poem like my dog doggerel makes you laugh, this reaction does not alert you to any sadness in the poem; it draws your attention instead to its comic ineptitude (assuming you have a generous sense of humour). The contrast with a poem such as Coleridge's 'Dejection: An Ode' is like night and day. Coleridge's poem is a genuine Romantic expression of melancholy in a persona (indeed in Coleridge himself), and it gets readers to feel what it is like to be melancholy in the precise way expressed by the poem. But it is also reasonable to say that the poem has the *expressive quality* of melancholy. In other words, in addition to being a melancholy poem, it also induces certain emotions—melancholy, wistfulness, and so on—in those who read it with understanding, and furthermore, it may very well be through the melancholy and wistfulness it induces that the reader is alerted to the melancholy in the poem.

This is not to say that expressive qualities in artworks simply *are* qualities that arouse corresponding emotions[60] in audiences, only that (I am suggesting) a good criterion for what should count as *expressive qualities* is that they evoke corresponding emotions in audiences and that these emotions can alert audiences to the expressive qualities in the work. Similarly, the Romantic expression of emotion in artworks is not *the same thing* as the arousal of emotion in audiences. However, a good criterion of successful artistic expression is that it arouses appropriate emotions in audiences. To borrow Coleridge's words in the Dejection Ode, the hope of genuine expression for both artist and audience is 'from outward forms to win | The passion and the life, whose fountains are within'.

The art that in many ways succeeds best in communicating emotions in this way is the art of music, to which the rest of this book is devoted.

Part Four

Music and the Emotions

Part Four is devoted to music. Chapters 10 and 11 are about musical expression, and Chs. 12 and 13 are about the arousal of emotions by music.

In Ch. 10 I show how in many ways song—more especially the Romantic *lied*—is the quintessential art of Romantic expression. For the past hundred years or so music theory has been dominated by a formalistic aesthetic that has tended to denigrate the importance of emotion in music. For the contemporary descendants of this line of thinking, expression in music is simply an *appearance* worn by music, much as the sad face of the St Bernard or basset-hound is an appearance that has nothing to do with the expression of any actual emotion the dog might be feeling. But in fact, contrary to what the doggy theory asserts, some Romantic music is an expression of emotion in the full Romantic sense I outlined in Ch. 9. In particular many Romantic lieder express the emotions of their dramatic protagonists. Music, like emotion, is a process, and so it is peculiarly well suited to express not only particular emotional states but also blends of emotion, conflicts between emotions, ambiguous emotions, and the way one emotion transforms into another. I illustrate these themes with a reading of Brahms's lied, 'Immer leiser wird mein Schlummer'.

In Ch. 11 I argue that in Romantic instrumental music it is often appropriate to posit a persona in the music, whether this is a persona of the composer or a character created by the composer to play a role in a kind of wordless drama. On this assumption it turns out that some 'pure' instrumental music is also an expression of emotion in the full Romantic sense. Instrumental music can express emotions in just the same way as 'Immer leiser'. I illustrate this idea with a reading of Brahms's Intermezzo Op. 117 No. 2.

Chapters 12 and 13 are about the arousal of emotions by music. In Ch. 12 I argue that some of the emotions aroused by music can play an important role in helping us to understand it—both its structure and what it expresses. This chapter parallels Ch. 4 where I made a comparable argument about literature. I use some results from the psychology of music to help make my case.

The final substantive chapter is Ch. 13 and it deals with the vexed question of *how* music can arouse emotions at all. According to the popular 'judgement theory' of emotion, it is completely incomprehensible how music can evoke emotions, with the exception of those emotions that appear to be based on some judgement about the music. I show that there are multiple ways in which music arouses emotions. In particular, music, more than any of the other arts, has a powerful effect on our physiology. Music arouses mood states from which we readily enter into emotional states. Once in a suitable bodily state, we *label* it with a tag from the folk psychology of emotion. This mechanism of emotional arousal by music also explains the powerful quasi-religious effects that some people attribute to it. It also lends support to the theory of emotion with which I began in Part One.

10

Emotional Expression in Music

> ... all nuances of cheerfulness and serenity, the sallies, moods and
> jubilations of the soul, the degrees of anxiety, misery, mourning,
> lament, sorrow, grief, longing etc., and lastly of awe, worship,
> love, etc., become the peculiar sphere of musical expression.
>
> G. W. F. Hegel, *Aesthetics: Lectures on Fine Art*

The Hanslick Legacy

The modern discussion of the expression of emotion in music really
begins with Eduard Hanslick, Richard Wagner's arch-enemy, who in
1854 published his *Vom Musikalisch-Schönen* (*On the Musically Beautiful*), a polemical tract which argued that the beautiful in music consists
solely in beautiful musical forms, especially melodies, and that we
should resist the idea that music is *about* or *represents* human feelings.
The content of music is 'tönend bewegte Formen' glossed by Payzant
as 'forms dynamically related, the relationships being those inherent
in the diatonic (i.e. tonal) musical system'.[1] The 'content of music,
that which musical art presents in its works'[2] is not feelings, but music
itself.

Hanslick anticipates the judgement theory of emotion, arguing
that music cannot express or represent 'definite feelings', because it
cannot represent the 'specific representations or concepts' that define
particular emotions.

The feeling of hope cannot be separated from the representation of a future
happy state which we compare with the present; melancholy compares past
happiness with the present. These are entirely specific representations or

concepts. Without them, without this cognitive apparatus, we cannot call the actual feeling 'hope' or 'melancholy;' ... If we take this away, all that remains is an unspecific stirring, perhaps the awareness of a general state of well-being or distress.[3]

Similarly, the specific emotion of love cannot be represented without 'the representation of the beloved person, without desire and striving after felicity, glorification and possession of a particular object', in short, without specific thoughts, wishes, and appraisals.

Music can represent only the dynamic aspect of feelings. [Love's] dynamic can appear as readily gentle as stormy, as readily joyful as sorrowful, and yet still be love. This consideration by itself suffices to show that music can only express the various accompanying adjectives and never the substantive, e.g., love itself.[4]

Music can represent ideas 'which relate to audible changes in strength, motion, and proportion; and consequently they include our ideas of increasing and diminishing, acceleration and deceleration, clever interweavings, simple progressions, and the like'.[5] But this is not enough to represent emotions themselves.

Not surprisingly Hanslick also denies that music can express the emotions of the composer. 'We can say of any theme at all that it sounds noble or sad or whatever. We cannot say, however, that it is an expression of the noble or sad feelings of the composer.'[6] Yet, in his own music criticism Hanslick sometimes *sounds* as if he is doing just that. Here, for example, is a very flowery description of the first movement of Schubert's then recently discovered 'Unfinished Symphony'.

When, after the first few introductory measures, clarinet and oboe in unison began their gentle cantilena above the calm murmur of the violins, every child recognized the composer, and a muffled 'Schubert' was whispered in the audience. He had hardly entered, but it seemed that one recognized him by his step, by his way of opening the door. And when, after this nostalgic cantilena in the minor, there followed the contrasting G major theme of the violon–cellos, a charming song of almost *Ländler*-like intimacy, every heart rejoiced, as if, after a long separation, the composer himself were among us in person. The whole movement is a melodic stream so crystal clear, despite its force and genius, that one can see every pebble on the bottom. And everywhere the same warmth, the same bright, life-giving sunshine![7]

Notice, however, that Hanslick is here talking always about the style of the music and the aesthetic qualities of the music: first he says that it is characteristically *Schubertian* music; next he describes it using adjectives such as 'charming', 'gentle', and 'nostalgic'; finally, he uses a metaphor to try and convey an important aesthetic quality in the music: its limpidity and warmth. Nowhere does he imply that the piece is *about* any of these things or that it expresses or represents anything about the inner life of the composer. He is not saying that the piece *portrays* nostalgia or that it *represents* pebbles on the bottom of a stream.

In short, Hanslick thinks that music cannot present or express emotions themselves, but only the dynamic aspects of emotion. Music can be accurately described as 'majestic, graceful, tender, dull, hackneyed', but all these expressions simply 'describe the musical character of the passage'. Just as we describe music by using terms from our emotional life, 'arrogant, peevish, tender, spirited, yearning', so we also 'take our descriptions from other realms of appearance ... and speak of fragrant, vernal, hazy, chilly music'.[8] The vocabulary of feelings is just one resource among others for the description of purely musical characteristics. Using an emotion vocabulary is harmless provided we do not think it implies that music portrays feelings.

Hanslick's argument has had a major influence on all subsequent theories of musical expression.[9] Susanne Langer agrees with almost everything Hanslick says except, crucially, that she thinks that representing the dynamic *aspects* of emotion is enough to represent *emotions*, at least in a general way. Peter Kivy and Stephen Davies have largely accepted Hanslick's conclusions but have argued that some emotions can be expressed without conveying any 'cognitive content', any wishes, thoughts, or appraisals. I myself think that music is the pre-eminent art of expression in the sense I described in Chs. 8 and 9. Consequently I think that Hanslick's ideas on expression must be rejected pretty much in their entirety. This chapter and the next present an extended defence of the view that music is the pre-eminent art of Romantic expression in the sense that I described in Chs. 8 and 9. In this chapter I criticize contemporary Hanslickians and illustrate what musical expression is capable of by illustrating with a Brahms lied, 'Immer leiser'. And in Ch. 11 I go on to apply these lessons to instrumental music. After that I take up the issue of whether and how the listener's own emotions are evoked when listening to music and what role the emotions might play in how we understand music.

The Expression of Inner Emotional Development: Susanne Langer

Susanne Langer differs fundamentally from Hanslick in that she thinks that music is *about* feelings. Music gives us a '*formulation and representation* of emotions, moods, mental tensions and resolutions—a "logical picture" of sentient, responsive life, a source of insight, not a plea for sympathy'.[10] But although she sounds as if she is diametrically opposed to Hanslick, the reason why she thinks that music functions as a 'language of feeling'[11] is that she believes that music is a special non-discursive kind of symbolism that symbolizes or represents in virtue of structural similarities between the symbol and what it symbolizes, in this case, music and feelings. And the similarity of structure that Langer sees between music and feelings is precisely the similarity that Hanslick noted, namely the similarity between music and 'certain dynamic patterns of human experience'.[12] '[T]here are certain aspects of the so-called 'inner life'—physical or mental—which have formal properties similar to those of music—patterns of motion and rest, of tension and release, of agreement and disagreement, preparation, fulfillment, excitation, sudden change, etc.'[13] She thinks this is sufficient to establish that music is a symbolism that imparts knowledge and insight into the life of feeling. By sharing their dynamic structure, music reveals 'the rationale of feelings, the rhythm and pattern of their rise and decline and intertwining'.[14] Moreover, music has a special cognitive role, she thinks, because the forms it articulates are forms '*which language cannot set forth*'.[15] 'Because the forms of human feeling are much more congruent with musical forms than with the forms of language, music can *reveal* the nature of feelings with a detail and truth that language cannot approach.'[16]

Langer thinks that music cannot represent specific emotions but only '*the morphology of feeling*',[17] since—as Hanslick points out—very different emotions, such as joy and sadness, may have a similar morphology: there can be intense joy and intense sadness, calm joy and calm sadness, turbulent joy and turbulent sadness. But Langer sees it as an advantage to music that it can represent only 'the forms of human feeling'.[18] 'The real power of music lies in the fact that it can be 'true' to the life of feeling in a way that language cannot; for its significant forms have that *ambivalence* of content which words cannot have.'[19] Because Langer thinks that music articulates the dynamics of our inner life, she pays attention to the way in which music 'reveals' not just isolated emotions of this or that sort, but the way that our inner life unfolds over time. Music 'can have not only a content, but a transient play of contents.'[20] In short, Langer thinks that musical expression is ambiguous, not expressing any specific emotions that can be named or articulated in language but representing how our emotional life develops over time. What music gives us is, 'in very naive phrase, a knowledge of "how feelings go"'.[21]

Some of Langer's ideas must be rejected but others are very valuable. The idea that symbolism in general requires isomorphism of structure between a symbol and what it symbolizes has not been taken seriously since Wittgenstein's *Tractatus*. One of the earliest reviews of Langer's *Philosophy in a New Key* by Ernest Nagel takes her to task on this very point.[22] Nevertheless, although symbolism in general does not work this way, it may well be true that musical expression works this way, i.e. that music expresses emotional life by mirroring its dynamic structure in some sense.

Secondly, Langer thinks that music is not an art of self-expression because self-expression '*requires no artistic form*', but her examples of self-expression—'a lynching-party howling round the gallows-tree, a woman wringing her hands over a sick child, a lover who has just rescued his sweetheart in an accident and stands trembling, sweating, and perhaps laughing or crying with emotion'[23]—make it clear that she is talking about the betrayal of emotion, not expression in the Romantic sense I laid out in previous chapters. Her claim that music reveals and thereby gives us knowledge of human feeling is consistent with my view that Romantic expression consists in reflection upon or cognitive monitoring of an emotional experience and not just the betrayal of emotion.

Thirdly, when Langer says that only the 'dynamic aspects' of emotional experience can be conveyed by music, it is unclear exactly what she means, but if it is that music reveals the way emotions change and develop, then music does indeed accomplish this very beautifully, as we shall see. It is an important and valuable observation that music reflects emotional *processes*, not just states such as sadness and joy, and the way emotions shift and are modified over time. On the other hand, we can often give at least a rough approximation of the particular emotions involved. A song moves from sorrow to acceptance, or from hope to despair. Music can express particular nameable emotions, not just the 'movement' of emotions. At the same time, it is unlikely that the description 'It moves from sorrow to acceptance' is an adequate 'paraphrase' of what a piece of music expresses. In this sense, Langer is right to say that what is expressed cannot be named in words.

The Doggy Theory of Musical Expressiveness

Peter Kivy

The most widely accepted theory of musical expressiveness today is probably Peter Kivy's. In his celebrated book, *The Corded Shell*, Kivy argues that to hear music as expressive is in the first instance to anthropomorphize or 'animate' the music: 'we must hear an aural pattern as a vehicle of expression—an utterance or a gesture—before we can hear *its* expressiveness in it'.[24] Kivy takes as his chief exemplar of expressiveness the face of the St Bernard dog in which, because of our tendency to animate our surroundings, we naturally see sadness, just as we naturally hear sadness in certain expressive 'contours' in music. Following Tormey, Kivy maintains that music can be *expressive of* an emotion without being an *expression of* anyone's emotion, just as the St Bernard's face is expressive of sadness without being an expression of its own sadness: he just happens to look that way. Music is expressive 'in virtue of its resemblance to expressive human utterance and behavior'.[25]

Sometimes music mimics expressive human *utterance*. The musical line at the beginning of *Arianna's Lament* from Monteverdi's *Arianna* is 'a kind of musical icon'[26]—a weeping figure—that resembles the passionate speaking voice expressive of grief. And in Handel's *Messiah* the opening phrase of the soprano solo 'Rejoice Greatly' 'resembles the voice rising in joy'.[27] Sometimes music mimics expressive human *gestures* and *bodily movements*. Kivy contrasts the 'Pleni sunt Coeli' from Bach's *Mass in B Minor* which is said to express 'exuberant' or 'leaping' joy with Handel's 'I know that my Redeemer liveth' from *Messiah* to which he attributes a 'confident but more subdued joy'.[28] He ascribes the difference to the fact that the Bach passage 'maps' bodily motion and gesture 'of tremendous expansiveness, vigor, violent motion', whereas the Handel passage 'suggests, rather, a dignified public declaration of faith: a speaker firm, confident, stepping forward, gesturing expressively, but with a certain circumspection'.[29] In both cases what is 'mapped' by the motion of the music are bodily gestures that in a human being would be expressive of the states indicated.

Not all expressiveness in music can be explained in terms of the resemblance between musical 'contours' and expressive human speech and behaviour. Kivy augments his account of musical expressiveness by allowing that some musical phrases, melodies, rhythms, and so on are 'a function, simply, of the customary associations of certain musical features with certain emotive ones, quite apart from any structural analogy between them'.[30] Thus there is no resemblance between the minor key and a sad human voice or posture; there is only a *conventional* connection between the minor key and the negative emotions.[31] Kivy christens his theory the 'contour and convention theory' of musical expressiveness: a musical phrase can be expressive of sadness (say) either because it has the contour of human speech or behaviour that is expressive of sadness or because it is conventionally linked to sadness in our culture.

In a later book, *Music Alone*, Kivy argues that not all emotions can be expressed by 'pure' instrumental music, only 'garden variety emotions, fear, grief, joy, and the like',[32] which have '*standard* behavioral responses'[33] and which do not have to have 'intentional objects'.[34] Music can be expressive of joy, for example, because one can be joyful without being joyful *about* something in particular, and because joy has a standard *behavioural expression* that can be mimicked by energetic, 'expansive' music.[35] By contrast, cognitively complex emotions,[36] such as pride and respect, always require 'objects'.[37] The only way such an emotion could be expressed by music would be if it were 'capable of expression in broad accent or gesture' and is 'customarily . . . so expressed'.[38] Thus pomposity (which he claims— implausibly—is an emotion) has a standard behavioural expression of strutting and posturing and since musical gestures can also strut and posture, music can express pomposity. By contrast, to a suggestion that the opening of Elgar's First Symphony is expressive of 'the pride of an imperial race at the apex of its power',[39] Kivy replies that it cannot be *expressive* of pride, since there is no standard behavioural manifestation of pride and hence pride cannot be heard as 'part of the aesthetic or musical fabric', but could be perceived in the music only by 'someone acquainted with the composer and his social milieu'.[40]

Kivy stresses that his theory is a theory about musical 'expressiveness', not musical 'expression',[41] and like Tormey, he thinks that 'expressiveness' can be explained perfectly adequately in terms of 'expressive properties'. Unlike facts about what, if anything, the composer is expressing in his work, which we have to go 'outside' the work to discover, expressive properties are part of the musical structure itself, and their function is 'to be musically exploited, musically developed, musically played with, musically built with and built upon, along with the rest of the musical qualities [they] may be in company with'.[42] In other words expressiveness is an aspect of the *form* of a piece of music and can therefore be appreciated with a clear conscience.

Problems with Kivy's Version of the Doggy Theory

Like Langer's theory, Kivy's theory of expressiveness contains some valuable observations, especially about the grounds of musical expressiveness. It is true that we sometimes hear musical gestures as expressive of particular emotions based on their resemblance to expressions of emotion in ordinary life, whether vocal or behavioural. And it is true that there are cultural conventions underlying much musical expressiveness. On the other hand, there is a lot that the theory fails to explain.

It has often been remarked that Kivy's examples in *The Corded Shell* are mostly examples of music with words, whereas he is supposed to be giving us a general theory that will apply also to 'pure' instrumental music.[43] Moreover, he sticks to a narrow range of examples of emotion—mostly varieties of joy, sorrow, calm, and restlessness, and claims that only somewhat general emotions can be expressed.[44] If music has to express emotions by mimicking expressive gestures, then this is not a surprising claim. Many people, however, agree with Langer that one of the marks of musical expressiveness is its subtlety, its capacity to express emotions that cannot be named in language.

Again, all Kivy's examples in *The Corded Shell* are of short phrases. Even when in *Music Alone* he gives a longer example of expressiveness from the final movement of Brahms's First Symphony and notes that there is a succession of different 'expressive properties,' he does not focus on the way one transforms into another or why such transformations might be psychologically as well as musically satisfying. But if Langer is right, music expresses subtle changes and modifications in our emotional life. Kivy's theory ignores or underemphasizes the way in which musical expressiveness is a function of musical *process*, of the way in which themes interact, harmonies modulate, rhythms transform, etc.[45] This is particularly true of his discussion of harmony. Kivy restricts himself to saying that conventionally the minor key signifies negative emotions and the major key positive emotions. But expressiveness is typically the result not of the effect of a single key, but of a changing sequence of keys or key areas. In the Brahms song I discuss shortly, there is an interplay between references to E minor and to E major, before the song reverts to the tonic C sharp minor, and at the end there is a magical transformation from C sharp minor to D flat major. There is nothing in Kivy's theory to explain why there should be any change in feeling between two different major keys or two different minor keys, or why there is anything special about the particular key change at the end of the piece.

Kivy implicitly denies that there is any such thing as musical expression in the Romantic sense I explicated in Chs. 8 and 9. In his view we call music 'expressive' not because composers are expressing anything in it, but because listeners hear it as expressive: they 'animate' or 'anthropomorphize' what they hear. The composer's job is to provide musical gestures that can be readily animated in this way. But as I argued earlier, that is not normally what expressing an emotion means. Expressiveness is not primarily something perceived by perceivers. The only reason people perceive weeping as expressive of melancholy is that it *is* normally an expression (or, more correctly, a betrayal) of melancholy. Similarly, when a composer expresses some emotion in his music, it is primarily something that he *does* or that he makes it *appear* that he does. In this respect the doggy theory is profoundly misleading: the St Bernard's expression simply doesn't play any comparable role in its psychology.

The St Bernard's face is said to be expressive of melancholy because that's how it is perceived by human observers. It has nothing to do with its actual inner psychological states. By analogy, Kivy analyses expressiveness in music as something perceptible by human perceivers, who have a tendency to anthropomorphize their surroundings, including their pets: human beings *animate* the doggy face and they *animate* music.[46] The weeping figure in Arianna's Lament is heard as melancholy because it sounds like weeping, just as the drooping jowls of the St Bernard are expressive of melancholy because they look like a melancholy human face. For Kivy expressiveness is a surface phenomenon, a matter of how something looks or sounds.

But expression is not just a matter of appearances: a melancholy human face is perceived as such because it is usually the result of melancholy. Moreover, human facial and vocal expressions are not just signs of emotion but contribute to the emotion process itself. As we saw in Ch. 2, the deliberate expression of a basic emotion such as joy or sadness can induce physiological changes corresponding to the emotion expressed. Facial expressions and motor activity can themselves result in affective appraisals and cognitive changes.

Finally, Kivy's defence of the idea that 'music alone' cannot express such emotions as pride or neuroticism on the grounds that these states cannot be heard as 'part of the aesthetic or musical fabric' relies on a narrowly formalist conception of what 'the musical fabric' is. The whole notion of what is 'in' a work of art is deeply problematic, and depends upon the conception of the work that a listener brings to it. If we think of the work as nothing but a structure of musical forms, and expression as nothing but the possession of expressive properties, then perhaps it is indeed inappropriate to find pride or neuroticism in a work of music, but, as we will see, there are other models of musical interpretation that permit us to find all kinds of things 'in' the work, including the expression of cognitively complex emotions such as pride. In particular if it reasonable to find a *persona* 'in' the work, then we can hear in it all the emotions—simple and complex—that the persona expresses in it. In Ch. 11 I will talk about this possibility in more detail.

Stephen Davies

In his book *Musical Meaning and Expression* Stephen Davies develops a theory of musical expressiveness that is similar to Kivy's.[47] Like Kivy, Davies thinks that 'the expressiveness of music consists in its presenting emotion characteristics in its appearance',[48] and like Kivy, he illustrates the point by reference to a sad doggy face, in his case the basset-hound. Davies thinks that emotion words such as 'sad' or 'nostalgic' have a primary usage in which they refer to emotional experiences, but they also have a secondary use in which they refer to the 'look' of a person. 'Emotion characteristics are attributed to the appearances people present and not, as is true of emotions, to the people themselves. It is faces and the like that are sad-looking. Faces do not feel emotions and do not think thoughts; they are nonsentient.'[49] Musical expressiveness depends partly on similarities between music and the passionate speaking voice, but mostly on 'a resemblance we perceive between the dynamic character of music and human movement, gait, bearing, or carriage'.[50] Davies also acknowledges that convention plays an important role in musical expressiveness: 'Naturally expressive elements are taken up within traditions of musical practice and style . . . that are highly conventionalized.'[51]

Davies makes a sharp distinction between emotions as *experiences* and emotion characteristics in appearances. Unlike experiences, 'the emotions expressed in music are not of the kind that depend on thoughts and, crucially, not of the kind that need be felt'.[52] This passage gives the unfortunate impression that there are two kinds of emotions, one that is felt and one that isn't. But, as we have seen, emotions are processes that usually involve both thoughts and expressions. To talk about expressions as though they were a different sort of thing altogether from felt emotions is misleading.[53]

Despite the similarities between Davies's and Kivy's theories, Davies goes beyond Kivy in some important respects. In particular,

1. Davies stresses that musical movement, 'like human action and behavior (and unlike random process) . . . displays order and purposiveness' and 'provides a sense of unity and purpose': 'We recognize in the progress of music a logic such that what follows arises naturally from without being determined by, what preceded; in this, musical movement is more akin to human action than to random movement or to the fully determined movements of a nonhuman mechanism.'[54]

2. Perhaps for this reason, Davies is much more optimistic than Kivy about the possibility of music's expressing cognitively complex emotions, such as 'hope, embarrassment, puzzlement, annoyance, and envy.' Davies 'suspects' that Kivy is right to regard 'higher' or cognitively complex emotions as lacking 'emotion characteristics in appearances', in so far as such emotions 'do not possess characteristic behavioral expressions inextricably bound to the propositional attitudes that mark them as the emotions they are'.[55] However, Davies thinks it might be possible for a piece of music to express hope, for example, if the emotion characteristics in a longish piece or passage of music were judiciously ordered. A natural progression of feelings might be conveyed by an appropriate sequence of emotional characteristics in appearances.

Such progressions might be used by the composer to articulate in his music emotions other than those that can be worn by appearances without regard to feelings. Thus, by judiciously ordering the emotion-characteristics presented in an extended musical work the composer can express in his music those emotional states not susceptible to presentation in mere appearances. . . . In this way hope, for example, may be expressed in music, although hope cannot be presented as the emotion-characteristic in an appearance. Thus the range of emotions that can be expressed in music . . . goes beyond the range of emotion-characteristics that can be worn by appearances. Nevertheless, the expression of such emotional states as hope in a musical work depends directly upon and is controlled by the emotion-characteristics in sound presented in the musical work. Before hope can be expressed in a musical work that work must have sufficient length and expressive complexity to permit the emotions presented in its 'appearance' to form a progression in which hope occurs naturally.[56]

Thus, 'just as music might present the characteristic of an emotion in its aural appearance, so too it might present the appearance of a pattern of feelings through the order of its expressive development'.[57]

3. Davies attacks Kivy for insisting that music is never *about* anything and is therefore not about emotions. After all, the faces of basset hounds and St Bernards do not *mean* anything. They are just God's gift to basset hounds and St Bernards. However, in Davies's view, music 'does not merely present emotion; it "comments" or may "comment," on the expressions so expressed'. Composers intentionally choose 'sounds with one expressive potential rather than another' and this suggests that 'it is not inappropriate that we find significance in the appropriations that occur'.[58] Composers have 'much more to 'say' about emotions than those emotions have to 'say' about themselves under standard conditions'.[59]

Limitations of the Doggy Theory

Much of what Davies wants to say about musical expression seems to me to be exactly right: (1) yes, music can convey 'a pattern of feelings', and 'a sense of order and purposiveness',[60] not just particular feelings such as sadness and joy; (2) yes, music can express some cognitively complex emotions; (3) yes, music is sometimes *about* the emotions it expresses. Unfortunately, these conclusions are inconsistent with the doggy theory.

  1. If musical expressiveness is solely a matter of emotion characteristics in appearances, then the only way in which it can convey 'a pattern of feelings' is by presenting one emotion appearance after another, for example, gloom followed by joy followed by more gloom, and ending in tranquility. But a sequence of this sort hardly substantiates the claim that music conveys a sense of order and purposiveness, since there is no organic connection between one state and the next, and so no *development* from one state to the next: the states are simply concatenated. This is insufficient to warrant talk of a teleological quality in musical expressiveness.

  2. A similar problem besets the idea that emotion characteristics in appearances can convey cognitively complex emotions. Davies suggests that progressions of this sort 'might be used by the composer to articulate in his music emotions other than those that can be worn by appearances without regard to feelings',[61] in particular, cognitively

complex emotions such as hope. Thus although hope 'cannot be presented as the emotion-characteristic in an appearance', maybe it can be expressed in music by the joy in the sequence of 'feelings' outlined in my example above. But again Davies is claiming more than his view allows. There is no 'progression in which hope occurs naturally',[62] as Davies claims. Perhaps hope usually occurs after a blow, and so after sadness, but hope may lead to despair or steadfast joy or anxiety or any number of other states. Furthermore, even if we grant that hope 'naturally' occurs in a particular sequence of states (perhaps, sadness, anxiety, transient joy?), there will be no way to tell the difference between cheerfulness and hope if all we have to go by is a sequence of emotion characteristics in appearances. Hope requires the expression of desires and thoughts.[63] Merely coming after sadness and before tranquility, for example, isn't enough to distinguish hope from transient joy or a fit of ebullience or from the representation of some non-emotional event such as a break in the clouds or the arrival of a long-lost friend.

3. I think Davies is right to say that music can be about emotions and that composers can 'comment' on and 'say' things about emotions in their works, but, again, Davies's theory does not allow him to say this. There is no way that emotion characteristics in appearances can *say* anything and even though a composer can arrange emotion characteristics in appearances in interesting sequences, that's all they are: interesting sequences. Without connections between one emotional state and another, nothing much can be 'said'.

In a more recent paper, Davies tries to answer the objection that his theory cannot 'avoid treating changes in the work's mood merely as a procession of unconnected expressions'.[64] He replies by saying that in some cases 'attention to the work's formal features is likely to be sufficient to explain its coherence and integrity if the work is one in which expressiveness is not the prime concern'.[65] This may be so, but the controversial cases are those where there does seem to be emotional development in the music and where we may need to hear the expressive or emotional progression in order to grasp the 'purely musical' progression. In these cases, where 'the expressive progress of the work is central to its character', Davies says that we can explain its 'unity and closure'—the sense of an inevitable expressive development—'as resulting from the composer's control of the material'.[66]

Because the expressive material is being 'shaped and ordered by the composer', it is therefore 'appropriate to look for a connection between [the expressive appearances] and for the possibility of reference through them to the world of human feeling'.[67]

This reply is inadequate. The problem is this: given that the music conveys a sense of emotional progression, what is it that is responsible for that sense, and what is the source of the emotional coherence of the piece? That it is composed by a human being is hardly an explanation. We need to know according to what principles the composer has shaped his material. Why is one sequence of emotion characteristics in appearances emotionally satisfying and not another? Simply to say that the composer orders them in a particular way does not explain anything.

In summary, there are several fundamental problems with the doggy theory. To begin with, the theory does not recognize that music can express emotions in the full-blooded Romantic sense I outlined in Chs. 8 and 9. Another problem is that it assumes an impoverished theory of emotions, according to which there is no connection between the expression of emotion and the rest of an emotion process. The doggy theory does not pay adequate attention to what emotions are: there are not two kinds of emotion, inner feelings and outer expressions, but one complex process in which a non-cognitive appraisal can set off bodily processes that in turn influence our view of the world: the bodily processes and the view of the world are two aspects of the same phenomenon.

In my discussion of Davies, I have focused on three more particular problems with the theory. First, it does not account for the way music is able to express the organic development of emotional processes from one to another. Secondly, it does not explain how music can express or articulate cognitively complex emotions. And thirdly, it does not take account of how music can be *about* or comment on the emotions it expresses.

Before leaving the doggy theory, I would like to point out that in addition to denying or ignoring (1) the expression (in the sense of articulation) of particular emotions by a piece of music, the doggy theory does not adequately distinguish between (2) the possession of emotional qualities such as sadness and cheerfulness by music, and

(3) emotional *expressiveness* in music. The basset hound's face is indeed sad and it is sad because we see it as sad, and we see it as sad because it resembles human faces when they are sad. But a sad *expression* is not necessarily very *expressive*. If, as in one of Davies's examples, I work in a factory making tragic masks, I suppose I might get depressed, just as I might get depressed if I spend my days surrounded by basset hounds. But on the other hand—maybe there is something wrong with me— I suspect I would be more likely to find the situation humorous. There is something comical about the basset hound's sad face, after all: although it *looks* sad, it doesn't make me *feel* sad.[68] One good reason for this is that I am well aware that the dog's expression is not an expression of his sadness; it is merely a comical reminder of a sad human face. In short, although his face seems to be an expression of sadness, it is not very expressive. We can say much the same thing of the smiley face and its counterpart, the upside-down smiley face. The upside-down smiley face is clearly a sad expression, but it is not expressive and hence very unlikely to make anyone feel sad.

Kivy seems to be half aware of this distinction. He remarks in passing that Telemann wrote 'yards and yards of mournful music'[69] which is not *moving*. It is presumably mournful in Kivy's view because it resembles mournful human vocal or behavioural expressions and/ or because it has some of the conventional marks of musical mournfulness, but at the same time it is not *expressive*, and because it is not expressive it does not move me: it does not evoke any emotion in me. I will return later to the connection between musical expressiveness and how music causes listeners to *feel* as they listen.

Emotion as Process, Music as Process

In Ch. 3 I described how an emotional response is a physiological response to something important in the environment, the wonderful, the strange, the unexpected, the enemy, the friend, the loss, the threat, the offence, and so on. The emotional response is an automatic and immediate response that initiates motor and autonomic activity and prepares us for possible action. After the initial response cognition kicks in and corroborates or modifies our affective appraisal. And later still we may label our state with an emotion word from our folk psychology in an attempt to understand what has happened to us. The whole series of events is a *process* and each element in the process feeds back into it and affects its development.

One emotion process can thus *transform* into another as grief gives way to rage or fear to amusement. Moreover, many of these emotion processes are not easily nameable in terms of folk psychology: they are *blends* of different named emotions or they are *conflicts* between one named emotion and another, or they are *ambiguous* between one emotion label and another. As Phoebe Ellsworth says, our emotional life occurs in *streams*, which change all the time in response to ever-changing affective appraisals, ever-evolving thoughts, ever-changing actions and action tendencies, bodily states, and feelings. It is well-nigh impossible to capture accurately in language how these streams of experience flow along and interweave.

But if emotions are processes and if our emotional life occurs in streams, then it is reasonable to think that music, which is itself a process or a series of processes occurring in streams, would be peculiarly well-suited to mimic or mirror emotions. How exactly does it do this? Clearly there are some aspects of emotion—facial expressions, hormonal secretions—that music would be hard-put to reflect, but most of the important aspects of an emotion process can be mirrored by music.

The doggy theory suggests one way in which this might happen: music can mirror the vocal expressions and the motor activity—including expressive bodily gestures and action tendencies—that characterize particular emotions. Music can sigh and wail; it can freeze or frolic. It can creep menacingly or stride angrily. It can also mirror autonomic changes, as when an agitated or irregular rhythm mimics an agitated heart or irregular breathing.

More significantly, music can mirror the cognitive or evaluative aspects of emotion. Most obviously, there are many ways in which music can mirror *desire*, aspiration, or striving. A theme may struggle to achieve resolution, fail, try again, fail again, try a third time, and finally achieve closure. Or one theme may gradually and with apparent difficulty transform into another with a different character. Music can also mirror the effects of *memory*, as when a musical idea harks back to or seems to remember an earlier moment in the work either with nostalgia for a pleasanter past that has now vanished or with horror at a miserable past that threatens to return.[70] Finally, in addition to mirroring desire and memory, music can also mirror *evaluations* of the environment in that music can convey—very roughly— a sense that the world is a sunny place and that things are going well, or that the world is a gloomy, stormy, menacing place and that things are going badly.

Most importantly of all, music can mirror the streams of emotional experience: the many interrelated currents going on simultaneously, perhaps reinforcing one another, perhaps in conflict. Music can express the way one emotion morphs into another over time, how the stream turns in another direction or returns peaceably to its original channel. Music can convey changes and modifications in emotion, a sense that things are going from good to bad or from bad to good, a sense that desires are gratified or disappointed, a sense that memories have engulfed a person or been swept away. Music can also convey blends of emotion, a bittersweetness that is a blend of hope and resignation or sadness and nostalgia. It can convey emotional ambiguities—hope or wistfulness? serene resignation or leaden despair? It can convey emotional conflicts—between sexual passion and devotion to knightly duty, between the desire for pastoral innocence and the desire for glitzy urban life.[71]

It can achieve this through complex movements of harmony, melody, and rhythm. The mimicking of physiological or motor tendencies or vocal expressions can evolve and undergo modification: a cry of woe can transform into a scream of pain; a light-hearted frolicsome theme or rhythm can evolve into a heavy-hearted, plodding one. A theme that seems to hark back longingly to something in the past can change its character and become cheerful. A theme with melancholy minor harmony can transform into a related theme in a related major key. Music changes in chameleon-like ways, just like our emotional life.

This may all sound pretty implausible in the abstract. So I'd like to illustrate my suggestions by reference to a Brahms song, where we will be able to detect detailed interactions between what the protagonist is expressing in words and what she is expressing through musical means. Notice that the song is not just a sequence of emotional contours, but emanates from a protagonist who is in a genuine emotional state and is expressing that state in her musical utterance.

Then in the next chapter I will suggest that, given certain assumptions, pure instrumental music without words can also mirror emotional life in just the same ways. I choose Brahms for my examples partly because I am talking about Romantic expression in music, partly because I get a certain perverse satisfaction in illustrating my thesis with Hanslick's favourite exemplar of pure music, and partly because the pieces I discuss are personal favourites of mine.

Brahms's 'Immer leiser'

In the previous chapter we saw how in poetry the dramatic speaker of a poem expresses his emotions not only by showing how the world looks to him and articulating the thoughts that characterize his emotion but also by conveying in rhythm and tone of voice how the emotion expressed affects him physically. Dance, by contrast, expresses a character's emotions chiefly through gesture and action. Music, as Edward T. Cone puts it, is 'both poetry and dance',[72] expressing emotion through gesture and movement like dance, as well as through tone of voice and through the articulation of thoughts and points of view like poetry. For this reason song, especially Romantic song, is perhaps the quintessential form of Romantic artistic expression. In what follows I will try to make the case that Brahms's song 'Immer leiser' is a paradigm of Romantic expression in the sense I defined in Chs. 8 and 9.

'Immer leiser', the second of Brahms's Opus 105 set of songs, was written in 1886 for Hermine Spies, a young woman with whom Brahms had formed a romantic attachment. It is the song of a woman near death who longs for her lover to come to her once more before it is too late. The piece is for low voice and we can hear in the melody an echo of the lovely cello solo in the slow movement of Brahms's B flat Piano Concerto, which has something of the same quality: dark, poignant, yet ultimately serene. It is a simple two-stanza song with a beautiful haunting melody, but its greatness lies in the magical ways in which Brahms transforms the first stanza in his treatment of the second. Overall the transformation is from profound sorrow to something like serene acceptance, which is mirrored broadly in the harmonic development from C sharp minor to the parallel major. But

Fig. 10.1. Johannes Brahms, Op. 105 No. 2, 'Immer leiser wird mein Schlummer'

(*Continued*)

Fig. 10.1. *Continues*

(Continued)

Fig. 10.1. *Continues*

the transformation is accomplished without any sudden or jarring changes in tempo, rhythm, or melody, as though throughout the piece there is no great psychological or musical distance between the major and the minor, the sorrowful and the serene. Overall the piece has a bittersweet quality, which reflects the closeness between these two psychological and musical areas.

The opening melody has the quality of a lullaby or cradle-song. The gentle, dotted rhythm in the voice and the way the left hand of the piano follows slightly behind the melody lend it a tentative, halting quality. The tone of voice is mournful and weary, with repeated use of a 'sighing figure', the descending minor second. The woman tells how she often dreams of her lover calling her outside her door, but 'no-one wakes; no-one opens the door to you. I wake up and weep bitterly.' Melodically the first fourteen bars are permeated by descending minor thirds. Then in bars 15–20— at 'niemand wacht, und öffnet dir, ich erwach [und weine]'—the hitherto descending minor thirds move upward. But at the same time there is a stepwise descent from G♯ to G to F♯ to F to E in the middle voice of the right hand on the piano, and in the left hand there is a descent from D ♮ (bar 16) to C ♮ (bar 18) to B at the beginning of bar 20, so that the overall effect is not of soaring but of an effortful attempt to rise that is being resisted by sinking tendencies. By the time we reach the concluding phrases of the stanza in bars 21–4 the melodic line is once more falling, and by the end of the stanza it has descended despairingly (on the word 'bitterlich') to the tonic C sharp minor.

Harmonically, the first stanza stays mostly in C sharp minor, with poignant Brahmsian dissonances at 'Schleier', 'liegt', 'Kummer', and elsewhere, reinforcing the melancholy effect of the descending minor thirds. Similarly, in bars 10–14, there are dissonances on 'Traume', 'dich', and 'meiner'. The dissonance usually lasts only a moment but it is enough to be unsettling. As the melodic line rises to 'Tür' at the end of the phrase, we get a cadential E major root-position chord which for a moment gives a glimmer of hope. But in the succeeding bars, with the melody striving to rise on 'Niemand wacht und öffnet dir' but always weighed down, the piano makes a stepwise descent of six-four chords on G at 'wacht', on F at 'dir', and on 'wach' we get a six-four on E minor. At 'weine bitterlich' the melody rises as if in a cry of sorrow and despair, and the verse ends with a repeat of the words 'weine bitterlich' as a low moan descending to the tonic C sharp minor. This harmonic movement from a suggestion of E major to a suggestion of E minor and then a return to the tonic minor reinforces the effect of attempting to climb out of grief and despair only to sink back into it.

Rhythmically, the melodic line with its minor third descending phrases is set against a gently lilting syncopated piano accompaniment, reminiscent of a lullaby. In the section beginning 'Niemand wacht', arpeggios in the left hand of the piano work together with the vocal line and against the breathless, syncopated chords in the right hand of the piano. The effect, along with the harmonic changes, is to establish a troubled, uneasy feeling.

The second stanza seems at first to be simply a variation of the first. It begins with the melody in the upper voice of the piano, and the singer silent. Ivor Keys suggests that it is 'as though the singer can sing no more'.[73] Perhaps she is lost in remembrance or too overcome by grief to go on. When 'she finds the strength to join in the second phrase',[74] and enters with 'Ja, ich werde sterben müssen; eine Andre wirst du küssen' ('Yes, I will have to die; you will kiss another'), the effect is unutterably moving.[75] The melodic line moves into a lower register, forcing the singer (at least if she is a mezzo-soprano) to sing more softly, even a little hoarsely, as she contemplates her ageing and imminent death, which will come before the May breezes blow, before the thrush sings in the forest.

In the first part of the second stanza, there is a similar melodic line and the same pattern of descending minor thirds. Bars 37–41 exactly mirror bars 10–14, with the same gentle rise at the end of the phrase and the same E major root-position chord, this time on 'Wald'. But at this point there is a magical transformation of the first stanza. The minor thirds, which have been falling hitherto, instead rise, from G♯ to B on 'Willst du mich', from B to D♮ on 'noch einmal seh'n', and finally and triumphantly from D♮ to F♮ on 'komm', o kom-me.' At the same time Brahms moves from the root-position E major chord on 'Wald' to a six-four chord on G at 'mich', a six-four chord on B flat at 'seh'n', and then on 'komme' in bar 47, the climax of the piece, there is a six-four chord in D flat major, the enharmonic of C sharp major, which is the parallel major of the piece. Where in the previous verse we had a stepwise movement in the bass down from G to F to E, ending with a grief-stricken return to the tonic of C sharp minor, in the second verse there is stepwise ascent from E to G to B♭ in the piano, ending with a radiant transformation into D flat major with the soloist singing the highest note of the piece (reached with the maximum effort), a glorious F♮ at the top of the D flat major chord. C sharp minor and the flirtation with E minor are banished, as the protagonist expresses her hope that her lover might come again soon ('Komm', o komme bald'). After the impassioned climax the melody descends again, but this time into an area of calm and stability, and the song ends peacefully on a five-one cadence in D flat major, suggesting that the woman will now die in peace, whether or not her lover hears her plea. Macdonald refers to the 'other-worldly calm'[76] of the ending.

Throughout the song there is oscillation between major and minor, as if the protagonist is torn between acceptance and grief, between hope and despair. Some of the minor passages have an undercurrent of major and the major passages of minor. This Brahmsian ambiguity is what gives the piece its bittersweet quality, and what enables the protagonist to express ambiguity between sorrow and hope, yearning and acceptance.

In both the words and the music of 'Immer leiser' Brahms represents the woman expressing her emotions partly by mirroring the way the body moves under the influence of emotion, and partly by tone of voice, but most importantly by mirroring how she is thinking, how she evaluates her situation, and how it affects her deepest desires. We can hear her sinking feelings in the sinking minor thirds as she sings of her impending death, just as we hear her more hopeful feelings in the rising thirds at the end, as well as, of course, in the transformation from minor to major, in her cry of 'Come, come soon!' In short, we can hear the unfolding of her emotional state in the gradual development of melody, harmony, and rhythm.

When we hear 'Immer leiser' as an expression of emotion, as a passionate utterance, our experience of the music is organized in a particular way. Details of the music that might seem to be unrelated—such as a sighing figure, a syncopated rhythm, and a key change from tonic minor to parallel major—now fit into a coherent pattern. Once we hear 'Immer leiser' as an expression of the anguished emotions of a dying woman, then all these details come together as part of that expression: the sighing figure is heard as a sigh of misery (a vocal expression), a syncopated rhythm is heard as an agitated heart (autonomic activity), a change from tonic minor to parallel major is heard as a change of viewpoint (a cognitive evaluation) on the situation from unhappiness to happiness, or unease to serenity, and given the close connection between the two keys and the fact that the melody remains largely the same, we readily hear the evaluation as ambiguous or as shifting: the situation can be seen as both positive and negative. When we hear the bass descending and the melody rising, we may hear an effortful attempt to rise out of passivity—an action tendency—resisted by sinking tendencies or a tendency to abdicate from action, to give up trying. Overall we may hear the piece as moving from grief and anguish to serene resignation, all of which are cognitively complex emotions.[77]

This music is a genuine expression of emotion by the dramatic 'speaker' of the song, not just a series of expressive 'contours' or 'emotion characteristics in appearances'. It expresses emotion in many ways, corresponding to the various aspects of the emotion process.[78] The music itself consists of processes that mirror emotion processes. It conveys 'a pattern of feelings', and the 'sense of order and purposiveness' it conveys is due in large part to the overall expressive structure of the piece, from sorrow or anguish to serene acceptance or hope. What's more, the music expresses cognitively complex emotions. The emotions expressed are much more specific than mere sadness or joy. Finally, the song is *about* the emotions it expresses. Brahms himself is commenting on the emotions his protagonist expresses. We can hear the movement from sorrow to acceptance as something he sympathizes with and perhaps experiences vicariously. In short, the ways in which the song expresses the emotions of its protagonist are far more complex than anything permitted by the doggy theory.

To my mind 'Immer leiser' is a paradigm of Romantic expression. It is a short lyrical piece in which the protagonist is explicitly articulating in a number of different ways what her emotions are and how they change and develop.[79] However, in 'Immer leiser' we can connect the minor thirds with the girl's state of mind, because the words tell us that the girl is in a minor-thirdish state of mind. But without words, how can we tell what is being expressed in the music? Can a piece of pure instrumental music ever express emotion in the same or a similar way? Does it even make sense to give a psychological reading of a Brahms Intermezzo, for example? In the next chapter I shall argue that it does, that there are pieces of pure or absolute music that lend themselves to psychological interpretation, and that there are reasonable ways of engaging in such interpretation.[80] I do not think that *all* music in *all* styles is fruitfully to be considered in this way. But there are, I believe, many Romantic pieces that not only can but should be given a psychological interpretation, and that do not reveal all their meaning and profundity unless they are given such a reading.

11

The Expression of Emotion in Instrumental Music

music can only be understood in forms drawn from a relationship to life, or an expression of life ...

Richard Wagner, 'On Franz Liszt's Symphonic Poems'

Edward T. Cone and the Persona in Music

In his groundbreaking book, *The Composer's Voice*, Edward T. Cone
advocates the idea that instrumental music can be appropriately heard
as the expression of emotions in a musical 'persona'. Cone starts from
the premise that 'a basic act of dramatic impersonation' underlies all
poetry and literary fiction.[1] He then suggests that 'all music, like all
literature, is dramatic; that every composition is an utterance
depending on an act of impersonation which it is the duty of the
performer or performers to make clear'.[2] The point is easy to establish
in relation to vocal music. 'Immer leiser' is an utterance by a performer who is playing the role of a dying woman in a dramatic
monologue. A ballad is an utterance by the narrator of a story, with
perhaps dramatic interjections by the characters, as in Schubert's 'Der
Erlkönig'. Cone also applies his idea to programme music, arguing
that Berlioz's *Symphonie Fantastique* expresses the reactions of a persona to the sequence of events outlined in the programme for the
symphony. Like the narrator of a story, this persona expresses his
reactions through the 'characters' which appear in the symphony.
Characters are often individuated as instruments or groups of
instruments, but Cone thinks that they can be 'any recognizably

continuous or distinctively articulated component of the texture: a line, a succession of chords, an ostinato, a pervasive timbre'.[3]

Cone then generalizes this 'lesson from Berlioz' to pure instrumental music: 'In every case there is a musical persona that is the experiencing subject of the entire composition, in whose thought the play, or narrative, or reverie, takes place—whose inner life the music communicates by means of symbolic gesture.'[4]

Cone suggests that pure instrumental music is 'a form of utterance' emanating from musical personas or characters.

Qua poetry, a song is a kind of verbal utterance; qua music, its medium is the human voice, independent of verbal meaning—a vocal, symbolic, nonverbal utterance. Instrumental music, whether alone or accompanying the voice, goes one step further in the direction of abstraction from the word and constitutes a form of purely symbolic utterance, an utterance by analogy with song.[5]

Music is not, strictly speaking, a language, since linguistic utterances have conventional meanings that music does not aspire to—with the possible exception of national anthems and operatic or programmatic leitmotifs—but they do carry meaning by means of intonation, tone of voice, timbre, and so on. This is the 'gestural aspect' of utterance and it is this aspect that music simulates and symbolizes in Cone's view. 'The vocal utterance of song emphasizes, even exaggerates, the gestural potentialities of its words. Instrumental utterance, lacking intrinsic verbal content, goes so far as to constitute what might be called a medium of pure symbolic gesture.'[6] Here Cone anticipates the doggy theory in arguing that how music expresses is by musical gestures that simulate human expressive vocal and bodily gestures, but unlike the doggy theory, Cone thinks that the music does not get its expressiveness simply from individual gestures. He points out that the formal development of motifs, harmony, and rhythms, can mirror the psychological development of the 'characters' or agents in the music. It is the whole piece that functions as an utterance, not just the odd phrase here and there.

Cone argues that the expressive content of a musical gesture is 'humanly expressive content',[7] and it cannot be grasped unless we know the context in which it occurs. Just as an expressive gesture such as a sigh or a chuckle depends on its context to disambiguate its meaning, so the expressiveness of a musical sigh or chuckle is dependent on the words that provide its context. In 'Immer leiser' the words of the song tell us that the weeping gestures are to be heard as the lament of a dying woman. In the *Symphonie Fantastique* the programme tells us that the structure of the piece is to be heard as the unfolding series of events in the life of the persona, a lovelorn artist. But what of pure instrumental music, where there are no helpful words to disambiguate the content?

Cone suggests that the expressive or psychological structure in a piece of instrumental music is consistent with a number of different 'stories' or dramas. A piece of music has an 'expressive potential', which will be realized in different ways in different contexts, but which sets broad limits on what a piece of music can be said to express. If we ignore the words of 'Immer leiser', for example, the music is consistent with a number of different stories or dramas, including psychological stories or dramas, but I doubt it is consistent with a tale in which a militaristic hero wins a number of glorious battles before sinking into drunken sloth and dying a wretched and inglorious death, or a psychological drama in which cheerful enthusiasm turns into deep despair or light-hearted innocence is overcome by mean-spirited narrow-mindedness.

Cone is urging that all music should be heard as a kind of utterance in 'the composer's voice', and in a sense this has to be right: works of music, like all works of art, are in some sense utterances by their makers and potentially able to express (in Vermazen's sense, that is, to *betray*) something about the psychological attributes of their makers. But Cone seems to make no distinction between the composer as the author or implied author of a work and the composer as a character or persona inside the work, like a character in a literary drama.[8] Not all instrumental music is usefully experienced as an expression of emotion in characters in the work. As I said about expression in general in Ch. 9, once the notion of Romantic expression in music has been introduced, then we can, if we wish, listen to different kinds of music *as if* it were an expression by some character in the music,[9] but much music was not intended by its author to be an expression of emotion in some persona. Furthermore, among music that does seem to express somebody's emotions, the degree to which it articulates and individuates the emotion expressed varies greatly. For these reasons

I do not want to be committed to Cone's view that *all music* should be experienced as an utterance by a persona in a work and hence potentially an expression of that persona in the full Romantic sense.

Elsewhere I have suggested that one way of specifying content is in terms of how the composer broadly intended the piece to be construed, the structural metaphor or metaphors in terms of which he or she construed the music.[10] Thus Cone is urging that all music should be heard as a kind of dramatic utterance by some character or persona, but I would say that this is but one metaphor in terms of which we can construe music. Some music is best heard as dance music, other music as pictorial, other music again as primarily mathematical structure.[11] Even among pieces that are reasonably construed as rhetorical utterances, there are many different kinds of utterance, such as orations, conversations, narratives, and dramas.[12] Thus some Haydn string quartets can plausibly be heard as conversations among the players, while Beethoven's later symphonies are perhaps best construed as psychological dramas. Some music can be reasonably heard as belonging to more than one appropriate context. Hearing a piece of music in different contexts may reveal different aspects of the 'expressive potential' of the piece. Thus the witty, conversational quality in Haydn's Opus 33 quartets can be best appreciated if the instruments are heard as characters in conversation. At the same time, the metaphor reaches only so far. Not every aspect of the work is rewardingly heard in terms of the conversation metaphor.[13]

Despite these qualifications, I believe Cone is right to point out that there are works of music especially in the Romantic period that it is appropriate to hear as psychological stories or dramas about characters or personae in the music, and that these works lend themselves to being experienced as expressions of emotion in their characters or personae. If this is correct, then it will be possible to hear an instrumental piece of pure music as an expression of emotion in some protagonist in the full Romantic sense in almost exactly the same way as in 'Immer leiser'. The music can mirror the desires, memories, and 'evaluations' or points of view of the protagonist (or protagonists) as well as his or her vocal expressions, expressive movements, action tendencies, and so on. Musical processes can mirror emotion processes, the *transformation* of one emotion into another, *blends* of emotion, *conflicts* between emotions, and *ambiguities* in emotion.[14]

The suggestion that we can hear a piece of pure instrumental music as the expression of psychological states in a persona or character has at least four appealing consequences.

1. First of all, on Cone's conception of music, an entire piece of music can be thought of as an expressive utterance or as a psychological drama, so that the 'meaning' or expressiveness of a particular passage is a function of 'the significance of the entire composition'.[15] This is in striking contrast to the doggy theory which is stuck with the idea that only individual gestures can be heard as expressive, since only individual gestures are heard as similar to some particular human vocal or behavioural expression. If a whole piece of music is heard as a wordless song, then expressiveness is indeed a function of musical process as I have been urging. It is not just isolated gestures that are expressive, but the way one theme or harmony transforms into another, the way that the end of the piece sheds new light on the beginning, and so on and so forth. (Of course this kind of analysis is much more appropriate to dramatic music of the classic and Romantic eras rather than to minimalist or even Baroque music.)

As we saw in the previous chapter, Davies points out that musical works often express emotions in series: 'we expect development, connections, and integration within the music'.[16] Cone's way of hearing music 'emphasizes the extent to which the listener's impression of overall structure depends as much on awareness of the pattern of the musical work's expressive character and development as on knowledge of formal features, narrowly construed'.[17] The view explains nicely why the expressive and purely formal structures of a piece of music are sometimes interdependent: the form of the piece develops as it does partly because of the psychological story that is being told.

This is a theme that has often been sounded by the musicologist Anthony Newcomb, who argues that in some symphonic works the 'musical structure' is also a 'plot structure', a psychological storyline that is common to a number of different works. Newcomb calls such a storyline a 'plot archetype'.

The conception of music as composed novel, as a psychologically true course of ideas, was and is an important avenue to the understanding of much nineteenth-century music . . . Thus we may find at the basis of some symphonies an evolving pattern of mental states, much as the Russian formalists and the structuralists find one of several plot archetypes as the basis of novels and tales.[18]

According to Newcomb, Schumann's Second Symphony has the same plot archetype as Beethoven's Fifth: 'suffering leading to healing or redemption'.[19] Newcomb goes so far as to claim that in music 'formal and expressive interpretation are in fact two complementary ways of understanding the same phenomena'.[20] Expressive interpretation must concern itself with 'the way the piece presents itself to the listener as successiveness, as a temporal unfolding, as a large-scale process'.[21] Newcomb emphasizes the expressive importance of transitions from one section of a piece to another,[22] as well as of 'thematic metamorphosis' that 'leads us to hear the intrinsic meaning of each theme as colored by what it has been'.[23] In this respect Newcomb's view is reminiscent of Langer's, but unlike Langer, Newcomb thinks that an extended piece of music can express a sequence of particular emotional states and not just the ebb and flow of unspecified inner feelings.

2. A second important consequence of Cone's idea that music can contain agents or characters or personae is that it shows how cognitively complex emotions can be expressed by instrumental music without words. The pioneer here is Jerrold Levinson, who, in his 'Hope in *The Hebrides*', argues that if we postulate a persona in music, we can then attribute to that persona cognitively complex emotions, and not just the old favourites, joy and sorrow.[24] However, Levinson thinks it is enough for some cognitively complex emotion to be expressed by music that the music signify or bring to mind some of the non-cognitive aspects of emotion, such as 'qualitative feels, desires, and impulses, varieties of internal sensation, degrees of pleasure and pain, patterns of nervous tension and release, patterns of behavior (gestural, vocal, postural, kinetic)'.[25] While all these aspects of emotion are certainly important, they normally won't be enough to identify a particular emotional state as being of one sort rather than another. We usually need to know how the world is affectively and cognitively appraised, and what wants, goals, and interests are at stake in the emotional encounter. Levinson thinks that music can sometimes convey a general sense of 'a psychological state's being

intentional'[26] and may even 'regularly call to mind in culturally back-grounded listeners certain thoughts, even ones of some complexity',[27] but he does not say much about how this can happen.

In an essay on Shostakovich's Tenth Symphony, Gregory Karl and I argued that the music tells a psychological story about a persona, whom for various reasons we should think of as the composer himself, and that we should interpret the musical persona as longing for, desiring, trying to achieve, regretting, feeling nostalgia, and so on.[28] Thus in order to express the cognitively complex emotion of hope or hopefulness, the music needs to be able to express some of the so-called 'cognitive content' of hope, especially the desires and thoughts characteristic of hope. We argued that the incremental changes in the hopeful theme that finally produce the cheerful main theme of the final movement convey a sense of effort and purposeful-ness as the persona strives to realize the hopeful future he envisages. Similarly, the recurrence of an early idyllic theme later in the sym-phony surrounded by darker material suggests a memory of—perhaps nostalgia for—a past happy time that contrasts with a threatening present. In these ways the music is actually able to *articulate* a specific cognitively complex emotion (roughly describable as 'hope') by articulating desires, points of view, action tendencies, and so on in the musical persona.

3. Thirdly, if we postulate a persona in music, we are in a position to say, as Davies is not, that pure instrumental music can be *about* the emotions it expresses. The composer, in creating the persona or personae or characters in the music is able to comment on their emotions and convey his attitudes towards them. So Brahms char-acterizes the dying woman in 'Immer leiser' as suffering, yet as ultimately resigned to her fate. Moreover, to me at least, he seems to be commenting on more than just the situation of his character. He also seems to be expressing his own attitude to love and death. The transformation at the end is not just a shift in the *character's* perspec-tive, but also a shift in Brahms's conception of life, love, and death: like much of Brahms's late music it has a certain serenity indicating perhaps that Brahms has accepted his fate and the loneliness at the heart of his life.

4. Finally, if there is a persona or set of characters in a piece of instrumental music, then a piece of 'music alone' can be a genuine

Romantic expression of emotion in a protagonist, just like a song, and not just a sequence of expressive contours. In the last chapter we saw how 'Immer leiser' is a passionate utterance that expresses the unfolding, ambiguous, shifting emotions of the dramatic protagonist, by mirroring aspects of her emotion processes, evolving evaluations, thoughts, desires, and action tendencies, as well as the vocal and gestural expressions emphasized by the doggy theory. If there is a persona or character in a piece of Romantic instrumental music, then perhaps it too can express the emotions of that persona or character in just the same way.

Why Postulate Personae in Music?

I have just listed four advantages to accepting the idea of a persona in instrumental music, but of course, the fact that there are advantages to this idea doesn't make it true. What positive reasons are there for interpreting music along these lines? What grounds are there for thinking that interpretations of the sort I have been suggesting are interpretations *of the music* and not just fanciful fabrications using the music as a taking-off point?

One answer is that this way of interpreting music can sometimes explain what appear to be anomalies in a piece when it is interpreted as a 'purely musical' structure of tones. For example, in an essay entitled 'Once More "Between Absolute and Program Music": Schumann's Second Symphony', Newcomb argues that very often if a critic looks only at the purely musical structure of a work in isolation from expression, he or she cannot figure out a coherent interpretation because there are anomalous elements that do not fit into a coherent whole. Newcomb points out that Schumann's Second Symphony has been widely condemned by twentieth-century critics who have tried to understand it on purely structural grounds while ignoring its expressive content.[29] By contrast, contemporary writers and musicians thought it was one of Schumann's crowning achievements.

Similarly, in our study of Shostakovich's Tenth, Gregory Karl and I focus on the apparently anomalous horn call which sounds out of nowhere in the middle of the third movement and seems to have no purely structural raison d'être.[30] We suggest that an interpretation of the horn call in terms of its significance in the psychological drama is crucial to understanding the third movement and the thematic transformations that lead from the third movement to the main lively theme of the fourth. In our interpretation[31] we endorse Newcomb's idea that form and expression are interdependent, that expression is not just embroidery upon form but may itself motivate form.

A third example is Charles Fisk's account of Schubert's last sonata, in which Fisk takes as his starting point the puzzling trill at the very beginning of the first movement. The trill is puzzling because of 'its chromatic pitch, its low register and its rhythmic placement'.[32] 'Instead of merely reinforcing an already participating note or gesture the way most trills do, it brings a foreign tonal region—one centered in the chromatic Gb—into play, uncertainly yet emphatically revealing it, suggesting its presence through a tremulous whisper.'[33] Fisk then gives a psychological reading of the sonata that shows the role of the trill in the psychological drama that he thinks the first movement exemplifies. An anomalous formal element is justified in terms of its expressive role in the musical structure.

Now, Schumann, Shostakovich, and Schubert may just have written incoherent works. The anomalous elements may be just that—anomalous—and it may be simply perverse to try to explain them away.[34] But there are a number of reasons why it is appropriate to accept these *kinds* of readings (even if listeners may disagree about the details of what's expressed). These reasons hark back to the general view of interpretation that I presented in earlier chapters on literature (especially Chs. 4 and 6).

First, these readings are consistent with what is known about the author and what the author probably intended. Thus it is reasonable for Newcomb to find coherence in Schumann's Second Symphony by attributing to it a psychological content because there is good evidence that Schumann himself, like other Romantic composers, did in fact think of his instrumental works in this way. 'Music for Schumann was an expressive enterprise and a form of communication, reflecting in some way the experience of its creator. . . . it embodies the emotions or interior attitudes attendant upon experienced objects or events.'[35] In other words, Schumann subscribed to some version of the Romantic expression theory I outlined in Ch. 9.

Indeed Newcomb claims that in the Second Symphony Schumann wanted to convey not just a series of moods, but 'an evolving story':[36] his music articulates the evolving emotional states of a persona who 'owns' those states. Likewise, other instrumental pieces by Schumann contain duelling personae that reflect different aspects of his own personality, the vigorous, active Florestan and the dreamy, poetic Eusebius.[37]

In a similar way, in our essay on Shostakovich, Gregory Karl and I showed that it is reasonable to interpret the Tenth Symphony as containing a persona of the composer, Shostakovich. This is partly because Shostakovich uses within it a 'signature' motif, consisting of D—E♭—C—B, corresponding to the German transliteration of the initials 'D. Sch.' for 'Dimitri Shostakovich'. (In German E♭ is represented by the syllable *es*, and H is used for B♮.) This signature reappears in other Shostakovich works, such as the String Quartet No. 8. Moreover, Solomon Volkov in his biography of Shostakovich reports that Shostakovich claimed that the second movement of the Tenth contained 'a musical portrait of Stalin'.[38] It seems reasonable, then, to interpret the symphony as expressing Shostakovich's reaction to the Stalin years and their aftermath. Such an interpretation is not only rich, rewarding, and coherent, it is also consistent with Shostakovich's apparent intentions.

Secondly, I observed in a footnote in Ch. 4 that interpretations should obey Beardsley's principles of 'congruence' and 'plenitude'. In other words, you should make your interpretations fit as much of the work as possible in as consistent a way as possible.[39] Again, the interpretations I have been discussing meet these criteria. Newcomb, for example, explicitly argues in his Schumann paper that if we interpret the Second Symphony in the way that Schumann's contemporaries mostly did and in a way consistent with Schumann's own compositional practices, we discover that the piece is in fact coherent. His thesis is, he says, that 'a shift in critical methods'—that is, away from interpretation in terms of psychological content and towards purely formal 'analysis'—led to a 'shift in critical evaluation' of the symphony, roughly from admiration to condemnation. In tying the formal development of the final movement to the dramatic development of the 'plot', Newcomb's interpretation makes the piece out to be consistent in a way that more formalistic interpretations deny, and it takes account of aspects of the work that such formalistic interpret-ations omit. Similarly, our interpretation of Shostakovich's Tenth construes it as internally consistent and we explain anomalous aspects ignored by more purely formal interpretations.

So far, however, I have been arguing that it's all right to postulate characters or personae in music if doing so explains anomalous aspects of a piece. But many instrumental pieces do not have anything particularly anomalous about them. There is no particular problem finding a purely musical interpretation of a Brahms Intermezzo, for example. So why insist on populating pure instrumental music with characters and personae when we don't *need* to do this in order to understand the music?

The short answer is that the interpretation of instrumental music should obey the same principles of interpretation I have just enunci-ated (and which I defended in more detail in connection with literary interpretations). An interpretation of a piece of music should be consistent with what is known about the composer—including his compositional practices, beliefs, and attitudes—and it should account for as much of the piece as possible in a consistent way. Hence, even if there are no anomalies in the music requiring special explanation, it is appropriate to interpret a piece of instrumental music as containing characters if this interpretation is consistent with what is known about the composer, including his compositional practices and beliefs, and if interpreting the piece in this way is part of a consistent interpretation that makes sense out of the piece as a whole.

The Persona under Attack

Several objections are commonly made to the idea that music—or some music—should be interpreted as the expression of emotion in a persona or characters. The best argument for the prosecution that I know of is by Stephen Davies.[40] Davies distinguishes different ver-sions of the persona theory. He thinks the most interesting is the strongest version: 'that, to understand and appreciate some musical works fully, the listener *must* hypothesize a persona and hear the unfolding of the formal and expressive elements of the music as actions and feelings of, or events affecting, that persona'.[41] He contrasts this strong version with a slightly weaker version of the theory: that 'we should hypothesize a persona in listening to music', and that so doing 'leads to a proper understanding of the music for what it is', but that 'other styles or methods of listening' are also 'viable', and 'might lead equally to a sympathetic appreciation of the works involved'.[42] Davies points out that the various different defenders of the theory actually hold slightly different positions.

My own view is that some Romantic pieces of music *should* indeed be experienced as containing a persona whose unfolding emotional life is portrayed in the music. By saying they should be so interpreted, I mean that important aspects of the work are likely to be inaccessible to listeners who do not listen in this fashion. To this extent we *must* listen in this way in order to detect the work's expressive structure. I do not, however, like to put the point by saying that hypothesizing a persona is necessary for appreciating a work 'fully', in Davies's terms, since talking about the 'full' interpretation of a work seems to imply that interpretations differ from one another in how fully they match up to some ideal interpretation, whereas, as I've argued earlier, there can be multiple incompatible interpretations of the same work, which are all in some way appropriate to it. There are no doubt appropriate ways of experiencing these works that do not involve experiencing them as the development of the emotional life of a persona. We can experience them as purely musical structures; we can experience them as musical structures with some notable emotional qualities; or we can experience them as psychological dramas or narratives in which a character or characters articulate and elucidate their conflicting or ambiguous or shifting emotions. But although much can be gained from a purely musical interpretation, or even an interpretation in terms of emotion characteristics in appearances, there are subtleties in the musical development that will escape such readings.

As with literature, there are many appropriate interpretations of the same piece, and as with literature, there are different *types* of interpretation. Some interpretations of music focus on form in abstraction from expressive content, while others focus on expression. Just as different types of interpretation in literature uncover different aspects of a text, so different types of interpretation of music uncover different aspects of the music. Moreover, not every interpretation can focus on every aspect of a text or a piece of music. A Schenkerian analysis, for example, focuses on harmonic development, whereas Rudolph Reti's analyses focus on theme and thematic development and transformation. An analysis of a piece as the expression of emotions in a persona or character(s) will foreground aspects of the piece that may receive less emphasis in a purely formal analysis. In short, you don't have to listen to a Brahms Intermezzo as a psychological drama in order to appreciate it in some way or other, but if you do hear it as a psychological drama, you will hear things in it that you wouldn't hear otherwise.

But are you actually hearing what is *in* the music? Davies objects that personae are not *in* the music in the way that melodies and harmonies are. They are imported from the outside. As he puts it: 'the listener interjects, instead of uncovering, the ideas that fuel her imagination'.[43] While an analysis by Schenker or Reti emphasizes different aspects *of the music*, those critics who interpret music in terms of the expression of emotion by characters or personae in it are not emphasizing some interesting features that are really there in the music, although hitherto unnoticed; they are not talking about aspects *of the music* at all, but simply letting their imaginations run wild.

In some cases this charge is easily rebutted. As we have seen, Schumann explicitly admits that some of his music represents the two different parts of his personality, the Florestan aspect and the Eusebius aspect. Shostakovich plants his signature DSCH all over the Tenth Symphony, so it is hardly far-fetched to imply an autobiographical intention. Furthermore, the interpretations I have discussed of Schumann's Second and Shostakovich's Tenth obey the principles of plenitude and congruence. But what of other music in which there is no explicit evidence that the composer meant his music to contain characters or a persona? Davies says: 'It seems straightforwardly false' that there are 'practices or conventions calling on the listener to hypothesize a persona in the music'.[44] It follows that there is no reason to think that composers should be understood as having intended to invoke such practices and conventions. I question this conclusion.

There is as a matter of fact a long tradition in Western music of populating music with characters, where, as Cone says, a musical character can be a particular instrument or theme or any 'recognizably continuous or distinctively articulated component of the texture'.[45] I have already briefly mentioned the rhetorical tradition in Western music, very strong in the Baroque and continuing to be influential in the Classical period, according to which it was a commonplace to think of music as a rhetorical discourse of some kind, in which characters took part in conversations, participated in dramas of various kinds, and even delivered orations. Much Baroque music was based on dance forms, and it is natural to hear such music as the movements performed by some person or character who is dancing to the music. Even in Peter Kivy's favourite example of 'music alone', the fugue, the different strands of the fugue are often described as voices or as characters.[46] C. P. E. Bach wrote a set of descriptive pieces for keyboard called 'Character Pieces', illustrating the indecisive person, the complacent person, and so on.[47] In the Romantic period, where the idea of art as expression gained widespread currency, and which also saw the invention of the tone poem and of elaborate forms of programme music, it was natural for composers to think of their music in the way described by Cone, as utterances by characters or personae in the music. Today, Elliott Carter is but one notable example of a composer who thinks of his main musical ideas as characters and thinks of their development as the development of characters.

The Romantics, however, gave a special twist to the tradition of characters in music: they put *themselves* into their music as characters or personae. In programmatic works such as the *Symphonie Fantastique*, this is quite explicit, and it is almost as explicit in Shostakovich with his signature DSCH or in Schumann with his two partial self-portraits, Florestan and Eusebius. Not all Romantic composers wear their hearts on their sleeves to this extent, however. Brahms is a far more reticent, introspective composer, at least in his later works—and he hasn't left any diary entries saying of his Intermezzi 'This is me!' Nevertheless, it is perfectly consistent with the Romantic aesthetic that he should conceive of an Intermezzo as dramatizing a psychological or emotional conflict that could well have been a conflict in his own psyche, and as expressing conflicting emotions that could well have been his own.

In view of this long tradition of hearing characters in music and in view of the Romantic aesthetic of self-expression in music, it is

eminently reasonable to interpret at least some Romantic instrumental music as expressions of emotions in characters or personae in the
music. There are indeed 'practices and conventions' calling on listeners to hear characters in music.

Davies's second main objection to the idea of hypothetical personae in music is that, even granting that it is legitimate to interpret
some instrumental music as containing personae, interpretations in
terms of narratives or dramas containing characters or personae are
too idiosyncratic to count as interpretations *of the music* rather than
fanciful free associations to it: 'music is too indefinite to constrain the
contents of such narratives to the required extent'.[48] Now, it is true
that music is not constrained to the same degree that poetry is, but, as
Cone suggests, music has an 'expressive potential' realized in different
ways in different contexts that nevertheless sets broad limits on the
kinds of emotional narrative or drama that the music can exemplify
and the kinds of emotional process that the music can express. Shortly
I'll be giving an interpretation of a particular Brahms Intermezzo, but
this interpretation is just *one* possible interpretation that is consistent
with the expressive potential of the music. I will not be claiming to
have found the one and only meaning of this nuanced piece. Indeed
in general the best such interpretations in this genre seem to me to be
ones that avoid very specific readings. Neither Newcomb's interpretation of Schumann's Second Symphony nor Karl's of Shostakovich's
Tenth are highly specific (except where the composer's programmatic intentions seem clear from external sources).

Cone's idea of the expressive potential of a piece of music that
becomes more specific in particular contexts allows him to recognize
the possibility of a set of nested dramatic interpretations that increase
in specificity. This is a useful way of thinking about these kinds of
interpretations, but when he applies the idea to a Schubert 'Moment
Musical', we can see the dangers of extending an interpretation to a
very specific level. Cone interprets the piece as in a general way
dramatizing 'the injection of a strange, unsettling element into an
otherwise peaceful situation'.[49] Given the context which Cone himself 'brings' to the music, which presumably includes an understanding of Schubert's life and personality, he says he 'can go further and
suggest a more specific interpretation of that context: it can be taken
as a model of the effect of vice on a sensitive personality'.[50] Finally, in

a context that he thinks Schubert himself might have 'adduced', he offers a reading of the piece as expressing Schubert's 'sense of desolation, even dread' that arose from his discovery that he had syphilis.[51] Presumably this is the kind of thing Davies has in mind when he says that interpretations in terms of personae are too idiosyncratic to be genuine interpretations of the music. To be fair, however, Cone is explicit that this specific reading is one that he thinks the music permits, not one that it demands.

I conclude that although music permits a wider variety of appropriate interpretations than literature does, since the expressive potential of a piece allows for diverse interpretations, nevertheless there are constraints on these kinds of interpretations. In addition to the general ones I have already discussed—they should be consistent with what is known about the author's compositional practices, and they should account for as much of the work as possible in a consistent way—there are constraints imposed by the expressive potential of the music. Not every reading is equally appropriate. Some are more idiosyncratic and indefensible than others.

The Expression of Emotion in a Brahms Intermezzo

To illustrate these ideas, I turn now to another late piece by Brahms, the Intermezzo in B flat minor, Opus 117 No. 2. This piece is in a ternary A-B-A′ form, with a conclusion in which A and B are brought together. Malcolm Macdonald points out that the piece 'traces a miniature sonata design',[52] but it does not adhere very exactly to sonata form. There is an initial statement of the first theme (a) in bars 1–9 in the tonic B flat minor, then a variation on (a), (a′), in bars 9–22. In bars 22–38 the B theme is introduced in the relative major of D flat. There follows an extended development section in bars 38–51 in which only the A theme figures. At 51–60 there is a restatement of the a theme, as in bars 1–9, and at 61 we think we are heading for the coda, but instead there is further development of the A theme leading to the climax of the piece at bar 69. At bar 72 the coda finally arrives, with the return of the B theme in B flat major. The final section, in bars 72–85, is marked più adagio. The B theme intertwines with the A theme, and the key is ambiguous between B flat minor and B flat major before finally resolving into the tonic minor. The ambiguity is underlined by an 'uneasy pedal F',[53] which sounds all the way from bar 70 to the end.

Melodically the A theme is 'evolved from the first and last note of semiquaver groups of four' which are 'arranged in waving arpeggio style'.[54] The theme is built primarily from descending seconds and rising fourths. Interestingly, the B theme is closely related melodically to the A theme. In particular, the opening of the B theme is strikingly similar to the phrase in bars 1–2; indeed, it is a transposed version of the very same phrase but in a different key and rhythm. (See Figs. 11.1 and 11.2.) Nevertheless, the A and B themes have a very different character. The A theme is arpeggiated, and ranges over a wide register—from a very low Bb to a high Eb at bar 69. The B theme comprises a single 16-bar period, with its two 8-bar phrases divided into two 4-bar sub-phrases, like a question and answer. The most important notes in the melody are on the downbeat, unlike the more rhythmically off-beat A theme, and the predominant rhythmic activity is twice as slow as that of the A theme. On the other hand, despite its ostensibly sturdier quality, the inner voices of the B theme reflect the restless chromaticism of the A theme.

Rhythmically the piece is in 3/8 time, with characteristic Brahmsian hemiolas that give a sense of metrical ambiguity. The B theme, for example, at least in some performances, almost has a duple feeling. Brahms referred to the three Intermezzi of his Opus 117 as 'three cradle-songs of my sorrows',[55] and the A theme certainly has a gentle, lilting lullaby feel to it, although the shifts in harmony and register prevent it from having a calming effect.

The most striking feature of the harmony is how Brahms continually curtails or postpones resolution to the tonic, while leading us to expect it. The first convincing cadence in any key is that to the relative major (D flat) at the beginning of the B theme. Thus although in the statement of the A theme there are tonic B flat minor chords on the downbeats of both bars 1 and 2, the harmony does not *sound* stable or resolved because these chords are in first inversion (so that the root of the chord is not in the bass) and they are not preceded by the dominant. Moreover, all the chords in the A theme from the end of the second bar are dissonant: when each chord is resolved by the one that succeeds it, it is immediately replaced by another equally strong

Fig. 11.1. Johannes Brahms, Intermezzo, Op. 117 No. 2. Example 1. A theme

dissonance.[56] In the development section there are continuous modulations, and in the coda Brahms keeps the harmony ambiguous until the very end. The climax of the piece comes in bar 69. We have been listening to a low B (which can be read as C♭)[57] sounding all through measures 67 and 68 in the bass while in the upper voice in bar 68 there is a descent from A to G♯ to F♯, leading us to expect an E (F♭). But at bar 69 unnervingly[58] the bass line moves up to C which grounds a dominant 7th chord on F (the dominant of B flat),

Fig. 11.2. Johannes Brahms, Intermezzo, Op. 117 No. 2. Example 2. B theme

re-establishing the B flat minor harmony in a jarring, unexpected way. In the ensuing coda, as the A and B themes intertwine, the harmony is ambiguous between B flat minor and major before finally resolving unambiguously into B flat minor at the very end.

If we think in terms of the expressive qualities of this music, then overall it is certainly not a jolly piece, and we might even call it 'sad', although 'bittersweet' might capture its mood more accurately. But like all complex Romantic music, it does not express just a single emotional state. The music develops and changes in its character as it progresses. The A-B-A' structure is not just the result of Brahms's wanting a convenient way of writing a piece with a high degree of unity and coherence; it is also a dramatic structure, and the two themes with their two distinct harmonic associations and strong motivic relations interact with one another to create a mini-drama, rather like the mini-drama of 'Immer leiser'. Indeed, in both pieces a dramatic interplay of themes and—especially—of major and minor modalities helps to create an overall bittersweet character. We may say that the overall bittersweet character of the piece *emerges* from this dramatic interplay between melodies and harmonies.

The arpeggiations of the A theme feature prominent weeping or sighing contours, in the manner of the doggy theory, whereas, ostensibly at least, the B theme has a more dignified, serious, sturdy quality to it: each four-bar 'question' is tentative but the four-bar 'answering' phrases seem to be firmly and reassuringly asserting a response to the question. But however we interpret the piece, it would be a mistake to hear it as a succession of unrelated expressive qualities. I have noted that the B theme grows out of the A theme, and that the A theme is in B flat minor while the B theme is in the relative major of that key. In other words, we hear an organic connection between these two themes, as if they were two ways of experiencing the same material. This effect is reinforced by a suggestion of the A theme restlessness in the inner voices of the B theme (where chromatic minor seconds abound).

If, now, we think of the piece as a psychological drama, then the A-B-A′ structure turns out to be not just a conveniently unified musical form, but a dramatic psychological structure. One way of construing this structure would be as a conflict between two different characters in the music. However, since the two themes are so closely related harmonically and melodically, I think it makes more sense to hear them as a single character, responding in two different ways to the same material. The overall experience of the persona or character in the music is bittersweet because the music goes back and forth between the two themes and between the major and minor modalities.

The arpeggios surrounding the A theme and the way that the tonic is constantly foreshortened give it a questing, yearning quality, as if it were striving to reach a goal which is perennially out of reach. Firm resolution is only achieved with the arrival of the B theme, which treats the melodic material in a more deliberate and calmer way (on the downbeat), as the restless arpeggios give way to a dense chordal structure. At the same time, however, there is intense chromaticism in the inner workings of the B theme. Moreover, the A theme with its insistently striving quality dominates the work: apart from the sixteen bars stating the B theme, the entire work up until the coda is devoted to the A theme and its development. In the development section the A theme is interwoven with its inversion, as it becomes ever more excited and obsessive and reaches ever further into the upper and (especially) the lower register of the piano. It is as if the character in the music is becoming ever more intense and impassioned, and ever more insistent and urgent in his search. Harmonically, in venturing into relatively distant territories the character seems to be yearning towards something difficult to reach, and perhaps unattainable, and rejecting the calmer, more sober assessment of the B theme. But at bar 69 the character is brought up short, and as the melodic line slowly descends (in bars marked *ritardando*) the quest too seems to slow down. But that is not where the piece ends.

In the final fourteen bars, marked *più adagio*, the somewhat calmer B theme returns, interwoven with the passionate questing A theme. (See Fig. 11.3.) The major interpretative question, as I see it, concerns the conclusion and the way in which the two themes and the two modes

Fig. 11.3. Johannes Brahms, Intermezzo, Op. 117 No. 2.
Example 3. Final section, marked *Più Adagio*

of major and minor are ultimately reconciled. The A theme throughout has been associated with the minor key, chromaticism, and
yearning. The B theme is more robust and calmer, because it is
introduced on the downbeat and in the major key. In the coda just
as there is ambiguity between major and minor, so there is interplay
between the A and B themes. The last ten bars are given over to the A
theme but in a much steadier rhythm than hitherto, the rhythm of the
B theme. Harmonically, the final chord is unambiguous: D flat major,
the key of the B theme, has been banished by B flat minor, the key of
the A theme.

How are we to understand this conclusion? There is clearly some
kind of contrast or conflict between the two themes, although if we
listen to those inner voices in the B theme, we can hear that the A
theme has to some extent infiltrated the B theme from the start.
I myself hear the sturdier B theme as in a sense overwhelmed by
the A theme, but not entirely so: the B theme, although vanquished,
has left its mark on the A theme. Its inner restlessness has always had
some affinity for the A theme but its outward calm has affected the A
theme and has reduced the A theme's restless questing. On the other
hand, the B theme has certainly not tamed the restlessness completely.
I hear the B theme as modifying to some degree the quality of the
passionate A theme, as though the character has accepted that
yearning is to be his fate, has recognized that he will not achieve his
desire, and sorrowfully, reluctantly, has resigned himself to that realization. The B theme's absorption by the A theme is not a foregone
conclusion: the music fluctuates between minor and major and it
seems possible that the B theme will predominate with both its
rhythm and its major tonality. But at bar 81 it becomes clear that
although the A theme has taken on the calmer rhythm of the B
theme, the dark minor tonality will predominate.

Because the piece ends up back in the tonic of B flat minor and
sounding a variant of the A theme but in the rhythm of the B theme,
it sounds as though the A theme's passionate yearning has been
neither satisfied nor conquered, but it has to some extent been
subdued. The final resolution shows how far the character still is,
however, from simple acceptance. It comes in the tonic B flat minor,
the key of the A theme, but the resolution is hardly very resolute,
since it occurs in an arpeggio that extends over three bars, beginning

on the lowest B flat on the piano and rising to the highest. The insistent passionate questing has been transmuted into a certain degree of calm and resignation, but it has not been utterly *resolved* either musically or psychologically. The persona is only partly reconciled to his fate. Indeed it would also be possible, I think, to hear the ending as despairing, as the first theme crushed into the recognition that it never will achieve its goals. Possibly different pianists could perform the piece in each of these different ways and thus arrive at a different resolution to the psychological drama.[59]

Why Interpret the Intermezzo as an Expression of Emotion in a Persona?

How do I justify my psychological, dramatic reading of the Intermezzo? After all the music does not have any particularly *anomalous* features that cry out for interpretation in dramatic or psychological terms, like Schumann's Second Symphony or Shostakovich's Tenth. A purely musical interpretation is available in the A–B–A' form and its suggestions of a truncated sonata form. So what is the justification for interpreting the Intermezzo as a psychological drama, a kind of interior dramatic monologue much like 'Immer leiser', in which the protagonist expresses his conflicting emotions?

I have argued in general terms that it is not anachronistic or inappropriate in any other way to interpret an instrumental piece by Brahms as an expression of emotion in a character or characters. I have tried to give an interpretation that is consistent with what we know about Brahms and how he thought of these late piano works. My interpretation is consistent over all; it takes into account all or most of the musical developments in the piece; and it does not leave out of account any striking aspects of the music that ought to be addressed by any interpretation (although of course I have not given a detailed enough analysis to be fully justified in saying this).

More specifically, the interpretation has a number of advantages.

First, the expressiveness of particular passages is a function of the expressive significance of the whole piece. The formal and expressive structures of the piece are interdependent. In the Intermezzo what is expressed in the *più adagio* section, for example, is a function of everything that has come before formally and expressively. We have seen how the piece as a whole is dominated by the passionately yearning A theme, that the A and B themes are closely related motivically and harmonically, and that in the final section the passionate A theme adopts the rhythm of the B theme. What is expressed in the *più adagio* section is, I suggested, a reluctant acceptance that the character's yearning will never be satisfied. This interpretation is unavailable to those like the doggy theorists who do not hear the piece as an expressive whole, as a psychological mini-drama.

Secondly, the Intermezzo is able to express cognitively complex emotions. The passionately striving A aspect of the persona is influenced by the at least apparently calmer B aspect, so that we can say that the character arrives at a partial resignation to his fate, but it is a resignation of a subtle sort: it is not whole-hearted acceptance and peaceful reconciliation to one's lot, but troubled, reluctant and still to some extent yearning towards the unattainable. Alternatively, I suggested we can hear the piece as despairing, as the character realizes that he will never be free of striving and yearning. Both these interpretations ascribe complex emotional states to the persona in the music.

Thirdly, the music is a genuine Romantic expression—the articulation and clarification—of emotion in a character, not just a sequence of expressive contours. The emotional state of the protagonist unfolds as the music unfolds, and the music mirrors the psychological development of the protagonist. The A theme is yearning partly on doggy theory grounds: it has a restless contour and its seemingly unstable harmonies suggest uneasiness. Similarly the B theme's greater stolidity is suggested by the more dignified way in which it moves. But the music also mirrors the way the protagonist's emotion processes develop and change over time. It expresses continuous yearning (the A theme) in conflict with calmer proclivities (in the B theme), but a calm that is itself undermined by a certain restlessness (since the B theme sounds calm but also has some restlessness in its inner voices), and that only partly succeeds in calming the striving and yearning (by bringing it into its own calmer rhythm) but that does not succeed in turning the yearning into acceptance (since the tonic minor key wins out in the end). The music mirrors these conflicts and ambiguities in the emotions expressed by the protagonist, the conflict between yearning and acceptance, and the ambiguity between despair that intense desires will be for ever unfulfilled and resignation to this fate. It conveys some sense of the conflicting desires and evaluations between which the protagonist is torn, as the protagonist moves back and forth between B flat minor and D flat major, and between the minor and major of B flat in the *più adagio* section. The piece has the dramatic structure of a psychological drama, and this remains true even if you reject the specifics of my account and the particular way I construe the drama.

If we hear the Intermezzo as a psychological mini-drama, then we can detect qualities in the music that otherwise we might miss, such as the conflict between restless striving and calm acceptance in the coda, the ambiguity in the concluding arpeggio, and the intimate yet troubled relationship between the A and B themes throughout the piece and especially at the end. Even more important perhaps, if we do not interpret the piece as a psychological drama in which powerful emotions are traced and expressed, we cannot understand why the piece is so powerfully moving. Without paying attention to the piece as a psychological drama I would suggest that we cannot appreciate its poignancy or its profundity. Why is this music poignant, and why profound? The answer is that it records and expresses a poignant and profound psychological experience. Music in A-B-A' form is not poignant and profound just because it is in that form. It is, in Newcomb's words, the 'metaphorical resonances' of the music, in particular what it means psychologically, that makes it poignant and profound.

Finally, I have explained how music is often *about* the emotions it expresses. Composers can 'comment' on the emotions expressed in their music: the composer can manipulate the unfolding emotions expressed in the music just as a dramatist does in a play. Is there any evidence that Brahms was saying something about the emotions his protagonist is expressing in the Intermezzo? I would say that we can find in Brahms's biography ample justification for his thinking of these late piano pieces as conveying his own deepest, most intimate thoughts and feelings. I have already noted that Brahms referred to the three Intermezzi of his Opus 117 as 'three cradle-songs of my sorrows'. Never a man to pour out his feelings in words, Brahms communicates what he has to say in his music. At this point in his life much of the music he writes has a kind of tragic radiance, a dignified acceptance of the losses and failures in his life, and in particular the failure to find a satisfying reciprocal romantic relationship.

Jan Swafford in his biography of Brahms speculates:

Maybe all the [Opus 117, 118, and 119] pieces with their delicate lyricism are love songs to lost women in Brahms's life, to Ilona and Clara and Agathe and Hermine and Alice, to Elisabet for whom he wrote the rhapsodies of Opus 79, and to all the others known and unknown to history. And no less he may have composed the pieces to try and keep Clara Schumann going in body and soul. Since she could only play a few minutes at a time now, and because she loved these miniatures so deeply, maybe they did keep her alive.[60]

But their 'main significance' was that they are 'a summation of what Brahms had learned, almost scientific studies of compositional craft and of piano writing, disguised as 'pretty little salon pieces'.[61] As Collingwood said, what makes an artistic masterpiece is not mere craft but the way a composer puts his craft to use in the expression of unique, individual emotions.

12

Listening with Emotion: How Our Emotions Help Us to Understand Music

Emotion in aesthetic experience is a means of discerning what properties a work has and expresses.

Nelson Goodman, *Languages of Art*

The Arousal and Expression of Emotions in Music

We saw in Ch. 4 how the emotional responses evoked or aroused by a novel can help us to understand the novel and serve as a basis for an interpretation of it. In this chapter I'll argue that our emotional experiences of music very often operate in the same way: much music evokes emotional responses, and by cognitively monitoring or reflecting upon those responses, we can come to grasp the *structure* of the music as well as what it *expresses*. As before I will concentrate on complex 'art' music, which best exemplifies what I want to talk about. As with literature, the relevant emotional responses are not the result of idiosyncratic associations that you or I happen to have to the music, as when 'Jingle Bells' makes me weep because it reminds me of the vanished Christmases of yesteryear. The relevant responses are the result of listening carefully to the music itself, and they are the responses of more or less *qualified listeners*. By 'qualified listeners', I mean listeners who have some understanding of the aesthetic and stylistic principles governing the music they are listening to: not necessarily trained music theorists, but not people who never listen to 'art' music (so-called 'classical' music) either.[1] As we'll see, the emotional responses of such listeners can alert them to aspects of the music, both expressive and structural, that they might otherwise overlook.

What I'll be focusing on in this chapter, then, is something fairly specific: the way that our emotions operate as a *guide to understanding* music. One of the things I'll be interested in, of course, is whether the emotions a piece of music arouses in listeners have anything to do with what the music expresses. If the Romantic theory of expression is correct, then at least sometimes the emotions a piece of music arouses in qualified listeners will be those very emotions that it expresses. But the emotions music arouses are not always the same as those it expresses. As we'll see, even when the emotions that the music arouses in us *help us to grasp* what the music expresses, the emotions aroused may not be the very same as those expressed.[2]

Nor surprisingly, Peter Kivy thinks that the emotions music arouses *cannot* help us to understand what music expresses, for the simple reason that music simply cannot arouse the 'garden-variety' emotions that it expresses. The emotions music arouses are quite distinct from those it expresses. I begin the chapter by briefly considering Kivy's view. Then I consider a view at the opposite extreme, the view that not only does music arouse garden-variety emotions, but that the expression of these emotions in music is *nothing but* the arousal of those same emotions in listeners. Few people hold the view in this extreme form, but there are milder versions of this view that do have adherents. I will discuss Aaron Ridley's views, with which I am partially in sympathy, and Kendall Walton's version, which I find unnecessarily baroque. In general, although I do not think that we can *define* expression as the arousal of emotions in listeners, nevertheless, the emotions that we feel as we listen to music can sometimes mirror and thereby reveal to us what the music expresses.

In Ch. 4 I invoked the literary theorist Wolfgang Iser as showing that having appropriate emotions evoked can alert the reader to the narrative structure of a novel. Something similar is true of music. As Leonard Meyer has shown, having 'the right emotions' evoked at 'the right moments' can alert us to the *structure* of a complex piece of tonal music. I examine his views and then extend them: having the right emotions at the right moments can also alert us to what a piece *expresses*, if anything. But the emotions thus evoked—surprise, bewilderment and so on—are not emotions that are necessarily expressed by the piece.

I'll end the chapter by describing a recent experiment by psychologist Carol Krumhansl which seems to show, contrary to Kivy, that music really does arouse garden-variety emotions, and that confirms my view that paying attention to the emotions music arouses may often alert us to important features of the structure and expressiveness of the music. It also suggests, however, that what's appropriately felt in response to music is much less specific than what's appropriate to literature. There is a wider range of appropriate emotional responses to a piece of music than there is to a novel.

Being Moved by Music: the Kivy Emotions

In his book *Music Alone* Peter Kivy rejects the idea that music can *arouse* the 'garden variety emotions, fear, grief, joy, and the like'[3] that he thinks music can *express*. Real-life garden-variety emotions have 'cognitive objects' that are simply not available in our experience of music. To illustrate his point, Kivy describes how his Uncle Charlie always gets him angry by telling self-serving lies about Aunt Bella, and he notes that in this and other emotional states in ordinary life there is always something like Uncle Charlie whom I'm angry *with* or afraid *of* or happy *about*. But when it comes to music there is no obvious candidate for the object of emotion, what I'm sad or happy or nostalgic or anguished *about*. 'Where's the Uncle Charlie?'[4] as Kivy pointedly asks.

Kivy is assuming here some version of the judgement theory of emotions. An emotion has to have a cognitive object, something that it is directed towards or is about. Music in his view cannot evoke garden-variety emotions such as sadness and fear because listeners do not have the cognitions that he thinks are essential to emotions. He complains that many theorists, including Descartes, assume that music functions as a 'stimulus object', that can directly stimulate pleasure, sadness, or some other garden-variety emotion. But if music were able to directly stimulate pleasure or any other emotional state, this would be tantamount, he thinks, to viewing music as a drug, a conclusion he vehemently opposes. Music, he thinks, 'is not a stimulus object but a cognitive one'. It is 'an object of perception and cognition'[5] and our pleasure in music derives from comprehension of it, not mere stimulation by it.

Kivy does recognize, however, that we do respond emotionally to music on occasion. He thinks that when this happens the music itself is the cognitive object of our emotion. We may be emotionally *moved* by the beauty of a piece of music, by the 'incomparable craftsmanship' of its counterpoint, or by its daring way of overcoming constraints. We can be moved in all these ways by a section of Josquin's *Ave Maria* in which the composer writes a very beautiful canon at the fifth with the voices only one beat apart.[6] In such examples we are responding emotionally to aspects of the music itself, its beauty and its graceful solution to a musical problem.

One of the things we might be moved by in an expressive piece of sad music is the sadness that we recognize in it, but Kivy wants to insist that being moved by sadness in the music is not at all the same thing as being made sad by the music.

we must separate entirely the claim that music can arouse emotion in us from the claim that music is sometimes sad or angry or fearful: in other words, we must keep apart the claim that music is expressive (of anger, fear, and the like) and the claim that music is arousing in the sense of moving. . . . a piece of sad music might move us (in part) because it is expressive of sadness, but it does not move us by making us sad.[7]

By the same token, although we might be moved by expressive properties in a piece of music, the emotion of 'being moved' is not normally what is expressed by the music. The emotions expressed are quite different from the emotions aroused (if any), and independent of them.

There are a number of problems with Kivy's view. First, 'being moved' is not the *only* possible emotional response to music. As we'll see, people do in fact report feeling happy, sad, excited, wistful, nostalgic, and so on as a result of listening to music, and there is good evidence that they are right. 'Being moved' is just one of many possible emotional responses that people have to music. Secondly, it is unclear what being moved amounts to. It seems to mean simply being in some emotional state or other, or perhaps being in a state of emotional arousal. In other words, Kivy can be taken to be saying that music evokes some emotional state or other without specifying what that state is. It's not clear, therefore, that what is evoked in these cases isn't some kind of garden-variety emotion. Indeed, since Kivy is talking about an emotional state aroused by the *beauty* and *craftsmanship* of the music, perhaps 'being moved' could be interpreted as a blend of admiration, awe, and delight, or something of this sort. These, however, are presumably garden-variety emotions of the sort Kivy denies music can evoke.[8] Thirdly, the fact that music is sometimes a cognitive object of emotion does not rule out the possibility that it can also be a stimulus object. As we'll see later (especially in Ch. 13), although music is sometimes a cognitive object, it can also function as a stimulus object of emotion.

Finally, Kivy thinks that being moved by the beauty or craftsmanship of a piece of music is unconnected to the specific emotions, if any, that the music expresses. But even if being moved by music is sometimes irrelevant to what the music expresses, it could often happen that when we are moved by a particular harmonic modulation or change in rhythm, or the reiterated fragment of an earlier melody, we are in fact being moved partly by what the music *expresses*.[9] Indeed, in his own example, we may be moved partly by Josquin's *expression* of awed reverence for the Virgin. What's more, being moved in this way may *draw our attention* to what is being expressed. We are moved by and so are led to focus on not only Josquin's craftsmanship and the beauty and complexity of his music, but also what he expresses in this piece.

Feeling What the Music Expresses: Aaron Ridley

Whereas Kivy claims that the arousal of emotion by music has nothing whatever to do with the expression of emotion by music, there are those at the opposite end of the spectrum who claim that expression is nothing but the arousal of emotion. Few hold the view in this bald form. On the one hand, it certainly seems as if a piece of music can arouse emotions it does not express, as when I get all upset and teary-eyed on hearing 'Jingle Bells' because it reminds me of the lost Christmases of yesteryear. Even if 'Jingle Bells' makes me feel sad, it does not express sadness. And on the other hand, even if lots of people agree that 'Jingle Bells' expresses gaiety or cheerfulness, they do not all respond to it with cheerfulness—many of us greet the well-known tune with irritation or boredom. Still, the idea that musical expression must have something to do with the arousal of feeling dies hard. There have been several recent attempts to show that the arousal theory, suitable modified, has a kernel of truth to it.

Aaron Ridley, in his book *Music, Value and the Passions*, defends what he calls a 'weak arousal theory' of musical expression. He thinks that the emotions *induced* by music help to identify the emotions that the music *expresses*. Ridley argues that we become aware of expressive musical gestures by means of responding to them sympathetically. For example, when I am listening to the Funeral March from Beethoven's *Eroica* symphony, 'in attending to the musical gestures I come to be aware of their heavyhearted, resolute quality through the very process of coming myself to feel heavyhearted but resolute'.[10]

Ridley focuses on 'melismatic gestures', that is, musical gestures that resemble 'items in the expressive repertoire of extramusical human behavior, either physical or vocal'.[11] He agrees with the doggy theory that music often resembles 'the tone, inflections and accents of the expressive human voice',[12] or 'the motions character-istic of certain forms of passionate experience'.[13] However, for Ridley a melismatic gesture is not expressive solely by virtue of this resem-blance. We may all agree that 'Jingle Bells' is cheerful music because of the sprightly way it moves, but it doesn't follow that 'Jingle Bells' is particularly expressive music. Music can be sad or cheerful without moving us emotionally: to be expressive is not the same thing as to have a sad or cheerful 'contour'.[14] For Ridley, whether a musical gesture is expressive or not depends on whether or not it *moves us emotionally*, and what the musical gesture expresses is partly a function of the exact shade of emotion it arouses in listeners.

To hear music as expressive is to have an experience of the music that has affective aspects, such that the melismatic gestures are heard as being expressive of the state, which, sympathetically, we experience. In the responsive listener, such states, because they are a mode of experiencing infinitely particular musical gestures, are themselves infinitely particular; and the states so conveyed, the expressive qualities of the music, may be described in as precise a manner as the nature of those states, and the possibilities of the listener's language, permit.[15]

Ridley thinks that we recognize the peculiar kind of sadness in the music as a result of being saddened by it in this peculiar way:[16] just as I come to understand the states of mind of other people by sympathetically responding to them, so I understand a musical melisma by sympathetically responding to it. We come to understand another person's melancholy partly by *feeling* it: I come to realize 'what it would be like to be in the state that his gestures reflect'.[17] Similarly with music: we never merely recognize dispassionately what music expresses; we identify what a piece of music expresses partly by the way it makes us feel. Ridley adds that in the case of *unfamiliar* melismatic gestures, we *have* to be able to feel them in order to have any idea what they express.

This does not mean, however, that sympathetic responses to musical melisma are mere idiosyncratic associations to the music, since 'the experience of sympathetic response . . . is ineliminably an experience of the music which occasions it',[18] and hence open to public assessment. If I say that Beethoven's Funeral March makes me want to frolic joyfully, you can point out that I cannot in that case be responding to the music itself (rather than some peculiar idiosyncratic associations I may have in regard to the music), because the melismatic gestures in the music are in fact heavy-hearted and resolute. 'Melismatic gestures are the features of a musical work that through sympathetic response are grasped as expressive features; and the expressive attributions made on the basis of sympathetic response are elucidated by appeal back to those melismatic gestures.'[19]

Ridley thinks his theory explains Mendelssohn's enigmatic saying that what music expresses is not too ambiguous for words but 'too definite', for when I experience a piece of expressive music that is expressive of some kind of melancholy, the precise nature of the melancholy expressed is revealed in the way it makes me feel. What the music is heard as expressing is partly due to the state of mind it induces in me. So in listening to the Funeral March from Chopin's B minor Piano Sonata, I feel a very precise sadness that is different from that which I encounter—and feel—in Beethoven's Funeral March, and these different sadnesses are *what the music expresses*. Furthermore, because the states of which we take the two Funeral Marches to be expressive 'are both in fact *our* states, it explains why the experience of music as expressive is often felt to be the most intimate of all aesthetic experiences'.[20]

Ridley's theory is ingenious and he has answers to some of the perennially puzzling features of musical expression. For example, he has an explanation for the connection between music's being expressive and its being emotionally moving: expressive music, he thinks, *is* music that is emotionally moving, that is, music that evokes the fine-tuned emotional experiences he identifies. I am also sympathetic to one of the motivations underlying his view. It's probably true that unless many people had responded with emotion to musical melisma, 'music would never have become a context into which the application of expressive predicates [was] extended'.[21]

Nevertheless, there are problems. One objection to his view might be that it focuses only on melisma and ignores other important musical parameters such as harmony and rhythm. As we've seen, harmonic changes can be the most expressive moments in music. But Ridley openly acknowledges that music has many ways of arousing feelings other than those he discusses.

Another potential problem lies in Ridley's examples. As we'll see shortly, there is plenty of evidence that music makes people happy and sad, but how can a piece of music make me feel more fine-grained emotions? How can it make me feel *resolute*, for example? Normally one might think it takes particular kinds of cognitive states—intentions, desires, goals—plus a certain moral courage and so on, things that music does not seem capable of initiating. As Kivy would no doubt point out, as we listen to the Funeral March of the *Eroica* symphony, what's there to be resolute about?

This objection I think Ridley can rebut. The empirical evidence seems to suggest that what music can do is induce physiological changes, movements, gestures, and action tendencies. So perhaps music can get us to straighten our shoulders, to tighten the jaw, to move—or be disposed to move—in a certain solemn way, and perhaps this will induce a feeling of resoluteness.[22] Or perhaps we are positing a Beethoven-persona or a Napoleon-persona or more generally a struggling-hero-persona in the music—in the way I suggested in Ch. 11—so that one is identifying with the resoluteness of this persona in the music. And of course one can identify with the resolute persona by having just the behavioural tendencies—straightened shoulders, tense muscles, and so on—that, as I was just mentioning, the music can induce. Similarly, when Ridley asserts that different funereal music evokes subtly different feelings of sadness in him, he may be right in that the different music may induce different physiological states, action tendencies, and gestures, which in turn make him *feel* different.

Jerrold Levinson has another objection. Since, in Ridley's view, the finely discriminated emotions or feelings that the music makes me experience are the very emotions or feelings that the music expresses, Levinson pronounces Ridley guilty of 'creeping narcissism': for Ridley, what a piece of music expresses is 'the listener's self-expression',[23] whereas expressiveness, according to Levinson, is something public, not something determined by individual listeners. What seems to be bothering Levinson is the idea that what a piece of music expresses is *determined* by the way it makes individual listeners feel. This makes it sound as if Ridley is *defining* expression as the arousal of emotion in individual listeners.

But Ridley does not think that listeners' states of mind on listening to music *completely determine* what the music expresses, because expressiveness for him is partly a matter of doggyish expressive contours. For Ridley all that's determined by individual listeners is the exact *shade* of an emotion that we know—on independent doggy grounds—the music expresses. It is only the fine-grained quality of the melisma that is determined by individual emotional responses in his view. So to accuse Ridley of saying that musical expression is always 'the listener's self-expression' is misleading.

My own take on Ridley's theory is that we should not think of it as a theory of what expression *is*. After all, I have just spent four chapters arguing for a quite different—'Romantic'—theory of expression. Expression cannot be even partly *defined* as the arousal of emotion: expression is something accomplished by artists and composers, not something determined by readers and listeners.[24] On the other hand, as I urged in Ch. 9, if composers succeed in expressing (articulating and elucidating) emotions in a piece of music, then a good criterion of their success will be that qualified audiences will in turn feel appropriate emotions in their encounters with the music. So in a sense what Ridley says is quite right: what a piece of music expresses is a function of what sequence of emotions a composer articulates in the piece, as *experienced* and subsequently *interpreted* by particular listeners. So how a listener responds to two subtly different melancholy pieces will very likely be subtly different, corresponding to the subtle differences in what's expressed, even though the listener's experience is not what *determines* what's expressed by the music.

If we interpret Ridley as making some observations about how listeners *come to understand* and *interpret* what music expresses, what he says is both interesting and insightful. He is suggesting that when a person listens to the Beethoven or the Chopin funeral marches, a sequence of emotional or affective states is evoked that are different and so *feel* different in various ways. And yes, we may very well feel differently when listening carefully to these two pieces precisely because the music expresses subtly different emotions or has subtly different expressive qualities. Furthermore, our subtly different feelings of melancholy may alert us to differences in the music that are responsible for the differences in the way we feel. What's more, the *same* music may elicit somewhat different responses in different qualified listeners, and how these listeners interpret the music (including what it expresses, if anything) will probably vary depending on exactly how they feel in response to it. There is a continual interaction between how we feel in listening to a piece of music and what we interpret it as expressing.

In this respect music is quite like literature and painting. How we feel in response to music affects our understanding of it, just as how we feel in response to *The Reef* or *The Large Enclosure at Dresden* affects our understanding of those very different works. Reflecting on our emotional responses is likely to get us focused on those aspects of the music that (we think) are responsible for our reactions. How different qualified readers or listeners or spectators interpret an artwork depends partly on how it affects them emotionally. And, as I argued in Ch. 9, in a successful work of artistic *expression*, the artist has carefully constructed a work so as to articulate a particular emotion; and audience members are actively encouraged to respond emotionally to the work in such a way that their own emotional responses help them to understand what the work expresses.

There are probably fewer constraints on what counts as an appropriate emotional response to a piece of expressive pure instrumental music than there are for responses to *The Reef* or *The Large Enclosure at Dresden*. But as with literature and painting, not every emotional response will be appropriate and not every emotional response will alert us to aspects of the music itself. It would not be appropriate to respond to Beethoven's Funeral March by frolicking around the concert hall, and such a reaction would lead away from the work rather than deepening our understanding of it.

My own main reservation about Ridley's idea is that he insists that the response to music is a *sympathetic* one, that the feeling I experience is the very one that I attribute to the music as what it expresses. He overlooks the fact that what is expressed is not always or even usually what is aroused in listeners.[25] In listening to 'Immer leiser', for example, I may feel longing and anguish *with* the protagonist in the music, but I may feel pity and hopelessness as I contemplate her fate. In listening to the Brahms Intermezzo Opus 117 No. 2, I may feel *with* the conflict between the two points of view I pointed out, identifying now with one and now with the other, but I may also feel heavy-hearted and compassionate as I contemplate the musical conflict in the persona: I may feel *for* him rather than *with* him.[26] And we can say similar things about music that has expressive qualities, but does not express emotions in the full-fledged Romantic sense I discussed in Ch. 9: a piece of music may, I think, express *nostalgia* although the emotion it evokes in me is *melancholy*; a piece may express *fear* while evoking in me only *anxiety*.

In summary, Ridley is right that experiencing music as expressive of some emotion requires an emotional response to the music, and he is right that the exact shade of emotion felt will affect how we interpret the music, including what it expresses. But his theory does not successfully *define* expression; it is better interpreted as a theory about how listeners come to understand what a piece of music expresses. And as a theory of how listeners come to understand what a piece of music expresses, it faces the problem that the emotions evoked in (qualified) listeners may not always be exactly the same as the emotions they hear the music as expressing.

Listening with Imagination: Kendall Walton

Kendall Walton agrees with Ridley that music sometimes evokes feelings in listeners, but he thinks that it also typically invites us to exercise our imaginative capacities rather than getting us to experience actual emotions. So, for example, a song such as 'Immer leiser' creates a 'world' in which a protagonist expresses her anguish and yearns for her beloved. For Walton this means that in listening to the song we are to *imagine* the protagonist expressing anguish and yearning for the beloved. I might also respond emotionally: on Walton's view I am likely to have an empathetic response to the protagonist of 'Immer leiser', (in imagination) feeling with her in her anguish and longing.

But it is not only in regard to song that we imagine ourselves to be feeling something in response to the music. Pure instrumental music—if it is *expressive*—can induce us to 'imagine feeling or experiencing exuberance or tension ourselves—or relaxation or determination or confidence or anguish or wistfulness'.[27] Furthermore, Walton explains the peculiar intimacy that he thinks we feel with the music so experienced by suggesting that 'anguished or agitated or exuberant music' can not only induce one 'to imagine feeling anguished or agitated or exuberant' but can also induce one 'to imagine of one's auditory experience that it *is* an experience of anguish or agitation or exuberance'.[28] In 'Immer leiser', there is a 'work-world', which exists independently of whomever happens to be listening to it, in which it is 'fictionally true' that there is a protagonist urging her lover to return. Pure instrumental music has no work-world in this sense. As Walton sees it, when I imagine of my auditory experiences that they are in fact experiences of emotion, my imaginings are due solely to my own personal interactions with the music: 'it is as though I am inside the music, or it is inside me'.[29]

Walton defends his view that we imagine of our auditory experiences of the music that they are experiences of 'anguish or agitation or exuberance' by pointing out analogies between feeling and hearing, for example, that we think of sounds as 'independent entities separate from their sources',[30] as coming over us and permeating our consciousness, as waxing and waning, intensifying and diminishing, and so on.[31] But this is not much of an argument. As I have said before, there are endless analogies between musical sounds and other phenomena (weather, landscapes, and so on) and analogies alone cannot ground a theory of what our musical experiences are experiences of.[32] I suspect that it is only because music *actually* arouses emotions that Walton is led to suppose that it also arouses emotions in imagination. As we will see in great detail later on, music is capable of directly evoking many of the emotions that Walton thinks we only imagine feeling.

I suppose that boisterous music can induce me to *imagine* that I am feeling boisterous, but other things being equal, boisterous music does not induce imaginings of boisterousness; it just makes me feel boisterous. Nor do I typically imagine of my auditory experience of boisterous music that it is an experience of feeling boisterous. On the contrary: the feelings I experience are simply feelings of boisterousness. Similarly, exuberant music tends to make us feel exuberant and agitated music tends to make us feel agitated. Anxious, unsettled, nervous-sounding music makes us anxious, unsettled, and nervous. Calm music calms us down. Sad music saddens us. Happy music cheers us up. These are all emotion states that music can induce pretty straightforwardly without the intervention of imagination. We do not need to invoke the imagination in order to explain how music produces these emotional reactions in listeners. We will see plenty of evidence of this at the end of this chapter and in Ch. 13.[33] And if a simpler explanation of the phenomena is available, we should probably adopt it.

Bewilderment, Surprise, and Relief: The Meyer Emotions

According to my version of Ridley, if the qualified listener pays attention to the emotions that he or she experiences in listening carefully to a piece of music, that can help the listener to reach an understanding of what the music *expresses*. Not all qualified listeners will understand the music in exactly the same way, partly because their responses will differ somewhat and so will the expressive qualities that they detect in the music. It is also true, however, that the emotions a piece of music evokes can help listeners understand the more purely *structural* aspects of the piece. This is an idea that goes back to Leonard Meyer and has more recently been taken up by Eugene Narmour.[34]

The theory Meyer defends in *Emotion and Meaning in Music* is a theory about understanding musical *structure*. It is not a theory about musical expression, as some have thought. Meyer does have views about expression, but he explains it in terms of associations and relegates his discussion of it to a final chapter, entitled 'Note on Image Processes, Connotations, and Moods', which is a kind of afterthought. Meyer thinks that the music theorist confronted with a complex piece of Western tonal music can *understand* it by 'cognizing' the way it develops melodically, rhythmically, harmonically, and so on. But someone who is not trained in music theory—but has listened to a lot of music—may still be able to grasp the musical structure if she experiences appropriate emotional responses at appropriate moments in the musical development. Meyer suggests that even if I cannot describe the musical structure in a technical, music-theoretical way, I still genuinely *understand* the music, provided I feel the appropriate responses at appropriate moments in the music. 'Whether a piece of music gives rise to affective experience or to intellectual experience depends upon the disposition and training of the listener. . . . Thus while the trained musician consciously waits for the expected resolution of a dominant seventh chord the untrained, but practiced, listener feels the delay as affect.'[35] For Meyer, responding emotionally to the musical structure as it unfolds over time is one way of *understanding* the musical structure.[36] The structure of a piece of (Western tonal) music can be cognized by the cognoscenti, but it can also be felt 'as affect' by the rest of us.

According to Meyer, emotions such as surprise, bewilderment, anxiety, relief, and satisfaction can be induced by our expectations about a piece of (Western tonal) music given our implicit understanding of the norms of its style. We are *surprised* and possibly *bewildered* at unexpected key shifts, made *anxious* by prolonged periods in keys that modulate ever further from the tonic, *relieved* and *satisfied* when the harmony returns to 'normal', and so on. Moreover, all these emotions—surprise, bewilderment, anxiety, relief, satisfaction—are emotions directed towards the music as its 'cognitive object' in Kivy's phrase.

For example, as we listen attentively to Brahms's 'Immer leiser', we may be *surprised* when the tonic minor moves to the parallel major and *satisfied* by the resolution at the end. In listening to the development section of the Brahms Intermezzo we may be *bewildered* by the way the piano ranges into ever more distant keys, *unnerved* by the sudden shift in harmony at bar 69, and *relieved* by the arrival of the *più adagio* section with its return to the B theme. But then we may find that we are *puzzled* and *unsettled* by the ambiguity between B flat major and minor at the end.

Meyer's theory takes off from the premise that 'emotion or affect is aroused when a tendency to respond is arrested or inhibited'.[37] Music in the Western tonal tradition arouses expectations of certain sorts. Harmonically, we expect that a certain cadence will lead to the tonic or that a piece which begins in C minor will not modulate immediately to C sharp minor. In general, Meyer claims that 'affect or emotion-felt is aroused when an expectation—a tendency to respond—activated by the musical stimulus situation, is temporarily inhibited or permanently blocked'.[38] Although this won't do as a general account of emotion (since among other things it fails to fit positive emotions such as happiness), it is certainly true that having one's expectations blocked or inhibited is *one* good way of eliciting emotion.

There has been some empirical support for the Meyer–Narmour theory. People really do have expectations about how a line of music will develop, based on their internalized understanding of the musical style and the probabilities it incorporates. For example, on the Meyer view, the fluctuating sense of key—its 'instability and stability, ambiguity and clarity'[39]—as a musical piece develops will be very important to the emotional responses of the listener. Carol Krumhansl has demonstrated that people really do have such a sense of key, and that their sense of key changes as a sequence of chords unfolds over time. In one experiment, for example, she used ten different chord sequences consisting of nine chords each. Some of the sequences were designed to suggest key changes from one chord to another and some of the modulations were to more distant keys than others. First of all a chord was sounded, followed in turn by each of the twelve probe tones of the chromatic scale, and listeners were asked to say how well the various tones fitted with the preceding chord. Then the first and second chords were sounded in succession, followed by each probe tone, and so on until all nine chords had been sounded. Her results showed that 'listeners were integrating information about the possible functions of the chords across multiple chords, and arriving at a sense of the intended key that was stronger than each individual chord would predict'.[40] This sense of key 'changes as subsequent events occur that suggest another key'.[41] Moreover, when keys are more distantly related, 'listeners tend to resist the change to the new key longer, and then suddenly jump to the new key, suppressing the sense of the initial key'.[42] Krumhansl did not study the affective aspects of what listeners were registering, but she does establish that listeners respond predictably to stable, unstable, clear, and ambiguous chord sequences, and that they have an internal 'sense of key' that affects how they hear the development of the sequences.

Many people report feeling 'thrills' or 'chills' at significant moments in the development of a piece of music. It may be that this phenomenon too can be explained in terms of the expectations formed by listeners familiar with the style of the piece in question. The psychologist of music, John Sloboda, has studied the features of music that tend to elicit such responses and has found that they include 'syncopations, enharmonic changes, melodic appoggiaturas, and other music-theoretical constructs, which have in common their intimate relationship to the creation, maintenance, confirmation, or disruption of musical expectations'.[43] However, since almost every musical event is in some respect expected or unexpected, Sloboda argues that there must be other factors contributing to the emotional effect. He suggests that these include 'density of eliciting events, positioning within the compositional architecture, and what [he] has called "asynchrony of levels"—an event which simultaneously confirms an expectation on one level while violating it on another'.[44] In any event, if Sloboda is right, emotional thrills and chills are the result of the way the music plays with our expectations: mixing the interestingly unexpected with the satisfyingly expected.[45]

Thrills and chills that affect us at 'structural high points' in the music alert us to the existence of those high points. If Sloboda is right, thrills and chills are induced by structurally significant events, including changes in rhythm, key, timbre, melodic direction, tempo, dynamics, etc., and these physiological responses—the thrills and the chills—alert us to the corresponding structural changes, although we may not be *aware* of this until after the event.

It has been found that music hotspots usually involve particular structural events which tease structural expectancies. They do this by repeatedly creating and resolving tensions, or by manipulating timing parameters that cause expected events to happen earlier or later than expected. Emotional response to music is thus an integral outcome of the intuitive structural analysis that goes on while listening.[46]

In short, feeling surprised, bewildered, relieved, and so on—as well as being thrilled and chilled—as the musical events unfold, is a way of understanding the structure of the music. My cognitive evaluations may be impoverished (if I don't know much about music theory) and I may not be able to explain in words much about the musical structure. But if I am surprised, bewildered, and relieved at the 'right' moments while listening to a piece of music, then in some sense I have understood the piece.

Meyer's picture of what happens when we listen to music fits nicely with the theory of emotions I outlined in Part One. When we are surprised or bewildered or relieved by what is going on in the music, we are affectively appraising a musical event as surprising or puzzling or satisfyingly unexpected—**That's weird! That's unexpected! That satisfies my goals!**—and this appraisal immediately produces a physiological reaction. Thrill and chills are perhaps the most dramatic responses of this sort.[47] As in any emotion process, affective appraisals give way to cognitive evaluations. And one of the things I'm likely to reflect on is what it is in the music that caused me to respond emotionally (physiologically) in the way that I did. Why was I surprised? Why bewildered? Why relieved? And why did I feel that thrill? Upon reflection I may figure out that I was surprised by an unexpected key shift, bewildered by a passage of uncertain tonality, relieved when the wandering harmony returned to the tonic, and that the thrill came when the orchestral build-up was accompanied by a magical harmonic and melodic shift. Even if I don't know enough about music to figure this out, I may still be able to say that I was surprised by a strange moment when things suddenly seemed to get dark, or that I was relieved when I heard the melody sounding in a familiar way (that is, in the tonic).

Significantly, something very similar is true about the way we understand literature, as I explained in Ch. 4. Indeed, Meyer's 'listener-response theory' of musical understanding is the musical equivalent of Iser's reader-response theory of literary understanding. Both are theories about how we come to understand the structure of a work by having appropriate emotions evoked at appropriate times. Both raise the same questions about whether there is an 'ideal' listener or reader who has the *right* responses at the *right* time. On this point, I would say about music what I said earlier about literature. Our emotional responses are interactions between reader or listener and work, and there can be many different appropriate responses corresponding to subtle or not so subtle differences in our interpretations of how the work is structured.[48] *Appropriate* emotional responses need to take into account the historical context in which the work was written, its genre, perhaps its history of performance practice and so on, but there is no one ideal set of responses to any musical work.[49]

Interestingly, the picture I have painted of how we respond emotionally to musical structure helps to explain the 'Meyer paradox'. One of the puzzles that Meyer thought his theory spawned was that even though 'affect' is supposed to be aroused by thwarted expectations, we still experience affect even when we know the piece well and know exactly what is going to happen and when it is going to happen.[50] This is the musical version of the paradox of suspense to which I alluded briefly in Ch. 4. The solution to this puzzle is that the appraisal that one's expectations have been violated is a non-cognitive affective appraisal. It occurs subconsciously. The brain processes the music automatically so that 'however well one knows the piece, expectation, suspense, and surprise can still occur within the processor, because the processor is always hearing the piece "for the first time"'.[51] The emotions discussed by Meyer rely on knowledge of certain norms, but once these norms are internalized, the relevant emotions are evoked automatically or non-cognitively. However clearly your cognitive system anticipates the harsh dissonance on the horns or the sudden key change, your affective system is always taken by surprise when it happens.

How Emotions Help Us Understand Musical Expressiveness

Meyer's theory is about how listeners can grasp musical structure by having their emotions aroused: our emotional responses of surprise, bewilderment, relief, and so on alert us to what is going on in the musical structure. But there is another consequence of Meyer's view that he does not address. The emotions evoked by a piece of music may also alert listeners to what is *expressed* in the music. In Brahms's 'Immer leiser', I may be disturbed not only by all the descending minor thirds, but also by the descent into pessimism that the minor thirds seem to express. I may be *relieved* and *surprised* not only by the key change at the end of the piece, but also by the dramatic trans- formation from sorrow to radiant acceptance that the key change helps to establish. In other words, when I cognitively monitor my affective responses, I may realize that I am responding to what is *expressed* by the music as well as to its purely musical structure.

As Ridley stresses, when we listen to music, we do not just grasp intellectually what is being expressed; we understand expressiveness partly through the emotions it evokes in us. Thus, although Meyer does not explicitly make this connection, the emotions that he thinks music *evokes* alert the listener not only to the *structure* of the music, but also to its *expressiveness*—both what it expresses in the full Romantic sense, where that is appropriate, and what its expressive qualities are.

In the Brahms Intermezzo Opus 117 No. 2, the A theme makes me feel *anxious* and *uneasy*, which helps me to recognize the yearning quality in the theme. When the B theme arrives I am *relieved* and *pleased*, and this helps me realize that the B theme is more stolid and reassuring than the A theme it replaces, although at the same time I may experience an edge of uneasiness that alerts me to the uneasy reflection of the A theme in the B theme's inner voices. During the development section, I may become *unsettled* by the harmonic modu- lations, and *puzzled* by a vague sense that something is wrong which (I may on reflection discover) is caused by the fact that the questing A theme continues throughout the development with no allusion to the B theme. In bar 69 I am *startled* and *unnerved* by the unexpected change in harmony. In the *più adagio* section when the B theme returns intertwined with the A theme, I am kept *uneasy* because I cannot tell which melody and which key will win out. These unsettled emotions help me to *feel* the conflict that the piece is about and to grasp what the piece expresses. At the same time, however, if my account of the piece in Ch. 11 is at all plausible, then what is being *expressed by the music* is a reluctant acceptance of unsatisfied longing, whereas the emotions *aroused in me* are puzzlement, anxiety, uneasiness, and so on.[52]

Earlier I endorsed Aaron Ridley's view that the specific state of feeling that a piece of music induces in a listener affects what that listener hears the music as expressing, but I also urged that the feelings *induced* may not be the same as the emotions *expressed* by the piece. In general, the Meyer emotions evoked by a piece of music are not normally those that the music expresses, despite the fact that these Meyer emotions—surprise, bewilderment, anxiety, relief, and so on—do play an important role in getting us to understand and to experience what is expressed by the music. I am *surprised* when the harmony modulates from minor to major near the end of 'Immer leiser', but the song does not express surprise; it expresses radiant acceptance (as I hear it). I am *bewildered* by the harmonic shifts in the development section of the Intermezzo, but the music expresses unassuaged longing, or something of this sort. On the other hand, there may sometimes be a coincidence of emotions expressed and emotions aroused. The development section of the Intermezzo could perhaps be said to both express and arouse *anxiety* and *unease*.

As far as it goes, Meyer's theory is very helpful in exploring how our emotional responses to music help us to understand both musical form and musical expressiveness. But there are other ways in which our emotional experiences of a musical work can help us to understand it. When I listen to 'Immer leiser', or an instrumental minidrama such as the Brahms Intermezzo, I am not just surprised and bewildered by the musical events; I also respond emotionally to the drama enacted by the song. I respond emotionally to the dying woman's expression of her feelings. I respond in the same sort of way as I respond to Anna Karenina, with sadness and compassion for the dying woman's anguish in the first stanza and perhaps with relief that she arrives at resignation in the second. At the end of the song I may feel some of the radiant hope that the protagonist expresses, or

I may simply feel the calm that descends on the protagonist and that is reflected in the calm ending. Whatever the exact sequence of my emotions, if I am paying attention and cognitively monitoring what I feel, my emotional responses may alert me to what the song is about and what the protagonist is expressing.

In this respect, understanding the mini-drama of 'Immer leiser' is quite like understanding a literary drama. As is the case in literature, the emotional responses evoked by the music may or may not be the same as the emotions that are expressed by it. Likewise, my emotional responses to the Brahms Intermezzo may alert me to aspects of its 'story', but whereas the music (if I am right) expresses tragic resignation (or something of the sort), I may respond with heartfelt sympathy or grief or even (if the performance is overly sentimental perhaps) impatient contempt. The emotional experiences I have as I listen to the music help me to understand what is going on musically and expressively, but the emotions I feel don't have to be the very same as the emotions the music expresses.

Some expressive music—music with expressive qualities—does not tell a story or enact a drama or express emotion in the full Romantic sense of Ch. 9, but nevertheless evokes emotional responses without appealing to our musical expectations in the way described by Meyer. What I have in mind are cases in which I am calmed by calm music, made nervous or agitated by agitated music, cheered up by jolly music, and the like. If the music calms me down, and I then reflect upon how I feel, I may thereby come to recognize the calm quality of the music. If I am made nervous and anxious by a piece, this may lead me to recognize the nervous, anxious quality in the music. If I begin to feel cheery, then cognitive monitoring of my emotional state may alert me to the cheerfulness in the music. But once again, the expressive qualities I hear in the music may not be best described by simply labelling them as the way I feel. As I pointed out in the discussion of Ridley, nostalgic music may make me melancholy, music that expresses optimism may make me light-hearted, and as we'll see shortly, music that expresses fear may make me anxious rather than afraid. Similarly, a piece of music may have the expressive qualities of being witty and cheeky without its making me feel witty and cheeky. Nevertheless I may be alerted to the wit and cheekiness by the fact that it makes me smile.[53]

Like Iser, Meyer implicitly assumes that, in responding emotionally to music, there is a norm of understanding that we all more or less approach.[54] In earlier chapters I have argued that the distinctive emotional experiences of audiences—whether readers of literature, or listeners to music, or viewers of works of visual art—affect their interpretation of what they are reading or listening to or viewing, and that understanding a work of art always involves an interaction between a work and a reader or listener or viewer. And as Ridley suggests, if music makes us feel a particular shade of light-heartedness or melancholy, this will affect what we hear it as expressing. But there will probably be substantial individual differences among responses to music of this sort. While the Beethoven Funeral March may not make any qualified listener feel frolicsome, it is highly unlikely to induce exactly the same physiological changes and accompanying feelings in every listener. And because how we feel in response to music affects what we hear the music expressing, it is not surprising that there are differences both in how music makes people feel and in what expressive qualities they attribute to the music.[55] Likewise, different listeners may respond somewhat differently to the structure of a piece: we are not all surprised or bewildered or relieved in exactly the same places.

Krumhansl's Experiment

In the debate between Kivy and Ridley, Kivy claims that music cannot arouse the garden-variety emotions that it typically expresses, and Ridley presumably thinks that music can arouse any emotions that it expresses, including most of the garden-variety ones.[56] Recently the psychologist Carol Krumhansl has set out to test Kivy's hypothesis that 'the emotion is an expressive property of the music that listeners recognize in it, but do not themselves experience'.[57] In her experiment she selected pieces of music with distinctive expressive qualities[58] and sought to find out whether or not those pieces aroused the emotions they expressed. She chose two pieces of *sad* music (the famous Albinoni and Barber adagios), two pieces of *happy* music ('Spring' from Vivaldi's *Four Seasons* and *Midsommarvaka* by Hugo Alfven), and two pieces that she classified as representing *fear*

(Mussorgsky's *Night on Bald Mountain* and 'Mars, the Bringer of War' from Holst's suite *The Planets*). All the subjects in the experiment had had several years of musical training (usually vocal or instrumental) and were familiar with classical music (so they were 'qualified listeners'), but they were not music theorists or even music majors.

Subjects were divided into two groups. The first group—the 'dynamic emotion' group—recorded their emotional state as it changed over time as they listened to these pieces. This group was divided into four subgroups, each of which was assigned a different emotion, sadness, fear, happiness, and tension. The members of the 'sad' subgroup were asked to adjust a slider on a computer display to indicate the amount of sadness they experienced while listening to the six pieces. And similarly for the 'happiness', 'fear', and 'tension' subgroups.

The second group—the 'physiological' group—was monitored continually for the physiological changes that occurred while they listened to the six pieces. Twelve different measures were used, including heart rate, breathing rate, blood pressure, skin conductance, and finger temperature.

As soon as the listening part of the experiment was over, both groups were given a questionnaire and asked for a self-report of the *emotional effect* the music had on them, using a rating scale of 0–8 and a specific set of choices: afraid, amused, angry, anxious, contemptuous, contented, disgusted, embarrassed, happy, interested, relieved, sad, and surprised.

Krumhansl found that in their self-reports (their answers to the questionnaires) the subjects in both groups gave very similar responses: they rated their response to the 'sad' music to be strongest for the emotion of 'sadness', their response to the 'fear' music to be strongest for the emotions of 'anxious, afraid, and surprised', and their response to the 'happy music' to be strongest for the emotions of 'happy, followed by amused and contented'.[59]

In the dynamic emotions group, the dynamic emotion ratings over time also showed the intended emotions of the music excerpts, and the emotion in question was sustained at a fairly high level throughout the listening experiment. The amount of sadness felt was highest for the sad music, the amount of fear was highest for the fear excerpts and so on. Interestingly, those in the 'tension' group felt the most tension in the places where the fear group felt the most fear, but to a lesser extent they also felt tension where the happy group felt most happy and the sad group most sad. Krumhansl observes that this 'suggests that tension is a multivalent quality, influenced by the predominant emotional response to the music'.[60]

In the 'physiological study', Krumhansl found that there were distinct physiological changes associated with listening to the different types of excerpt. To give some idea of the differences found, the sad excerpts (Albinoni and Barber) produced the largest differences in heart rate, blood pressure, skin conductance, and finger temperature, and the happy excerpts (Vivaldi and Alfven) produced the largest differences in respiration.

Moreover, there were also significant correlations between the dynamic emotion ratings made by the subjects in the dynamic emotion group and the dynamic physiology measures taken from the physiological group. Again, what correlated best with the sad ratings were measures of heart rate, blood pressure, skin conductance, and finger temperature in the physiology group subjects. What correlated best with the happy ratings were various respiration measures. Interestingly, 'the strongest physiological effects for each emotion type generally tended to increase over time, or at least did not strongly return toward baserate levels'.[61]

When self-reports (in answers to the questionnaire) of the strength of the emotions felt were compared with *average* physiological measures for each excerpt, however, the correlations were mostly insignificant. Krumhansl speculates that these negative results suggest that

averaging the physiological measures across the entire excerpts gives far less systematic results than considering how the physiological measurements change dynamically over time. In other words, it would seem that dynamic variations in the measures are important indicators of musical emotions, and this information is lost when the physiological measures are averaged over whole excerpts.[62]

Another 'negative' result was that 'emotion-specific changes in physiology did not clearly map onto those found in studies of non-musical emotions'.[63] Thus, Krumhansl's results were not entirely consistent with Ekman and Levenson's data, which I reported in Ch. 2, on the physiological identifying characteristics of happiness, sadness, and fear. Interestingly, 'the effects of music on a number of physiological measures were similar to the suppressed emotion condition' in a study by Gross and Levenson. 'These similarities,' comments Krumhansl, 'suggest that suppression of overt action during music listening may also affect physiological measures'.[64] I have remarked before that people listening to classical music do not typically dance around or behave in ways typical of particular emotional states: they suppress their action tendencies and motor activities. It is therefore not surprising that the physiological symptoms of the emotions felt while listening to music are to some extent different from those emotions when experienced in normal life situations. Krumhansl notes some support for this idea in the fact that her physiological measures match those of some other experimenters doing experiments using film manipulation, in which again normal behavioural symptoms of the emotion are suppressed.

In summary, Krumhansl found that music with different expressive or emotional qualities does indeed produce statistically significant differences in such autonomic measures as heart rate, blood pressure, respiration rate, skin temperature, and skin conductance. Moreover, physiological effects *changed dynamically over the listening period*, and these dynamic physiology measures correlated significantly with dynamic emotion ratings (made by those pushing the slider). And in self-reports, 'emotion adjectives' were consistently assigned to the excerpts that 'matched the intended emotions', subjects reporting feeling sad when they listened to the sad excerpts and so on.[65] Within the dynamic emotions group, responses among the various members of each subgroup were strongly correlated, and very similar judgements were made of the two excerpts in each category (happy, sad, fearsome). Krumhansl concludes that Kivy is wrong to defend a 'cognitivist' position that holds that listeners recognize emotions in music but do not actually experience them.

It is true that Krumhansl's study was carried out with a small sample (forty subjects in the dynamic emotion group and thirty-eight in the physiological study group), and that the subjects were, as usual in psychology experiments, college students. But there is no reason to suppose that college students have peculiar attitudes to classical music. In general, as experiments in psychology of music go, this one is extremely thorough, well designed, and meticulously carried out.

From my point of view, this experiment produced a number of interesting results that shed light not only on Kivy's position but on Meyer's and Ridley's as well.

1. First, the experiment shows that, when asked if they feel some distinct emotion in the process of listening to a piece of music that expresses some particular emotion, listeners report that they do. They report feeling 'happy', 'amused', or 'contented' when listening to the happy music, 'anxious', 'afraid', or 'surprised' when listening to the music expressing or representing fear, and 'sad' when listening to sad music. That they feel some distinct emotion is confirmed by the dynamic emotion ratings, given as the music unfolds. Even more significant, perhaps, music with a distinct emotional or expressive character really does evoke distinct physiological changes, and the dynamically felt emotions correlate with the physiological changes. These results show that subjects are indeed experiencing emotions or affective states and that these emotions or affective states are distinct.

2. According to Meyer's theory, our emotions change all the time as we listen to music, depending upon the exact sequence of structural and expressive events. The experiment seems to show that Meyer is right about this. There are continuous physiological changes as people listen to expressive excerpts and these changes correlate with the dynamic emotions subjectively experienced (as indicated by when the dynamic emotions subjects pushed the slider). In fact, it is *because* the physiological changes correlate with changes in experienced emotion that we can be reasonably confident that the physiological responses to the music are in fact *emotional responses* (rather than just some physiological changes unrelated to emotion). It is equally unsurprising, however, that an *average* of physiological measures would be uninformative, since it is the way that various physiological measures *change over time* that seems to map emotional changes.

3. The experiment demonstrates that it is the expressive character of music ('what the music expresses') that is responsible, at least in part, for emotional responses in listeners. But if this is true, then it seems reasonable to infer that cognitive monitoring of the emotional (physiological) state the listeners find themselves in may well in turn alert them to the expressive qualities in the music that are apparently responsible for their emotional state.[66] Thus listeners who reported

feeling *anxiety* when listening to Mussorgsky's *Night on Bald Moun-tain*, maybe became alerted thereby to the *fearsome* quality in the music. Listeners who felt amused or happy might be led to notice the happi-ness in the Vivaldi 'Spring' concerto. And so on. Furthermore, the tension the subjects felt in response to the most anxiety-provoking passages in the Mussorgsky or the most happiness-provoking passages in the Vivaldi was quite likely to make them sit up and take notice of what is being expressed in these passages. Tension in listeners seems to reflect tension in the music, no matter what expressive qualities they are responding to. In short, it seems reasonable to suppose that the emotions evoked by the ongoing flow of music will indeed alert listeners to the expressive character of the music as it unfolds. Of course, in listening to music we may also be *noticing* expressive contours and *figuring out* how the expressive character of the music unfolds, but these cognitive modes of understanding are most prob-ably aided by the way the music makes us *feel*.

4. There was some interesting variation in the emotion words subjects picked out to characterize the emotion they felt while listening to the various excerpts. This was particularly striking in the case of the excerpts said to 'represent fear', Holst's 'Mars' from *The Planets* and Mussorgsky's *Night on Bald Mountain*. The most popular word to describe what this music aroused was 'anxious', interestingly enough an emotional state that does not require an 'intentional object': music can make me anxious without making me anxious about anything in particular.

But some listeners said that they felt 'fear' when listening to the fear excerpts and others said they felt 'surprise'. Significantly, both these pieces are semi-programmatic, and it makes sense to postulate a persona in them. The Holst can be heard as expressing the *fear* of someone who contemplates the fearsome planet, Mars, 'The Bringer of War', and the Mussorgsky can be heard as expressing the *fear* of a witness to the witches on the bare mountain. It makes sense that a listener might take on the role of such a witness and respond sympathetically with fear to these pieces. In that case, these pieces arguably *express* fear in what I have called the full Romantic sense. Similarly, perhaps the Mussorgsky could also be said to express *surprise*, namely the surprise of an onlooker happening upon the witches.

Krumhansl construes the fact that different subjects describe their emotional state somewhat differently as indicating that emotions aroused by music 'are not differentiated at fine-grained levels within basic emotion categories'.[67] Whereas in real life fear, surprise, and anxiety are significantly different emotional responses, in the context of music listening they are submerged into a larger category. (It's perhaps worth recalling that in some of Ekman's experiments, subjects from other cultures could not distinguish fearful from surprised facial expressions.)

Ridley, however, would presumably draw a different moral: that different listeners do feel different fine-grained emotions in response to music. I agree. Different fine-grained emotions experienced in response to music reflect different interactions between listener and music. If, for example, I hear the Holst excerpt as containing a persona, I am much more likely to feel fear rather than simply anxiety. Unfortunately, however, we do not know how the subjects in the experiment would have described what the music *expresses*; and so we cannot tell whether differences in the emotions they reported—'anxious', 'surprised', 'fearful'—really reflect differences in the expressive qualities they found in the music.

I do, however, draw some tentative corroboration for my view that the emotions that music expresses are not always exactly the same as the emotions the music arouses. Although I might be *amused* by the Alfven and Vivaldi pieces and find them *amusing*, I find it a little odd to say that either of these pieces 'expresses amusement'. Similarly, I might be *surprised* by some of the unexpected developments in the Mussorgsky or Holst pieces, without thinking that they *express* surprise (especially if I do not think of them as containing a surprised persona). More generally, all the emotions reported by the listeners are clearly *appropriate* to the music they heard, whether or not they match exactly the emotions they heard the music as expressing. Perhaps we should reach the suitably modest conclusion that there is a greater range of appropriate emotional responses to music than to some of the other arts.

5. Finally, Krumhansl's results suggest an answer to an old puzzle about music. Both Ridley and Walton point out that we feel a peculiar sense of *intimacy* with the music we attend to, and both want to explain this intimacy. Ridley says that the fine-grained

emotions we actually feel in response to a musical melisma are what the music expresses. Walton thinks that expressive music induces us to imagine of our experience of it (the music) that it is an experience of our own feelings. But Krumhansl's experiment suggests that there is a much simpler reason why we feel we are 'inside' the music and it is 'inside us'. The music affects us on the inside; it affects us physiologically and motorically. The rhythm of the music is mirrored in our heart rhythms; the tension in the music is felt as tension in our muscles. This *is* an intimate connection. Paintings can cause us to see the world in a new way and to some extent can cause us to feel in a new way, as we saw in the discussion of Friedrich's landscapes. Novels and poems can give us new points of view on the world as well as to some extent inducing physiological changes and action tendencies. But none of the other arts affects us so powerfully in the direct physiological way that music does. I suspect that this is the most important reason why music is often said to be the most emotionally moving of all the arts.

Going with the Flow

What I've been mainly trying to establish in this chapter is that we do experience emotion in response to music and that the emotions we experience in listening to music help us to *understand* it: they reveal to us musical structure and musical expression. Listening to music is an emotional business. This is not just a Romantic myth but an established empirical fact.

This conclusion confirms my suggestion at the end of Ch. 9 that the appropriate evocation of emotions is a good criterion for successful artistic expression. If works of music successfully express emotions, then it seems we do respond to them emotionally. Moreover, Ridley is right that the emotions we feel may often alert us to subtleties in the musical fabric.

In discussing the Meyer emotions, I emphasized how a piece of complex music induces a sequence of emotional or affective responses, which probably map onto musical parameters, developments in melody, rhythm, and harmony. When we respond to the telling of a story or the expression of emotion in a song or to an unfolding

psychological drama in an instrumental piece, our emotional responses also change as the story or the drama unfolds. In these cases
of complex music, the changing emotions we feel direct our attention
to the unfolding of the musical fabric. When we cognitively monitor
our affective responses, we may detect the structural and expressive
features of the music that were responsible for them. In short, if we go
with the flow of our emotions, they can play an important role in
uncovering the flow of the music.

Meyer thought that responding emotionally in an appropriate way
is just one method of understanding music; the music theorist understands in a different way. No doubt there is much that the untrained
music lover misses when she listens to music. But by the same token
the theorist who feels no emotion in listening to music may be able to
grasp the purely musical structure, but is unlikely to grasp the subtleties in what the music expresses and hence is unlikely to be able to
detect an expressive structure in the music. Listening to music without having one's emotions evoked is an impoverished way of
listening. It will prevent the listener from detecting some of the
ways in which both musical structure and musical expression gradually emerge as the music unfolds.

There is some suggestive work in music therapy that seems to
confirm my picture of how cognitive monitoring of our emotional
responses to music as they change and develop can alert us to
important features of the music as it gradually unfolds. The music
therapists Leslie Bunt and Mercedes Pavlicevic assert that there are
many examples in music therapy practice when 'connections can be
observed between the emotional experiences of the patients and both
surface and deep structural aspects of the music'.[68] In the 'guided
imagery in music (GIM)' approach patients listen to 'specifically
programmed sequences of recorded music in a deeply relaxed state'.
Besides triggering personal associations, memories and images, and
inducing 'iconic associations … between aspects of the music and
non-musical events,' this approach evokes 'intrinsic connections
between layers of musical expectations and deep structures and the
forms and patterns of their internal emotions'.[69] The effect of one
such sequence involving excerpts from Beethoven, Vivaldi, J. S.
Bach, Fauré, and Wagner, is described as follows:

The overall order of the pieces created a mood of expectancy and deepening feelings of awe and wonder. Body-based reactions—changes in breathing, shudders, tension in the stomach, or feelings of lightness, etc.—were closely entrained with the formal aspects of the music—phrasing, changes in pitch, sudden harmonic shifts, shifts in loudness levels, density of the textures, etc. The climactic moments of the Prelude to Lohengrin corresponded with the most illuminating and profoundly moving moments of the session, the powerful memory of which has proved long lasting and in many ways transformative.[70]

In the next chapter I will have more to say about the power of music to 'transform' us. Meanwhile, what's right about the picture painted by Bunt and Pavlicevic is that the physiological changes induced while listening to complex music do map onto the dynamic emotions we feel as we listen, as Krumhansl showed, and it therefore seems likely that they also map the structure and the expressiveness of the music. In this way our emotional responses guide us listeners through the music and help us to identify important structural and expressive passages. Just as the form of a literary work guides and manages our emotional responses to that work, so the musical structure guides and manages our emotional responses to it. Cognitive monitoring of these moment-to-moment responses can teach the attentive listener about both formal and expressive structure. Indeed part of our pleasure in music may come from having our emotional experiences of it managed and guided by the musical form in the way I described for literature in Ch. 7. And of course we may also be moved by the beauty and intricacy of the musical (and expressive) structure.

13

Feeling the Music

For rhythm and harmony penetrate deeply into the mind and have a most powerful effect on it...

Plato, *Republic*, Book III

The Puzzle of Musical Emotions

The idea that music arouses powerful emotions is a very old one, going back at least as far as Plato. In Book III of the *Republic*, when he is discussing the education of the future guardians of the state, Plato inveighs against most of the modes and rhythms of Greek music as inducing the wrong sorts of emotion. Laments and dirges are to be discouraged because they focus attention on death and thus weaken a person's moral fibre. Similarly, the Lydian mode is to be discouraged because it tends to make people 'drunk and soft and idle'.[1] Only the Dorian and Phrygian modes are exempt from Plato's criticism. The Dorian mode is appropriate to 'the voice of a man who, even when he fails and faces injury or death or some other catastrophe, still resists fortune in a disciplined and resolute manner'. And the Phrygian mode is suited to such a man when he is 'engaged in peaceful enterprises', such as trying to win over somebody to his own point of view or when he is 'praying to the gods'.[2]

Instruments that are too sensuous, such as psalteries, harps, and reed-pipes, are out. The lyre and the cithara are in, 'as instruments which serve some purpose in an urban setting', and in the country 'the herdsmen can have wind-pipes'. Plato also inveighs against 'complexity of rhythm and a wide variety of tempos'.[3] Sounding much like a contemporary parent discoursing on rap or heavy metal, Plato identifies some kinds of rhythm as suiting 'meanness and promiscuity or derangement'. In general, goodness and equanimity are to be encouraged by harmony and grace in both music and poetry. Plato is clear that music can have profound emotional and moral effects, and that its use should be monitored accordingly.

But although Plato warned of the dangers inherent in music's power to arouse the passions, most of the musical tradition considers this power to be one of music's virtues. The rhetorical tradition in music, which flourished in the seventeenth and eighteenth centuries, emphasized the arousal of 'affects' as the principal function of music. Just as an oration should be designed to influence its hearers emotionally, so too should music.[4] In the Baroque period, the evocation of a specific affect—sadness, hate, love, joy, anger, fear, etc.—was a principle of unity for a particular piece, or for a section of a longer piece such as a suite.[5] The idea that music should arouse emotions survives into the classical period. Haydn stressed that the composer was a craftsman whose job is to arouse 'sentiments', including moral sentiments.[6]

In the Romantic period, as we have seen, music is thought of as a means of expression, in which the composer expresses his unique individual emotions, but the Romantic artist or composer was also supposed to communicate to an audience the emotions he was expressing so that listeners could recreate these emotions in their own experience. I have been suggesting that a good criterion for successful Romantic expression is the evocation of appropriate emotions in listeners.

Even the arch-formalist, Eduard Hanslick, who famously denied that the function of music was to evoke emotions and thought that we should resist the temptation to think that either the expression or the arousal of feeling plays any role in truly musical appreciation, pays eloquent tribute to music's ability to evoke our emotions.

Even if we have to grant all the arts, without exception, the power to produce effects upon the feelings, yet we do not deny that there is something specific, peculiar only to it, in the way music exercises that power. Music works more rapidly and intensely upon the mind than any other art. With a few chords, we can be transported into a state of mind that a poem would achieve only through lengthy exposition, or a painting only through a sustained effort to understand it...The effect of tones is not only more rapid but more immediate and intensive. The other arts persuade, but music invades us. We experience this, its unique power over the spirit, at its most powerful, when we are severely agitated or depressed.[7]

Today there is plenty of empirical evidence that music does indeed evoke emotions. The psychologist of music David Huron observes that people 'self-medicate' with music, listening to specific kinds of music in order either to confirm or to change the emotional states in which they find themselves.[8] Carol Krumhansl's experiment, which we looked at in Ch. 12, strongly suggests that people experience emotions that are aroused by the music they hear. There has also been some study of the 'thrills and chills' and other physiological symptoms of emotion that some people experience when listening to music. Many people claim to find their emotional experiences of music to be powerful and profound, even life-changing.[9]

If all music told a story as 'Immer leiser' does, perhaps we could explain the arousal of emotion by music in the same way as the arousal of emotion by literary fictions. As I explained in Ch. 5, we respond emotionally to thoughts about fictional characters. But not all music tells a story and not all music contains characters. There is much instrumental music that cannot be appropriately interpreted as containing a persona whose emotional ups and downs we follow as we listen. And in any event, even story-telling music seems to have a power that goes beyond the telling of the story. Furthermore, lots of instrumental music that doesn't tell a story has just as powerful an emotional impact as story-telling music.

So there is a problem. In ordinary life our emotions are evoked when we sense some important wants, goals, or interests to be at stake: wants, goals, and interests that affect the survival or well-being of me and mine. Yet listening to music does not typically seem to involve any powerful wants, needs, or interests of this sort. I may *want* the theme to resolve back to the tonic or the strings to turn the melody over to the winds, but not much seems to be at stake for me in whether or not my wants are satisfied. Emotions are reactions to a stimulus appraised as good or bad, as satisfying or failing to satisfy my goals or interests, as an offence, a loss, or a threat. I am angry when I sense that I or those close to me have been offended, afraid when I or those close to me are under threat, happy when good things happen to me and mine, sad when bad things happen. But in listening to music, the emotions that I feel often do not seem to be in response to anything bad or good that's happening to me or mine. If the tonic fails to return, so what? My life will go on pretty much the same, unaffected by this event.

Krumhansl's experiment appears to demonstrate that happy music can make us happy and sad music sad, but how can this be? Happy and sad music, as Peter Kivy reminds us, doesn't provide anything to be happy or sad *about*, unless there are some helpful accompanying words. I have suggested that happy and sad music makes us happy and sad by affecting us physiologically. I'll develop this idea in much greater detail in this chapter. But if this solves one problem, it opens up another: if all that music does is to induce physiological changes characteristic of happiness or sadness, how does that explain why so many people claim to have profoundly meaningful experiences in response to music?

The judgement theory has particular difficulty dealing with our emotional experiences of music. As Phoebe Ellsworth observes:

Explaining emotional responses to instrumental music is a real problem for appraisal theories, and may be a real threat to the generality of appraisals as elicitors of emotion. Appraisal theories can account for *some* emotional responses to music, as attention and valence certainly occur in listening to music just as they do in responding to other stimuli. ... Nonetheless, many people report responses to music that are far more elaborate than a simple sense of pleasure or displeasure.[10]

As we have seen, Kivy concludes that since garden-variety emotions require cognitive objects, and music does not provide them, therefore music does not evoke such emotions—whatever anyone claims.[11] According to my theory of emotion, the more accurate conclusion is that emotions simply do not require cognitive objects. But even if you do not think that emotions must involve judgements or cognitive evaluations, it remains true that an emotion is stimulated by something or other. The basic problem reappears, even if you are not a judgement theorist, in the form of the question: what is it about music that causes an emotional response? All those who believe that music evokes emotions have to answer this challenge.

In this chapter I will review a number of proposals designed to solve the puzzle. I think that almost all of them point to important ways in which music can arouse emotions or moods: there are multiple sources of our emotional responses to music. I'll show that recent results from the psychology of music lend support to the theory of emotion I defended in Part I, and knock additional nails into the coffin of the judgement theory of emotion. My theory of emotion, with its emphasis on automatic affective appraisals and resultant physiological responses, can explain *how* music evokes moods and emotions, even ones of some complexity. Our most powerful emotional reactions to music are often richly ambiguous. I'll end with a new proposal for explaining why people claim to have such powerful and profound emotional experiences in listening to music.

The Role of Personal Associations

The most obvious solution to the puzzle of musical emotions is that people respond emotionally to music because of the associations they have to it. But this does not explain why different people respond with powerful emotions to the very same music. If the only reason I get a nice warm feeling inside when listening to the Samuel Barber *Adagio for Strings* is that it was playing on the radio when you proposed to me, this doesn't explain why other people are just as moved by the Barber *Adagio* even though it has no such associations for them. And, of course, if you proposed to a background of 'The Girl from Ipanema' instead, I might be profoundly moved by a piece of music that leaves other people feeling just slightly mellow or mildly upbeat. It will turn out, I think, that associations do play a role in the evocation of emotions by music, but it is not this straightforward kind of role.

On the other hand, it may be significant that 'music, like odours, seems to be a very powerful cue in bringing emotional experiences from memory back into awareness'. Klaus Scherer speculates that this is partly due to the fact that music is associated with many significant events in life such as weddings, funerals, dancing, and other festivities, but also because 'music, like odours, may be treated at lower levels of the brain that are particularly resistant to modifications by later input, contrary to cortically based episodic memory'.[12] (Scherer explicitly has in mind here LeDoux's studies of emotional memory that I discussed in Ch. 3.) Consequently it may be no accident that music evokes associations in a powerful, unconscious way and that part of our emotional response to music is based on emotional memories that are the more insistent for being only vaguely understood.[13]

The Kivy and Meyer Emotions

In Ch. 12 we saw that Kivy thinks music can evoke emotion if the music itself is a cognitive object of the emotion concerned, as when we are emotionally moved by the beauty and craftsmanship of Josquin's 'Ave Maria'. We don't need to accept the implicit judgement theory assumptions he's making here in order to understand how such emotions get evoked. The arousal of Kivy emotions is in any case unproblematic: it is not puzzling that people do indeed get pleasure from beauty and feel admiration for fine craftsmanship, especially when the craftsmanship produces something beautiful.

The Meyer emotions are more troubling. In listening to a piece of music in sonata form, I may be *surprised* by a sudden change from tonic minor to relative major, *bewildered* by a prolonged excursus into distant keys, and *relieved* by the eventual reappearance of the tonic. As we saw in Ch. 12, these emotions—surprise, bewilderment, relief, and so on—are emotions that are stimulated by the music itself (and are directed towards the music as their 'object') and the expectations we have as we listen. Listeners are appraising the musical development in terms of their expectations (given their knowledge of the music's style), as surprising, bewildering, satisfying, and so on. But there is an apparent puzzle here. Emotions are evoked only when our wants, goals, and interests are felt to be at stake. It seems perfectly natural that we have an interest in the beautiful and so respond emotionally to a beautiful melody or a beautiful harmonization of the melody, but why should a mere modulation from B flat minor to D flat major, as in the Brahms Intermezzo, arouse emotion? In the large scheme of things such an event does not seem to be of great personal significance to me or mine.

One explanation might focus on the extent to which our sense of tonality and our internalization of the rules of 'good continuation' and so on, that according to Meyer are characteristic of tonal music, evoke powerful *desires* in us, notably the desire for closure and resolution. Those of us who are sensitive to music just do have powerful desires that, for example, the Brahms Intermezzo should not just continue to modulate indefinitely but return to B flat minor. But the pleasure of having such desires satisfied cannot provide the whole solution to the problem, because we enjoy the tension that comes from delayed modulation to the tonic just as much as we enjoy the return to the tonic. Perhaps we even enjoy the uncertainty of the tonal journey more than the certainty of arrival. Musical tension seems to be emotionally exciting in itself and for that very reason enjoyable.

John Sloboda and Patrik Juslin have a better explanation. They link Meyer's view with Nico Frijda's theory of emotion according to which emotion is generated by appraisals of match or mismatch with the agent's goals or interests.

Most compositional systems, such as the tonal system, provide a set of dimensions that establish psychological distance from a 'home' or 'stability' point. Proximity or approach to this resting point involves reduction of tension; distance or departure involves increase of tension. Distance can be measured on a number of dimensions, including rhythm and metre (strong beats are stable, weak beats and syncopations are unstable), and tonality (the tonic is stable, non-diatonic notes are unstable). There is now much experimental evidence that the human listener is sensitive to such features, and represents music in relation to them. . . . These features provide reference points against which the emotional system can plausibly compute match or mismatch in terms of envisaged end points.[14]

This way of thinking is consistent with my own view that emotions are generated by automatic appraisals of the significance of something to one's wants, goals, and interests. Although the music does not present me with situations of particular significance to me and mine, it does present me with events—albeit *musical* events—that I am programmed to respond to affectively: the novel, the unexpected, and that which either gratifies or thwarts my desires and goals.

As we saw in Ch. 3, Damasio explains how we are born responding emotionally to events of certain kinds, such as the novel and the weird. We then learn to respond emotionally to novel events in new domains (such as music). Although it may not be particularly useful to be skilled at responding with surprise, bewilderment, and so on at appropriate moments in a Brahms Intermezzo, it is in general important for us to respond emotionally to the novel, the bewilderingly complex, the surprising, and so on. In many life situations it is important that we respond emotionally to the weird and unexpected, and our response to the weird and unexpected in music—such as unexpected modulations or melodic sequences—is a by-product of this general feature of our constitution. Similarly, we respond in general with pleasure when our desires are satisfied, so it is not surprising that we feel relief and satisfaction when the tonic returns.

Suppose, for example, that I respond with pleased surprise to the modulation from B flat minor to D flat major at the introduction of the second theme in Brahms' Intermezzo. My attention is drawn to something strange but pleasant in the musical environment. I appraise this stimulus as novel, unexpected, and pleasing. The non-cognitive affective appraisal or appraisals cause physiological changes, expressive gestures, motor activity, action tendencies, and so on, that cement my focus of attention on the stimulus. If I then monitor cognitively what is going on, I might realize that it is the shift from B flat minor to D flat major that is causing my response. And I might also describe my experience: 'I was *surprised* when the key changed but *delighted* by the beauty of the transition', or something of this sort. (Of course there is a lot more to respond to in this passage than the mere key change I'm focusing on here.)

A similar explanation may partially account for the thrills and chills that many people report feeling at key moments in the development of a piece of music, and which, if Sloboda is right, are the result of the way the music plays with our expectations, mixing the interestingly unexpected with the satisfyingly expected.[15] However, as we'll see later, this is not the whole story where thrills and chills are concerned.

Contagious Reactions to Musical 'Doggy' Expressions

Kivy and Meyer are both talking about emotions that are evoked by paying attention to the musical structure. But music also has the power to affect us more directly. In Kivy's terminology, music does not have to be a cognitive object of emotion; it can also act as a stimulus object.

It is well documented that people respond automatically to other peoples' expressions of emotion by mirroring the emotion expressed. People very readily 'catch' each other's facial expressions. Think of what happens when you join a friend who is smiling or laughing: you find yourself smiling too even if you don't know why. This phenomenon is known as 'emotional contagion'.

Stephen Davies has suggested that *music* can evoke emotions by a kind of contagion. Musical 'emotion characteristics in appearances' can communicate emotion directly to audiences by means of mirroring responses that rest on 'the recognition of the expressive character of the music'.[16] If I hear a sad expression in the music, I mimic the expression I hear and thus acquire the corresponding feeling. According to Davies, 'The expressiveness of music can be powerfully moving. It moves us not only to admire the composer's achievement but also, sometimes, to feel the emotions it expresses. Expressive "appearances" are highly evocative, even where one does not believe that they relate to someone's occurrent emotion.'[17] If my companion looks miserable, he can infect me with his apparent misery, regardless of whether he is actually miserable or not. Similarly, the sad face of the basset hound as well as music that sounds and moves in a sad way can infect us with sadness, he thinks, even if they are not expressions of anyone's sadness, but only 'appearances' of emotion.

Davies's account cannot be quite right for two reasons. For one thing, emotional contagion normally occurs automatically without our being aware of what's happening: the expression is acquired automatically by some form of motor mimicry. *Recognition* of the expression is not necessary as Davies stipulates, and may even prevent or moderate the effect of contagion.

Secondly, on Davies's account music is *like* an expression of emotion—just as is the configuration of the basset hound's face—but it isn't one really. We are programmed to respond with sadness to an expression of sadness in another human being. The fact that we are probably programmed to respond to other *human* faces (on the grounds that sad human expressions usually indicate sad humans) probably has no implications for our responses to doggy faces. (After all, if living with a basset hound were like living with a depressed person, would normal folk choose a basset hound as their life's companion?) And by parity of reasoning we are probably not programmed to respond to musical sounds by virtue of the fact that they are *like* expressions of emotion in some way. Indeed this brief discussion once again underlines how misleading the basic doggy theory analogy is.

Patrik Juslin has come up with an explanation for musical contagion that does not depend on the recognition of an expression. Juslin's idea is that 'music performers are able to communicate emotions to listeners by using the same acoustic code as is used in vocal expression of emotion'.[18] Thus just as a baby's cry of distress automatically elicits emotion in the caregiver, so a musical cry of distress—which has the same timbre, loudness, and tempo, among other things—elicits the same sort of response in listeners. Interestingly, there is some evidence that timbre, loudness, and tempo have emotional significance that is relatively independent of culture (unlike, say, harmony). Juslin speculates that an explanation for the similarity in our responses to the baby's cry and the music is that the simple, automatic, independent brain systems—or 'modules'—that respond to cries of distress 'do not "know" the difference between vocal expression of emotion and other acoustic expression but will react in the same way as long as certain cues (e.g. high speed, loud dynamics, fast attack, many overtones) are present in the stimulus'.[19]

Juslin has proposed a plausible mechanism for emotional contagion through music. Notice, however, that it has very limited application. It applies only to music that *sounds like* a vocal expression of emotion.

Moreover, when emotional expressions infect us in this way, the emotions we are infected with do not always or even typically *mirror* the emotions expressed. The automatic, inbuilt response to a baby's distress cry is as likely to be tenderness and love as distress, just as the inbuilt response to another person's anger or hostility is as likely to be fear as anger or hostility.[20] Emotions are interactions between organism and environment: we are attuned to other people's expressions (some people being more attuned than others), so that we can respond appropriately, and an appropriate response is not always a mirroring response.

The Dance of Love

The doggy theorists treat expressiveness in music *as if* it were a genuine expression of emotion even though they think that no one is actually expressing their emotions in the music. And Juslin's explanation is of the evocation of emotion by music that sounds *as if* it is a vocal expression of emotion. But there are many occasions in ordinary life when people genuinely do interact emotionally through music. One of the most moving occasions is when mothers bond with their babies through singing to them. Isabelle Peretz observes that accurate communication between mothers and their infants is essential to survival, and that 'music plays an important role in emotion regulation and emotional communication between caregivers and infants'.[21]

When caregivers sing to their newborn infants, the infants pay very close attention. The infants pay 'more sustained attention' to their mums when they are singing than when they are merely speaking (even when they are talking 'baby talk'). Infants are 'hypnotized' by their mothers' singing. In turn the mothers or caregivers

nicely mirror infants' perceptual abilities by singing more slowly, at higher pitch, with exaggerated rhythm, and in a more loving or emotionally engaging manner than when singing alone. . . . Responsiveness to such infant-directed singing appears inborn. Two-day-old hearing infants, born from congenitally deaf parents (who sign and do not sing or speak), prefer infant-directed singing to adult-directed singing.[22]

In other words, maternal singing is an expression of love, and the infant's emotional response is a reciprocal loving response: the baby isn't just responding to an emotional 'appearance', a 'doggy expression', but to a genuine expression of maternal love.

Furthermore, as Bunt and Pavlicevic report, the response to maternal singing is part of a broader pattern of communication between mother and infant:

newborn infants are neurologically predisposed to identifying, and responding to, contours and rhythms of movements, gestures, and vocalizations in their mothers' gestures, vocal sounds, and facial expression. . . . In addition, they 'tune in' to subtle shifts in vocal timbre, tempo, and volume variations, and with their mothers negotiate and share a flexible musical pulse between them, constantly adapting their [sic] tempo, intensity, motion, shape, and contour of their sounds, movements, and gestures in order to 'fit' and to communicate with one another. . . . Mother and infant develop and share a rich musical 'code' that has interactive significance.[23]

Bunt and Pavlicevic see this interaction as anticipating later 'interactional synchrony', the 'dance between persons'[24] that occurs when we interact with each other socially, adapting our gaze, and coordinating head movements, hand gestures, and so on. They also see the 'dance' between mother and baby, in which each is sensitive to the changes in emotional expression of the other and adapts their own behaviour accordingly, as a model for their own work in music therapy.

Peretz reports that the 'dominant view' about the adaptive value of music is that it is best explained at the group level: music helps to promote group cohesion. Music encourages harmonization both literally and metaphorically, and regular rhythm promotes 'motor synchronicity'.[25] Basically, the idea is that dancing and singing together helps to cement the social group. We see this in modern Western culture at rock concerts, square dances, and many other venues. And perhaps mother–baby musical interaction is an early example of this. One of the researchers on maternal singing puts the point this way: 'Maternal singing is likely to strengthen the emotional ties between mother and infant just as singing in other circumstances reduces the psychological distance between singer and listener. Indeed, maternal singing may set the stage for the subsequent role of music in group bonding.'[26]

Art music today, however, is typically heard in solitude or in the silent concert hall, where singing along and swaying back and forth to the music are discouraged. Yet even 'Immer leiser' and the Brahms

Intermezzo promote emotional interaction between performer and listener. I have argued that 'Immer leiser' is an expression of emotion in the full Romantic Collingwoodian sense. The music evokes an emotional response partly because it *is* an expression of emotion, and is not merely heard *as if* it were an expression of emotion. An appropriate response to this song *ought* to be partly emotional: I may feel empathetically with the protagonist in her sense of loss and eventual acceptance of loss, or I may respond with sympathy and compassion to her expression of these emotions. Of course, I am also cognitively monitoring my responses, figuring out what I am responding to, and perhaps 'cataloguing' my emotional responses in reflection as 'sorrow' or 'compassion'. My affective appraisal of the music involves a good deal of cognitive activity, whereas the besotted baby listening to his mummy singing a lullaby may be making solely non-cognitive, affective appraisals: '**Yum**' or something of the sort! Nevertheless, part, at least, of my response to 'Immer leiser' involves an immediate emotional response to the protagonist's cries of distress.

The Jazzercise Effect

Emotional contagion is supposed to work through feedback from mimicry of other people's expressions of emotion. It probably isn't true that we are emotionally affected by *recognizing* emotional doggy expressions in music, as Davies thinks. But it does seem to be true that music directly affects us physiologically and acts directly on the motor system, and that our subjective feelings change as a result of being influenced in these ways by the music. As in genuine emotional contagion, these reactions get caused *without* our recognizing what causes them.

Elaine Hatfield and her colleagues have summarized the mechanism of emotional contagion in ordinary life in three propositions:

> Proposition 1. In conversation, people tend automatically and continuously to mimic and synchronize their movements with the facial expressions, voices, postures, movements, and instrumental behaviors of others.

Proposition 2. Subjective emotional experiences are affected, moment to moment, by the activation and/or feedback from such mimicry.

Proposition 3. Given Propositions 1 and 2, people tend to 'catch' others' emotions, moment to moment.[27]

In other words, the mechanism of emotional contagion relies on feedback from motor mimicry. In a sense music does induce us to mimic its movements. More generally, however, music affects our emotions through affecting our motor and other bodily systems.

There is lots of evidence that happy music does cheer people up and sad music saddens them, that restless music makes people restless and calm music calms them down *without* there being any prior 'cognitive evaluation' (or even any prior *affective* evaluation) of the music. I call this the 'Jazzercise effect'. In the Jazzercise effect, a happy response to happy music is not based on an evaluation of the music or of anything else. Nor is it necessarily a result of hearing the music as someone's *expression* of happiness. Happy music can affect us directly even if it is not heard as an expression of happiness. 'Jingle Bells' is 'happy music' and it can in the right context make people happier, but it isn't particularly expressive music nor is it typically heard as an expression of anyone's happiness.

Granted, it is not always clear whether music is giving us *pleasure* just because it is beautiful or interesting or expressive, or whether music is infecting us with *happiness* because of a direct response to the way it sounds or moves. Many experiments in the psychology of music fail to distinguish between pleasure as an emotion directed at the music as cognitive object and happiness as an emotion directly induced by emotional qualities in the music. And of course in real life these two phenomena no doubt frequently exist side by side.

There are only a few emotion qualities in music that have been shown to induce the corresponding emotional state. In the literature it is happiness, sadness, restlessness, and calm that come up over and over again. Interestingly, these are psychological states that do not have to be *about* anything, as the judgement theorists might say, nor do they have to be stimulated by a specific affective appraisal (such as **The situation is bad** or **The situation is good**). This suggests that music induces not emotions per se, but *moods*. Indeed, serenity and restlessness don't seem to be emotions in the normal sense at all, although they are often classified as moods.[28] Happiness and sadness are used both as terms for regular emotional responses—'I was happy when Jane won the prize and sad when the dog died'—and as mood terms—'I've been feeling happy/sad all day and I don't know why.'

Moods and emotions both involve physiological changes, changes in action readiness, changes in point of view and characteristic subjective feelings. But, according to most theorists, moods are more *global* and *diffuse* than emotions; they are of *longer duration* and *lower intensity*.[29] Moods can be caused in ways that do not involve an appraisal of external events, for example by drugs or the weather (and, as we will see, also by music). Both Nico Frijda and Paul Ekman propose that moods *lower the threshold* for being in emotional states. Frijda says that moods are 'states of lowered thresholds for appraising events as having pleasant or unpleasant aspects to them'.[30] He is clearly thinking here only of positive and negative moods. Speaking more generally, Ekman says that moods 'lower the threshold for arousing the emotions, which occur most frequently during a particular mood'.[31] So in a nervous mood I am more likely to fly off the handle when something goes wrong; in a happy mood I am more likely to shrug off adversity.

Several philosophers have said that the emotions music evokes are truncated or etiolated in some way. Stephen Davies says that we do have emotional responses to music that mirror what it expresses, but they are 'less thought-founded'[32] than standard object-directed emotional responses, and they lack objects: 'The response to music is comparable to objectless reactions of the garden variety,'[33] such as sadness, joy, and fear. Aaron Ridley concurs: what music evokes are not actual episodes of emotion since they lack a 'material object'. Rather what is evoked is a 'feeling', by which he means an emotion 'shorn of [its] cognitive aspect'.[34] It is not enough, however, simply to assert that emotions can be evoked 'shorn' of their cognitive aspect. We need to know how it can be that emotions survive being shorn in this way. More troubling, in my view, is the fact that these emotional states seem to be evoked by music without any *affective appraisal*, yet an affective appraisal is normally the *sine qua non* of emotional responses.

The obvious solution is to say that music evokes moods rather than emotions per se,[35] but Davies at least resists this conclusion: 'the response to music is not like an objectless mood, for the former involves close attention to the music and is a reaction to that close attention, whereas the latter is objectless not only in lacking an emotional object but also in lacking a specific cause and focus'.[36] Davies's discussion suggests that what he has in mind are the kind of rich, aesthetic responses we have to serious 'art' music such as 'Immer leiser', which may indeed require focused attention on the details of the music for its emotional effect. But these are not the *only* responses we have to music. Music also induces moods without our having to pay much, if any, attention to it: its powers of mood induction seem to operate largely below conscious awareness. Indeed, if you start paying attention to the music in elevators or grocery stores, you are likely to end up heading for the exit. Much popular music gets its listeners into a joyful, melancholy, sexually aroused, or belligerent state without the listener having to know how the trick is turned. And even though an adequate emotional response to 'Immer leiser' requires paying close attention to it, this does not mean that the song is not simultaneously affecting us in a subliminal way *as well*.

How can happy music make people happy, and calm music calm people down? The answer in a nutshell is that music with a happy, sad, calm, or restless character causes *physiological changes, motor activity*, and *action tendencies*, that are experienced as happiness, sadness, seren-ity, or restlessness. These states are *emotional* rather than merely physiological states in that they bring in their wake not only charac-teristic subjective feelings but also characteristic cognitive activity: people have a tendency to view the world in characteristic ways. However, although the world gets 'regestalted', so that we are more inclined to take a certain point of view on things or view the world in a certain way, there is no affective appraisal of some particular event or situation (and certainly no 'cognitive object' of emotion) that sets off the emotion process. The points of view we take tend to be global: we view ourselves and the world in general in a positive or negative, reassuring or uncertain way.

What, then, is the evidence that music evokes moods? There is an area of research in psychology called human factors research that includes studies of the effect of music in the workplace, on shoppers, and so on. I, however, am going to focus on the evidence from psychologists of music who are interested not so much in getting people to calm down in hospital or buy more in the supermarket but in music itself and how it functions. First, I'll focus on the evidence that music does cause bodily changes and in the following section I'll present the evidence that these bodily changes are experienced and described as emotional or mood changes, with consequences for various aspects of cognition.

Evidence for the Jazzercise Effect

Evidence that Music Affects Physiology

It is well documented that music has a direct effect on the body. I have already discussed Carol Krumhansl's experiment that showed pretty clearly that music has physiological effects on listeners. But there is plenty of other evidence too. Dale Bartlett looked at over 130 research studies from the early 1900s to 1994 on the ability of music to effect physiological changes, and concluded that 'the majority' of them 'demonstrate physiological responses in reaction to experimental settings of music and sound stimuli'.[37] He found that, despite many differences between the studies he looked at, there is good evidence that 'test stimuli (either music or sound sources) that may be categorized as stimulative (e.g. march-style music, rhythmic melodies, high loudness conditions, white noise, fast tempos, stimulative rhythm, and auditory onset)' produced an *increased* heart or pulse rate, and 'test stimuli that may be categorized as sedative' (e.g. 'depressing' music, slow tempo or relaxation-type music, sedative classical music, chordal harmony, etc.) produced *decreased* rates.[38] Among the pieces that raised heart or pulse rate were the Toreador song from *Carmen* and the 'Stars and Stripes'; among those that decreased heart or pulse rate were Tchaikovsky's *Pathétique* symphony.

The clearest evidence that music can arouse people or calm them down comes from measures of skin conductivity: exciting music produces decreased resistance in skin conductivity and calming music produces increased resistance.[39] Other measures studied include respiration rate, blood pressure, muscular tension and motor activity, finger or peripheral temperature, and stomach contractions. Unfortunately, the experiments used so many different types of musical stimuli and so many different experimental formats that there are no consistent results over a number of studies that might tie specific mood states to specific musical parameters. Nevertheless it does establish—unsurprisingly—that the right kind of music arouses people physiologically or calms them down.

Although this is somewhat interesting to have empirically confirmed, it is not enough to show that music arouses specific moods. In discussing the fight or flight syndrome—the classic 'arousal' syndrome—in Ch. 2, we saw that arousal is characteristic of several different negative emotions, and is also characteristic of some positive emotions. I can be aroused and happy (excited and ebullient) or aroused and unhappy (nervous and agitated). I can also be calm and happy (serene) or calm and unhappy (leaden or dejected). Other studies of physiological changes induced by music are more informative.

A study by Nyklicek et al. using classical music excerpts judged independently to be happy, sad, serene, and agitated respectively, found that the emotions induced by such music could be reliably differentiated on the basis of cardio-respiratory activity.[40] In experiments using musical examples with a marked happy, sad, serene, or agitated character, Witvliet and associates found that agitated music evoked marked arousal effects on the autonomic measures of skin conductance and heart rate.[41] More significantly, perhaps, using facial myography techniques, they discovered that happy music induced subliminal *smiles* and sad music induced subliminal *frowns*. In other words, here is evidence that music with a particular happy or sad character induces expressions characteristic of the corresponding emotional states. Lundqvist et al. report essentially the same thing but in more technical language. In their experiment 'The happy music elicited larger zygomatic activity [smiles], larger skin conductance, lower finger temperature, more (self-reported) happiness and less sadness compared with the sad music.'[42]

Music also apparently has direct effects on hormonal activity. Peretz reports that there is some data to suggest that music is 'effective in eliciting [neurochemical] responses, as suggested by the action of the antagonists of endorphins...and cortisol measures'.[43] For example, the infants who listened to maternal singing showed marked arousal-modulation effects in the cortisol in their saliva.[44]

The neurophysiologist Walter Freeman has also suggested that oxy-
tocin may be released while listening to music.[45] There is very little
data so far on this question, however. Moreover, some of this hormonal activity may be part of a pleasurable response to music just
because it sounds good, or a pleasurable response to a moment of
heightened tension in the unfolding of a complex musical structure.

There is a better case to be made for the effect of music with a
specific type of emotional character on movement and action tendencies. The connection between music and movement has been
emphasized since Aristotle and was part of the Cartesian legacy to the
Baroque theorists. According to Descartes, music directly induces
movements of the animal spirits which then act upon the muscles.
Much music has been written to facilitate specific activities: brisk,
martial music for military marches, sad, dignified music for funeral
processions, gentle, tender music for lullabies, and arousing music of
various sorts and degrees for various sorts of dances, work tunes, and
so on. All of this seems intuitively obvious. But Sloboda and Juslin do
cite some sources claiming empirical support for the idea that music
induces movement. They point out, too, that 'even when suppressing an overt response to music, listeners may still be engaging in
subliminal physical action'.[46]

An aspect of music that appears to be genuinely 'contagious' is
rhythm. One interesting study showed that adults while listening to a
lullaby had markedly decreased heart rates and their 'breathing
rhythm became synchronized with the rhythm of the music.'[47] (No
such effects were found in the control group who were listening to
jazz!) Scherer comments that 'susceptible individuals' find it difficult
not to move to music, and cites studies that seem to show that 'such
coupling of internal rhythms to external drivers . . . might be present
at a very early age'.[48]

In a sense, then, music *is* contagious, but it is contagious not
because we recognize an expression of emotion in music, and are
influenced by that, as Davies thinks. Music is contagious by virtue of
the Jazzercise effect: it affects people directly in their physiology. It
is pretty clear, then, that contrary to what Kivy claims, music can act
as a stimulus object, very much like a drug. Arousing music really
does arouse people and calm music really does calm them down, as
measured by motor and autonomic activity. What's more, music

induces physiological changes and action tendencies characteristic of happiness and sadness. But is this enough to show that people are actually in a different *mood*? Remember that this involves not just physiological changes, motor activity, and states of action readiness, but also a *shift in point of view*, a *tendency to view the world in a characteristic way* (such as pessimistically or optimistically).

Evidence that Music Manipulates Mood

In Ch. 12 we saw that in Krumhansl's experiment physiological changes were correlated with reports by the subjects that they did indeed experience distinct emotions on listening to different types of music.[49] But as is well-known, self-reports are not always reliable. It would be nice if we could confirm by other means that the physiological effects of music also bring about changes in people's points of view or ways of viewing the world.

The idea that bodily changes alone can produce cognitive changes, such as of outlook or point of view, goes back to William James:

There is no more valuable precept in moral education than this, as all who have experience know: if we wish to conquer undesirable tendencies in ourselves, we must assiduously, and in the first instance cold-bloodedly, go through the *outward movements* of those contrary dispositions which we prefer to cultivate. The reward of persistency will infallibly come, in the fading out of the sullenness or depression, and the advent of real cheerfulness and kindliness in their stead. Smooth the brow, brighten the eye, contract the dorsal rather than the ventral aspect of the frame, and speak in a major key, pass the genial compliment, and your heart must be frigid indeed if it do not gradually thaw![50]

Significantly, one of the main therapies for depression is behavioural: engaging in activities that in former times you enjoyed is a good recipe for improving your mood.[51] David Watson, the mood specialist, confirms that the best way to improve your mood is simply by engaging in some activity or other.[52] Similarly, as I reported in Ch. 2, Paul Ekman has found that getting people to put on a particular facial expression will induce corresponding physiological activity and subjective feelings.

Psychologists who have no particular interest in music per se frequently use music as a method of mood-induction and then proceed to measure what happens when one is in the given mood, positive or negative. There are some interesting results. In one study 'participants who felt depressed after listening to sad music perceived more rejection/sadness in faces with ambiguous emotional expressions and less invitation/happiness in faces with clear, unambiguous expressions'.[53] Paula Niedenthal and her colleagues have found that happy (sad) music makes subjects quicker to detect happy (sad) facial expressions in other people and quicker to recognize words like 'happy' ('sad').[54] Music also has effects on memory. One mood-induction study, in which moods were purportedly induced by playing appropriate music, showed that events that one has memorized under the effect of a certain mood are recalled more easily when that mood or a similar one is evoked (in this case by music). Scherer comments that it is mostly 'the valence dimension of the emotional state that triggers the effect':[55] the emotions in question are simple positive and negative affect or 'happiness' and 'sadness'.

One experimenter has found that 'a music mood-induction procedure yielded significant effects on behavioural measures, such as decision-time, distance approximation, and writing speed (behaviours believed to be affected by moods)'.[56] In another study, after suitable music was played to induce 'positive, negative, or neutral affect', listeners were asked to evaluate their own 'specific qualities and characteristics (How smart are you? How kind are you?). It was found that subjects rated themselves more favorably after listening to happy compared with sad music.'[57] This experiment is reported by Scherer who comments: 'Interestingly, this effect was stronger for subjects with low self-esteem, suggesting greater sensitivity to mood manipulation for this particular group.'[58] And in a pleasing footnote to Plato, an experiment by Fried and Berkowitz has shown that when four groups of people were played examples of soothing, stimulating, or 'aversive' music (or—for the control group—no music), 'those who heard the soothing music were most apt to show altruistic behavior immediately afterwards'.[59] The mood ratings for the various groups suggested that 'the soothing and stimulating music created somewhat different positive moods'.[60]

We are all familiar with the mood-altering effects of Jazzercise or other exercise, not to mention the effects of taking 'mind-altering' substances. Usually happiness or euphoria is what is aimed at, although as we also know only too well, some drugs such as alcohol have a depressive effect. Music with a pronounced happy or sad character seems to work in a not dissimilar way. It induces bodily changes which, as James suggests so eloquently, in turn lead to a disposition to evaluate the world positively or negatively. Such effects are unlikely to counterbalance tendencies to happiness or sadness caused by affective evaluations that something good has happened or that one has suffered a loss. Happy music probably won't cheer me up if I have just learnt that my mother has died—indeed it may irritate me precisely because it tends to cause bodily effects that do not match my point of view on the world. The effects I am talking about may also not last very long. Nevertheless, however weak and transient they may be, these effects seem to be real.

Labelling the Jazzercise Emotions

In the normal way, emotions are the result of *affective* appraisals, such as **Threat!** or **Loss!** or **Goal Achieved!** But music—whether it be Western art music, rock, or African drum music—is able to induce physiological changes, facial expressions, and action tendencies, which in Jamesian fashion are all by themselves capable of putting listeners into a particular mood. However, listeners do not just describe themselves as in a state of arousal or a mood. They regularly attribute *emotions* to themselves as a result of listening to music. In Krumhansl's experiment, for example, people described themselves as feeling 'contented' or 'amused' as well as 'happy'; 'fearful' and 'surprised' as well as 'anxious'. We don't know why different listeners described their affective experiences somewhat differently, even though the music affected them physiologically in very similar ways, but a good conjecture would be that listeners *labelled* their physiological/affective state differently depending on the different contexts they brought to the music. As we saw in Ch. 11, Edward T. Cone says that music is consistent with a number of different 'contents', each distinguished by a different 'context'. Something similar may be true of our emotional reactions to music. Music induces a mood—of excitement or calm, of happiness or sadness—which is then interpreted in different ways depending on the context the listener brings to the music. In the Krumhansl experiment one obvious context is the programme that accompanies some of the pieces. Another obvious context would be the cultural associations that surround these pieces: in particular, the Barber *Adagio* and *Night on Bald Mountain* have associations with specific melancholy or spooky events.[61]

Towards the end of Ch. 3, I discussed the research of the psychologist Stanley Schachter, the expert on 'misattribution', who in a series of experiments demonstrates that if people are in a state of arousal for which they have no adequate explanation, they experience what he calls 'evaluative needs'.[62] In other words, they feel a need to make sense out of and understand their state of arousal in the most *appropriate* way. Consequently, people tend to label some inexplicable state of arousal with an emotion word that seems appropriate to the context in which they find themselves. In the famous Schachter and Singer experiment, subjects were in a state of arousal for which they had no adequate explanation; they sought an explanation for their state of arousal; and they labelled their state depending on the social context in which they found themselves. Different people in the same state of arousal labelled their state differently because they interpreted their state in the light of the different contexts they adduced.[63]

How is all this relevant to music? My proposal is that at least sometimes music plays a role similar to that which the epinephrine played in Schachter's famous experiment. It *arouses* listeners and puts them into a bodily or mood state. But, as in the experiment, listeners have no good explanation for their state of arousal. Why, after all, should music make me feel anxious or fearful? There's nothing to warrant an affective appraisal of **Threat**! In such circumstances of unexplained arousal, listeners experience evaluative needs. So what they do is what the subjects in the Schachter experiment did: they look around for an appropriate label for their vaguely felt affective state, and they *label* their state of arousal depending on the context they bring to the experience. Consequently, different people label their states of arousal in different ways, depending on the different contexts they bring to the music. If it is objected[64] that I don't need to look around for an explanation for my state of arousal when I'm listening to music, since I am perfectly aware that what I'm doing is *listening to music*, I suggest that, given how the emotions work, it *is* puzzling to us when an emotion seems to have been aroused in us and yet we cannot find any affective appraisal that might be responsible for it. For one thing, the Jazzercise effect operates below the level of conscious awareness and outside our control. I have to pay attention in order to figure out how the music is affecting my body. And secondly, even if we consciously *feel* ourselves aroused and we *feel* ourselves to be in some mood state, we will still be puzzled, because nothing is happening in the actual world to justify an emotional reaction of fear or grief or contentment: all that's happening is that music is playing.[65]

As I explained in Ch. 3, the Schachter and Singer experiment is often described as an example of simple 'misattribution':[66] people think they are angry or euphoric, but (perhaps) they are mistaken. But, as I pointed out earlier, labelling our emotions frequently becomes a self-fulfilling prophecy. If I am in a physiologically aroused state and I label my state 'anxious', then I will most likely begin to make anxious affective appraisals, to act anxiously, and so on. If, on the other hand, I label myself 'afraid', or 'surprised', I am likely to begin making different affective appraisals and arriving at somewhat different emotional states.[67] Labelling the experience is part of *cognitive monitoring*, and cognitive monitoring itself *alters the nature of the experience*, feeding back upon bodily changes, action tendencies, and affective appraisals.

Oatley and Jenkins note that 'Emotion, or arousal, acquired in one situation, can affect behavior and intensity of emotions in other situations, particularly if the people concerned do not know the source of their mood.'[68] One example of the effect of arousal is seen in a famous experiment by Dutton and Aron, who found that subjects 'became more amorous after crossing a high and rather scary suspension bridge'.[69] Oatley and Jenkins see this as an example of 'misattribution'. But it's also true that if I label myself 'amorous' because I'm aroused and I don't know why, and being amorous seems to be the best explanation on offer for my state of arousal, then likely as not I will quickly *become amorous*: my act of labelling affects my emotional state. Similarly, when we listen to music a state of arousal is induced and how we label that state of arousal affects how we feel to some degree. That is why it is not just mood terms that I employ when describing the affective state that music has induced in me. I also attribute *emotions* to myself even though my feeling state may not be the result of any affective appraisal. Strictly speaking, I should not attribute any emotions to myself unless and until I start to make appropriate affective appraisals. But once I've interpreted my feelings as being of a particular emotional state, this tends to become a self-fulfilling prophecy: I start to view the world in the appropriate way and I begin to make the corresponding affective appraisals. In short, emotion begins in bodily changes which in turn induce a mood and make us readier to get into some emotional state. Which emotional state we get into is the result of interpreting our bodily state by reference to the context in which we find ourselves.[70] We can describe this process as 'confabulation', but what starts out as a fable may end up coming true.

If this picture is correct, then there will be general agreement about which passages of music are particularly arousing emotionally but disagreement about what exactly they signify and what emotion exactly they provoke. As I've tried to demonstrate, my proposal is consistent with what is known about how moods and emotions work. But there is also some other evidence that supports the view more directly. First there is the suggestive fact noted by Waterman that in an experiment in which listeners pressed a button whenever they 'felt something' in response to an unfolding piece of music, different listeners 'felt something' at the *same point* in the music, but their 'stated reasons' for pressing the button 'were very different from one another'.[71] This strongly suggests that people are aroused by music at more-or-less the same places in its development (assuming some familiarity with the style of the music in question), but that they do not label their experiences in the same way. To paraphrase Collingwood, they feel something they know not what.

Secondly, evidence from ethnomusicology suggests that in different cultures the same sort of music will be labelled differently. Judith Becker notes that 'Emotional responses to music do not occur spontaneously, nor "naturally," but rather, take place within complex systems of thought and behavior concerning what music means, what it is for, how it is to be perceived, and what might be appropriate kinds of expressive responses.'[72] She points out that when people say they are 'happy' while listening to music, this is often the effect of simple arousal. 'We tend to feel better when we are musically aroused and excited.'[73] But in specific cultural contexts this 'arousal' or 'happiness' may be interpreted in very different ways.

Finally, a number of psychologists have noticed the 'ambiguity and cue-impoverishment' that characterizes our emotional experiences of music. As Sloboda and Juslin put it,

a great deal of what looks like emotional responses to music is not accompanied by any strong sense of where the significance lies. A person can be reduced to tears by a particular passage of music, yet be completely unable to specify, even in outline, any objective feature of the music which would account for its grief-inducing qualities.

They go on to cite LeDoux and Zajonc as showing that 'people often perceive and process emotional information in a pre-conscious or automatic manner',[74] as indeed I have emphasized throughout my discussion. In listening to music we often feel that we are in some kind of emotional state, but it is not immediately obvious how we should label it.

What, then, are the contextual factors that influence how we label our emotional experiences of music? One of them is probably personal associations and emotional memories. You feel nostalgia and I feel wistfulness, she feels melancholy and he feels loneliness and abandonment. Differences such as these may be partly due to differences in the personal experiences and memories associated with the music. Appropriate affective appraisals may arise from the fact that I start to think about some significant emotional event from the past. The insistence of emotional memory may also be responsible for the sense we often have that the musical experience is powerful and deep.

Another important contextual factor is what the music expresses, if anything.[75] In listening to the opening of 'Immer leiser', I probably feel, in broad terms, 'sad'. If I pay attention to the words of the song, I am likely to label my sad feelings in a way appropriate to the emotions expressed by the protagonist of the song. I may say I feel 'yearning' or 'longing' because I feel as she does, or I may say I feel 'nostalgic' or 'wistful' about my own lost youth or love, or I may feel 'sorrowful' and 'compassionate' as a result of contemplating the protagonist's situation.[76] In the case of instrumental music, we may sometimes posit a persona in the music to whose expressions of emotion we respond. For example, in discussing Krumhansl's experiment, I suggested that those who heard the Mussorgsky as a full Romantic expression of emotion were more likely to say they felt 'fear' in response to it, because they could have been identifying with a fearful persona in the music witnessing the terrifying witches on Bald Mountain.

Cultural context is also important in how we label our emotions. This is a general truth about emotions in different cultures, but it has special application to music. In ordinary life situations we label our emotions partly depending on what is deemed appropriate in the light of the cultural context and the emotion concepts available to us in our particular language. Music's ambiguity simply allows more leeway for what counts as an 'appropriate' label for our emotional experience. The emotions that music evokes in us are labelled in pretty different ways, depending partly on cultural norms of various sorts. In our culture, for example, as DeNora has noticed,[77] music plays a role in the creation of self-image, especially among teenagers, and it is to be expected that how one responds emotionally to particular kinds of music will partly depend on how it affects one's self-image. The labelling of emotions is a thoroughly social and cultural affair.

The Power of Music

The Jazzercise effect is a quite general capacity of music—whether Brahms, rock, or folk music—to 'infect' us with a mood by a kind of contagion or motor mimicry. Music evokes moods by means of effecting autonomic changes, motor activity, and action tendencies, so as to put listeners into a mood state, a state in which they more readily ascribe emotions to themselves. Different listeners label their states by reference to different contexts, and that is one big reason why different people say they feel somewhat different emotional states in response to the very same music. However, my account also explains a more deeply puzzling phenomenon. Many qualified listeners—music lovers who are not necessarily musical experts—

when listening to good music[78] sometimes feel themselves suddenly overwhelmed emotionally without knowing why. This can happen when we're listening to Brahms or Mahler, but also when we're listening to good rock music or other popular genres. People describe themselves as getting the chills or feeling their hair stand on end.

I noted in Ch. 12 that John Sloboda identifies these moments of intense emotional experience as occurring at structural high points or climaxes or moments of maximum tension in the musical development. It is not surprising that they occur at moments of high tension in the music, since, as we have seen, tense music is *arousing*: it affects our autonomic and motor systems in various ways. But even if Sloboda is right that these thrills or chills occur at structural high points, this does not explain why such moments are experienced with such great passion. Even if I figure out that it was when the key changed that the goose bumps came over me, I may be puzzled about *why* such a powerful emotional experience would be evoked just because the key changed. I am more likely to attribute my emotion to something else. It's not just the six-four chord in D flat that I heard but the reconciliation of man and nature, the voice of God, or the cry from *outre-tombe* of a long-lost beloved. Again, although people report feeling some powerful emotion at these climactic moments, they may have quite different descriptions of what exactly this powerful emotion is.

Sometimes, I have a better explanation at hand for my experience: I am responding emotionally to what is *expressed* by the music.[79] If I am excited by the triumph of Beethoven Hero[80] or I am suffering in anguished sympathy with the pessimistic Shostakovich persona at the beginning of the Tenth Symphony or I am feeling resignation along with the conflicted persona of the Brahms Intermezzo, this seems to explain why I might get so extraordinarily worked up.[81] But it's also true that the story alone doesn't explain the power of these responses. The poem to 'Immer leiser', for example, necessarily tells the same story as the song, but it has far less emotional effect alone than in Brahms's musical setting. What's more, not all great music does tell a story or express the emotions of a suffering or triumphing persona. For this music there is no obvious explanation as to *why* it should move us so profoundly. Think of the Introduction and Allegro by Ravel, for example, or the theme from the *Goldberg Variations*. Such pieces may of course be very beautiful, which accounts for some of their power to move us, but some pieces and passages that evoke chills may be powerful without being particularly beautiful. (It is easy to get the chills when listening to some popular music that isn't especially striking.) Again, such music may have expressive *qualities*, which, I have suggested, are qualities that—for one reason or another—evoke our emotions, but why should mere expressive qualities affect us so profoundly?

Interestingly, in studies that measured cerebral blood flow in response to music that induces chills, Anne Blood found that

> subjective reports of chills [in response to music] were accompanied by changes in heart rate, electromyogram, and respiration. As intensity of these chills increased, cerebral blood flow increases and decreases were observed in brain regions thought to be involved in reward/motivation, emotion, and arousal, including ventral striatum, midbrain, amygdala, orbitofrontal cortex, and ventral medial prefrontal cortex. These brain structures are known to be active in response to other euphoria-inducing stimuli, such as food, sex, and drugs of abuse.[82]

It is remarkable that people make the same kinds of claim about music as are made by those in the throes of sexual ecstasy or on a heroin high: they too avow that they have heard the voice of God, or in a blinding flash have suddenly comprehended the Meaning of Life.

I suggest that on these chilling musical occasions, music is once again playing much the same role as the epinephrine in the Schachter and Singer experiment. The music is powerfully arousing, but we cannot understand *why*. It just does not seem possible that the state of extreme excitement that the music produces should be merely a physiological effect; surely something more powerful and profound must have caused it! When we experience structural high points, we are intensely stirred physiologically, but we cannot account for the way we feel. So we interpret our emotional state in a way that seems to us commensurate with its power and its intensity: we are feeling religious ecstasy at receiving a missive from God or we are feeling overpowering joy at a moment of profound insight into the meaning of life.

Sloboda suggests that one reason why people attribute such powerful emotions to the effect of music is that the music is inherently ambiguous:

In such a state of ambiguity and cue-impoverishment we may well expect the profound and semi-mystical experiences that music seems to engender. Our own subconscious desires, memories, and preoccupations rise to the flesh of the emotional contours that the music suggests. The so-called 'power' of music may very well be in its emotional cue-impoverishment.[83]

This may be part of the explanation: each person includes their own emotional memories and associations as part of the context they bring to the music. But music is not 'a kind of emotional Rorschach blot',[84] as Sloboda says: it is not *just* personal associations that determine what we feel in response to music: they are just one part of the total context a listener brings to the music. My proposal explains why different listeners tend to experience these mysterious states at the *same moments* in the music, why these are moments of *high tension* in the music, and why 'cue impoverishment' should lead to powerful emotional experiences. The reason is that we are intensely stirred up physiologically at moments of high musical tension, but there is nothing apparently to be so stirred up *by*; and so we seek an explanation that is commensurate with the intensity of the experience.

As I suggested before, exactly how we interpret our states of arousal will depend on the context we bring with us. Certainly, if the music expresses some powerful emotion, then that will be a prominent part of the context in which we label our emotion. But again not all music expresses emotions, and even when it does, the emotions expressed may not be compelling enough to explain the apparent profundity of our emotional response to it. 'Immer leiser' may be powerfully expressive, but much lesser music can also induce the chills.

I chose 'Immer leiser' as one of my prime examples of an expression of emotion in the full Romantic sense. The composer is articulating an individual emotion and hoping that the attentive listener responds appropriately to what is expressed, perhaps with an individual emotional state of their own that approximates the one expressed in the work.[85] One reason why music seems to be such a powerfully expressive medium is that in responding to an expression such as we find in 'Immer leiser', it's not just what we pay close attention to that evokes our responses—it's not just the Kivy and Meyer emotions and not just what we *notice* about what's being expressed. Part of the reason we feel so deeply in response to music is that it affects us physiologically in a way that we don't quite understand. Our deep feelings in response to music are partly due to the chills and thrills of the 'primitive' Jazzercise effect.

How we label these powerful experiences will depend on the context we bring to the music. If I experience a thrill while listening to the *Missa Solemnis*, maybe I will interpret it as a thrill of religious awe. If I (an English person living in the USA) experience a chill in listening to Peter Butterworth's *A Shropshire Lad*, maybe I will interpret it as a feeling of nostalgia for the Old Country. And so on. Again, Fred Maus points out that gospel and soul music have much in common musically:[86] the very same piece of music may evoke either religious or sexual ecstasy.

Cultural context is also important. Becker gives a nice example of how cultural context affects the labelling of powerfully intense arousing music. In listening to music of great intensity, the Sufi mystic may experience 'the ultimate joy of a direct and personal knowledge of Allah',[87] whereas the member of the Pentecostal congregation may be 'expectant, alert, and waiting' to be transported, to experience 'the Holy Spirit in his or her own body'.[88] By contrast the Balinese *bebuten* trance induced by exciting music 'is not ecstasy. It is a feeling of rage directed toward the witch Rangda, and may leave the trancer feeling embarrassed later by his behavior during the trance and with an exhaustion that may last for several days.'[89] Becker's idea fits nicely with my suggestion: arousing music will be labelled differently according to the cultural context in which it is heard.

At the same time, the anthropological perspective reminds us that these 'peak experiences' in response to music may take different forms in different cultures. In the modern Western concert hall these experiences tend to be intensely emotional but essentially private. Such experiences may well be a feature of post-Romantic high culture in the West. We are all under the influence of the Romantic ideas I examined in earlier chapters. We expect music to give us powerful private emotional experiences; it's part of the lore in our culture that that's what music is supposed to do. But not all cultures encourage the suppression of emotional expression in response to music. In other cultures with other kinds of music, and even in more popular culture in our own society, where music is embedded in social activities, 'peak experiences' may well take a very different, more public form.

The Emotional Richness of our Musical Experiences

In this chapter I have described multiple sources of the emotions we experience when listening to music. We may be *delighted* and *moved* by the beauty and craftsmanship of the music (the Kivy emotions); *surprised*, *bewildered*, and *relieved* by the structural and expressive development of the music (the Meyer emotions); and we may experience *nostalgia*, *resignation*, or *anguish* as we feel with or for the protagonist in a song or in an instrumental piece who is expressing his or her emotions in the music. On many of these occasions we are aware of what we are responding to emotionally: it is because we are paying close attention to the music that we are *moved* by the clever canon at the fifth, *surprised* by an unexpected harmonic modulation, or *grieved* by the poignant lament of the protagonist in a song. Sometimes, however, we are not aware that we are being influenced emotionally by the music (or at least not, perhaps, until we are interrogated by some inquisitive psychologist). We may be under the influence of an unconscious emotional memory, or unbeknownst to us, the music may affect us as if it were the forlorn cry of an unhappy child. More commonly, music unconsciously affects us in a *bodily* way: it induces autonomic changes, facial expressions, action tendencies and so on that in turn can change our outlook and put us into a distinctive *mood*. Contagious effects of music are likely to be more powerful when they are not noticed or fully understood. Because there are multiple mechanisms for arousing emotion and because the emotions aroused may be different from one another, it is not surprising that music is ambiguous in its emotional effects.

Moreover, as Krumhansl demonstrates, the physiological changes that a complex piece of music evokes are changing all the time as we listen: we respond over time to changes in the music in a way that to some extent *maps* the unfolding musical structure. The experience of listening to a long and complex piece such as Beethoven's Third or Shostakovich's Tenth Symphony is often as physically tiring or emotionally draining as it is cognitively challenging. At the end we may feel as if we have undergone a powerful series of experiences, a significant emotional drama occurring not just to the persona in the music but to ourselves. But because our affective experiences are changing all the time as we listen, it may be very difficult to say at the end of the work what mood or emotion on the whole I have experienced. When we listen to 'Jingle Bells', it may be clear to us that it makes us feel jolly (or irritable, as the case may be), but in listening to a long and complex piece in which the emotional landscape is itself shifting and ambiguous, our own reactions are likely to be shifting and ambiguous too.

Finally, whether or not music is an expression of emotion in some protagonist, whether or not it moves us by its beauty or craftsmanship, whether or not we respond emotionally to its structural and expressive development, music of all sorts—highbrow and lowbrow, Baroque and Romantic, folk and rock—affects us emotionally by affecting our bodies. The Jazzercise effect operates in every kind of music, inducing autonomic changes, smiles and frowns, motor activity, and action tendencies, which in turn appear to influence people's outlook on life, how much sadness and happiness they detect in other people's expressions, how positively or negatively they assess themselves, and so on. Once in such a physiological or mood state, we are more ready to label ourselves as in some emotional state. And if the state of arousal we are in is powerfully intense, we may attribute it to a deep and abiding joy or a state of religious ecstasy.

It remains to be said that all these different emotional mechanisms may be functioning at the same time. In listening to a complex piece of 'art' music, I may have personal memories evoked; I may be moved by the beauty and craftsmanship of the music, as well as temporarily bewildered, then pleasantly surprised and delighted by the clever harmonic, melodic, and rhythmic development; I may also be responding to what sounds like an expression of cheerful emotion in a singer or persona in the music; in addition, the music may induce in me a happy mood, by means of its rhythm, timbre, and dynamic qualities, and it may put me into a state of arousal that seems to me appropriately labelled 'high-spirited' or 'good-humoured', and indeed I may have a tendency to think better of myself and the world while listening to the music. All of these sources of emotion have their effect on me and reinforce my feelings of good cheer.

On the other hand, rather than reinforcing one another, the various sources of emotion may *contradict* one another, thereby contributing to the effect of ambiguity and making me unsure how to label my emotional state. As we have had occasion to see, music can express *blends* of emotion, *ambiguous* emotions and emotions that *shift and modify* from one moment to the next. It seems that music can also *arouse* blends of emotion, ambiguous emotions, and emotions that shift and modify.

An example where multiple sources of emotion seem to confirm one another and to intensify the musical effect is Henry Purcell's anthem, 'Hear my Prayer, O Lord'. In me it induces the full range of emotions I have discussed in this chapter. It arouses Kivy emotions: I am moved by its beauty and the craftsmanship of its eight-part polyphony. It arouses Meyer emotions: its dissonances are surprising and unsettling, and the ultimate resolution a source of relief. It is also an *expression* of anguished pleading, and the eight voices sound like voices expressing anguished pleading. My emotional response to it is partly a response to this expression. The piece is perhaps most notable, however, for the way in which it slowly increases in volume and intensity until the end. (Usually the final bar is sung somewhat more softly.) The build-up of tension is powerfully arousing, affecting me physiologically along a number of dimensions. At the points of marked dissonance I feel chills. If asked what I feel when listening to this piece, I might say 'sad', but this label strikes me as woefully inadequate. Since there are words to this piece, they provide the context in which to find a label that is appropriate to the intensity and power of the experience I am having: it makes me feel 'the anguish of frail and vulnerable human beings who implore God's help in their hour of need'. In this way I attempt to do justice to its intense, powerful, and profound effect.

14

Epilogue

This book has examined some of the important ways that emotions interact with the arts. It does *not* present a 'theory of art', and it does *not* argue that all art or all good art has to have something to do with the emotions. There are all sorts of marvellous artworks that do not traffic in emotions. To understand much of the world's art it is probably more important to investigate the mechanisms of perception rather than the mechanisms of emotion.

The art I have mainly focused on is Western art dating from the Renaissance or later. My central examples have been from the great works of nineteenth-century realism and Romanticism: Tolstoy, Henry James, Edith Wharton, Delacroix, Friedrich, Beethoven, and Brahms. I have had a lot more to say about literature and music than about photography, sculpture, or dance. This is partly out of simple preference on my part, but also because the temporal arts are peculiarly well suited to deal with emotions, which are temporal processes. Much of what I say could be adapted to the temporal art of film, for example, although I have had little to say about this genre of art.

Today we are in an era of falling public subsidies for both the arts and the humanities. Part of my subtext has been to show why it's so important to continue to engage with the great novels and poems and pieces of music I discuss, which are some of the greatest achievements of Anglo-European culture. It's not just that these works engage our emotions. After all, Harlequin romances, dime-store horror novels, and run-of-the-mill pop songs all evoke our emotions. But the works I'm talking about not only evoke emotions that are more complex and ambiguous but also—most importantly—they actively encourage us to reflect about our emotional responses and to learn from them.

The book draws out some implications of the theory of emotion I presented in Part I. Suppose the theory is shown to be false? Does this invalidate my entire enterprise? I hope not. Even if the theory of emotion is not correct in all its details, there are aspects of it that I hope will in any event win broad agreement: the importance of physiological changes to emotion, the fact that emotional 'appraisals' are automatic and in some sense immune to 'higher' cognitive intervention, the concomitant idea that cognitive monitoring and labelling of emotions occurs subsequent to an initial gut reaction, and the fundamental notion that emotions are not primarily things or states but *processes*.

Throughout the book I have tried to stress how the judgement theory of emotions distorts our understanding of a number of issues in aesthetics and that my own process-based account with its emphasis on automatic processing and physiological arousal does a much better job of explaining them. In this respect the whole book is an argument for the theory presented in the first three chapters.

Finally, it has been my ambition in this book to marry C. P. Snow's 'Two Cultures', the scientific and the humanistic. On the one hand I have offered detailed accounts of particular literary and musical works. And on the other hand I have relied heavily on scientific research, mainly by psychologists. I hope to have illustrated that the two approaches are symbiotic. An appeal to science lends credibility to my thesis about the functions of emotions, and the analysis of how emotions function in relation to particular works of art confirms the importance of the arts in a fully human life.

Notes

INTRODUCTION

1. I say 'in the West' because I am mainly going to be talking about Western culture, but these ideas are not confined to the West. There is an old tradition in Indian aesthetics, for example, of associating works of literature and music with particular emotions.

CHAPTER 1

1. The judgements in my examples are crude. Gabriele Taylor, *Pride, Shame, and Guilt: Emotions of Self-Assessment* (New York: Oxford University Press, 1985) has far more subtle analyses. For the views of non-philosophers about how these concepts should be used, see June Price Tangney and Kurt W. Fischer, *Self-Conscious Emotions: The Psychology of Shame, Guilt, Embarrassment, and Pride* (New York: Guilford, 1995).
2. See Cheshire Calhoun and Robert C. Solomon, *What Is an Emotion?: Classic Readings in Philosophical Psychology* (New York: Oxford University Press, 1984). For Aristotle's views on emotion see especially the *Rhetoric*. The passage I quote is from the *Rhetoric*, as glossed by W. W. Fortenbaugh, *Aristotle on Emotion* (London: Duckworth, 1975), 12. Descartes's theory is to be found in René Descartes, 'The Passions of the Soul', in *The Philosophical Writings of Descartes* (Cambridge: Cambridge University Press, 1985), Spinoza's in Baruch Spinoza, *Ethics* (Indianapolis: Hackett, 1992), and Hume's in David Hume, *A Treatise of Human Nature*, ed. L. A. Selby-Bigge (London: Clarendon, 1967). Relevant passages are excerpted in Calhoun and Solomon, *What Is an Emotion?*.
3. In fairness to Gordon, he implicitly acknowledges that beliefs and wishes are not sufficient for emotion by saying that beliefs and wishes together with *some other unspecified conditions* are sufficient for emotion. Philosophers will recognize in Gordon's account the influence of Donald Davidson's theory of action. See especially Donald Davidson, 'Actions, Reasons, and Causes', in *Essays on Actions and Events* (New York: Oxford University Press, 1980).
4. Taylor, *Pride, Shame, and Guilt*, 41.
5. Robert C. Solomon, *The Passions*, 1st edn. (Garden City, NY: Anchor Press/ Doubleday, 1976), 187.
6. Robert C. Solomon, 'Emotions and Choice', in Amélie Rorty (ed.), *Explaining Emotions* (Berkeley: University of California Press, 1980); Solomon, *The Passions*.

7. William E. Lyons, *Emotion*, Cambridge Studies in Philosophy (Cambridge: Cambridge University Press, 1980), 58.

8. Ibid. 71.

9. Ibid. 59.

10. Solomon, *The Passions*, p. xvii.

11. There are a number of other philosophers who defend judgement theories that I haven't explicitly discussed. Notable among more recent additions to the literature are Aaron Ben-Ze'ev, *The Subtlety of Emotions* (Cambridge, Mass.: MIT, 2000); Peter Goldie, *The Emotions: A Philosophical Exporation* (Oxford: Clarendon, 2000); and the neo-Stoic Martha Craven Nussbaum, *Upheavals of Thought: The Intelligence of Emotions* (Cambridge: Cambridge University Press, 2001).

12. Richard S. Lazarus, *Emotion and Adaptation* (New York: Oxford University Press, 1991), 177.

13. Ibid. 122.

14. Ibid. 121.

15. Andrew Ortony, 'Value and Emotion', in William Kessen, Andrew Ortony, and Fergus Craik (eds.), *Memories, Thoughts, and Emotions: Essays in Honor of George Mandler* (Hillsdale, NJ: Erlbaum, 1991). See also Andrew Ortony, Gerald L. Clore, and Allan Collins, *The Cognitive Structure of Emotions* (Cambridge: Cambridge University Press, 1988).

16. Solomon, *The Passions*, 187.

17. Ibid. 188.

18. Solomon, 'Emotions and Choice', 264–5.

19. In terms of a distinction that used often to be made about the emotions, Lyons thinks that it's a *conceptual* necessity that an emotional response is a physiological response *caused* by a particular evaluation.

20. Another excellent account along these lines is Daniel Farrell's analysis of jealousy in Daniel Farrell, 'Jealousy', *Philosophical Review* 89 (1980).

21. Paul Rozin is perhaps the leading researcher on disgust and he has a much more sophisticated account of the concept. See e.g. Paul Rozin and A. E. Fallon, 'A Perspective on Disgust', *Psychological Review* 94 (1987).

22. Marian Engel, *Bear* (New York: Atheneum, 1976).

23. Lyons, *Emotion*, 100.

24. Patricia S. Greenspan, 'A Case of Mixed Feelings: Ambivalence and the Logic of Emotion', in Amélie Rorty (ed.), *Explaining Emotions* (Berkeley: University of California Press, 1980); ead., *Emotions & Reasons: An Inquiry into Emotional Justification* (New York: Routledge, 1988).

25. Greenspan, 'A Case of Mixed Feelings', 237.

26. Resistance to summing is closely linked to two other features of emotions that they share with desires: tolerance of inconsistency and resistance to change. See Jenefer Robinson, 'Emotion, Judgment, and Desire', *Journal of Philosophy* 80 (1983).

27. Greenspan, *Emotions & Reasons*, 14–19.

28. See ibid.

29. However, although a thought all by itself is not enough for emotion, we do often respond emotionally to thoughts. In fact, this idea will loom large in the discussion of the 'paradox of fiction' in Ch. 5.

30. Greenspan, *Emotions & Reasons*, 48. See Jenefer Robinson, 'Startle', *Journal of Philosophy* 92/2 (1995), 74.

31. Amélie Rorty, 'Explaining Emotions', in ead. (ed.), *Explaining Emotions* (Berkeley: University of California Press, 1980).

32. Ibid. 112. Rorty's formulation has found echoes in Ronald de Sousa's idea that we think of emotions as 'species of determinate patterns of salience among objects of attention, lines of inquiry, and inferential strategies'. Ronald de Sousa, *The Rationality of Emotion* (Cambridge, Mass.: MIT, 1987), 196.

33. Robert Kraut, 'Objects of Affection', in K. D. Irani and G. E. Myers (eds.), *Emotion: Philosophical Studies* (New York: Haven, 1983).

34. For a *locus classicus*, see R. E. Nisbett and T. D. Wilson, 'Telling More Than We Can Know: Verbal Reports on Mental Processes', *Psychological Review* 84 (1977).

CHAPTER 2

1. William James, *The Works of William James*, ed. Frederick H. Burkhardt, 3 vols. (Cambridge, Mass.: Harvard University Press, 1981), ii. 1065–7. All quotations are from this edition.

2. In a subsequent paper James admits that his earlier formulation had a 'slapdash brevity' that could lead to misunderstanding. William James, 'The Physical Basis of Emotion', *Psychological Review* 1 (1894), 519. As Ellsworth points out, because his vivid allusions to 'the bear' stuck in people's minds, 'James's actual claim—that the sensation of bodily changes is a *necessary condition* of emotion—was simplified and quickly crystallized into the idea that emotions are *nothing but* the sensation of bodily changes.' Phoebe Ellsworth, 'William James and Emotion: Is a Century of Fame Worth a Century of Misunderstanding?', *Psychological Review* 101 (1994), 222.

3. Nico Frijda, *The Emotions* (Cambridge: Cambridge University Press, 1986), 155.

4. Theodore D. Kemper, 'Power, Status, and Emotions: A Sociological Contribution to a Psychophysiological Domain', in Klaus Scherer and Paul Ekman (eds.), *Approaches to Emotion* (Hillsdale, NJ: Erlbaum, 1984), 377, citing, among others, A. F. Ax, 'The Physiological Differentiation between Fear and Anger in Humans', *Psychosomatic Medicine* 15 (1953).

5. Frijda, *The Emotions*, 133–5.

6. For this and ensuing references, see ibid. 163.

7. Robert Levenson, 'The Search for Autonomic Specificity', in Paul Ekman and Richard J. Davidson (eds.), *The Nature of Emotion: Fundamental Questions* (New York: Oxford University Press, 1994), 255.

8. A variation on this idea is suggested by LeDoux: 'in any condition involving strong emotional arousal there is . . . a backdrop of undifferentiated autonomic activity, reflecting a generalized state of nonspecific arousal, against which more specific changes are expressed'. Joseph LeDoux, 'Emotion-Specific Physiological Activity: Don't Forget About CNS Physiology', in Ekman and Davidson (eds.), *The Nature of Emotion*, 249. Thanks to Michael Sontag for this reference.

9. Frijda, *The Emotions*, 165.

10. Ibid.

11. See e.g. Paul Ekman, 'An Argument for Basic Emotions', *Cognition and Emotion* 6 (1992); Paul Ekman, *Emotions Revealed* (New York: Henry Holt, 2003); id. 'Expression and the Nature of Emotion', in Scherer and Ekman (eds.), *Approaches to Emotion*; id. 'Facial Expression and Emotion', *American Psychologist* 48 (1993). Confirmation comes from, among others, Carroll Izard, e.g. in *The Face of Emotion* (New York: Appleton-Century-Crofts, 1971). There are a few dissenters, notably Alan Fridlund. See e.g. Alan Fridlund and Bradley Duchaine, 'Facial Expressions of Emotion and the Delusion of the Hermetic Self', in R. Harré and W. G. Parrott (eds.), *The Emotions: Social, Cultural and Biological Dimensions* (London: Sage, 1996).

12. Ekman, *Emotions Revealed*, 58. In the past he has been less sure that the facial expressions for contempt and disgust can be distinguished, and in one preliterate culture there seemed to be no distinction between the expressions for fear and surprise (although fear/surprise was distinguished from anger, sadness, disgust, and happiness). See ibid. 10.

13. Ibid. 58.

14. Ekman, 'An Argument for Basic Emotions', 172.

15. Ibid. 176.

16. Similar research on vocal expressions by e.g. Klaus Scherer and others is less well advanced. See Klaus R. Scherer, *Facets of Emotion: Recent Research* (Hillsdale, NJ: Erlbaum, 1988); id., 'Vocal Affect Expression: A Review and a Model for Future Research', *Psychological Bulletin* 99 (1986); and id et al., 'Vocal Cues in Emotion Encoding and Decoding', *Motivation and Emotion* 15 (1991).

17. See Ekman, 'Expression and the Nature of Emotion', 320–1.

18. Ibid. 322–3.

19. Antonio R. Damasio, *Descartes' Error: Emotion, Reason, and the Human Brain* (New York: G. P. Putnam, 1994), 140. Guillaume-Benjamin Duchenne noticed as early as the mid-nineteenth century that a genuine smile required different muscles to move than a deliberate smile. In both the muscles around the mouth are involved, but only in a genuine smile is there involuntary contraction of the orbicularis oculi, a muscle at the corner of the eyes. See ibid. 142. Also Ekman, 'Expression and the Nature of Emotion', 321–4.

20. Ekman, *Emotions Revealed*, 15.

21. Paul Ekman, *Telling Lies: Clues to Deceit in the Marketplace, Politics, and Marriage* (New York: Berkley Books, 1985). An interesting *New Yorker* article explains some of the applications of Ekman's work to law inforcement: Malcolm Gladwell, 'The Naked Face', *The New Yorker*, 5 August 2002.

22. Richard A. Friedman, 'A Peril of the Veil of Botox', *New York Times*, 6 August 2002.

23. Ekman, 'Expression and the Nature of Emotion', 324–8.

24. It is conceivable that when facial manipulation produces the physiological changes characteristic of a particular emotion, at the same time there is produced an 'emotional' appraisal of the environment. So making a face which is, unbeknownst to the subject, an angry face may produce not only the ANS changes typical of anger (as far as we can specify them), but also an 'angry frame of mind', a tendency to think angry thoughts or to get angry with whoever happens to be around. But the subjects in Ekman's experiments seemed to be perfectly aware that there is actually nothing for them to be angry about.

25. Ekman uses this term in 'Biological and Cultural Contributions to Body and Facial Movement in the Expression of Emotions', in Amélie Rorty (ed.), *Explaining Emotions* (Berkeley: University of California Press, 1980), 80. It is taken up by Paul Griffiths in *What Emotions Really Are: The Problem of Psychological Categories* (Chicago: University of Chicago Press, 1997), 77.

26. John B. Watson, *Psychology, from the Standpoint of a Behaviorist*, 2nd edn. (Philadelphia: J. B. Lippincott, 1924), 229–31.

27. A. N. Meltzoff and M. K. Moore, 'Imitation of Facial and Manual Gestures by Human Neonates', *Science* 198 (1977); Tiffany Field et al., 'Discrimination and Imitation of Facial Expressions by Neonates', *Science* 218 (1982); A. N. Meltzoff and M. K. Moore, 'Imitation in Newborn Infants: Exploring the Range of Gestures Imitated and the Underlying Mechanisms', *Developmental Psychology* 25 (1989); A. N. Meltzoff and M. K. Moore, 'Infants' Understanding of People and Things: From Body Imitation to Folk Psychology', in J. Bermúdez, A. Marcel, and N. Eilan (eds.), *The Body and the Self* (Cambridge, Mass.: MIT, 1995).

28. Alan L. Sroufe, 'The Organization of Emotional Development', in Scherer and Ekman (eds.), *Approaches to Emotion*, 112.

29. Klaus R. Scherer, 'On the Nature and Function of Emotion: A Component Process Approach', in Scherer and Ekman (eds.), *Approaches to Emotion*; Scherer, *Facets of Emotion*.

30. Frijda reports on many of these studies in id., *The Emotions*, 272–3.

31. Robert Zajonc, 'Feeling and Thinking: Preferences Need No Inferences', *American Psychologist* 35 (1980); W. R. Kunst-Wilson and R. B. Zajonc, 'Affective Discrimination of Stimuli That Cannot Be Recognized', *Science* 207 (1980); Robert Zajonc, 'On the Primacy of Affect', *American Psychologist* 39 (1984); S. T. Murphy and R. B. Zajonc, 'Affect, Cognition, and Awareness:

Affective Priming with Suboptimal and Optimal Stimulus', *Journal of Personality and Social Psychology* 64 (1993); Robert Zajonc, 'Evidence for Nonconscious Emotions', in Ekman and Davidson (eds.), *The Nature of Emotion*.

32. Kunst-Wilson and Zajonc, 'Affective Discrimination of Stimuli that Cannot Be Recognized', 558.
33. Murphy and Zajonc, 'Affect, Cognition, and Awareness', 726.
34. Richard S. Lazarus, *Emotion and Adaptation* (New York: Oxford University Press, 1991), 155–6.
35. J. Garcia and K. W. Rusiniak, 'What the Nose Learns from the Mouth', in D. Muller-Schwarze and R. M. Silverstein (eds.), *Chemical Signals* (New York: Plenum Press, 1980).
36. Zajonc, 'On the Primacy of Affect', 120. Zajonc tries to overwhelm the reader with data. Some of it, however, although it sounds impressive, is really inconclusive. I discuss his results in more detail elsewhere.
37. Lazarus, *Emotion and Adaptation*, 177.
38. For the dispute see R. B. Zajonc, 'Feeling and Thinking'; Richard S. Lazarus, 'Thoughts on the Relations between Emotion and Cognition', *American Psychologist* 37 (1982); and Zajonc, 'On the Primacy of Affect'.
39. Lazarus, *Emotion and Adaptation*, 153, 156.
40. Ibid. 190.
41. Ibid. 158.
42. Phoebe Ellsworth, 'Levels of Thought and Levels of Emotion', in Ekman and Davidson (eds.), *The Nature of Emotion*, 193.
43. cf. Frijda who distinguishes two meanings of 'cognition', namely 'conscious awareness and complex information processing'. Nico Frijda, 'Emotions Require Cognitions, Even If Simple Ones', in Ekman and Davidson (eds.), *The Nature of Emotion*, 197. Frijda himself claims there is a difference between 'affect' which can be elicited non-cognitively and 'emotion' which he thinks always requires cognition, in the sense of 'information processing', even if the information processing is not very complex. For example, he thinks that the evocation of emotion by 'unexpected intense stimuli', and 'body restraint and other interference in self-initiated movement', among others, involves 'more than a single localized stimulus' as well as 'comparing a stimulus against schemata or expectations' (ibid. 200–1), both of which involve cognition. I am less convinced that responding to such stimuli involves 'complex information processing' and hence cognition.
44. Keith Oatley, *Best Laid Schemes: The Psychology of Emotions* (Cambridge: Cambridge University Press; Paris: Éditions de la Maison des Sciences de l'Homme, 1992), 53.
45. Ibid. 54.
46. Joseph LeDoux, *The Emotional Brain: The Mysterious Underpinnings of Emotional Life* (New York: Simon & Schuster, 1996), 126–7.
47. Joseph LeDoux, 'Cognitive-Emotional Interactions in the Brain', *Cognition and Emotion* 3 (1989), 271.

48. LeDoux, *The Emotional Brain*, 149.
49. LeDoux thinks the concept of a 'limbic system' is actually ill-defined.
50. LeDoux, *The Emotional Brain*, 163.
51. Ibid. 163–5.
52. Dean G. Purcell, Alan L. Stewart, and Richard B. Skov, 'Interference Effects of Facial Affect', in Robert R. Hoffman, Michael F. Sherrick, and Joel S. Warm (eds.), *Viewing Psychology as a Whole: The Integrative Science of William N. Dember* (Washington DC: American Psychological Association, 1998), 434. The reference is to William N. Dember, *The Psychology of Perception* (New York: Holt, Rinehart, & Winston, 1960), 321.
53. LeDoux, *The Emotional Brain*, 162.
54. LeDoux, 'Cognitive-Emotional Interactions in the Brain', 272.
55. LeDoux, *The Emotional Brain*, 69.
56. LeDoux, 'Cognitive-Emotional Interactions in the Brain', 279.
57. Joseph LeDoux, 'Cognitive-Emotional Interactions in the Brain', in Ekman and Davidson (eds.), *The Nature of Emotion*, 221.
58. Of course we do not know the exact neural pathways for 'hostility' rather than fear, although fear certainly seems to be playing a role in Jonah's response.
59. Robert C. Solomon, *The Passions*, 1st edn. (Garden City, NY: Anchor Press/Doubleday, 1976), 188.
60. Robert C. Solomon, 'Emotions and Choice', in Amélie Rorty (ed.), *Explaining Emotions* (Berkeley: University of California Press, 1980), 264–5.

CHAPTER 3

1. Paul Ekman gives a similar formulation. In his most recent book he asserts: 'Emotion is a process, a particular kind of automated appraisal influenced by our evolutionary and personal past, in which we sense that something important to our welfare is occurring, and a set of physiological changes and emotional behaviors begins to deal with the situation.' Paul Ekman, *Emotions Revealed* (New York: Henry Holt, 2003), 13.
2. In Jenefer Robinson, 'Startle', *Journal of Philosophy* 92/2 (1995) I argued that the startle response is a good model for emotional response in general.
3. Paul Ekman, 'Expression and the Nature of Emotion', in Klaus R. Scherer and Paul Ekman (eds.), *Approaches to Emotion* (Hillsdale, NJ: Erlbaum, 1984), and Paul Ekman and Wallace V. Friesen, 'Is the Startle Reaction an Emotion?', *Journal of Personality and Social Psychology* 49 (1985), 1416–26. Whether the startle response is 'automatic' turns out to be more complicated than Ekman or I assumed. See Michael E. Dawson, Anne M. Schell, and Andreas H. Bohmelt (eds.), *Startle Modification: Implications for Neuroscience, Cognitive Science, and Clinical Science* (Cambridge: Cambridge University Press, 1999).

4. C. Landis and W. A. Hunt, *The Startle Pattern*, 2nd edn. (New York: Johnson Reprint Corp., 1968), 136.

5. Franklin B. Krasne and Jeffrey J. Wine, 'The Production of Crayfish Tailflip Escape Responses', in Robert C. Eaton (ed.), *Neural Mechanisms of Startle Behavior* (New York: Plenum, 1984), 180.

6. Ibid., 181.

7. Similar startle reactions have been observed in teleost fishes. See Eaton (ed.), ibid. 213–66.

8. Joseph E. LeDoux, *The Emotional Brain: The Mysterious Underpinnings of Emotional Life* (New York: Simon & Schuster, 1996), 100.

9. Richard S. Lazarus, *Emotion and Adaptation* (New York: Oxford University Press, 1991), 54.

10. See Keith Oatley, *Best Laid Schemes: The Psychology of Emotions* (Cambridge: Cambridge University Press; Éditions de la Maison des Sciences de l'Homme, 1992), 60.

11. James A. Russell, 'Culture and the Categorization of Emotions', *Psychological Bulletin* 110 (1991), 431.

12. An alternative would be to construe these different negative emotions as consisting in different cognitive evaluations—such as 'This is an offence,' 'This is a threat,' 'This is a loss,' or 'This is nauseating'—plus the very same non-cognitive 'trigger' appraisal **I don't like it!** I find this implausible, as the physiological states that result from the respective affective appraisals are so different in each case.

13. Klaus R. Scherer, 'On the Nature and Function of Emotion: A Component Process Approach', in Scherer and Ekman (eds.), *Approaches to Emotion*, 310.

14. Klaus R. Scherer, *Facets of Emotion: Recent Research* (Hillsdale, NJ: Erlbaum, 1988), 58.

15. Phoebe Ellsworth and C. A. Smith, 'From Appraisal to Emotion: Differences among Unpleasant Feelings', *Motivation and Emotion* 12 (1988).

16. Notice that this is one of Scherer's 'components'.

17. Lazarus, *Emotion and Adaptation*, 149. Lazarus distinguishes primary appraisals from secondary appraisals. I will have more to say about secondary appraisals later in this chapter and in Ch. 7.

18. Interestingly, some of the intuitively plausible candidates for 'componential' non-cognitive appraisals might also be capable of being dealt with by the goal-oriented view. 'This is a friend/enemy' can be thought of as 'This is a person who is conducive to my interests.' 'This is uncertain,' 'This is novel,' or 'This is weird' are all variations on the theme of surprise and curiosity. 'This is an obstacle' and 'I can't control this' are both analysable as 'This is contrary to my goals.' However, these redescriptions are much less fine-grained that the componential analyses they replace. As in the case of the pleasure–aversion hypothesis, the goal-orientation analysis makes cognitive evaluation the major player in distinguishing one emotional response from another.

19. Another less charitable way to construe Lazarus's view is that he has a variety of different and inconsistent theories of what the 'primary appraisal' consists in.

20. Jaak Panksepp has studied neural circuits implicated in rage, fear, love, grief, and joy. See id., *Affective Neuroscience* (New York: Oxford University Press, 1998).

21. See Joseph LeDoux, 'Emotion, Memory and the Brain', *Scientific American* 270 (1994). See also work by Larry Squire and Daniel Schachter, for example L. R. Squire, B. Knowlton, and G Musen, 'The Structure and Organization of Memory', *Annual Review of Psychology* 44 (1993). LeDoux recounts the story about Claparède in LeDoux, *The Emotional Brain*, 180–2. It is also mentioned by Oliver Sacks, *An Anthropologist on Mars* (New York: Vintage Books, 1995), 53.

22. Patricia S. Greenspan, *Emotions & Reasons: An Inquiry into Emotional Justification* (New York: Routledge, 1988); Robinson, 'Startle'.

23. Amélie Rorty, 'Explaining Emotions', in ead. (ed.), *Explaining Emotions* (Berkeley: University of California Press, 1980).

24. R. B. Zajonc and Hazel Markus, 'Affect and Cognition: The Hard Interface', in Carroll E. Izard, Jerome Kagan, and Robert B. Zajonc (eds.), *Emotion, Cognition, and Behavior* (New York: Cambridge University Press, 1984).

25. Antonio R. Damasio, *Descartes' Error: Emotion, Reason, and the Human Brain* (New York: G. P. Putnam, 1994), 138.

26. The psychologist Paula Niedenthal has also argued that emotions categorize stimuli. See P. M. Niedenthal and J. B. Halberstadt, 'Emotional Response as Conceptual Coherence', in Eric Eich et al. (eds.), *Cognition and Emotion* (New York: Oxford University Press, 2000).

27. Damasio, *Descartes' Error*, 216–17.

28. Ibid. 221.

29. Phoebe Ellsworth, 'William James and Emotion: Is a Century of Fame Worth a Century of Misunderstanding?', *Psychological Review* 101 (1994), 227.

30. Ibid.

31. Ibid. 228.

32. James D. Laird and Nicholas H. Apostoleris take a Jamesian view of feelings as perceptions of bodily changes and behaviour, and postulate a functional role for feelings as (unconsciously) providing 'information about behavior'. Rom Harré and W. Gerrod Parrott, *The Emotions: Social, Cultural and Biological Dimensions* (London: Sage, 1996), 289. See also Antonio Damasio, *Looking for Spinoza: Joy, Sorrow, and the Feeling Brain* (Orlando, Fla.: Harcourt, 2003).

33. When I first began reading psychologists on emotion I was scandalized by their tendency to say that 'an emotion' lasts only a few seconds, when what they meant was that an emotional expression typically lasts only a few seconds. As a philosopher interested in 'evaluations', it sounded very odd to me that an evaluation could last only a few seconds, especially evaluations as important as those involved in fear and love. Now I acknowledge that emotional non-cognitive appraisals happen very fast, and so do the expressions they elicit, but

we have to remember that the evaluations that result from cognitive monitoring of an affective evaluation may endure for a lifetime.

34. Keith Oatley and Jennifer M. Jenkins, *Understanding Emotions* (Oxford: Blackwell, 1996), 44; June Price Tangney and Kurt W. Fischer, *Self-Conscious Emotions: The Psychology of Shame, Guilt, Embarrassment, and Pride* (New York: Guilford, 1995), 490.

35. Catherine Lutz, *Unnatural Emotions: Everyday Sentiments on a Micronesian Atoll and Their Challenge to Western Theory* (Chicago: University of Chicago Press, 1988), 119.

36. Russell, 'Culture and the Categorization of Emotions'.

37. John Benson, 'Emotion and Expression', *Philosophical Review* 76 (1967).

38. William James, *The Works of William James*, ed. Frederick H. Burkhardt, 3 vols. (Cambridge, Mass.: Harvard University Press, 1981) ii. 1077–8.

39. Stanley Schachter and Jerome Singer, 'Cognitive, Social, and Physiological Determinants of Emotional State', *Psychological Review* 69 (1962), 381.

40. Ibid. 398.

41. Michael Sontag, 'Emotion and the Labeling Process' (Cincinnati: University of Cincinnati, 2005); cf. Rainer Reisenzein, 'The Schachter Theory of Emotion: Two Decades Later', *Psychological Bulletin* 94 (1983).

42. In *What Emotions Really Are: The Problem of Psychological Categories* (Chicago: University of Chicago Press, 1997), Paul Griffiths argues that the Schachter and Singer case is merely an example of confabulation. The example is in many ways hard to gloss. The subjects in the experiment *behaved* angrily or euphorically, but when asked they did not describe themselves so unambiguously.

43. Paul Ekman discusses the differences among emotions and moods in id., 'Expression and the Nature of Emotion', and id., 'Moods, Emotions, and Traits', in Paul Ekman and R. Davidson (eds.), *The Nature of Emotions: Fundamental Questions* (New York: Oxford University Press, 1994). I'll have more to say about moods in Ch. 13.

44. What's odd about the 'mood' in this case is that it is as likely to produce anger as euphoria.

45. Daniel Farrell, 'Jealousy', *Philosophical Review* 89 (1980).

46. James R. Averill, *Anger and Aggression: An Essay on Emotion*, Springer Series in Social Psychology (New York: Springer-Verlag, 1982), 175.

47. Ibid. 191.

48. Ibid. 208.

49. In my example of being abandoned by my husband, labelling my emotion 'indignation' could itself be part of the way that I *cope* with the situation.

50. Averill, *Anger and Aggression*, 219.

51. Griffiths, *What Emotions Really Are*. Griffiths also discusses a third variety of emotion, derived from Robert Frank: 'an irruptive pattern of motivation', ibid. 120. See Robert H. Frank, *Passions within Reason: The Strategic Role of the Emotions* (New York: W. W. Norton, 1988).

52. See the discussion of Paul Ekman on display rules in Ch. 2.

53. On this point I have changed my position since Jenefer Robinson, 'Emotion, Judgment, and Desire', *Journal of Philosophy*, 80 (1983).

54. Exactly what this notion of 'alertness' will turn out to be is not clear, however, since the 'thoughts' which prompt emotion may be unconscious.

55. Ekman, 'Moods, Emotions, and Traits', 57.

56. Since I wrote these chapters, a book has appeared with a view that is not dissimilar to that defended here. Unfortunately it appeared too late for me to discuss it. See Jesse Prinz, *Gut Reactions: A Perceptual Theory of Emotion* (Oxford: Oxford University Press, 2004).

57. Farrell, 'Jealousy'.

58. Greenspan, *Emotions & Reasons*.

CHAPTER 4

1. The main difference is that when we read a novel or watch a movie or play, our responses are manipulated by the *formal* devices that the author employs to tell the story. This is the theme of Ch. 7.

2. See F. R. Leavis, *The Great Tradition: George Eliot, Henry James, Joseph Conrad* (London: Chatto & Windus, 1948).

3. Leo Tolstoy, *Anna Karenina*, trans. Rosemary Edmonds (Harmondsworth: Penguin, 1971), 566.

4. Lawrence Blum, 'Compassion', in Amélie Rorty (ed.), *Explaining Emotions* (Berkeley: University of California Press, 1980), 509.

5. Ibid. 512.

6. In John Morreall, 'Fear without Belief', *Journal of Philosophy* 90 (1993) Morreall stresses the importance of *vividness* in the mental representations that cause fear.

7. Shaun Nichols *Sentimental Rules: On the Natural Foundations of Moral Judgment* (New York: Oxford University Press, 2004, ch. 2) disagrees. He thinks that altruistic behaviour does not depend on perspective-taking. Although I implicitly endorse Blum's view in my discussion, the correct analysis of compassion is tangential to my concerns in this chapter.

8. William Shakespeare, *Macbeth*, ed. Kenneth Muir, 9th edn., *Arden Shakespeare* (London: Methuen, 1962), IV. iii. 216–19.

9. Perhaps he has become the type of creature that Noël Carroll identifies as 'interstitial', i.e. existing between species, since he is no longer fully human. Being 'interstitial' in this way is, according to Carroll, the mark of a 'monster' that arouses the emotion of 'art-horror'. See id., *The Philosophy of Horror: Or Paradoxes of the Heart* (Routledge, 1990). I should add that Macbeth is not the chief focus in this scene. Our main emotion is compassion for Macduff. Thanks to Alex Neill for discussion of this example.

10. All quotations are from Henry James, *The Ambassadors*, Signet Classics (New York: 1960), 12.

11. Thanks to Cathryn Long and Ellen Peel for helping me draw out the implications of this example.

12. The references are to Sophocles' *Oedipus the King* and Euripides' *Hippolytus*.

13. Much has been written about the role of *imagination* in our understanding of novels. I sidestep these issues here. There will be some further discussion in Ch. 5.

14. I will have more to say about such matters in Ch. 6.

15. See Wolfgang Iser, *The Implied Reader: Patterns of Communication in Prose Fiction from Bunyan to Beckett* (Baltimore: Johns Hopkins University Press, 1974); Wolfgang Iser, *The Act of Reading: A Theory of Aesthetic Response* (London: Routledge & Kegan Paul, 1978); and Wolfgang Iser, *Prospecting: From Reader Response to Literary Anthropology* (Baltimore: Johns Hopkins University Press, 1989).

16. Richard J. Gerrig, *Experiencing Narrative Worlds: On the Psychological Activities of Reading* (New Haven: Yale University Press, 1993), 27.

17. Ibid. 40.

18. Ibid. 31, quoting G. McKoon and R. Ratcliff, 'Inference During Reading', *Psychological Review* 99 (1992), 441. Compare Jerrold Levinson's account of understanding music in Jerrold Levinson, *Music in the Moment* (Ithaca, NY: Cornell University Press, 1997).

19. Gerrig, *Experiencing Narrative Worlds*, 39. In his writings Iser sometimes seems to suggest that there is an ideal reader who will respond 'properly'. This restricted variety of reader-response criticism has come under attack by theorists such as Holland and Fish. At other times Iser seems quite aware that individual readers fill in the gaps in their own way, for example Wolfgang Iser, 'The Reading Process: A Phenomenological Approach', in Jane P. Tompkins (ed.), *Reader-Response Criticism:From Formalism to Post-Structuralism* (Baltimore: Johns Hopkins University Press, 1980), 55. I will be discussing these issues in more detail in Ch. 6.

20. All quotations are from Gerrig, *Experiencing Narrative Worlds*, 40–6.

21. Noël Carroll, *Beyond Aesthetics: Philosophical Essays* (Cambridge: Cambridge University Press, 2001), 126–7.

22. Described by Gerrig, *Experiencing Narrative Worlds*, 46–7.

23. Ibid. 47, quoting C. R. Fletcher, J. E. Hummel, and C. J. Marsolek, 'Causality and the Allocation of Attention During Comprehension', *Journal of Experimental Psychology: Learning, Memory, and Cognition* 16/233–40 (1990), 239.

24. Gerrig, *Experiencing Narrative Worlds*, 47, quoting Fletcher, Hummel, and Marsolek, 'Causality and the Allocation of Attention During Comprehension', 233.

25. Gerrig, *Experiencing Narrative Worlds*, 48.

26. Ibid. 66.

27. Ibid. 69.

28. Ibid.

29. Ibid. 76.

30. Gerrig cites Andrew Ortony, Gerald L. Clore, and Allan Collins, *The Cognitive Structure of Emotions* (Cambridge: Cambridge University Press, 1988), 131.

31. Gerrig, *Experiencing Narrative Worlds*, 66–7.

32. One last point: Gerrig notes that most of the research he discusses applies equally well to the understanding of real and of narrative worlds, fiction and non-fiction. My discussion of emotion also applies equally well to fiction and non-fiction. It's just that in great realist novels the authors exploit the appeal to our emotions in many ways, both subtle and unsubtle.

33. Leonard Meyer's account of understanding music is very similar to Iser's account of understanding narratives. In Leonard B. Meyer, *Emotion and Meaning in Music* (Chicago: University of Chicago Press, 1956), 37–8, Meyer distinguishes 'hypothetical meanings', which 'arise during the act of expectation'; 'evident meanings', which are apparent only 'when the relationship between the antecedent and consequent is perceived'; and 'determinate meanings', which arise 'only after the experience of the work is timeless in memory'. An interpretation in my view corresponds to what Meyer calls 'determinate meaning'. I discuss Meyer's views on music in Ch. 12.

34. The same is true of some music, as we'll see in Ch. 12.

35. The idea is due to Berlyne. See D. E. Berlyne, *Aesthetics and Psychobiology* (New York: Appleton-Century-Crofts, 1971). See also Gerrig, *Experiencing Narrative Worlds*.

36. A theme that runs through Susan L. Feagin, *Reading with Feeling: The Aesthetics of Appreciation* (Ithaca, NY: Cornell University Press, 1996).

37. Cf. Noël Carroll, 'Art, Narrative, and Emotion', in Mette Hjort and Sue Laver (eds.), *Emotion and the Arts* (New York: Oxford University Press, 1997), 192: 'The emotions in life and in art have the function of focusing attention.' Carroll cites my essay, 'Startle', *Journal of Philosophy*. 92 (1995), in support of this contention. The view that emotions are primarily devices for focusing attention has been most forcefully defended in Ronald de Sousa, *The Rationality of Emotion* (Cambridge, Mass.: MIT, 1987).

38. Peter Salovey et al., 'Current Directions in Emotional Intelligence Research', in Michael Lewis and Jeannette M. Haviland-Jones (eds.), *Handbook of Emotions*, 2nd edn. (2000), 506.

39. A lot of people have argued that we need to explain 'mind-reading' in terms of the concept of 'simulation'. By contrast, I am stressing here the role of emotional responses to what we *perceive* in other people's expressions and gestures, and what we are *told* about other people's thoughts and ways of seeing the world (as well as what we are told about their expressions and gestures). More on this in Ch. 6.

40. Much has been written recently about people with autism, who typically have severe problems with social interaction. One of the deficits associated with autism lies in the ability to 'mind-read', i.e. to understand what other people are feeling and thinking. In certain kinds of autism most cognitive abilities remain intact, yet

even high-functioning autistic people fail to respond with appropriate emotions to others. It is possible, therefore, that such people have difficulty understanding others because, although they can grasp cognitively what is going on around them, they cannot understand emotionally what other people are feeling and thinking. On the other hand, Shaun Nichols (personal communication) has pointed out to me that the research over the last decade or so has shown that children with autism and Asperger's are actually competent at identifying simple emotions and seem to experience at least some distress at others' suffering. Where they show clear emotional deficiencies is in the attribution of complex emotions such as pride. It is therefore possible that it is *cognitive* demands that interfere with success and that autism should be treated as a cognitive psychopathology rather than an emotional one. But all of this is contested territory.

41. Gregory Currie and Ian Ravenscroft (*Recreative Minds: Imagination in Philosophy and Psychology* (Oxford: Clarendon, 2002), 198), link these two abilities by suggesting that both involve 'modelling' in imagination: 'while your resentment is real, my imaginative modelling of it represents it as mine'. While I agree there is very probably a connection between these two abilities, I do not make the connection in this way. In particular, I reject the assumption that when emotionally grasping your resentment, I necessarily feel resentment myself. Emotional intelligence does not *consist* in mirroring other people's emotions. But see also Ch. 9, n. 35.

42. See Annette Barnes, *On Interpretation: A Critical Analysis* (Oxford: Blackwell, 1988) for a very intellectualized theory of interpretation.

43. The examples or similar ones are taken from Edward Bullough, J. O. Urmson, and Jerome Stolnitz. The tradition of aesthetic disinterestedness goes back to Shaftesbury and is prominent in Hume and Kant. For a very interesting essay on how some contemporary analytic philosophers have to some extent distorted the eighteenth-century ideas of 'taste' and 'disinterestedness' see Paul Guyer, 'History of Modern Aesthetics', in Jerrold Levinson (ed.), *The Oxford Handbook of Aesthetics* (Oxford: Oxford University Press, 2003).

44. Jerome Stolnitz, *Aesthetics and Philosophy of Art Criticism; a Critical Introduction* (Boston: Houghton Mifflin, 1960), excerpted in Philip Alperson, *The Philosophy of the Visual Arts* (New York: Oxford University Press, 1992), 7–14.

45. Alperson, *The Philosophy of the Visual Arts*, 10.

46. J. O. Urmson, 'What Makes a Situation Aesthetic?', in Joseph Margolis (ed.), *Philosophy Looks at the Arts: Contemporary Readings in Aesthetics*, (New York: Charles Scribner's Sons, 1962).

47. In fact for most eighteenth-century thinkers, disinterested attention to a good work of art would produce feelings of pleasure.

48. Monroe Beardsley (*Aesthetics: Problems in the Philosophy of Criticism* (New York: Harcourt Brace, 1958), 144), proposed two criteria of correctness for interpretations, the principle of congruence (make your interpretation of the parts of the text consistent), and the principle of plenitude (make your interpretation fit as much of the text as possible). His advice remains sound. Adjusting his view

to my emotional reader-response perspective, I would propose that a 'dispassionate' interpretation should take into account as many of our emotional responses as possible, provided that they are consistent with an overall reading of the text. I return to Beardsley's principles in Ch. 6.

CHAPTER 5

1. S. R. Vrana, B. N. Cuthbert, and P. J. Lang, 'Processing Fearful and Neutral Sentences: Memory and Heart Rate Change', *Cognition and Emotion* 3 (1989).
2. Paul L. Harris, *The Work of the Imagination* (Oxford: Blackwell, 2000), 70. Lang was one of Vrana's collaborators in the 1989 study cited above.
3. Richard J. Gerrig, *Experiencing Narrative Worlds: On the Psychological Activities of Reading* (New Haven: Yale University Press, 1993), 81, citing P. E. Jose and W. F. Brewer, 'Development of Story-Liking: Character Identification, Suspense, and Outcome Resolution', *Developmental Psychology* 20 (1984).
4. See Ch. 12.
5. Thanks to Susan Feagin for pressing me on this point.
6. Susan L. Feagin, *Reading with Feeling: The Aesthetics of Appreciation* (Ithaca, NY: Cornell University Press, 1996). See also Roger Scruton, *Art and Imagination* (London: Methuen, 1974), 131.
7. Recall Beardsley's principles of congruence and plenitude. See Ch. 4 n. 48.
8. In Ch. 6 I discuss in more detail the constraints upon interpretation, including the role of the author's intentions.
9. Noël Carroll is an exception. He follows William Lyons. See Noël Carroll, 'Art, Narrative, and Emotion', in Mette Hjort and Sue Laver (eds.), *Emotion and the Arts* (New York: Oxford University Press, 1997).
10. I refer to a series of children's books by Alison Uttley.
11. Oliver Sacks, *The Man Who Mistook his Wife for a Hat* (New York: Harper & Row, 1987), 208–9.
12. Harris, *The Work of the Imagination*.
13. All examples are from Paul Rozin and A. E. Fallon, 'A Perspective on Disgust', *Psychological Review* 94 (1987), 30–1.
14. Colin Radford, 'How Can We Be Moved by the Fate of Anna Karenina?', *Proceedings of the Aristotelian Society*, suppl. vol. 49 (1975).
15. She describes her case of mixed feelings as 'perfectly rational in light of the special relationship between emotions and behavior'. Patricia S. Greenspan, 'A Case of Mixed Feelings: Ambivalence and the Logic of Emotion', in Amélie Rorty (ed.), *Explaining Emotions* (Berkeley: University of California Press, 1980), 238.
16. Ibid. 236.
17. Ibid. 238.

18. Greenspan, 'A Case of Mixed Feelings', 240.
19. Ibid. 240–1.
20. Jerrold Levinson, 'Emotion in Response to Art: A Survey of the Terrain', in Hjort and Laver (eds.), *Emotion and the Arts* see n.9 p.429 , 22–3. There are other ways of construing it, but this is a very clear statement of what is usually meant by the paradox of fiction.
21. Ibid. 23.
22. See Jenefer Robinson, 'Startle', *Journal of Philosophy* 92 (1995).
23. Levinson, 'Emotion in Response to Art', 23.
24. I'll be exploring this idea in more detail in Ch. 7.
25. Levinson, 'Emotion in Response to Art', 23. Adherents to this view include Peter Lamarque, 'Fear and Pity', in *Fictional Points of View* (Ithaca: Cornell University Press, 1996), and Noël Carroll in *The Philosophy of Horror: Or Paradoxes of the Heart* (Routledge, 1990). Currie and Ravenscroft argue that 'there can be emotional responses to what is merely imagined', including fictional characters and events. Gregory Currie and Ian Ravenscroft, *Recreative Minds: Imagination in Philosophy and Psychology* (Oxford: Clarendon, 2002), 196.
26. Levinson, 'Emotion in Response to Art', 23. Kendall Walton has a similar criticism: *Mimesis as Make-Believe: On the Foundations of the Representational Arts* (Cambridge, Mass.: Harvard University Press, 1990), 203.
27. See J. C. Gosling, 'Emotion and Object', *Philosophical Review* 74 (1965), for an old but still useful survey of some of the many possible meanings of the term 'object of emotion'.
28. Levinson, 'Emotion in Response to Art', 23.
29. Ibid. 24.
30. See also John Morreall, 'Fear without Belief', *Journal of Philosophy* 90 (1993).
31. Levinson, 'Emotion in Response to Art', 24. In a series of articles on the paradox of fiction Alex Neill has argued that while some reactions to fiction are not fully emotional (in his view), being more like non-cognitive reactions of startle or shock, other such reactions, such as pity for Anna Karenina, are genuinely emotional because they involve taking a certain perspective on fictional characters without having to commit to those characters' existence. See Alex Neill, 'Fear, Fiction, and Make-Believe', *Journal of Aesthetics and Art Criticism* 49 (1991); Alex Neill, 'Fiction and the Emotions', *American Philosophical Quarterly* 30 (1993), and 'Fear and Belief', *Philosophy and Literature* 19 (1995).
32. Levinson, 'Emotion in Response to Art', 24.
33. See the discussion of Lawrence Blum and Anna Karenina in Ch. 4.
34. Levinson, 'Emotion in Response to Art', 25.
35. Ibid. cf. Alex Neill, 'Fiction and the Emotions'.
36. Barring special circumstances, such as the situation in which I have bet a large sum of money that e.g. Desdemona won't come to grief in *Othello*.
37. Levinson, 'Emotion in Response to Art', 26. The idea originated in Kendall Walton, 'Fearing Fictions', *Journal of Philosophy* 75 (1978), and was further developed in Walton, *Mimesis as Make-Believe*.

38. There is a huge literature on this issue, of which I have mentioned only a few samples. For a good recent bibliography see Hjort and Laver (eds.), *Emotion and the Arts*.

39. For an interesting recent account, see Peter Goldie, *The Emotions: A Philosophical Exporation* (Oxford: Clarendon, 2000), Ch. 7.

CHAPTER 6

1. This is a theme that runs through her essays on Henry James. See 'Flawed Crystals: James' *The Golden Bowl* and Literature as Moral Philosophy', and 'Finely Aware and Richly Responsible: Literature and the Moral Imagination' in Martha Craven Nussbaum, *Love's Knowledge: Essays on Philosophy and Literature* (New York: Oxford University Press, 1990), 125–67.

2. For example, in her first 1993 Gifford Lecture, 'Emotions as Judgements of Value', Nussbaum defended the view that emotions are judgements of certain sorts. In Martha Craven Nussbaum, *Upheavals of Thought: The Intelligence of Emotions* (Cambridge; New York: Cambridge University Press, 2001), she has developed with great subtlety a cognitive theory of emotion that she characterizes as neo-Stoic.

3. Edith Wharton, *The Reef* (New York: Macmillan (Collier Books), 1987), 3.

4. Ibid. 11.

5. As we saw in Ch. 1, Greenspan argues that emotions, which she sharply distinguishes from beliefs, are affective states (states of 'comfort' or 'discomfort') directed towards propositions or thoughts that they serve to keep in mind. Part of their motivational force, as she sees it, is to continue the comfort or put an end to the discomfort they afford. See Patricia S. Greenspan, *Emotions & Reasons: An Inquiry into Emotional Justification* (New York: Routledge, 1988), 53.

6. Wharton, *The Reef*, 138.

7. Ibid. 139.

8. Ibid. 146.

9. Ibid. 145.

10. Ibid. 141.

11. Ibid.

12. Ibid. 147.

13. Ibid. 161–2.

14. Ibid. 180.

15. Ibid. 179.

16. Ibid. 251.

17. Ibid. 253.

18. Ibid. 254.

19. Wharton, *The Reef*, 302.
20. Ibid. 76.
21. Ibid. 302–3. Some readers will find Darrow's speech self-serving: as Ellen Peel pointed out to me, in saying that 'we' are 'all' blunderers, he is implicitly abrogating some responsibility for his own actions.
22. Ibid. 83.
23. Ibid. 91. One is reminded of Isabel Archer's fate in Henry James's novel, *Portrait of a Lady*.
24. Ibid. 89.
25. Ibid. 96–7.
26. Ibid. 106.
27. Ibid. 107.
28. Ibid. 109.
29. Ibid. 112.
30. Ibid. 178.
31. Ibid. 233.
32. Ibid. 243–4.
33. Ibid. 260.
34. Ibid. 263.
35. Ibid. 265.
36. Ibid. 272.
37. Ibid. 282.
38. Ibid. 283.
39. Ibid. 275–6.
40. Ibid. 277.
41. Ibid. 279.
42. Ibid. 281.
43. Ibid.
44. Ibid. 283.
45. Ibid. 280.
46. Ibid. 289.
47. Ibid. 306
48. Ibid. 304.
49. Ibid. 325.
50. Ibid. 323.
51. Ibid. 331.
52. Ibid. 343.
53. In the introduction to the Collier Books edition of *Summer*, Marilyn French writes that 'in a peculiar final scene, Anna discovers the true root of her attitudes—her profound sexual disgust. In this scene, Anna visits Sophy's older sister, who lives a loose sexual life. Anna's horror is out of proportion to what she sees: what she is envisioning is a conclusion she finds ugly and inevitable to Sophy's free ways.' But Wharton nowhere says that Anna is horrified or disgusted. She merely presents the scene as Anna sees it, without

commenting on Anna's attitude towards what she sees. French is filling in the gaps in her own way. See Edith Wharton, *Summer* (New York: Macmillan (Collier Books), 1987), p. xxviii.

54. Cf. R. K. Elliott, 'Aesthetic Theory and the Experience of Art', in Alex Neill and Aaron Ridley (eds.), *The Philosophy of Art: Readings Ancient and Modern* (Boston: McGraw-Hill, 1995).

55. The expression is Susan Feagin's, but she uses it in a slightly different way: see *Reading with Feeling: The Aesthetics of Appreciation* (Ithaca, NY: Cornell University Press, 1996).

56. However, although Wharton gets us to think or conceive of her characters and situations in certain ways, to focus attention on them so conceived, and to have certain wants with respect to them, we do not have to form *beliefs* about them in order to have such thoughts, conceptions, and wants. Of course, if we think of the characters in appropriate ways, we are likely to arrive at the corresponding beliefs by the end of the novel.

57. I don't want to continue putting quotation marks around Wharton's name, but note that when I discuss what Wharton describes in the novel and how she treats her subject, I am really referring to the author as she seems to be, i.e., to the implied author.

58. Wharton, *The Reef*, 10. The technique is known as 'free indirect discourse'.

59. Ibid. 303.

60. Ibid. 6.

61. In saying this, I do not mean to imply that 'constructing' or making inferences about the implied author is any different in principle from making inferences about the *theme* of a novel or what it expresses or exemplifies.

62. Noël Carroll, 'Art, Narrative, and Emotion', in Mette Hjort and Sue Laver (eds.), *Emotion and the Arts* (New York: Oxford University Press, 1997), 202.

63. Ibid. 203.

64. Ibid. 204.

65. This is not surprising, since he cites approvingly my 'Startle', *Journal of Philosophy* 92 (1995), in the elaboration of his own view. But I suspect he was unaware of my 'L'Éducation Sentimentale', *Australasian Journal of Philosophy* 73 (1995), 212–26.

66. Carroll, 'Art, Narrative, and Emotion', 208.

67. Wolfgang Iser, 'The Reading Process: A Phenomenological Approach', in Jane P. Tompkins (ed.), *Reader-Response Criticism: From Formalism to Post-Structuralism* (Baltimore: Johns Hopkins University Press, 1980), 50, endorses Roman Ingarden's idea that, as Iser puts it: 'The convergence of text and reader brings the literary work into existence.'

68. Wharton, *The Reef*, 304.

69. Jerrold Levinson, *The Pleasures of Aesthetics: Philosophical Essays* (Ithaca: Cornell University Press, 1996), 186.

70. Ibid. 179–80.

71. Levinson, *The Pleasures of Aesthetics*, 185. Notice that the meaning of 'A Country Doctor' that Levinson proposes is what might be called the *theme* of the story; it is not just the literal linguistic meaning of a sequence of 'utterances'. In a similar way, I use the term 'meaning' to include the theme of an artwork, as well as what it represents, expresses, and exemplifies (if anything). In short, I take 'meaning' to include all those aspects of an artwork that are typical objects of 'interpretation'. The relationships between the meaning of the sentences or utterances in a novel and meaning in this broader sense is beyond the scope of my discussion here. See Robert Stecker, *Interpretation and Construction: Art, Speech and the Law* (Oxford: Blackwell, 2003).

72. Levinson, *The Pleasures of Aesthetics*, 185.

73. The disputants are Gary Iseminger, 'Actual Intentionalism Vs. Hypothetical Intentionalism', *Journal of Aesthetics and Art Criticism* 54 (1996), and Levinson.

74. I am trying hard to avoid defending a full-fledged theory of interpretation here. My main assumption is that interpretation is a matter of figuring out the meanings (broadly speaking) communicated—wittingly or unwittingly—by an implied author. See n. 71. I acknowledge, however, that there are other goals of other kinds of interpretation in which the author or implied author does not loom so large. See n. 89 below.

75. For more on betrayal and the difference between betrayal and expression, see Chs. 8 and 9.

76. Darrow says to Anna: 'When you've lived a little longer you'll see what complex blunderers we all are.' See n. 21 above.

77. Marilyn French would perhaps disagree. Although far from claiming that Wharton was a Marxist, French observes that 'Wharton's [genius] was socio-logical and psychological,' and that, as a woman, she was more aware than Henry James of 'the power of the environment over the individual'. Wharton, *Summer*, p. xxxix.

78. The idea of the implied author was introduced by Wayne C. Booth: see *The Rhetoric of Fiction* (Chicago: University of Chicago Press, 1961). I have relied on this idea in Jenefer Robinson, 'Style and Personality in the Literary Work', *Philosophical Review* 94 (1985).

79. Stuart Gilbert identifies Mandeville, Malory, Sir Thomas Browne, and a host of others. This section is not 'narrated' at all in the usual sense. See Stuart Gilbert, *James Joyce's Ulysses: A Study* (Harmondsworth: Penguin (Peregrine Books), 1963), ch. 14.

80. Wharton, *The Reef*, p. vii.

81. Norman Holland, *Five Readers Reading* (New Haven: Yale University Press, 1975). His study is not scientifically rigorous.

82. Stanley Fish, *Is There a Text in This Class?: The Authority of Interpretive Communities* (Cambridge, Mass.: Harvard University Press, 1980).

83. Ibid. 346.

84. Ibid. 347.

85. Judith Fetterley, *The Resisting Reader: A Feminist Approach to American Fiction* (Bloomington: Indiana University Press, 1981), 49.

86. Jacques Derrida *Of Grammatology*, trans. Gayatri Chakravorty Spivak (Baltimore: Johns Hopkins University Press, 1976).

87. Interpretation is very problematic when we have no idea about the origins of a text.

88. Cf. Beardsley's principles of plenitude and congruence.

89. But not everything is an 'interpretation of the text'. Roland Barthes's exuberant paean to the individual reader and her pleasure in the text is no longer, I think, about interpreting what an author communicates. See Roland Barthes, *The Pleasure of the Text*, trans. Richard Miller (New York: Noonday Press and Farrar, Strauss, & Giroux, 1975).

90. In this respect my perspective is closer to Holland's than to Fish's. But I am not denying that our emotional responses will be affected by the background assumptions of our cultural communities. And of course I differ from Holland in stressing that interpretation should be focused on what the implied author communicates.

91. But although this is how I *understand* the novel, I am perhaps too inclined to sympathize with Darrow to count as responding emotionally in a truly feminist way!

92. Wharton, *The Reef*, Introduction, p. xiii.

93. Maybe a clever teacher can make connections between the loneliness and frustrations experienced by these characters and a kind of loneliness and frustration that teenagers can recognize and feel for themselves, but I should imagine that this is a challenge.

CHAPTER 7

1. Clive Bell, *Art* (London: Chatto & Windus, 1914).

2. Charles Darwin, *The Expression of the Emotions in Man and Animals*, ed. Paul Ekman (New York: Oxford University Press, 1998), 43–4.

3. Phoebe Ellsworth and C. A. Smith, 'From Appraisal to Emotion: Differences among Unpleasant Feelings', *Motivation and Emotion* 12 (1988).

4. Klaus R. Scherer, 'On the Nature and Function of Emotion: A Component Process Approach', in Klaus R. Scherer and Paul Ekman (eds.), *Approaches to Emotion* (Hillsdale, NJ: Erlbaum, 1984).

5. Richard S. Lazarus, *Emotion and Adaptation* (New York: Oxford University Press, 1991), 39.

6. For further details, see my discussion in Ch. 1.

7. Lazarus, *Emotion and Adaptation*, 145.

8. Ibid. 39.

9. On the other hand, Lazarus's list of emotions with 'core relational themes' is much longer than Ekman's list of 'basic emotions'.
10. Lazarus, *Emotion and Adaptation*, 39.
11. Ibid. 112.
12. Richard S. Lazarus, 'Universal Antecedents of the Emotions', in Paul Ekman and Richard J. Davidson (eds.), *The Nature of Emotion: Fundamental Questions* (New York: Oxford University Press, 1994), 166.
13. Lazarus, *Emotion and Adaptation*, 112.
14. Ibid. 113.
15. See e.g. Richard S. Lazarus and Elizabeth Alfert, 'Short-Circuiting of Threat by Experimentally Altering Cognitive Appraisal', *Journal of Abnormal and Social Psychology* 69 (1964).
16. Lazarus, *Emotion and Adaptation*, 114.
17. Ibid. 155.
18. Ibid. 113.
19. Ibid. 163.
20. If this is right, however, it sheds doubt on the idea that both fear and anger are 'basic emotions'.
21. Although, as we have seen, we may not *behave* the same way in life and in the theatre (say), because cognitive monitoring modifies the effects of affective appraisals.
22. Phoebe Ellsworth, 'Levels of Thought and Levels of Emotion', in Ekman and Davidson (eds.), *The Nature of Emotion*, 194.
23. Norman Holland, *The Dynamics of Literary Response* (New York: Oxford University Press, 1968), 28–9.
24. Norman Holland, 'Unity Identity Text Self', in Jane P. Tompkins (ed.), *Reader-Response Criticism: From Formalism to Post-Modernism* (Baltimore: Johns Hopkins University Press, 1980), 126.
25. Holland, *The Dynamics of Literary Response*, 75.
26. Ibid. 105.
27. See ibid. 58. In comments on a precursor to this chapter, Daniel Herwitz notes that not all of those who call themselves Freudians today are likely to accept Holland's version of Freud (for example, the followers of Melanie Klein). Comments on 'Norman Holland's Reader-Response Theory', American Society for Aesthetics Pacific Division meetings, 1992.
28. Ibid. 131.
29. Holland, 'Unity Identity Text Self', 126.
30. Ibid. 124.
31. One of the apparent inconsistencies in Holland's thought is that authors are supposed to have identity themes that are 'revealed' in the texts they write, but at the same time readers are supposed to respond to authors in terms of their own identity themes, and hence presumably to construct—at least in part—the identity themes of the authors they read. See ch. 6.

32. See Holland's remarks on different ways of experiencing *Hamlet* in Holland, 'Unity Identity Text Self', 124–5.
33. Holland, *The Dynamics of Literary Response*, 114. Compare my discussion of Iser and Gerrig in Ch. 4.
34. There is a large literature on the paradox of tragedy. For an interesting recent account with a good bibliography, see Aaron Ridley, 'Tragedy', in Jerrold Levinson (ed.), *The Oxford Handbook of Aesthetics* (Oxford: Oxford University Press, 2003).
35. William A. Madden, 'Arnold the Poet (I) Lyric and Elegiac Poems', in *Matthew Arnold*, ed. Kenneth Allott (Athens, Ohio: Ohio University Press, 1976), 64.
36. J. D. Jump, *Matthew Arnold* (London: Longman's, Green & Co., 1955), 80.
37. Holland, *The Dynamics of Literary Response*, 117.
38. Ibid. 125.
39. Ibid. 123.
40. Of course these ways of reading the poem would be construed by Holland as themselves defensive readings.
41. Holland, *The Dynamics of Literary Response*, 128.
42. Ibid. 106. Holland (ibid. 131) cautions us, however, that the distinction between form and content is not hard and fast. In a poem, he says, 'any given element may serve as a representation of content or as a part of a formal and defensive manœuver'. I should add that my treatment of coping devices in literature is not meant to mirror Holland's exactly; I use his ideas merely as a jumping-off point.
43. Gérard Genette, *Narrative Discourse: An Essay in Method* (Ithaca, NY: Cornell University Press, 1980).
44. Roland Barthes, *S/Z*, trans. Richard Miller (New York: Hill & Wang, 1974).
45. Edith Wharton, *The Reef* (New York: Macmillan (Collier Books), 1987), 218–19.
46. Or, to put it more crudely, kill the son in order to marry the father.
47. The fact that character and setting function as principles of structure is to some extent conventional. In novels of the sort I am discussing we expect it.
48. Stephen Booth, *An Essay on Shakespeare's Sonnets* (New Haven: Yale University Press, 1969), 84.
49. Ibid. 120.
50. Ibid. 124.
51. Ibid. 170.
52. Ibid. 171.
53. Ibid. 172.
54. Ibid. 187.
55. Ibid. 125.
56. Ibid.
57. Ibid. 126.
58. Ibid. 127.

59. Booth, *An Essay on Shakespeare's Sonnets*, 129.
60. Ibid. 130.
61. Susan Folkman and Richard S. Lazarus, 'Coping and Emotion', in Nancy Stein, Bennett Leventhal, and Tom Trabasso, (eds.), *Psychological and Biological Approaches to Emotion* (Hillsdale, NJ: Erlbaum, 1990), 320. As they refined their view of coping in the 1980s, Folkman and Lazarus identified eight different coping strategies, six of which are 'emotion-focused' rather than 'problem-focused', and which include 'distancing, escape-avoidance, accepting responsibility or blame, exercising self-control over the expression of feelings, seeking social support, and positive reappraisal'. Folkman and Lazarus, 'Coping and Emotion', 317.
62. I am grateful to Miles Rind and James Shelley for pressing me on the question of whether Shakespeare is helping us to cope by avoidance strategies or by getting us to confront death.
63. Booth, *An Essay on Shakespeare's Sonnets*, 171.
64. Thanks to Edward Nowacki for this example.
65. Edward Bullough, ' "Psychical Distance" as a Factor in Art and an Aesthetic Principle', in Morris Weitz (ed.), *Problems in Aesthetics* (London: Macmillan, 1970).
66. George Dickie, 'The Myth of the Aesthetic Attitude', *American Philosophical Quarterly* 1 (1964).
67. Strictly speaking, it is the author as he seems to me to be, i.e. the implied author, who is a master manipulator.
68. McEwan's *Atonement* is once more a particularly interesting case.

CHAPTER 8

1. David H. Richter (ed.), *The Critical Tradition: Classic Texts and Contemporary Trends* (New York: St Martin's, 1989), 295.
2. Elizabeth Gilmore Holt (ed.), *From the Classicists to the Impressionists: Art and Architecture in the 19th Century*, 2nd edn. (New Haven: Yale University Press, 1986), 84.
3. Lorenz Eisner (ed.), *Neoclassicism and Romanticism 1750–1850: Sources and Documents*, 2 vols. (Englewoods Cliffs, NJ: Prentice-Hall, 1970), ii. 54.
4. Sam Morgenstern (ed.), *Composers on Music: An Anthology of Composers' Writings from Palestrina to Copland* (New York: Random House (Pantheon Books), 1956), 87.
5. G. W. F. Hegel, *Aesthetics: Lectures on Fine Art*, trans. T. M. Knox, 2 vols. (Oxford: Clarendon, 1975), i. 38.
6. Eugene Delacroix, *The Journal of Eugène Delacroix*, trans. Lucy Norton, 3rd edn. (London: Phaidon, 1995), 36.

7. The best guide to this fascinating terrain remains M. H. Abrams's classic study *The Mirror and the Lamp: Romantic Theory and the Critical Tradition* (Oxford: Oxford University Press, 1953). Although the two are closely related in various ways, Romanticism is not consistent with every aspect of Hegel's Idealism. In particular, Hegel's system is based on the idea of reason, whereas Romantic artists by and large emphasized emotion at the expense of reason. As we'll see, however, the Romantic notion of expression combines conscious reflection with emotion, although not in a way that Hegel would necessarily have endorsed.

8. For further evidence of the oddities of Romantic thought, try rereading Johann Wolfgang von Goethe, *The Sorrows of Young Werther*, trans. Michael Hulse (London: Penguin, 1989), first published 1774, or Penelope Fitzgerald, *The Blue Flower* (London: HarperCollins, 1995), about the poet Novalis.

9. Alan Tormey, *The Concept of Expression. A Study in Philosophical Psychology and Aesthetics* (Princeton, NJ: Princeton University Press, 1971), 103.

10. R. G. Collingwood, *The Principles of Art* (Oxford: Clarendon, 1963), 27.

11. Ibid. 109–10.

12. Ibid. 110. Collingwood's point relies on a particular interpretation of *catharsis*. If Martha Nussbaum is right and catharsis means 'cleaning' or 'clearing up' in the cognitive sense of getting clear about something, then Collingwood's meaning is closer to Aristotle's than he thought. At the same time, however, there is still a difference between Aristotelian catharsis and Collingwoodian expression in that Aristotle is talking about how the *audience* to a tragedy achieves clarification or purgation of its emotions, whereas Collingwood is talking about the *artist*. See Martha Craven Nussbaum, 'Tragedy and Self-Sufficiency: Plato and Aristotle on Fear and Pity', in Amélie Oksenberg Rorty (ed.), *Essays on Aristotle's Poetics* (Princeton, NJ: Princeton University Press, 1992), 281.

13. Collingwood, *The Principles of Art*, 111–12.

14. Ibid. 112.

15. Ibid. 113.

16. Ibid. 119.

17. Ibid. 311.

18. Ibid. 312.

19. Ibid. 110–11.

20. Aaron Ridley has made this point forcefully, see 'Not Ideal: Collingwood's Expression Theory', *Journal of Aesthetics and Art History* 55 (1997).

21. Collingwood, *The Principles of Art*, 122.

22. Ibid. Collingwood singles out the end of Hardy's *Tess of the D'Urbervilles* for particular castigation. See Ch. 7.

23. Ibid. 249–50. Collingwood had his own theory of emotion. He distinguished 'psychic emotions' (emotional charges on sensations) from emotions of consciousness (emotional charges on acts of consciousness of our feelings) and intellectual emotions (emotional charges on acts of higher thinking). Psychic

emotions can only be expressed 'psychically', i.e. by automatic bodily responses such as sweating. Our other emotions, however, can be expressed either psychically or in 'language', linguistic expression being an imaginative activity whereby we become conscious of emotions of which we were formerly only dimly aware. There 'are no unexpressed emotions', ibid. 238. Following Croce, Collingwood held that language includes any self-conscious bodily gesture—including speech and writing—by which emotion is expressed, such as a child's self-conscious expression of rage. For Collingwood art is language in that it is a bodily gesture that expresses an emotion by bringing it to consciousness. Speech, painting, dance, and instrumental music are among the many different forms of 'language'. Since we can experience emotions only through expressing them in language, art is an important source of self-knowledge. Collingwood's talk of 'emotional charges' is vague and metaphorical. But he is right that there are no unexpressed emotions, in the sense that even 'psychic emotions' have a bodily expression, and the idea that emotions are brought to consciousness through language is just another way of saying that we learn about our emotions by expressing—articulating or elucidating—them.

24. John Dewey, *Art as Experience* (New York: Capricorn Books, 1959).

25. O. K. Bouwsma, 'The Expression Theory of Art' in William Elton (ed.), *Æsthetics and Language* (Oxford: Basil Blackwell, 1954); John Hospers, 'The Concept of Artistic Expression', *Proceedings of the Aristotelian Society* (1954–5). reprinted with minor changes in Morris Weitz (ed.), *Problems in Aesthetics: An Introductory Book of Readings* (New York: Macmillan, 1970), 221–45; Tormey, *The Concept of Expression*.

26. Weitz (ed.), *Problems in Aesthetics*, 241–2.

27. Ibid. 226.

28. It might be thought that I am wasting my time attacking a 30-year-old theory, but it has been given a new lease of life by Peter Kivy in *The Corded Shell* and is still widely accepted.

29. Tormey, *The Concept of Expression*, 103.

30. Ibid.

31. Ibid. 104 n. 17.

32. Ibid. 104.

33. Ibid. 104–5.

34. Ibid. 105.

35. Ibid. 106.

36. Ibid. 30.

37. But surely pain can be expressed, even though pain is not directed towards anything? It is just a sensation like hunger or thirst. And what about moods? Can't they be expressed even though they may not be about anything in particular? On pain, Tormey responds that it is not the objectless *sensation* of pain that is expressed but the 'attitude or feeling' of distress or dislike, 'having the sensation as its object', ibid. 27. And as for moods, he denies that moods lack

objects: the objects are just 'unknown, unrecognized, or repressed', or 'too diffuse to be easily located or precisely described', ibid. 34. I find these responses unconvincing. For one thing, I find the concept of intentionality hopelessly vague, and secondly, there is no reason why 'inner' psychological states cannot be expressed in 'outer' behaviour, regardless of how precisely or imprecisely those states are delineated. However, I will not pause to argue the case any further.

38. Ibid. 58.
39. The example is Stephen Davies's. Peter Kivy prefers the St Bernard, a dog which has a similarly 'sad face', regardless of whether it is actually happy or sad. See Ch. 10 for more on the doggy theory of musical expression.
40. Tormey, *The Concept of Expression*, 121.
41. Ibid. 128.
42. Actually Tormey says that non-expressive qualities 'ambiguously constitute' expressive qualities, since 'a given set of nonexpressive properties may be compatible with, or constitutive of, any one of a range of expressive properties', ibid. 132–3.
43. Ibid. 111.
44. Ibid.
45. Ibid. 118.
46. Ibid. 118–19.
47. Ibid. 120.
48. Ibid.
49. Ibid. 122.
50. Ibid. 124.
51. Guy Sircello has argued for something similar in Guy Joseph Sircello, *Mind & Art: An Essay on the Varieties of Expression* (Princeton, NJ: Princeton University Press, 1972), as have I in Jenefer Robinson, 'Art as Expression', in Hugh Mercer Curtler (ed.), *What Is Art?* (New York: Haven, 1983).
52. Tormey, *The Concept of Expression*, 120.
53. E. H. Gombrich, *Art and Illusion* (London: Phaidon, 1962), ch. 11.
54. Jonathan Kramer, 'Unity and Disunity in Nielsen's Sixth Symphony', in Mina Miller (ed.), *The Nielsen Companion*, (Portland, Oregon: Amadeus Press, 1994), 321.
55. Ibid. 323–4.
56. Ibid. 324. Many commentators have been puzzled by the Sixth. Povl Hamburger's view ('Carl Nielsen: Orchestral Works and Chamber Music', in Jurgen Balzer (ed.), *Carl Nielsen: Centenary Essays* (London: Dennis Dobson, 1966), 45–46) is typical: 'The *Humoresque* in particular was a hard nut to crack when the symphony made its first appearance, with its many strikingly grotesque ideas, such as a repeatedly occurring trombone *glissando*. Was this meant seriously, or was it irony—and if so, was it perhaps a parody of certain extremist tendencies in contemporary music?' He concludes: 'Even today it is difficult to give a definite answer to this question, and altogether the sixth is generally considered the weakest of all Nielsen's symphonies. The view is echoed in

almost identical language in Jean-Luc Caron, *Carl Nielsen: Vie et Œuvre 1865–1931* (Lausanne: Éditions l'Âge d'Homme, 1990). Tormey may have had in mind an interpretation of this general sort: the Sixth Symphony reveals Nielsen's 'exasperation' at the 'new' atonal music and his 'bitterness' at failing to be as successful as Schoenberg and Stravinsky. Jonathan Kramer has a much more interesting and convincing interpretation, seeing it as 'the most profoundly post-modern piece composed prior to the post-modern era', 'Unity and Disunity in Nielsen's Sixth Symphony', 293. In playing with different styles, Nielsen is not commenting adversely on atonality, but using it as one of the many styles to which he alludes. On the other hand, Kramer too reads it as a pessimistic work, as exemplifying an 'expressive paradigm' (or 'plot archetype' as we will discuss in Ch. 11) in which 'sunny innocence . . . gives way gradually to darker complexity' followed by 'a resolution to a newly won simplicity, analogous—but usually not similar—to the initial gesture', ibid. 294. Later he comments: 'The process of destruction of innocence, of loss of . . . simplicity, is the essence of this fundamentally dark work,' ibid. 322.

57. As we will see in Ch. 11, the music may be an expression of pessimism in Nielsen's musical persona in this piece, rather than Nielsen himself.

58. Francis Sparshott, *The Theory of the Arts* (Princeton, NJ: Princeton University Press, 1982), 623.

59. The term 'expressive qualities' is unfortunate, since a picture or a poem can be 'sad' or 'happy' without being expressive, as I demonstrated with my poem above. Yet in the literature the term 'expressive qualities' is usually taken to refer to (at least) qualities such as sadness and happiness that are named by emotion words, and in this instance I am following that usage.

60. Weitz (ed.), *Problems in Aesthetics: An Introductory Book of Readings*, 242–3.

61. Quoted by Hospers, ibid. 244.

62. Leonard G. Ratner, *Classic Music: Expression, Form, and Style* (New York: Schirmer Books, 1980).

63. Human beings tend to see many of their encounters with the environment in emotional terms, in terms of their own wants, wishes, values, and interests, hence they are inclined to attribute emotional qualities to things, to anthropomorphize the world. This may explain why Nelson Goodman thinks that non-emotional qualities as well as emotions can be expressed by works of art. Even when we attribute non-emotional properties such as warmth, iciness, flamboyance, dullness, buoyancy, or weight to the world, we are describing the world as experienced in terms of its human significance. That is why there is some justification for Goodman's treating such properties, like more psychological ones, as *expressed* by a work of art. See Nelson Goodman, *Languages of Art: An Approach to a Theory of Symbols* (Indianapolis: Bobbs-Merrill, 1968), ch. 2.

64. In *On the Spiritual in Art*, in Kenneth C. Lindsay and Peter Vergo (eds.), *Kandinsky: Complete Writings on Art* (New York: Da Capo, 1982), 182.

65. Ibid. 180–1. More recently, 'human factors' research has identified colours that are soothing to patients in hospital or invigorating to workers.

66. And of course the cultural and the natural or physical often mutually reinforce one another.

67. Richard Wollheim, *Painting as an Art*, A. W. Mellon Lectures in the Fine Arts, 1984 (Thames & Hudson, 1987), 91.

68. Sparshott, *The Theory of the Arts*, 224.

69. cf. Leo Treitler, 'Language and the Interpretation of Music', in Jenefer Robinson (ed.), *Music and Meaning* (Ithaca: Cornell University Press, 1997), 37, from which I borrow the Kennedy example.

70. This is a word that Wollheim favours. However, Wollheim himself may reject the assimilation of 'correspondences' to associations, since he thinks correspondences answer to a human psychological capacity for *projection*. See Wollheim, *Painting as an Art*, 80–7.

71. Morris Weitz, 'The Role of Theory in Aesthetics', in Joseph Margolis (ed.), *Philosophy Looks at the Arts*, (New York: Scribner's Sons, 1956).

72. After all, Keats famously stressed the importance of 'negative capability' in a poet, which suggests that he thought a poet did not express just his own personal emotions in his work.

73. As we'll see in Ch. 9, Bruce Vermazen talks of 'layers of personae' in a literary work, with the implied author being the source of what the work as a whole expresses.

74. Croce called the intuitions artists have 'lyric' intuitions. Benedetto Croce, *Guide to Aesthetics*, trans. Patrick Romanell (Indianapolis: Bobbs-Merrill, 1965), 27.

75. A realistic novel does not typically emphasize the expression of emotion or personality in the author, or his persona, even where there is a characterful 'voice' telling the story. There are exceptions, often humorous, such as *Tristram Shandy*.

CHAPTER 9

1. Bruce Vermazen, 'Expression as Expression', *Pacific Philosophical Quarterly* 67 (1986), 197. Tormey wants to restrict expression to intentional states, but there is no need for this limitation. See Ch. 8 n. 37.

2. Vermazen's account of artistic expression is not unlike the concept of expression I employed in Jenefer Robinson, 'Style and Personality in the Literary Work', *Philosophical Review* 94 (1985). As we'll see, it is also similar in some respects to the theory I developed in ead., 'Art as Expression', in Hugh Mercer Curtler (ed.), *What Is Art?* (New York: Haven, 1983). Ismay Barwell defends a similar idea in 'How Does Art Express Emotions?', *Journal of Aesthetics and Art Criticism* 45 (1986).

3. Vermazen, 'Expression as Expression', 207.

4. Ibid. 208–9. Some of these properties are *presupposed* in the act of interpretation. In imagining the persona we naturally make assumptions about him (her?) usually based on knowledge of the actual author or the period or place where the object was produced. We assume that the persona is basically rational. And we also make more specific assumptions, usually based on what we know about the actual author of the object, assumptions, for example, about 'whether he was human, European, of the thirteenth century, acquainted with the works of Machaut, employing a certain convention about correspondences between modes and humors, and so on', ibid. 209. The object does not, however, express mental properties, which are presupposed in the act of interpretation. Vermazen's more circumspect version of his theory is as follows: 'An object expresses a mental property if and only if (subject to certain constraints) attributing that property to an utterer of the object would explain the object's having the features it has, and the property is not one of those presupposed in the attempt to interpret', ibid.

5. Ibid. 200.

6. Ibid. 197.

7. Ibid. 216. Vermazen uses the term 'persona' to refer indiscriminately to characters, narrators, and implied authors, assuming rightly that in different works the locus of expression will be different.

8. Ibid. 197.

9. Robert Stecker makes this suggestion in 'Expression of Emotion in (Some of) the Arts', *Journal of Aesthetics and Art Criticism* 42 (1984).

10. Vermazen, 'Expression as Expression', 222.

11. Ibid. 197.

12. Ibid. 209.

13. We can even say, perhaps, that Albers's 'Homage to the Square', while clearly not a work of Romantic expression, nevertheless *expresses* in Vermazen's sense a rejection of Romantic expression.

14. Indeed, in his essay 'Musical Expressiveness' Jerrold Levinson defines expressiveness in music (roughly) in terms of its *hearability* by 'an appropriately backgrounded listener' *as* an expression by a musical persona. Levinson, *The Pleasures of Aesthetics: Philosophical Essays* (Ithaca: Cornell University Press, 1996), 90–125. His definition is on p. 107.

15. Ibid. 102. Levinson is writing specifically about 'musical expressiveness' rather than expressiveness—or expression—in general.

16. See Guy Sircello, *Mind & Art: An Essay on the Varieties of Expression* (Princeton, NJ: Princeton University Press, 1972), esp. ch. 6. This book remains a fascinating attempt to devise a theory of expression in the spirit of Collingwood.

17. Of course it might help if we were to study facial expressions more carefully, as Paul Ekman encourages us to do in *Emotions Revealed* (New York: Henry Holt, 2003).

18. Robinson, 'Art as Expression'.

19. Ibid. 110.

20. Ibid. 110–11.
21. Both the idea that expression is intentional and the idea that certain sounds and colours 'correspond' to emotions derive from Richard Wollheim. On 'correspondences' see e.g. Richard Wollheim, *Art and Its Objects. An Introduction to Aesthetics* (New York: Harper & Row, 1968), 31; Richard Wollheim, *On Art and the Mind* (Cambridge, Mass.: Harvard University Press, 1974), 95; and Richard Wollheim, *Painting as an Art*, A. W. Mellon Lectures in the Fine Arts 1984 (Thames & Hudson, 1987), 82. Wollheim himself rejected my view. One reason is that for him it is important that what is expressed is projected by the artist and derives from the artist's own psychology. Wollheim seems to want nothing to do with the idea of a persona. In this respect his theory is more 'Romantic' than mine. However, its real roots lie in a Kleinian version of Freudian psychology that I see no reason to accept.
22. I ignore here the complications derived from my taking as central the case where the artist himself is expressing his very own emotion, and treating as only secondary those cases where the emotion expressed is that of a persona.
23. What I said was that the emotion causes the work to be the way it is. Vermazen's formulation of the idea in terms of 'providing evidence for' is more perspicuous and therefore preferable.
24. Robinson, 'Art as Expression', 110–11.
25. I am not alone in this. Most modern writers on artistic expression just assume we all know what emotions are. Collingwood and Dewey actually had their own theories of emotion, which are quite interesting, although of course both are largely speculative. See Ch. 8 n. 23 for a brief summary of Collingwood's theory.
26. Some might object to my saying that *appraisals* appraise the environment rather than that *I* appraise the environment. I find this locution harmless, however, because these non-cognitive appraisals are below the level of awareness, hence 'making an appraisal' is not an action that I perform. See Ch. 3.
27. I ignore the complication that only *part* of an artwork might be an expression.
28. Arthur Danto, 'The Artworld', *Journal of Philosophy* 61 (1964).
29. For example in his discussion of Peter Kivy's views on musical expression at Levinson, *The Pleasures of Aesthetics*, 106.
30. See Ch. 3.
31. But see n. 35 below. Facial and gestural expressions may indeed allow the spectator to know what it feels like to be in the state expressed, and to that extent they 'clarify' what the experience is like.
32. Later I will have more to say about how expressions induce emotions in audiences.
33. Kendall Walton, 'Style and the Products and Processes of Art', in Berel Lang (ed.), *The Concept of Style* (Philadelphia: University of Pennsylvania Press, 1979).
34. As before, I would prefer not to talk about *imagining* feeling an emotion; if the process works as Collingwood envisages, the responding reader will feel genuine emotions. Either way, of course, some kind of bodily response is necessary if the experience is truly an *emotional* one. The evidence cited in n. 35

below confirms my hunch that we do not need the concept of 'imagination' to help us understand our emotional reactions to artworks.

35. Fascinating new results in neurophysiology have shown that mirror neurons respond virtually the same way when we see a facial expression of emotion (e.g. disgust) and when we make that facial expression ourselves. Similarly, mirror neurons respond virtually the same way when we feel our leg touched with a stick and when we watch someone else have their leg touched with a stick. It is therefore unsurprising that we respond to pictures of people expressing emotions and to dance works in which people express their emotions by feeling the very same emotions that are being expressed. Moreover, when we observe, predict, or hear the consequences of some action, the motor system activates as if we were performing the action. Papers by Vittorio Gallese and Ralph Adophs delivered to a session on 'The Social Brain' at the American Philosophical Association Central Division meetings, Chicago 2004.

36. As we saw in Chs. 4–5, the emotions I feel for a character may mirror either those of the character or the different emotions of the (implied) author who is himself (herself) responding emotionally to the character, *or both*.

37. What particular people feel as they read a poem, look at a painting, or listen to music will depend upon how they interpret the poem, painting, or music, and how it affects them emotionally. We cannot hope to mirror exactly what Keats or Beethoven had in mind when they 'expressed an emotion' in their work, but within the constraints of our own belief and value systems, our own wants and goals, our own ways of looking at things, we can to some degree approximate what great Romantic artists from the past probably wanted us to experience in experiencing their works. And of course we have to understand as much as we can of the context in which they worked, including the artistic conventions that they observed.

38. This point was eloquently defended in John Benson, 'Emotion and Expression', *Philosophical Review* 76 (1967).

39. Epic poetry—indeed narrative poetry in general—may express the emotions and attitudes of the (implied) author of the poem or of the narrator or of the various characters. In this respect epic poetry is like other narrative forms such as the novel.

40. Jean Clay, *Romanticism* (Secaucus, NJ: Chartwell Books, 1981), 199.

41. Wollheim, *Painting as an Art*, 133.

42. Michele Hannoosh, *Painting and the Journal of Eugène Delacroix* (Princeton, NJ: Princeton University Press, 1995), 91. Kenneth Clark notes that Delacroix 'agreed with Leonardo that the first requisite of the painter of histories is the power of seizing those fleeting gestures in which men reveal their emotions'. He quotes Delacroix as saying to Baudelaire, 'if you can't make a drawing of a man who has thrown himself out of a fourth floor window before he hits the ground, you will never be able to paint 'de grandes machines'. Kenneth Clark, *The Romantic Rebellion: Romantic Versus Classic Art* (New York: Harper & Row, 1973), 203.

43. Clay, *Romanticism*, 154.

44. Ibid.

45. This is also true of his celebrated depiction of *Liberty Leading the People*, in which the way that the figures in the painting are depicted expresses the enormous excitement of the artist himself and his sympathetic revolutionary fervour. Delacroix 'sided with the revolting oppressed, those who storm forward across the corpses in a dusky whirlwind'. Walter Friedlander, *David to Delacroix*, trans. Robert Goldwater (Cambridge, Mass.: Harvard University Press, 1952), 113. At the same time the expression of Delacroix's emotions becomes an unforgettable frozen image that sums up revolutionary republican fervour so that we can contemplate ('cognitively monitor') it.

46. Lorenz Eisner (ed.), *Neoclassicism and Romanticism 1750–1850: Sources and Documents*, 2 vols. (Englewoods Cliffs, NJ: Prentice-Hall, 1970), ii. 127.

47. Delacroix thought that 'from an emotional point of view, the experience of the effect of a painting was identical to the experience of music'. Petra ten-Doesschate Chu, ' "A Science and an Art at Once" ', in Beth S. Wright (ed.), *The Cambridge Companion to Delacroix*, (Cambridge: Cambridge University Press, 2001), 94.

48. Eugène Delacroix, *The Journal of Eugène Delacroix*, trans. Lucy Norton, 3rd edn. (London: Phaidon, 1995), 213. As for communicating with an audience, Delacroix famously pronounced in his *Journal* on 8 October 1822, that 'in painting it is as if some mysterious bridge were set up between the spirit of the persons in the picture and the beholder', ibid. 6. Over thirty years later, on 20 October 1853, he endorses the same idea: 'The figures and objects in the picture, which to one part of your intelligence seem to be the actual things themselves, are like a solid bridge to support your imagination as it probes the deep mysterious emotions, of which these forms are, so to speak, the hieroglyph, but a hieroglyph far more eloquent than any cold representation, the mere equivalent of a printed symbol,' ibid. 213.

49. Delacroix was an important influence on Van Gogh and in turn on the Expressionist movement.

50. I use the masculine pronoun because the character depicted seems to be Munch himself. Katherine Nahum reports that 'Munch's diary entry that is often coupled with this image provides a chilling narrative': *'I was walking along the road with two friends. The sun set. I felt a tinge of melancholy. Suddenly the sky became a bloody red. I stopped, leaned against the railing, dead tired (my friends looked at me and walked on) and I looked at the flaming clouds that hung like blood and a sword (over the fjord and city) over the blue-black fjord and city. My friends walked on. I stood there, trembling with fright. And I felt a loud, unending scream piercing nature.'* Katherine Nahum, ' "In Wild Embrace": Attachment and Loss in Edvard Munch', in Jeffery Howe (ed.), *Edvard Munch: Psyche, Symbol and Expression* (Boston: McMullen Museum of Art, Boston College, 2001), 39–40. Nahum notes that Reinhold Heller translates and includes all the versions of the narrative. This one is dated 22 January 1892. See Reinhold Heller, *Edvard Munch: The Scream* (New York: Viking, 1972).

51. Kirchner painted many street scenes. I am thinking of the one from 1907 that hangs in the Museum of Modern Art in New York.

52. Wollheim, *Painting as an Art*, 95.

53. That is, the *implied* Michelangelo is reverential and sorrowful.

54. *The Burghers of Calais* represents an incident in the Hundred Years War between England and France. After Edward III laid siege to the city of Calais in 1346–7, six burghers of the city—the leading citizens—agreed to sacrifice their lives and hand over the keys of the city if the king would spare the city. Although the sculpture (of which there are several versions) is a monument to patriotism, Rodin did not represent the burghers in a conventionally heroic fashion. For one thing they look starved and weak after suffering the siege for so long. Rodin said of them, 'I have not shown them grouped in a triumphant apotheosis; such glorification of their heroism would not have corresponded to anything real.' Nelly Silagy Benedeck, *Auguste Rodin: The Burghers of Calais* (New York: Metropolitan Museum of Art, 2000), 20.

55. See Ch. 8 for a discussion of Tormey and music played *espressivo*.

56. Recall Ekman's experiments as well as the neurophysiological results reported in n. 35.

57. But we should remember the qualifications from earlier chapters. The spectator, listener, or reader must be 'qualified', that is, familiar with the genre and style of the work, with the conventions invoked, and so on. Different emotional responses may be equally 'appropriate', given differences between the maker of the work and the audience. Nevertheless, if a work of genuine Romantic expression succeeds in its goal, it will be possible for audiences to be able to some degree to 'recreate' for themselves the emotions expressed. If I am beginning to sound like Tolstoy, I should remind readers that the expression of emotion in the Romantic sense involves articulation and elucidation of emotion—cognitive monitoring of it—not merely infection by it. See Leo Tolstoy, *What Is Art?*, trans. Aylmer Maude (Indianapolis: Bobbs-Merrill, 1960), for the 'infection' theory.

58. See Ch. 8.

59. Although it may make you sad about my poetic abilities. And certainly it is a sad excuse for a poem.

60. Notice that the expressive quality of melancholy does not necessarily induce melancholy but other related emotions such as, perhaps, wistfulness. See Ch. 12 for more on this topic.

CHAPTER 10

1. Eduard Hanslick, *On the Musically Beautiful*, trans. Geoffrey Payzant (Indianapolis: Hackett, 1986), 102.

2. Ibid. 3.

3. Ibid. 9.
4. Ibid.
5. Ibid. 10.
6. Ibid. 47.
7. Eduard Hanslick, *Hanslick's Music Criticisms*, trans. Henry Pleasants (New York: Dover, 1950), 102.
8. Hanslick, *On the Musically Beautiful*, 32. Peter Kivy ('Something I've Always Wanted to Know About Hanslick', *Journal of Aesthetics and Art Criticism* 46 (1988), 416, 417) takes Hanslick to be saying that 'music has no expressive qualities' and argues that in his music criticism Hanslick simply 'forgets himself, and lapses into...talking about music in emotive terms'. But Hanslick is explicit that it is all right to describe the character of music in emotive terms; he just denies (as indeed do I) that this amounts to the 'expression of emotion' in music.
9. We have already heard strong echoes of it in Tormey's account of expression which I discussed in Ch. 8.
10. Susanne K. Langer, *Philosophy in a New Key*, 3rd edn. (Cambridge, Mass.: Harvard University Press, 1976), 222.
11. Ibid. 221.
12. Ibid. 226.
13. Ibid. 228.
14. Ibid. 238.
15. Ibid. 233.
16. Ibid. 236.
17. Ibid. 238.
18. Ibid. 235.
19. Ibid. 243.
20. Ibid.
21. Ibid. 244.
22. Ernest Nagel, 'Review of Susanne K. Langer, *Philosophy in a New Key*', *Journal of Philosophy* 40 (1943), 323–9.
23. Langer, *Philosophy in a New Key*, 216.
24. Peter Kivy, *The Corded Shell: Reflections on Musical Expression* (Princeton University Press, 1980), 59. This book was reissued with additional essays as Peter Kivy, *Sound Sentiment: An Essay on the Musical Emotions* (Philadelphia: Temple University Press, 1989).
25. Kivy, *Corded Shell*, 56.
26. Ibid. 20.
27. Ibid. 51.
28. Ibid. 53.
29. Ibid. 54.
30. Ibid. 77. See also my discussion of *topoi* in Ch. 8, as described by Leonard Ratner. Ch. 8 n. 62.

31. On the other hand, Kivy hypothesizes that 'all expressiveness by convention was originally expressiveness by contour, either as the thing itself, or as ingredient', as, for example, the minor key may derive its sadness from the minor triad, once an 'active, dissonant chord', which may have connected to a restless, unfinished quality that—at one time—could have been experienced as an expressive contour of the darker emotions. See ibid. 82–3.

32. Peter Kivy, *Music Alone: Philosophical Reflections on the Purely Musical Experience* (Ithaca, NY: Cornell University Press, 1990), 175.

33. Ibid. 177.

34. Ibid. 175. This idea is probably derived from Hanslick's argument that emotions are defined by 'specific representations or concepts'. In contemporary debate the idea goes back at least as far as A. J. P. Kenny, *Action, Emotion and Will* (London: Routledge & K. Paul; New York: Humanities Press, 1966). I have studiously avoided the concept of an intentional object in my theory of emotion. As we have seen, emotions are always *evoked by* something or other in the external or internal environment, although *moods* of joy or sadness need not be.

35. Kivy borrows from Daniel Putman the idea that 'emotions that *require* objects in non-musical contexts are precisely those which pure instrumental music cannot express'. *Music Alone*, 176, whereas emotions that can occur without objects in ordinary contexts, such as sadness and joy, are those that pure instrumental music *can* be expressive of. See Daniel A. Putman, 'Why Instrumental Music Has No Shame', *British Journal of Aesthetics* 27 (1987), 55–61.

36. Kivy borrows Julius Moravcsik's concept of 'Platonic attitudes'. See Julius Moravcsik, 'Understanding and the Emotions', *Dialectica* 36 (1982).

37. When we talk about Mr Darcy as a proud man, his pride does not require an object, but presumably Kivy would say that pride in this instance is a character trait rather than an emotion or emotional episode. See Gabriele Taylor, *Pride, Shame, and Guilt: Emotions of Self-Assessment* (New York: Oxford University Press, 1985), for varieties of pride.

38. Kivy, *Music Alone*, 178.

39. Ibid.

40. Ibid. 180. Kivy treats the supposed expression of neuroticism in Mahler's symphonies in a similar way. Since there is no standard way of expressing neuroticism in ordinary behaviour, there are no standard expressive gestures for music to mimic and hence music cannot express neuroticism, and neuroticism is not part of the 'musical fabric'.

41. He thinks that music only very rarely expresses the emotions of its composer (or anyone else). An exception, he suggests, is Mozart's *Requiem*, which in places expresses Mozart's 'terror of death'. Kivy, *Corded Shell*, 15.

42. Kivy, *Music Alone*, 185–6.

43. Among the critics are Renée Cox, 'Varieties of Musical Expressionism', in George Dickie, Richard Sclafani, and Ronald Roblin (eds.), *Aesthetics:*

A Critical Anthology (New York: St Martin's, 1989), and myself in 'The Expression and Arousal of Emotion in Music', *Journal of Aesthetics and Art Criticism* 52 (1994).

44. Gross expressive properties (geps) and moderate expressive properties (meps), not subtle expressive properties (seps). See 'Newcomb's Problems', in Kivy, *Sound Sentiment*, 177–209. In this essay Kivy criticizes an essay by Anthony Newcomb, which I will be discussing in Ch. 11. See Anthony Newcomb, 'Sound and Feeling', *Critical Inquiry* 10 (1984), and Kivy's further discussion in Peter Kivy, 'A New Music Criticism?', *The Monist* 73 (1990).

45. Kivy tries to answer this objection in Kivy, *Sound Sentiment*, but I do not think he addresses clearly the issue of how musical process can itself be expressive. Compare the structural/psychological relations in 'musical plots' identified by Gregory Karl in 'Structuralism and Musical Plot', *Music Theory Spectrum* 19 (1997), 13–34. One theme, key area, or rhythm, for example, can *subsume* another, or *interrupt, disrupt,* or *subvert* its development, or it might *integrate* with another, *realize* it more fully, or *transform* it.

46. Jerrold Levinson points out that Kivy does not distinguish very clearly between giving an analysis of what musical expressiveness is and stating the grounds for musical expressiveness. He himself thinks that Kivy should be interpreted as holding that expressiveness should be defined as 'animation' of the music by listeners. Jerrold Levinson, *The Pleasures of Aesthetics: Philosophical Essays* (Ithaca, NY: Cornell University Press, 1996), 106.

47. The two theories were developed independently and simultaneously, by Kivy in *The Corded Shell*, and by Davies in 'The Expression of Emotion in Music', *Mind* 89 (1980).

48. Stephen Davies, *Musical Meaning and Expression* (Ithaca, NY: Cornell University Press, 1994), 228.

49. Ibid. 223.

50. Ibid. 229.

51. Ibid. 242.

52. Ibid. 221.

53. Davies has responded (in correspondence) that his turn of phrase here is indeed somewhat misleading. He thinks that strictly speaking 'there are no emotions in or expressed by pure music [as opposed to opera, for example]; there are emotion-characteristics, which are neither'. See also Stephen Davies, 'The Expression Theory Again', *Theoria* 52 (1986).

54. Davies, *Musical Meaning and Expression*, 229.

55. Ibid. 226.

56. Ibid. 262, quoting from his 1980 article 'The Expression of Emotion in Music', 78.

57. Davies, *Musical Meaning and Expression*, 263.

58. Ibid. 265.

59. Ibid. 273. Another important difference between Kivy and Davies that I will consider in Chs. 12 and 13 is that whereas Kivy thinks we only ever notice or

452 NOTES TO CHAPTER 10

recognize the emotions expressed in music, Davies thinks that listeners at least sometimes sympathetically feel the emotions expressed by a piece of music.

60. Ibid. 229.

61. Ibid.

62. Ibid. 262.

63. Gregory Karl and I explicitly defend this view in Gregory Karl and Jenefer Robinson, 'Shostakovich's Tenth Symphony and the Musical Expression of Cognitively Complex Emotions', *Journal of Aesthetics and Art Criticism* 53 (1995).

64. Stephen Davies, 'Contra the Hypothetical Persona in Music', in Mette Hjort and Sue Laver (eds.), *Emotion and the Arts* (New York: Oxford University Press, 1997), 98.

65. Ibid.

66. Ibid.

67. Ibid.

68. Kivy says 'Of course.' It's Davies's version I am attacking here. But there again Davies's version is, in my view, superior to Kivy's in that he (Davies) at least acknowledges that the arousal of feeling has something to do with musical expression or expressiveness. For Davies's example of the tragic mask factory, see Davies, *Musical Meaning and Expression*, 303–4.

69. Kivy, *Music Alone*, 162.

70. See e.g. Karl and Robinson, 'Shostakovich's Tenth Symphony', and Anthony Newcomb, 'Action and Agency in Mahler's Ninth Symphony, Second Movement', in Jenefer Robinson (ed.), *Music and Meaning* (Ithaca, NY: Cornell University Press, 1997).

71. I am thinking of Wagner's *Tannhäuser* and Anthony Newcomb's reading of the second movement of Mahler's Ninth in Newcomb, 'Action and Agency'. Of course, the opera has words as well as music to help convey emotions.

72. Edward T. Cone, *The Composer's Voice*, Ernest Bloch Lectures (Berkeley: University of California Press, 1974), 164.

73. Ivor Keys, *Johannes Brahms* (London: Christopher Helm, 1989), 288.

74. Ibid.

75. Steven Cahn has suggested (in conversation) that it is as if the protagonist has only a tenuous hold on life. Jennifer Judkins (in comments on a version of this chapter delivered at the 2003 Pacific Division meetings of the American Society for Aesthetics, Pacific Grove, California) notes that the 'late' vocal entrance is simply a convention in Romantic 'art music'. It may be true that this is a conventional 'trope', but nevertheless Brahms puts the convention to expressive use. I would like to thank Steven Cahn, Jennifer Judkins, Gregory Karl, and Severine Neff for helpful discussion of this piece.

76. Malcolm Macdonald, *Brahms* (London: J. M. Dent & Sons, 1990), 350.

77. Moreover, if we experience the music in this way we are also invited to have certain emotions and attitudes towards it—to feel *sympathy* for the dying protagonist and perhaps to empathize with her sorrow and her attempts to

rise out of it, and *gladness* for her new-found serenity at the end. Indeed these feelings that are evoked by hearing the music in this way may be one important reason why we hear this music as both moving and psychologically profound. More on the arousal of feeling by music in Chs. 12 and 13.

78. In his comments on an abridged version of this chapter given at the American Philosophical Association Pacific Division meetings in Pasadena, 2004, Andrew Kania argues that what I suggest is not inconsistent with the doggy theory: 'someone could see the light in Robinson's theory of emotions and become a born-again doggy theorist, rejecting the dog-ma that the only aspects of emotions music can mirror are publicly accessible behavioral ones, and appealing to our common experience of the physiological and cognitive aspects of emotion to ground our recognition of their contours in music's appearance'. But thoughts, desires, and 'experiences' are not the sorts of things that have observable 'contours', as behavioural and vocal expressions of emotion do. The 'born-again doggy theorist' seems to me to have given up the central claim of orthodox doggy theory.

79. And it also arouses the listener's own emotions.

80. Perhaps the doggy theorists would argue that 'expression' in song is a very different kettle of fish from expression in pure instrumental music, and that a song *can* be a genuine expression of emotion by a dramatic 'speaker'. But even if this is true, they would not agree that the expression of emotion by a dramatic speaker in a song is paradigmatic of musical expression in general, that is, musical expression not just in song but in pure instrumental music as well.

CHAPTER 11

1. Edward T. Cone, *The Composer's Voice, Ernest Bloch Lectures* (Berkeley: University of California Press, 1974), 2.

2. Ibid. 5.

3. Ibid. 95.

4. Ibid. 94.

5. Ibid. 160.

6. Ibid. 164.

7. Ibid. 165.

8. Stephen Davies has emphasized the importance of this distinction in Stephen Davies, 'Contra the Hypothetical Persona in Music', in Mette Hjort and Sue Laver (eds.), *Emotion and the Arts* (New York: Oxford University Press, 1997).

9. Indeed Jerrold Levinson elevates this principle into a theory of expressiveness. See Jerrold Levinson, *The Pleasures of Aesthetics: Philosophical Essays* (Ithaca, NY: Cornell University Press, 1996), 107. Levinson's theory is plausible for

some pre-Romantic music which *seems* to be an expression of emotion by an 'agent' in the music, although it is unlikely that the composer had any such idea specifically in mind. For example, some of Bach's heartbreaking sarabandes, such as the 25th variation from the *Goldberg Variations,* or the sarabande from the unaccompanied Cello Suite in D minor (No. 2) can be *heard as* outpourings from the soul—maybe of an agent in the music and maybe of the performer. But not all music is plausibly to be construed in this way.

10. Jenefer Robinson, 'Can Music Function as a Metaphor of Emotional Life?', *Revue Française d'Études Americaines* 86 (2000). An expanded and updated version of this essay will appear in Kathleen Stock (ed.), *Philosophers on Music: Experience, Meaning, and Work* (Oxford: Oxford University Press, 2007).

11. And some music can be heard in a number of different ways. In n. 9, I acknowledged that some of Bach's sarabandes—which, after all, are (stylized versions of) dances—can appropriately be heard as expressive utterances. Other Baroque music originating in dances is appropriately heard as pictorial, for example, parts of Vivaldi's *Four Seasons* concerti.

12. See Mark Evan Bonds, *Wordless Rhetoric: Musical Form and the Metaphor of the Oration* (Cambridge, Mass.: Harvard University Press, 1991), for a very interesting account of how the idea of music as a 'wordless oration', which was so pervasive in the eighteenth century, gradually gave way to the idea of music as an 'organism' in the nineteenth.

13. Thanks to Frank Samarotto for pressing me on this point.

14. Monroe Beardsley once argued that the trouble with Langer's theory that music mirrors or is an 'iconic sign' of emotional life is that music mirrors all kinds of other things as well. Examples might include journeys, battles, and the weather. Now, it's true that the 'expressive potential' of a piece of music may allow for various different interpretations of it. But what I am suggesting is that there are conventions that determine whether in particular cases a piece of music should be heard as an actual or an emotional journey (or both, as in *Winterreise*), as a picture of the changing moods of the sea (*La Mer*), or as an expression of a person's changing moods. See Monroe C. Beardsley, *Aesthetics: Problems in the Philosophy of Criticism* (New York: Harcourt Brace, 1958), 332–7, for a discussion of music as an 'iconic sign'.

15. Cone, *The Composer's Voice,* 165.

16. Davies, 'Contra the Hypothetical Persona in Music', 97. Davies argues there that his own theory can endorse this point, but I argued in Ch. 10 that he is wrong about this.

17. Ibid.

18. Anthony Newcomb, 'Once More "Between Absolute and Program Music": Schumann's Second Symphony', *19th Century Music* 7 (1984), 234. Similarly, Fred Maus has argued that the musical structure of the opening measures of Beethoven's String Quartet Opus 95 is its dramatic structure or 'plot'. Fred Everett Maus, 'Music as Drama', in Jenefer Robinson (ed.), *Music and Meaning* (Ithaca: Cornell University Press, 1997), 128.

19. Newcomb, 'Once More "Between Absolute and Program Music"', 237.
20. Anthony Newcomb, 'Sound and Feeling', *Critical Inquiry* 10 (1984), 636.
21. Ibid. 627.
22. For example, in his discussion of the second movement of Mahler's Ninth in Anthony Newcomb, 'Action and Agency in Mahler's Ninth Symphony, Second Movement', in Jenefer Robinson (ed.), *Music and Meaning* (Ithaca, NY: Cornell University Press, 1997), he emphasizes the importance of transitional passages.
23. Newcomb, 'Once More "Between Absolute and Program Music"', 240.
24. 'Hope in *The Hebrides*', in Jerrold Levinson, *Music, Art, and Metaphysics: Essays in Philosophical Aesthetics* (Ithaca, NY: Cornell University Press, 1990), 336–75.
25. Ibid. 347.
26. Ibid.
27. Ibid. 346. His own example is a passage from Mendelssohn's Overture to *The Hebrides*, which he claims expresses the cognitively complex emotion of hope or hopefulness. He refers to the way in which the melody takes leaps of a fourth and fifth, which he claims we hear as 'reaching for something—for something higher', and which help to account for 'a quality of *aspiration*', Levinson, *Music, Art, and Metaphysics*, 367, 368. He also suggests that the passage in question positioned 'as general counterpoise to the worrisome tenor of the overture's first section' perhaps suggests 'some of the pure conceptual content of hope—its favorable assessment of future in relation to present', ibid. 373. For criticism of his interpretation of *The Hebrides* overture, see Gregory Karl and Jenefer Robinson, 'Levinson on Hope in *The Hebrides*', *Journal of Aesthetics and Art Criticism* 53 (1995).
28. Gregory Karl and Jenefer Robinson, 'Shostakovich's Tenth Symphony and the Musical Expression of Cognitively Complex Emotions', *Journal of Aesthetics and Art Criticism* 53 (1995). Reprinted in Jenefer Robinson (ed.), *Music & Meaning* (Ithaca, NY: Cornell University Press, 1997), 154–78.
29. For example, Mosco Carner's influential judgement on the symphony is that it is 'deeply flawed', largely because of the 'perceived formal incoherence' of the last movement which Carner hears as a sonata with an exposition of 118 bars, a 'telescoped' development and recapitulation of roughly 160 bars, and a coda of 310 bars. Armin Gebhardt also condemns the last movement, although he gives a different formal interpretation from Carner's. '[Gebhardt] interprets the movement as an extremely sectional, patchy pair of interlocking rondos, with fourteen sections rolling past as functionally undifferentiated as the cars of a freight train.' Newcomb, 'Once More "Between Absolute and Program Music"', 239.
30. Karl and Robinson, 'Shostakovich's Tenth Symphony'.
31. Throughout I will talk of 'our' interpretation, since our essay was co-authored, but in fact the interpretation is largely due to Gregory Karl.
32. Charles Fisk, 'What Schubert's Last Sonata Might Hold', in Robinson (ed.), *Music and Meaning* (Ithaca: Cornell University Press, 1997), 183.

33. Fisk, 'What Schubert's Last Sonata Might Hold', 179.

34. On the other hand, Wolfgang Iser notes that *all* interpretations of literary works contain 'alien associations' that do not fit into the pattern of meaning that a reader discerns in the work. Wolfgang Iser, 'The Reading Process: A Phenomenological Approach', in Jane P. Tompkins (ed.), *Reader-Response Criticism: From Formalism to Post-Structuralism* (Baltimore: Johns Hopkins University Press, 1980), 60.

35. Newcomb, 'Once More "Between Absolute and Program Music"', 233.

36. Ibid. 234.

37. They both appear, for example, in *Carnaval*.

38. Dmitri Dmitrievich Shostakovich, *Testimony: The Memoirs of Dimitri Shostakovich, as Related to and Edited by Solomon Volkov*, trans. Antonina W. Bouis (New York: Harper & Row, 1979), 141. There has been some dispute about the authenticity of this memoir, however. One of the chief sceptics is Laurel Fay. See Laurel E. Fay, *Shostakovich: A Life* (Oxford: Oxford University Press, 2000).

39. Of course, some good pieces may consistently aim for a certain kind of inconsistency. Perhaps postmodern works such as some of Schnittke's would be a case in point.

40. In his 'Contra the Hypothetical Persona in Music', Davies both attacks the persona theory and tries to defend his own doggy theory against the persona account. I have already considered and rejected his pro-doggy theory arguments in Ch. 10.

41. Ibid. 101.

42. Ibid. 99.

43. Ibid. 105.

44. Ibid. 101.

45. Cone, *The Composer's Voice*, 95.

46. Notice that in a canon or a fugue there is the *dux* (the voice that enters first) and the *comes* (the imitative voice), the leader and the companion(s). Indeed even the doggy theory attests to the widespread practice of hearing characters in music: on this view music conveys the appearance of a person behaving in certain ways.

47. In the liner notes to his CD of character pieces by C. P. E. Bach, Tom Beghin points out that the term 'character' at this period can mean either a particular type of temperament or a particular person or persona. Tom Beghin, *The Characters of C. P. E. Bach* (Leuven: Eufoda, 2003).

48. Davies, 'Contra the Hypothetical Persona in Music', 107.

49. Edward T. Cone, 'Schubert's Promissory Note: An Exercise in Musical Hermeneutics,' *Nineteenth-Century Music* 5 (1982), 239. Note how similar Cone's reading of the *Moment Musical* No. 6 is to Fisk's reading of the last sonata. Other examples also come to mind, such as the *Wanderer* fantasy. It seems likely that this characteristic psychological theme in Schubert's music reflects something real in his psychology.

50. Ibid. 240.

51. Ibid. 241.
52. Malcolm Macdonald, *Brahms* (London: J. M. Dent & Sons, 1990), 357.
53. Ibid.
54. Edwin Evans, *Brahms' Pianoforte Music Handbook* (London: William Reeves, 1936), 232.
55. Quoted by Swafford in Jan Swafford, *Johannes Brahms: A Biography*, 1st edn. (New York: Alfred A. Knopf: distrib. Random House, 1997), 587.
56. Technically, what Brahms has done is to create a chain of 7th chords progressing in a circle of fifths.
57. Bars 66–70 are in F flat (E) major.
58. The word is Steven Cahn's. I would like to thank him as well as Gregory Karl, Severine Neff, and the late Allen Sapp for helping me with the analysis of this complex piece.
59. Harald Krebs has insisted (in a personal communication) on the importance of the performer's role in interpreting a piece. Strictly speaking, I should analyse particular performances of the works I discuss. It is always the performer who represents the protagonist of a piece if there is one. When emotions are expressed by a persona or characters in a piece of music, it is performers who enact the personae or characters. In solo performance especially it often seems to be the performer whose emotions are being expressed.
60. Swafford, *Johannes Brahms: A Biography*, 587.
61. Ibid.

CHAPTER 12

1. In fact, there is some evidence that trained musicians process music differently from other people. Renée Cox reports that there is evidence that 'melodies are most likely to be processed in the right hemisphere (left ear) by nonmusicians, but more likely to be processed in the left hemisphere (right ear) by musicians'. See Renée Cox, 'Varieties of Musical Expressionism', in George Dickie, Richard Sclafani, and Ronald Roblin (eds.), *Aesthetics: A Critical Anthology* (New York: St Martin's, 1989), 623–4. The people I have in mind as 'qualified listeners' are people who have grown up listening to Bach, Haydn, Beethoven, and so on, so that they have some understanding of the style of the music, even if they have never studied music theory. In Levinson's terminology, they are 'suitably backgrounded'. Henceforth when I talk about 'the listener', I shall mean 'the qualified listener' in this sense. If I am talking explicitly and exclusively about trained music theorists, I will say so.
2. See Jenefer Robinson, 'The Expression and Arousal of Emotion in Music', *Journal of Aesthetics and Art Criticism* 52/1 (1994), where I first argued that sometimes the emotions a musical work *arouses* can alert us to what it

expresses, although the emotions aroused may be different from the emotions expressed. For further discussion, see the sections on the Meyer emotions below.

3. Peter Kivy, *Music Alone: Philosophical Reflections on the Purely Musical Experience* (Ithaca, NY: Cornell University Press, 1990), 175.
4. Ibid. 149.
5. Ibid. 40–1. For the judgement theory of emotion, see Ch. 1.
6. Ibid. 159–60.
7. Ibid. 153.
8. To be fair, Kivy is mainly concerned to deny that we are moved to feel *the garden-variety emotions that the music expresses.*
9. Maybe Kivy recognizes this: he does say that we can be moved by *beautifully expressive* music. But, as Stephen Davies (*Musical Meaning and Expression* (Ithaca, NY; London: Cornell University Press, 1994), 286) argues, 'there is no room in [Kivy's] account for the claim that the listener responds directly to the fact that the music expresses, say, sadness rather than happiness, or to the quality of the sadness expressed. Kivy's theory allows that *how* the sadness is expressed affects the listener's response—she reacts to the felicity or otherwise of the expressive achievement—but the theory makes no allowance for the idea that *what* is expressed shapes the response.'
10. Aaron Ridley, *Music, Value, and the Passions* (Ithaca, NY: Cornell University Press, 1995), 128.
11. Ibid. 192.
12. Ibid. 76.
13. Ibid. 94.
14. I think this is right about 'expressive qualities' in general, as I observed in Ch. 9.
15. Ridley, *Music, Value, and the Passions*, 138.
16. Contrast Stephen Davies who thinks that we are saddened by sad music as a result of recognizing the sadness in the music. Davies, *Musical Meaning and Expression*, Ch. 6.
17. Ridley, *Music, Value, and the Passions*, 131.
18. Ibid. 135.
19. Ibid. 140.
20. Ibid. 138.
21. Ibid. 133.
22. I'll develop this idea more fully in Ch. 13.
23. Jerrold Levinson, *The Pleasures of Aesthetics: Philosophical Essays* (Ithaca, NY: Cornell University Press, 1996), 97.
24. At this point I probably part company from Levinson. See ibid. 107 for Levinson's definition of musical expressiveness.
25. Ridley acknowledges that we sometimes hear instrumental music as containing a persona on a 'soul journey' but he still seems to believe that the listener's understanding response to such a persona is basically sympathetic or perhaps

'empathetic', i.e. that we feel what the persona feels: we feel *with* him or her, not *for* him or her.

26. I acknowledge that many Romantic lieder and many 'introspective' lyric pieces such as the Intermezzo may encourage the listener to identify with a persona in the music. Similarly, in my examples at the end of Ch. 9, such as Keats's 'Ode' and Friedrich's *Large Enclosure*, the reader or viewer may typically enter into the feelings of the apparent 'utterer' of the works, and feel *with* the painter or dramatic speaker. That is because these are 'lyric' works of (apparent) self-expression by a painter, poet, or composer.

27. Kendall Walton, 'Listening with Imagination', in Jenefer Robinson (ed.), *Music and Meaning* (Ithaca, NY: Cornell University Press, 1997), 73.

28. Ibid.

29. Ibid. 71. For Walton the music itself does not generate the 'fictional truth' that I am feeling anguished or agitated or exuberant; it merely supplies me with the personal auditory experiences that generate this fictional truth. In Ch. 13 I give an alternative and, I think, more plausible explanation for this phenomenon.

30. Ibid. 77.

31. Ibid. 78.

32. See Ch. 11 n. 14, on Beardsley on music as an 'iconic sign' of emotion.

33. In Ch. 13 I also discuss how music induces more complex emotions such as anguish.

34. For example in Eugene Narmour, 'The Top-Down and Bottom-up Systems of Musical Implication: Building on Meyer's Theory of Emotional Syntax', *Music Perception* 9 (1991).

35. Leonard B. Meyer, *Emotion and Meaning in Music* (Chicago: University of Chicago Press, 1956), 40.

36. See Hébert, Peretz, and Gagnon on the 'implicit knowledge that all listeners share when listening to tonal music'. Sylvie Hébert, Isabelle Peretz, and Lise Gagnon, 'Perceiving the Tonal Ending of Tune Excerpts: The Roles of Pre-existing Representation and Musical Expertise', *Canadian Journal of Experimental Psychology* 49 (1995), 207.

37. Meyer, *Emotion and Meaning in Music*, 14.

38. Ibid. 31.

39. Carol L. Krumhansl, *Cognitive Foundations of Musical Pitch* (New York: Oxford University Press, 1990), 214.

40. Ibid. 219.

41. Ibid. 225.

42. Ibid. 226.

43. John A. Sloboda and Patrik N. Juslin, 'Psychological Perspectives on Music and Emotion', in eid., *Music and Emotion: Theory and Research*, (Oxford: Oxford University Press, 2001), 91. See also Alf Gabrielsson, 'Emotions in Strong Experiences with Music', in Juslin and Sloboda (eds.), *Music and Emotion*, 433. The most frequently cited papers on this topic seem to be Jaak Panksepp,

'The Emotional Sources of "Chills" Induced by Music', *Music Perception* 13 (1995), and A. Goldstein, 'Thrills in Response to Music and Other Stimuli', *Physiological Psychology* 8 (1980).

44. Sloboda and Juslin, 'Psychological Perspectives on Music and Emotion', 92.

45. Jerrold Levinson thinks that more is involved in the production of chills and thrills than Sloboda recognizes. See his 'Varieties of Musical Pleasure: Musical Chills and Other Delights' (paper presented as the Monroe Beardsley lecture, Temple University, Philadelphia, 2002). I will have more to say about Levinson's view in Ch. 13.

46. John A. Sloboda, 'Music—Where Cognition and Emotion Meet', *The Psychologist* 12 (1999), 452.

47. Later in this chapter and in the next we will be examining some empirical evidence that music does indeed cause physiological changes. In the next chapter I will examine whether these physiological changes are genuinely emotional. Why, after all, should a delayed move to the tonic be regarded as 'something significant to me or mine'?

48. Here as elsewhere I am abstracting from questions of performance. Clearly different performances of the same piece can find different structures within it, and underline them by differences in phrasing, differences in emphasis on particular melodic lines, differences in timbre, dynamics, and so on.

49. And of course there can be *inappropriate* responses, as when I am *bored* by Beethoven's Third because I don't understand Beethoven very well or I've heard the piece ten times already today or I'm distracted or inattentive or in a bad mood and unwilling to listen to anything 'difficult', etc. See Ch. 4.

50. 'On Rehearing Music', in Leonard B. Meyer, *Music, the Arts, and Ideas* (Chicago: University of Chicago Press, 1967), 42–53.

51. Sloboda and Juslin, 'Psychological Perspectives on Music and Emotion', 92, citing R. Jackendoff, 'Musical Processing and Musical Affect', in M. R. Jones and S. Holleran (eds.), *Cognitive Bases of Musical Communication* (Washington, DC: American Psychological Association, 1992).

52. Stephen Davies objects that having such emotions aroused is not enough for us to be able to follow musical structure or expressiveness in any detail. This may be true. All I am asserting is that having our emotions evoked plays an *important role* in figuring out and experiencing what is being expressed. See Stephen Davies, 'Contra the Hypothetical Persona in Music', in Mette Hjort and Sue Laver (eds.), *Emotion and the Arts* (New York: Oxford University Press, 1997), 105–6.

53. In Ch. 13 I have more to say about these cases, especially about the apparent lack of any 'affective appraisal' to set off the emotions evoked.

54. In discussing literature I distinguished the reader-response theory of Iser from the more radical views of Holland and Fish. Meyer gives us a 'listener-response' theory of music listening which is similar to Iser's. What I am doing here is adumbrating a listener-response theory of musical understanding that

allows for greater variety of appropriate emotional responses than Meyer seems to want to allow, but obeys the strictures on 'appropriateness' that I outlined in my discussion of interpretation in literature in Chs. 4–7.

55. And again there will always be inappropriate responses by some listeners. If I'm feeling low and bored, I might find even the greatest music tedious or pretentious.

56. More accurately, Ridley says that music evokes 'feelings', that is, emotions 'shorn of their cognitive aspect'. Ridley, *Music, Value, and the Passions*, 32. I'll amplify this point in Ch. 13.

57. Carol L. Krumhansl, 'An Exploratory Study of Musical Emotions and Psychophysiology', *Canadian Journal of Experimental Psychology* 51 (1997), 338.

58. A word on terminology: for Kivy, an 'expressive property' is simply a property named by an emotion word that correctly describes the music. However, as we'll see, the experiment shows that the pieces Krumhansl selects also have 'expressive qualities' in my sense and Ridley's: they are not only named by an emotion word, but also evoke a corresponding emotion.

59. Krumhansl, 'An Exploratory Study of Musical Emotions and Psychophysiology', 347–8.

60. Ibid. 348.

61. Ibid. 345.

62. Ibid. 349.

63. Ibid. 351.

64. Ibid. 350.

65. Ibid.

66. However, as bruce mcclung points out (personal communication), the pieces that Krumhansl chose have marked cultural associations, at least for American listeners: the Barber *Adagio* is associated with the death of J.F.K., for example, and the *Night on Bald Mountain* with Hallowe'en. Some of the emotion that listeners feel may also be partly due to these associations. How music with a particular expressive quality arouses a corresponding emotion in listeners is something I discuss further in Ch. 13.

67. Krumhansl, 'An Exploratory Study of Musical Emotions and Psychophysiology', 348.

68. Leslie Bunt and Mercedes Pavlicevic, 'Music and Emotion: Perspectives from Music Therapy', in Juslin and Sloboda (eds.), *Music and Emotion* 185.

69. Ibid.

70. Ibid. 186.

CHAPTER 13

1. Plato, *Republic*, trans. Robin Waterfield (Oxford: Oxford University Press, 1993), 110.

2. Plato, *Republic*, 116.
3. Ibid.
4. Thus Aristotle's theory of the emotions is given mainly in the *Rhetoric*, where Aristotle is describing ways for the orator to influence his hearers most effectively.
5. The *New Grove* tells us that although many writers have talked about 'the doctrine of the affections' or 'Affektenlehre' in the Baroque period, 'in fact no one comprehensive, organized theory of how the Affects were to be achieved in music was ever established in the Baroque period'. Stanley Sadie (ed.), *The New Grove Dictionary of Music and Musicians* (London: Macmillan, 1980), xxi. 269.
6. See Carl Dahlhaus, *The Idea of Absolute Music*, trans. Roger Lustig (Chicago: University of Chicago Press, 1989), 4. For a very interesting account of the influence of the rhetorical tradition in eighteenth-century music, see Mark Evan Bonds, *Wordless Rhetoric: Musical Form and the Metaphor of the Oration* (Cambridge, Mass.: Harvard University Press, 1991).
7. Eduard Hanslick, *On the Musically Beautiful*, trans. Geoffrey Payzant (Indianapolis: Hackett, 1986), 50. It is interesting to note that Hanslick is aware that music affects our moods and is most evocative when we are depressed. What he says is consistent with the idea that music works through 'non-cognitive' channels and evokes at least some aspects of emotion, such as physiological changes, in an automatic way. As we'll see, he's right about all these things.
8. David Huron, 'How Music Evokes Emotion' (paper delivered to University of Cincinnati College Conservatory of Music, 2001). Later, in discussing the Jazzercise effect, we'll see how this can happen.
9. Recall the large claims for the power of music made by Bunt and Pavlicevic, the music therapists, whom I quote in Ch. 12.
10. Phoebe Ellsworth, 'Levels of Thought and Levels of Emotion', in Paul Ekman and Richard J. Davidson (eds.), *The Nature of Emotion: Fundamental Questions* (New York: Oxford University Press, 1994), 195.
11. This argument could be taken as a reduction to the absurd of the view that emotions require cognitive objects.
12. Klaus R. Scherer and Marcel R. Zentner, 'Emotional Effects of Music: Production Rules', in Patrik N. Juslin and John Sloboda (eds.), *Music and Emotion: Theory and Research* (Oxford: Oxford University Press, 2001), 369.
13. There are other interesting connections between mood and memory, which I'll discuss later in the chapter.
14. John A. Sloboda and Patrik N. Juslin, 'Psychological Perspectives on Music and Emotion', in eid. (eds.), *Music and Emotion*, 92–3, citing Nico Frijda, *The Emotions* (Cambridge: Cambridge University Press, 1986). They also appeal to J. J. Bharucha, 'Tonality and Expectation,' in R. Aiello and J. A. Sloboda (eds.), *Musical Perceptions* (New York: Oxford University Press, 1994), and Carol L. Krumhansl, *Cognitive Foundations of Musical Pitch* (New York: Oxford University Press, 1990), for confirmation of this view.

15. See Ch. 12.

16. Stephen Davies, *Musical Meaning and Expression* (Ithaca, NY: Cornell University Press, 1994), 315. Davies does not argue that expressiveness in music can be analysed in terms of the arousal of emotion in listeners, but that *perceiving* or *recognizing* an emotion characteristic in appearances is what prompts the arousal of the corresponding feeling. Notice that this is not the same as Aaron Ridley's view that I discussed in Ch. 12. Ridley thinks we recognize what music expresses (partly) by virtue of what it makes us feel. Davies thinks we recognize what music expresses and *as a result of this recognition* feel the same way. His position contains echoes of Jerrold Levinson, 'Music and Negative Emotion', in Jenefer Robinson (ed.), *Music and Meaning* (Ithaca: Cornell University Press, 1997), 228–9.

17. Davies, *Musical Meaning and Expression*, 271.

18. Patrik N. Juslin, 'Communicating Emotion in Music Performance: A Review and Theoretical Framework', in Juslin and Sloboda (eds.), *Music and Emotion*, 321.

19. Ibid. 329.

20. But recall Lazarus's theory that suggests a close connection between fear and anger: both may be hostile responses.

21. Isabelle Peretz, 'Listen to the Brain: A Biological Perspective on Musical Emotions', in Juslin and Sloboda (eds.), *Music and Emotion*, 114.

22. Ibid.

23. Leslie Bunt and Mercedes Pavlicevic, 'Music and Emotion: Perspectives from Music Therapy', in Juslin and Sloboda (eds.), *Music and Emotion*, 193. See also Daniel N. Stern, *The Interpersonal World of the Infant: A View from Psychoanalysis and Developmental Psychology* (New York: Basic Books, 1985).

24. Bunt and Pavlicevic, 'Music and Emotion: Perspectives from Music Therapy'. 194.

25. Peretz, 'Listen to the Brain: A Biological Perspective on Musical Emotions', 115.

26. Sandra Trehub, 'Musical Predispositions in Infancy: An Update', in R. J. Zatorre and Isabelle Peretz (eds.), *The Cognitive Neuroscience of Music* (Oxford: Oxford University Press, 2003), 13.

27. Elaine Hatfield, John T. Cacioppo, and Richard L. Rapson, *Emotional Contagion* (Cambridge: Cambridge University Press; Paris: Éditions de la Maison des Sciences de l'Homme, 1994), 10–11.

28. For example, by David Watson: see *Mood and Temperament*, (New York: Guilford, 2000).

29. See e.g. Nico Frijda, 'Moods, Emotion Episodes, and Emotions', in M. Lewis and J. M. Haviland (eds.), *Handbook of Emotions* (New York: Guilford, 1993), and Keith Oatley and Jennifer M. Jenkins, *Understanding Emotions* (Oxford: Blackwell, 1996).

30. Frijda, 'Moods, Emotion Episodes, and Emotions', 384.

31. Paul Ekman, 'Moods, Emotions, and Traits', in Paul Ekman and Richard J. Davidson (eds.), *The Nature of Emotion: Fundamental Questions* (New York: Oxford University Press, 1994), 57.

32. Davies, *Musical Meaning and Expression*, 315.
33. Ibid. 302. An important precursor is Jerrold Levinson who once argued that the 'cognitive (or thoughtlike) component' in our emotional responses to music is 'etiolated by comparison to that of real-life emotion'. Levinson, 'Music and Negative Emotion', 229.
34. Aaron Ridley, *Music, Value, and the Passions* (Ithaca NY: Cornell University Press, 1995), 32. These 'feelings' are, however, distinguished by 'a disposition to experience the world under the description given by the formal object' of the corresponding emotion, so that sad music prompts a disposition to view the world sadly, as well as 'characteristic forms of behavior' and 'an identifying experiential character (which is what a given feeling is like, and how we know we're having it)', ibid. 136. Ridley's view is consistent with the idea that he is talking about moods rather than emotions.
35. Later I'll modify this view.
36. Davies, *Musical Meaning and Expression*, 302–3.
37. Dale L. Bartlett, 'Physiological Responses to Music and Sound Stimuli', in Donald A. Hodges (ed.), *Handbook of Music Psychology*, 2nd edn. (San Antonio, Tex.: Institute for Music Research, 1996), 375.
38. Ibid. 355.
39. For example, G. H. Zimny and E. W. Weidenfeller, 'Effects of Music Upon GSR and Heart Rate', *American Journal of Psychology* 76 (1963).
40. I. Nyklicek, J. F. Thayer, and L. J. P. van Doornen, 'Cardiorespiratory Differentiation of Musically-Induced Emotions', *Journal of Psychophysiology* 11 (1997). For a discussion see Scherer and Zentner, 'Emotional Effects of Music: Production Rules', 376.
41. C. V. Witvliet and S. R. Vrana, 'The Emotional Impact of Instrumental Music on Affect Ratings, Facial Emg, Autonomic Response, and the Startle Reflex: Effects of Valence and Arousal', *Psychophysiology Supplement* 91 (1996). C. V. Witvliet, S. R. Vrana, and N. Webb-Talmadge, 'In the Mood: Emotion and Facial Expressions During and after Instrumental Music, and During an Emotional Inhibition Task', *Psychophysiology Supplement* 88 (1998). Discussed by Juslin, 'Communicating Emotion in Music Performance', 329, and Scherer and Zentner, 'Emotional Effects of Music', 376.
42. Cited by Scherer in Scherer and Zentner, 'Emotional Effects of Music', 376.
43. Peretz, 'Listen to the Brain', 126.
44. Trehub, 'Musical Predispositions in Infancy: An Update', 11.
45. Reported by David Huron in David Huron, 'Is Music an Evolutionary Adaptation?', in R. J. Zatorre and Isabelle Peretz (eds.), *The Biological Foundations of Music* (New York: New York Academy of Sciences, 2001), 57.
46. Sloboda and Juslin, 'Psychological Perspectives on Music and Emotion', 88.
47. Scherer and Zentner, 'Emotional Effects of Music', 378.
48. Ibid. 371–2. A pioneer in this area is Manfred Clynes: see e.g. his 'Neurobiologic Functions of Rhythm, Time and Pulse in Music,' in id. (ed.), *Music, Mind, and Brain* (New York: Plenum, 1982).

49. Sloboda and Juslin also list a number of other studies that 'provide evidence from self-reports that listeners experience emotions in relation to music', 'Psychological Perspectives on Music and Emotion', 84.

50. William James, *The Works of William James*, ed. Frederick H. Burkhardt, 3 vols. (Cambridge, Mass.: Harvard University Press, 1981), ii. 1077–8. I already quoted from this passage in Ch. 3.

51. Peter M. Lewinsohn et al., *Control Your Depression* (New York: Prentice-Hall, 1986), esp. ch. 6.

52. Watson, *Mood and Temperament*, 102.

53. Scherer and Zentner, 'Emotional Effects of Music: Production Rules', 374, citing A. L. Bouhuys, G. M. Bloem, and T. G. Groothuis, 'Induction of Depressed and Elated Mood by Music Influences the Perception of Facial Emotional Expressions in Healthy Subjects', *Journal of Affective Disorders* 33 (1995).

54. See e.g. P. M. Niedenthal and M. B. Setterlund, 'Emotion Congruence in Perception', *Personality and Social Psychology Bulletin* 20 (1994); P. M. Niedenthal, M. B. Setterlund, and D. E. Jones, 'Emotional Organization of Perceptual Memory', in P. M. Niedenthal and Shinobu Kitayama (eds.), *The Heart's Eye* (San Diego, Calif.: Academic Press, 1994); P. M. Niedenthal and M. Brauer, J. B. Halberstadt and A. H. Innes-Ker, 'When Did Her Smile Drop? Facial Mimicry and the Influences of Emotional State on the Detection of Change in Emotional Expression', *Cognition and Emotion* 15 (2001).

55. Scherer and Zentner, 'Emotional Effects of Music', 373.

56. Sloboda and Juslin, 'Psychological Perspectives on Music and Emotion', 84.

57. Reported by Scherer and Zentner, 'Emotional Effects of Music', 380.

58. Ibid.

59. Ibid. 378, citing R. Fried and L. Berkowitz, 'Music That Charms . . . and Can Influence Helpfulness,' *Journal of Applied Social Psychology* 9 (1979). This 'altruistic behavior' consisted in volunteering for another study!

60. The aversive music 'tended to arouse negative feelings'. Scherer and Zentner, 'Emotional Effects of Music: Production Rules', 378. Psychologists writing about these matters constantly talk as though finding pleasure or displeasure in music is the same sort of 'emotional effect' as being put into a calm or aroused state or a happy or sad mood by music. But disliking the music is an affective state directed at the music, not a state caused by the music and not directed at anything in particular.

61. See Ch. 12 n. 66.

62. See Stanley Schachter, *The Psychology of Affiliation: Experimental Studies of the Sources of Gregariousness* (Stanford, Calif.: Stanford University Press, 1959), for interesting work on how—in a kind of contagion effect—groups come to create a consensus on what response is appropriate to their situation. Thanks to Michael Sontag for this reference. Schachter also refers to 'evaluative needs' in Stanley Schachter and Jerome Singer, 'Cognitive, Social, and Physiological Determinants of Emotional State', *Psychological Review* 69 (1962).

63. Today many theorists think that the Schachter and Singer experiment is discredited, because it has never been exactly replicated. But I am not relying on any consequences it has for the 'theory of emotion'. I treat it as one of many experiments conducted by Schachter into how we attribute emotional states to ourselves in specious ways in ambiguous situations. But, as I'll be emphasizing, in treating it as an example of 'confabulation', we should always bear in mind that labelling one's emotional state actually has the effect of altering one's emotional state.

64. Jerrold Levinson made this point in his remarks on a version of this chapter which I read at an invited symposium on Philosophy of Music at the Eastern Division meetings of the American Philosophical Association in Washington, 2003. I am grateful for Levinson's thoughtful comments.

65. Notice that I'm confining my attention here to the Jazzercise effect and abstracting for the time being from other possible sources of emotion, such as the Kivy or Meyer emotions, or the emotion that might result from hearing the music as an emotional expression in some protagonist. These will all be part of the *context* in which we hear the music, however.

66. For example, by Paul Griffiths, *What Emotions Really Are: The Problem of Psychological Categories* (Chicago: University of Chicago Press, 1997).

67. To feel 'afraid', I must be frightened by something or other if only by a frightening *thought*, such as the thought of witches on a Bald Mountain, so the context I bring to the music must allow for this.

68. Oatley and Jenkins, *Understanding Emotions*, 281.

69. Ibid.

70. Notice, however, that this cognitive monitoring may not result in much insight into the *music*. The Jazzercise effect, as I keep emphasizing, is a very broad effect that occurs in any music, good or bad, simple or complex. Hence the *labelling* of Jazzercise effects is probably not a particularly insightful way of responding to music and may of course be positively misleading. On the other hand, if one is listening to good and complex music, paying attention to the state of one's body as one listens may help us recognize developments in the music, as I argued in Ch. 12.

71. Sloboda and Juslin, 'Psychological Perspectives on Music and Emotion', 91.

72. Judith Becker, 'Anthropological Perspectives on Music and Emotion', in Juslin and Sloboda (eds.), *Music and Emotion*, 137.

73. Ibid. 145.

74. Sloboda and Juslin, 'Psychological Perspectives on Music and Emotion', 85.

75. Scherer notes that, when asked, subjects have no difficulty distinguishing between the emotions expressed by a piece and those it evokes in the listener. I am not claiming anything to the contrary. The emotions expressed *affect* how we label what we feel, but they are not necessarily identical to the emotions we feel.

76. Perhaps it will be objected that if I am responding emotionally to a Romantic expression of emotion in some protagonist, I don't need to invoke the Jazzercise effect to explain my reactions. I would suggest that any emotional

response to an expression of emotion is almost certainly influenced by the direct physiological effects of the music.

77. Sloboda and Juslin, 'Psychological Perspectives on Music and Emotion', 97.

78. I say 'good music', rather than 'great music', because I am not convinced that musical chills exactly correlate with moments of musical greatness. Given how I think musical chills originate, this should not be too surprising.

79. Being moved by the beauty and power of the music (as Kivy describes) will also be part of this experience, no doubt.

80. Cf. Scott Burnham, *Beethoven Hero* (Princeton, NJ: Princeton University Press, 2000).

81. It is interesting that Jerrold Levinson thinks that musical chills and thrills ('frissons') are evoked by narratives that we attach to the music. If he is right, this is a good example of just the sort of labelling process I am talking about. See Jerrold Levinson, 'Varieties of Musical Pleasure: Musical Chills and Other Delights' (paper presented as the Monroe Beardsley lecture, Temple University, Philadelphia, 2002). Notice, too, that if a person thinks he understands why he is having an emotional response to a piece of music, e.g. he has recognized a Meyerian structural high point, then he may not seek any further explanation for his state of feeling. When Peter Kivy hears the culmination of the Brahms Intermezzo as a complex interplay of B flat minor and major, he may simply recognize what is happening structurally, and admire it. He has no need to search around for a further explanation of his experience. He was moved (if he was), and moved by the way the music unfolded. But for those who do not know what caused the tension and uncertainty, there will be a search for a reasonable explanation of what could be an intense emotional experience.

82. From the abstract to A. J. Blood and R. J. Zatorre, 'Intensely Pleasurable Responses to Music Correlate with Activity in Brain Regions Implicated in Reward and Emotion', *Proceedings of the National Academy of Sciences of the U.S.A.* 98 (2001). Subjects in the experiment chose their own selections, from rock music to Beethoven. Blood comments: 'This finding links music with biologically relevant, survival-related stimuli via their common recruitment of brain circuitry involved in pleasure and reward.' Interestingly, Tia Denora, a sociologist of music, has noted the ways in which music lovers behave like drug users when preparing for an aesthetic experience: 'The music "user" is . . . deeply implicated as a producer of his or her own emotional response.' Listeners are 'active in constructing their "passivity" to music—their ability to be "moved"'. Tia Denora, 'Aesthetic Agency and Musical Practice: New Directions in the Sociology of Music and Emotion', in Juslin and Sloboda (eds.), *Music and Emotion*, 168–9.

83. Sloboda and Juslin, 'Psychological Perspectives on Music and Emotion', 96, citing John Sloboda, 'Musical Performance and Emotion: Issues and Developments,' in S. W. Yi (ed.), *Music, Mind, and Science* (Seoul: Western Music Research Institute, 2000), 226.

84. Sloboda, 'Musical Performance and Emotion', 96.
85. Although, as I noted in Ch. 12, different listeners paying close attention to the music may nevertheless appropriately respond to it in somewhat different ways. In particular, not all listeners respond by identifying with the protagonist.
86. Personal communication.
87. Becker, 'Anthropological Perspectives on Music and Emotion', 146.
88. Ibid. 150.
89. Ibid. 146.

Bibliography

ABRAMS, M. H., *The Mirror and the Lamp: Romantic Theory and the Critical Tradition* (Oxford: Oxford University Press, 1953).

ALPERSON, PHILIP, *The Philosophy of the Visual Arts* (New York: Oxford University Press, 1992).

ARISTOTLE, *Rhetoric*, trans. W. Rhys Roberts, 2nd edn. (New York: Random House, 1984).

—— *Poetics*, trans. Richard Janko (Indianapolis: Hackett, 1987).

AVERILL, JAMES R., *Anger and Aggression: An Essay on Emotion*, Springer Series in Social Psychology (New York: Springer-Verlag, 1982).

AX, A. F., 'The Physiological Differentiation between Fear and Anger in Humans', *Psychosomatic Medicine* 15 (1953), 433–42.

BARNES, ANNETTE, *On Interpretation: A Critical Analysis* (Oxford: B. Blackwell, 1988).

BARTHES, ROLAND, *S/Z*, trans. Richard Miller (New York: Hill & Wang, 1974).

—— *The Pleasure of the Text*, trans. Richard Miller (New York: Noonday Press; Farrar, Strauss, and Giroux, 1975).

BARTLETT, DALE L., 'Physiological Responses to Music and Sound Stimuli', in Donald A. Hodges (ed.), *Handbook of Music Psychology* (San Antonio, Tex.: Institute for Music Research, 1996), 343–85.

BARWELL, ISMAY, 'How Does Art Express Emotions?', *Journal of Aesthetics and Art Criticism* 45 (1986), 175–81.

BEARDSLEY, MONROE C., *Aesthetics: Problems in the Philosophy of Criticism* (New York: Harcourt Brace, 1958).

BECKER, JUDITH, 'Anthropological Perspectives on Music and Emotion'. in Patrik N. Juslin and John A. Sloboda (eds.), *Music and Emotion: Theory and Research* (Oxford: Oxford University Press, 2001), 135–60.

BEGHIN, TOM, CD: *The Characters of C. P. E. Bach* (Leuven: Eufoda, 2003).

BELL, CLIVE, *Art* (London: Chatto & Windus, 1914).

BENEDECK, NELLY SILAGY, *Auguste Rodin: The Burghers of Calais* (New York: Metropolitan Museum of Art, 2000).

BENSON, JOHN, 'Emotion and Expression'. *Philosophical Review* 76 (1967), 335–57.

BEN-ZE'EV, AARON, *The Subtlety of Emotions* (Cambridge, Mass.: MIT, 2000).

BERLYNE, D. E., *Aesthetics and Psychobiology* (New York: Appleton-Century-Crofts, 1971).

BHARUCHA, J. J., 'Tonality and Expectation', in R. Aiello and J. A. Sloboda (eds.), *Musical Perceptions* (New York: Oxford University Press, 1994), 213–39.

BLOOD, A. J., and ZATORRE, R. J. 'Intensely Pleasurable Responses to Music Correlate with Activity in Brain Regions Implicated in Reward and Emotion', *Proceedings of the National Academy of Sciences of the U.S.A.* 98 (2001), 11818–23.

BLUM, LAWRENCE, 'Compassion', in Amelie Rorty (ed.), *Explaining Emotions* (Berkeley: University of California Press, 1980), 507–17.

—— *Friendship, Altruism and Morality*, International Library of Philosophy (London: Routledge & Kegan Paul, 1980).

BONDS, MARK EVAN, *Wordless Rhetoric: Musical Form and the Metaphor of the Oration* (Cambridge, Mass.: Harvard University Press, 1991).

BOOTH, STEPHEN, *An Essay on Shakespeare's Sonnets* (New Haven: Yale University Press, 1969).

BOOTH, WAYNE C., *The Rhetoric of Fiction* (Chicago: University of Chicago Press, 1961).

BOUHUYS, A. L., BLOEM, G. M., and GROOTHUIS, T. G. 'Induction of Depressed and Elated Mood by Music Influences the Perception of Facial Emotional Expressions in Healthy Subjects', *Journal of Affective Disorders* 33 (1995), 215–26.

BOUWSMA, O. K., 'The Expression Theory of Art', in William Elton (ed.), *Aesthetics and Language* (Oxford: Blackwell, 1954), 73–99.

BUDD, MALCOLM, *Music and the Emotions: The Philosophical Theories* (London: Routledge & Kegan Paul, 1985).

—— *Values of Art: Pictures, Poetry and Music* (London: Penguin, 1995).

BULLOUGH, EDWARD. ' "Psychical Distance" as a Factor in Art and an Aesthetic Principle', in Morris Weitz (ed.), *Problems in Aesthetics* (London: Macmillan, 1970), 782–92.

BUNT, LESLIE, and PAVLICEVIC, MERCEDES, 'Music and Emotion: Perspectives from Music Therapy', in Patrik N. Juslin and John Sloboda (eds.), *Music and Emotion: Theory and Research* (Oxford: Oxford University Press, 2001), 181–201.

BURNHAM, SCOTT, *Beethoven Hero* (Princeton, NJ: Princeton University Press, 2000).

CALHOUN, CHESHIRE, and SOLOMON, ROBERT C., *What Is an Emotion?* Classic Readings in Philosphical Psychology (New York: Oxford University Press, 1984).

CANNON, WALTER B., *Bodily Changes in Pain, Hunger, Fear and Rage: An Account of Researches into the Function of Emotional Excitement.* 2nd edn. (New York: Harper & Row, 1963).

CARON, JEAN-LUC, *Carl Nielsen: Vie Et Œuvre 1865–1931* (Lausanne: Éditions l'Age d'Homme, 1990).

CARROLL, NOËL, *The Philosophy of Horror: Or Paradoxes of the Heart* (London: Routledge, 1990).

—— 'Art, Narrative, and Emotion'. in Mette Hjort and Sue Laver (eds.), *Emotion and the Arts* (New York: Oxford University Press, 1997), 190–211.

—— *The Philosophy of Art* (New York: Routledge, 1999).

CARROLL, NOËL, *Beyond Aesthetics: Philosophical Essays* (Cambridge: Cambridge University Press, 2001).

—— and BORDWELL, DAVID, *Post-Theory: Reconstructing Film Studies*, Wisconsin Studies in Film (Madison: University of Wisconsin Press, 1996).

CHU, PETRA TEN-DOESSCHATE, ' "A Science and an Art at Once" ', in Beth S. Wright (ed.), *The Cambridge Companion to Delacroix* (Cambridge: Cambridge University Press, 2001), 88–107.

CLARK, KENNETH, *The Romantic Rebellion: Romantic Versus Classic Art* (New York: Harper & Row, 1973).

CLAY, JEAN, *Romanticism* (Secaucus, NJ: Chartwell Books, 1981).

CLYNES, MANFRED, 'Neurobiologic Functions of Rhythm, Time and Pulse in Music', in Manfred Clynes (ed.), *Music, Mind, and Brain* (New York: Plenum, 1982), 171–216.

COLLINGWOOD, R. G., *The Principles of Art* (Oxford: Clarendon, 1963).

CONE, EDWARD T. *The Composer's Voice*, Ernest Bloch Lectures (Berkeley: University of California Press, 1974).

—— 'Schubert's Promissory Note: An Exercise in Musical Hermeneutics', *Nineteenth-Century Music* 5 (1982), 233–41.

COOK, NICHOLAS, *Music, Imagination and Culture* (Oxford: Clarendon, 1990).

—— 'Theorizing Musical Meaning', *Music Theory Spectrum* 23 (2001), 170–95.

COOKE, DERYCK, *The Language of Music* (Oxford: Oxford University Press, 1959).

COX, RENÉE, 'Varieties of Musical Expressionism', in George Dickie, Richard Sclafani, and Ronald Roblin (eds.), *Aesthetics: A Critical Anthology* (New York: St Martin's, 1989), 614–25.

CROCE, BENEDETTO, *Guide to Aesthetics*, trans. Patrick Romanell (Indianapolis: Bobbs-Merrill, 1965).

—— *The Aesthetic as the Science of Expression and of the Linguistic in General*, trans. Colin Lyas (Cambridge: Cambridge University Press, 1992).

CURRIE, GREGORY, *The Nature of Fiction* (Cambridge: Cambridge University Press, 1990).

—— and RAVENSCROFT, IAN, *Recreative Minds: Imagination in Philosophy and Psychology* (Oxford: Clarendon, 2002).

CURTLER, HUGH MERCER, *What Is Art?* (New York: Haven, 1983).

DAHLHAUS, CARL, *The Idea of Absolute Music*, trans. Roger Lustig (Chicago: University of Chicago Press, 1989).

DAMASIO, ANTONIO R., *Descartes' Error: Emotion, Reason, and the Human Brain* (New York: G. P. Putnam, 1994).

—— *Looking for Spinoza: Joy, Sorrow, and the Feeling Brain* (Orlando, Fla.: Harcourt, 2003).

DANTO, ARTHUR, 'The Artworld', *Journal of Philosophy* 61 (1964), 571–84.

—— *The Transfiguration of the Commonplace* (Cambridge, Mass.: Harvard University Press, 1981).

DARWIN, CHARLES, *The Expression of the Emotions in Man and Animals*, ed. Paul Ekman (New York: Oxford University Press, 1998).

DAVIDSON, DONALD, 'Actions, Reasons, and Causes', in *Essays on Actions and Events* (New York: Oxford University Press, 1980), 685–700.

DAVIES, STEPHEN, 'The Expression of Emotion in Music'. *Mind* 89 (1980), 67–86.

—— 'The Expression Theory Again'. *Theoria* 52 (1986), 146–67.

—— *Musical Meaning and Expression* (Ithaca, NY: Cornell University Press, 1994).

—— 'Contra the Hypothetical Persona in Music', in Mette Hjort and Sue Laver (eds.), *Emotion and the Arts* (New York: Oxford University Press, 1997), 95–109.

DAWSON, MICHAEL E., SCHELL, ANNE M., and BÖHMELT ANDREAS H. (eds.), *Startle Modification: Implications for Neuroscience, Cognitive Science, and Clinical Science* (Cambridge: Cambridge University Press, 1999).

DELACROIX, EUGÈNE, *The Journal of Eugène Delacroix*, trans. Lucy Norton, 3rd edn. (London: Phaidon, 1995).

DEMBER, WILLIAM N., *The Psychology of Perception* (New York: Holt, Rinehart, & Winston, 1960).

—— 'Motivation and the Cognitive Revolution', *American Psychologist* 29 (1974), 161–8.

DENORA, TIA, 'Aesthetic Agency and Musical Practice: New Directions in the Sociology of Music and Emotion', in Patrik N. Juslin and J. A. Sloboda (eds.), *Music and Emotion: Theory and Research* (Oxford: Oxford University Press, 2001). 161–80.

DERRIDA, JACQUES, *Of Grammatology*, trans. GAYATRI CHAKRAVORTY SPIVAK (Baltimore: Johns Hopkins University Press, 1976).

DESCARTES, RENÉ. 'The Passions of the Soul', in *The Philosophical Writings of Descartes* (Cambridge: Cambridge University Press, 1985).

DEWEY, JOHN, *Art as Experience* (New York: Capricorn Books, 1959).

DICKIE, GEORGE, 'The Myth of the Aesthetic Attitude', *American Philosophical Quarterly* 1 (1964), 56–65.

EATON, ROBERT C., *Neural Mechanisms of Startle Behavior* (New York: Plenum, 1984).

EISNER, LORENZ (ed.), *Neoclassicism and Romanticism 1750–1850: Sources and Documents*, 2 vols. (Englewoods Cliffs, NJ: Prentice-Hall, 1970).

EKMAN, PAUL, *Darwin and Facial Expression* (New York: Academic Press, 1973).

—— 'Biological and Cultural Contributions to Body and Facial Movement in the Expression of Emotions', in Amélie Rorty (ed.), *Explaining Emotions* (Berkeley: University of California Press, 1980), 73–101.

—— 'Expression and the Nature of Emotion', in Klaus R. Scherer and Paul Ekman (eds.), *Approaches to Emotion* (Hillsdale, NJ: Erlbaum, 1984), 319–44.

—— *Telling Lies: Clues to Deceit in the Marketplace, Politics, and Marriage* (New York: Berkley Books, 1985).

—— 'An Argument for Basic Emotions', *Cognition and Emotion* 6 (1992), 169–200.

EKMAN, PAUL, 'Are There Basic Emotions? A Reply to Ortony and Turner', *Psychological Review* 99 (1992), 550–3.

—— 'Facial Expression and Emotion', *American Psychologist* 48 (1993), 384–92.

—— 'Moods, Emotions, and Traits', in Paul Ekman and Richard J. Davidson (eds.), *The Nature of Emotion: Fundamental Questions* (New York: Oxford University Press, 1994), 56–8.

—— *Emotions Revealed.* (New York: Henry Holt, 2003).

—— and DAVIDSON, RICHARD J. (eds.), *The Nature of Emotion: Fundamental Questions* (New York: Oxford University Press, 1994).

—— and FRIESEN, WALLACE V., 'Is the Startle Reaction an Emotion?', *Journal of Personality and Social Psychology* 49 (1985), 1416–26.

ELLIOTT, R. K., 'Aesthetic Theory and the Experience of Art', in Alex Neill and Aaron Ridley (eds.), *The Philosophy of Art: Readings Ancient and Modern* (Boston: McGraw-Hill, 1995), 154–64.

ELLSWORTH, PHOEBE, 'William James and Emotion: Is a Century of Fame Worth a Century of Misunderstanding?', *Psychological Review* 101 (1994), 222–9.

—— 'Some Reasons to Expect Universal Antecedents of Emotion', in Paul Ekman and Richard J. Davidson (eds.), *The Nature of Emotion: Fundamental Questions* (New York: Oxford University Press, 1994), 151–62.

—— 'Levels of Thought and Levels of Emotion', in Paul Ekman and Richard J. Davidson (eds.), *The Nature of Emotion: Fundamental Questions* (New York: Oxford University Press, 1994), 192–6.

—— and SMITH, C. A. 'From Appraisal to Emotion: Differences among Unpleasant Feelings', *Motivation and Emotion* 12 (1988), 271–302.

ELSTER, JON, *Alchemies of the Mind: Rationality and the Emotions* (Cambridge: Cambridge University Press, 1999).

ELTON, WILLIAM (ed.), *Æsthetics and Language* (Oxford: Basil Blackwell, 1954).

ENGEL, MARIAN, *Bear* (New York: Atheneum, 1976).

EVANS, EDWIN, *Brahms' Pianoforte Music Handbook* (London: William Reeves, 1936).

FARRELL, DANIEL, 'Jealousy', *Philosophical Review* 89 (1980), 527–59.

FAY, LAUREL E., *Shostakovich: A Life* (Oxford: Oxford University Press, 2000).

FEAGIN, SUSAN L., *Reading with Feeling: The Aesthetics of Appreciation* (Ithaca, NY: Cornell University Press, 1996).

FETTERLEY, JUDITH, *The Resisting Reader: A Feminist Approach to American Fiction* (Bloomington: Indiana University Press, 1981).

FIELD, TIFFANY, et al., 'Discrimination and Imitation of Facial Expressions by Neonates', *Science* 218 (1982), 179–81.

FISH, STANLEY, *Is There a Text in This Class?: The Authority of Interpretive Communities* (Cambridge, Mass.: Harvard University Press, 1980).

FISK, CHARLES, 'What Schubert's Last Sonata Might Hold', in Jenefer Robinson (ed.), *Music and Meaning* (Ithaca, NY: Cornell University Press, 1997), 179–200.

FITZGERALD, PENELOPE, *The Blue Flower* (London: HarperCollins, 1995).

FLETCHER, C. R., HUMMEL, J. E., and MARSOLEK, C. J. , 'Causality and the Allocation of Attention During Comprehension', *Journal of Experimental Psychology: Learning, Memory, and Cognition* 16 (1990), 233–40.

FOLKMAN, SUSAN, and LAZARUS, RICHARD S., 'Coping and Emotion', in Nancy Stein, Bennett Leventhal, and Tom Trabasso (eds.), *Psychological and Biological Approaches to Emotion* (Hillsdale, NJ: Erlbaum, 1990), 313–32.

FORTENBAUGH, W. W., *Aristotle on Emotion* (London: Duckworth, 1975).

FRANK, ROBERT H., *Passions within Reason: The Strategic Role of the Emotions* (New York: W. W. Norton, 1988).

FRIDLUND, ALAN, and DUCHAINE, BRADLEY, ' "Facial Expressions of Emotion" and the Delusion of the Hermetic Self', in R. Harré and G. Parrott (eds.), *The Emotions: Social, Cultural and Biological Dimensions* (London: Sage Publications, 1996), 259–84.

FRIED, R., and BERKOWITZ, L. 'Music That Charms…and Can Influence Helpfulness', *Journal of Applied Social Psychology* 9 (1979), 199–208.

FRIEDLANDER, WALTER, *David to Delacroix*, trans. Robert Goldwater (Cambridge, Mass.: Harvard University Press, 1952).

FRIEDMAN, RICHARD A., 'A Peril of the Veil of Botox', *New York Times*, 6 August 2002.

FRIJDA, NICO, *The Emotions* (Cambridge: Cambridge University Press, 1986).

—— 'Moods, Emotion Episodes, and Emotions', in M. Lewis and J. M. Haviland (eds.), *Handbook of Emotions*, 2nd edn. (New York: Guilford, 1993).

—— 'Emotions Require Cognitions, Even If Simple Ones', in Paul Ekman and Richard J. Davidson (eds.), *The Nature of Emotion: Fundamental Questions* (New York: Oxford University Press, 1994), 197–202.

GABRIELSSON, ALF, 'Emotions in Strong Experiences with Music', in Patrik N. Juslin and John A. Sloboda (eds.), *Music and Emotion: Theory and Research* (Oxford: Oxford University Press, 2001), 431–49.

GARCIA, J., and RUSINIAK, K. W. 'What the Nose Learns from the Mouth', in D. Muller-Schwarze and R. M. Silverstein (eds.), *Chemical Signals* (New York: Plenum, 1980), 141–56.

GENETTE, GÉRARD, *Narrative Discourse: An Essay in Method* (Ithaca, NY: Cornell University Press, 1980).

GERRIG, RICHARD J., *Experiencing Narrative Worlds: On the Psychological Activities of Reading* (New Haven: Yale University Press, 1993).

GILBERT, STUART, *James Joyce's Ulysses: A Study* (Harmondsworth: Penguin (Peregrine Books), 1963).

GLADWELL, MALCOLM, 'The Naked Face', *The New Yorker*, 5 August 2002: 38–49.

GOETHE, JOHANN WOLFGANG VON, *The Sorrows of Young Werther*, trans. Michael Hulse (London: Penguin, 1989).

GOLDIE, PETER, *The Emotions: A Philosophical Exporation* (Oxford: Clarendon, 2000).

GOLDSTEIN, A., 'Thrills in Response to Music and Other Stimuli', *Physiological Psychology* 8 (1980), 126–9.

GOMBRICH, E. H., *Art and Illusion* (London: Phaidon, 1962).

GOODMAN, NELSON, *Languages of Art: An Approach to a Theory of Symbols* (Indianapolis,: Bobbs-Merrill, 1968).

GORDON, ROBERT M., *The Structure of Emotions* (New York: Cambridge University Press, 1987).

GOSLING, J. C., 'Emotion and Object', *Philosophical Review* 74 (1965), 486–503.

GREENSPAN, PATRICIA S., 'A Case of Mixed Feelings: Ambivalence and the Logic of Emotion', in Amélie Rorty (ed.), *Explaining Emotions* (Berkeley: University of California Press, 1980), 223–50.

—— *Emotions & Reasons: An Inquiry into Emotional Justification* (New York: Routledge, 1988).

GRIFFITHS, PAUL, *What Emotions Really Are: The Problem of Psychological Categories* (Chicago: University of Chicago Press, 1997).

GUYER, PAUL, 'History of Modern Aesthetics', in Jerrold Levinson (ed.), *The Oxford Handbook of Aesthetics* (Oxford: Oxford University Press, 2003), 25–60.

HAMBURGER, POVL, 'Carl Nielsen: Orchestral Works and Chamber Music', in Jurgen Balzer (ed.), *Carl Nielsen: Centenary Essays* (London: Dennis Dobson, 1966), 19–46.

HANNOOSH, MICHELE, *Painting and the Journal of Eugene Delacroix* (Princeton, NJ: Princeton University Press, 1995).

HANSLICK, EDUARD, *Hanslick's Music Criticisms*, trans. Henry Pleasants (New York: Dover, 1950).

—— *On the Musically Beautiful*, trans. Geoffrey Payzant (Indianapolis: Hackett, 1986).

HARRÉ, ROM, *The Social Construction of Emotions* (Oxford: Blackwell, 1986).

—— and GERROD PARROTT, W., *The Emotions: Social, Cultural and Biological Dimensions* (London: Sage, 1996).

HARRIS, PAUL, L., *The Work of the Imagination* (Oxford: Blackwell, 2000).

HATFIELD, ELAINE, CACIOPPO, JOHN T., and RAPSON, RICHARD L., *Emotional Contagion* (Cambridge: Cambridge University Press; Éditions de la Maison des Sciences de l'Homme, 1994).

HATZIMOYSIS ANTHONY, (ed.), *Philosophy and the Emotions*, Royal Institute of Philosophy Suppl. 52 (Cambridge: Cambridge University Press, 2003).

HÉBERT, SYLVIE, PERETZ, ISABELLE, and GAGNON, LISE, 'Perceiving the Tonal Ending of Tune Excerpts: The Roles of Pre-Existing Representation and Musical Expertise', *Canadian Journal of Experimental Psychology* 49 (1995), 193–209.

HEGEL, G. W. F., *Aesthetics: Lectures on Fine Art*, trans. T. M. Knox, 2 vols. (Oxford: Clarendon, 1975), i.

HELLER, REINHOLD, *Edvard Munch: The Scream* (New York: Viking, 1972).

HIGGINS, KATHLEEN MARIE, *The Music of Our Lives* (Philadelphia: Temple University Press, 1991).

HJORT, METTE, and LAVER, SUE (eds.), *Emotion and the Arts* (New York: Oxford University Press, 1997).

HODGES, DONALD A. (ed.), *Handbook of Music Psychology*, 2nd edn. (San Antonio, Tex.: Institute for Music Research, 1996).

HOLLAND, NORMAN, *The Dynamics of Literary Response* (New York: Oxford University Press, 1968).

—— *Five Readers Reading* (New Haven: Yale University Press, 1975).

—— 'Unity Identity Text Self', in Jane P. Tompkins (ed.), *Reader-Response Criticism: From Formalism to Post-Modernism* (Baltimore: Johns Hopkins University Press, 1980), 118–33.

HOLT, ELIZABETH GILMORE, (ed.), *From the Classicists to the Impressionists: Art and Architecture in the 19th Century*, 2nd edn. (New Haven: Yale University Press, 1986).

HOSPERS, JOHN, 'The Concept of Artistic Expression', *Proceedings of the Aristotelian Society* (1954–5), 313–44.

HUME, DAVID, *A Treatise of Human Nature*, ed. L. A. Selby-Bigge (London: Clarendon, 1967).

HURON, DAVID, 'How Music Evokes Emotion', Paper delivered to University of Cincinnati College-Conservatory of Music, 2001.

—— 'Is Music an Evolutionary Adaptation?', in R. J. Zatorre and Isabelle Peretz (eds.), *The Biological Foundations of Music* (New York: New York Academy of Sciences, 2001), 43–61.

ISEMINGER, GARY (ed.), *Intention and Interpretation, The Arts and Their Philosophies* (Philadelphia: Temple University Press, 1992).

—— 'Actual Intentionalism Vs. Hypothetical Intentionalism', *Journal of Aesthetics and Art Criticism* 54 (1996), 319–26.

ISER, WOLFGANG, *The Implied Reader; Patterns of Communication in Prose Fiction from Bunyan to Beckett* (Baltimore: Johns Hopkins University Press, 1974).

—— *The Act of Reading: A Theory of Aesthetic Response* (London: Routledge & Kegan Paul, 1978).

—— 'The Reading Process: A Phenomenological Approach', in Jane P. Tompkins (ed.), *Reader-Response Criticism: From Formalism to Post-Structuralism* (Baltimore: Johns Hopkins University Press, 1980), 50–69.

—— *Prospecting: From Reader Response to Literary Anthropology* (Baltimore: Johns Hopkins University Press, 1989).

IZARD, CARROLL, *The Face of Emotion* (New York: Appleton-Century-Crofts, 1971).

—— KAGAN, JEROME, and ZAJONC, ROBERT (eds.), *Emotion, Cognition, and Behaviour* (Cambridge: Cambridge University Press, 1984).

JACKENDOFF, R., 'Musical Processing and Musical Affect', in M. R. Jones and S. Holleran (eds.), *Cognitive Bases of Musical Communication* (Washington, DC: American Psychological Association, 1992), 51–68.

JAMES, HENRY, *The Art of the Novel* (New York: Scribner's, 1934).

—— *The Ambassadors*, Signet Classics (New York: New American Library, 1960).

JAMES, WILLIAM, 'The Physical Basis of Emotion', *Psychological Review* 1 (1894), 516–29.

—— *The Works of William James*, ed. Frederick H. Burkhardt, 3 vols. (Cambridge, Mass.: Harvard University Press, 1981).

JEFFERSON, ANN, and ROBEY, DAVID (eds.), *Modern Literary Theory* (Totowa, NJ: Barnes & Noble, 1982).

JOSE, P. E., and BREWER, W. F., 'Development of Story-Liking: Character Identification, Suspense, and Outcome Resolution', *Developmental Psychology* 20 (1984), 911–24.

JOYCE, JAMES, 'Dubliners', in Harry Levin (ed.), *The Portable James Joyce*, (New York: Viking, 1966), 19–242.

JUMP, J. D., *Matthew Arnold*. (London: Longman's, Green & Co., 1955).

JUSLIN, PATRIK N., 'Communicating Emotion in Music Performance: A Review and Theoretical Framework', in Patrik N. Juslin and J. A. Sloboda (eds.), *Music and Emotion: Theory and Research* (Oxford: Oxford University Press, 2001), 309–37.

—— and SLOBODA, JOHN A. (eds.), *Music and Emotion: Theory and Research* (Oxford: Oxford University Press, 2001).

KARL, GREGORY, 'Structuralism and Musical Plot', *Music Theory Spectrum* 19 (1997), 13–34.

—— and ROBINSON, JENEFER, 'Levinson on Hope in the Hebrides', *Journal of Aesthetics and Art Criticism* 53 (1995), 195–9.

———— 'Shostakovich's Tenth Symphony and the Musical Expression of Cognitively Complex Emotions', *Journal of Aesthetics and Art Criticism* 53 (1995), 401–15.

KEMPER, THEODORE D., 'Power, Status, and Emotions: A Sociological Contribution to a Psychophysiological Domain', in Klaus Scherer and Paul Ekman (eds.), *Approaches to Emotion* (Hillsdale, NJ: Erlbaum, 1984), 369–83.

KENNY, ANTHONY JOHN PATRICK, *Action, Emotion and Will* (London: Routledge & Kegan Paul; New York: Humanities Press, 1966).

KERMAN, JOSEPH, *Contemplating Music* (Cambridge, Mass.: Harvard University Press, 1985).

KEYS, IVOR, *Johannes Brahms* (London: Christopher Helm, 1989).

KIVY, PETER, *The Corded Shell: Reflections on Musical Expression* (Princeton, NJ: Princeton University Press, 1980).

—— 'Something I've Always Wanted to Know About Hanslick', *Journal of Aesthetics and Art Criticism* 46 (1988), 413–17.

—— *Sound Sentiment: An Essay on the Musical Emotions* (Philadelphia: Temple University Press, 1989).

—— *Music Alone: Philosophical Reflections on the Purely Musical Experience* (Ithaca, NY: Cornell University Press, 1990).

—— 'A New Music Criticism?', *The Monist* 73 (1990), 247–68.

KRAMER, JONATHAN, 'Unity and Disunity in Nielsen's Sixth Symphony', in Mina Miller (ed.), *The Nielsen Companion* (Portland, Oreg.: Amadeus, 1994), 293–344.

KRASNE, FRANKLIN B., and WINE, JEFFREY J., 'The Production of Crayfish Tailflip Escape Responses', in Robert C. Eaton (ed.), *Neural Mechanisms of Startle Behavior* (New York: Plenum, 1984), 179–211.

KRAUT, ROBERT, 'Objects of Affection', in K. D. Irani and G. E. Myers (eds.), *Emotion: Philosophical Studies* (New York: Haven, 1983), 42–56.

KRUMHANSL, CAROL L., *Cognitive Foundations of Musical Pitch* (New York: Oxford University Press, 1990).

——'An Exploratory Study of Musical Emotions and Psychophysiology', *Canadian Journal of Experimental Psychology* 51 (1997), 336–52.

KUNST-WILSON, W. R., and ZAJONC, R. B. 'Affective Discrimination of Stimuli That Cannot Be Recognized', *Science* 207 (1980), 557–8.

LAIRD, JAMES D., and APOSTOLERIS, NICHOLAS H., 'Emotional Self-Control and Self-Perception: Feelings Are the Solution, Not the Problem', in Rom Harré and W. Gerrod Parrott (eds.), *The Emotions: Social, Cultural and Biological Dimensions* (London: Sage, 1996), 285–301.

LAMARQUE, PETER, 'Fear and Pity', in *Fictional Points of View* (Ithaca, NY: Cornell University Press, 1996), 113–34.

—— *Fictional Points of View* (Ithaca, NY: Cornell University Press, 1996).

—— and OLSEN, STEIN HAUGOM, *Truth, Fiction and Literature* (Oxford: Clarendon, 1994).

LANDIS, C., and HUNT, W. A., *The Startle Pattern*, 2nd edn. (New York: Johnson Reprint Corporation, 1968).

LANE, RICHARD D., and NADEL, LYNN (eds.), *Cognitive Neuroscience of Emotion* (New York: Oxford University Press, 2000).

LANG, BEREL, *The Concept of Style* (Philadelphia: University of Pennsylvania Press, 1979).

LANGER, SUSANNE K., *Feeling and Form* (New York: Scribner's, 1953).

—— *Problems of Art* (New York: Scribner's, 1957).

—— *Philosophy in a New Key*, 3rd edn. (Cambridge, Mass.: Harvard University Press, 1976).

LAZARUS, RICHARD, S., 'Thoughts on the Relations between Emotion and Cognition', *American Psychologist* 37 (1982), 1019–24.

—— *Emotion and Adaptation* (New York: Oxford University Press, 1991).

——'Universal Antecedents of the Emotions'. in Paul Ekman and Richard J. Davidson (eds.), *The Nature of Emotion: Fundamental Questions* (New York: Oxford University Press, 1994), 163–71.

—— and ALFERT, ELIZABETH, 'Short-Circuiting of Threat by Experimentally Altering Cognitive Appraisal', *Journal of Abnormal and Social Psychology* 69 (1964), 195–205.

LEAVIS, F. R., *The Great Tradition: George Eliot, Henry James, Joseph Conrad* (London: Chatto & Windus, 1948).

LEDOUX, JOSEPH, 'Cognitive-Emotional Interactions in the Brain', *Cognition and Emotion* 3 (1989), 267–89.

LeDoux, Joseph, 'Cognitive-Emotional Interactions in the Brain', in Paul Ekman and Richard J. Davidson (eds.), *The Nature of Emotion: Fundamental Questions* (New York: Oxford University Press, 1994), 216–23.

——'Emotion-Specific Physiological Activity: Don't Forget About CNS Physiology', in Paul Ekman and Richard J. Davidson (eds.), *The Nature of Emotion: Fundamental Questions* (New York: Oxford University Press, 1994), 248–51.

——'Emotion, Memory and the Brain', *Scientific American* 270 (1994), 50–7.

——*The Emotional Brain: The Mysterious Underpinnings of Emotional Life* (New York: Simon & Schuster, 1996).

Levenson, Robert, 'The Search for Autonomic Specificity', in Paul Ekman and Richard J. Davidson (eds.), *The Nature of Emotion: Fundamental Questions* (New York: Oxford University Press, 1994), 252–57.

Levinson, Jerrold, *Music, Art, and Metaphysics: Essays in Philosophical Aesthetics* (Ithaca, NY: Cornell University Press, 1990).

——*The Pleasures of Aesthetics: Philosophical Essays* (Ithaca, NY: Cornell University Press, 1996).

——*Music in the Moment* (Ithaca, NY: Cornell University Press, 1997).

——'Music and Negative Emotion', in Jenefer Robinson (ed.), *Music and Meaning* (Ithaca, NY: Cornell University Press, 1997), 215–41.

——'Emotion in Response to Art: A Survey of the Terrain', in Mette Hjort and Sue Laver (eds.), *Emotion and the Arts* (New York: Oxford University Press, 1997), 20–34.

——'Varieties of Musical Pleasure: Musical Chills and Other Delights', Monroe Beardsley lecture, Temple University, Philadelphia, 2002.

Lewinsohn, Peter M., Muñoz, Ricardo F., Youngren, Mary Ann, and Zeiss, Antonette M. *Control Your Depresssion* (New York: Prentice-Hall, 1986).

Lewis, Michael and Haviland-Jones, Jeannette M. (eds.), *Handbook of Emotions* (New York: Guilford, 1993).

Lewis, Michael and Haviland-Jones, Jeannette M. (eds.), *Handbook of Emotions*, 2nd edn. (New York: Guilford, 2000).

Lindsay, Kenneth C., and Vergo, Peter (eds.), *Kandinsky: Complete Writings on Art* (New York: Da Capo, 1982).

Lutz, Catherine, *Unnatural Emotions: Everyday Sentiments on a Micronesian Atoll and Their Challenge to Western Theory* (Chicago: University of Chicago Press, 1988).

Lyons, William E., *Emotion*, Cambridge Studies in Philosophy (Cambridge: Cambridge University Press, 1980).

Macdonald, Malcolm, *Brahms* (London: J. M. Dent & Sons, 1990).

McKoon, G., and Ratcliff, R., 'Inference During Reading', *Psychological Review* 99 (1992), 440–66.

Madden, William A., 'Arnold the Poet (I) Lyric and Elegiac Poems', in Kenneth Allott (ed.), *Matthew Arnold* (Athens, Ohio: Ohio University Press, 1976).

MANSTEAD, ANTHONY S. R., FRIJDA, NICO, and FISCHER, AGNETA (eds.), *Feelings and Emotions: The Amsterdam Symposium* (Cambridge: Cambridge University Press, 2004).

MATRAVERS, DEREK, *Art and Emotion* (Oxford: Clarendon, 1998).

MAUS, FRED EVERETT, 'Music as Drama', in Jenefer Robinson (ed.), *Music and Meaning* (Ithaca, NY: Cornell University Press, 1997), 105–30.

MELTZOFF, A., and MOORE, M. K., 'Infants' Understanding of People and Things: From Body Imitation to Folk Psychology', in J. Bermúdez, A. Marcel, and N. Eilan (eds.), *The Body and the Self*, (Cambridge. Mass.: MIT Press, 1995), 43–69.

——and MOORE, M. K., 'Imitation of Facial and Manual Gestures by Human Neonates', *Science* 198 (1977), 75–8.

——————'Imitation in Newborn Infants: Exploring the Range of Gestures Imitated and the Underlying Mechanisms', *Developmental Psychology* 25 (1989), 954–62.

MEYER, LEONARD B., *Emotion and Meaning in Music* (Chicago: University of Chicago Press, 1956).

——*Music, the Arts, and Ideas* (Chicago: University of Chicago Press, 1967).

MILLER, MINA F., *The Nielsen Companion* (Portland, Oreg.: Amadeus, 1995).

MORAVCSIK, JULIUS, 'Understanding and the Emotions', *Dialectica* 36 (1982), 207–24.

MORGENSTERN, SAM (ed.), *Composers on Music: An Anthology of Composers' Writings from Palestrina to Copland* (New York: Random House (Pantheon Books), 1956).

MORREALL, JOHN, 'Fear without Belief', *Journal of Philosophy* 90 (1993), 359–66.

MORSBACH, H., and TYLER, W. J. 'A Japanese Emotion: Amae', in Rom Harré (ed.), *The Social Construction of Emotions* (Oxford: Blackwell, 1986), 289–307.

MURPHY, S. T., and ZAJONC, R. B., 'Affect, Cognition, and Awareness: Affective Priming with Suboptimal and Optimal Stimulus', *Journal of Personality and Social Psychology* 64 (1993), 723–39.

NAGEL, ERNEST, 'Review of Susanne K. Langer, Philosophy in a New Key', *Journal of Philosophy* 40 (1943), 323–9.

NAHUM, KATHERINE, ' "In Wild Embrace": Attachment and Loss in Edvard Munch', in Jeffery Howe (ed.), *Edvard Munch: Psyche, Symbol and Expression* (Boston: McMullen Museum of Art, Boston College, 2001), 31–47.

NARMOUR, EUGENE, 'The Top-Down and Bottom-up Systems of Musical Implication: Building on Meyer's Theory of Emotional Syntax', *Music Perception* 9 (1991), 1–26.

NEILL, ALEX, 'Fear, Fiction, and Make-Believe', *Journal of Aesthetics and Art Criticism* 49 (1991), 47–56.

——'Fiction and the Emotions', *American Philosophical Quarterly* 30 (1993), 1–13.

——'Fear and Belief', *Philosophy and Literature* 19 (1995), 94–101.

NEWCOMB, ANTHONY, "Sound and Feeling", *Critical Inquiry* 10 (1984), 614–43.

—— 'Once More "Between Absolute and Program Music": Schumann's Second Symphony', *19th Century Music* 7 (1984), 233–50.

NEWCOMB, ANTHONY, 'Action and Agency in Mahler's Ninth Symphony, Second Movement', in Jenefer Robinson (ed.), *Music and Meaning* (Ithaca, NY: Cornell University Press, 1997), 131–53.

NICHOLS, SHAUN, *Sentimental Rules: On the Natural Foundations of Moral Judgment* (New York: Oxford University Press, 2004).

NIEDENTHAL, P. M., and HALBERSTADT, J. 'Grounding Categories in Emotional Response', in Joseph P. Forgas (ed.), *Feeling and Thinking: The Role of Affect in Social Cognition* (Cambridge: Cambridge University Press; Édition de la Maison des Sciences de l'Homme, 2000), 357–86.

—— and SETTERLUND, M. B., 'Emotion Congruence in Perception', *Personality and Social Psychology Bulletin* 20 (1994), 401–10.

—— —— and JONES, D. E., 'Emotional Organization of Perceptual Memory', in P. M. Niedenthal and Shinobu Kitayama (eds.), *The Heart's Eye* (San Diego, Calif.: Academic Press, 1994), 88–113.

—— and BRAUER, M., HALBERSTADT, J. B., and INNES-KER, A. H., 'When Did Her Smile Drop? Facial Mimicry and the Influences of Emotional State on the Detection of Change in Emotional Expression', *Cognition and Emotion* 15 (2001), 853–64.

NISBETT, R. E., and WILSON, T. D., 'Telling More Than We Can Know: Verbal Reports on Mental Processes', *Psychological Review* 84 (1977), 231–59.

NOVITZ, DAVID, *Knowledge, Fiction and Imagination* (Philadelphia: Temple University Press, 1987).

NUSSBAUM, MARTHA CRAVEN, *Love's Knowledge: Essays on Philosophy and Literature* (New York: Oxford University Press, 1990).

—— 'Tragedy and Self-Sufficiency: Plato and Aristotle on Fear and Pity', in Amélie Oksenberg Rorty (ed.), *Essays on Aristotle's Poetics* (Princeton, NJ: Princeton University Press, 1992), 261–90.

—— *The Therapy of Desire: Theory and Practice in Hellenistic Ethics* (Princeton, NJ: Princeton University Press, 1994).

—— *Upheavals of Thought: The Intelligence of Emotions* (Cambridge: Cambridge University Press, 2001).

NYKLICEK, I., THAYER, J. F., and VAN DOORNEN, L. J. P., 'Cardiorespiratory Differentiation of Musically-Induced Emotions', *Journal of Psychophysiology* 11 (1997), 304–21.

OATLEY, KEITH, *Best Laid Schemes: The Psychology of Emotions* (Cambridge Cambridge University Press; Paris: Éditions de la Maison des Sciences de l'Homme, 1992).

—— and JENKINS, JENNIFER M., *Understanding Emotions* (Oxford: Blackwell, 1996).

ORTONY, ANDREW, 'Value and Emotion', in William Kessen, Andrew Ortony, and Fergus Craik (eds.), *Memories, Thoughts, and Emotions: Essays in Honor of George Mandler* (Hillsdale, NJ: Erlbaum, 1991), 337–53.

——CLORE, GERALD L., and COLLINS, ALLAN, *The Cognitive Structure of Emotions* (Cambridge: Cambridge University Press, 1988).

PANKSEPP, JAAK, 'The Emotional Sources of "Chills" Induced by Music', *Music Perception* 13 (1995), 171–207.

——*Affective Neuroscience* (New York: Oxford University Press, 1998).

ISABELLE, PERETZ, 'Listen to the Brain: A Biological Perspective on Musical Emotions', in Patrik N. Juslin, and J. A. Sloboda (eds.), *Music and Emotion:Theory and Research*, (Oxford: Oxford University Press, 2001), 105–34.

PLATO, *Republic*, trans. Robin Waterfield (Oxford: Oxford University Press, 1993).

PRINZ, JESSE, *Gut Reactions: A Perceptual Theory of Emotion* (Oxford: Oxford University Press, 2004).

PURCELL, DEAN G., STEWART, ALAN L., and SKOV, RICHARD B., 'Interference Effects of Facial Affect', in Robert R. Hoffman, Michael F. Sherrick, and Joel S. Warm (eds.), *Viewing Psychology as a Whole: The Integrative Science of William N. Dember*, (Washington DC: American Psychological Association, 1998), 433–47.

PUTMAN, DANIEL A., 'Why Instrumental Music Has No Shame', *British Journal of Aesthetics* 27 (1987), 55–61.

RADFORD, COLIN, 'How Can We Be Moved by the Fate of Anna Karenina?', *Proceedings of the Aristotelian Society*, suppl. vol. 49 (1975), 67–80.

——'Muddy Waters', *Journal of Aesthetics and Art Criticism* 49 (1991), 247–52.

RATNER, LEONARD G., *Classic Music: Expression, Form, and Style* (New York: Schirmer Books, 1980).

REISENZEIN, RAINER, 'The Schachter Theory of Emotion: Two Decades Later', *Psychological Bulletin* 94 (1983), 239–64.

RICHTER, DAVID H. (ed.), *The Critical Tradition: Classic Texts and Contemporary Trends* (New York: St Martin's, 1989).

RIDLEY, AARON, *Music, Value, and the Passions* (Ithaca, NY: Cornell University Press, 1995).

——'Not Ideal: Collingwood's Expression Theory', *Journal of Aesthetics and Art History* 55 (1997), 263–72.

——'Tragedy', in Jerrold Levinson (ed.), *The Oxford Handbook of Aesthetics* (Oxford: Oxford University Press, 2003), 408–20.

RINCK, M., and BOWER, G. H., 'Anaphora Resolution and the Focus of Attention in Situation Models', *Journal of Memory and Language* 34 (1995), 110–31.

ROBINSON, JENEFER, 'Emotion, Judgment, and Desire', *Journal of Philosophy* 80 (1983), 731–40.

——'Art as Expression', in Hugh Mercer Curtler (ed.), *What Is Art?* (New York: Haven, 1983), 93–121.

——'Style and Personality in the Literary Work', *Philosophical Review* 94 (1985), 227–48.

ROBINSON, JENEFER, 'The Expression and Arousal of Emotion in Music', *Journal of Aesthetics and Art Criticism* 52 (1994), 13–22.

—— 'L'Education Sentimentale', *Australasian Journal of Philosophy*, 73 (1995), 212–26.

—— 'Startle', *Journal of Philosophy*, 92 (1995), 53–74.

—— (ed.), *Music & Meaning* (Ithaca, NY: Cornell University Press, 1997).

—— 'Theoretical Issues in the Role of Appraisal in Emotion: Cognitive Content Versus Physiological Change', in Robert R. Hoffman, Michael F. Sherrick, and Joel S. Warm (eds.), *Viewing Psychology as a Whole: The Integrative Science of William N. Dember* (Washington, DC: American Psychological Association, 1998), 449–69.

—— 'Can Music Function as a Metaphor of Emotional Life?', in Kathleen Stock (ed.), *Philosophers on Music: Experience, Meaning, and Work* (Oxford: Oxford University Press, 2007). An abridged version has appeared in *Revue Française d'Études Americaines* 86 (2000), 77–89.

—— 'Emotion: Biological Fact or Social Construction?', in Robert C. Solomon (ed.), *Thinking About Feeling: Contemporary Philosophers on Emotion* (New York: Oxford University Press, 2004), 28–43.

RORTY, AMÉLIE, *Explaining Emotions* (Berkeley: University of California Press, 1980).

—— 'Explaining Emotions', in ead (ed.), *Explaining Emotions* (Berkeley: University of California Press, 1980), 103–26.

ROZIN, PAUL, and FALLON, A. E., 'A Perspective on Disgust', *Psychological Review* 94 (1987), 23–41.

RUSSELL, JAMES A., 'Culture and the Categorization of Emotions', *Psychological Bulletin* 110 (1991), 426–50.

SACKS, OLIVER, *The Man Who Mistook His Wife for a Hat* (New York: Harper & Row, 1987).

—— *An Anthropologist on Mars* (New York: Vintage Books, 1995).

SADIE, STANLEY (ed.), *The New Grove Dictionary of Music and Musicians* (London: Macmillan, 1980).

SALOVEY, PETER, BEDELL, BRIAN T., DETWEILER, JERUSHA B., and MAYER, JOHN D., 'Current Directions in Emotional Intelligence Research', in Michael Lewis and Jeannette M. Haviland-Jones (eds.), *Handbook of Emotions*, 2nd edn. (New York: Guilford, 2000), 504–20.

SCHACHTER, STANLEY, *The Psychology of Affiliation: Experimental Studies of the Sources of Gregariousness* (Stanford, Calif.: Stanford University Press, 1959).

—— and SINGER, JEROME, 'Cognitive, Social, and Physiological Determinants of Emotional State', *Psychological Review* 69 (1962), 379–99.

SCHERER, KLAUS, R., *Facets of Emotion: Recent Research* (Hillsdale, NJ: Erlbaum, 1988).

—— 'On the Nature and Function of Emotion: A Component Process Approach', in Klaus R. Scherer and Paul Ekman (eds.), *Approaches to Emotion* (Hillsdale, NJ: Erlbaum, 1984), 293–317.

SCHERER, KLAUS, R., 'Vocal Affect Expression: A Review and a Model for Future Research', *Psychological Bulletin* 99 (1986), 143–65.

—— and EKMAN, PAUL (eds.), *Approaches to Emotion* (Hillsdale, NJ: Erlbaum, 1984).

—— and ZENTNER, MARCEL R., 'Emotional Effects of Music: Production Rules', in Patrik N. Juslin and John Sloboda (eds.), *Music and Emotion: Theory and Research* (Oxford: Oxford University Press, 2001), 361–92.

—— et al., 'Vocal Cues in Emotion Encoding and Decoding', *Motivation and Emotion* 15 (1991), 123–48.

SCRUTON, ROGER, *Art and Imagination* (London: Methuen, 1974).

—— *The Aesthetic Understanding: Essays in the Philosophy of Art and Culture* (London: Methuen, 1983).

—— *The Aesthetics of Music* (Oxford: Oxford University Press, 1997).

SHAKESPEARE, WILLIAM, *Macbeth*, ed. Kenneth Muir, 9th edn. Arden Shakespeare (London: Methuen, 1962).

SHOSTAKOVICH, DMITRI DMITRIEVICH, *Testimony: The Memoirs of Dimitri Shostakovich, as Related to and Edited by Solomon Volkov*, trans. Antonina W. Bouis (New York: Harper & Row, 1979).

SIRCELLO, GUY JOSEPH, *Mind & Art: An Essay on the Varieties of Expression* (Princeton, NJ: Princeton University Press, 1972).

SLOBODA, JOHN, 'Musical Performance and Emotion: Issues and Developments', in S. W. Yi (ed.), *Music, Mind, and Science* (Seoul: Western Music Research Institute, 2000), 220–38.

—— 'Music—Where Cognition and Emotion Meet', *The Psychologist* 12 (1999), 450–5.

—— and JUSLIN, PATRIK N., 'Psychological Perspectives on Music and Emotion', in Patrik N. Juslin and John A. Sloboda (eds.), *Music and Emotion: Theory and Research* (Oxford: Oxford University Press, 2001), 71–104.

SOLOMON, ROBERT C., *The Passions*, 1st edn. (Garden City, NY: Anchor Press/ Doubleday, 1976).

—— 'Emotions and Choice', in Amélie Rorty (ed.), *Explaining Emotions* (Berkeley: University of California Press, 1980), 251–81.

—— 'On Emotions as Judgments', *American Philosophical Quarterly* 25 (1988), 183–91.

—— 'The Politics of Emotion', In *Midwest Studies in Philosophy: Philosophy of Emotions*, (Notre Dame: University of Notre Dame Press, 1998), 1–20.

—— *Not Passion's Slave: Emotions and Choice* (New York: Oxford University Press, 2003).

—— (ed.), *Thinking about Feeling: Contemporary Philosophers on Emotions* (New York: Oxford University Press, 2004).

SONTAG, MICHAEL. 'Emotion and the Labeling Process' (Cincinnati: University of Cincinnati, 2005).

SOUSA, RONALD DE, *The Rationality of Emotion* (Cambridge, Mass.: MIT, 1987).

SPARSHOTT, FRANCIS, *The Theory of the Arts* (Princeton, NJ: Princeton University Press, 1982).

SPINOZA, BARUCH, *Ethics* (Indianapolis: Hackett, 1992).

SQUIRE, L. R., KNOWLTON, B., and MUSEN, G., 'The Structure and Organization of Memory', *Annual Review of Psychology* 44 (1993), 453–95.

SROUFE, ALAN L., 'The Organization of Emotional Development', in Klaus R. Scherer, and Paul Ekman (eds.), *Approaches to Emotion* (Hillsdale, NJ: Erlbaum, 1984), 109–28.

STECKER, ROBERT, 'Expression of Emotion in (Some of) the Arts', *Journal of Aesthetics and Art Criticism* 42 (1984), 409–18.

——*Interpretation and Construction: Art, Speech and the Law* (Oxford: Blackwell, 2003).

STERN, DANIEL N., *The Interpersonal World of the Infant: A View from Psychoanalysis and Developmental Psychology* (New York: Basic Books, 1985).

STOCK, KATHLEEN (ed.), *Philosophers on Music: Experience, Meaning, and Work* (Oxford: Oxford University Press, 2007).

STOLNITZ, JEROME, *Aesthetics and Philosophy of Art Criticism: A Critical Introduction* (Boston: Houghton Mifflin, 1960).

SULEIMAN, SUSAN, and CROSMAN INGE, (eds.), *The Reader in the Text: Essays on Audience and Interpretation* (Princeton, NJ: Princeton University Press, 1980).

SWAFFORD, JAN, *Johannes Brahms: A Biography*, 1st edn. (New York: Alfred A. Knopf: distrib. Random House, 1997).

TANGNEY, JUNE PRICE, and FISCHER, KURT W., *Self-Conscious Emotions: The Psychology of Shame, Guilt, Embarrassment, and Pride* (New York: Guilford, 1995).

TAYLOR, GABRIELE, *Pride, Shame, and Guilt: Emotions of Self-Assessment* (New York: Oxford University Press, 1985).

TOLSTOY, LEO, *What Is Art?*, trans. Aylmer Maude (Indianapolis: Bobbs-Merrill, 1960).

——*Anna Karenina*, trans. Rosemary Edmonds (Harmondsworth: Penguin, 1971).

TOMPKINS, JANE P., *Reader-Response Criticism: From Formalism to Post-Structuralism* (Baltimore: Johns Hopkins University Press, 1980).

TORMEY, ALAN, *The Concept of Expression: A Study in Philosophical Psychology and Aesthetics* (Princeton, NJ: Princeton University Press, 1971).

TREHUB, SANDRA, 'Musical Predispositions in Infancy: An Update', in R. J. Zatorre and Isabelle Peretz (eds.), *The Cognitive Neuroscience of Music* (Oxford: Oxford University Press, 2003), 3–20.

TREITLER, LEO, *Music and the Historical Imagination* (Cambridge, Mass.: Harvard University Press, 1989).

——'Language and the Interpretation of Music', in Jenefer Robinson (ed.), *Music and Meaning* (Ithaca, NY: Cornell University Press, 1997), 23–56.

URMSON, J. O. 'What Makes a Situation Aesthetic?', in Joseph Margolis (ed.), *Philosophy Looks at the Arts: Contemporary Readings in Aesthetics* (New York: Charles Scribner's Sons, 1962), 13–27.

VERMAZEN, BRUCE, 'Expression as Expression', *Pacific Philosophical Quarterly* 67 (1986), 196–224.

VRANA, S. R., CUTHBERT, B. N., and LANG, P. J., 'Processing Fearful and Neutral Sentences: Memory and Heart Rate Change', *Cognition and Emotion* 3 (1989), 179–95.

WALTON, KENDALL, 'Fearing Fictions', *Journal of Philosophy* 75 (1978), 5–27.

—— 'Style and the Products and Processes of Art', in Berel Lang (ed.), *The Concept of Style*, (Philadelphia: University of Pennsylvania Press, 1979), 45–66.

—— *Mimesis as Make-Believe: On the Foundations of the Representational Arts* (Cambridge, Mass.: Harvard University Press, 1990).

—— 'Listening with Imagination', in Jenefer Robinson (ed.), *Music and Meaning*, (Ithaca, NY: Cornell University Press, 1997), 57–82.

WATSON, DAVID, *Mood and Temperament* (New York: Guilford, 2000).

WATSON, JOHN B., *Psychology, from the Standpoint of a Behaviorist*, 2nd edn. (Philadelphia: J. B. Lippincott, 1924).

WEITZ, MORRIS, 'The Role of Theory in Aesthetics', in Joseph Margolis (ed.), *Philosophy Looks at the Arts*, (New York: Scribner's Sons, 1956), 48–60.

—— (ed.), *Problems in Aesthetics: An Introductory Book of Readings* (New York: Macmillan, 1970).

WHARTON, EDITH, *The Reef* (New York: Macmillan (Collier Books), 1987).

—— *Summer* (New York: Macmillan (Collier Books), 1987).

WITVLIET, C. V., and VRANA, S. R., 'The Emotional Impact of Instrumental Music on Affect Ratings, Facial Emg, Autonomic Response, and the Startle Reflex: Effects of Valence and Arousal', *Psychophysiology Supplement* 91 (1996).

—— —— and WEBB-TALMADGE, N., 'In the Mood: Emotion and Facial Expressions During and after Instrumental Music, and During an Emotional Inhibition Task', *Psychophysiology Supplement* 88 (1998).

WOLLHEIM, RICHARD, *Art and Its Objects. An Introduction to Aesthetics* (New York: Harper & Row, 1968).

—— *On Art and the Mind* (Cambridge, Mass.: Harvard University Press, 1974).

—— *Painting as an Art*, A. W. Mellon Lectures in the Fine Arts 1984 (London: Thames & Hudson, 1987).

ZAJONC, ROBERT, 'Feeling and Thinking: Preferences Need No Inferences', *American Psychologist* 35 (1980), 151–75.

—— 'On the Primacy of Affect', *American Psychologist* 39 (1984), 117–29.

—— 'Evidence for Nonconscious Emotions', in Paul Ekman and Richard J. Davidson (eds.), *The Nature of Emotion*, (New York: Oxford University Press, 1994), 293–97.

—— and MARKUS, HAZEL, 'Affect and Cognition: The Hard Interface', in Carroll E. Izard, Jerome Kagan, and Robert B. Zajonc (eds.), *Emotion, Cognition, and Behavior*, (New York: Cambridge University Press, 1984), 73–102.

ZATORRE, R. J., and PERETZ, ISABELLE, *The Cognitive Neuroscience of Music* (Oxford: Oxford University Press, 2003).

ZIMNY, G. H., and WEIDENFELLER, E. W., 'Effects of Music Upon GSR and Heart Rate', *American Journal of Psychology* 76 (1963), 311–14.

Index

Engel, Marian, *Bear* 18, 416
enjoyment 33, 285
envy 13, 59, 68, 87, 171
espressivo 243, 248, 286–7
ethnomusicology 403
  see also Becker, Judith
euphoria 84–7, 400, 407
Evans, Edwin 457
expression of φ vs. φ expression 241–4,
  247–8, 250
  in music, 300–2
expression of emotion, artistic 231–92
  in "Art as Expression" 266–70
  as articulation and elucidation of
    emotion 262–4, 267–86, 357
  as cognitive monitoring of emotional
    responses 256–7, 264, 269, 272–7
  in dance 286–7
  defined 270–1
  as intentional 268, 270
  in painting 276, 279–84
  in poetry 277–9
  as a property of artworks 240–1
  as recollection in tranquility 232, 238,
    264, 287
  and recreation of emotion
    expressed 289–91
  new Romantic theory of 270–92
  in sculpture and architecture 284–6
  Vermazen's theory of 258–65
  see also expression theory of art;
    expression of emotion in music
expression of emotion in music 293–347
  arousal theories of 237, 292, 349, 352–8,
    375–6, 380
  and cognitively complex
    emotions 301–2, 304–6, 309, 320,
    327–8, 345
  Davies's theory of 305–10
  doggy theory of 300–310
  and emotion as process 303, 309–13,
    320–1, 325–6, 333, 341–4
  and expressive potential 324–5, 336–7,
    454 n.14.
  vs. expressiveness 240, 248, 251, 264–5,
    300–310
  Hanslick on 295–8
  in instrumental music 322–47

  Kivy's theory of 300–5
  Langer's theory of 297–300
  and psychological drama 322–6, 329–36,
    340–6, 367–8, 376–7, 411
  Ridley's theory of 353–60, 366–9, 375–6,
    373, 393
  Romantic conception of 309, 312–13,
    328–30, 345, 349 (check)
  Walton's theory of 359–360
  see also "Immer leiser wird mein
    Schlummer;" Intermezzo op. 117,
    no.2; expressive qualities; espressivo;
    expression theory of art; expression
    of emotion artistic
expressionism 232, 241, 254, 282–3,
  447 n.49
expressive qualities 232, 261, 269, 351, 366,
  368–9, 407
  in Brahms's Intermezzo op. 117 no.2:
    340–3
  defined 291–2
  in Kivy's theory of musical
    expression 302–4
  and Krumhansl's experiment 373–5
  vs. qualities named by an emotion
    word 309–10
  in Ridley's theory 354, 357–8, 360
  in Tormey's theory 240–51,
expression theory of art 234–50, 253–7, 258
  Collingwood's version of 235–9
  defended against Tormey 244–50
  features of summarized 256–7
  modified version of defended 253–7,
    270–7
  Tormey's critique of 239–44
  Tormey's definition of 240
  see also expression of emotion artistic

facial expressions of emotion *see* emotion,
  facial expressions of
fago 80
fantasy 196, 203–6, 209, 456
Farrell, Daniel 87, 97, 416, 424–5
Fauré, Gabriel 377
Fay, Laurel 456 n.38
Feagin, Susan 141, 427, 429, 433
fear:
  as affect program 92–3

Weitz, Morris 254, 443
Wharton, Edith, 157, 158–78, 190–3, 196,
    212, 216–19, 413, 431, 432, 433, 434,
    437
  as implied author 178–188, 193–4, 212,
    291
  Ethan Frome 194
  House of Mirth, The 187
  Summer, 187, 432–3 n.53, 434 n.77
  see also The Reef
Wilson, T. D. 417 n.34
Wilson, W. R. *see* Kunst-Wilson, W. R

Wittgenstein, Ludwig, *Tractatus
    Logico-Philosophicus* 299
Witvliet, C. V. 396, 464
Wollheim, Richard 252, 266, 280, 284, 443,
    445, 446, 448
Wordsworth, William 232, 238,
    264
Wuthering Heights 255

Zajonc, Robert 38–45, 48, 53, 55, 63, 72,
    86, 404, 419, 420, 423
Zatorre, R. J. 463, 464, 467